Inside

Adobe® Photoshop® 4

Gary David Bouton

Co-Authors
Barbara Mancuso Bouton
Gary Kubicek

New Riders

New Riders Publishing, Indianapolis, Indiana

Inside Adobe® Photoshop® 4

Gary David Bouton

Co-Authors
Barbara Mancuso Bouton
Gary Kubicek

Published by:
New Riders Publishing
201 West 103rd Street
Indianapolis, IN 46290 USA

Copyright ® 1997 by New Riders Publishing

Printed in the United States of America 1 2 3 4 5 6 7 8 9 0

Library of Congress Cataloging-in-Publication Data

CIP data available upon request

Warning and Disclaimer

PUBLISHER	Don Fowley
PUBLISHING MANAGER	David Dwyer
MARKETING MANAGER	Mary Foote
MANAGING EDITOR	Carla Hall

PRODUCT DEVELOPMENT SPECIALIST
Alicia Buckley

ACQUISITIONS EDITOR
John Kane

SOFTWARE SPECIALIST
Steve Flatt

SENIOR EDITORS
Sarah Kearns
Suzanne Snyder

DEVELOPMENT EDITOR
Marta Partington

PROJECT EDITOR
Gail S. Burlakoff

COPY EDITOR
Marta Partington

TECHNICAL EDITOR
Gary Kubicek

ACQUISITIONS COORDINATOR
Stacey Beheler

COVER DESIGNER
Karen Ruggles

COVER PRODUCTION
Aren Howell

BOOK DESIGNER
Anne Jones

PRODUCTION TEAM SUPERVISORS
Laurie Casey
Joe Millay
Gina Rexrode

GRAPHICS IMAGE SPECIALISTS
Wil Cruz
Tammy Graham
Oliver Jackson
Dennis Sheehan

INDEXERS
Erik Brinkman
Kevin Fulcher
Brad Herriman

PRODUCTION TEAM
Kim Cofer
Ann Dickerson
Maureen Hanrahan
Linda Knose
Elizabeth SanMiguel
M. Anne Sipahimalani
Deirdre Smith
Ian Smith

About the Authors

Gary David Bouton is an author and illustrator who adopted the personal computer after 20 years of creating artwork at a traditional drafting table. *Inside Adobe Photoshop 4* is Gary's fifth book on Adobe Photoshop; he has written six other books on computer graphics for New Riders Publishing, in addition to being a contributing author to three books on CorelDRAW! These titles include *Inside Extreme 3D 2, Photoshop Filters & Effects,* and *CorelDRAW! Experts Edition.* He also recently wrote the book, *The Official Multimedia Publishing for Netscape,* for Netscape Press.

Gary has won several international awards in desktop publishing and design and was a finalist in the 1996 Macromedia People's Choice Awards. A contributing writer to *Corel Magazine* and other publications, Gary is also moderator of the CorelXARA discussion list on CorelNet (http://www.corelnet.com/hyper/xaratalk).

Gary can be reached at:
Gary@TheBoutons.com.

Barbara Mancuso Bouton has co-authored all editions of *Inside Adobe Photoshop* and is the editor of the *New Rider's Official World Wide Yellow Pages, 1996 Edition.* She is also the author of Netscape Press' *Official Netscape Power User's Toolkit.* Barbara is a desktop publishing and electronic and Internet document production professional, and systems consultant for Fortune 500 firms.

"Photoshop 4 brings to the graphics community a perfect blend of production tools and creative features," said Barbara. "Regardless of your level of expertise, you can get right down to work in version 4. Much of the interface has changed, but at the same time, Photoshop 4 has taken on an appearance more consistent with other products by Adobe Systems. Adobe has provided an easier-to-use program; what *you* need to bring to the application is a concept. In this book we concentrate on how to use Photoshop's tools to successfully execute your concept and express what you see in your mind's eye."

Barbara can be reached at:
Barbara@TheBoutons.com, or at
bbouton@dreamscape.com.

Gary and Barbara maintain their own Internet site (http://www.TheBoutons.com) as a repository of book listings, essays on computer graphics, and as an art gallery of current images.

Gary Kubicek has been the technical editor for New Riders books on Photoshop; this is the second book for which he is a contributing author. A professional photographer for more than 20 years, Gary was an early adopter of Photoshop and the "digital darkroom" as an extension of the self-expression he finds in his traditional photographic work.

"The limitations and confines of conventional photography led me to electronic imaging," said Gary. "If you come from a traditional imaging background, you will have the time of your life in Photoshop 4. The workspace might feel a little unfamiliar at first, but Photoshop has the digital equivalents to many real-world tools, and…many that don't even exist in the physical darkroom. Together, these digital tools enable you to freely produce the special effects images you always wanted to create in the camera or in the darkroom, but couldn't."

Gary Kubicek can be reached at: gary@kubicek.com.

Trademark Acknowledgments

All terms mentioned in this book that are known to be trademarks or service marks have been appropriately capitalized. New Riders Publishing cannot attest to the accuracy of this information. Use of a term in this book should not be regarded as affecting the validity of any trademark or service mark.

Dedication

This book is dedicated to the artists—the designers, the dancers, and other practitioners of self-expression—who *share* what they have learned with others. Secrets are weapons; communication is power.

Acknowledgments

By all rights, you should not be holding this book. This *does not* mean that you didn't choose the best book on Photoshop! We simply mean that the task of delivering a book on the world's most popular image editing application within only a few months after Photoshop 4 shipped—and doing it without informational or creative compromise—required a *lot* of support! Support in the form of input and other valuable contributions by the authors, a magnificent collection of friends (who also happen to be professionals) who fine-tuned seemingly countless pages of MS-Word manuscript, and other individuals who fulfilled hardware, software, and occasionally emotional needs while the book was being written. The Boutons and Gary Kubicek want to thank the following folks for their graciousness, their time, and their effort in making *Inside Adobe Photoshop 4* everything we expected, and—most important—we hope, everything *you* expect:

◆ Gail Burlakoff, Project Editor, who made real-world sense (see, Gail? we remembered the hyphen!<g>) of a sea of documents, figures, and schedules that required incredible amounts of sifting and organizing to bring this book to press on time. Gail has (somewhat masochistically, we believe) edited no less than five of the Boutons' books, and we realize that either we are getting better at this stuff, or Gail's thinking is becoming more like ours. A frightening thought, Gail, but thank you from the bottom of our hearts for your invaluable work.

◆ Marta Partington, Development Editor, who ensured that what we wrote was what we meant, for translating techno-gibberish into user-accesible prose on more than a few occasions, and for believing in the concept of this book. Marta, thank you for your support on the color signature, the style we used to explain priciples in this book, and for being a friend who genuinely listens when the issue at hand is an artistic call.

◆ Thanks to David Dwyer and Don Fowley for continuing to let us tell a story whose primary value for the reader concerns art, and not how a specific application tool is displayed. Photoshop 4 is in many ways larger than a computer program, and we thank our publishers for understanding that a book about Photoshop needs to be more than simple program documentation.

◆ The Boutons thank Gary Kubicek, Technical Editor and Co-Author, for the persistent, often irksome thoroughness with which he edited our work. This is *exactly* what a good tech edit should be, Gary, and we hope you take this in the same spirit as when you ordered pizzas delivered to our home at 2:30 in the morning! Thank you, friend, for the fine work we're all proud of.

◆ Thanks to John Kane, Acquisitions Editor, for choreographing the long-distance process by which authors in Upstate New York communicate with editors in Indy and New York's Hudson Valley, and then bring it on back home to New Riders. Writing this book took 10 extremely intense weeks, and Citizen Kane approached the challenge with aplomb and courtesy! Thanks, John!

◆ Suzanne Snyder, Senior Editor, who dove into the production process of this book at the 11th hour and helped us straighten out the figures, pages, and supplemental material. Thank you, Suzanne—and we never did learn what happened to the plastic ducks and alligators…

◆ Stacey Beheler, Acquisitions Coordinator, our "air traffic controller" for the Photoshop 4 book. Thanks, Stacey, for handling the "paper chase," both physical and electronic, and for keeping the wheels rolling.

◆ MCP Production, for bringing the documentation to physical format and for allowing the authors to contribute to the book's finished appearance.

◆ Steve Flatt, Software Specialist, for ensuring that the Companion CD was mastered correctly and that the contents are easy to access on both the Macintosh and Windows platforms.

◆ At Adobe Systems, Sonya Schaefer and John Leddy, for the answers and the product in its early development cycle. Thanks, Sonya, for the opportunity to work with you people on an incredibly advanced application that none of us thought could possibly get better after version 3.0.5. Special thanks to Kellie Bowman and Patty Pane at Adobe Systems for providing us with related tools, such as Illustrator and Acrobat Exchange, as they were used to compile the Companion CD. Thanks to Kevin Conner for Windows support on Photoshop 4, and extra thanks to Peter Card, for PageMaker 6.0, used to compile the Acrobat documentation on the CD.

◆ Daryl Wise and Jon Bass at Fractal Design Corporation, for the use of Painter 4 and Poser, shown in examples in this book and in many of the resource files on the Companion CD.

◆ Special thanks to Charles Moir and Dave Matthewman at XARA, Ltd., for access to the advance versions of CorelXARA, which was used to illustrate and annotate many of this book's figures.

◆ A big thanks to Rix Kramlich and Steve Kusmer at Macromedia, for their support on Extreme 3D, the application used to model many of the figures, example images, and the pictures in the color signature.

◆ J. Scott Carr at Digimarc, for an advance copy of the watermark plug-in for Photoshop, and also for providing background information in Chapter 3.

◆ Mark Law at Extensis, for the use of PageTools and PhotoTools, wonderful add-on programs for Adobe products.

◆ Thanks to Renee at Capitol Filmworks for great work processing our film and transferring the images onto PhotoCDs. These are the same folks who have extended a special offer to our readers in the back of the book. Thanks for great turnaround times, and quality work.

◆ Thanks to John Niestemski and Susan Bird at Graphic Masters, the folks who bring you the offer in the back of this book for exceptional film recording work (see Chapter 16) from your Photoshop files. For more than four years, Graphic Masters has been the professional choice of the authors for getting 35mm and larger format film copies of our work, and for good reason. It's called *quality*.

◆ Our ISP, Scott Brennan, President of Dreamscape On-Line, PLC., for the type of bandwidth and service we needed to get massive amounts (we *are* talking larger than a floppy here!) of work to Indianapolis faster than overnight. Dreamscape's success here on the East Coast is rooted in personal service, and Scott is yet another business professional we've had the pleasure of calling a friend.

◆ Lauriellen Murphy Vitriol was kind enough to allow us to use her image in Chapter 11. Thank you, Laur; this smacks of largesse, you know! Thanks also to Carol DiSalvo, who took the photograph, for the use of the image in this book.

◆ Thanks to David Bouton, closely related to Gary and Barbara, for the use of his image in Chapter 13. Dave, you get your picture in these books more often than *we* do. What's your secret? Thank you, brother!

◆ Thanks to Jim Gosch, the "son" in Chapter 14, for letting us use the photo of your father, and for being a model. We hope your mom enjoys the image!

◆ Gary K. thanks his wife, Theresa, and two daughters, Rachael and Bethany, for their support and distractions during those many 18-hour workdays.

◆ Gary and Barbara Bouton want to thank their parents, Jack, Eileen, John, and Wilma, for putting up with *another* year's absence from family functions, while we diligently completed three books, and occasionally asked ourselves whether the hermit-hood that accompanies author-dom is worth it. You've told us that what we're doing is important, and it is your faith in our talents that makes you all that much more dear to us. Thanks, mom. Thanks, pop.

Contents at a Glance

Table of Contents

New Riders Publishing

The staff of New Riders Publishing is committed to bringing you the very best in computer reference material. Each New Riders book is the result of months of work by authors and staff who research and refine the information contained within its covers.

As part of this commitment to you, New Riders invites your input. Please let us know if you enjoy this book, if you have trouble with the information and examples presented, or if you have a suggestion for the next edition.

Please note, however: New Riders staff cannot serve as a technical resource for Photoshop 4 or for questions about software- or hardware-related problems. Please refer to the documentation that accompanies your software or to the applications' Help systems.

If you have a question or comment about any New Riders book, there are several ways to contact New Riders Publishing. We will respond to as many readers as we can. Your name, address, or phone number will never become part of a mailing list or be used for any purpose other than to help us continue to bring you the best books possible.

You can write us at the following address:

New Riders Publishing
Attn: Publisher
201 W. 103rd Street
Indianapolis, IN 46290

If you prefer, you can fax New Riders Publishing at:

317-817-7448

You can also send electronic mail to New Riders at the following Internet address:

jkane@newriders.mcp.com

New Riders Publishing is an imprint of Macmillan Computer Publishing. To obtain a catalog or information, or to purchase any Macmillan Computer Publishing book, call 800-428-5331 or visit our Web site at http://www.mcp.com.

Thank you for selecting *Inside Adobe Photoshop 4*!

INTRODUCTION

INTRODUCTION

The last few times we've heard the term "Photoshop" mentioned in conversations, it has been used as a verb ("I Photoshopped it"), an adjective ("That must be a Photoshop image"), and as a home—"I live in Photoshop." Clearly, Adobe Photoshop—the imaging software application—has become more than an integral part of graphic designers' working tools. Photoshop has earned the reputation of being a mysterious, magical environment where reality is twisted and reshaped, where disintegrating family photos are returned to perfect condition, and where the line between illustration and photography is freely crossed.

Inside Adobe Photoshop 4 removes the mystique from Photoshop, without taking away from the excitement we all find in a well-presented magic trick. If you picked up a copy of Photoshop 4 recently because friends and colleagues recommended it, but you have no idea where to begin, keep your expectations high and be prepared for a lot of surprises in this book. The "magic" you find in Photoshop depends in large part on how well you play the role of magician; we start you off with a few parlor tricks at the beginning of this book, progress to feats of levitation (see Chapter 7), and round out your education in image editing with World Wide Web wonders and pre-press basics.

If you're already a Photoshop user, *Inside Adobe Photoshop 4* is an excellent, peer-to-peer guide to the new features in this version, as well as an important resource for advanced techniques you can apply to your current assignments. Most of the information in this book is presented in the context of real-world examples; step-by-step instructions demonstrate not only a technique, but also *why* things work in Photoshop. The authors believe that when you provide a solution, you give fellow Photoshop users a leg up in their work. But when you explain *why* the solution works, you provide a background to the information that a designer or photographer can build on. Professionals and hobbyists alike are *results-oriented*, and we've made every effort in writing this book to pave the smartest, quickest path, while mapping the "back roads"—the undocumented shortcuts—for you to achieve the goals you have in mind.

What Should I Pack for the "Photoshop Safari"?

Clearly, the trip from the foothills to the highlands of computer graphics described in this book is not a one-pager. For the excursion and adventures that lie ahead in Photoshop, with *Inside Adobe Photoshop 4* as your guide, you need to bring along a few mental provisions. Previous experience with Photoshop is not a prerequisite, but you should at least be familiar with a few personal computer concepts.

In this book we presume that you are familiar with your operating system's interface. This includes knowing how to copy, save, and delete files, create directories (*folders*), and back up your work. Being fairly comfortable navigating an extended keyboard and using a mouse helps, too. But you also need to get comfortable with how to follow the steps in this book, and how to execute many of the keyboard actions and mouse or digitizing tablet moves you make in Photoshop.

Okay, I'm Packed. Where Are the Directions?

Most of the examples described in the book are documented in a step-by-step format. If you follow along, your screen should look exactly like this book's figures, except that your screen will be in color. Each chapter leads you through at least one set of numbered steps, with frequent asides explaining why we asked you to do something. The figures show the results of an action, and we explain what the effect should look like.

Most of Photoshop's tools have different, enhanced functions when you hold down the Shift, Alt, or Ctrl keys (Shift, Opt, ⌘ Command keys, for Macintosh users) while you click with the mouse or press other keyboard keys. These commands are shown in the steps as Ctrl(⌘)+click, Alt(Opt)+click, Ctrl(⌘)+D, and so on. *Inside Adobe Photoshop 4* is a bi-platform documentation of the application; Windows key commands are shown first in the steps, followed by the Macintosh key equivalent (enclosed in parentheses). For example, the step for loading the dialog box for the last-used filter in Photoshop looks something like this:

1. Press Ctrl(⌘)+Alt(Opt)+F to load the dialog box for the filter you used in step x.

Translation... you hold down the first key while you press the second and third keys. Then release all three keys to produce the intended result in Photoshop. Function keys appear in this book as F1, F2, F3, and so on.

If the steps in an application that's available in both Windows and Macintosh formats are significantly different, we fully explain the steps used in this book.

The Photoshop interface itself is practically identical on all operating platforms. The only real differences lie in the system "padding"—the screen elements that the Macintosh OS and different versions of MS Windows add to windows, palettes, and menus—and the system font used to display text. In figure I.1, you can see the Windows 95 presentation of Photoshop 4.

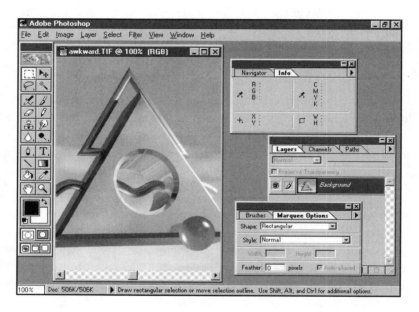

figure I.1
Photoshop 4 running under Windows 95.

Figure I.2 shows the same document you see in figure I.1, but loaded in the PowerPC version of Photoshop 4 for the Macintosh. The 68 KB version of Photoshop is identical in appearance.

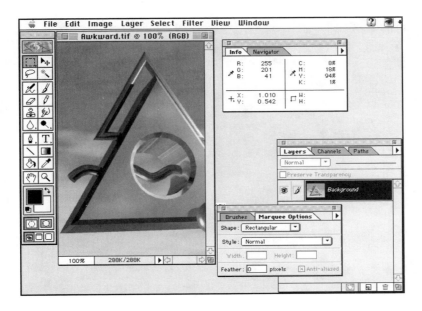

figure I.2
The Photoshop interface running on a Power Macintosh.

If you compare these two figures, you'll note that there is a nominal difference between the two interfaces; there is no difference in the *features* offered in the two versions of Photoshop, however. In figure I.3, you can see the Windows 3.1x layout of Photoshop's interface. Except for the Close Box on the title bar, the menu and palette system text display, and element padding, there is no difference in the appearance of interface features between these versions.

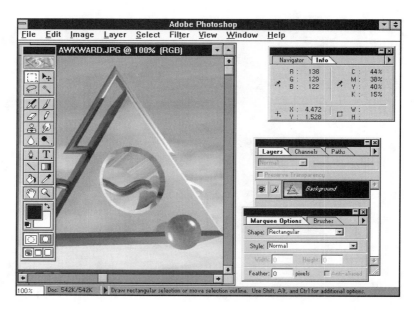

figure I.3
Photoshop 4 running under Windows 3.1x.

With a few exceptions, the screen captures shown in this book were taken in Windows 95; there simply isn't the room in this book to show all the versions of Windows, Unix, and Macintosh interfaces! Again, where there is a significant difference in the way something is accomplished on a specific platform, this book details specific steps to be used.

A Note to Southpaws

This book was written a little chauvinistically, in that we assume you are right-handed. The Macintosh platform uses a single-button mouse, and which hand you use to click makes no difference. Many commands and shortcuts in Photoshop 4 can be accessed in Windows by clicking on the secondary mouse button, however, and the steps in this book's chapter are written on the assumption that this is the right-mouse button. If you are left-handed and have specified reverse ordering of the primary and secondary mouse buttons, the term *right-click* in the chapter steps means *click on the secondary mouse button.* When we say "right-click," Macintosh users should hold Ctrl and click, as written in this book's steps. Every function in the Windows and Macintosh versions of Photoshop is equal, but certain features are not accessed identically.

Terms Used in This Book

The term *drag* in this book means to hold down the primary mouse button and move the on-screen cursor. This action is used in Photoshop to create a marquee selection, and to access tools on the toolbox flyout. On the Macintosh, dragging is also used to access *pull-down menus*; Windows users do not need to hold the primary mouse button to access flyout menus and main menu commands.

Click means to press and release the primary mouse button once.

Double-click means to press quickly the primary mouse button twice. Usually you double-click to perform a function without the need to click on an OK button in a directory window. Additionally, when you double-click on a tool in Photoshop's toolbox, the Options palette appears.

Shift+Click means that you should hold down the Shift key while you click with the primary mouse button.

Conventions Used in This Book

Throughout this book, conventions are used clarify certain keyboard techniques and to help you distinguish certain types of text (new terms and text that you type, for example). These conventions include the following:

Special Text

Information you type is in **boldface**. This rule applies to individual letters, numbers, and text strings, but not to special keys, such as Enter (Return), Tab, Esc, or Ctrl(⌘).

New terms appear in *italic*. Italic text is used also for emphasis, as in "*Don't* unplug your computer at this point."

Text that is displayed on-screen but is not part of the Photoshop application, such as dialog and attention box text, appears in a special monospace typeface.

Our Use of Product Names

Inside Adobe Photoshop 4 would be an even larger book than it already is if every reference to a specific graphics product or manufacturer included the full brand manufacturer, product name, and version number. For this reason, you'll occasionally see Adobe Photoshop 4 referred to as simply "Photoshop" in the text of this book. Similarly, Adobe Illustrator is referred to as "Illustrator," and other products are mentioned by their "street names."

New Riders Publishing and the authors acknowledge that the names mentioned in this book are trademarked or copyrighted by their respective manufacturers; our use of nicknames for various products is in no way meant to infringe on the trademark names for these products. When we refer to an application, it is usually the most current version of the application, unless otherwise noted.

Contents at a Glance

The authors recommend that you use *Inside Adobe Photoshop 4* as a reference guide, but it was also written as a sequential, linear, hands-on tutorial. And this means that you might benefit most from the information in the book by reading a little at a time, from the first chapter to the last. We are aware, however, that this is not the way everyone finds information—particularly in an integrating graphics environment such as Photoshop's, where one piece of information often leads to a seemingly unconnected bit of wisdom. For this reason, most chapters offer complete, self-contained steps for a specific topic or technique, with frequent cross-references to related material in other chapters. If you begin reading Chapter 9, for example, you will learn a complete area of image editing, but you can build on what you've learned if you thoroughly investigate Chapter 2, as well.

Part I: Exploring Features, Old and New

In Chapter 1, "Changing the Way You Work with the New Photoshop," experienced Photoshop users quickly get up to speed with new features and new locations for traditional tools. For those of you who are new to Photoshop, we explore the functions of the tools, and provide working examples of how to accomplish the editing of images by using shortcuts. We recommend ways to display the interface so that the most-used elements are only a click away. Shortcuts are listed for new and current Photoshop users alike.

Chapter 2, "Leveraging Photoshop's New Capabilities," is a hands-on extension of Chapter 1. It's a step-by-step application of the tools discussed in the first chapter, with emphasis on technique and the best way to accomplish a specific assignment. Learn how to define custom, multicolor fills with transparency options with the new Gradient tool, and build a kiosk interface from the ground up, complete with a seamless tiling background and 3D navigation controls.

Part II: Up and Running

Chapter 3, "Personalizing Photoshop: Preferences and Options," provides in-depth documentation on setting up Photoshop's workspace, specifying user preferences, memory allocation—all the things you need to know to keep your work and Photoshop running smoothly. If system memory and resources are not properly allocated and managed, Photoshop can indeed run out of resources; this chapter shows you how to fine-tune Photoshop to make it an optimized graphics tool.

Chapter 4, "Using Paths, Selections, and Layers," explores the power of Photoshop's different selection capabilities. Version 4 makes it easier to accomplish the task of selecting image areas, and the way many common selection tasks are performed has changed between versions 3 and 4. New users and experienced professionals alike will want to check out this chapter to see how layers and the Paths feature can offer quick, flawless image-compositing capabilities.

Part III: Image Retouching

Chapters 5, "Restoring an Heirloom Photograph," and 6, "Retouching an Heirloom Photograph," demonstrate the digital equivalent in Photoshop of the traditional art of image restoration. If you have a family photo, or an image from a client that looks more like a candidate for the "circular file" than for publishing, bring it along—you'll learn how to perform miracles with a damaged photograph.

In Chapter 7, "Combining Photographs," without the assistance of a fork lift you will make a sports car float six feet off the ground. Impossible? Or course! But Photoshop excels at creating photorealistic fantasy images, and making objects appear to fly in an otherwise humdrum image can be your personal career-saver when you need to create an inspired piece from pedestrian stock photos.

Part IV: Advanced Imaging

Chapter 8, "Correcting Images," is where you learn how to create the perfect image, and where we as artists qualify "perfect" as a relative term. Images you might see as perfect can be viewed as something quite different by your audience. In this chapter, we address some workarounds and inspired editing techniques for making an image suit different commercial needs. An image that is "perfect" for printing, for example, will need "correction" if it is to be used as a web graphic. This chapter also covers backgrounds that overwhelm a photograph's foreground content, and how to correct the dimensions of an image to suit different output needs.

Chapter 9, "Working with Adjustment Layers," takes a look at how Photoshop 4's new Adjustment layers can be best used in everyday imaging assignments. See how to extend the capability of Photoshop's Paintbrush tool to not only apply color, but also to apply color and tonal *corrections* to images. It's as easy as painting Contrast or stroking Hue into a photograph. Learn how to leverage the special property of Adjustment layers in Chapter 9.

Chapter 10, "Enhancing Images," shows you how to add photorealistic reflections to your images. You'll learn how to place a sailboat into a scene, and then add reflections in the water that look so authentic that viewers of the image will never suspect the scene was not photographed. Also, you'll see how to perk up a scene by adding a new sky, and how to add text to an image, to complement the existing elements in a composition.

Chapter 11, "Black and White…and Color," documents the different color modes for images. Have a color image that must reproduce well in grayscale? Need to hand-tint a black-and-white photograph? Chapter 11 has the steps you'll want to take to making every image look its best, regardless of its color capability.

Part V: Photoshop Special Effects

Chapter 12, "Working with Text as Graphics," shows you how images for advertisements, product promotions, and any photograph that contains text can be edited to present a fresh graphical idea. See how to use Photoshop's Type tool and an outside vector illustration program to create elegant text that enhances the commercial value of a digital image.

Photoshop 4 ships with more than 100 plug-in filters, over 40 of them new, and geared toward the creative, artistic embellishment of images. Chapter 13, "Creative Plug-Ins," looks at what these filters are good for in your work, and shows you how to use your own creative input, in combination with plug-ins, to accent, enhance, and transform images. Plug-in filters do *not* "do it all." See how your supervision of a filter can lead to the best special effect you can imagine.

Chapter 14, "Special Effects with Ordinary Photographs," presents a challenge few traditional photographers would accept. How do you integrate an image of a man, photographed last week, with an heirloom image of his father, taken 30 years ago? Learn how to travel through time in Chapter 14, and bring emotional content to your work through techniques, extended Photoshop features, and most important, artistic insight.

Chapter 15, "The Artistic Side of Photoshop 4," shows a unique aspect of Photoshop's features—how to create Art for Art's Sake. This chapter features a surrealistic image, "Water Street," that is both visually provoking and defies examination for hints that the busy street *isn't* actually submerged at the bottom of a lake! If you have some stock photography, and want to convey a personal idea, bring your resources along as we "play" in Photoshop 4.

Part VI: Production, Web-Worthy Imaging, and Beyond

Chapter 16, "Outputting Your Input," covers essential steps and procedures for optimizing electronic images for traditional printing. Whether your output is to laser paper or to glossy, four-color magazine stock, you need to know how many pixels your image should contain, what the correct color space is, and how to accurately convert your existing images for the intended output. Do not press Ctrl(⌘)+P without first checking out Chapter 16!

Chapter 17, "Mixed Media and Photoshop," covers the transformation of a cartoon, from its beginnings on a piece of paper to a glorious, color, electronic Photoshop file. Photoshop, in combination with outside hardware and software, can bring traditional artwork into the computer, where special fills, minute corrections to hand-drawn lines, and out-of-this-world textures can happily co-exist. Chapter 17 shows key principles for combining classically taught art techniques with advanced, digital image-editing secrets.

The term "3D" is a buzzword in design circles today, and you might think that you have to learn a modeling and rendering application to participate in the new wave of photorealistic imaging. Not so! Chapter 18, "3D and Photoshop," shows you how Fractal Design Poser, used in combination with Photoshop, can produce stunning, dimensional human figures to add to advertisements, Web pages, or simply to keep you company! Expressing yourself in the third dimension is easier than you think, and Chapter 18 provides you with the step-by-step answers.

Chapter 19, "Web Site Construction," takes you beyond the canvas of a document window, and gets you thinking about how to create the elements of an HTML page for the World Wide Web. You'll need navigation control buttons, background images, and you'll need to convert images into a format suitable for the Web. See how to use Photoshop 4's Actions List to batch-process photographs for the Web or traditional output, and use the example files to learn how to create the graphics for *several* linked Web pages.

In Chapter 20, "Animations and SFX on the Web," you'll learn how to prepare animation sequences in several file formats for use as Web media objects, or for multimedia presentations. Photoshop is the home base for your work, as animated textures for VRML worlds, and animated GIFS are created in step-by-step, comprehensive documentation.

On the CD

Don't you hate reaching the end of a good book, only to find that the authors skimped on the research they put into it?! Everyone who works with a computer has a natural curiosity about where to learn more, where to find the best sources for more tools, and what stuff means when they read it out of context.

This is precisely what the *Inside Adobe Photoshop 4 Companion CD* is all about. On the CD, you will find a number of important resources for your continuing adventures in Photoshop, long after you've poured through the pages in this book:

◆ Resource files for the chapter examples. We recommend that you work through the steps shown in this book, using files (carefully prepared by the authors) that demonstrate specific procedures and effects. The files, located in the EXAMPLES folder on the Companion CD, are platform-independent and can be used on any Macintosh or Windows system with Photoshop 4 installed. Sorry, Photoshop 4 itself is not included on the Companion CD! You need to bring *some* ingredients in the recipe for imaging fame and fortune to the party yourself!

◆ *The Inside Adobe Photoshop 4* OnLine Glossary. This Acrobat PDF file contains color examples, shortcuts, definitions, and other material pertaining to this book, to Photoshop, and to computer graphics in general. We recommend that you install the OnLine Glossary on your system, and then launch Adobe Acrobat Reader 3 when you need a quick explanation of a technique or interface element in your Photoshop work.

◆ *The Argyle Pages*, Volume II, also in Acrobat format, is a hyperlink document from which you can easily access over 100 professional resources for software, hardware, educational institutions, services, and more. If you have an Internet connection open, you can click on any of the links in *The Argyle Pages* and surf to the scores of commercial sites that provide up-to-the-minute information on their offerings.

◆ Textures, fonts in Windows and Macintosh formats, a stupendous collection of cloud and sky images, and more. The authors have produced a fairly extensive collection (in our opinions) of frequently needed resource material for Web pages, traditional publication, and other types of media construction. Check out the documentation and the license agreement in the BOUTONS folder on the Companion CD; these are completely unique, one-of-a-kind, Photoshop-oriented files and programs.

◆ Shareware and utilities provided on the Companion CD are hand-picked items the authors have used and that we recommend. There are certain restrictions on some of the shareware, and please don't confuse "shareware" with "freeware." If you find something on the Companion CD that is useful in your professional work, please read the Read Me file in the folder where you found the utility or file, and register (pay a small fee) to the creator of the program.

Folks Just Like You

Although Chapter 3 is intended to help you sort out any system configuration problems, we think it only fair to tell you what systems *the authors* used to prepare this book and the CD. Nothing out of the ordinary—we used Photoshop 4, a few outside applications, and systems configured to what we believe are middle-of-the-road specifications. For the photographic images, we used available lighting most of the time, a 35mm SLR camera, and family and friends as patient subjects. We believe that business professionals will see where these examples can lead in their own work, and that novices won't be intimidated by a super-polished compendium of imaging work. The systems include an Intel 486 DX50 with 32 MB of RAM; Pentium 166 mHz machines with 128 MB of RAM, running Windows 3.1x and Windows 95; and a PowerMacintosh 8500 with 48 MB of system RAM, running System 7.5.3. All machines have 200–500 MB of empty hard disk space on hard disks of different sizes.

Electronic imaging is such a wonderful, enchanting thing that it's impossible to keep the child in us quiet. For that reason, many of the examples in this book are a little whimsical—they stretch reality a tad, in the same way you'll learn to stretch a pixel or two, using Photoshop. We want to show you some of the fun we've had with a very serious product, and hope that perhaps we will kindle or fan the flame of the creative spark in you, as well.

Wanna get started now?

PART

I

EXPLORING FEATURES, OLD AND NEW

CHANGING THE WAY YOU WORK WITH THE NEW PHOTOSHOP

This is not "The Beginner's Chapter!" Often, people skip the first chapter in a book, believing that it contains an overview of an application, or that the author thinks creating a selection of a circle is a worthwhile place to begin a book.

But there is nothing "simple" about Photoshop; in fact, Adobe Systems worked quite hard to put advanced commands and features in easy reach—so that all of us could get on with the more complicated stuff. If you're new to Photoshop, we will get you up and running in this chapter with the directions for advanced image editing. And if you're proficient with Photoshop 3.0.5, this chapter is especially useful as a guide to the new commands and features. At least 70 percent of the methods you have used in the past *have changed* in version 4—from moving selections to different layers to how selections are no longer what they appear to be— even toolbox locations for your favorite tools have moved.

There are three things to remember in Photoshop 4 that will make your work go faster, with fewer unexpected mishaps:

◆   There are at least two ways, sometimes three, to do almost anything in Photoshop, from picking a tool to a command. We show several different methods for editing in this book. The technique you choose should be the one that makes the most sense with the way you presently work.

◆   Photoshop 4 is object-driven. This means that you can perform many commands by dragging one interface element on top of another interface element. Almost everything you can access from the main menu can be accessed more quickly by using icons, accessing the Context menu, and generally confining your cursor to a smaller work area. Ergonomically, Photoshop's new interface significantly reduces repetitive motions and "long reaches" for menu and palette items. The trick is to learn where all the useful interface objects are located. Throughout this book we stress the quickest way to accomplish a task in Photoshop, with emphasis on the most common tasks in this chapter.

◆   A selection marquee and the image area it surrounds are *not* equivalent. There is indeed something in Photoshop we call an "empty selection"; a marquee without image contents. Chapter 4, "Using Paths, Selections, and Layers," contains extensive documentation on working with selections, and we discuss this somewhat in this chapter. Selection capabilities are the true strength of Photoshop as an image editor. If you become proficient in creating, saving, and manipulating selections, you are well on your way to mastering Photoshop.

Most of all, don't be intimidated by new terms, concepts, or procedures. This book focuses on goals and techniques, and not simply on the names and locations of tools. Now it's time to see where the new features are located, and for you to get comfortable with some of the procedures you will use in the chapters to follow.

Accessing the Tools

Photoshop's toolbox is one of the three most-used workspace locations, and version 4 brings with it a reorganization of tools by function. The toolbox not only contains editing and painting tools, but also determines how an image—and to a limited extent, the workspace—is displayed. Figure 1.1 shows the Windows and Macintosh versions of Photoshop's toolbox; only the "padding" that the operating system adds to the toolbox, document window, and palette borders is different between operating platforms.

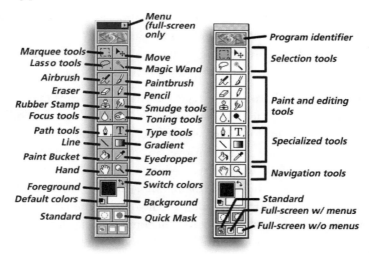

figure 1.1
The tools in Photoshop's toolbox are organized according to function.

The Selection Group of Tools

The uppermost area on the toolbox contains selection tools. The Marquee, Magic Wand, and Lasso tools are used to create a selection in an image, but the selection marquee only defines an area (the image content is only highlighted). To move, copy, or cut the image area encompassed by a marquee, you must perform an additional operation. Also, the Crop tool is now located on the Marquee tool flyout, and Single Row and Single Column, formerly options on the Options palette, are now full-fledged tools.

To copy or cut an image area, you can choose the familiar keystroke combinations, Ctrl(⌘)+C and Ctrl(⌘)+X, respectively. Alternatively, you can choose these commands from the Edit menu. To access them when your cursor is within a marquee, right-click to access the Context menu. The Macintosh currently does not support a right mouse button; to display the context menu in Photoshop for the Macintosh, you hold Ctrl and click.

To move a selected image area in Photoshop, you must either switch from the selection tool to the Move tool, or hold Ctrl(⌘). With the exception of the Hand tool and the Pen tools, holding Ctrl(⌘) toggles the current tool to the Move tool; release the Ctrl(⌘) key and the cursor reverts to the last-used tool.

All toolbox tools have a single keystroke shortcut to select them. For the most part, the mnemonic for a tool is straightforward: *T* is for Type, *L* is for Lasso, and so on. Using shortcuts for tools can be an invaluable technique when the toolbox cannot be seen on-screen. Palettes can overlap the toolbox, and pressing Tab clears all interface elements from the screen—but you can still work with tools in this mode, if you know how to shortcut to them. *Inside Adobe Photoshop 4*'s hands-on examples frequently list a shortcut to a tool, and if you run through the steps we outline, the task of memorizing shortcut keys will come to you subliminally! Check Adobe's documentation for a complete list of the toolbox shortcuts.

Photoshop's Painting and Editing Tools

Located beneath the selection tools are Photoshop's paint application and editing tools. In actuality, the Type tool, the Line tool, the Paint Bucket, and the Gradient tool should be included in this area; these are "specialty" tools, however—ones that apply paint, but require dragging or clicking the cursor instead of stroking.

The most common tool for painting in Photoshop is the Paintbrush tool, followed by the Airbrush tool for design situations in which you do not want a visible brush stroke in your work. The Pencil tool, unlike other Photoshop tools, leaves a hard, aliased edge, and you cannot change this option. The Pencil tool is good for creating hard-edged borders (good for interface design), but it is not the tool of choice for photographic image retouching.

The Rubber Stamp tool does not use colors, but instead depends upon a sampling point in an image, which duplicates image areas wherever you stroke with the tool. This sampling point can move as you move the Rubber Stamp tool (the aligned Option), or the sampling point will reset itself to the original point you specify with every new brush stroke (nonaligned Option). Additionally, the point at which you sample with the Rubber Stamp tool can be taken from a different image window; it can be stored in memory (From Saved or From Snapshot options). The From Snapshot option requires that you choose Edit, Take Snapshot with the current image before you choose this option.

The Focus tools, Toning tools, and Smudge tools do not apply paint. Instead, they modify (edit) existing image areas. You can access tool groups on the toolbox in any of the following three ways:

◆ Press the shortcut key for a tool more than once. For example, pressing **O** several times will choose the Toning tools group, cycling through the Dodge, Burn, and Sponge tools.

◆ Drag on the face of the tool in a group. Tool groups are indicated on the toolbox with a triangle in the corner. Dragging displays a flyout, and you release the cursor on the tool in the flyout you seek.

◆ Choose a specific tool in a group from the Options palette's tool drop-down list.

TIP

The Options palette is displayed in the workspace when you double-click on any tool. The Options palette is context-sensitive; it offers extended features relating to the tool you choose.

The Options palette can also be displayed by choosing Window, Show Options.

The Specialized Tools

Do not assume that tools at the top of the toolbox are used more often than those in the middle or at the bottom. The specialized tools area offers text, vector paths, and a redesigned Gradient tool that can create multicolor blends.

The Type tool is now a group in Photoshop 4. By default, text is applied automatically to a new layer in the active document; text cannot be accidentally deselected as a floating selection in version 4. Users of earlier versions should also be aware that, by default, the Preserve Transparency option is enabled for new text layers—before you apply an effect to text, uncheck this option on the Layers palette. The Type Mask tool is the alternate text tool; it creates a marquee selection above the current image (or image layer) in a document. You can reposition the marquee and then apply color, paste into the marquee from a clipboard copy of an image, or apply the Layer Mask feature (discussed in this chapter) to automatically remove image areas on layers that lie outside the text marquee.

The drawing tools for path creation have been moved off the Paths palette in version 4; all five path tools are now located on the Pen tool flyout. Path operations—saving paths, stroking paths, and so on— are still accomplished by using the Paths palette, however.

The Eyedropper tool is perhaps the least-used tool on the toolbox; all tools that apply color toggle to the Eyedropper when you hold Alt(Opt). Because sampling image colors is not an extensive, work-related function, you will do well to remember Alt(Opt)=Eyedropper when painting.

The Gradient tool has undergone a dramatic improvement over earlier versions. Although Photoshop's Gradient tool does not replace Kai's Power Tools' Gradient Designer, the Gradient tool now supports multicolor fills in Linear and Radial types, it supports transparency, and you can save collections of custom Gradient patterns to a file that can be shared with other users. The Gradient Editor can be displayed by clicking on the Edit button on the Options palette when the Gradient tool is the current tool in Photoshop.

The Navigation Tools

The Hand and Zoom tools are useful for quickly viewing a specific image area; however, they can be *accessed* more quickly through keyboard toggles than from the toolbox.

The spacebar is the toggle key for the Hand tool, and a combination of keyboard shortcuts exist for toggling to the Zoom tool.

Ctrl(⌘)+spacebar toggles to the Zoom tool from every current tool, and Ctrl(⌘)+Alt(Opt)+spacebar toggles to the Zoom out tool. Unlike previous versions of Photoshop, zoom controls are offered in stepless increments; marquee dragging with the Zoom tool zooms you to any viewing resolution from 1600 percent down to .19 percent—all resolutions to two decimal places between these amounts can be defined.

Clicking, instead of marqueeing in a document, zooms you into the image in steps. Below 100 percent (1:1 viewing resolution), you zoom in at 33-percent increments; with zoom resolutions greater than 100 percent, clicking increases the viewing resolution by additional 100 percents (for example: 200%, 300%, 400%). Holding Alt(Opt) while you click with the Zoom tool decreases viewing resolution; there are no separate zoom in and zoom out tools.

Color Controls

If you're familiar with an image editing program other than Photoshop, there are no real surprises with the color control area of the toolbox. The current Foreground color overlaps the Background color selection box. Click on either area to display the color picker, where you can define colors in different color modes and spaces. Above and to the right of the Foreground/Background colors is the Switch colors icon, which switches the current foreground and background colors when you click on it. To the left and bottom of the color selection boxes is the Default colors icon. This icon sets the current foreground color to black and the background to white. Both icons have keyboard shortcuts: D sets the colors to default, and X switches current foreground/background colors.

It is worth noting that the background color applies to nonlayered images and the Background layer of a Photoshop PSD document. When you use the Eraser tool or delete a selection, the area in the image changes to the current background color *unless* you are working on an image layer. Image layers do not have a background; when you erase the contents of a layer, you usually wind up with transparent areas. Only if the Preserve Transparency option (on the Layers palette) is checked for a layer, will erasures or deleted areas change to the current background color.

TIP

To instantly convert a Background layer to a Photoshop layer, choose the Move tool, and then press a keyboard arrow key. You can also drag in the document window to convert the Background to a Photoshop layer.

We do not recommend this technique, because you necessarily move the image within the document window. The image can be moved back to its original position by first pressing an arrow key, and then pressing the opposing arrow key an equal number of times. Layer images must be saved in Photoshop's native PSD format.

Quick Mask and Standard Viewing Modes

Below the color controls on the toolbox are icons that represent the editing state of the current image. By default, every image you open is in Standard editing mode. When Standard editing mode is active, selections can be made to an image and paint can be applied. In Quick Mask mode, none of the image is selected; applying paint results in a tinted overlay on top of the image. This is a Quick Mask—an on-screen indicator of image areas that will be surrounded by a selection marquee when you click on the Standard editing mode icon. All selection tools and painting tools can create the Quick Mask overlay in an image. With selection tools, you must fill the selection marquee with foreground color, and then deselect the marquee to define an area you want selected in Standard editing mode.

Quick Masks can be saved to an image channel, but if you switch to Standard editing mode and then deselect the resulting marquee, the Quick Mask selection information is gone forever.

NOTE

Do not evaluate the extent of a selection based upon a marquee selection, when it was created using percentages of black in Quick Mask mode. The authors calculate that areas brighter than 60% (with 100% representing white) are not included in a marquee selection on-screen.

Screen View Controls

The screen controls in Photoshop operate a little differently in Windows than those on the Macintosh because the Macintosh OS requires an application to show the desktop, whereas Windows allows applications to display a workspace, hiding the desktop.

Standard screen mode is the icon at the bottom left of the toolbox, and is the default application state when you open Photoshop. If you want to remove the application title in Windows and maximize the current image window to full screen, use the Full Screen with menu icon to the right of the Standard icon. On the Macintosh, the Full Screen with menu button maximizes the image window, but this also hides the desktop. The advantage to working in Full Screen with menus is that your workspace is maximized; the disadvantage is that you can no longer work between multiple image windows.

You activate Full Screen without menus mode by clicking on the far right button on the toolbox. This is an excellent presentation mode when clients drop by. In Full Screen without menus, palettes and the toolbox are still displayed, but the menu at the top of the interface is gone, and single images can be displayed, framed against a black background (which makes the colors in the image appear more intense). Press Tab in any of the screen modes to remove palettes and the toolbox from the screen, creating a completely uncluttered showcase for your work. You can select tools by using shortcut keys after you press Tab, and palettes can be selectively called by shortcut keys, as well. Pressing Tab a second time restores the toolbox, and from there, you can switch back to other screen modes.

There's one icon on the toolbox we have yet to explore: the program identifier icon.

The Program Identifier Icon

Because Adobe products are available worldwide, and because the fastest worldwide distribution avenue at present is the Web, for users who have access, Adobe decided to create a link in Photoshop to Adobe's home page. The official story is that future versions of Adobe products will look more and more alike, and the program identifier icon at the top of the toolbox is a visual reference for users as to which Adobe application they are working in.

But the real purpose of the program identifier icon, as far as users are concerned, is that you click on it to display Adobe's splash screen, with an unmarked Adobe logo in the upper left (see fig. 1.2); clicking on the logo launches the Web browser you have designated for your system.

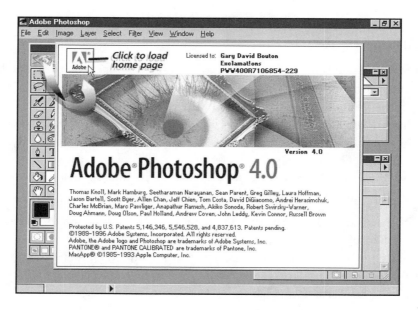

figure 1.2
If you want to get on the World Wide Web and check out Adobe's site, click on the
program identifier icon.

The Web browser does *not* automatically establish a link to the Internet or take you to Adobe's site, however. This sort of dynamic control over your communications connections might not be welcome, especially if your system resources were tied up working on a large image file!

The Photoshop link to Adobe's site is intended to provide users with up-to-the-minute product information, downloads of future patches and updates, and to serve as a general dissemination point for tricks and techniques. The page that loads in your Web browser is merely a local HTML document (PshpLink.htm, in the folder in which you installed Photoshop). When you click on any of the URLs listed on the page, your computer will make a connection to the Web, and you will be off to any of the areas you chose. Figure 1.3 shows the Adobe site as this book was being written; a click on Home on the local Photoshop document established a link to Adobe's top page at their site.

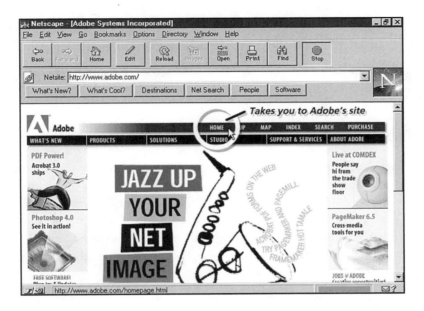

figure 1.3
Click on an URL or anywhere on the menu in the PshpLink.htm document to launch a
connection to Adobe's site.

When you're working with the toolbox you cannot accidentally request an Internet connection, but it can be annoying to see the splash screen pop up when you *intended* to click on the Move tool! The only real peril to this new Web connection on the toolbox is forgetting to close the connection after you go to Adobe's site. If you access information, remember to close the link outside Photoshop when you finish.

Document Information Is a Click Away

If you have ever ground your system to a halt while working on a 25 MB image, and wished Photoshop had flagged you that your resources were low prior to the event, the Document Info pop-up in Photoshop 4 is the answer to your problems. To the right of the Zoom percentage field (on the status line in Windows, and on the horizontal scroll bar of an image window on the Macintosh) is an arrow; when you click on it, it provides four different settings for image sizes and memory (Document Sizes, Scratch Sizes, Efficiency, Timing) that continuously display and update.

The following sections take a look at Document Info and how to choose the best setting for your work.

Document Sizes

When you click on the document Info triangle and choose Document Sizes from the pop-up list, the current document size is displayed to the right of the Zoom percentage field as a fractional amount. The left side of the fraction tells you the size of the current document as it would be spooled to a printer. This number is often less than the amount at the right (the file as held in memory) because a printed file cannot contain layer or alpha channel information, both of which contribute heavily to saved file sizes.

The fractional amount at right is not the current image size as saved to file; this amount indicates how much hard disk space and RAM is being used at the moment for working with the image. If this amount seems too large, or it looks as though you might be running out of resources, choose File, Save, and Photoshop will release some of the system resources it is holding to store multiple versions of the current file for Undo and Restore commands. Check out Chapter 3, "Personalizing Photoshop: Preferences and Options," for detailed information on system requirements, fine-tuning Photoshop's memory allocation, and setting up a scratch disk that Photoshop uses to store files while you work.

Scratch Sizes

If you haven't specified Scratch Disk and Memory and Image Handling in Photoshop 4, right now is a good time to press Ctrl(⌘)+K and do so. By default, Photoshop uses your startup disk for the scratch disk, and you might not have sufficient space on this drive for the files Photoshop writes in an editing session. Additionally, Adobe's documentation warns Windows users *not* to use the boot drive, usually the drive that contains the Windows operating system, as the drive for the scratch disk location.

The Scratch Sizes setting for Document Info tells you, as a fractional expression, how much scratch disk is being used versus how much you have defined for

Photoshop to use. When the number on the left approaches the number on the right, it is time to save your work and quit Photoshop. After that, it is time to specify a larger scratch disk on your system, and to read Chapter 3 for strategies for optimizing your system to work better with Photoshop.

Efficiency

Photoshop can measure how often it needs to swap segments of a file in and out of RAM while you work. When you do not have enough available RAM, Photoshop writes to file on your hard disk. Basically, the less often Photoshop needs to write to media whose access time is measured in milliseconds, compared to the nanoseconds by which we measure RAM, the faster you will work. In figure 1.4, you can see the Document Sizes and Efficiency fields as displayed in Photoshop. The figure shows that Photoshop is at 100% Efficiency when working with a 2 MB image. The PowerMacintosh we used to take the screen shot used in this figure has 48 MB of system RAM, with 25 MB assigned to application RAM for Photoshop. This not only more or less requires that Photoshop should run alone without other applications running in the background, but it also means that Photoshop has enough environment space in memory not to write to disk.

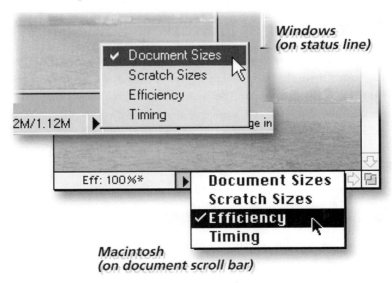

figure 1.4
Photoshop's Document Info feature lets you see at a glance how well it is handling memory and file sizes.

Timing

The Timing setting for Document Info is bound to appeal to trade paper writers and magazines, but it might be of little use to you in everyday work. Timing reports how long a specific action takes—for example, if you apply the Gaussian Blur to a 10 MB image, the timing field shows how long the process took.

TIP

To reset the timer in the Timing display, hold Alt(Opt), place the cursor over the triangle at the bottom of the status line (Macintosh: at the bottom of the document window), hold down the mouse button, and then choose Timing from the document Info menu drop-down list.

Of all the settings for the Document Info field, the authors recommend the default, Document Sizes, as providing the most useful information in your daily work. Document Sizes tells you how much RAM and hard disk space the current image requires, and if you know how much memory you have dedicated to Photoshop, you will always have a clear idea of how far you can take your editing without fear of a system halt.

A Taxi Driver's Tour of Photoshop Editing

Although *Inside Adobe Photoshop 4* contains a wealth of real-world examples, we felt that Chapter 1 would be a good place to start one's education, and re-education, as to how selections and working between document windows are accomplished. The tasks we have chosen could be performed in Photoshop 3.0.5, but with far more steps and possible mistakes. The following sections walk you through some fairly sophisticated image editing techniques, to show you how new key commands and Photoshop's object-oriented workspace work together.

The Mark's Cookies Assignment

Selecting, then copying, and finally masking are the progressive steps that Photoshop users typically make in image composition work. We have taken the most time-intensive step out of the process in this section—that of selecting a foreground object from its background—to better focus on how selections, layers, and masking are integrated in Photoshop 4. There are many examples in Chapter 4 of how to create selections and refine them.

A fictitious client, Mark, comes to you with a need for a package design. He wants an image of cookies to appear on his packages (a natural enough request). And he wants to look over your shoulder while you work to advise you on the appearance and placement of the cookies (a common—and irritating—request).

CD-ROM On the Companion CD are two image files, Marks.tif and Cookies.psd, in the Photoshop PSD file format. The cookies in the Cookies file are on two separate image layers, each layer labeled for convenient reference. Although keeping image elements on separate layers provides you with editing flexibility, you now need to copy the separate elements and position them. In the following steps, you will see how quickly this can be accomplished in Photoshop 4. You will also pick up some insights on how to do advanced editing, using a combination of tools and interface objects.

TRANSPLANTING COOKIES

1. Open the Marks.tif image from the CHAP01 folder on the Companion CD. Then press Ctrl(⌘)++ or – until the title bar tells you that the document viewing resolution is 50%. The Ctrl(⌘)++/– keyboard shortcuts are yet a third method for quickly adjusting your view of an image.

2. Drag the document borders away from the image so that you can see the document without scroll bars.

3. Open the Cookies.psd document from the CHAP01 folder; double-click on the Hand tool to zoom the viewing resolution of the document to fit to screen without scroll bars. Position the Cookies window to the left of the Marks image window, without overlapping the windows.

4. Press F7 to display the Layers/Channels/Paths grouped palette. Because the Cookies image is in the foreground in the workspace, the Layers palette displays the contents of this image window. Cookie 1 and Cookie 2 are the layers contained in the image, and the Cookie 1 layer is the current editing layer in the document. Only one layer can be active at a time in a document, and only the Photoshop PSD file format can contain layers.

5. Click on the icon space directly to the left of the layer thumbnail image on the Cookie 2 title, on the Layers palette. The space now displays a chain link icon, which means that it is linked to the underlying layer. This space on each layer title displays the properties of the layer in the image. Note that the Cookie 1 layer has a paintbrush icon in the property space; this represents the current editing layer.

6. Press **V** (Move tool), place the cursor in the Cookies.psd window, and then drag from the cookies window into the Marks.tif window (see fig. 1.5). Because the layers are linked in the Cookies image, both cookies are copied to the Marks.tif image, and their names and layer order are preserved through copying.

figure 1.5
Linking image layers allows the contents of the layers to be moved simultaneously.

Our client Mark is amazed at this feat, and starts thinking that there is no end to the miracles you can perform in Photoshop (not realizing that you're only reading Chapter 1 here). He asks whether you can add a drop shadow to the cookies. The cookies are on separate layers in the Marks.tif image, but creating a drop shadow for both cookies can be accomplished in a single step by using Photoshop's feature for adding to selections.

7. Close the Cookies.psd file without saving. Click on the link icon on the Cookie 2 title. The two cookies can be repositioned independently of one another, if you want to contribute some of your own creative flair to this assignment. When you finish, click on the Cookie 1 title on the Layers palette to make this layer the current editing layer.

8. Press Ctrl(⌘) and click on the Cookie 1 layer title. This loads the nontransparent areas of the layer as a marquee selection.

9. Press Ctrl(⌘)+Shift and click on the Cookies 2 layer title (see fig. 1.6). Note that the hand cursor features a plus sign. When clicking over a layer title, Ctrl loads a selection

marquee, holding Shift adds to the current marquee, and holding Alt(Opt) subtracts from the current selection. The outline of both cookies is now described by a marquee selection.

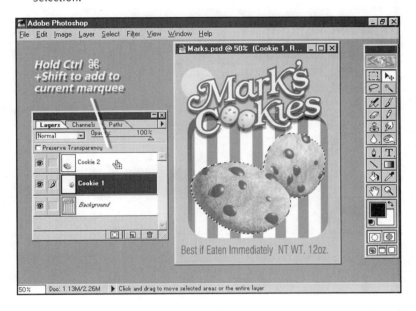

figure 1.6

Photoshop 4 displays over 100 cursors, each one an indication of the task you are performing.

10. Click on the Background layer title on the Layers palette to make it the current editing layer. Click on the Create new layer icon (the page with the folded corner) at the bottom of the palette. This creates a new layer in the document, automatically numbered as Layer 1, directly above the layer that was previously the current editing layer.

11. Press **D** (Default colors) and then press Alt(Opt)+Delete (Backspace) to fill the selection marquee with foreground color. Press Ctrl($\mathcal{H}$)+D to deselect the marquee now.

12. Drag in the document window downward and to the right, until you can see the black shape the cookies are hiding. You're repositioning the nontransparent contents of Layer 1.

13. Drag the Opacity slider on the Layers palette to about 50% (see fig. 1.7). This decreases the opacity of the black on Layer 1, and allows the Background of the image to show through.

figure 1.7
Every layer in an image can have an opacity assigned to it.

14. Choose File, Save As, and save your work to your hard disk as Marks.psd, in the Photoshop file format. Keep the image open; our client is contemplating more revisions to the work.

Photoshop's cursors are always a good visual hint as to the action that's about to be performed. Become familiar with what the cursors represent, and you will work more quickly in the program.

Client Mark is getting to like this program as much as you do. He now asks whether you can make one of the cookies look partially eaten. In the following section, this assignment (a thinly disguised excuse to demonstrate new Photoshop features) shows how to create masks by using the Layers Palette in combination with marquee selections.

TIP

You might never need to access the selection mode that creates an intersection between marquees, but you can do so by holding Alt(Opt) and Shift with a selection tool and an active marquee.

For example, by dragging with the Elliptical Marquee tool to intersect an existing elliptical marquee selection while you hold Alt(Opt)+Shift, you create a marquee shaped like the side view of a clam shell.

Creating and Moving Complex Selections

As mentioned earlier, selection marquees *describe* an underlying image area; there is the *potential* for creating change based upon a marquee, but nothing happens to the image until you apply changes in the marquee. You can create a half-eaten cookie in the Marks.psd image by adding selection marquees together, and then masking the area the marquee is located over. In the following set of steps, the entire image window is available for creating a complex selection that will be used to hide part of the Cookie 2 layer. You can work anywhere as you create the selection, because selection marquees can be moved without altering the image. Only the Move tool creates changes to a layer's contents.

Here's how to use the Elliptical Marquee tool with the keyboard extender features you used in the previous example to create a selection that masks part of the cookie:

CREATING A SELECTION FOR MASKING

1. Press **M** several times until the Elliptical Marquee tool appears on the toolbox.

2. Double-click on the Zoom tool to change your viewing resolution of the Marks.psd image to 100%. Drag the image window borders away from the image until the image window is maximized. Windows users can click on the Maximize/Restore button on the title bar to maximize the window.

3. Drag an ellipse in the image a little larger than one of the chocolate chips in the image. Then, holding Shift, drag a second ellipse that intersects the first. The result is a marquee that resembles a view through binoculars.

4. Drag a third, and then a fourth marquee, overlapping the ellipses and creating an overall arc shape, until you have a selection that looks like the one in figure 1.8. Precision design is not important here; in fact, the more the selection describes a caricature of a row of teeth, the more clearly the cookie will represent a half-eaten cookie when the marquee is turned into a mask.

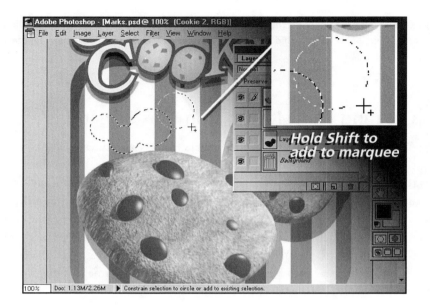

figure 1.8
Add to the previous ellipse marquee by holding Shift as you drag.

5. Drag within the marquee selection until it is positioned on the cookie (see fig 1.9). Users experienced with version 3 and earlier should not fret about moving the underlying image; selection marquees are nondestructive in version 4.

6. Press **L** (Lasso tool); then, while holding Shift, drag around the top of the cookie to add the top portion of the cookie to the selection.

7. Click on the Cookie 2 layer title on the Layers palette to make this the current editing layer.

8. Press Ctrl(⌘)+Shift+I to reverse the selection marquee so that everything except the area over the cookie is selected. Layer masks allow only those areas encompassed by a marquee to "peek through" the selection; everything else is hidden.

9. Click on the Create Layer Mask icon (see fig. 1.10). The image area on the Cookie 2 layer inside the selection marquee is now hidden, and the selection marquee lines are no longer visible.

10. Press Ctrl(⌘)+S to save your work.

figure 1.9
Move a marquee, but not the image contents, by dragging inside the selection.

figure 1.10
The Layer Mask feature hides image areas inside marquee selections.

The Layers palette displays a handy visual device for telling at a glance which image areas are masked. The icon to the right of the layer thumbnail image (refer to fig. 1.10) displays black where image areas are hidden, and white where image areas remain visible.

Mark, a perceptive fellow, notices that a half-eaten cookie in the design that has a drop shadow of an *entire* cookie, looks wrong.

This is an oversight, but not a problem as long as a Layer Mask already exists in the image. In the following section, you copy the mask information and apply it to the drop-shadow layer.

Layer Mask Transparency Information

The monochrome Layer Mask thumbnail on the Layers palette is a visual metaphor used to indicate which parts of the layer are visible, and which are transparent. Because this mask defines a geometric area within the layer, it can be used to create a selection marquee of an identical shape.

Here's how to load the areas not masked on the Cookie 2 layer, to define a selection area to be masked on the drop-shadow layer (Layer 1):

COPYING LAYER MASK INFORMATION

1. Right-click (Macintosh: hold Ctrl and click) on the Cookie 2 Layer Mask thumbnail image, and then choose Select Layer Transparency from the Context menu (see fig 1.11). This loads the visible areas (the areas displayed as white on the thumbnail) as a marquee selection.

2. Click on the Layer 1 title to make Layer 1 the current editing layer in Marks.psd.

3. Click on the Create Layer Mask icon at the bottom of the Layers palette. The cookie drop shadow disappears in the area where it's masked on the Cookie 2 layer. This is not entirely correct lighting; the drop shadow should cast slightly to the right of where it's eaten.

4. Click on the link icon between the image thumbnail and the Layer Mask thumbnail on the Layer 1 title (see fig. 1.12). Usually, you will want a Layer Mask to hide areas that directly correspond to the image. The Layer Mask is a Photoshop object, however, and it can be moved anywhere on the layer to hide areas other than the one where it was created. The link icon is on, by default, every time you create a Layer Mask.

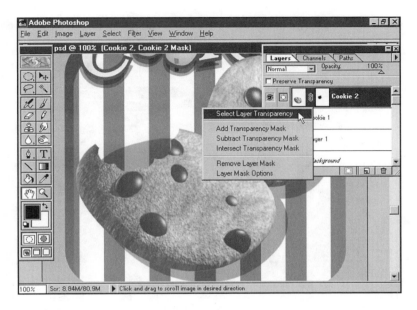

figure 1.11
Load the layer areas that are visible in Layer Mask mode as a selection marquee.

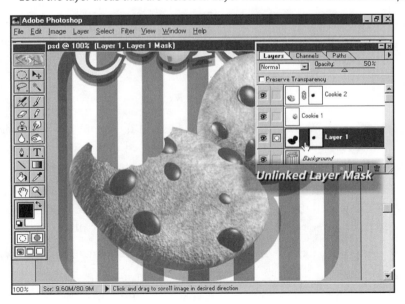

figure 1.12
A Layer Mask can be unlinked from its parent layer and repositioned anywhere on the layer.

5. With the Move tool, drag to the right in the image until you see the drop shadow peeking through the masked area on the Cookie 2 layer (see fig. 1.13).

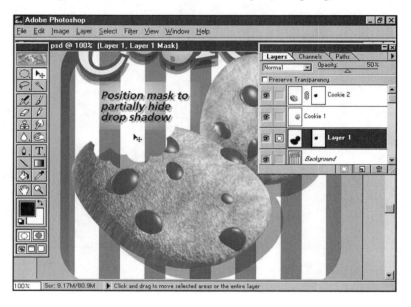

figure 1.13

The Move tool is the only toolbox tool that can move images within selections, nontransparent layer contents, and Layer Masks.

6. Press Ctrl(⌘)+S to save your work.

The changes you have made to the Marks.psd image are not permanent ones. A Layer Mask is actually a *preview* state for image editing; you can decide at any time to discard the Layer Mask and return the image to its original state.

Let's stretch reality here and pretend that your client is completely happy with the design now, and that he wants to run the design off to the commercial printer. You need to do three things before you hand Mark a floppy disk:

◆ Apply the Layer Masks and make the edits permanent to the image.

◆ Flatten the image to a single Background layer so that it can be saved in a bitmap format that others can view and print. Photoshop's PSD format is a proprietary one.

◆ Ask for a check from a bank that's within walking distance.

Here's how to do the first two things:

STANDARDIZING PHOTOSHOP IMAGING WORK

1. Click on the thumbnail icon for the Layer Mask on the Cookie 2 layer; then choose Layer, Remove Layer Mask from the main menu. An attention box appears, where you can click on Apply, Discard, or Cancel (to cancel the operation).

2. Click on Apply. The Layer Mask thumbnail disappears from the Layers title for Cookie 2. Everything that was hidden on this layer has been deleted.

3. Perform steps 1 and 2 with the Layer 1 (the drop shadow) layer.

4. Choose Layer, Flatten Image from the main menu. Then press Ctrl(⌘)+Shift+S (File, Save As), and save the file in TIFF format to hard disk as Marks.tif. You can close the image at any time now.

In your own work, the Save A Copy command on the File menu is useful when you want to continue editing an image with layers. Save A Copy writes a copy of the image to hard disk (not the workspace), and you have the options of deleting alpha channels, flattening the image, and saving to file formats that support the color capability and other properties of the image.

In addition to changing marquee selections into masked layer areas, you can also hide layer areas by using Photoshop's paint tools in Layer Mask mode. (For more information on working with layers, see Chapter 4.)

TIP

You can apply shades of black to a Layer Mask to partially hide image areas. For example, applying 50% black in Layer Mask mode makes the underlying image area half-transparent. Don't confine your editing work to the use of black and white only!

Palette Organization

The palettes have been reorganized in this new version of Photoshop. Also, some new palettes have been added and the Scratch palette—where you used to mix colors and save samples—is gone. Chapter 11, "Black and White…and Color," shows you how to work with the Swatches palette to save colors, and Chapters 2 and 5

("Leveraging Photoshop's New Capabilities" and "Restoring an Heirloom Photograph," respectively) discuss the new Navigator/Actions palette.

With the abundance of palettes, you may find Photoshop's workspace a little cramped when you're working on a document; an 800 by 600 video resolution is recommended if your system has the video drivers to support higher resolutions. But even increasing the screen size will not help you work more quickly unless you organize the palettes to accommodate the way you work. The following section guides you through the customization of Photoshop's palette arrangements.

Examining the Most-Used Palettes

The figures in this book do *not* represent Photoshop's default configuration for palette display. *Inside Adobe Photoshop 4* is a collection of real world, working examples, and the authors took the time to customize Photoshop to reflect our own work styles.

A logical question when you begin working with Photoshop is, "What can stay and what can go in the workspace?" As mentioned earlier, you can remove some, or all, interface elements in Photoshop by choosing a screen mode from the toolbox and pressing Tab to hide the palettes. This is a legitimate solution, but not a workable one if you're unfamiliar with Photoshop's shortcut keys for accessing tools and displaying palettes. A much better alternative is to limit the number of grouped palettes on-screen at any time, and to arrange these palettes so that they offer the features you use the most.

In version 3.0.5, the Brushes palette and the Options palette were grouped; these palettes are in near-constant use for defining the size of painting tools, and the Options palette is indispensable for extending the features of any specific tool. We recommend reuniting the Brushes and Options palettes and keeping the group on-screen while you work.

The Layers/Channels/Paths palette from version 3.0.5 has an addition in version 4: the Actions list. The Actions list doesn't take up much room in this group, but because we seldom use it for design and editing work, we prefer to separate it from the grouped palette and make it a stand-alone palette. Whether it's in the default group or located on its own, press F9 to display the Actions palette. The Layers/Channels/Paths palette is another palette that's good to have on-screen at all times. Without this palette, you cannot see which image elements are located on layers, nor can you switch to different editing layers.

The authors use Brushes/Options and Layers/Channels/Paths as the two persistent workspace elements, and display other palettes as we need them.

These two changes can be made in about two steps. If you're unhappy with this arrangement, press Ctrl(⌘)+K to display the General Preferences dialog box, click on Reset Palette Locations to Default, and all palettes will return to their original configuration.

Here's how to change the configuration of the palettes to offer the smallest intrusion on the workspace, but offer the most commonly used editing and painting features:

REORGANIZING THE PALETTES

1. Press F5 and double-click on any toolbox tool. This displays the Colors/Swatches/Brushes grouped palette and the Navigator/Info/Options grouped palette. Pressing F6 also displays the Colors/Swatches/Brushes palette, but double-clicking on a tool is easier to remember.

2. Drag the Options tab away from the grouped palette and then drop it in a clear area of the workspace (see fig. 1.14). The palette becomes a stand-alone palette, and the F6 shortcut to display Options no longer works.

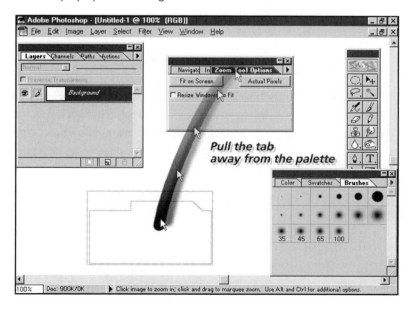

figure 1.14
Drag a palette by the title tab to remove it from its position in a group.

3. Drag the Brushes palette by the tab from the Navigator/Info/Brushes grouped palette, and drop it onto the Options palette to create a new group: Options/Brushes.

4. Press F7 to display the Layers/Channels/Paths/Actions palette; then drag the Actions tab away from the palette and drop it on the workspace. Close the Action palette by clicking on the Close Box on the palette.

Whether you choose to keep the palettes in their default configuration or go with our recommendations, there are shortcuts for displaying all palettes that do not change unless you reassign commands, using the Actions palette (see Chapter 3). Table 1.1 lists the shortcut keys to display palettes; the palettes can also be accessed through the Window main menu command.

Table 1.1

Shortcuts to Palettes

Command	Palette
F5	Brushes
F6	Colors/Swatches
F7	Layers/Channels/Paths
F8	Info/Navigator
F9	Actions
Double-click on a tool	Options

Changing palette contents is only one of the customizations you can perform in Photoshop. Chapter 3 shows you how to control other screen elements, handle memory, and other aspects of Photoshop that can have a direct impact on your productivity.

Good-Bye Commands, Hello Actions Palette

The Commands palette in Photoshop 3.0.5 was a wonderful, customizable feature that offered quick access to the commands you used the most. Adobe Systems replaced the Commands palette with the Actions palette (also known as the Actions List) in version 4. You can assign keyboard shortcuts to the Actions list, but you can also run a script of commands to batch-process images that would otherwise take repetitive, manual intervention to accomplish.

CD-ROM

The Actions list is covered in detail in Chapters 3 and 19 ("Web Site Construction") but the CHAP01 folder on the Companion CD holds a gift from the authors for use with Photoshop 4 (it might remind you of Photoshop 3.0.5's Commands palette). In figure 1.15 you can see the Photoshop 3.0.5 Commands palette and, on the right, the Actions list, loaded with settings from Default3.atn, a file in the CHAP01/ACTIONS folder on the Companion CD. Additionally, we have ported the Design, Favorite, Retouch, Layout, and PrePress commands from the Commands palette to Actions list files.

Photoshop 3.0.5
Commands palette

Inside Photoshop 4
Commands Actions list

figure 1.15
If you want Photoshop 3.0.5's Commands palette in version 4, check out the ACTIONS folder on the Companion CD.

To load any of the command groups into the Actions palette, follow these steps:

LOADING CUSTOM ACTIONS COMMANDS

CD-ROM

1. Press F9 to display the Actions palette if it's not already on-screen.

2. Click on the menu flyout icon (the triangle) on the Actions palette, and choose Replace Actions from the menu. Don't worry—this does not delete the default Actions list; you can choose Reset Actions from the flyout menu at any time to restore the factory settings.

3. In the Load dialog box, choose a path to the CHAP01/ACTIONS folder on the Companion CD. Click on the Default3.atn file, and then click on Open.

4. The Default3 Actions list now appears on the Actions list. To take up less screen space and to display the keyboard shortcuts associated with these commands, click on the menu flyout icon and choose Button Mode from the menu.

We realize that not all the commands on the Actions list might be your own all-time favorites; to create your own Actions list, see Chapter 19.

Further Exploration of New Features

There are so many new features (and different locations for Photoshop's traditional features) that this chapter can hold only the most essential ones. Before moving to Chapter 2 where there are more work-through examples than hints and tips, you will see how Photoshop modes and context-sensitive commands can make everyday image editing an inspired task.

New Filters and the New Fade Option

Photoshop 4 ships with 40 new plug-in filters, re-engineered from Adobe's Gallery Effects, a separate line of products that produce painting and other natural media versions of original digital images or designs. Because the Filters menu can hold only so many third-party plug-ins, Adobe has reorganized the Filters menu to separate native filters from those you purchase and add to Photoshop, and has created submenus for native filters, organized in 14 categories.

If you're familiar with any plug-in filters, you realize that they are separated into two distinct camps. There are those that display a dialog box, where you can customize a filter's settings, and those that automatically execute (there are no options). Regardless of the type of filter you choose for a specific assignment, Photoshop 4 now includes the Fade option (Ctrl(⌘)+Shift+F). After applying a filter, you now have the opportunity to blend the effect with the original image. Adobe has turned the procedure of mixing original pixel colors with filtered pixel colors into High Art. Not only can you specify the percentage of the original/filtered mixture, but you can also specify a mode in which the pixels are combined. In Photoshop, there are three locations where you can specify modes under which images are blended together:

◆ On the Layers palette—Pixels on one layer combine with underlying layers in any of 17 modes. Multiply, Screen, Color Burn, and Color are only a few of the options that produce unique effects. See Chapter 6, "Retouching an Heirloom Photograph," for complete explanations of the different blending modes.

◆ On the Options palette—Whenever you apply color with a painting tool, you can choose how the color is blended with the surface. You can wind up with some wonderfully strange and occasionally redundant blending combinations by painting in a blending mode on a layer that is also in a blending mode.

◆ On the Filters menu.

In the next example, you apply one of the Artistic filters to an image and then apply the Fade command in a blending mode. Let's see how creative flexibility and speed can come together when you use filters.

APPLYING A FILTER IN A BLEND MODE

CD-ROM

1. Open the Bridge.tif image from the CHAP01 folder on the Companion CD.

2. Choose Filter, Artistic, Watercolor (see fig. 1.16). In this figure you can see our collection of third-party plug-ins, neatly organized, alphabetically, below Photoshop's native plug-ins.

   Watercolor is perhaps the most popular of Photoshop's plug-ins; it makes practically every image on earth look soft, eye-pleasing, and compositionally richer.

3. Drag the Brush Detail slider to 14 (maximum fidelity when the filtered image is compared to the original).

4. Drag the Shadow Intensity slider to 0. This option adds contrast to images at areas of color contrast, similar to the way actual watercolors block up when they dry in areas of pigment concentration. This particular image would not benefit visually from Shadow Intensity.

5. Drag the Texture slider to 2. This option adds a mild amount of abstract interpretation to the filtered image—a human touch. Click on OK to apply the filter.

6. Press Ctrl(⌘)+Shift+F to display the Fade dialog box.

7. Choose Overlay from the mode drop-down list, and drag the Opacity slider to about 85% (see fig. 1.17). On this slider, 0% represents the original image, and 100% represents 100-percent application of a specific filter.

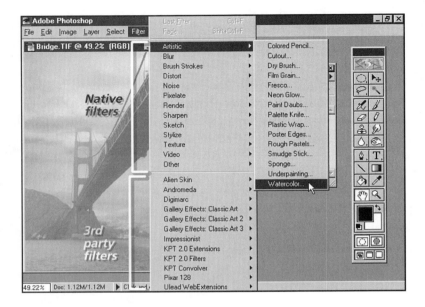

figure 1.16
Photoshop's new plug-in filters are located in submenus at the top of the Filters list.

figure 1.17
Overlay blending mode intensifies the highlights and shadows in an image, screening lighter colors and multiplying darker ones.

8. You might choose to save the file at this point, but the authors will not feel hurt if you close the image without saving.

Modes play an important part in image composition; shadows and special effects are easy to create when you select the appropriate blending mode. See Chapter 13, "Creative Plug-Ins," for the creative use of many other Photoshop plug-in filters.

The Photoshop 3.0.5 Quick Reference Cheat Sheet

It can be very frustrating for experienced Photoshop users to get right down to work in this new version. On one hand, there are fantastic new features, and on the other, the shortcuts you learned in the past don't always work!

The authors compiled the brief list shown in table 1.2 as an equivalency table between version 3.0.5 shortcuts and version 4. If you're new to Photoshop, read on anyway; the less frequently you visit the main menu, the more time you can save.

Table 1.2

Photoshop 3.0.5 Shortcuts in Photoshop 4

Feature	Photoshop 3 Shortcut	Photoshop 4 Shortcut
Select Inverse	Shift+F7	Shift+F7, or Ctrl(⌘)+Shift+I
Load selection from channel	Alt(Opt)+click on load channel icon	Ctrl(⌘)+click on channel title
Load layer as selection	Ctrl(⌘) +Alt(Opt)+T	Ctrl(⌘)+click on layer title
Move marquee, not image	Ctrl(⌘)+Alt(Opt)+ drag (with selection tool)	Drag (with selection tool)
Float a selection	Drag (with selection tool)	Drag with Move tool
Drag and float a duplicate	Alt(Opt)+drag (with selection tool)	Ctrl(⌘)+Alt(Opt)+drag (with selection tool)
Cropping an image	Edit/Crop	Image/Crop
Paste Layer	Edit/Paste Layer	Edit/Paste

continues

Table 1.2, *continued*

Photoshop 3.0.5 Shortcuts in Photoshop 4

Feature	Photoshop 3 Shortcut	Photoshop 4 Shortcut
Contrast/Brightness	Ctrl(⌘)+B	Image/Adjust/Contrast/Brightness
Color Balance	Ctrl(⌘)+Y	Ctrl(⌘)+B
Defringe	Select/Matting/ Defringe	Layer/Matting/Defringe; Floating a selection is no longer required
Scale, Skew, Distort, Perspective	Image/Effects	Layer/Transform; Ctrl(⌘)+T for Free Transform
Color composite view	Ctrl(⌘)+0	Ctrl(⌘)+~(tilde)

There are different menu locations for several commands, but basically, if you're working on a layer, look in the Layer menu for a familiar command that might have been moved. If you want to apply changes to all layers, or to the Background of an unlayered image, the Image menu is where to find that elusive command.

Look to the Context Menu

The functionality of Photoshop 4 in a production environment is divided between palettes, menus, and tools. The authors discovered through months of working with version 4 that the Context menu provides invaluable relief from repetitive motions, and can help keep your cursor where the action is—in an image window.

A "context" menu means exactly that, however; menu items change on the context menu, depending on where your cursor is located when you right-click (Macintosh: hold Ctrl and click). The Zoom tool is chosen in figure 1.18; this composite figure shows the Context menu options when the cursor is over the image window, the thumbnail image on the Layers palette, and the title for the layer on the Layers palette. Many different sets of options are at your command, depending upon the current tool and the place on-screen from which you access the Context menu.

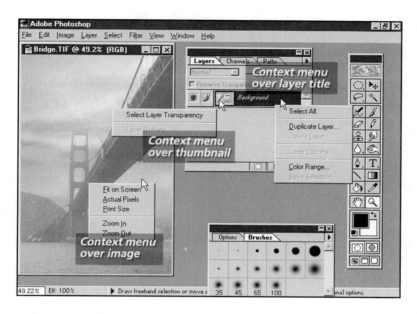

figure 1.18

Many of the main menu options are at your fingertips when you access the Context menu with a specific tool.

Additionally, the Context menu options change according to whether a marquee is present in an image, or whether the current editing zone in the image is the Background or an image layer. Use shortcut keys, keyboard commands for common tasks such as copying and pasting, and save the mileage you put on your muscles and your cursor for image editing.

Summary

This chapter is intended to provide new and experienced Photoshop users with the basic structure of the new interface: where commands and features are located, and the best, quickest way to access them. Obviously, we haven't gotten down to business yet (the business of image editing). Chapter 2 builds on this chapter, providing practical demonstration examples related to the principles behind the tools. Read on, and tap into the power of Photoshop 4.

CHAPTER

LEVERAGING PHOTOSHOP'S NEW CAPABILITIES

In Chapter 1, "Changing the Way You Work with the New Photoshop," you

took a look at Photoshop 4's new features in somewhat of a creative vacuum.

This limited viewpoint was offered so that you could concentrate on how

things work, and see how to apply your own concept, style, and techniques to

the tools. Now, to integrate what you know with what is possible in the

program, this chapter looks at examples of the smartest, most efficient ways to

work with features. You begin, as you would begin any assignment, by setting

up criteria: What are you trying to accomplish? How do you create an effect?

How do you arrive at the intended goal? You're going to establish a design

procedure to use with Photoshop 4.

The Lighting Enhancement Assignment

Lighting is an important, yet subtle quality in all images, be they photographs or illustrations. The audience is not supposed to remark at the exquisite lighting conditions suggested in art, and yet, if the lighting is incorrect or looks flat, the *content* of the image is less attractive.

The Morning.tif image you will work with in this section has good color and interesting geometric composition. The image lacks atmosphere, however. The lighting makes the image look as though it were photographed for a catalog, not as an expressive, artistic image. Photoshop's Lighting Effects filter might seem an obvious choice of tools to enhance the lighting, but you will use the new Gradient tool instead. The concept here is that the scene—of a morning cup of coffee or tea— suggests that light coming through a window would be at a steep angle, and that most people would keep the blinds slightly closed during the early hours. You will add a venetian blind shadow to the scene, thus contributing to the geometry of the image and also adding an element that partially obscures the view of the scene. Sometimes the audience works harder to appreciate, and looks longer at an image whose visual content is moody, a little secretive, and contains messages at both the obvious and subliminal levels. The Gradient Editor is used for its transparency feature in the following sections, to "sculpt" lighting conditions into the image.

Working with the Gradient Editor

Applying a gradient fill in Photoshop isn't nearly as interesting or complicated a task as *defining* the progression of the colors used in a fill. Unlike previous versions of Photoshop, foreground and background colors for a gradient fill in Photoshop 4 are simply the beginning and end of the process! The fun lies in what you put in the *middle* of a gradient fill. Here are the steps for prepping the Morning image for a complex fill overlay. These steps show you how to use the Gradient Editor to define an elegant venetian blind pattern.

GOOD MORNING!

CD-ROM

1. Open the Morning.tif image from the CHAP02 folder of the Companion CD. Double-click on the Zoom tool to change the viewing resolution of the document to 100%, and drag the window borders away from the image so that you can see the complete image.

2. Press F7 to display the Layers palette, and click on the Create new layer icon at the bottom of the palette. The new layer is the current editing layer in the file; it's labeled "Layer 1" by default.

3. Double-click on the Gradient tool to select the tool and to display the Options palette.

4. Press **D** (Default colors), choose Foreground to Background as the Gradient type on the Options palette, choose Linear from the Type drop-down list, and then click on Edit (see fig. 2.1). The Edit button on the Gradient Tool Options palette is the only location in Photoshop where you can display the Editor and define a custom fill.

figure 2.1
Add a layer to the composition so that the gradient fill you add will not be a permanent change until you're happy with the effect.

5. In the Gradient Editor, click on New, type **Venetian Blinds** in the Name field, and click on OK. Both the top (the color blend) preview strip and the bottom (the transparency blend) preview strip turn solid black, which is the default foreground color you defined in step 4.

6. Click on the Transparency button; the color markers on the left of the Editor are replaced with the Opacity field. You're not going to design a color gradient in this example; you're creating a solid fill whose opacity alternates, like a view through venetian blinds.

7. Click on the far left marker and type **0** in the Opacity field. The color strip now has a transition between white and black (see fig. 2.2), and the transparency preview strip fades from Photoshop's transparency grid (the pale checkerboard design) to solid black.

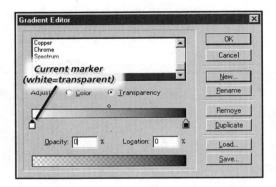

figure 2.2
White on the color strip represents transparent; black represents opaque.

8. Hold Alt(Opt) and drag the black marker to the left; this duplicates the marker and puts it in a different position on the color strip. The location of the marker on the strip is not important at this point.

9. Repeat step 8 until you have a total of eight black markers on the color strip anywhere on the strip. The markers, wherever you have chosen to place them, will be arranged later in this example.

10. Perform steps 8 and 9 to the white strip marker (see fig. 2.3) until you have seven white markers.

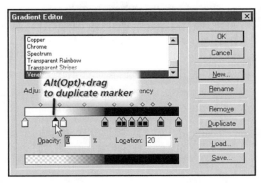

figure 2.3
Hold Alt(Opt) and drag to duplicate a specific color marker in the Gradient Editor.

11. Alternate the markers between black and white (see fig. 2.4). You can click on a marker to highlight it (the arrow on the marker turns black), and then type a number in the location field (type multiples of 7 to evenly space 15 markers from 0 to 100 locations). It might be easier in this example, however, to "eyeball" the even spacing needed to create the venetian blind effect.

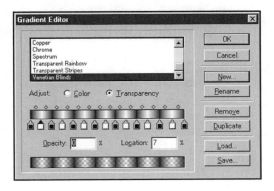

figure 2.4
Alternating the white and black markers creates a fill whose opacity alternates.

12. Click on OK to return to the workspace. The Venetian Blinds Gradient fill is displayed on the preview strip on the Options palette.

13. Check the Mask check box. This Options palette feature applies transparency and color information when you use the Gradient tool. Unchecked, the tool would apply the color (which is entirely black in the Venetian blinds fill) without the transparency scheme you defined, creating a solid fill in the image.

14. Maximize the Morning.tif image window so that at least one to two screen inches of document background are displayed; then, beginning outside the image, drag the cursor from the top left to the bottom right, slightly outside the image (see fig 2.5).

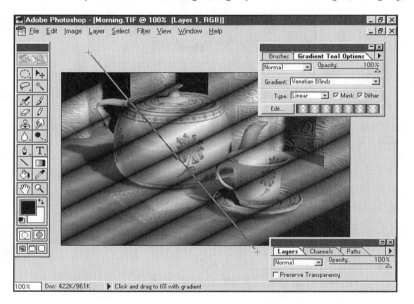

figure 2.5
Create venetian blind shading in the image by applying the custom gradient you defined.

15. If you're not satisfied with the direction or the overall effect, press Ctrl(⌘)+Z to Undo the gradient fill, and try again. Unlike opaque fills, you cannot apply one transparency blend over another; the transparent areas will fill in as alternating opaque information is applied to the image.

16. Press Ctrl(⌘)+Shift+S (File, Save As), and save the file as Morning.psd, in the Photoshop file format, to your hard disk.

The Dither option on the Options palette, something you weren't asked to switch on or off in the preceding example, is useful only when you output your work to PostScript printers. PostScript language cannot handle more than 256 bands of unique colors in a transitional blend between two or more colors. Although this limitation does not apply to on-screen presentations and certain output devices, such as Scitex publishing systems, the Dither option breaks up colors to a 256-unique-value limit. You might not even notice the dithering on-screen; Photoshop uses diffusion type dithering, but if you're a purist about image fidelity, you might want to uncheck this option.

The perk to using a layer as a place within the document for the gradient fill is that you can now adjust the opacity and the mode in which the fill will eventually become a permanent part of the composition. Notice that the venetian blind effect is striking, but perhaps a little too intense to fit comfortably with other image content. Here's how to soften the gradient fill.

ADJUSTING THE BLINDS

1. With Layer 1 as the current editing layer, choose Multiply from the modes drop-down list on the Layers palette, and drag the Opacity slider to about 65 (see fig. 2.6).

2. Choose Filter, Blur, Blur More. The Blur More filter averages the brightness of pixels on the layer without the bell-shaped distribution pattern that the Gaussian Blur filter creates. (Gaussian Blur in this example would make the dense regions of the venetian blind look thin.)

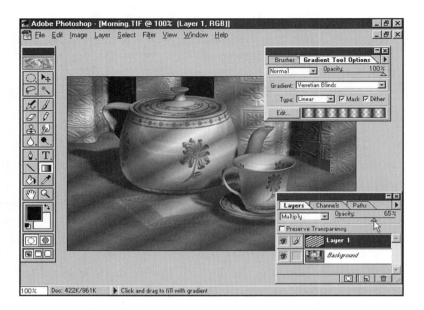

figure 2.6
Multiply mode emphasizes the darker tones on an image layer.

3. Press Ctrl(⌘)+S to save your work. You can choose File, Save A Copy, choose the TIFF file format for the copy, and the layer will be automatically merged (*flattened*) so that the copy of your work can be displayed on machines that do not have Photoshop.

Custom gradient fills are limited to the Linear and Radial types, but this does not mean that you should confine your *concept* of multicolor fills to that of straight and circular pattern-making. The following section looks at ways to use other Photoshop features in combination with the Gradient tool to produce unusual effects.

Changing the Midpoint and Mapping of Fills

The diamond marker on the top of the color strip in the Gradient Editor defines the point between color markers at which a 50% blend of two colors (or the midpoint between two degrees of transparency) is located. By shifting the midpoint marker, you can create a banding effect between two colors and simulate textures that look like wood or ocean waves.

The next assignment is to create the pattern found on a child's pinwheel. You need to use the midpoint Gradient Editor feature along with a Photoshop distort filter, however, because the Gradient tool does not support a spiral type of blend. Here's how to design a texture that can represent anything from a pinwheel to a space warp.

BLENDING A SPIRAL FILL

1. Press Ctrl(⌘)+N to open the New dialog box. Windows users can hold Ctrl and double-click on the workspace to display the dialog box.

2. Specify a new document that is 300 pixels wide by 300 pixels high, in RGB color Mode, with a resolution of 72 pixels/inch. The Contents of the new image should be White. Click on OK to create the new document.

3. Choose the Gradient tool, and click on the Edit button on the Options palette to display the Gradient Editor.

4. Click on New, name the new gradient **Pinwheel,** and then click on OK to return to the Editor.

5. Click on the Color button, not the Transparency button. Click on the left marker on the color preview strip, and then click on the black color swatch beneath the color strip. This swatch displays the color picker.

6. Drag the color field marker, and then the color strip marker, to define a bright reddish-orange color. Click on OK to return to the Gradient Editor. You can see that the left of the color strip is the color you defined, and it makes a transition to black, from left to right on the strip.

7. Click on the right marker, and then click on the color swatch. Define a bright gold in the color picker and click on OK to return to the Editor.

8. Press Alt(Opt) and drag on the orange marker to duplicate the marker to the right of the original's location. Do this two more times, for a total of four orange markers on the color strip.

9. Press Alt(Opt) and drag to the left on the gold marker, to make four gold markers on the color strip.

10. Alternate the markers between gold and orange.

11. One at a time, drag the midpoint markers located to the left of the orange markers all the way to the right, as far as they will go (see fig. 2.7). This creates the banding effect you will use to create the pinwheel.

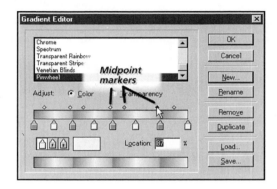

figure 2.7

Move the midpoint markers between gold and orange to the right, to create an abrupt transition between colors.

12. Click on OK to return to the new document. Uncheck the Mask box on the Options palette, and then drag the Gradient tool from the upper-left to the lower-right corner of the image window (see fig. 2.8).

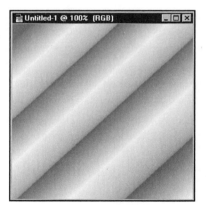

figure 2.8

Sharp transitions created by moving the midpoint markers can create effects, such as tubes.

13. Choose Filter, Distort, Twirl. Drag the Angle slider to 712 (see fig. 2.9) and then click on OK to apply the filter.

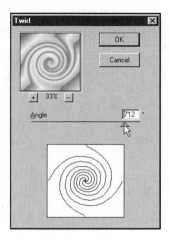

figure 2.9

The Twirl filter twists an image in increasing intensity, from the outside of the selection toward the center.

14. Press Ctrl(⌘)+S, and save the image to your hard disk in the Photoshop file format, as Pinwheel.psd.

If you're looking for an image that is only pinwheel with no undistorted areas, create a file larger than the final image dimensions and then crop the image after you apply the Twirl effect.

If you remember that geometry class where an understanding of Cartesian coordinates and a package of graph paper were prerequisites, the Polar Coordinates filter will seem familiar. Polar Coordinates plots rectangular image information around an imaginary cylinder whose center is the center of the image. The Polar Coordinates filter has a Polar to Rectangular option also, in case you own any of the anamorphic lens art reproductions from the 1700s and want to view them without those mirrored cylinders.

In the following steps, you "misuse" the Polar Coordinates filter—use it on artwork that has *not* been anamorphically distorted—to create an interesting variation on the pinwheel artwork. Need to create a flowing fabric look? Here's how to do it.

POLAR COORDINATES DISPLACEMENT MAPPING

1. Choose Filter, Distort, Polar Coordinates.

2. Click on Polar to Rectangular (see fig. 2.10) and then click on OK.

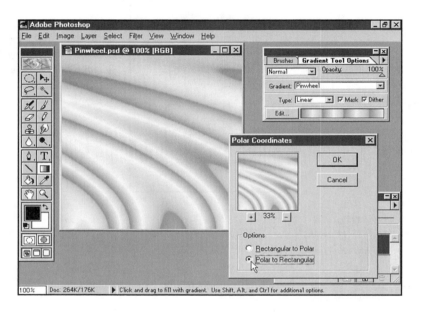

figure 2.10
Polar Coordinates treats the image as though it were round, and "peels" and flattens it to conform to a rectangular surface.

3. Choose File, Save As, and save the image as Fabric.psd in the Photoshop file format.

You can follow the preceding steps several times to further distort the pinwheel gradient fill. Press Ctrl(⌘)+F to apply the last-used filter. Also, before the fill has been distorted to the point of disintegration, try pressing Ctrl(⌘)+Shift+F to access the Polar Coordinates dialog box without applying the filter, and then click on the Rectangular to Polar setting. All progressive filter applications move the image content farther from the original, but switching Polar Coordinate settings tends to "freshen" the resulting image, with novel twists and bends, to a pattern that becomes static after many filter applications.

There are many more tools to explore in this chapter, and many new features that make complicated tasks easier to accomplish. The following sections describe a fairly substantial assignment that highlights several new features in concert.

The GeoPrimitive Kiosk Assignment

CD titles and Web pages aren't the only places that Photoshop can be used to make electronic media stand up and shout. If you're a programmer, a Macromedia Director author, or simply want to present a rough idea as a presentation to a client, we walk you through the construction of a kiosk interface—a stand-alone, interactive terminal popular in malls and other public places. From interface background to selection buttons, Photoshop 4 is the creation tool of choice for electronic, as well as traditional media.

Creating a Textured Interface

The intricacy of an actual kiosk interface has been scaled back in this chapter to a background image, a title, and three interface buttons, so that we can concentrate on the construction process in Photoshop. What you learn can be used to create dozens of menu pages and hundreds of buttons, but to work from bottom up, a distinctive background pattern is the first task.

When you design electronic presentations, it's a good idea to decide whether text will be light or dark. You don't want the background fighting for attention with the text message; it should be muted in tone, and the pattern should be apparent but not visually overwhelming. Additionally, you will use a monochromatic color scheme for the interface and the controls, to better highlight the kiosk title and text.

Figure 2.11 is the Geotile.tif image from the CHAP02 folder on the Companion CD, from which you will create a textured, dimensional background. This image was created by using XAOS Tools, Inc.'s Terrazzo filter, a handy plug-in to Photoshop for creating kaleidoscopic, seamless image tiles. In the following steps, you will create a texture from the tile by filtering the image.

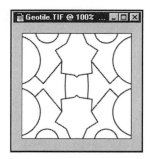

figure 2.11
Any pattern image that is seamless can be modified to make a seamless, textured image.

Here's how to use a combination of filters to create an interface background that looks like concrete.

DIMENSIONALIZING A LINE DRAWING THROUGH FILTERS

CD-ROM

1. Open the Geotile.tif image from the CHAP02 folder on the Companion CD.

2. Choose Filter, Other, Minimum. The Minimum filter performs an operation that can be compared to creating a *spread* (a mask that overlaps darker printing colors to close a gap between lighter printing colors) in traditional prepress.

3. Drag the slider to 1 pixel (see fig. 2.12) and click on OK. The Minimum command makes the thin pattern outline into a thick pattern outline that will make a better dimensional pattern.

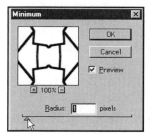

figure 2.12
Use the Minimum command on patterns or drawings whose visual content lacks boldness and contrast.

4. Choose Filter, Distort, Glass. The Glass filter displaces visual content according to preset image maps found in the Texture drop-down list, or you can choose your own Photoshop (PSD) image.

5. Drag the Distortion slider to 2. This controls the amount of displacement created by the map you choose in the Texture drop-down list. The default, Frosted, works fine for this example, so don't change it.

6. Drag the Smoothness slider to 4. Smoothness is the "amplitude" of the Distortion option. At this amount, the edges of the pattern will be rough, and characteristic of the edges of worn concrete slabs.

7. Drag the Scaling slider down to about 80% (see fig. 2.13). Usually, 100% is the best scaling choice, but because this is a small pattern image, scaling the effect down creates more visual interest in the filtered design. Click on OK to apply the Glass filter.

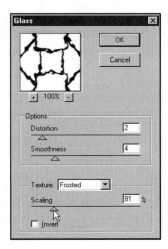

figure 2.13

The Glass filter distorts an image according to a predefined displacement map. Create organic textures and then roughen smooth edges.

8. Click on the Foreground color selection box on the toolbox and then use the color picker to define a light, warm tone (H: 20, S: 2, and B: 70 is a good color). Click on OK to return to the workspace.

9. Click on the Background color selection box. In the color picker, define a warm tone, slightly darker than the current foreground color. (H: 0, S: 20, and B: 42 is a good choice.) Click on OK to close the color picker and return to the workspace.

10. Choose Filter, Sketch, Note Paper. Drag the Graininess slider to 7, and then drag the Relief slider to 13 (see fig. 2.14). The Note Paper filter uses the current foreground/background colors to create a textured, dimensional version of the original image. Click on OK to apply the filter.

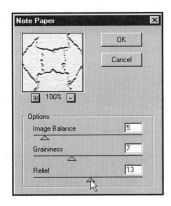

figure 2.14

Use the Note Paper filter to create a colorized, high-contrast, embossed version of your work.

Although the Geotile image displays many more photorealistic qualities now, the texture and contrast are a little too much for the kiosk background, and the image will overwhelm the message in the foreground.

11. Choose Filter, Blur, Blur More. There are no options for the Blur More filter; the image is thrown slightly out of focus.

12. Choose Image, Adjust, Brightness/Contrast. Drag the Contrast slider to –55, drag the Brightness slider to –14, and then click on OK. You're finished with the texture for the interface design.

13. Press Ctrl(⌘)+Shift+S (File, Save As), and then save the image to your hard disk in the TIFF file format, as Geotile.tif. Keep the image open in Photoshop.

One of the benefits of using a seamlessly tiling image to create interface backgrounds is that the resource file (Geotile.tif) is quite small—less than 100 KB, in this example. In the following section, you create the background image and add the title for the kiosk.

Creating the Foundation for the Kiosk

You have done some hard work up to this point; now it's the authors' turn to contribute to the kiosk creation! In the following steps, you fill a new document window with the pattern you created, and then drag the title we have provided on the Companion CD into the composition.

Designing an Interface Background

CD-ROM

1. Press Ctrl(⌘)+A (Select, All) and choose Edit, Define Pattern. Close the Geotile image now.

2. For this example, we use a document window smaller than one that might be displayed on a kiosk. This enables you to zoom in and out of the document with a minimum amount of scrolling. Press Ctrl(⌘)+N (Windows users can press Ctrl(⌘) and double-click on the workspace). In the New document dialog box, type **600** in the Width field, type **400** in the Height field, choose RGB Color from the mode drop-down list, type **72** in the Resolution field, and then click on OK to create the document.

3. Press Ctrl(⌘)+A, and then right-click (Macintosh: hold Ctrl and click) over the Background title on the Layers palette (press F7 if it isn't currently on-screen) to display the Context menu. Choose Fill from the Context menu, choose Pattern from the Use drop-down list, and then click on OK to apply the pattern.

4. Press Ctrl(⌘)+D to deselect the marquee; then choose Edit, Purge, Pattern from the main menu. Whenever you have a Clipboard copy for which you have no further use, or a pattern stored in memory that's served its purpose, it's a good idea to purge the information.

5. Open the Geohead.psd file from the CHAP02 folder of the Companion CD.

6. Press **V** (Move tool), and then drag from the Geohead image window into the Untitled-1 image window (see fig. 2.15). The title for the kiosk is copied, and you can see the default name, Layer 1, appear on the Layers palette. Close the Geohead.pdf file at any time now.

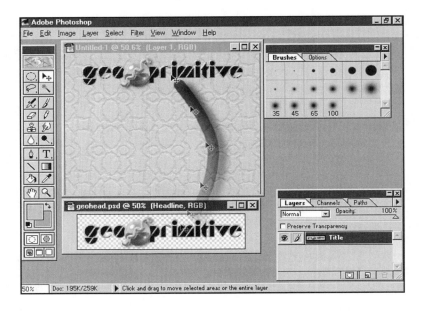

figure 2.15
Use the Move tool to drag the contents of a layer into a different document window to copy the information.

7. With the Move tool, drag the title for the kiosk to the top center of the document. Press Ctrl(⌘)+S, and save the image to your hard disk as GeoPage.psd, in the Photoshop file format. Keep the image open.

The next phase of the assignment calls for measuring and fitting the foreground elements into the composition. (Before Photoshop 4, this might have been a signal to move your work to a desktop publishing or drawing application.) The following sections show you how to create some smart-looking buttons for the interface, and how rulers and the grid in Photoshop are defined and used.

The Grid, Rulers, and Snap-To Design Work

Aligning the nontransparent contents of Photoshop layers was not the easiest of tasks in earlier versions, but all this has changed in version 4. By the end of this chapter, you may even feel as though you're working in PageMaker or Illustrator.

Buttons need to be created for the kiosk to offer customers a variety of selections. The following sections show you how to use Photoshop's native features in combination with the snap-to grid and guides to accomplish a creative and precise task.

Setting Up a Grid

Because a kiosk is an electronic presentation, you do not need to concern yourself with how many inches wide or high the background is when you define grid increments. Everything is measured in pixels. When pixels are measured against pixels, the measurements you define will be absolute ones; there is no ambiguity when only one unit of measurement is used.

The default color for the grid feature in Photoshop is a 50% black. Unfortunately—and this *will* happen in your own design work—the background against which you create buttons is also a medium tone. The first step is to specify a unique color for the grid, but before you begin you need to decide also what size and shape the kiosk buttons should be. A 60-pixel-square, 3D button will fit nicely within the dimensions of the background; at 60 pixels on a side, there will be room for a dozen or so buttons, depending upon how many selections the client needs, and how much text accompanies the buttons.

Here's how to set up the grid for button creation, and how to begin the button design.

PLANNING A DESIGN AGAINST A GRID

1. Double-click on the Zoom tool to change the viewing resolution of GeoPage.psd to 1:1 (100%). Maximize the window; drag the window borders as far away from the image as possible. (Windows users: click on the title bar Maximize button.)

2. Press Ctrl(⌘)+R to display the rulers around the document window. By default, inches are displayed on the rulers. But we want pixels.

3. Press F8 to display the Info palette, click on the plus sign at the bottom left, and choose Pixels from the drop-down list. Press F8 again to hide the Info palette. Ruler units can also be specified in General Preferences, or by double-clicking on a ruler.

4. Press Ctrl(⌘)+K, and then choose Guides & Grid from the drop-down list on the Prefer-ences dialog box.

5. Type **20** in the Gridline every field, type **5** in the Subdivisions field, and click on the color swatch to the right of the Grid field in the dialog box. This displays the color picker.

6. Choose a bright green or purple in the color picker, and click on OK to return to the Preferences box.

7. Check out figure 2.16. If the Guides & Grid looks like this on-screen, click on OK; the current document window is displayed with heavy gridlines every 20 pixels. The five dotted, lighter subdivision lines between each grid mark will not be visible until you zoom to a viewing resolution higher than 100%, due to the frequency of the subdivisions in this example.

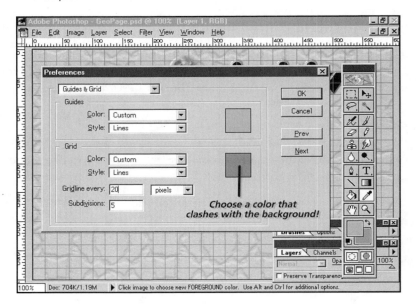

figure 2.16

The Guides color is visible against the background, but the gridlines are not. Choose a contrasting grid color.

8. On the Layers palette, click on the Create new layer icon. Layer 2 is now the current editing layer; nothing you do will mess up the title or the background in the composition.

9. Choose View, Show Grid, and then choose View, Snap to Grid from the main menu. With the Rectangular Marquee tool, drag a square three grid spaces wide and high (see fig. 2.17). The grid can be repositioned by changing the zero origin of the document; drag the zero origin (the box at the convergence of the horizontal and vertical rulers) into the window to define 0,0 coordinates for the rulers and the grid.

figure 2.17
When you use the "snap to" property for the grid, creating perfect squares is simply a matter of dragging with the Marquee tool.

10. Zoom in to 200% viewing resolution for the document. The quickest way to do this is to press Ctrl(⌘)++.

11. Press I (Eyedropper tool), and then click over the darkest area of the background. This defines a new foreground color on the toolbox.

12. Hold Alt(Opt) and click on a lighter area of the background. You have defined a new background color on the toolbox.

13. Choose the Gradient tool, choose Foreground to Background from the Gradient drop-down list on the Options palette, and make sure that Linear is the Type. The color strip on the Options palette should now show the foreground color blending to the background color.

14. Drag at a 45° angle from bottom left to top right, slightly outside the marquee (see fig. 2.18). The cursor is attracted to the grid subdivisions, which keeps the cursor aligned to the corners of the selection; the selection now has a shaded fill.

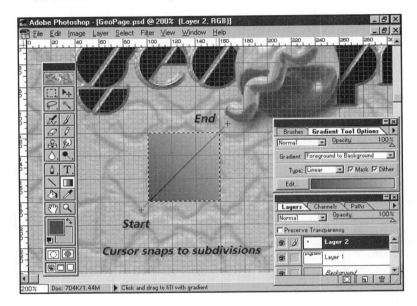

figure 2.18
The grid makes it easy to make gradient fills at precisely the angle you want.

15. Press Ctrl(⌘)+D to deselect the marquee, and then press Ctrl(⌘)+S. Keep the image open in Photoshop.

Grids are for designing, not simply aligning objects. The button doesn't really look like a button, but the preceding steps were an important start. An easy way to dimensionalize a shape is to create an inset shape whose apparent lighting is in an opposing direction to the "parent" shape. Because the lighting on the square is from the upper right, a smaller, inside shape with lighting from the lower left will make your work on Layer 2 look more like a button. The subdivisions on the document make it easy to design a marquee that is 16 pixels smaller in height and width than the square you created in the previous steps. Here's how to create a chiseled look for the button.

USING REVERSE LIGHTING

1. With the Rectangular Marquee tool, drag inside the square, starting top left, two subdivision rows and columns inside the gradient-filled square, and ending bottom right, two rows and two columns inside the gradient square.

2. With the Gradient tool, drag from the upper right of the selection marquee to the bottom left (see fig. 2.19). The closer to the inside of the marquee you begin and end the Gradient tool, the steeper the transition you create in the selection.

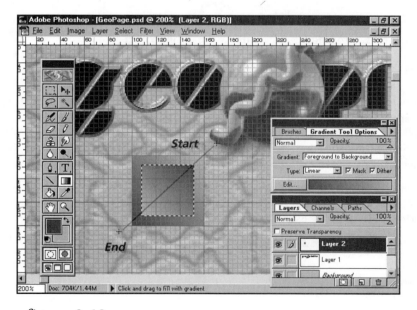

figure 2.19
Drag the Gradient tool cursor in the opposite direction to the direction you originally used to fill the first square.

3. Press Ctrl(⌘)+D to deselect the marquee, and then press Ctrl(⌘)S. Keep the document open.

The button looks a little too flawless to look real, compared to the concrete background. In the following section, you use the Pen tool and the Fade option in combination with the Paintbrush tool to create a realistic highlight on the edge of the button.

Stroking Paths and Fading Paint

As you will see throughout this book, the Pen tool can be used to define a vector, nonprinting shape that can then serve as the basis for a selection, the container for a fill, or a stroked outline. Paths in Photoshop can be stroked with paint application tools and with editing tools such as the Smudge tool.

One of the interesting effects you can create by stroking a path is to limit the length of the stroke. The Paintbrush, the Pencil, and Airbrush tools all offer a Fade option on the Options palette. When you click on the Fade check box and enter a number of steps, stroking a path creates a streaking, comet-like effect.

TIP

The number of steps you define for the Fade option do *not* correspond to pixels. The length of the fade is determined by the size of the brush tip and how much spacing is defined for the tip. Spacing is determined by double-clicking on a brush tip on the Brushes palette to display the Brushes Options dialog box. By default, all Brushes palette tips are spaced 25% of the tip's diameter.

Trying to determine how long a fade lasts for a stroked path is headache-inducing! Life is too short! What's the point of calculating that at a 10-step fade, a 20-pixel diameter brush with 25% spacing (5 pixels) will be 65 pixels long?

20 (pixel diameter tip) + (**5** pixel spacing × **9** steps in addition to the original)=**65** pixels

The authors heartily recommend trial and error when you are trying to achieve a faded stroke effect.

Here's how to create a highlight on the upper-right corner of the button, using the snap-to grid feature, the Pen tool, and the Fade Options feature:

STROKING A HIGHLIGHT

1. Choose the Pen tool from the toolbox.

2. Press Ctrl(⌘)++ to zoom in to 300% viewing resolution, and then hold the spacebar to access the Hand tool. Drag in the window until the button is centered on-screen, and then release the spacebar.

3. Click a point on the upper-right corner of the square within the square and then click a second point at the bottom right of the smaller square (see fig. 2.20). Paths can be open or closed to qualify for stroking.

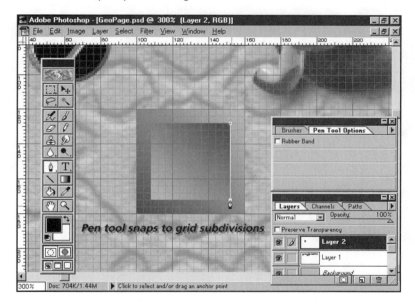

figure 2.20

The Pen tool, like the selection tools, snaps to the grid and its subdivisions.

4. Press **D** (Default colors) and then press **X** (Switch Foreground/Background colors).

5. Choose the Paintbrush tool and click on the Paths tab on the Layers palette.

6. On the Options palette, check the Fade check box and type **40**, using the number keys at the top of the keyboard (not the numeric keypad). (The keypad keys are reserved in Photoshop for entering Opacity settings, and it's nearly impossible to type Fade values by using the keypad keys.)

7. Choose the first row, second from left Brushes palette tip (see fig. 2.21), and then click on the Strokes path with the foreground color icon at the bottom of the Paths palette. A highlight appears vertically where you drew the path.

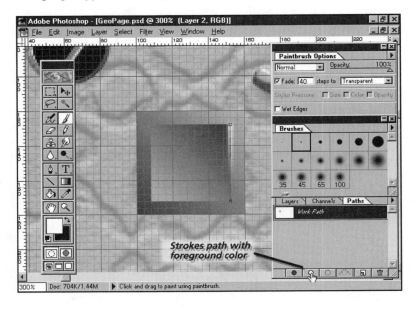

figure 2.21
Stroke the path, using white as the foreground color to add a highlight to the button.

8. Drag on the Pen tool to reveal the tool flyout, and then choose the Direct Selection tool (the arrowhead icon).

9. Click on the bottom anchor point on the path, and drag the anchor point to the upper-left corner of the smaller button shape.

10. Press **B** (Paintbrush tool) and click on the Strokes path with foreground color icon. Now the highlight is complete.

11. It's not necessary to delete the Work Path; paths do not display in bitmap images in programs other than Photoshop. Because the path *does* intrude on the view of your highlight work, however, click on an empty space on the Paths palette (below the Work Path title) to hide the path.

12. Press Ctrl(⌘)+S to save your work.

The button looks dimensional now, but it doesn't really appear to be *part* of the interface. The reason is that it has no graphical association with the interface. Objects in the real world cast shadows or create some other lighting effect on a surface close to them. In the next section, you create a "pillow emboss" effect to make the button appear to be pushed into the background surface.

Creating the Pillow Emboss Effect

Shortly after the "Gaussian Blur drop shadow" effect was discovered in Photoshop, designers began creating variations on this visual effect. The pillow emboss effect can be created inside or outside of an object to suggest that the surface an object is resting upon is soft, like a pillow. Essentially, to create this effect, you need to define a feathered selection and then paint opposing sides around a shape using darker and lighter colors. To make the visual effect a photorealistic one, the lighting of the pillow emboss effect needs to be the opposite of the object that is resting on the surface. In this example, the lighting of the button is from 2 o'clock, so the pillow emboss effect you create needs to have highlights at 8 o'clock (and shading at 2 o'clock).

Here's how to use the Behind painting mode in combination with the Expand and Feather features to integrate the button with the background:

CREATING A PUSH-BUTTON LOOK

1. Double-click on the Hand tool to zoom your view out to 100% (1:1 resolution). Press Ctrl(⌘)+R to hide the rulers, and then press Ctrl(⌘)+" (quotation marks) to hide the grid. When the grid is invisible, the snap to feature is automatically turned off. The Airbrush, Pencil, and Paintbrush tools don't snap to grids, so don't worry when you paint with grids on or off.

2. Double-click on the Layer 2 title on the Layers palette, type **Button** in the Name field of the Layer Options dialog box, and then click on OK to apply this name change. You will duplicate this layer in this chapter to make more buttons; if you name it now, Photoshop will default to the user name when it makes duplicates ("Button copy," "Button copy 2," and so on).

3. Press Ctrl(⌘) and click on the Button title on the Layers palette to load the nontransparent areas (the *layer content*) as a selection marquee.

4. Choose Select, Modify, Expand. In the Expand Selection dialog box, type **7** in the pixels field and click on OK.

5. Press Ctrl(⌘)+Shift+D to display the Feather dialog box. Type **5** in the pixels field and click on OK.

6. Choose the Airbrush tool, press **D** (Default colors), and on the Options palette, choose Behind from the modes drop-down list. The Behind painting mode affects only the transparent and semitransparent areas of a layer. If you try to paint over an opaque part of a layer, you appear to be painting behind the object.

7. Drag the Pressure slider to about 20, and choose the middle row, far right tip on the Brushes palette for the Airbrush tool.

8. Drag along the top and right edges within the marquee selection (see fig. 2.22). Be careful not to paint into the bottom and left edges; these areas need white paint, and you cannot paint on top of areas in Behind mode.

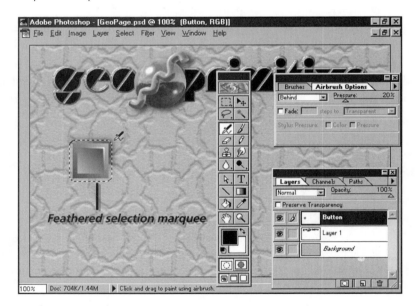

figure 2.22
Use the Behind paint mode to add shading to the button without the need to create a new layer.

9. Press Ctrl(⌘)+H to hide the edges of the marquee; the selection is still active, it simply doesn't show the on-screen marquee indicator.

10. Press **X** (Switch Foreground/Background colors), and then paint white in the bottom and left areas (see fig. 2.23). Precision is not required at this point. The feathered selection softens your painting work, and the Behind mode will not let you paint into the black areas you added in step 8.

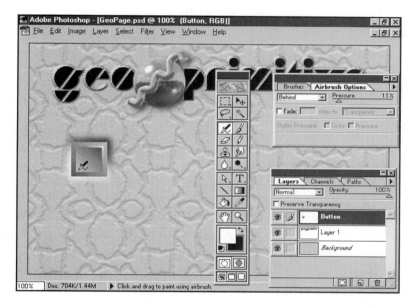

figure 2.23
Create the source of lighting for the pillow emboss in the opposite direction from that displayed on the button, to create a recess effect for the button.

11. Press Ctrl(⌘)+D, and then press Ctrl(⌘)+S to save your work. Keep the image open.

When you have created one button in Photoshop, you're only a few steps away from owning a gaggle of them. In the following section, you duplicate the buttons, position them, and then precisely align them by using the new guides feature.

Working in 3D in Photoshop

Users of Photoshop 3.0.5 understand that the Move tool has traditionally been used to move objects on layers across a plane—2D movement, if you will. With Photoshop 4, however, more emphasis has been placed on the Move tool as a positioning tool that you can use to move elements in any of three directions: top to bottom, left to right, *and* front to back.

Now you will see how to use the Move tool in combination with the Layers palette and guides feature to quickly populate the interface with buttons.

COPYING AND MOVING BETWEEN LAYERS

1. Drag the button title on the Layers palette on top of the Create new layer icon at the bottom of the palette. Doing this creates a new button, on a layer on top of the Button layer, with the name "Button copy."

2. Right-click (Macintosh: hold Ctrl and click) on the Button copy title on the Layers palette; from the Context menu, choose Duplicate Layer. This is a slower way to duplicate a layer; however, you get the opportunity to name the layer as it is being created.

3. Accept the default name (Button copy 2), click on OK, and a new button on its own layer is added to the top of the layer stack in the composition.

4. With the Move tool, drag in the image window. You will notice that one of the buttons comes out of hiding from behind the others. It makes no difference whether you drag on an object on a layer or the layer itself. The Move tool moves all nontransparent elements on a layer.

5. Drag the button to the bottom of the interface, below the rest of the buttons.

6. Right-click (Macintosh: hold Ctrl and click) on the remaining buttons. The Context menu offers you three options: Button, Button copy, and Background. Choose Button copy, and then drag in the window until the button appears above the bottom button. When you make a selection from the context menu by using the Move tool, the current layer in the image changes. You can see this happen if you look at the Layers palette while you make the selection.

7. Right-click (Macintosh: hold Ctrl and click) on the button you have not yet moved. You have the option of moving to the Button layer or the Background. The Context menu is location-specific in the document; only layers that have nontransparent elements exactly where you click are options. Click on the Button option (see fig. 2.24), and then drag in the window until the button is approximately vertically aligned with the other two buttons.

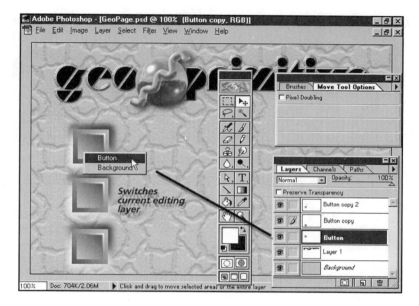

figure 2.24
The Context menu for the Move tool only offers to switch the current editing layer to one that has nontransparent content under the point at which you click.

8. Press Ctrl(⌘)+R to display the rulers and then drag a vertical guide out of the left ruler. You cannot add guides to an image without first displaying the rulers. Guides can remain visible, however, after they have been added without displaying rulers.

9. Drag the guide to touch the "g" in "geoPrimitive" (see fig. 2.25). Choose View, Snap To Guides, and then, one at a time, select the layer for the button you want to align to the guide, and drag the button to touch the guide. The buttons will snap into place.

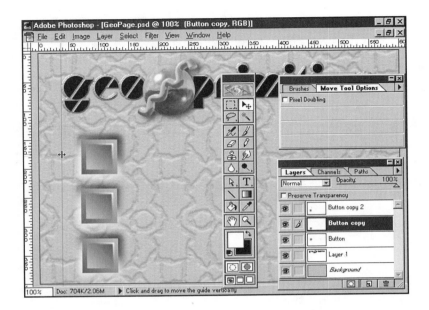

figure 2.25
The Move tool is the only tool that can reposition a guide; any tool can be used to drag
a guide from the rulers.

10. Press Ctrl(⌘)+S and keep the document open in Photoshop.

Note that guides can be locked (from the View menu) so they don't accidentally
move when you use the Move tool to reposition objects. This is unlikely, however,
because guides cannot be moved until the Move tool cursor changes to a "move
guide" cursor (illustrated in fig. 2.25), and this requires a slow and deliberate action,
unlike the way you would move layer contents.

Creating a Spherical Button

Because the buttons are on separate layers, modifications to this composition can
be made at any time by editing only those areas you decide need change. Suppose,

for example, that one button on the interface does something more important than the others, and deserves a different shape, but should have the same colors as the three you have created.

No problem. The easiest way to accomplish this is to define a custom gradient fill. In the following steps, you create a fill that suggests a roundish shape. When added to a circular marquee, the button is finished before you know it!

CREATING A SPHERICAL BUTTON

1. The current foreground color should be white. If it isn't, press **D** and then press **X**.

2. Drag on the Marquee tool to access the flyout, and then choose the Elliptical Marquee tool.

3. Hold Shift to constrain the tool to creating circles, and drag a marquee that is approximately the same width as the buttons. The current editing layer should be the Button layer. If it is not, click on the Button title on the Layers palette to switch to this layer.

4. Choose the Gradient tool and click on Edit on the Options palette. Click on New in the Editor, and type **Sphere** in the Name field. Click on OK to return to the Editor. The color strip is entirely white.

5. Drag the far right color marker to the left until the location field reads 75%.

6. Place the cursor outside the Gradient Editor, and click on the darker area of one of the buttons in the GeoPage.psd document (see fig. 2.26). The Eyedropper tool is the current cursor, and you can sample colors from any image window, the Swatches or Colors palette (if open), or the color strip itself (but not the interface itself or the desktop).

7. Click below the color strip to add a new marker, whose current color is the color indicated on the color selection box (to the left of the Location field). The new marker is highlighted, which means that it's available to change.

8. Click on the far left of the color strip to make the new marker color the same as the far left one: white.

9. Drag the new marker to the 100% Location position and then drag the midpoint marker (to the left of the color marker) as far right as it will go. The Location field reports that 87% is the maximum position on the strip for the midpoint marker (see fig. 2.27).

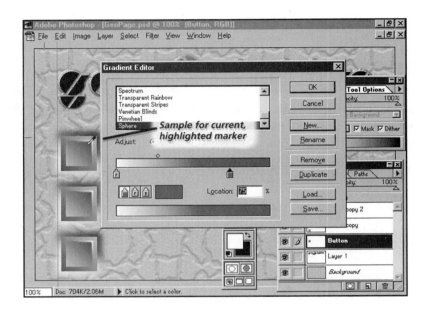

figure 2.26

When a marker on the color strip is highlighted, you can sample colors from open document windows, active or inactive.

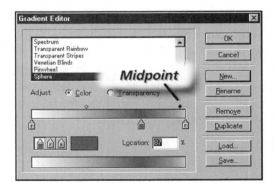

figure 2.27

Create a sharper transition at the end of the blend, and a more gradual one from the middle to the right, by changing the midpoint marker location.

10. Click on OK to exit the Gradient Editor, and then choose Radial Type from the drop-down list.

11. Drag from inside the marquee, at a 1 o'clock position, to outside the marquee at about 7 to 8 o'clock (see fig. 2.28). If you were to end the fill inside the selection, a harsh band would be apparent inside the selection; the transition between the middle color and the white end color is quite sharp toward the end of the fill. If you keep the end of the fill outside the marquee, however, you wind up with a pleasing catch-light effect on the bottom left of the shape, enhancing its roundish appearance.

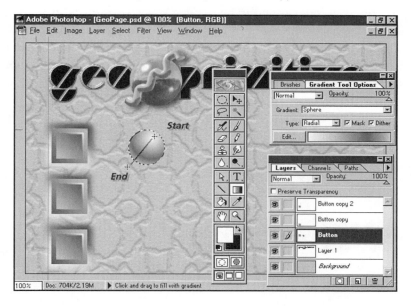

figure 2.28
Create Sphere shapes with a Gradient fill whose colors are weighted toward the end of the fill.

12. Press Ctrl(⌘)+D to deselect the marquee, and then choose the Lasso tool.

13. Draw a marquee around the top button (the square on the Button layer) and press Delete (Backspace).

14. Press Ctrl(⌘)+S to save your work.

To complete the shading of the round button, you need to follow the steps described earlier for creating a pillow emboss effect. Having done that, use the Move tool to position the round button flush left with the square ones, against the guide. Without the pillow emboss surrounding the button, the layer contents will not align properly to the rest of the buttons.

You now have a document that can used in a variety of design situations. We have been a little fuzzy on what "GeoPrimitive" manufactures in this chapter—the specific client is not a concern here. What you have learned can be applied to *many* different services in need of a kiosk, an on-screen presentation, or a Web site (see Chapters 19 and 20 for the finer points of Web site construction). In figure 2.29, you can see that text has been added to the interface; a second guide was used to align separate text layers to the buttons.

figure 2.29

From the background to the highlight on a button, Photoshop offers the flexibility of designing in bitmap format with the precision of a desktop publishing program.

Summary

Magic tricks aside, this chapter has shown you how to work in Photoshop; the *method* is as important as the techniques and tools to achieve the intended design results. If you learned a new procedure here, that's good, but if you have adopted a "rhythm"—you pick a tool, you define an option on a palette, you shortcut here, you zoom there—then you're on your way to better work, accomplished more quickly.

Chapter 3, "Personalizing Photoshop: Preferences and Options," covers some of the system and application optimization you will want to address before you move on to more complicated editing and larger images. Photoshop is like a sports car, and you definitely want to pack provisions for the ride and check under the hood to make certain that everything is fine-tuned before you step on the gas.

PART  II

UP AND RUNNING

CHAPTER 3

PERSONALIZING PHOTOSHOP: PREFERENCES AND OPTIONS

When designing Photoshop for the personal computer, Adobe Systems had no idea who you, the person in personal, might be—your preferences, the way you want to see cursors display on-screen, what brand of monitor you use, how much room you have left on your hard disks, and so on. That's why Adobe Systems made Photoshop 4's workspace and user preferences open-ended—so that you can create a personalized environment that suits your needs.

Optimizing Photoshop to offer the best features for you, and for your computer, is no more difficult than choosing a different color scheme for your desktop wallpaper. The secret to designing Frank's or Susan's Photoshop, then, lies in knowing where the controls for the customizable features are, and what they do.

Fine-Tuning Your Monitor

Calibrating (adjusting your monitor's settings) might sound as entertaining as arranging one's sock drawer at home, but if you don't invest the time to calibrate your video, you will produce work of inconsistent quality through time. Calibrating your monitor helps ensure that the images you see will look the same on other computers, and print with closely matched color values. Calibration is critical to creating work in Photoshop that can be accurately reproduced as hard copy.

Having stressed this, we need to let you know that the *reality* of computer design is that even if you calibrate your monitor perfectly, your finished image may not look so great when it's processed by a service bureau or viewed on another monitor. The reason is that the personal computer does not use the same materials for display as images rendered to paper or film do. Screen pixels simply do not equal dots of pigment on a surface. Although system calibration does not guarantee accurate image editing and output, Photoshop's calibration features are much better than using no system calibration at all.

Every computer monitor, printer, scanner, and film recorder has its own inherent range of colors it can express (its *gamut*), and its own calibration settings. And in this sense, monitor calibration is relative. You might find through experience that when you send your file to a specific output source (printer, film recorder) everything prints too dark or too light, or that blues turn into purples. If this is the case, you may want to calibrate your monitor to more closely match a particular output medium. Adobe has made calibrating your monitor easy, and you can save and recall different sets of custom calibration information that match different situations. When calibrating your monitor, you will want to make relative adjustments that fit your own needs, while maintaining consistency with the world of clients and suppliers to whom you send your files.

Methods of Calibration

The method Photoshop provides for calibrating your monitor is not the most scientifically precise method available. Photoshop's method relies on the user trying to match things by eye. The most precise and objective way to calibrate a monitor or other output device requires expensive equipment that actually reads the wavelengths of light produced or measures the density and color values of printed output. These physical calibration systems (such as Barco produces) are often used with proprietary color-management software, which helps ensure that the settings for *all* devices—your scanner, your monitor, and your printer or imagesetter—are tuned to match each other.

If you have a physical color-calibration system, you should use it instead of Photoshop's eyeball method. If you don't own third-party calibration software and hardware, this chapter walks you through the steps, using Photoshop's features. If your clients also use Photoshop, you can adjust their monitors' settings, if necessary, so that they can view your work accurately.

Setting Up the Monitor

One part of calibrating your monitor for use with Photoshop is to load a video driver for your system, a driver that displays the maximum color capability offered by your video adapter card. The steps required are different for every card; many video drivers come with special software, whereas others allow the operating system to change video drivers. Check the documentation that came with your video card for information about changing color display modes.

After the monitor has warmed up (don't perform calibration until at least one-half hour after you turn on the monitor), and you have the correct video driver installed, you need to refer to your monitor's documentation, which should include important information you need for Photoshop's Monitor Setup command. In particular, you need to know the brand of your monitor and the type of phosphors used in its screen. If your monitor is an OEM (Original Equipment Manufacturer) unit that you bought as part of a system package, you may not have access to these details. There is a workaround, however, that you can use to get the right settings.

The following steps show you how to tell Photoshop what kind of monitor you have, and how to make only those changes that apply to your monitor:

PHOTOSHOP'S MONITOR SETUP

1. In Photoshop, choose File, Color Settings, Monitor Setup.

2. Click on the Monitor drop-down list. This list contains preset calibrations for more than 45 different brands of monitor, most of them for the Macintosh. Additionally, NTSC Standard is available, in case you use Photoshop extensively for editing digital television media; also, Barco Calibrator is available, in case you own a Barco video system (an extremely accurate, expensive, high-end system).

3. Choose from the list of preset monitors, or stick with Default, or choose Other (see fig. 3.1). If you choose Default, the monitor settings don't change. If you choose Other, you must set the Monitor and Room Parameters manually by choosing one of the options from the drop-down boxes next to each parameter. Be sure to read the following section on Monitor Parameters before you make these changes.

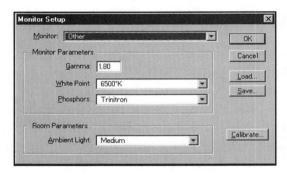

figure 3.1
The Monitor Setup dialog box.

4. Keep the Monitor Setup dialog box open for the following section.

If you select a monitor other than the one you use from the Monitor drop-down list, you will not harm your PC, your monitor, or Photoshop. Monitor Setup and the following calibrations in this section simply define the parameters within which Photoshop displays contrast, colors, and values.

For example, the specification sheet for the authors' own Philips 17-inch monitor, which is not listed in the Monitor drop-down list, is almost identical to a specific model of Nanao monitor, which is listed. When we included the Nanao as part of the setup that follows, it resulted in a dramatic difference in viewing and editing of images in Photoshop.

After the author chose the incorrect monitor make and model, the gamma of the display was lowered, and the colors on the monitor now more closely matched source material—scans of physical material and artwork from other applications — that the authors work with. In addition, Photoshop work now *imported* into other programs, such as PageMaker, with more color accuracy when compared to the images viewed in Photoshop.

Photoshop for the Macintosh offers global settings for Gamma adjustment (discussed later in this chapter). All applications respond to the Gamma control panel—found on the Apple menu—after you install Photoshop 4. Gamma is only one of the parameters that make up accurate monitor calibration. In Windows, none of the changes you make with your monitor settings in Photoshop affect other applications or your system's workspace. Although you can save indefinitely any changes to the Photoshop environment, you can reset them at any time, also, in Windows or on the Macintosh.

WARNING

If you use a third-party calibration program, do not perform Photoshop calibration in addition to the third-party calibration. This is a particular problem with Photoshop for the Macintosh because the third-party calibration software will update Photoshop's color space descriptor file, and the work of one software will be undone by the other.

Gamma

In the Gamma field (in Windows), and in the Gamma control panel (on the Macintosh), you specify the setting that might make the most difference for viewing your Photoshop work. *Gamma* is the measurement of the nonlinear relationship between brightness and voltage output. There is much misinformation in computer graphics circles concerning the term, and for all practical purposes, "gamma" has come to mean the contrast displayed within the midtones of images displayed on your monitor.

There are two problems associated with defining the correct gamma for your video system, in Photoshop or any other application. First, software programmers tend to presume linearity, when writing how an application displays an image. This means that no voltage to the monitor electronics should display black, that 50% voltage displays half-brightness for any given color, and that full voltage sent to the electronics represents full brightness for a color. In actuality, there is a drop-off that forms a curve as colors are defined as brighter and brighter, and there is *no* linear relationship between brightness and voltage sent to the monitor. In theory, this power–curve relationship changes brightness as the square of voltage at any given moment, so in theory, monitors should have a gamma of 2. In reality, computers are digital but video subsystems are analog, and many video subsystems do not translate brightness as a perfect power function of voltage. Television, for example, is more brilliant than digital computer displays; engineers frequently use a gamma of 2.2 to calibrate television output. The Macintosh video subsystem and IBM-PC video displays are lower than television, and although much documentation will tell you to always set gamma to 1.8, you need to define the gamma for Photoshop with your own eyes, using your own images.

Second, designers tend to change the data in a file until it looks right, instead of adjusting the gamma of the display or changing the monitor's own Brightness/Contrast controls. The authors recommend that if an image looks funny on-screen, your first action should be to adjust the monitor settings (before changing the image information). Bitmap images undergo progressive changes when you alter the hue, contrast, or other properties, and you can never restore these after two or more changes have been made. Look outside—to your hardware and software—for display problems before you touch a single pixel of a client's image.

Scientific explanations aside, the artistic quality you notice about images displayed on a system whose gamma is off is that the midtones—the areas that usually contain the most visual information in an image—are either too faint (gamma is too high) or too blocked in (gamma is too low).

Although the Gamma option is located in different places on both platforms, even one-tenth of a percent difference in the Gamma setting for your monitor will show a discernible on-screen difference. You can honestly evaluate the best gamma for your monitor display only after you spend some time working with different images. The perfect gamma is not realized with one image in five minutes.

WARNING

Although the authors recommend adjusting gamma first, and then adjusting image content to arrive at a perfectly exposed image, the gamma on your display will affect your finished work in two situations.

First, if you're working in Photoshop for Windows on a file that originated from a Macintosh machine, you must match the gamma of that particular Mac to get consistent results in your imaging.

Second, if you're editing a file to be used on an imagesetter, film recorder, or video output device, you must also set your monitor's gamma to match the gamma of that particular device.

Monitor Parameters

If your monitor isn't listed in the Monitor drop-down list, and you choose Other, Adobe recommends that you choose a White Point of 6500 degrees Kelvin. This setting complies with most new monitors.

If your whites don't look as white as you think they should with this setting, try the following before you change it:

◆ Wipe your monitor screen with a damp cloth. Your screen attracts dust and other airborne matter, which accumulates and dims your view faster than you realize.

◆ Adjust your monitor's brightness and contrast. These dials are usually located on the monitor in a place where it's easy to nudge them out of position accidentally. Taping the dials in position when you have them properly adjusted is an excellent idea, especially if your work environment requires that you move your monitor from time to time.

When you select different setup settings, you actually change the way Photoshop responds to your image editing, so before you change the setting, make sure that a less-than-ideal monitor view truly is caused by the wrong white point color temperature, and not by dust or a turned-down knob on your monitor.

Click on the Phosphors drop-down list. If your monitor is one of the six listed, choose it. Otherwise, leave the setting at its default of Trinitron. Many modern monitor tubes are Trinitrons. If, however, your monitor uses red, green, and blue phosphors not manufactured according to Sony's Trinitron standards, this setting allows Photoshop to compensate. And you do have to be a rocket scientist to give Photoshop custom phosphor information in the Phosphors dialog box that pops up when you choose Custom. A "good" owner's manual for a monitor will provide monitor phosphor information, but good OEM documentation is up there with gold with respect to its abundance on earth!

Room Parameters

Adobe included the Room Parameters window in the Monitor Settings dialog box with the most finicky folks in mind. In theory, the high, medium, and low options can compensate for bright, dim, or average lighting in your work environment. These obviously are not precise settings, and you should pick the Ambient Light setting that seems to describe your situation the best.

But instead of pondering over Photoshop's Room Parameters, it's better to ask yourself a question at this point: why would a serious imaging person want bright lights bouncing off his or her monitor? Or lighting conditions that change dramatically throughout the day? Unless your employer is a tyrant, you can do something *yourself* about harsh, dim, or inconsistent lighting conditions that will make a *much* greater difference than choosing one of the Ambient Light settings.

Saving Your Settings

Even before you're certain that the settings you entered in the Monitor Setup dialog box are final, you can save them to an AMS file. AMS is the Windows file extension that Photoshop gives to files that contain monitor settings. You will appreciate this feature if you decide to reinstall Photoshop, or if an unexpected system halt corrupts your one and only file.

Here's how to save your monitor settings.

SAVING A PHOTOSHOP SETTING

1.   Click on the Save button on the Monitor Setup dialog box to display the Save directory dialog box.

2. If you have a folder on your hard disk where you keep invaluable information, choose this from the directory dialog box. If not, Photoshop installs a folder called Calibrat (Calibration files). You can find this under the Photoshop folder on your hard disk.

3. In the File name text box, enter a name for the monitor setting that you will be able to remember easily (see fig. 3.2). One of us still has Photoshop 3.0.5 on his machine, and you can see that the monitor setting for version 3.0.5, along with settings for his favorite film recording service bureau and others, are stored in a DATASAFE folder on hard disk.

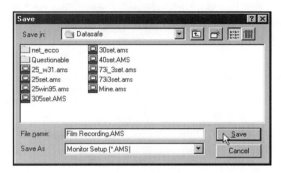

figure 3.2
Name the Monitor Setup file something you can easily remember and load it later.

4. Click on OK to return to the Monitor Setup dialog box, and save the current setting to file. Keep the Monitor Setup dialog box open.

Now, every time you experiment with your monitor settings you can return to any setting you made and saved earlier, simply by clicking on Load from the Monitor Setup dialog box and then clicking on the AMS file of your choice. If you ever need to reinstall Photoshop, or if Photoshop crashes, taking your Monitor Setup preferences with it, the monitor settings you saved to disk will save you minutes of work re-establishing your viewing environment. You will be surprised at how accustomed you become to specific display conditions, and how irritating it is to suddenly work without them!

TIP

The Save and Load options are available in several of Photoshop's dialog boxes, not just the Monitor Setup dialog box. As you will see throughout this book, you can save Calibration, Levels, Variations, and other global changes to Photoshop and your images, and then load them at any time.

Saved settings are very useful in Photoshop work, and the saved files are very small (typically 50 to 200 bytes). You should take advantage of this Photoshop feature when it's offered in a dialog box because it often enables you to backtrack when you make a mistake.

Monitor Calibration

Your monitor's color temperature, its make, and the phosphor characteristics are only part of setting up the monitor to provide accurate, consistent viewing conditions. Balancing the contrast, the color channels, and black and white points for your monitor are important calibration steps also, to make your monitor faithfully represent your images. You need to set up your monitor so that its display capability is optimized when you edit images.

In the Monitor Setup dialog box, click on the Calibrate button to display the Calibrate dialog box. This section explains how the settings in this dialog box affect your imaging.

At the top of the dialog box is the Gamma area, which consists of checkered stripes alternating with 67% black, solid stripes, with a slider beneath the stripe pattern. This option enables you to manually refine the gamma value in the Gamma window of the Monitor Setup dialog box (Macintosh: on the Gamma control panel). If you fine-tune the gamma for your monitor, people who view your images from other workstations will see color values that are closer to those you intend. This solution, although not perfect, is the best available, short of buying a monitor-calibration package. Now to show you how to use this feature of the Calibrate dialog box.

The stripes above the slider are something like an eye test, in which you try to blend the stripes together by moving the slider in either direction. First, click on the Balance button, which controls the balance between the black point and white point. For the authors, the stripes are pretty well blended together at 72 (see fig. 3.3). This does not mean that *you* should choose 72; your monitor and ours are probably not identical (and yours is surely a newer model!). The value 78 doesn't correspond to the absolute value of the gamma; it's merely a Photoshop reference number.

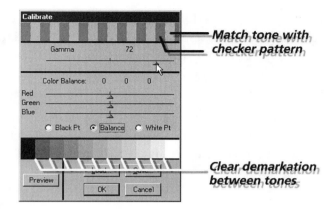

figure 3.3

To set the best gamma balance for your monitor, adjust the slider until the banding between solid tones and patterns disappears.

Do the same for the black point and the white point. First, click on the White Pt button, and then adjust the slider so that the stripes at the top invisibly blend. Also note that the density swatches at the bottom of the dialog box (refer to fig. 3.3) will become clearly defined or blend together, depending on the direction in which you drag the Gamma slider. The idea is to be able to see the pattern swatches at the top fade into the tone solids, while at the same time, the density swatches at the bottom should display clear demarcations between tones. Each density swatch should look distinctly different from its neighbors. Now click on the Black Pt button and perform the same balance. Finally, click on the Balance button again and readjust the balance, if necessary, to blend the stripes together.

On Color Balance

Some monitors today still have a bluish color cast to them. This is obviously a problem when you try to do precise retouching to a color image. To compensate for a color cast from your monitor, Photoshop offers a color-correction feature. This feature enables you to achieve color balance in the same way you correct gamma, except that you use Red, Green, and Blue sliders instead of the Gamma slider to make the stripes match at the top of the dialog box.

Most monitors manufactured in the last two years don't display a noticeable color cast, however, and you won't need to reset the color balance for Photoshop. But you should check to make sure, and *don't touch a thing* or save the settings to file until everything is balanced. If you notice a color cast, try sliding the little triangles from the zero point; if this causes the stripes at the top of the dialog box to blend better, your monitor needs calibration. If the stripes' contrast increases, you should leave the settings alone.

Again, when you have the best settings for gamma calibration, click on the Save button to save them; then you can always recall them, as you can the monitor settings. Windows users need to specify the AGP extension at the end of the saved gamma settings file.

NOTE

The settings in the Calibrate dialog box affect Photoshop differently than those in the Monitor Setup dialog box do. Whereas the Monitor Setup settings—Monitor type, Phosphors, and the like—change your view of the image, the Calibrate settings change an image file's color properties.

Monitor calibration has a direct impact on the way Photoshop translates the RGB color model (the model your monitor uses to display color) into the CMYK color model (used in the creation of color separations for four-color process printing). The CMYK color model has four channels (Cyan, Magenta, Yellow, and Black), compared to RGB's three channels. Accurate CMYK imaging depends on having accurate RGB information to start with. Calibration is designed to help ensure that the RGB information is correctly displayed.

Calibration is not critical for displaying an RGB image in its native RGB monitor mode, but a badly calibrated monitor will affect the color information generated and written to a file for an image that has been translated into CMYK.

Whenever image data is translated, it adheres to the old computer adage: *GIGO* (garbage in, garbage out). Don't expect great results if you don't feed your computer great information.

Additionally, if your monitor setup is not optimized, the result will be less than perfect when you try to blend a selection area into a background image. The brightness of the overall image is affected as well.

Keep all these concerns in mind if you ever doubt that fine-tuning your monitor is worth the hassle.

Expressing Your General Preferences

After the preferences for your monitor's gamma and other parameters have been defined, it's time to take a tour of Photoshop's General Preferences. In version 4, all the preferences from previous versions, plus some new ones, are neatly organized on a single dialog box that toggles forward and backward according to subcategory of preferences. Preferences are used to define the way you see and work with different Photoshop elements: palettes, cursors, your selection of a color model from which to choose colors, and many other things that indirectly relate to the quality of the finished image. Figure 3.4 shows the new layout of the Preferences dialog box.

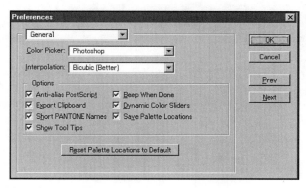

figure 3.4

The File/General/ Preferences dialog box.

The following sections describe the General Preferences options. You should press Ctrl+K (or choose File, Preferences, General) in Photoshop now, and choose the options that will be most worthwhile in your own work. The General Preferences can be respecified at any time; if you find that a Preference simply isn't working out, General Preferences is the place to change something.

Using Photoshop's Color Picker

Photoshop not only supports the system color pickers native to the different operating system versions of Photoshop 4, but also comes with an incredibly full-featured color picker of its own (see fig. 3.5). By default, when you first launch Photoshop after installation, Photoshop's Color Picker is loaded. The Color Picker drop-down list is at the top of the General Preferences dialog box.

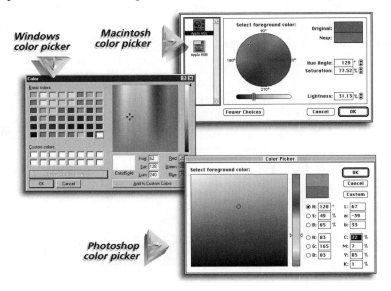

figure 3.5
System color pickers are fine for applications that don't provide one, but Photoshop's color picker is a complete, color-matching system for on-screen and prepress productions.

Unless you are handed color specifications from the Windows or the Macintosh color pickers, there is no logical reason to choose a color picker other than Photoshop's. The Windows color picker specifies HSB color model colors on a scale from 0 to 240; this scale is incompatible with Photoshop's color specification and most other graphics programs. The Macintosh color picker similarly defines HSB and RGB colors in percentages (0–100), not on a brightness scale from 0 to 255, as does Photoshop. Photoshop's color picker is the one shown in figures throughout this book. You access the color picker by clicking on the foreground/background colors on Photoshop's toolbox.

Why is Photoshop's color picker a better general preference than your operating system's? Because Photoshop's color picker displays HSB, RGB, CMYK, and LAB color models from which you can specify a color. Additionally, you can choose from Custom color palettes that represent the digital equivalents of the PANTONE, FOCOLTONE, TOYO, TRUEMATCH, and other physical color-matching systems (see fig. 3.6).

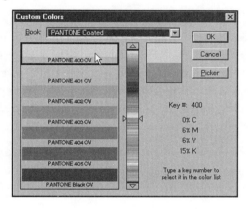

figure 3.6
Photoshop's Color Picker is the only choice when you need to precisely match color printing inks used in traditional printing.

Photoshop's color picker is also aware of illegal video colors—colors that might display on-screen but cannot be created with process colors on a commercial printing press. If you specify in the Color Picker a color that cannot be printed, an exclamation button appears in the Color Picker's dialog box, indicating that a color is out of CMYK gamut. If you then click on the color swatch beneath the exclamation button, you tell Photoshop to calculate the closest, "legal" color in the CMYK printing gamut. This attention feature also appears on the Color palette when you specify an out-of-gamut color. If you work at a commercial printer, or frequently send your work to a commercial printer, Photoshop's color picker is a must, to ensure that CMYK colors are faithfully represented in your work and on-screen.

Interpolation

Photoshop uses interpolation rather than diffusion to make the changes you specify for an image's new dimensions, resolution, or other edits you specify in images while you work with RGB (*TrueColor, millions of colors*) images. Interpolation may seem to rearrange color pixels in an image, but it actually adds and deletes pixels to complete an action or edit, and then reassigns different colors to existing pixels to execute a particular command. The quality of Photoshop's interpolation calculations depends on the speed with which you choose to accomplish them. Speed is the trade-off for accuracy, and you have three choices as to how Photoshop interpolates your editing work:

◆ The Bicubic option is the most accurate method of rearranging pixels and is the default setting. Photoshop calculates the average of pixels surrounding the pixel to be recolored, in all directions, and then calculates a weighted average (based upon color similarity in neighboring pixels) for the resulting color. It takes the longest for Photoshop to calculate, but on a Pentium or PowerMac, the wait is nominal, and the result is the highest quality image.

◆ The Bilinear option is the middle ground between quality and speed of interpolation. This type of interpolation calculates new pixel colors from an average of existing colors in a row and in a column surrounding the pixel that is reassigned a color.

◆ The Nearest Neighbor method of interpolation is Photoshop's on-the-fly estimate of what an altered pixel in your image should look like. This method is the surest way to introduce *aliasing*, the unwanted stair-step effect at the edges of color contrast in an image. You should reserve this option for the night you need to retouch 100 images by morning for a client with no taste in art.

General Options

Below the Interpolation and Color Picker selection areas are the general options setting up Photoshop's environment. The way the program works with the system, and the way import and export objects are handled are defined here.

Anti-Alias PostScript

The clipboard on both the Macintosh and Windows systems is a feature that is alternately prized and detested, depending upon what you're trying to accomplish. In Windows, Photoshop is an OLE client, and you can paste almost anything from the clipboard into a new or existing Photoshop document window. The only problem is that vector data is not anti-aliased, and the resulting pasted object looks like Etch-A-Sketch artwork rather than a refined computer graphic. (We own three different-sized Etch-A-Sketch tablets, and are not slamming the fine Ohio Arts product here.)

Similarly, the Macintosh clipboard converts everything to PICT format; there is no way, except for the Anti-Alias PostScript option, to paste vector information into a Photoshop window and keep a smooth look to objects with diagonal lines and curves in their geometry. If you have Adobe Illustrator on the Macintosh, you can copy from a design (because the design is translated to PostScript format as it is held on the clipboard) and then paste the design into a Photoshop document. Before importing the clipboard information, Photoshop displays a dialog box asking whether you want the clipboard information pasted as pixels (with or without anti-aliasing) or as a collection of Photoshop paths.

Because anti-aliased PostScript pasting from the clipboard is confined to Illustrator files, Windows users cannot use CorelDRAW, XARA, or FreeHand to work between Photoshop and a drawing program to retain path information, or enable anti-aliasing to occur in the imported design. Illustrator 4.0.1 for Windows cannot be considered a modern drawing application; Adobe Systems has not kept Illustrator equal on both platforms, as they have Photoshop. If Windows users want the flexibility of copying from a drawing program and pasting into Photoshop, however, version 4.0.1 works quite well with Photoshop. In figure 3.7, you can see the Paste box that appears only when an Illustrator file is on the clipboard; in the background, you can see a nicely anti-aliased design. If you turn off the Anti-Alias option in Preferences, the pasted image will look crude and unrefined.

figure 3.7
Use the clipboard for quick import/export of a drawing file, if you use Illustrator or other
PostScript products.

TIP

On both platforms, Adobe's TypeAlign and Streamline products can copy PostScript, vector-
type information and Type 1 text to the clipboard, and Photoshop 4 will import it.

Windows users should note that files with the extension EPS are not necessarily vector in
content, nor are they necessarily Illustrator-type files. To be certain that Photoshop can paste,
open, or place Illustrator vector data, be sure to name your file with the AI extension, whether
from Illustrator, or another drawing application that can export to Illustrator format. Saved
Illustrator files cannot be copied to the clipboard and into Photoshop by using an application
other than Illustrator. You must save the file and then choose File, Open or File, Place in
Photoshop for Windows to convert a generic EPS file (one not created in Illustrator) to bitmap
format.

Export Clipboard

The Export Clipboard option can be useful when you are working between
applications, but you should use the new Edit, Purge, Clipboard feature in
Photoshop immediately after you know that the clipboard copy has safely arrived

at its destination. System clipboards require system resources to hold an image, and this can impact on the speed and stability of Photoshop, particularly with files larger than 1–2 MB.

The Export Clipboard option causes Photoshop to query you upon exit as to whether you want the contents of the clipboard purged from the system. After considering this option and playing it both ways for a month or so, the authors have concluded that you should leave this option checked, with only two reservations:

◆   You make it a practice to purge the clipboard after copying large files

◆   You need to know in advance which applications can and cannot handle Photoshop media

Most programs will accept Photoshop images through the clipboard, except for those that use a "private" internal clipboard, such as Fractal Design Painter. If you copy a layer to the clipboard, it will arrive in the host application composited against a white background, the size of the background being the maximum height and width of the layer object's dimensions.

Short PANTONE Names

As shown earlier, you can choose and apply colors that approximate PANTONE colors in Photoshop. PANTONE colors (like those you find in the fanning swatch books) are color specifications for paints and inks. If your assignment calls for using a specific PANTONE color for corporate colors, for example, Photoshop is very good at approximating paint and ink values to the monitor.

When you use a genuine PANTONE color in a design, it is reproduced at press time as a combination of ink colors mixed to exacting standards. The purpose of the PANTONE color-matching system is to ensure that a design is faithfully reproduced from a printing press that could be a thousand miles away from the designer. Or when someone another thousand miles away wants you to design a graphic and has an exact shade of color in mind, they call you, tell you the ink name, and you're all set to do the design. If you check the Short PANTONE Names option in the More Preferences dialog box, the PANTONE colors you select can be matched when you export an image to other programs.

Adobe continually updates new PANTONE paint and ink *digital simulations* (the technical name for the on-screen display of PANTONE and other manufacturer's color mixtures) in releases of new products such as Photoshop and Illustrator. Although it's good to get the latest paint specs, other applications, such as Quark and CorelDRAW, cannot access the new, proprietary names from embedded EPS files. And so the color separations outside Photoshop will not represent the colors you have specified, say, for a corporate logo, where color-matching is critical.

If you choose Short PANTONE Names, Photoshop will use the traditional names used by other applications for the colors in Photoshop files. The additional benefit to using this option is that specifying the same color used in Photoshop for text in PageMaker, for example, becomes an easy task. You choose the same name in PageMaker's Colors palette as that which appears in Photoshop's PANTONE color chart—and your print is consistent in all areas displaying a PANTONE color.

Show Tool Tips

Photoshop 4 has many new interface elements. To provide at-a-glance help to identify them, Adobe added Tool Tips—an interface element reminiscent of both Windows pop-up help and the Macintosh Balloon Help. Tool Tips pop up on-screen whenever you hover your cursor over an element that has been coded to display a pop-up message defining the element. Tool Tips are not limited to the toolbox; the palettes also offer identifying pop-up tags.

Although you might think this is an annoying interface addition that brands you as a novice, it's really not that intrusive, and *everyone* is a novice with a new version of a program. We recommend that you leave Tool Tips checked, and review your need for them in a month or so.

Beep When Done

This option encourages users to leap up and make a beeping sound whenever they complete a task. Onnnnly kidding. For systems that support sound, this is an invaluable option to have checked. Plug-in filters, in particular, can take up to 30 seconds to execute on files larger than 2–3 MB, while other effects, such as slight sharpening, might not provide a visible effect at certain viewing resolutions. If you check this option and your computer has sound capability, Photoshop will alert you with a system sound (you cannot assign specific sound files in Photoshop) when it has finished a process.

If you work elbow to elbow in a large enterprise, your Information Technology administrator might decide to disable this feature for you.

Dynamic Color Sliders

Leave this box checked. This option is similar to Photoshop's LUT (Look-Up Table) Animation, discussed shortly. The sliders on the Color Picker and Colors palette change to reflect a change in one or more color components as you define a color. If you don't check this option, colors on the sliders in both Photoshop color-definition areas remain constant until you finish defining the color, and you will have to guess a little more often at a result color when you blend the components (such as Hue and Brightness) of a color.

Save Palette Locations

You should leave the Save Palette Locations option checked if you want to return to the same customized setup for palettes and features in future sessions of Photoshop. You will soon learn about the Photoshop palettes—you use them in combination with tools and effects, and often must complete your work in more than one Photoshop session. When you check this option, Photoshop notes the settings, location, and position of palettes whenever you exit the program, and puts them back in place when you next open the program. Unfortunately, this option has nothing to do with the last image you worked on; Photoshop always begins a session with an empty workspace (unless you launch Photoshop by clicking on an associated image file). If you leave Save Palette Locations checked, you will find that the examples in this book are easier to follow if you take a break from them.

Also, if you disagree with the recommendations made in this chapter or elsewhere in this book, you can return Photoshop to its factory settings for all palettes by clicking the Reset Palette Locations to Default button on the General Preferences dialog box. This does not change the options on the palettes themselves; it simply restores the grouping and location on which a palette displays on-screen.

Saving Files

Now, having covered the General Preference options, click on the Next button or choose Saving Files (Ctrl(⌘)+2) to move to Photoshop's options for saving files.

Image Previews

Saving image previews is perhaps bigger news for Windows users than for Macintosh users, who have always had the capability to preview an image file and display it as a desktop icon. The Windows Image Previews option works for displaying previews in Photoshop in all versions of Windows, but thumbnail icons cannot be displayed on the desktop in Windows 3.1x because Win 3.1x doesn't have an interface desktop. To see desktop icons, you must use a HiColor (32,768 colors) or TrueColor (16.7 million colors) video driver, and use Windows 95 with the Plus! Pack or Windows NT 4.0 as your operating system.

In figure 3.8, you can see the authors' desktop on a good day. The Lawnchair.psd thumbnail icon has been clicked on to provide a tabbed menu of information options that can be specified after the file's creation, outside Photoshop.

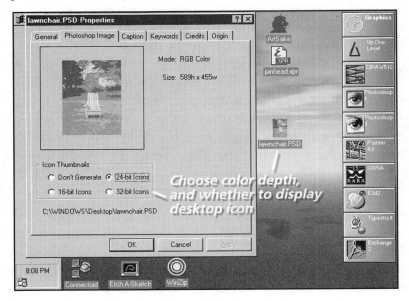

figure 3.8
Choose a color mode for thumbnail icon display and add text references in the header of the image file.

The information users can save is the same information you can add in Photoshop's File, File Info command, originally created so that users could send image information across the wires to news services. Because the Macintosh OS does not support property sheets, the Properties menu for Photoshop files is not available. To save desktop image icons in Windows, the file must be saved in Photoshop's PSD format; the picture icon will not display in a folder window, but only on the desktop. The options for saving with the Preview are Always, Ask When Saving, and Never Save in Photoshop for Windows.

The size of a saved image with preview capability does not increase significantly over images saved without preview images; you can expect an increase in file size of 1 or 2 KB.

On the Macintosh, you can choose to include an icon, a thumbnail image, a full-size preview, or any combination of the three. The Full size option is actually a 72 pixel-per-inch image embedded in Photoshop that can be used to place images in desktop publishing and other programs for position only. The format of this header image is PICT. We strongly recommend that you check this option only if your work calls for it; full-size images embedded as previews dramatically increase the saved file size.

2.5 Compatibility

This option stores a flattened version of your 4.0 document in the Photoshop 4.0 file, to be used with applications that don't understand the special 4.0 format. When the file is opened in a program that can only read a 2.5 image file, the image displays all the characteristics (such as alpha channels) it would have, had it been created in Photoshop 2.5. Guides, layers, and Adjustment layers will not display when the document is opened in Photoshop 2.5. This welcome, and fairly invisible, downward compatibility with Photoshop 2.5 comes with one penalty—the amount of disk space your files take is greater than if 2.5 compatibility were turned off.

There is one exception to this rule, however. If your 4.0 file has more than 16 channels, the file will not open in programs capable of handling only version 2.5 files. If you work with Photoshop 4.0 only, everyone you share files with uses either Photoshop 3 or 4, and you don't need the capability to create 2.5-compatible files, you can save a lot of disk space by turning off this feature.

Save Color Metric Tags

This option is of little use to most Windows users, where PageMaker is the dominant desktop publishing application; however, users of QuarkXPress can check this option to ensure that color separation tables prepared by using the EfiColor color-matching specification from Photoshop will export correctly.

Click on the Next button so that we can walk through the Display & Cursors options.

Display & Cursors

This area of preferences relates to the way cursors are displayed for the different tools, and the way images display on your monitor when you view color channels, or when your system video does not support 24-bit color or greater (*millions of colors*) (see fig. 3.9).

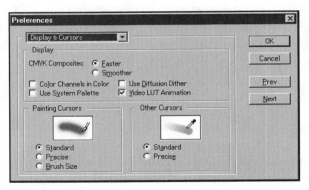

figure 3.9
The Display & Cursors dialog box.

CMYK Composites

If you're new to commercial printing or electronic imaging, CMYK may mean nothing to you. Before you choose a preference for the display of CMYK Composites, you need to understand what CMYK (pronounced *see-mac*) is.

Color models serve a very real purpose in the imaging world, and different models were invented for different reasons. Many artists like to describe color by using the Hue, Saturation, and Brightness (HSB) model. The Red, Green, Blue (RGB) color model serves a very useful purpose, enabling artists to communicate clearly with software engineers by describing color output to a monitor's red, green, and blue phosphors.

The Cyan, Magenta, Yellow, and Black (CMYK) model is used for color-separation printing. The mixture of these colors as ink, not light, makes up the color images you see in magazines and books. Also known as *process color*, CMYK is a subtractive color-creation process. As you may recall from school, pigments are subtractive colors and light is additive.

To make an RGB image printable on a commercial print press that uses the standard four process colors, the image must be converted to the CMYK color space. This is the reason that calibrating your monitor is important. Photoshop uses your monitor settings to perform RGB-to-CMYK conversions. A CMYK color file has four channels, as opposed to an RGB image's three, and a CMYK mode image can be stored as a TIFF, PSD, JPEG, Photoshop EPS (bitmap information only), or Scitex image.

You probably won't encounter a CMYK TIFF file unless it's been converted from an RGB image as part of the prepress process, or has been scanned directly from a CMYK-capable scanner. *Prepress* is the work and the procedures a commercial printer or service bureau goes through to take the elements (digital or otherwise) that make up a finished piece and create printing plates from them.

The reason Photoshop offers a choice of CMYK display is that Photoshop has to simulate CMYK values on-screen because your monitor isn't truly capable of displaying colors based on the CMYK color model. You have your choice of Smoother or Faster display simulations of an image based on commercial press colors. Like Interpolation, CMYK Composite display is another speed/accuracy trade-off. When you select Faster, Photoshop uses interpolation and a lookup table to assign CMYK color values to any color image you convert to the CMYK color mode or choose to view in CMYK Preview (under the View menu, which is covered later in this chapter). When you select Smoother, Photoshop takes its time to translate and assign more accurate CMYK color values to the RGB image on-screen.

If you work in the production department of a magazine or other publication, you want to display CMYK Composites by using the Smoother option. The Smoother option will show you potential problems that may occur when you use Photoshop to generate color separations from a digital image. To view a CMYK file that you intend to convert to RGB image mode by using the View menu command, select the Faster display option in the General Preferences dialog box before using View, CMYK Preview. CMYK has a smaller gamut than the RGB color model, and you don't get a better view of changes when you go from a less capable color mode to a more capable one. The CMYK Composites option determines the type of calculation Photoshop uses to generate the display of the image, not how it converts the image type when you change image modes from RGB to CMYK by using the Image, Mode menu commands.

TIP

The color mode change from RGB to CMYK, which is part of the prepress process, should take place *after* you have finished creating and enhancing an image in Photoshop. Each time you change an image's color mode (*color space*), Photoshop must interpolate the information to change from a three-channel color model (RGB) to a four-channel model (CMYK). Interpolation always causes some reduction in the quality of the image.

Do all your work in RGB mode, and when you finish your editing and enhancing, save the RGB mode file. Then save a *copy* of the RGB file with a different name. Finally, use the Image, Mode menu command to change the image type from RGB to CMYK mode.

Make any minor corrections in the CMYK mode file and then print your separations, or save the file for your service bureau. If you must make significant edits to the CMYK image, discard the CMYK file and make your changes in the original RGB copy. Repeat the previous procedure for saving the RGB file to a new name and converting the copy to CMYK.

Color Channels in Color

By default, when you use the Channels palette to look at the individual color channels in an image, color channel images (images containing more than 256 unique colors) are displayed as grayscale. The grayscale information, which indicates the relative strengths of an individual channel's contributions to the overall image, is combined to show a composite image in color. White in a channel indicates a strong color channel contribution, whereas black indicates no contribution; shades between white and black are different, partial strengths of channel color. Except when you investigate the coverage of channels in CMYK images (the amount of printing ink applied to a press plate, based upon an image channel), you have little reason to change the Color Channels in Color option.

Checking this option tells Photoshop to show you the channel in shades of the color that corresponds to the channel being viewed. Although it's easier to tell exactly which channel of an image you're viewing in Photoshop when the channel views are displayed in color, this option is bound to cause errors in advanced image editing because you're not truly seeing what the color channel information looks like. Try placing a colored gel in front of a grayscale image, and then consider how accurately you can edit the grayscale image. This is exactly the same effect you get when you check the Color Channels in Color check box—useful for prepress analysis of inks, but of little use in everyday image editing.

Use System Palette and Use Diffusion Dither

A system palette, as the name implies, is a palette of colors that is directly supported by your operating system and video card. When you choose Use System Palette in the Display & Cursors dialog box, you're telling Photoshop to use your computer's color support mechanism instead of a custom lookup table to display inactive image windows (images you have open, but aren't editing). The Use System Palette option can be helpful if you're running only a 256-color (hundreds of colors) video driver because Photoshop then can use most of the available display colors to show the active image window, and can let system colors represent the inactive document. (Photoshop doesn't read the lookup table for the inactive image windows.)

When you're running video drivers that can display at least 15 bits per pixel (AKA *HiColor, 32,768 colors,* or *thousands of colors*), you won't see a difference in display quality of images when this option is checked. Additionally, the Use Diffusion Dither option (covered next) works hand-in-hand with the Use System Palette option to better approximate display colors when you don't have a video driver capable of handling more than 256 colors.

Use Diffusion Dither

Here's your opportunity to decide how images are displayed when you're running a low color-depth video driver. If you check this option, the next time you run a 256-color driver while viewing an RGB image, the resulting color-depth mismatch will be diffused across the image. Although low color-depth and diffusion dithering are tedious ways to work with an image, using diffusion dithering is more visually relaxing than using a patterned dither, which is Photoshop's default when you leave this option unchecked.

Video LUT Animation

This option speeds up Photoshop screen redraws when you edit. Because the screen colors in an image change constantly as you perform color corrections and other editing, the Video LUT (Look Up Table) Animation option keeps the image you're working on updated on-screen (and in preview windows of dialog boxes) to reflect changes you make or propose making. LUT Animation is a dynamic updating of the color table used to display an image, and works only in a 16-bit or higher display mode. Leave Video LUT Animation checked. It asks more of your processor but will speed up your work because you can more accurately see what you're doing.

Painting and Other Cursors

Photoshop 4 gives you control over the way your tool cursors look on-screen. Uniquely shaped cursors can be a blessing when you have as many tools to work with as you do in Photoshop, but they can be a hindrance sometimes to precision editing. You can have it any of three ways in Photoshop, and the next section describes why you should have a strong preference as to what your cursor looks like.

Standard Cursors

You can see Photoshop's Standard cursors in the figures in this book—partially as a quick indicator of which tool is being used in an exercise, but mostly because Standard is Photoshop's default. As you will see on-screen, and throughout this book, the default cursors generally are shaped like the tool they represent. When you want the utmost precision, right down to the pixel, in selecting or painting an image area during a Photoshop session, you can switch between Standard and Precise cursors by pressing the Caps Lock key. You don't have to visit the Display & Cursors dialog box, but you *do* need to press Caps Lock again before you work in other applications, OR Your tEXT mIGHT lOOK lIKE tHIS!

TIP

Although Standard tool cursors appear to be handsomely crafted, overstated representations of the tools you choose, there is a hot spot you can identify on-screen for Standard tool cursors if you want to know exactly where a brush stroke begins, or where the Lasso tool begins its selection. Look carefully at a Standard cursor. One single pixel in the cursor shape is an inverted color: for example, when the Paintbrush tool is represented in black, a white pixel on its tip indicates the center of the Paintbrush's stroke. This is not an obvious feature of the Standard tool cursors, and we cannot recommend that you depend on the dot at the edge of the Standard cursors if you require precision in your editing work. Nevertheless, the Standard tool cursors provide an instant reference as to which tool is currently active. If you're new to Photoshop, you will benefit from the default settings for the tool cursors.

Precise Tool Cursors

When you choose the Precise option for the Painting tool cursors or Other tools, the cursor remains the same shape—it's a small crosshair, its center marked with a reverse-video color pixel. With this option checked, pinpoint accuracy is ensured in your editing, painting, and selection work; you must constantly reference the toolbox, however, to see which tool is currently chosen. An additional piece of helpful information about each tool is displayed on the Photoshop for Windows status line—each tool's *function* is described on the status line, but not the name of the tool itself.

If you choose the Brush Size tool cursor, discussed in the following section, you can toggle between Precise and Brush Size by pressing the Caps Lock key.

Brush Size Tool Cursors

When you choose Brush Size as the tool cursor for Painting tools, an empty circle appears over an active image window that signifies the approximate dimensions of the painting tool's tip. We must stress the word *approximate* here; most tips on the Brushes palette have soft edges, and the Brush Size tool cursor doesn't accurately reflect the *spread* that foreground color with a soft tip creates in an image.

The split screen in figure 3.10 shows the Precise cursor at left and the Brush Size cursor at right, both used to paint with the Airbrush tool. As you can see, at larger brush sizes, the Brush Size option can be a little visually overwhelming.

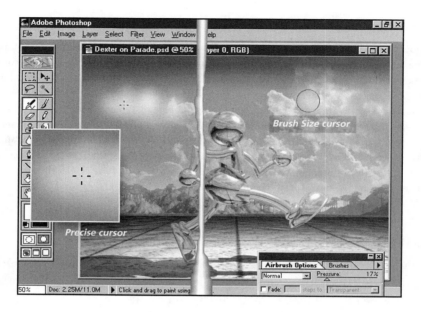

figure 3.10
You can use both options for painting tools, and Precise can also be used for editing and selection tools.

The disadvantage of working with the Brush Size tool cursor has to do with a drag you might feel when using a painting tool. Because Photoshop must redraw and constantly update the display of the Brush Size cursor, the circle (or other custom brush-tip shape) with which you paint can feel sticky and unresponsive. Some people don't mind the touch of a tool in an application, but more experienced users depend on the feedback of the mouse or digitizing tablet to guide brush strokes. If you're sensitive to the responsiveness of a tool cursor, you might want to skip Photoshop's Brush Size tool cursor option.

Transparency and Gamut

Click on Next, and we will look at the way Photoshop displays something you *cannot* see—transparency—and how an overlay on an image can alert you to colors that will not print as expected.

In the Transparency & Gamut dialog box, you have the option to display areas in image layers that contain no editable pixels as a checkerboard pattern, called the *transparency grid.* The transparency grid cannot be selected in an image; it's an on-screen placeholder in the same way a cursor such as the Paintbrush tool defines coordinates while you work. In figure 3.11, you can see the preferences for Transparency & Gamut.

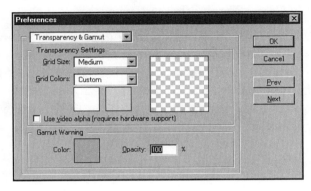

figure 3.11
The Transparency & Gamut dialog box.

The default Grid Size and Grid Colors work for much, but not all of your editing work. Once, the authors had an editing assignment where a checkered table cloth was on a layer, and the default options for Transparency *had* to be changed! If a target image has similar colors to those of the transparency grid, we recommend that you choose colors that are the opposite in this dialog box. Also, if you're working with very small objects on a layer, consider turning the Grid colors to the *same* color, to avoid the patterning effect of the transparency grid. Clicking on the color selection boxes in this dialog box will take you to the color picker, where you can define the colors you use.

Also, if you're running a high-resolution video or don't have 20/20 eyesight, you can increase the size of the grid in this dialog box. When you finish using the custom transparency grid you create, and want Photoshop's factory default for this feature, choose Medium from the Size drop-down list and choose Light from the Colors drop-down list. There is no option in Photoshop that automatically restores Transparency or Gamut preferences.

If you're using Photoshop to create or retouch images for a Web site or simply for viewing on your monitor, you do not need the Gamut Warning option, nor do you need to change it. Gamut Warning refers to the limitations of the CMYK (the commercial printing) color space. You can set the Gamut Warning preference to display a colored overlay on any image you intend to use for CMYK output. This is a handy visual reminder that your image will not print as it's displayed, and showing the Gamut Warning above an image is as easy as pressing Ctrl(⌘)+Shift+Y.

You have an option in this dialog box as to the Color and Opacity of the overlay that indicates out-of-gamut zones in an active image in Photoshop's workspace. As with Transparency, you should define a color that is clearly not in the image you want to view, and you might consider keeping the Opacity at 100% for Gamut Warning, to get a clear view of any problem areas in an RGB image when View, Gamut Warning is enabled.

Units & Rulers

As you will see in the examples throughout this book, Photoshop can express measurements in different kinds of units to help you size up your work. In two instances you want to specify the unit of your choice: when you check the Image Size and Canvas Size settings (both under the Image menu), and when you select the Show Rulers option (by pressing Ctrl+R) around an active image window.

Figure 3.12 shows the Unit Preferences dialog box, which you access by pressing Ctrl(⌘)+K, and then Ctrl(⌘)+5.

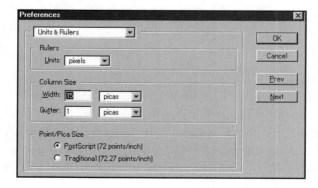

figure 3.12
The Units & Rulers dialog box.

The Rulers field at the top of the Units & Rulers dialog box controls the unit of measurement the rulers use in an active image. Inches and pixels will perhaps be the units you most often specify; when you need to measure an area for placing text, however, you should specify points as the unit of measurement for rulers.

TIP

A very quick way to choose units does not require a trip to the Preferences dialog box. When you press F8 in the workspace, the Info palette appears, and by clicking on the flyout icon next to the XY field, you can specify units here that apply to Photoshop's rulers, the Image Size and Canvas Size commands, and the Document Info field discussed in Chapter 2. Alternatively, you can double-click on rulers to display the Units & Rulers preferences box.

In the Column Size window of the dialog box, the Width and Gutter options show you how an image fits into a page layout of another application, such as a desktop publishing application. Set to inches, this unit of measurement is also used in the Image Size and Canvas Size options of the Image menu. You should set this option to inches unless your work calls for European or typographic standards.

Although it's becoming less and less used, if you work with phototypography or cold type (physical slugs of type), click on the Traditional button in the Point/Pica Size area of the Units Preferences dialog box. PostScript is the default, however, and we recommend that you leave this option at its default when using Type 1 digital typeface programs in Photoshop, and to make it easier to compare font sizes to those used in documents in other applications.

Guides & Grid

In figure 3.13, you can see the preferences for Guides & Grid display. It is here that you can specify the units between grid marks and the color of these interface elements.

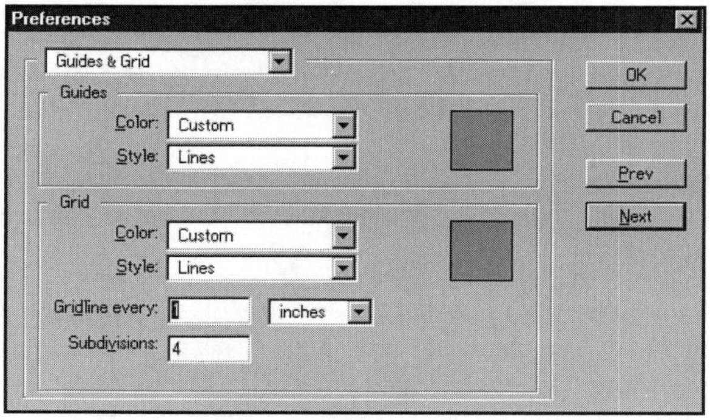

figure 3.13
The Guides & Grid setup dialog box.

As with Photoshop's other nonprinting screen elements, you have your choice of color for display of the guides and grid; choose a color that will stand out in the image in which you're working. You might also prefer a less intrusive view of guides or grids while you work, and the Style drop-down lists provide dashed lines and dots (grid only) to leave more original image displayed on-screen. To display guides and the grid in a document, use the new View command. You cannot add guides to a document without displaying the rulers first (Ctrl(⌘)+R) because you drag the guides in and out from the rulers.

After you have made the selection from the View menu to display the grid and guides, they will appear in every document you open or create. This somewhat annoying behavior needs to be turned off for each document in the workspace foreground. Click on the title bar to make a document window the current editing window, press Ctrl(⌘)+" (quotation marks) to hide the grid if it is visible, and press Ctrl(⌘)+; (semicolon) to hide the guides. Any tool can be used to pull a guide from the horizontal or vertical ruler; however, only the Move tool can be used to reposition a guide.

Plug-Ins

Although Adobe Systems has grouped the location of Photoshop's Plug-Ins Folder preferences with an important memory-handling option, filter locations are discussed as a separate issue here. Memory handling is of vital concern to Photoshop users, and the authors feel that the Scratch Disk setup belongs with the Memory & Image Cache preferences, discussed in the following section.

There is not much more than meets the eye to choosing a preference for the location of the Plug-Ins folder on the Plug-ins & Scratch Disk dialog box. When you click on the Choose button, a directory dialog box appears, in which you can specify the location of the filters you want to use in the *next* session of Photoshop. A change in the location of the Plug-Ins folder does not take immediate effect because Photoshop generates a new Filter menu that corresponds with what it finds in the designated Plug-Ins folder each time you open Photoshop. The authors recommend that you stick with the default folder, unless you plan to move all of Photoshop's native filters (located in the Filters folder in Plug-Ins) to a different location (hint: don't do this). If you have third-party filters from version 3 of Photoshop, you can either reinstall the filters and point the setup program to Photoshop 4's Plug-Ins folder (and the setup program may create a new folder here). Or you can copy the files to the Filters folder, which is what we did with KPT 2.0, Andromeda, and Alien Skin filters— and they function perfectly. Note that 16-bit and 32-bit third-party filters work with Photoshop 4, but 32-bit filters work faster.

Memory Considerations

When compared to the most popular commercial graphics applications on the market today, no single manufacturer realizes the importance of memory handling and adds this feature with such elegance and fault-tolerance as Adobe Systems has done with Photoshop. Photoshop can almost be considered to be a *scaleable* application; it works well on a Quadra, and the performance increases as you move to more expensive, faster hardware, such as the Power Macintosh and Pentium Pro processors.

Version 4 brings with it the capability to handle large images. Competing products have chosen a proxy scheme by which you work with a low-resolution image and then apply the editing commands to the larger original, but if you have the processing speed, RAM, and empty hard disk space on your computer, you can work with images in excess of 100 MB at a comfortable pace in Photoshop. The following sections describe what Photoshop needs from your system to transform your machine into a "Photoshop workstation," and what you can do to accommodate these application needs.

Scratch Disk Allocation and Optimization

If you press Ctrl(⌘)+K and then Ctrl(⌘)+7 now, you will move to the Plug-ins & Scratch Disk preferences dialog box. Note that you are offered both a primary and secondary location for defining a Scratch Disk—a location on the hard disk where Photoshop writes multiple copies of the image you are working on for effects and for Undo and Restore commands.

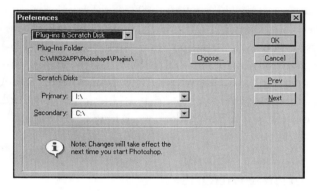

figure 3.14
The Plug-ins & Scratch Disk dialog box.

Understandably, every Photoshop user is anxious to get down to business in this new version, but if you haven't performed hard disk "housecleaning" recently, you will not get the performance from Photoshop that you anticipate. The reasons for this are not as clear as they could be, but they have to do with the way Photoshop accesses your system resources.

Photoshop uses a combination of RAM (memory) and hard disk space to perform its magic. If you have sufficient RAM on your system, Photoshop might never write to disk, but Photoshop has hard-coded instructions to request hard disk space for those occasions when system memory becomes fragmented. There is no way you can specify that Photoshop should use either RAM *or* hard disk space, and available hard disk space is tied to available RAM (*application RAM*) in the eyes of Photoshop. You can have a gigabyte of RAM installed on your machine (don't laugh—remember when 8 MB was an obscene amount?), but if your hard disk has only 100 MB of available space, Photoshop will use only 100 MB of application RAM. Check the Efficiency field on the Document Info box (see Chapter 2) to see whether you're always working in Photoshop at 100% efficiency. If the number is always lower than 100%, Photoshop is using RAM, but also a portion of your hard disk space.

This suggests two things you should do, most likely the first thing tomorrow morning, to make the best use of available RAM when in Photoshop:

◆ Move everything you have no immediate use for off of "expensive media" and onto cheaper media. Hard disks are inexpensive, but Zip disks and floppy disks are cheaper still for those multimedia titles and animation files. Nothing compares to the speed of a local hard disk, and this is where Photoshop looks to write scratch disk files. Users should *not* specify a network drive, a SyQuest, a removable disk, or other peripheral media storage as the scratch disk location in Photoshop. If possible, dedicate a large, fast, empty drive to Photoshop's scratch disk. If a dedicated disk is not available, choose the fastest hard disk you have that has a large amount of free space on it.

◆ Defragment your hard disk after you have moved nonessentials off of it. Windows 3.1x users can use a number of third-party utilities for defragmenting the hard disk, as can Macintosh users. Windows 95 users should use the Disk Defragmenter utility that came with the system, and should by no means use a third-party utility if they are using DriveSpace, the native, on-the-fly hard disk compression utility.

During defragmentation, or as a step prior to defragging, you should check the disk for logical and physical errors and allow the system to repair them. Windows users should also check for files with the extension CHK, TMP, ~TMP, and for BAK files in the root of your boot disk. CHK files are files written to disk when clusters on the hard disk have become indexed incorrectly (a corruption of the FAT, and/or VFAT tables). These files are hard disk error files that Windows often saves in the futile hope that the contents of the files include user information and can be retrieved by using a software utility, pliers from the local hardware store, or a séance. These files contain binary garbage 99% of the time, and take up a great deal of empty hard disk space that can be used for more important things. Be careful about deleting BAK files; files named PREFS.BAK, for example, are backups that an installation program has created from your previous settings. Files with names of user-created documents—artwork, spreadsheet, or word processing documents, for example—that end with the extension BAK are usually fair game for deletion.

Your primary scratch disk should be where you have the most open, uncompressed hard disk space. Windows users should specify a different drive or partition for Photoshop's primary scratch disk than the one Windows is using for its swap file. By default, both Windows and Photoshop will use your C drive. If possible, specify a different drive for one or the other. Macintosh users who use StuffIt Deluxe for compressing files should move compressed, user-created files to removable media. These files take up less space than their uncompressed originals, but they take up still less space on a Zip or other removable media. DriveSpace and Stacker for Windows are also wonderful compression schemes, but Photoshop will not work as quickly on drives specified as scratch disks as on an uncompressed, defragmented disk that is free of errors.

You have the option not to specify a secondary hard disk, but as you can see in figure 3.14, drive I is defined as the primary, and the other uncompressed system drive, boot drive C, is defined as the secondary location Photoshop can use for writing file scraps. If Photoshop runs out of primary disk space during an editing session, it will look for the secondary location. If it fails to find a secondary scratch disk, choose File, Save; choose Edit, Purge and then choose every highlighted option; quit Photoshop, and restart your system.

How Much Room Will Photoshop Need?

It's natural to ask, "How much is enough?" when you're defining scratch disk sizes. Unfortunately, however, this question has to be answered with another question. How large are the files that you typically work with, or want to work with? Adobe states that Photoshop requires up to three times the image size, in both RAM and in empty hard disk space, into which it writes multiple versions of an image, for the purposes of undoing the last-used command, for cloning from a Snapshot image or from the (last) Saved version, and the File, Revert command. After working with media both large and small, the authors have determined that three to five times the size of the image is a more reasonable estimate of system requirements. If you need to edit a 12 MB image, for example, you should have 36 to 60 MB of available application RAM and hard disk space at Photoshop's disposal. If you have less, you will work more slowly as Photoshop writes more image file components to hard disk. *Always,* when you're working with large data, check the Document Sizes box on the status line (Macintosh: at the bottom of the document window) to see whether the current file size (as held in system resources) is a figure close to the allocation you have provided Photoshop. When the Document Sizes number on the left of the fraction exceeds the number on the right, you're low on resources and should save your work. This allows Photoshop to purge other saved versions of the image, and you should consider at this point deleting alpha channels in the image and merging layers to make the file smaller.

TIP

Layers can add significantly to the file size of an image held in system resources. This is important because Photoshop 4 does not paste selections from the clipboard; it pastes layers, as does the Type tool. If you are using the clipboard and the Type tool a lot in a composition, when elements are arranged as you like, press Ctrl(⌘)+E to Merge Layers, and then choose Save to reduce the size of the file as held in RAM and on hard disk.

Memory & Image Cache Preferences

There are three things you can do to make your work in Photoshop a fast, fun, productive experience:

1. Allocate as much RAM as you can spare to Photoshop while in Photoshop.

2. Buy more RAM, and if your motherboard is full, buy a different motherboard. RAM prices are like stocks these days; they go down and then they go up again. Plan new system purchases when prices are low and even consider purchasing RAM for your new machine before you buy the new machine. The price of computers has fallen over the past eight years, whereas RAM prices have fluctuated.

3. Don't use other applications while you work in Photoshop. If you absolutely must have other programs running, start Photoshop *after* all the other programs have loaded.

Figure 3.15 shows you how the authors have set up the Memory & Image Caching settings. These are the default settings; in a moment, we will look at the conditions under which you might want to change them.

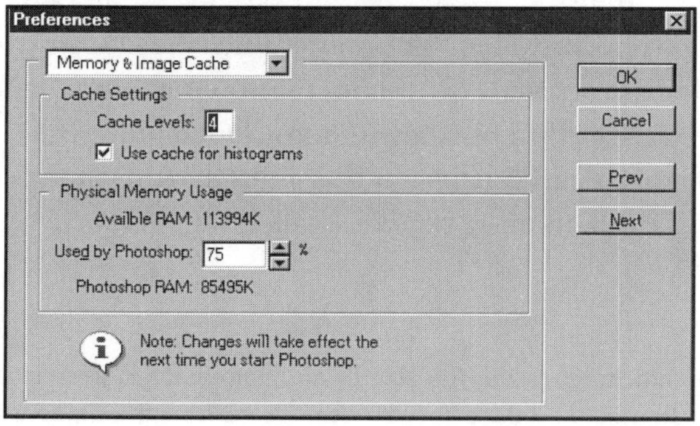

figure 3.15
Photoshop's Image Caching & Memory preferences.

Image Caching is a new Adobe technology by which images display on-screen in progressive resolutions. For example, when you apply the Free Transform operations to a selected area, the edges look coarse until you double-click in the center (or press Enter) to finalize the editing work. The selection then increases in resolution, anti-aliased edges appear, and the Photoshop calculations are applied to the image area. At higher caching levels (8 is the maximum) screen redraws during editing happen quickly, at the expense of application RAM usage. As a side note here, the pixel-doubling option on the Move Options palette enables screen redraws caused by moving image areas to occur more quickly, but without the quality preview of your actions. This is another example of display caching (you only have the on or off option for pixel-doubling). For smaller files, a setting of 2 or 3 is good; 4 is good for files around 10 MB. Use settings greater than 4 for files that are larger than 10 MB. The size of the Image Cache is a tradeoff between performance and the use of system resources.

The last preference setting that is made in the Cache section of Memory & Image Cache Preferences is whether you want Photoshop to use Image Caching to display histograms. When you open the Levels command, or choose Histogram from the Image menu, Photoshop takes a moment to calculate the histogram. The amount of time it takes to calculate and display the histogram can be reduced if the Use cache for histograms check box is checked. The authors recommend that you uncheck this box because when the histogram is created by using cache, it is not as accurate. We don't feel that the tradeoff in speed is, under most circumstances, worth the inaccuracy.

Memory settings for Photoshop are different in Windows and the Macintosh, and need to be discussed as separate issues. Please feel free to peruse *both* of the following sections; you never know when a design opportunity might require that you work on a different operating system.

Optimizing Windows Memory

The most important memory aspect to Windows 3.1x's users is the small pool of system memory that Windows 3.1x allots to handling the *graphical user interface* (GUI). Only 32 KB is allotted to handle the display of interface elements such as menus, brushes, and pens, in all running programs. If you have many applications open, or if programs you have closed didn't return all the resources they used, the behavior of currently running applications is affected and you might experience a system halt. To avoid running into problems caused by low system resources, don't run any programs you don't have to while you are using Photoshop. It is also a good practice to restart Windows 3.1x at least twice a day, or when screen elements start to disappear or only partially display. The only way to restore GUI memory resources is to save your work, close all applications, and restart Windows 3.1x. When the authors use Windows 3.1x, we always keep an eye on system resources by using Microsoft's system resource meter, Sysmon.exe (available for download from Microsoft, and on the Windows 3.1x Resource Guide disks).

Windows 95 has a much larger pool of GUI memory than 3.1x has, so running out of system graphical display memory happens much less often—but it does happen occasionally. To be aware of the current graphical display memory, put Windows 95's resource meter, Rsrcmtr.exe, in your Startup folder so that it is always on the desktop.

Even if your Win95 system has a lot of RAM, running out of memory is possible. Sometimes the system RAM is actually depleted, and at other times the system warning message you receive means that you have run out of disk space. The trick here is knowing what *type* of disk space Windows (3.1, 95, and NT) and Photoshop use, and where the disk space is located. For Windows to operate efficiently, it needs to have a permanent swap file. Windows uses the swap file to free up RAM by swapping currently unused sections of application from RAM to hard disk, creating what is called *virtual RAM*. Photoshop never uses the Windows swap file; it handles its own memory needs. This *doesn't* mean, however, that you don't need a Windows swap file. You need the Windows swap file for other applications that are running in the background, including parts of the operating system itself. Windows usually determines and sets aside adequate amounts of disk space for the swap file. If you think Windows is allocating too much of your hard disk space for the swap file (sluggish performance is a sign), set your swap file to twice the amount of physical RAM you have. For example, if you have 16 MB of RAM, set the swap file to 32 MB of disk space.

Another area to look at for optimizing Photoshop performance is application temp space. Again, Photoshop doesn't use the same temp space as Windows or other programs, but sometimes the third-party filters you use in Photoshop do. In Windows 3.1x, temp space is also used for print spooling and printing from Photoshop. The location of the temp directory is set in the Autoexec.bat file. If you are using Windows 3.1x or Windows 95, you should make sure that you have the following two lines in Autoexec.bat (in these lines, the x is replaced by the drive letter on which the temp and tmp directories are located):

```
Set temp=x:\temp
Set tmp=x:\tmp
```

In Windows 95, the hard disk to which files to be printed spool is always on the same drive where Windows 95 is installed. The location of the print spool cannot be changed. If you have limited space on the drive on which Windows was installed, and you are printing a large graphic to PostScript, you may not be able to print from Photoshop. The only solution here is to free up space on the drive by moving files and programs from that drive to another drive.

Now that you have a handle on Windows' memory needs, let's take a look at how Photoshop handles its memory needs. Unlike on the Macintosh, applications in Windows don't need to declare in advance how many MB of memory they will use. Image editing is a memory-intensive operation, and Photoshop needs all the memory it can get. Because Windows applications are allowed to continually ask for more memory as they need it, Photoshop could easily ask for and take so much of your RAM that there wouldn't be enough left for other applications or the operating system to run. To avoid this, load the programs you need (the fewer the better) before you load Photoshop. Then, when Photoshop loads, it looks at how much RAM is currently available, and limits its needs to the percentage you specify in the Image Caching & Memory dialog box.

Don't worry if the percentage of RAM you have allocated to Photoshop isn't enough to process a specific Photoshop task. As mentioned in the discussion on Scratch Disk space, when Photoshop runs out of physical RAM, it creates virtual RAM by swapping sections of the image or its own code to the scratch disk. This will downgrade performance, but it won't cause a system halt or keep you from running a filter or other process (unless you run out of disk space, too, or there is a hard disk error).

When you change any of the Image Caching & Memory options, remember to restart Photoshop so that the changes take effect.

Macintosh Memory Usage

Macintosh users are faced with a different set of options for optimizing Photoshop 4's memory usage, but it's the same game on both platforms—give Photoshop the resources it needs, and your imaging work will go smoothly and quickly. The Macintosh and Windows operating systems handle the allocation of application memory differently. Unlike Windows, when you use Photoshop on a Macintosh you must specify in advance exactly how many MB of RAM can be dedicated to Photoshop, rather than a percentage of available RAM. If the amount of RAM specified isn't enough, Photoshop cannot ask the operating system for more, and you will see an Out Of Memory message.

One way to increase the amount of RAM on your system is to use Connectix's RAM Doubler. Photoshop will only use physical RAM and won't use the virtual RAM that RAM Doubler creates, but other applications you have running will.

By default, Photoshop takes 9 MB of RAM for 68 KB Macintosh computers, and 15 MB for PowerMacs. If you have more RAM than is necessary for running the OS software and Photoshop, you can increase the allocation size for Photoshop, thus enabling you to work faster. System 7.5.x requires anywhere between 8–12 MB of RAM to load and run. In figure 3.16, you can see Photoshop Info for the authors' Power Macintosh. We have 48 MB of RAM installed, and have increased Photoshop's application RAM from the minimum to 25 MB. You can do this by clicking on the Photoshop icon (not the alias) and then choosing File, Get Info from the Apple menu.

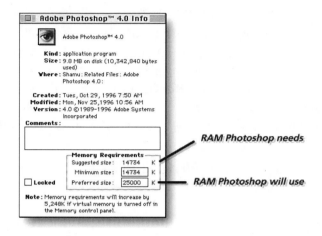

figure 3.16
Increase the amount of application RAM for Photoshop through File, Get Info on the Apple menu.

If you don't use RAM Doubler, there are two schemes we can offer to make Photoshop perform more efficiently with your current amount of RAM, but neither scheme is without its impact on the rest of the system and software you might own.

System 7.5.x and higher comes with Modern Memory Manager and Virtual Memory options. Although Photoshop 3.0.5 did not operate well with Virtual Memory turned on, Photoshop 4 works *excellently* with this option enabled. The problem, at least for Illustrator 6 users, is that Illustrator 6 runs like a slug with Virtual Memory turned on. In figure 3.17, you can see the Memory settings displayed by choosing File, Control Panels from the Apple menu. With Virtual Memory turned off and Illustrator and Photoshop running, we chose File, About this Macintosh, and the Largest Unused Block was only 520 KB, having allocated 25 MB to Photoshop and 14 MB to Illustrator. On the other hand, if we forgo using Illustrator and Photoshop concurrently, and only load Photoshop with Virtual Memory turned on, there is almost 67 MB of unused memory that can be assigned to Photoshop or applications that don't mind Virtual Memory handling.

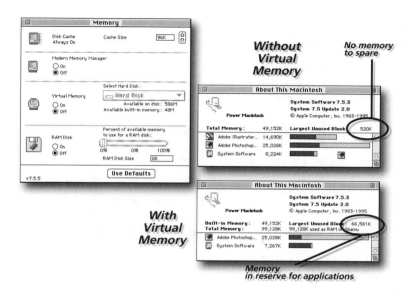

figure 3.17
Virtual Memory in System 7.0.x can add to the system application memory that
Photoshop can use to run faster.

"Dirty" applications are another problem that throws a monkey wrench into
Photoshop memory handling. Basically, your system's memory pool can become
fragmented; this happens on *all* operating systems, and Macintosh users would do
well not to listen to conflicting reports. Applications are supposed to notify the
operating system when they close and resources are returned to the general memory
pool. But they don't always, especially not 16-bit applications running under
Windows 95 and NT. When a program loads, the first continuous block of memory
is allotted to the program, and if a "dirty" application does not return all the
resources upon closing, a gap then exists in the general memory pool. When too
many applications are run that do not return all system resources, your system runs
out of continuous memory (largest unused block) and Photoshop will not load.

In Windows, all versions, the solution is to restart the system. On the Macintosh,
you might want to check out OS Purge, a freeware utility distributed on the Web
and commercial online services such as AOL. Created by E.K. Takeuchi, OS Purge
returns resources to the Mac OS memory pool so that you can return to working
with Photoshop and other programs without restarting. In figure 3.18, the OS

Purge program has been launched, the program displays the About This Macintosh box, and all memory resources except those used by the OS are returned for use.

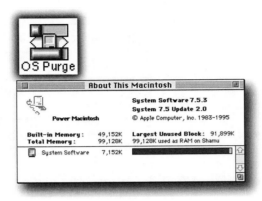

figure 3.18
OS Purge can return system resources that certain applications hang onto. Run this freeware application before running Photoshop.

Our advice for users of Photoshop 4, on both operating systems, is to practice prudent system conservation, leave as much uncompressed hard disk space for Photoshop's scratch disks as you can afford, and buy as much RAM as your budget can bear. You can open impossibly large images in Photoshop, where other applications would groan and crash. But you must let Photoshop do its own thing with memory. Don't tinker with the plumbing while the water's running!

From the Preference Menu to Workspace Options

You have learned how to ensure consistent viewing of an image, how to set the appearance of tools used to edit an image, and a good deal of prudent preparation work for the imaging experiences that lie ahead in this book and with Photoshop. So let's get out of the Preferences boxes and move onto the Photoshop workspace!

Brushes Palette Options

In addition to the default Brushes palette with which you will probably perform most of your imaging work, Photoshop ships with three other palettes: Assorted, Square, and (Drop) Shadows. The files for these palettes are all located in the BRUSHES subdirectory of Photoshop. The Windows version of these files uses the ABR extension; Macintosh users can load the custom palettes by selecting the long file names. Photoshop's default palette of round, soft tips cannot be deleted accidentally because the default palette of Brushes tips is stored in one of Photoshop's program files (users cannot access it).

Although the additional Brushes palettes are not loaded by default, they can be very useful in special situations if you know how to load them. Additionally, you can *create* a brush, or several of them, as an entire palette you can work with in Photoshop.

Loading and Resetting the Brushes Palette

The special palettes Adobe has created for your use consist of sampled, grayscale image areas. Unlike the default palette, where you have the option of adjusting the size and angle you may apply to a tip, the special palette tips, and those you create, are of a fixed size; you have only one option, spacing, to modify a special Brushes tip. Your choice of tools to use with user-defined or special brushes affects the quality of the brush strokes you make. For example (as mentioned in Chapter 1), the Pencil tool does not produce anti-aliasing wherever you stroke. On the other extreme, the Airbrush tool produces such a soft-edged stroke that the "novelty" tips offered in the BRUSHES folder in Photoshop produce vague, not dynamic, art when used with this tool. We recommend using the Paintbrush tool for your adventures with custom and user-defined brush tips, so that you always have control over opacity of the strokes, the choice of foreground color, and the spacing option.

Here's a "test drive" of Photoshop's special tips and palette options, to get you thinking about a collection of tips you would like to create for yourself:

LOADING AND WORKING WITH SPECIAL BRUSH TIPS

1. Press Ctrl(⌘)+N. In the New dialog box, specify a new document that is 300 pixels wide and high, at a resolution of 72 pixels/inch, in RGB Color mode, and whose Contents are white. Click on OK to create the document.

2. Double-click on the Paintbrush tool to select it and to display the Paintbrush Options palette. Press F5 to display the Brushes palette if you decided not to follow our recommendation in Chapter 2 to group the Brushes and Options palettes.

3. On the Brushes palette, click on the menu flyout button (the right-facing triangle) and then choose Replace Brushes. This displays the Load box, which shows your current hard disk's directory structure. Don't fret over the command "Replace Brushes." This merely means that new brushes are loaded without displaying the current brush tips on the palette.

4. Choose Assorted from the Photoshop/Brushes folder on your hard disk. The Brushes palette now loads with pictures and texture samples.

5. On the Options palette, make certain that Opacity is set to 100%, that painting mode is Normal, and that the Wet Edges and Fade options are unchecked.

6. Press D (Default colors), type **400** in the Zoom percentage field, and then press Enter to zoom to a 4:1 viewing resolution of the document.

7. Click on the Canadian goose tip on the Brushes palette, and then click, don't drag, in the document window. Instant art!

8. Check the Wet Edges check box on the Options palette, and then click to the right of the first goose. The Wet Edges option makes the silhouette of a brush stroke (or click) produce a dark outline of the brush tip, which makes a sharp tone transition toward the center of the mark to a lighter color (see fig. 3.19). Wet Edges is an option you might not use often because it doesn't produce a definitive stroke; this option is interesting to use with the custom brush tip collections.

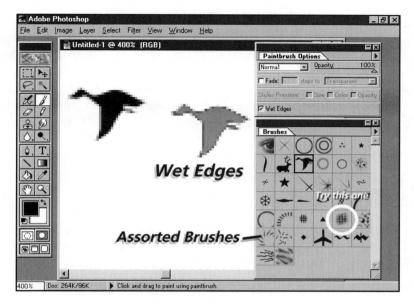

figure 3.19

Use the Assorted brush tips in combination with different foreground colors, opacity settings, and the Wet Edges option.

9. Click on the tip circled in figure 3.19 (the small woven texture swatch) and uncheck the Wet Edges option on the Options palette.

10. Drag in the image window and then stop. You can see that the tip, although intricate in design, fails to produce a huge, tiling sample of the texture tip. The reason? The default spacing for the tip is too small. Press Ctrl(⌘)+Z to Undo the paint stroke, and let's try this a different way.

11. Double-click on the tip on the Brushes palette. This displays the options for the brush tip. Type **77** in the Spacing field, and then click on OK.

12. Hold Shift while you drag the Paintbrush up in the window. Shift constrains most tools' movement to angles in multiples of 45°, so the stroke is a perfect vertical line. Because successive strokes are separated by a space three-quarters the size of the brush tip, the texture pattern nearly interweaves to create a straight texture pattern.

13. You do not have to save this masterpiece. If you are finished exploring the Assorted brush tip palette, choose Reset Brushes from the Brushes palette menu flyout, and then click on OK in the attention box to replace the current brush set with the default tips.

So how did Adobe Systems create these neat brush tips? It's simple; someone sampled an existing design in a document window. Read on, and we will create a custom brush tip.

Creating Your Own Brushes

There is one rule for creating brush tips in Photoshop, and two recommendations from the authors:

1. **Rule:** You must have an active selection marquee in an image to define the source for the new brush tip. Any of the selection tools can be used to make the marquee, and feathering can be applied to the selection edges to create a soft-tip custom brush.

2. **Suggestion:** Sample from a grayscale image and not from a color one. All brush tips are grayscale. You have 256 unique tones with which to define a tip, but if you sample from a color image, Photoshop automatically converts the sample to grayscale, and the tip might be lighter or darker than you intended. This happens because color causes tone-shifting when color is converted to grayscale without first balancing tone (see Chapter 11 for more details on this).

3. **Suggestion:** Keep the target size for the tip sample small; fewer than 50 pixels is best. You can have a lot of fun with custom-designed tips, but if you make them too large, you will get very few brush strokes to the document.

Although you can definitely use your own image in the following steps, we have provided you with a file, Ball.psd in the CHAP03 folder of the Companion CD. The Ball image produces a pretty interesting brush tip; it was created by using KPT Glass Lens Bright in combination with Alien Skin's Drop Shadow filters.

Here's the big secret to creating a brush tip that features a perfect drop shadow. With Gaussian blur shadows (you will see how to create them in future chapters) and ones you create with plug-in filters, the shadow blends to background color almost imperceptibly at the edges. And if you accidentally make the selection marquee for defining the tip even a pixel or two too small, the resulting brush tip will contain a hard edge where you truncated the shadow. Therefore, instead of using a selection tool in the following steps, you automatically load non-transparent layer information as a marquee selection to perfectly define the new brushes tip.

Defining a Brush Tip

CD-ROM

1. Open the Ball.psd image from the CHAP03 folder of the Companion CD, and then double-click on the Zoom tool to move your view of the window to 1:1 viewing resolution. Drag the window borders away from the image if you still cannot see the white ball against Photoshop's transparency grid.

2. On the Layers palette (press F7 if it isn't on-screen) hold Ctrl(⌘) and click on the Ball title on the palette to load the nontransparent pixels on the layer as a marquee selection.

3. On the Brushes palette, click on the flyout menu button and then choose Define Brush (see fig. 3.20). The new tip appears at the bottom of the default tips.

4. Create a new document and then drag the Paintbrush tool with the new tip around a few times. You will notice that like the weave pattern tip in the previous example, the spacing is too tight for the new brush tip. Press Ctrl(⌘)+Z to undo the brush stroke, or open a new document window.

5. Double-click on the brush tip, type **100** in the Spacing field (see fig. 3.21), and then click on OK in the Brush Options dialog box to apply the new spacing option.

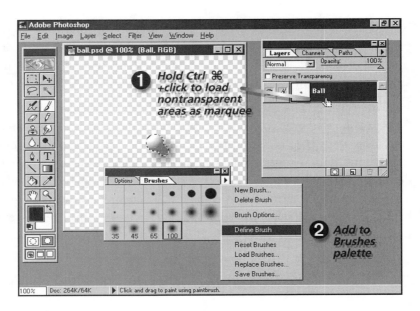

figure 3.20

Load a selection marquee based upon the non-transparent design area, then choose Define Brush from the Brushes palette menu flyout.

figure 3.21

Define spacing of 100% of the brush tip's dimensions to create a tiling effect, using the tip.

6. Paint a little more in the document window. As you can see in figure 3.22, this tip is not only fun to use, but can produce a design that looks like a pool table, choreographed by a marching band leader.

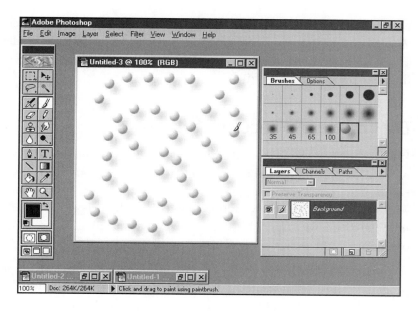

figure 3.22

Anything you can draw or copy from an image can be used as a custom Brushes palette tip.

7. Click on the Brushes menu flyout and choose Save Brushes. Then in the Save dialog box, choose the BRUSHES folder and save the palette a with a unique name. Maurice has always been our personal favorite.

Let us stress here that the target file for creating a tip does not *have* to be a Photoshop layered image; you can create a tip from an image Background by using any of the selection tools. You simply produce a more refined brush tip when you carefully select the design you want to use as a tip, and then move or copy the design to a layer.

If you had not saved the default palette to Photoshop's ABR file extension, the next time you switched to, say, the Drop Shadow collection and then restored the Brushes palette to its default, the ball tip would be gone. You can save entire collections of tips you create, and share them with co-workers and friends who also use Photoshop. We recommend that you try sampling an entire alphabet of tips by using a font you like, and perhaps adding a drop shadow to the characters. You can also customize Photoshop's default brush tips—make them larger, smaller, hard or 100% feathered (*soft*) or elliptical, by double-clicking on a tip and then choosing different Brush Options settings.

Digimarc: The Security Option

We have covered a lot of ground in this chapter. By now, you should have a fair idea of what is possible in Photoshop and how you can make your workspace a completely user-friendly place in which to work. We want to leave you, however, with a walk-through of a very important filter Photoshop has included; it has nothing to do with special effects, and everything to do with protecting the ownership of the things you will create in this program.

Digimarc, Inc., has developed the PictureMarc plug-in for use with Photoshop and programs that support Adobe's plug-in extension. Included on the Photoshop setup CD, and installed by default on your system, PictureMarc has two commands, located beneath Digimarc on Photoshop's native plug-in filters on the Filter list: Embed Watermark and Read Watermark. If you have tried these filters and nothing happened, here's the documentation.

The PictureMarc filter adds noise to an image. It's a very subtle amount of noise and a highly engineered noise type that is impossible to remove. Copying the image, filtering it, and even scanning a printed copy of a watermarked image will reveal the copyright information—the visible noise—embedded in the image. In the Embed Watermark filter dialog box, you are greeted with a Register button the first time you use the filter. This is a trial version of the Digimarc technology, and you must subscribe to the Digimarc service to use the filter with your images. We will get to the Registration process in a moment.

Also in the Embed Watermark dialog box is the Type of Use field, where you can specify that Royalty Free, Restricted usage, and Adult Content can be embedded in the image. Images marked by the Digimarc system display a copyright symbol on the title bar of the document window when opened or scanned into Photoshop. In figure 3.23, the Goldwyn.tif image in the CHAP03 folder is zoomed into by 600%, so you can see for yourself the mild amount of noise introduced by watermarking the image (right), compared to the original (left).

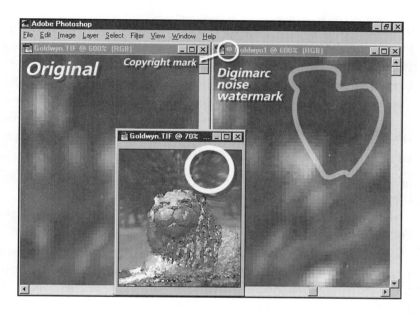

figure 3.23

Professional photographers and designers who do not want noise in images, but do want security on the Web, should watermark a copy of such images.

The watermark can be set to be more visible in the image, or less visible. The tradeoff here is that images watermarked with the less visible settings can lose embedded information if someone who is determined to remove the watermark runs it through several intentional defacing methods. Converting an image to an Indexed image format or using large amounts of JPEG compression on a watermarked image requires using the higher visibility settings.

There is no absolute guarantee against theft of images posted on the World Wide Web or used in print, nor are there ironclad assurances against theft of other types of media. What watermarking *does* do for you is advertise to others in a convenient and highly visible way that you created the image, and it gives the viewer a way to get in touch with you. When you sign your work with a Digimarc watermark, no one who might appropriate your work can plead ignorance of your ownership. Digimarc has made the process of watermarking and registering your ID with their server an easy, inexpensive task. Watermark the images you distribute, and you will rest a little easier knowing that for the first time you can protect your work.

The registration process takes a little more than five minutes over the Internet. Here's the deal: when you click on the Personalize button you display the Personalize Creator ID dialog box, where you can either click on the Register button (if you have Internet service) or call in your registration by dialing the 1-800 number displayed on the dialog box. After you complete the registration form, you are given a serial number for the Embed Watermark filter. Enter this number in the Creator ID field, and the PictureMarc Demo text is replaced with the last digits of your creator ID. Do *not* depend upon the Embed Watermark dialog box to remember your Creator ID! Write it down someplace safe! The first digits of the code do *not* display on-screen (to prevent unauthorized use of your watermark).

If you receive an anonymous image that displays a copyright symbol on the title bar and on the Document Info field, the first thing you will want to do is find out the creator's information. To do this, choose Filter, Digimarc, Read Watermark. You then click on the Web Lookup button, the connection is made to Digimarc's home page, and the information the creator of the image gave to Digimarc is displayed in your browser (see fig. 3.24).

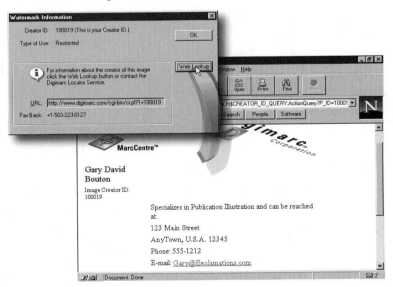

figure 3.24
Digimarc is a service that references complete creator information based upon a code embedded in your images.

The good news for Photoshop users is that Digimarc is offering three months of free reference service when you subscribe. At the time of this writing, the $150 annual subscription fee is discounted to $79. In figure 3.25, you can see Digimarc's home page. When you click on the Register button in the filter dialog box, this is what the browser displays to register with Digimarc.

figure 3.25
Photoshop users are "preferred customers" to Digimarc. If you need watermarking for the Web, the technology is a click away.

Web content creators will benefit the most from the Digimarc electronic watermarking technology. For you to successfully watermark an image, the image must contain at least 4,500 pixels. You can find out how many pixels are in an image by choosing Image, Histogram from Photoshop's main menu. Digimarc recommends that images be about 256 × 256 pixels or greater in size. An image must also contain colors other than pure black or pure white. Traditional publishers will find useful the technology's capability to transfer to physical media, scan back to electronic format, and still preserve the noise code that identifies an image. The amount of noise added by the watermarking process is much less than that produced by the conversion of the digital image to the half-tone image required for printing.

If you're into Photoshop for fun and not profit, you probably will not benefit from the services that Digimarc provides. If you subscribe, and then change your mind and do not re-subscribe the following year, your records at Digimarc are deleted, and your watermarked images will fail to display anything on another user's machine (except a cryptic Creator ID number, known only to you).

This is a wonderful advancement in a field of communications that has had no piracy insurance to date. If you make a living from your images, it only makes sense to protect your investment.

Summary

You have seen in this chapter that Photoshop 4 is more than an application. It's a creative environment, where scores of options are at your disposal to make "hanging your hat" inside the doors of the digital darkroom a more comfortable, predictable, and productive adventure. Before we move on to Chapter 4, we want to leave you with two thoughts that will make your Photoshop work more productive and less prone to error:

◆ Buy more RAM for your system than you think you can afford. Money is not the new medium of exchange these days; *time* is. With the time you save by working in Photoshop on a fast machine, you can *make* more money!

◆ Change the image data only as a last step if an image doesn't look quite right. Monitor settings can dramatically change your view of an image. Changing the gamma, the color balance, or any other property of an image itself produces a change you cannot usually restore.

The way you select image areas is discussed in Chapter 4. Photoshop has at least five ways you can create a marquee based upon geometry, color, tone, and other means. Let's take the first step toward advanced, professional, flawless image retouching.

CHAPTER

USING PATHS, SELECTIONS, AND LAYERS

The concept of a selection in a computer application has historically been fairly straightforward: you highlight or marquee an area on-screen, and when you move it, the contents of the selection moves—leaving a hole where the original area was.

Taking this idea to a new plateau, Adobe Systems made the Photoshop 4 selection marquee a distinct entity, separate from the underlying image area. This marquee can be refined, transformed to different visual formats, and saved indefinitely without touching a pixel of the original image. Add to the selection options the capability to move or copy image areas to discrete layers within the image, whose non-image areas are transparent. It then becomes evident that much of the power behind Photoshop lies in a visual metaphor similar to pushing shards of paper around a background frame to create an artistic composition.

This chapter clarifies the procedures you can use to reorganize the visual content of an image, and shows you the smartest way to select, copy, and move image areas to perform seamless image retouching. You will see also how different tools and modes in Photoshop are suited for specific retouching steps, and you might find a personal style of image manipulation that you can quickly master. Even if you are proficient in earlier versions of Photoshop, the examples in this chapter will acquaint you with different keystrokes and operations, as well as with some of the new features that make selection definition and image area duplication much easier.

Key Concepts Behind Layers and Selections

Photoshop's toolbox is organized by type of task, and all the tools used to select and move the contents of a selection are located on the top of the palette. If you base your approach to the image-editing process on previous experience with other graphics applications, the experience will be frustrating, and the results unexpected. You need to be able to distinguish between a *selection marquee* and a *selected image area*. A selection marquee marks an area above an image. (A marquee is sometimes referred to as "marching ants" because of the way the marked area looks.) In Photoshop, unlike other programs, the inside of the marquee is empty—it has no content—until you command Photoshop to lift or duplicate the image content contained within the marquee.

Layer content (also called an image layer) is yet another sort of selection in Photoshop. As a designer, the way you copy, cut, and paste the contents of a selection is more "layer-centric" in Photoshop 4 than in earlier versions of the program. A *layer* in Photoshop is an image area surrounded by an in-place mask. The layer mask is invisible, and the unmasked image areas are non-transparent (opaque, or partially opaque). This chapter shows you how to convert masked image layers, selections, marquees, and other definitions of image areas to different types, according to your design needs. You will take some tools out for a test spin with Games.psd on the Companion CD, and see how to use selection tools to make dramatic changes to the composition.

Working with Paths and the Pen Tool

Adobe Systems is in the process of converging application features, which means that if you are experienced with Adobe Illustrator, Photoshop's Paths tools will work much as you would expect them to work. For designers who come from drawing programs such as CorelDRAW or FreeHand, the finer points of vector path manipulation and creation in Photoshop might seem a tad foreign. For those of you who have *no* experience with vector design, the Pen tool is an important Photoshop feature for defining selections, and paths deserve a thorough explanation here.

Paths are nonprinting, inactive on-screen representations of shapes. Drawn with the Pen tool, paths can be modified by using the other tools beneath the Pen tool on the toolbox flyout. Paths can be stroked with foreground color to produce a permanent design on an image or an image layer, and paths can also be used as the basis of a marquee selection, from which an image area can be copied, cut, or duplicated.

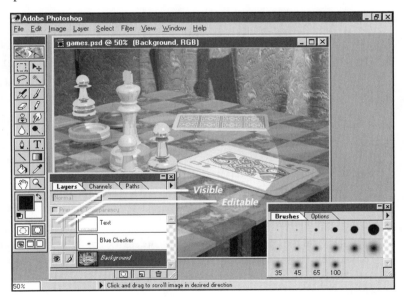

figure 4.1
Image layers can be hidden or displayed, but only one layer can be edited at a time.

In this section you will play around with the Games.psd image shown in figure 4.1, editing the image content to create a different composition. Take a moment now to note the callouts in this figure. Note also that elements are organized differently in the Layers palette than they are in other palettes. The eye icon represents visibility for an image layer—click on it to hide or show a layer in the image window. Directly to the right of the eye icon is the painting icon. You can have only one layer in painting "mode"; the chosen layer is referred to in this book as the *active*, or *current* layer. Notice that Games.psd has two hidden layers. They are used later in this chapter to demonstrate advanced image selection and editing features.

In the Games.psd image, whoever was playing cards seems to have dealt an uneven hand; one card is face down, yet several cards are face up on the table. To even the odds, duplicates of the face-down card can be made in the document by using the Pen tool. In this first example, working with the Pen tool and the modifier tools, you will accurately define the card.

WORKING WITH THE PEN TOOL

CD-ROM

1. Open the Games.psd image from the CHAP04 folder on the Companion CD.

2. With the Zoom tool, marquee around the face-down playing card to get this image area in clear view, filling the image window without cropping the card by the window.

3. Double-click on the Pen tool to display the Options palette for the Pen tool.

4. Check the Rubber Band option if this box isn't already checked.

    This step is optional; you can design paths on an image without the Rubber Band. What this feature does, however, is connect an anchor point—a point you click with the Pen tool—with a preview of what the path segment will look like before you click a point to establish the path segment. When you use this option, paths are displayed as they are in most vector drawing applications.

5. Click a point at the upper left of the playing card, to the right of where the card's rounder corner ends. This is called an anchor point in Photoshop (other drawing applications may use names such as nodes, connector points, and control points for the same screen element).

6. Click a point at the upper-right side of the card, to the left of the beginning of the card's upper-right rounded edge. A line is drawn between the first and second anchor points.

7. Click a point at the end of the upper-right rounded corner.

You are defining points along the outline of the card, where a path changes direction. These points of inflection roughly describe the outline. Yes, the corners of the card are excluded from the path segments you are drawing; they will be included after you use a path editing tool in the following section.

8. Continue clicking on the points of inflection—outline areas that change in path direction—in a clockwise direction until you arrive at the first point you clicked.

Because a picture is worth a thousand words, look at figure 4.2. As you can see, the Pen tool has completed the second corner of the card outline, and is coming to the third rounded corner.

figure 4.2
Single clicks with the Pen tool create anchor points; straight path segments are created automatically between anchors.

9. Move the Pen tool cursor directly above the first anchor point. When you see a small circle to the lower right of the cursor, click to close the path (see fig. 4.3).

10. Press Ctrl(⌘)+S and save the image as Games.psd to your hard disk. Keep the image open in Photoshop for the following examples.

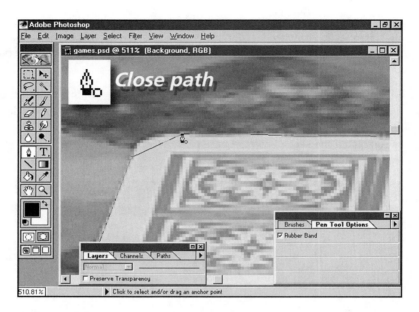

figure 4.3
A path can be closed by clicking with the Pen tool when the cursor displays a small circle to its lower right.

Using the Convert Anchor Point Tool

One of the reasons to design a path to serve as a template for a selection marquee (instead of using Photoshop's selection tools) is that a path is easy to edit and refine. A path is a connected series of components—path segments and anchor points—that can be changed to define a different shape than you originally created. Think of the polygonal shape you created in the previous example as a "pencil sketch" of the outline of the card, a sketch you will now refine to precisely match the card outline.

An anchor point determines the properties of the path segments it connects. Curved path segments, segments that meet at a 180° (*smooth*) angle, or those that meet at a small, sharp (*corner*) angle, are all determined by the property of the governing anchor point. The Convert Anchor Point tool, located on the Pen tool flyout, is used in the following example to redefine the properties of the anchor point located at the rounded corners of the playing card. You will change the anchor point property to make the path segment into a curved path.

Here's how to put one of the features of the Convert Anchor Point tool to good use in refining the path's shape:

CHANGING ANCHOR POINT PROPERTIES

1. Zoom into the upper-left corner of the path, where the beginning and end anchors were closed in the previous example. You can use the Zoom tool to zoom in (about 500% is a good viewing resolution), or you can type **500** in the Zoom percentage field, and then press Enter (Return). The Zoom percentage field is at the left of the status line in Windows, and at the bottom left of the document window on the Macintosh.

2. Drag on the Pen tool to reveal the flyout, and then release the cursor over the Convert Anchor Point tool (the icon on the far right of the flyout).

3. The first target anchor point to edit is the original anchor you created in the preceding example. Changing its property from corner to smooth affects both the segment preceding it and the one that follows. Click and hold on the anchor point with the Convert Anchor Point tool, and then drag directly to the right, until the segment that precedes the point begins to curve (see fig. 4.4).

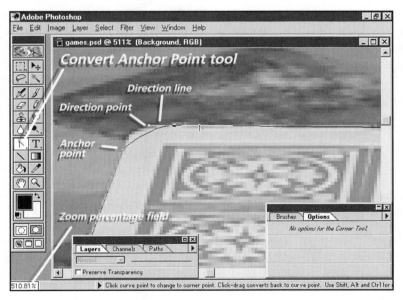

figure 4.4
Dragging on an anchor point with the Convert Anchor Point tool changes the way the connecting segments meet, and also changes the property of the segments.

Notice, as you drag on the anchor point, that you are no longer controlling this screen element, but instead your cursor is over a *direction point*. Direction points are the "handles" for an anchor that connect curved path segments. You can change the angle at which neighboring curved path segments meet anchor points. You can also define the direction in which a segment curves by changing the position of direction points in the image. How steeply a path segment curves is determined by changing the distance of a direction point from the parent anchor point.

4. Click and drag to the right on the anchor's right direction point, and then release the cursor. This changes the property of the anchor point from smooth to corner; now the direction handles can be manipulated independent of one another.

    On a smooth anchor, the direction points are always in 180° opposition to one another, which would fail to describe the rounded corner of the playing card outline. On a corner anchor point, each connecting path segment can be reshaped without changing the opposing path segment.

5. Hold Ctrl(⌘). This toggles the Convert Anchor Point tool to the Direct Selection tool (the tool that repositions anchor points and moves direction handles without changing an anchor point's properties).

6. Click and drag on the left direction point until you see the curved path segment to the left of the anchor conform to the shape of the rounded card corner. Then release the cursor.

7. Click and drag the right direction point so that it lies directly on the path segment to the right of the anchor point. It doesn't matter where along the segment the direction point rests; as long as it is located on the segment, the segment will be straight. Because the top side of the playing card outline is basically straight, you have manipulated the corresponding path segment to conform to the geometry of the card.

8. Perform steps 3–7 with the other anchors that govern the shape of the path segment, which should be curved to define the card's rounded corners.

    Hold the spacebar to access the Hand tool; then scroll the image within the window to work closely in the other image areas. Release the spacebar after you have scrolled. This saves you the additional steps of zooming in and out of the image.

9. When the path looks as though it describes the playing card, press Ctrl(⌘)+S to save your work.

The Path tools in Photoshop take a little getting used to, especially if you come from a drawing application other than Illustrator. As you gain experience, however, you will be able to define image areas you want selected, and the Path tools may become your selection tools of preference in Photoshop. The next section takes a look at the extended features of the Path tools.

Examining the Toggling Path Tools

In earlier examples you used three of the five tools on the Pen tool flyout—the Pen, Direct Selection, and Convert Anchor Point tools—to construct paths. The following sections describe the tools' extended functions and the way these tools can toggle anchor and path properties. Using the Path tools can be frustrating if you forget this concept:

To create complex paths, you must constantly switch Path tools.

The following descriptions explain what each tool on the Pen tool flyout does, how to access its extended features, and under which design circumstances you might want to use the tool's features.

The Pen Tool

The Pen tool operates in two modes: Bézier curve mode and straight-line mode. You used the straight-line mode earlier to create the "rough sketch" of the playing card outline. If you click and drag with the Pen tool, however, instead of simply clicking, you produce a Bézier path segment—a curve whose parent anchor point has direction points at 180° in opposition. You can use a combination of clicking an anchor with clicking and dragging a Bézier path segment when you use the Pen tool. Because this takes some getting used to, we recommend clicking single points of inflection around the desired image outline instead, and then using the Convert Anchor Point tool to refine the path.

The Pen tool can be toggled to the Direct Selection tool by holding Ctrl(⌘)while you click or drag. All the functionality of the Direct Selection tool can be used when you hold Ctrl(⌘).

Figure 4.5 illustrates Photoshop's creation and modification tools in action. As you can see in the example in the upper left, curved segments with smooth anchor points are created by clicking and dragging with the Pen tool.

The Direct Selection Tool

For designers unfamiliar with Adobe Illustrator, the "Direct" part of this tool's name means that a single path, or a single anchor on a path, can be selected. Shortly you will learn about saving paths, and you will see that many unconnected paths can be saved as a group. This tool is used to select one of a *collection* of paths.

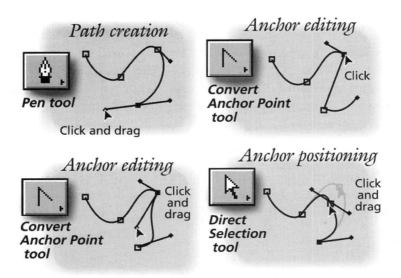

figure 4.5

The Path tools flyout in Photoshop offers tools for creating and modifying paths.

As you saw in figure 4.5, you can reposition an anchor point within a document by clicking and dragging on the anchor. You also expose an anchor's direction points by clicking on the anchor or the path segment associated with the anchor; the direction points can then be repositioned to change the curve of an associated path segment. Note, however, that you do *not* change the properties of an anchor with the Direct Selection tool; you cannot, for example, change a smooth anchor to a corner anchor with the Direct Selection tool in its default tool mode. But you can toggle the Direct Selection tool to the Convert Anchor Point tool by holding Ctrl(⌘) with this tool selected, and by changing anchor properties.

The current selected anchor in a path is a filled rectangle. Unselected anchors are represented by an empty rectangle along a selected path. To select all the anchors on a path, hold Alt(Opt) while you click with this tool. You can then move the entire path by releasing the Alt(Opt) key before you drag. To duplicate a path, keep holding Alt(Opt) while you drag on the selected path.

The Add and Delete Anchor Point Tools

You might never need to use these tools when you build a path to define as a selection, but there is no other method in Photoshop for removing or adding anchors to a path after you create it. The procedure is fairly straightforward for using either of these tools: to add an anchor you click over a path with the **Add Anchor Point** tool; to remove an anchor, you click over it with the **Delete Anchor Point** tool. A path does not have to be selected for you to use either of these tools. Interestingly, when you add an anchor, the anchor's property is smooth, producing curved connecting path segments, whether the original path segment is curved or straight.

Holding Ctrl(⌘) while you use the Add and Delete Anchor Point tools toggles the tool function to the Direct Selection tool.

NOTE

Pressing the Delete (Backspace) key while a path is selected removes that last-created anchor point. A second press on Delete (Backspace) removes the entire path. When one or more paths are unselected but visible on-screen, pressing Delete (Backspace) removes every path.

Choose Edit, Undo, or press Ctrl(⌘)+Z to restore the previous deletion, but only one deletion; you can undo only one edit in Photoshop.

The Convert Anchor Point Tool

This is an editing tool, not a creation tool, for path construction in Photoshop. The Convert Anchor Point tool operates in three ways, depending upon the property of the anchor you want to edit:

◆ Clicking and dragging on a corner-property anchor changes the anchor point to smooth; associated path segments become curved if the path segments were straight lines originally.

◆ Clicking on an anchor toggles the anchor property to corner if it was smooth (which changes curved associated path segments to straight segments). You must click and drag away from the new corner anchor point to return it to smooth with curved segments.

◆ Clicking and dragging on a direction point toggles a smooth anchor point to a corner anchor; the direction points will operate independently of one another.

Because the Convert Anchor Point tool changes anchor and path properties in an alternating fashion, this tool is the leading cause of frustration with inexperienced Photoshop designers; it simply doesn't work like editing tools in many other drawing applications. As a rule, you should press Ctrl(⌘) after you use the Convert Anchor Point tool. In this way you toggle the tool to the Direct Selection tool, which can then be used to reposition direction or anchor points whose properties have been changed (refer to fig. 4.5).

Loading and Using Selections from Paths

To return to the Games example—now that you have defined an outline around the playing card, it's time to base a selection marquee around the geometry of the path. By default, every new path you draw in a document window has the title "Work Path" on the Paths palette. A *work path* is not a *saved* path; you can delete it by clicking on the blank area below the Work Path title on the Paths palette and then drawing a new path. Fortunately, because you haven't had to work with the Paths palette yet in this Games example, the path is still intact.

Here's how to save the path for keeps, load it as a selection marquee, and duplicate the card area you have defined:

WORKING WITH PATHS AS SELECTIONS

1. Display the Layers/Channels/Paths grouped palette in Photoshop by pressing F7 (Window, Show Paths).

2. Double-click on the Work Path title on the Paths palette's list to display a Save Path dialog box.

3. Type **Card path** (or any similarly evocative name) in the Name field (see fig. 4.6) and then click on OK or press Enter (Return).

4. Click on the Loads path as Selection icon, the light, solid circle at the bottom of the Paths palette. This loads a marquee selection that is based on the shape of the currently selected path title on the Paths palette's list (see fig. 4.7).

5. Click on a blank area of the Paths palette's list to remove the path from view in the document. Paths are easy to delete accidentally; now that you have created the selection marquee, you don't need to see the path.

6. Press **V** (Move tool), hold Alt(Opt), and then drag inside the marquee selection. Two things have happened (see fig. 4.8): the inside of the marquee selection now contains a duplicate of the image area originally underneath the marquee, and if you click on the Layers tab, you will see that a new title, "Floating Selection," has been added above the Background layer title.

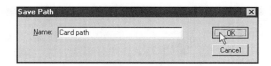

figure 4.6

Naming a path saves all the segments you have created as a Work Path to a permanent "layer" on the Paths palette's list.

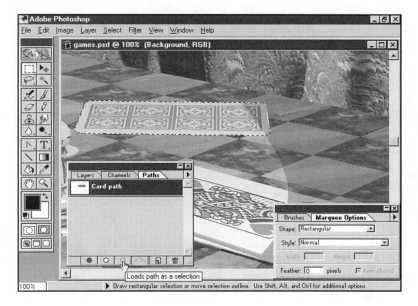

figure 4.7

The Loads path as a selection feature creates a marquee based upon the geometry of the current path.

It's very important to note here that a floating selection is not a permanent copy of an image area to a new layer. The floating selection will drop to the layer underneath it if you click anywhere outside the selection marquee—so *don't do it*, unless this is the effect you want to achieve.

7. Drag inside the marquee selection until the duplicate card inside the marquee is positioned about half its height beneath the original card, and about one card-pattern tile to the right of the original.

figure 4.8

Holding Alt(Opt) as you drag a selection marquee with the Move tool copies and floats
the area of the image the marquee surrounds.

Because the duplicate is where you want it to be in this example, you can drop the floating
selection onto the background at this point. But to save work and be a little creative with
this example, you will make another face-down card.

8. Hold Alt(Opt) while you drag the floating selection down and to the right. This drops the
    first duplicate onto the background. The image area beneath your cursor now contains
    a floating selection based upon the first (dropped) floating selection.

9. On the Layers palette, click on the Create new layer icon (the turned-down page symbol)
    at the bottom of the palette (see fig. 4.9). This puts the floating selection on its own layer.
    Because it is not merged with the background layer (as the first floating selection was),
    you can reposition and edit the new card at any time. Now Layer 1 is the current editing
    layer (the layer title is highlighted on the Layers palette).

10. Press Ctrl(⌘)+S to save.

figure 4.9
A floating selection is assigned its own layer when you click on the Create new layer
icon on the Layers palette.

TIP

You can create separate closed or open paths, and save them under one name in Photoshop.
Simply deselect the first path you have completed (or close the path), and then design a new
one. To load the path as a single marquee, deselect the current path segment, press Ctrl(⌘)+A
(Select, All), and then click on the Loads path as a selection icon.

Open paths that are used to create selections can be auto-closed by making a straight closure
line from the beginning to the end anchor points of the path.

Although the third face-down card appears to fit perfectly into the scene, it's not part
of the Background image layer at all—and this is where the wonder and power of
editing in Photoshop layers comes to light. The following sections show you how
to use this unusual on-screen metaphor for image masking (image layers) to arrange
the order of foreground-to-background objects in the Games.psd image.

Working with Image Layers

As explained earlier in this chapter, a Photoshop layer is actually a combination of an opaque (or semi-opaque) collection of pixels surrounded by masking pixels, which look transparent. Visually, what you see on a layer can be compared to a traditional acetate animation cell. The cartoonist paints on the acetate with pigment of different opacity; when the cell is placed over the background painting to be photographed and incorporated into the animation, the background shows through wherever the pigment is less than 100 percent opaque.

In the following sections, you will work with a layer-specific editing feature, the Layer Mask function, to specify that some of the opaque areas on the playing card layer should be transparent like the mask pixels on the layer. This will enable background image areas to show through, and create a convincing picture of background elements placed in front of the playing card on the layer.

Understanding Masks and Selections

Because varying degrees of opacity can be attributed to the content of a layer, this book distinguishes between layer content and the opaque areas of a layer. An image area that you copy or paint into a layer can be less that 100 percent opaque, and this chapter explores some of the creative uses for semi-opacity. As mentioned earlier, areas on a layer that are not visible are called *masks*. This is a perfect time to get working definitions for the terms *mask* and *selection* into the discussion.

A mask lies above an image area that you do not want to accidentally paint into, modify with filters, or display on-screen. A mask is *not* the opposite of a selection; the opposite of a masked area in an image is an unmasked area. *Unmasked areas* are visible, and you can modify them by using Photoshop's editing and painting tools. Often, as you edit images, you will want to use different types of visual representations for masked image areas. Photoshop offers layers, Quick Mask mode, and the exterior of a selection marquee as visual representations for image areas that cannot be edited, and you can use different tools to change the shape and the appearance of masked areas.

NOTE

Every type of bitmap image you can import is interpreted by Photoshop as a single layer image; the layer is labeled as the *Background layer*, and you cannot change this title. A Background layer, however, is different from layers you add to Photoshop's proprietary PSD and/or PDD image formats because when you remove foreground areas, the current Photoshop background color is displayed, not the transparent masking background you see when removing foreground areas from a user-defined Photoshop layer.

To convert an imported image with a Background layer to a Photoshop layer, double-click on the Background layer title on the Layers palette and either type a new name for the layer or accept the default name in the New Layer dialog box. The image can no longer be saved in its native format (TIFF, Targa, BMP, PICT, and so on), but you can mask the areas, place the converted layer in front of other layers, and use the layer's visual content in combination with other layers' content to create a composition.

If you paint on a layer, you change the shape of the invisible mask on the layer; the "transparent" pixels on this layer "protect" you from seeing the mask, but not from replacing masking pixels with layer content. To mask a layer's areas of "no image content" so that they cannot be seen or edited, check the Preserve Transparency box on the Layers palette when a specific layer is active.

A *selection* is the area inside a marquee that marks a geometric area of an image in order to copy the underlying image area or limit the editing to the area *inside* the selection. A selection doesn't necessarily hold image content.

Throughout this book the term *selection* is used to indicate image and layer areas that you want to move, copy, or edit. The term *mask* is reserved for image and layer areas that meet one or more of the following conditions: you cannot see, edit, copy, or move them. Several options in different interface areas of Photoshop enable you to transpose selected image areas and those that are masked (and vice versa). When these options are relevant in the context of an example, we point them out.

TIP

When you click on the Create new layer icon, new layers are assigned default, automatically numbered names (Layer 1, Layer 2, and so on). These default names are not very useful, however, in situations in which you must quickly choose many different elements on different layers.

To create a new layer (the hard way), and to get the opportunity to name the layer, choose New layer from the menu flyout on the Layers palette. A quick way to rename a layer that has a default name is to double-click on the layer title on the Layers palette's list area to display the Layer Options dialog box. Then, in this box, you can type the new name.

Positioning and Editing the Layer Card

In the analogy of a cartoon cell animator, movement of the contents of an animation cell is usually accomplished by moving the cell itself while the background remains static. Similarly, the Move tool can be used to change the location of layer contents relative to underlying layers and the background image. This procedure is much safer than moving a floating selection—there is no way to accidentally deselect layer content because no active selection is involved in the process.

In the next example you're going to move the face-down playing card to a position in front of the chrome pawn in the Games image. Naturally, having the card obscure the top of the pawn looks awkward—in real life, cards on a table cannot be positioned in front of a taller object. You will correct this oddity by using Photoshop's Layer Mask feature, which hides layer content from view. Layer Mask mode is a nondestructive feature; you can choose to restore visibility of layer content at any time, from session to session or month to month.

Here's how to perform your first advanced editing procedure in the Games image by using Photoshop's Layers:

USING LAYERS AND THE LAYER MASK

1. Double-click on the Zoom tool to change to a 100% viewing resolution of the Games image.

2. Press **V** (Move tool) and drag Layer 1 to the left, so that the card overlaps both the top of the pawn and part of the king's body (see fig. 4.10).

   If you drag slowly and deliberately when you use the Move tool, Photoshop automatically pans a window that is larger than your video resolution. This eliminates some of the need to adjust views frequently as you edit.

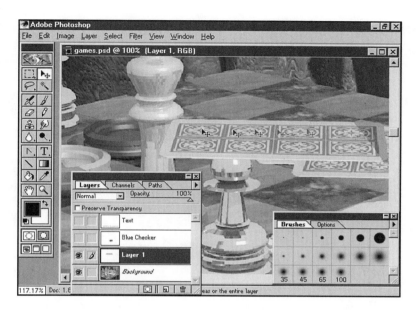

figure 4.10

Image content on layers can be repositioned without floating the image area.

3. Click on the Add Layer Mask icon, the button to the left of the Create new layer button on the Layers palette.

   A new thumbnail image appears to the right of the color thumbnail on this layer's title, and the painting icon to the left of the title changes to a circle (Photoshop's mask icon) The chain-link icon displayed between the layer mask thumbnail image and the color thumbnail image means that brushstrokes you create on the mask will correspond, pixel-to-pixel, to this layer's image content.

   Also, the Foreground/Background colors on the toolbox automatically switch from your current color selections to black foreground and white background. The colors you were using will return when you exit Layer Mask mode; Photoshop presumes that you want to begin with the "pure" masking colors of black and white.

4. Press **B** (Paintbrush tool) and then F5 to display the Brushes palette.

5. Click on the fourth brush tip (top row) on the Brushes palette.

   This nine-pixel tip is hard-edged (with a slight amount of feathering) and is a good choice for masking hard-edged areas such as the chess pieces in this example. For larger images, choose a correspondingly larger brush diameter from the palette or create your own. (See Chapter 3, "Personalizing Photoshop: Preferences and Options," for details.)

6. Paint over the area of the playing card where it overlaps the body of the king chess piece.

7. Paint around the top of the pawn. Do all of this masking slowly and don't worry about creating a clean separation between the top of the pawn and the layer areas you are hiding. (Cleanup comes later.) As you can see in figure 4.11, applying black to the Layer Mask hides the underlying areas on the layer. In Layer Mask mode you cannot touch the colors of the layer; all you can do is hide and reveal areas of this layer.

figure 4.11

In Layer Mask mode you hide layer content by applying black foreground color.

8. When you finish the rough masking work, press **X** (or click on the Swap colors icon, above and to the right of the foreground/background colors on the toolbox). White restores hidden areas of Layer Mask.

9. Type **300** in the Zoom percentage field and press Enter (Return). Hold the spacebar to access the Hand tool, scroll until you have a good close-up of the pawn's head in view, and then release the spacebar.

10. Click on the second tip on the top row of the Brushes palette and then paint around the edge of the pawn's head to restore the hidden areas of the playing card (see fig. 4.12).

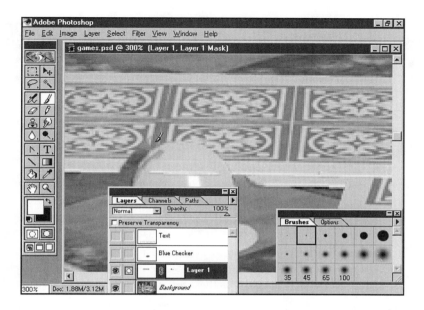

figure 4.12

Paint along the outside of the pawn's edge, between the pawn's head and the playing card, to restore the card areas to visibility.

11.   Press Ctrl(⌘)+S to save your work.

TIP

You don't have to click and drag directly upon the image content of a layer to reposition the image; you can drag anywhere within the image window to move layer content, just as an animator moves the entire acetate to move a design.

You can even move layer content outside the document window and then add image content to another area; the image mask you create on the layer can be larger than the document window! Areas outside the window on a layer are truncated (deleted) only when you crop the image or save a design to a file type other than Photoshop's native PSD format.

Using Layer Mask mode instead of the Eraser tool to eliminate unwanted image has obvious advantages. The Layer Mask can be kept indefinitely in a Photoshop format image file. Layer Masks contribute to overall saved file sizes, however; when you're certain that no more masking of the layer content is required, it's a good idea to commit to your editing work by applying the Layer Mask. When you apply the mask, the areas you have hidden by applying dark foreground color are permanently hidden—in effect, these areas are deleted.

To finalize the edited layer content for the playing card, follow these steps:

Applying a Layer Mask

1. Click on the Layer Mask thumbnail, to be certain that the mask (not the image) is active right now. The Layer Mask icon to the right of the eye icon confirms this. The paintbrush icon should not be displayed; if it is, click again on the mask thumbnail image.

2. Click and drag the thumbnail image into the trash icon at the bottom right of the Layers palette. In the attention box that appears (see fig. 4.13), click on the Apply button to remove the areas you masked on the layer.

figure 4.13
A Layer Mask can be applied or discarded at any time—from one session of working with an image to another session.

If you had clicked on Discard, you would have removed the effect of all your paint strokes on the layer, returning the image to its original state. If your decision to apply the mask was a hasty one, a few options exist that will return the layer to its masked state—but it's a far better practice to apply a mask with confidence, or to allow the Layer Mask to stay on the image until you are confident about the need to apply it. You can press Ctrl(⌘)+Z to Undo the application of the mask if you have made no other edits after applying it, or you can choose File, Restore to return the entire image to its previously saved state. This technique works only if you have saved the image with a Layer Mask. Ready to make that final commitment to your layer-editing work?

3. Press Ctrl(⌘)+S to save your work.

TIP

You almost never need to switch off the link icon while using the Layer Mask feature, but on occasion you might want to hide areas *other* than those you have painted on. To unlink and move a Layer Mask, click on the chain link icon to turn it off; then, with the Move tool, click and drag in the window.

Layer Transparency and Changing Editing Layers

The authors added a little something special to the Games document, to show you an advanced design principle—you can move the checker's *reflection* on the layer on top of the Background layer when you move the checker. The layer content was added to the document by copying and pasting, but the Layer Mask feature was then used to decrease the opacity of the checker's reflection.

An important trick to learn when you are editing images is how to simulate reflections; Chapter 10, "Enhancing Images," contains the secrets to creating mirror-like reflection areas. This trick is handy when you want to add an element to an image whose ground surface, such as the marble chess board in the Games image, contains reflections of the environment. To add an element such as the blue checker *without* a reflection would lead your viewing audience to dismiss the composition as edited. That would be a shame, because Photoshop's strength lies in tools that help you disguise retouching work. This set of steps examines the visual properties of the Blue Checker layer:

1. Double-click on the Hand tool to display the Games image window to fit the entire image to screen without scroll bars.

2. Click on the eye icon to the left of the "Blue Checker" title on the Layers palette's list. This makes the layer content on the Blue Checker layer visible; but because it's not the current editing layer, you cannot modify it now.

A feature new to version 4 helps you locate and select a layer for editing, based upon its visual representation in the document window. You can make any layer the current editing layer simply by clicking on an area in the image and choosing the layer from the Context menu.

3. Press **V** (Move tool) and then right-click (Macintosh: hold Ctrl and click) on the blue checker in the Games image. This pops up the Context menu and displays all the layers now under the cursor. In figure 4.14, the Move tool cursor is over the Blue Checker layer and the Background image. Click on the Blue Checker title on the Context menu. The Layers palette now displays the Blue Checker layer as the current, active layer in the document.

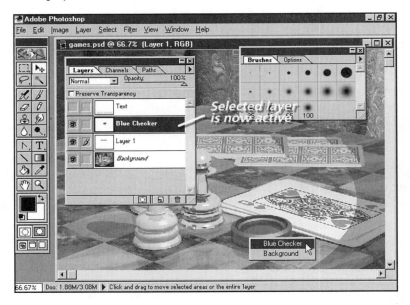

figure 4.14
When the Move tool is chosen, the Context menu displays all the layers that have image content beneath where you have clicked.

4. On the Layers palette, click on the eye icon and drag downward to Layer 1.
    This hides both Layer 1 and the Background layer from view; it's a quick
    technique for hiding multiple layers to display image content on layers
    above where you clicked and dragged.

The checkered background now visible behind the Blue Checker layer is Photoshop's
indicator that there is no image content behind what you are viewing—clear masking
pixels are difficult to display, and solid colors can hide areas of image content that
might be colored the same. This is called the *transparency grid* in Photoshop; you can
change the pattern size and colors under File\Preferences\Transparency and Gamut.
Notice in figure 4.15 (and on your monitor) that the reflection area of the checker
is partially transparent; you can see a faint transparency grid behind it.

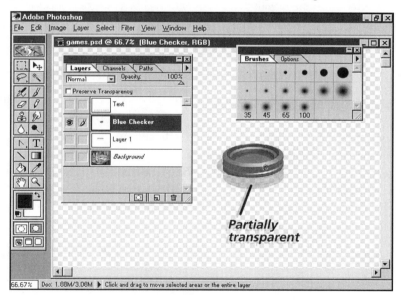

figure 4.15
The degree to which visual content on a layer obscures the transparency grid is
determined by the opacity of the image.

There's really no secret to designing a reflection such as this; you draw a path shaped
like a reflection, load the path as a selection, and then fill it with color. The *technique*
by which you then assign a partial opacity to the reflection image area is another

story, however. Earlier in this chapter, while working in Layer Mask mode, you applied black foreground color to areas of the playing card on a layer to hide visual content on the layer. You also applied white to areas to restore their visibility. Between black and white are 254 tones, shades of black, that when applied to image areas in Layer Mask mode, assign varying degrees of opacity to the visual contents. After the reflection was painted, Layer Mask mode was used on the layer, and about 40 percent black was applied to the image area. The mask was applied; now a semitransparent reflection travels with the (opaque) blue checker wherever it is moved.

The point is this: Don't limit your thinking to black and white when you tap into the power of layers in Photoshop. Different shades of a tone correspond to degrees of opacity in the same way that a slider control in a program specifies different font sizes or the level of zoom in a document.

Editing a Reflection with Quick Mask Mode

In addition to layer masking, Photoshop features Quick Mask mode, in which you describe a potential selection area on a layer as a tinted mask. You can paint foreground color of different shades to indicate a total or semitransparent selection of underlying image areas, but you can also use Photoshop's traditional selection tools to define an area to be filled with Quick Mask. The latter course of action is the focus of the following example, in which you remove part of the reflection area of the checker so that a reflection appears on the marble chess board, but not on top of a playing card.

Here's how to reposition the checker piece and work with Photoshop's Quick Mask mode:

EDITING A REFLECTION

1. Restore visibility of Layer 1 and the Background image layers by clicking on the layer visibility boxes on the Layers palette. When the eye icon is present, the corresponding layer is visible in the document window. Make certain that you do not click on the title of any layer other than Blue Checker. (Clicking on a layer's title makes that layer the current editing layer, and you want to edit the blue checker now.)

2. Press **V** (Move tool), and drag the checker to a position above the queen and to the left of the face-down cards so that the checker obscures parts of the face-down cards you duplicated earlier and so the reflection overlaps part of the queen playing card. (See fig. 4.16 for a more graphical idea of the checker's intended location.)

3. Type **200** in the Zoom percentage box in the left corner of status line (Macintosh: bottom left of document window), press Enter (Return), hold the spacebar, and then pan the window until you have a clear view of the checker.

   Although the reflection area of the blue checker looks appropriate on top of the marble chess board areas, it looks wrong on top of the playing card. Playing cards are shiny, but not really reflective. Notice also that the texture in the image makes it a little difficult to see the edge of the playing card. (And this edge is where you will create a selection.) No problem.

4. Press the number **5** on the keyboard. This is a shortcut to globally decrease the opacity on the current layer. You can also drag the Opacity slider on the Layers palette to 50%. Now you have a good view of the edge of the playing card around which you will define a selection area.

5. Drag on the Lasso tool, if it is the tool currently displayed on the toolbox, and then choose the Polygon Lasso tool.

   This new tool in Photoshop eliminates the need to hold Alt(Opt) while you click points in an image to define straight-edged selections with the traditional Lasso tool. To use the Polygon Lasso tool you click (instead of clicking and dragging) until you close the selection area at the beginning point. A circle at the bottom right of the cursor indicates that you are over a selection's beginning point. (This is similar to the Pen tool's close-path cursor.)

6. Click on the bottom edge of the playing card toward the right of the document, toward the character Q.

7. Click a point to the right and above the first point, creating a line that matches the edge of the playing card and is clearly above the faint reflection of the checker.

8. Click a third point down and to the right of the second point, creating a line that clears the reflection of the check. What you are doing here is encompassing only the part of the reflection that overlaps the playing card (see fig. 4.16). Click a fourth point and then take the Polygon Lasso tool cursor back to the beginning point of the selection.

9. Single-click on the beginning point of the selection to convert the area you have defined to an active selection marquee. The underlying image areas inside the marquee can be edited, and the areas outside of the marquee are protected, or masked, from any changes.

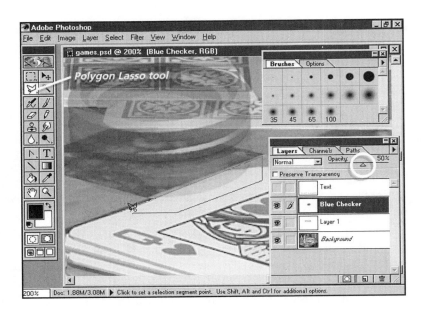

figure 4.16

Click points to encompass the area you want selected in the image. Photoshop automatically creates selection lines between the points.

It's not mandatory to single-click on the beginning point to close an active selection marquee with the Polygon Lasso tool. You can double-click anywhere in an image to enable Photoshop to automatically close the area you have defined. If you do this, Photoshop draws a straight path from the point at which you double-click to the beginning point.

10. Double-click on the Quick Mask mode button (the button on the right under the Foreground/Background colors on the toolbox) to display the Quick Mask options box.

Here's the story: Quick Mask is an editing mode in which areas of tinted overlay color are visible in a document. This tint color does not become part of your image—it's simply an indicator of where image areas are selected or masked. The beauty of this on-screen metaphor for a selection area is that both selection and paint tools can be used to edit the Quick Mask; after you finish editing, the areas of Quick Mask can be used to define a selection marquee.

Because you have a selection marquee active in the document as you enter Quick Mask mode, areas outside the marquee are tinted, by default, with the color overlay. This is not what you want here, however. The selection area, not the areas outside the selection, should be tinted in this example, because if you followed the steps, the selection marquee made with the Polygon Lasso tool encompasses areas of the checker selection that should remain in this image. It's easier to remove some of the unwanted Quick Mask if it defines the *selection* than to edit the entire outside, masked area within the image.

11. Below the Color Indicates line, click on the Selected Areas radio button and then click on OK (see fig. 4.17). The area inside the selection marquee now takes on a 50% red-tinted overlay, and the marquee selection disappears. Notice, on the Layers palette, that the Indicates painting icon is gone from the left of the layer title, and the Blue Checker title is dimmed. These two visual differences in Photoshop's interface tell you that you are editing selections, and not painting into image content, when you are in Quick Mask mode.

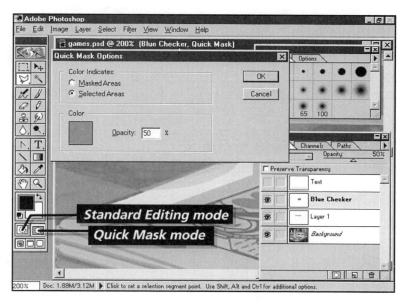

figure 4.17

Quick Mask mode replaces active selection marquees in the document with tinted overlay that depicts selections, or masked areas.

Admittedly, a semitransparent Quick Mask overlay on top of a semitransparent checker reflection is hard to show in a black-and-white book. This is why figure 4.18 is annotated with a dotted line where you want Quick Mask areas to remain in the image. The Polygon Lasso selection encompasses not only the interior of the playing card, but also a small area of the checker reflection that should remain in the image. What you need to do is remove Quick Mask outside the area marked in figure 4.18, to accurately define the inside edge of the playing card. When you return to Standard editing mode, the resulting selection marquee will encompass only those areas of the checker reflection that should not exist within the image.

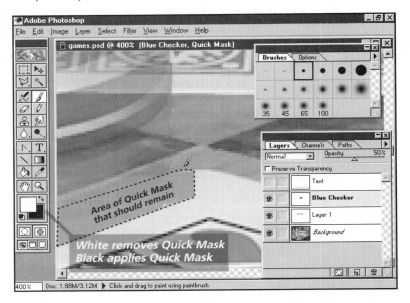

figure 4.18
Remove only Quick Mask areas that lie outside the interior of the playing card in the image.

12. Press **D** (Default colors) and then press **X** (switch colors) to make white the current foreground color on the toolbox. This can also be accomplished by clicking on the Default Colors icon and then clicking on the Switch Foreground and Background colors icon on the toolbox.

13. Choose the Paintbrush tool and then click on the third tip in the top row on the Brushes palette.

14. Carefully stroke around the outside edge of the playing card to remove any Quick Mask that lies on the exterior of the card. White foreground color removes Quick Mask overlay

in the document, and black applies Quick Mask. If you make a mistake, press X to swap foreground colors, and then apply Quick Mask where necessary.

15. When you have this Quick Mask area edited so that only the interior of the playing card has the overlay tint, click on the Standard editing mode button, to the left of the Quick Mask button on the toolbox. This exchanges the overlay color for a marquee selection in the document.

16. Double-click on the Zoom tool to take your viewing resolution of the Games image to 100%. Hold the spacebar to access the Hand tool, and then drag in the window to scroll your view so that the selection marquee is centered in the workspace.

17. Press Delete (Backspace). The area of checker reflection inside the playing card is now gone (see fig. 4.19). Press Ctrl(⌘)+D to deselect the active marquee selection.

18. Return the layer to 100-percent opacity by typing **o** on the numeric keypad; then press Ctrl(⌘)+S to save your work.

figure 4.19

Areas inside the marquee selection on the Blue Checker layer are deleted, providing an accurate representation of an object reflection in the composition.

TIP

In addition to choosing whether Quick Mask indicates selected or masked areas, the Quick Mask options box enables you to choose the color and opacity of the overlay tint. You can visit the options box at any time in Quick Mask mode to change all options. When you are working in Standard editing mode, double-click on the Quick Mask button to display the options box and put a document into Quick Mask mode automatically.

To change the color of the Quick Mask overlay, click on the Color swatch in the Quick Mask options box to display the color picker; then choose the exact hue, shade, and tone of the Quick Mask color. By default, the Opacity of the Quick Mask overlay is at 50%, which is a good opacity for most editing tasks. If you want more or less of the overlay obscuring your view as you work, type a different value in the Opacity field in the Quick Mask options box.

In the same way that you can decide whether the Quick Mask representation in a document describes masked or selected areas, you can easily invert a marquee selection. Say, for example, that you create a selection, change your mind, and want every area in an image that is masked to be selected, and vice versa. Version 4 has changed the key commands for Select, Inverse. The key command is now Ctrl(⌘)+Shift+I (version 3 was Shift+F7). This is a quick way to invert a selection marquee and has no effect when a selection marquee is not active in the document—pixel information in the document is not affected by Select, Inverse.

WARNING

Don't confuse Ctrl(⌘)+Shift+I (Select, Inverse) with Ctrl(⌘)+I, which is the command for Image, Adjust, Invert. The Invert command inverts the color order of an image, no selection marquee needs to be active in the document, and if you mistakenly choose this command you wind up with a photographic negative of your work instead of an inverse selection marquee.

Inverse selections and inverted image content are *not* the same thing!

Working with a Clipping Group

Yet another type of image mask you can work with in Photoshop, called a *clipping group*, can be used as both an editing and a creative tool. A clipping group assigns the bottom layer you specify as an image mask; subsequent layers you create or move above the base clipping group layer show through only the image content of the layer; areas of clear pixels on the base layer display no image information contained on layers on top of the base clipping group layer.

The following sections explore the use of Photoshop channels as a work area for creating additional visual content in the Games image, and show you how to create a special effects look for some text in the image.

What Are Image Channels?

Images whose pixel colors are organized as a composite of brightnesses for component color values are called *color channel images*. The distinction between color channel images and indexed color images is an important one because indexed color images cannot be manipulated easily in Photoshop. If you look on the Image, Mode menu, you see that the Games image is RGB color. This means that red, green, and blue are the color components of the image, and you can see the composite of these colors on-screen because of Photoshop's interpretation of brightness values in the red, green, and blue color channels in the image. When you view an indexed color image in Photoshop, there is only one channel in the image, and pixel colors are displayed through the use of a color look-up table in the header of the image file.

NOTE

Color channel images are not limited to RGB color in their construction. As you will see in subsequent chapters, CMYK and LAB color modes also contain multiple color channels.

Color channels, ironically, contain grayscale information; this is what you see in color channels through Photoshop's default configuration. The grayscale information is interpreted as relative contributions of component color strength to create the composite view of the full-color image. White depicts a high contribution of component color, whereas black depicts no color channel contribution.

To view the component brightness channels for red, green, and blue within a color channel image in Photoshop, click on the Channels tab on the Layers\Channels\Paths grouped palette, and then click on a title for the color channel you want to view. Channels are relevant to this discussion of Photoshop selections because color, channel-capable image file formats (such as TIFF, Targa, PICT, and Photoshop's PSD and PDD) can also hold a channel—called a *masking*, or *alpha, channel*—that contains information Photoshop does *not* read as image color information.

Alpha channels were first used in computer graphics programs as a way to store selection and other information within an image file. In reality, an application can interpret alpha channel information in any way the programmer chooses. In Photoshop, for example, alpha channel information can be interpreted as selected versus unselected areas in an image, but the Lighting Effects filter can also be used to interpret any visual content in an alpha channel as the bump height to be displayed through the use of this filter. (More on Lighting Effects in Chapter 13, "Creative Plug-Ins.")

The strength of an alpha channel as an editing tool has been significantly diminished by the advent of layers in Photoshop. After laboring over a selection definition, you no longer need to store it in an image channel—you simply apply the selection to the image, to copy or cut the image content within the selection marquee to a new layer. The alpha channel feature can be of great use, however, when you need to share an image file with a designer who doesn't own Photoshop. TIFF, Targa, and PICT image files can contain alpha channels, and many Windows and Macintosh applications can read this information correctly. And Photoshop understands alpha channel information written by other applications. Modeling applications, for example, usually write an alpha channel to a rendered file so that the creator can then strip areas out of the document that don't contain modeled images.

In the following sections, you get acquainted with Photoshop's Channels feature, and work with an alpha channel that you create to enhance the appearance of the as-yet-unexplored text layer in the Games image.

Loading and Saving Selections to Alpha Channels

An alpha channel can be created as a blank within a channel color image; then you fill in the information by painting shades of black within the blank alpha channel. But there's a much simpler (and more useful) method for storing the outline of layer content in an image such as Games.psd.

Shortcut key commands for loading a selection have changed in version 4. If you are accustomed to loading a selection with the Photoshop 3.0.x key command, Ctrl(⌘)+Shift+T, you are in for a surprise. In version 4, this command does nothing when an image layer (but not the background) is the current editing layer. The following example shows you how to load a selection based on a layer's visual content and save this selection information to an alpha channel.

WORKING WITH ALPHA CHANNELS

1. On the Layers palette, click on the Text title on the list. This restores visibility to the layer and makes it the current editing layer.

2. Hold Ctrl(⌘) and click on the title again. This time, you see a different cursor; the hand with its tiny, superimposed marquee rectangle means that the Text layer's contents will serve as the basis for a selection marquee. The long way to do this is to choose Select, Load Selection, and then choose Layer X (the layer's title) transparency from the Channel drop-down list.

3. Click on the Channels tab on the palette and then on the Save selection as channel button (see fig. 4.20). A new thumbnail image and title (#4, by default) are added to the channels list.

figure 4.20
Photoshop renders grayscale tones into a new alpha channel that corresponds to selected and masked areas in the image.

TIP

If you intend to create a number of alpha channels in images of your own, it's easy to assign each channel a unique name. Double-click on the title of an alpha channel and type a new name in the Name field.

And you can specify that you want black (and darker tones) to visually indicate either a selection area or the masked areas (the default configuration) of the selection saved to an alpha channel.

If for some reason the alpha channel appears to be white with black text, you have the Channel options defined as selected areas (rather than Photoshop's default of Color Indicates Masked Areas). This is not a problem. Instead of using the alpha channel information as selection information, you are going to copy the visual information out of this channel so that you can use it as a design element in Games. If you have the tonal inverse of white text on black now, press Ctrl+I (Image, Adjust, Invert) to make the alpha channel information correct.

4. Click on the #4 channel title on the Channels palette to switch document views to this channel. With the Rectangular Marquee tool, click and drag a marquee around the text in the alpha channel, leaving a space about half the text height at the top of the selection (see fig. 4.21). If the Rectangular Marquee tool isn't displayed on the toolbox, drag on the upper left button on the toolbox to display the marquee flyout, and then choose this tool.

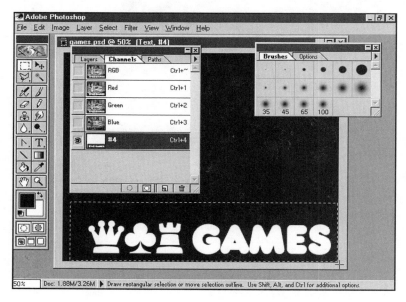

figure 4.21
Use the Rectangular Marquee tool to select the portion of the alpha channel that contains the text.

5. Press Ctrl(⌘)+X to cut the selected text from the alpha channel, and then press Ctrl(⌘)+ ~ (tilde) to return to the RGB color composite view of the document.

6. Click on the Layers tab on the grouped palette, and then press Ctrl(⌘)+V to paste the text onto a new layer in the Games image.

7. Press **V** (Move tool) and drag the contents of the new layer to a position slightly above the colored text in the Games image (see fig. 4.22). In a few steps, you will see how the colored text masks an edited version of this white text on black to create a carved drop-shadow look.

figure 4.22
Position the new layer's contents to slightly offset the position of the colored text.

8. Choose Filter, Blur, Gaussian Blur. Yes, this is the filter used on 99 percent of magazine covers to simulate a soft drop-shadow effect on text and other objects.

    The Gaussian Blur box contains only one control: the Radius of the effect, measured in pixels. The effect largely depends upon the size of the selection to be Gaussian blurred. Therefore, the amount specified in the following step is correct for the Games text layer; before you click on OK in your own work, use the preview box to see how much effect is applied.

9. Type **6** in the pixels field (or drag the slider) and click on OK (see fig. 4.23).

figure 4.23

The Gaussian Blur effect causes selected areas to be blurred in a bell-shaped curve distribution. The "core" of the selection is the most dense.

10. Hold Alt(Opt) and click between the Text title and the Layer 2 title (the layer containing the grayscale text) on the Layers palette's list. This specifies the Text layer as the clipping group base layer; on layers above the Text layer, any content that extends beyond the contents of the Text layer is clipped.

    A dotted line marks the top of the base clipping group layer on the Layers palette's list, and the title for the base layer is underscored. This is a handy visual reference if someone hands you a Photoshop file that you cannot edit correctly!

11. Click on the Layer 2 title, and choose Multiply from the modes drop-down list on the Layers palette. In Multiply mode, lighter colors can drop out to transparency, and darker colors are accentuated. The white text drops out now, exposing the colored text on the base clipping group layer, and the black areas outside the base layer lettering are invisible (clipped). (See fig. 4.24.)

12. With the Move tool, drag on Layer 2. Stop dragging when you can see the "fringe" created by the Gaussian Blur effect showing through the colored text from the upper right of the text characters. To place the text precisely, use the keyboard arrow keys to nudge the layer's contents into position.

13. Press Ctrl(⌘)+S to save your work.

figure 4.24
The base layer of a clipping group hides areas that fall outside the visual content of the layer.

Basically, you have finished the composition. If your image looks like figure 4.25 (in color, of course), you now have a pretty good handle on how selections, paths, layers, and masking are accomplished (and interrelated) in Photoshop 4.

As mentioned earlier in this chapter, the Photoshop format for image files is a proprietary one; only Photoshop 3 can read Photoshop 4 layers intact, and most image-viewing programs cannot understand or display the PSD or PDD format. Therefore, it's a good idea after you complete an assignment to save a copy of the image in a more conventional file format. To do this, follow these steps:

First, press Ctrl(⌘)+Alt(Opt)+S (File, Save a Copy) and then, from the Save As drop-down list in the Save a Copy dialog box, choose a file format you know that others can read on their systems. (On the Macintosh: the Format drop-down list contains the same file format choices as this Windows Save As list.)

The Save a Copy dialog box will not provide you with GIF or PCX image formats in which you can save a copy of your work, because these formats are indexed-color-type images, and the original (or a file duplicate) must be color-reduced before you can use the Save a Copy command.

figure 4.25
One of the keys to professional editing of digital images lies in Photoshop's selection tools.

If you want to save a copy to TIFF or Targa formats, this dialog box gives you the option to save or delete alpha channels from the saved copy. If you choose the Photoshop format in this dialog box (which defeats the purpose of these steps!), you can choose to flatten the image. This Flatten Image option is dimmed and the copy is flattened automatically if file formats other than Photoshop's are chosen. Additionally, Windows users can choose to Save Thumbnail, which means you can preview a thumbnail of an image before you open it in the Open dialog box in Photoshop. Macintosh users can specify in File, Preferences, Saving Files, whether to make image previews a desktop icon, a thumbnail preview, and/or a full size (512×512 by 72 pixel/inch) preview image. The full-size preview is intended for use in applications that can read only 72 pixel/inch resolution images; by default, the desktop icon and thumbnail options are turned on in Photoshop. If you're concerned about conserving hard disk space, don't choose to save with a full-size preview.

Finally, use the Save a Copy dialog box's directory controls to specify where you want this copy written, name the file Games.tif (or the file format of your choice), and then click on Save.

Games.psd is still the active image in Photoshop's workspace; the copy of the image is not in the workspace, but is now on your hard disk. The advantage of saving a copy instead of flattening a layered image is that you can come back to Games.psd on your hard disk and continue rearranging the playing cards, or create other layer-specific edits.

When you choose Flatten Image from the flyout menu on the Layers palette, the image becomes "standard," in the sense that you can save the image in TIFF or other format, and other image editors can read the file. The clipping group in this case removes areas outside the layer contents, the layers are merged in the currently chosen layer mode, and only the Background layer remains. Because this option eliminates any possibility of additional work with layers, however, you should flatten an image only when you're certain that you have finished editing.

WARNING

Images that are flattened and saved to file formats other than Photoshop's should be stripped of alpha channels, unless you're confident that another application can correctly read alpha channel information. BMP, PCX, GIF, JPEG, and other file formats that cannot support alpha information cannot be written to these formats from Photoshop—the option simply isn't displayed in the Save As dialog box—but be careful with files written to TIFF or Targa formats.

Many programs, such as Adobe Pagemaker, simply ignore alpha channel information; other programs fail to import files with alpha channels. To remove an alpha channel, click on the channel title on the Channels palette and drag the channel into the trash icon at the bottom of the palette. Alternatively, you can click on the channel title and click on the trash icon (and a confirmation box for this action will be displayed).

Summary

Having read Chapter 3 and this chapter, you should have Photoshop and your system up and running optimally, and have good working skills tucked away for the hardest part of image editing—selecting image areas. It's a good idea to pause occasionally before you execute editing steps to ensure that what you believe is selected is actually selected (that the selection is not inverse). Photoshop's selection capabilities can be converted easily from one on-screen representation to another, and depending on your working style, you're more than likely to develop a preference for at least one selection type.

In Part III, "Image Retouching," you shift into high gear and put what you have learned so far into practice, restoring and enhancing an heirloom photograph. Bring along what you have learned, and be prepared to explore some of Photoshop's new capabilities, as you see how to perform the digital equivalent of a craft that formerly required years of experience.

PART

IMAGE RETOUCHING

RESTORING AN HEIRLOOM PHOTOGRAPH

Traditional photographic retouching was an art on the wane before the advent of digital sampling of images and Adobe Photoshop. At its best, traditional image restoration was performed by a gifted craftsman with a background in both illustration and photography, whose tools included a magnifying glass, a collection of brushes, and semitransparent dyes. And the price commanded for such work could set your family back an amount equivalent to a new fridge or an air conditioner. At its worst, image restoration could ruin the original photo, or make the photo's subjects look as though they were created from shiny plastic; airbrushes, in the wrong hands, tend to do this stuff.

This chapter and Chapter 6, "Retouching an Heirloom Photograph," take you through the restoration, retouching, and enhancement of an image that a traditional retoucher would probably dismiss as damaged beyond repair. If you have an image of your own, get it out of the shoebox. You will see shortly that image recovery is well within your grasp, because the term "traditional" simply doesn't apply to the power found in Photoshop.

Lee at Age Three: Nice Kid, Disastrous Image

The image you will work with in this chapter is Lee.tif, found in the CHAP05 folder of the Companion CD. The original image—photographed more than 30 years ago—fell victim to a house fire, the subsequent water damage, and somewhat less than optimal care during the salvage process after the fire, and has perhaps suffered least of all from aging through the passing years.

The very first thing to do when you take on an assignment as demanding as the restoration of this image is to acquire a digital copy of it. In the case of Lee's picture, there was no image negative, and therefore the print had to be scanned. If you *do* own a film negative of a photo you want to restore, you should make arrangements with a photo-finisher to get the negative scanned to Kodak's PhotoCD, pronto. A PhotoCD file then becomes one generation closer to the original image, and you have more image content to work with. *Reflective scans*—those performed with hand-held or flatbed scanners—fail to acquire original image information as accurate as that acquired by *transparency scans*—those performed by Kodak for PhotoCDs—or by negative-scanning hardware such as Nikon's CoolScan.

Scanning Modes and Resolution

Regardless of whether a photo is in color or is a grayscale (or sepia tone image), you should acquire the digital sample of the image in RGB color mode. RGB color mode parallels the color capability of human vision, and you need as much original image information sampled as possible to restore the digital copy of the photo.

Image resolution—the number of pixels (*pi*cture el*e*ments)—should be defined as the greatest amount of digital information your system can handle. The fewer the samples (pixels) per inch at which you scan, the less original information is translated to digital image format—and you want every pixel you can get, to mend the photo. The Lee.tif image is a modest 1.8 MB in file size, and the authors do *not* recommend that you scan to achieve this small file size unless your system has modest RAM and processor specs. The techniques shown are valuable ones, and we went a little skimpy on the Lee.tif image's saved file size to enable users—of no matter what model and capability of computer—to follow along here. The authors scanned the image to get an 8 MB image file for the retouched image in the color signature of this book. Generally, you should scan an image to the final resolution of the piece as printed, but image restoration is an *exception* to the rule; scan at a resolution with which you can work comfortably in Photoshop. You can then make a copy of the retouched piece at different resolutions for output as necessary in the future.

Become a Detective Before Retouching

The term "re-creation" is often used to describe an event in which actors play out a historic scene from the American Revolution, or a monologue delivered by someone in makeup and clothes patterned after information about Mark Twain. Clearly, to preserve the fidelity of the image being conveyed, re-creation requires some *research*.

Because image restoration depends upon *adding* to areas of the original image that are beyond recovery, you should thoroughly examine the original before you pick up the Paintbrush tool. What are the problem areas? Which areas of the image can you resample, to mend damaged areas? In essence, the details that are not damaged in the current image should give you an indication of the style needed for areas that *are* damaged.

In figure 5.1, you can see two views of the Lee image. Open the file in Photoshop, and take a good look at different viewing resolutions. A superficial examination shows a crease running through the little girl's hair, water stains that have discolored her skirt, and many pinholes (dots of pure white) that are a combination of careless original printing (you're supposed to clean negatives before you print them) and dust that could not be removed because of the fragility of the print.

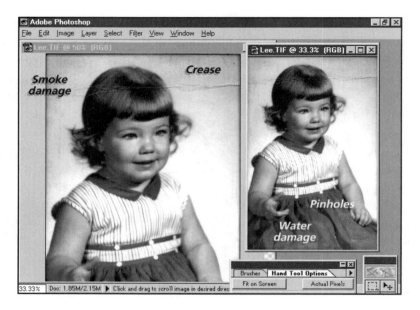

figure 5.1
Examine the image you want to restore for obvious problems, and then for not so obvious ones.

There are indeed certain areas of the image that are simply missing—areas of the hair, the background, and Lee's skirt need to be added to blend not only with the image content, but also with the grain and the focus of the photograph. The authors have come up with the "beneath the surface" observations discussed in the following sections.

A Shallow Plane of Focus Was Used

If you look carefully at the image, you can see that Lee's face is in near-perfect focus, and that the focus of the image drops off severely toward her hair and her hands. This lack of focus in image areas could have been done as an artistic effect, or it could have been caused by the lack of light and the type of camera used. For example, the *f-stop*, the depth of field used to capture an image, was not easy to define with *focal plane* (a.k.a. portrait) cameras in the 1950s.

This lack of focus will make areas of Lee's hair difficult to restore, and the course of action in Photoshop will be to add strands of hand-painted hair to the finished image.

It's Not a Color Image

When an image is damaged as severely as Lee's image was, it's difficult to tell whether the color in the image is natural or was added to the photo. Certainly, you can see some color in this image if you open Lee.tif in Photoshop. But was this a color image or a grayscale image that was hand-tinted? (To learn more about tinting grayscale images, read Chapter 11, "Black and White…and Color.")

If you zoom in to the image to more than 300%, you can see that the edges of Lee's profile are indistinct, suggesting that a tinted wash of color dye was used to color a grayscale version of this photo. Additionally, it seemed suspicious that a 3-year-old in the 1950s would wear makeup. Asked whether she had put lipstick on her child for the photographic session, Lee's mom said, "No."

This is wonderful news, at least pertaining to the reconstruction of the image. To retouch a grayscale image you need to match only 256 tones (max), compared to the 16.7 million unique colors possible in a color image. The color aspect of this image will be discarded in this chapter's restoration techniques; Chapter 6 will show you how to add color to the image after the grayscale version has been fixed.

Inconsistent Noise Is in the Image

There are three reasons for noise (the uneven dispersal of random colored pixels) in the digital image. The first is the hand-tinting. The dyes used either became separated from age and abuse, or were not mixed evenly. There are particles in some areas on the surface of the photo, but other areas are unaffected.

Scanning itself can produce noise in an image. At high levels of scanning resolution, the particles in photographic emulsion can sometimes reflect off the scanning element at an odd angle, producing noncontinuous zones of shading in the digitally acquired image. Also, the age of the photograph plays heavily into the noise present in the file of the scan. Scanners are extremely sensitive to changes in surface brightness, and the emulsion used in photographic imaging ages inconsistently. As you can see in figure 5.2, a close-up of Lee's right cheek shows noise caused by at least two of the factors described. Although noise might not be apparent at 1:1 viewing resolutions, it will interfere with the process of restoring image areas. The trick is to decide how much noise to filter from the image, and how much must remain to preserve photographic integrity.

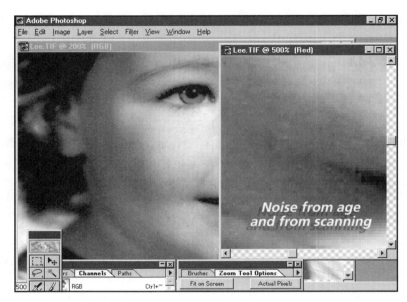

figure 5.2
An uneven amount of noise in the digital image makes it difficult to blend new areas into the photograph.

The sections to follow in this chapter demonstrate different techniques for restoring the image. You will learn more about the overall process if you tackle this chapter sequentially. Many examples in this book illustrate a principle; with the Lee.tif image, however, we recommend that you actually follow (*do*) the steps to build not only your knowledge, but also your *technique* in Photoshop.

Different Approaches for Different Problem Areas

Obviously, the first target in this image is Lee's hair. Thanks to a noticeable crack in the original photo's emulsion, her hair seems to be parted horizontally. Additionally, the pinholes in the image distract terribly from the image content, and the water stains in the image force the viewer to look at the surface of the picture instead of looking *into* it, to see the pretty girl. Each flaw in the image requires a different set of steps, a different Photoshop tool here and there, and a different conceptualization of what should appear in the finished image.

Changing Color Modes, Edgework, and Restoring the Hair

As mentioned earlier, the camera focus threw edges of Lee's hair into a blobby mass on photographic paper. Notice that the edge between her hair and the backdrop is actually a gradual transition between foreground and background. A soft-tipped tool can address the problem of restoring the edges, and Photoshop's Rubber Stamp tool can make quick work of cloning areas of Lee's hair into the damaged areas.

Here's how to remove the crease from Lee's hair:

STAMPING OUT PHOTO FLAWS

CD-ROM

1. Open the Lee.tif image from the CHAP05 folder on the Companion CD if you have not already done so.

2. Maximize the window area for the document, and type **200** in the Zoom percentage field; then press Enter (Return). If retouching looks okay at 200%, it will surely look fine at 1:1, normal viewing, and lower resolutions.

3. With the Hand tool, pan your view of the image so that Lee's hair is centered on-screen.

4. Choose Image, Mode, Lab Color. Press F7 to display the Layers\Channels\Paths palette if it isn't already on-screen.

5. Click on the Channels tab and then on the Lightness channel title. Choose Image, Mode, Grayscale from the menu, and click on OK in the attention box that tells you the other channels will be discarded. You have a faithful grayscale representation of the original image now. The document is also $1/3$ the original file size. See Chapter 12, "Working with Text as Graphics," for thorough explanations of how to convert between color modes.

6. Double-click on the Rubber Stamp tool, to choose it and to force the Options palette for this tool to the top of the workspace.

7. On the Options palette, make sure that Opacity is set to 100%, that the painting mode is Normal (from the drop-down list), and that the Style for the tool is set to Clone (aligned). Click on the Brushes tab on the palette, and then click on the second row, second from left tip.

8. Press Alt(Opt) and click in an undamaged highlight area of Lee's hair to specify the sample area in the image from which you will clone into damaged areas. In the Clone (aligned) style, the sampling point travels as you apply the Rubber Stamp tool to different image areas.

9. Drag the Rubber Stamp tool across an area damaged by the crease (see fig. 5.3). You should definitely follow the angle of the strands of Lee's hair. In other words, if you sample from the highlight area where the strands arc clockwise, apply this area only to an image area in which strands also arc clockwise.

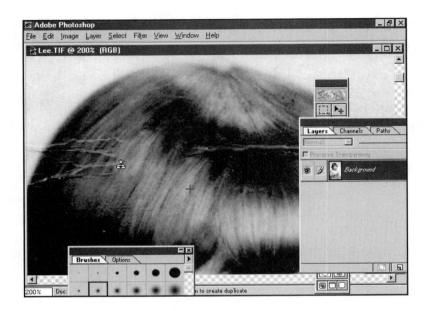

figure 5.3

Damaged hair can be restored by using a good conditioner...or the Rubber Stamp tool.

10. You will eventually run out of sampling areas with the Rubber Stamp tool; with the Clone (aligned) Option, the sampling point travels in tandem with the cursor. When you run out of sampling areas of highlighted hair, press Alt(Opt) and click on a different area from which to sample the hair; then continue melding the cloned Rubber Stamp strokes with the undamaged hair areas.

11. When the curve of the hair strands changes direction, resample the Rubber Stamp tool in an area that shows similar curves; then stroke into the damaged area to restore it.

12. When you reach the edge where the hair meets the backdrop, press Alt(Opt) and click on an undamaged hair area on the edge between hair and backdrop. Make certain that this sampling point is very close to the damaged area; otherwise, the curve of the hair silhouette will not be correct. Instead of dragging in this small area, simply click the tool over the damaged area. The Rubber Stamp tool provides a circular "burst" of replacement cloning, and you eliminate the problem of cloning into an area you do not want to change.

13. Choose File, Save As, and save the image to your hard disk as Lee.tif in the TIFF file format.

Rubber Stamp tool corrections are much easier to make in Grayscale mode than in a color image. Hair, for example, often contains many shades of color, but you can retouch hair successfully in Grayscale mode by using similar brightness values only. In your own work, scout around an image to find similar patterns for replacements. In a surprisingly large number of images, you can mend a not-so-perfect area by copying a perfectly good image area to it.

Advanced Editing with the Rubber Stamp Tool

The water stains on Lee's left cheek are easy to correct when the image is in Grayscale mode. One problem in retouching skin is that the human body is composed of many different types of skin, each with a unique coloration. Additionally, the shading caused by light striking human skin is usually fairly steep in transitional areas such as the cheeks and the nose, or anywhere the topology of a face curves and twists. But wait—there's more bad news. Because there's noise in the affected area, simply painting over the stain with the Paintbrush or Airbrush tool is out of the question. You need to match the tone and the noise to fix the stained area.

The authors tried several techniques to remove the water stain, and finally arrived at a novel solution: to measure the brightness value close to the stained area, and then define the Rubber Stamp tool's sampling point at an identical brightness area in the image. This technique requires using incredibly short strokes, but also gives you the opportunity to experiment with the usefulness of Photoshop's Info palette.

Here's how to get the toughest stains out of an image:

CALCULATING BRIGHTNESS WITH THE INFO PALETTE

1. The easiest way to zoom to 300% viewing resolution in the image is to click once with the Zoom tool in the document window. Next, hold the spacebar to toggle to the Hand tool, and pan your view so that you can see Lee's left cheek centered in the window.

2. Press F8 to display the Info palette. Click on the eyedropper flyout on the left field, and choose Grayscale from the flyout menu (see fig. 5.4). The Info palette offers dual displays so that you can see pixel colors displayed simultaneously in different color modes (RGB and CMYK, for example). Because all you need now is Grayscale information, adjusting both areas on the palette is not necessary in this example.

figure 5.4
The color mode you specify on the Info palette determines the pixel color displayed under your cursor at all times.

3. Move the cursor to an area extremely close to (but not directly on) the water stain in the image. Figure 5.5 shows a good target location for the cursor. You can use any tool to get color information (the Eyedropper tool was used in this figure, to visually reinforce a point). You will see that 12–13% black seems to be the tone surrounding the water stain that obscures the image area.

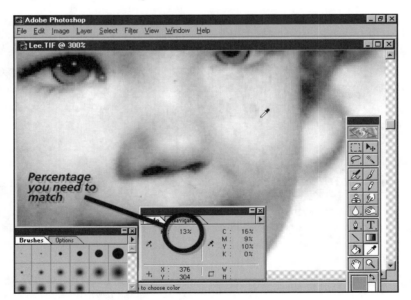

figure 5.5
The Info palette indicates the brightness of the location over which your cursor is located.

4. Choose the Rubber Stamp tool; then, with the same Options palette settings you used earlier in the chapter, hover the cursor over Lee's right cheek. Although the lighting is slightly different, the same general geometry and the way light casts on the cheek make it a suitable cloning source location. When the Info palette tells you that your cursor is over a location that's within one or two percent of 12%, press Alt(Opt) and click to define the sample point.

5. Click, don't drag, on the water stain area (see fig. 5.6). The water stain is replaced by a sampled area of the same brightness as surrounding image areas, and also contains the same type of image noise. Notice that three or four separate water stains are on Lee's left cheek. Take a brightness reading from the other areas close to the water stains, sample other areas on Lee's right cheek, and restore these areas.

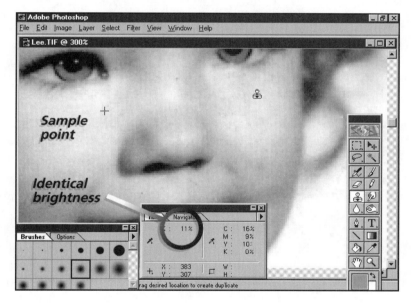

figure 5.6
Match the Rubber Stamp tool's sampling point to the brightness near stained image areas, to then restore them.

6. Press Ctrl(⌘)+S to save your work.

The Rubber Stamp tool is terrific for mending small areas of detail in an image, but a different strategy must be adopted when there are small flaws in a larger image area. The next section addresses solutions for reducing noise in the image.

Using the Dust & Scratches Filter

The name "Dust & Scratches Filter" suggests that this filter is a magic tool for removing pinholes and other areas of sudden pixel color changes in a digital image. In fact, the Dust & Scratches filter can *introduce* noise to an image; what the filter does depends upon the type of image area in which you work, and the settings you specify for the filter. The Dust & Scratches filter is used in the following set of steps to soften the noise on the right side of Lee's face, but not to eliminate the noise completely, because a smooth, flawless area looks artificial next to other areas that display some degree of noise. The trick is not to visually highlight a perfectly corrected area, but to restore an image to the highest quality displayed in the original.

Here's how to tone down the noise on Lee's right cheek:

AVERAGING BRIGHTNESS DIFFERENCES

1. Press Ctrl(⌘)+– to zoom out of the document to 200%. (This is the third method described in this chapter for zooming in and out; use the one that works best for you.)

2. Hold the spacebar to toggle to the Hand tool, and then drag in the document to pan your view to the right cheek area.

3. Choose the Lasso tool, and then drag to create a marquee that encompasses Lee's temple, the right cheek, and the part of her neck that displays noise. Figure 5.7 shows the location and shape of the marquee selection.

4. Right-click (Macintosh: hold Ctrl and click), and then choose Feather from the Context menu. In the Feather selection box, type **5** in the Feather Radius field; click on OK to apply the feathering to the selection. Depending on the overall image size in your own retouching work, you might need a higher or lower amount for the Feathering feature. Number 5 works in this example, to make a gradual transition between the interior of the marquee, which will be filtered, and the exterior of the marquee, whose pixels will not be changed.

5. Choose Filter, Noise, Dust & Scratches.

6. Type **2** in the Radius field. Photoshop will search by 2 pixels in distance to sample and reassign pixel brightness to bring the "out of place," noisy pixels back to a brightness displayed by most of the other pixels in the selection.

7. Drag the Threshold slider to about 6 (see fig. 5.7). The Threshold determines how similar in brightness value pixels must be to qualify for filtering. The higher the value, the more subtle the filtering effect, because more original brightness values are included in Photoshop's calculations. Lower Threshold values produce posterization in the selected image area.

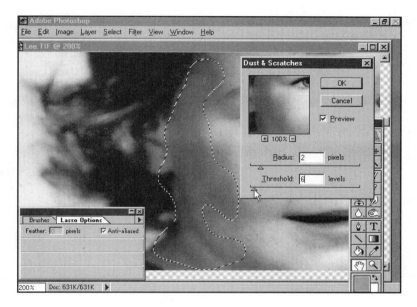

figure 5.7
Use the Dust & Scratches filter to reduce, but not totally eliminate, noise in the selected area.

8. Click on OK to apply the filter, press Ctrl(⌘)+D to deselect the marquee, and then press Ctrl(⌘)+S to save your work. Keep the image open in Photoshop.

One or two other areas in the Lee.tif image can benefit from the technique described in the previous steps. Look around the image, and reduce the noise in selected areas to blend them into the original image areas.

Using Different Selection Techniques

Restoring this image has led the authors to conclude that the way in which a selection marquee is defined is as important as the steps used to retouch or replace the selections. In the steps that follow, the pinholes on Lee's skirt and the water stains at the bottom of the image are removed by first *partially* selecting the affected areas. The Dust & Scratches filter and the Rubber Stamp tool are then used to mend the selected areas.

Photoshop's Quick Mask mode gives you the opportunity to *partially select* areas— that is, to make a selection of partial opacity. When you then apply the effect, it only partially affects the image area. The result is a subtle retouching effect, with some of the noise in the image retained to keep the overall image quality consistent.

Here's how to restore the pinhole areas in the image:

USING QUICK MASK TO DEFINE AREAS

1. Double-click on the Quick Mask mode icon toward the bottom of the toolbox. The Quick Mask options box appears. Make sure that the Color Indicates Selected Areas radio button is chosen, and click on OK to close the options box.

2. Click on the Foreground color selection box on the toolbox, and choose a medium black from the Color Picker. In the B field of the HSB area on the Color Picker, type **40** (a value that will work in this example). Press Enter (Return) and click on OK to close the Color Picker.

3. Press **B** (Paintbrush tool), and then click on the brush tip that is fourth from the left, top row, on the Brushes palette.

4. Hold the spacebar and drag upward in the document window to pan your view so that you can see the skirt area of the image.

5. Click on areas in the image where you see pinholes (see fig. 5.8). You have more latitude in the strength with which you apply the Dust & Scratches filter; the selections made in Quick Mask mode are only a little more than half-strength, and you can apply stronger filtering while retaining some of the original image content.

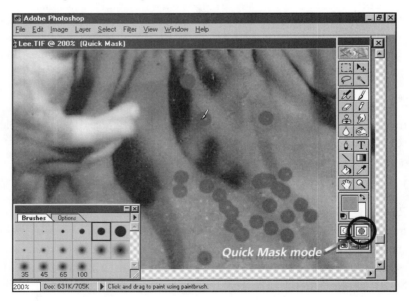

figure 5.8
The percentage of black with which you define Quick Mask overlay determines the opacity of the selection area.

6. Click on the Standard editing icon to the left of the Quick Mask mode icon to display on-screen the selections you have created as marquees ("marching ants").

7. Press Ctrl(⌘)+H to hide the marquee. In the filter dialog box, in preview, you need to compare the areas to be filtered with the original image areas—and marquees are generally a visual distraction. The hidden marquee is still active; you simply have no on-screen reminder!

8. Press Ctrl(⌘)+Alt(Opt)+F to access the dialog box for the last-used filter—the Dust & Scratches filter—without actually launching the last-used filter.

9. Drag the Radius slider to 3, and then drag the Threshold slider to 11. Look at the preview window in the Dust & Scratches dialog box. Play with the controls here; now is the time for experimenting on an image that you're not getting paid to retouch! When the pinholes have vanished in the preview window, click on OK to apply the effect.

10. Press Ctrl(⌘)+D to deselect the marquee selection, press Ctrl(⌘)+S to save your work, and keep the image open in Photoshop.

We might be getting a little ahead of ourselves, but all of the pinholes do *not* need to be filtered. When color is added to the image in Chapter 6, many of the pinholes will disappear; they will be filled in with color. But you now know the technique for repairing the most visible pinholes in the image. Look around at other areas and use the preceding steps to fix them.

Using the Rubber Stamp tool, you can clone over the water stains at the bottom of the image. Here's how to approach this restoration area.

REPLACING WATER-STAINED AREAS

1. Scroll the document window to the bottom, and click on the Quick Mask icon; then, with the Paintbrush tool, apply Quick Mask to the stained areas. (Peek ahead to fig. 5.9 to see which areas to select.)

2. Choose the Rubber Stamp tool, find an area close to one of the selected areas, and then press Alt(Opt) and click to define the source of the Rubber Stamp tool.

3. Drag in the selection area to replace the stained area (see fig. 5.9). Each stain obscures different tones in the image. Before moving to a different, isolated selection, be sure to resample with the Rubber Stamp tool an area that is close to the selection area.

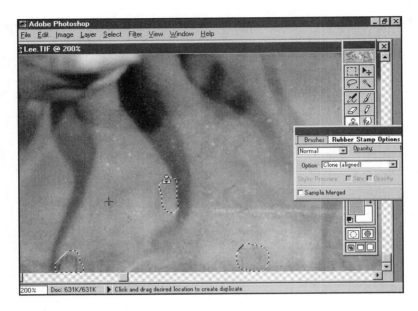

figure 5.9
Sample areas close to the area to be worked on, to ensure tonal consistency as you restore the image.

4. Press Ctrl(⌘)+S to save your work, but keep the document open in Photoshop.

As you work toward the bottom of the image of Lee, you will see a horizontal streak running the width of the image. Some areas do not require retouching, but the more obvious streak areas pose a problem. There is much variation in image detail, and none of the techniques you have used so far will mend the streak invisibly.

Copying Image Areas

The Rubber Stamp tool essentially serves as a local copying tool; samples are picked and applied by using a paintbrush on-screen metaphor. You might find, however, that simply copying an image area and pasting it into a damaged area can be quicker, and provides results that other techniques don't provide.

In the following set of steps, you copy a sliver of undamaged image area to use as a replacement for the streak in the image.

COPYING AND FEATHERING REPLACEMENT AREAS

1. With the Rectangular Marquee tool, drag a selection marquee around a wide, short area neighboring the streak area (see fig. 5.10 for the location).

2. Right-click (Macintosh: hold Ctrl and click) to access the Context menu, and then choose Feather. In the Feather Selection box, type **2** in the Feather Radius field. Click on OK to close the box.

3. Hold Ctrl+Alt (Macintosh: ⌘+Opt) and drag inside the selection marquee until the selection lies over the streak area (see fig. 5.10). You have duplicated and floated the selection. Because the selection is feathered, there is a gradual transition to transparency along the edge of the selection, which helps blend the duplicated area into its surroundings.

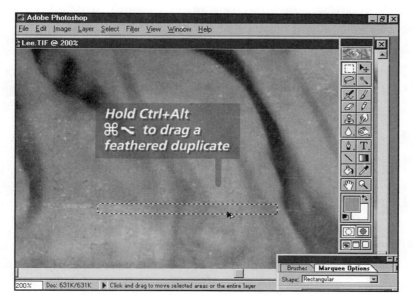

figure 5.10
A feathered duplicate of an area near the area to be replaced will blend the edges invisibly.

4. Apply steps 1–3 to other areas of the streak. The streak is inconsistent, appearing and disappearing horizontally across the image. Replace only areas that need replacing, and try to match image content from the source areas as closely in visual detail as possible to the damaged area.

5. Press Ctrl(⌘)+S to save your work, and close the image now.

Fortunately, the folds in the skirt help disguise any repeating pattern in the replacement work. If the skirt itself had a pattern, you would need to carefully align that pattern, as well as the folds in the fabric.

Replacing the Image Background

If you have read this far, you have at your disposal many of the methods for image restoration and can use them with your own images, or a client's. In this example, however, you have reached a crossroad—how to handle the backdrop in Lee.tif, which still shows signs of age and abuse. Should you invest the time in retouching an area that amounts to a blank space? Or would it be easier to replace the background, instead of cloning, blurring, and finessing this nonessential area?

The next sections show you how to create an accurate selection around the silhouette of Lee. The background can then be separated from the areas you have worked on, and a suitable replacement image can be added to the picture.

Becoming a Virtual Hair Stylist

Hair is perhaps the most difficult photographic detail to define accurately, because its appearance on film is inconsistent—in highlight areas it appears sharp, and as light on it diminishes, it loses clear focus. To compound the restoration challenges in Lee.tif, the edges of her hair have been further thrown out of focus by the camera.

Because much of the general shape of the hair will be masked in the image, our approach to defining the hair from the backdrop is unique—we separate the image from the backdrop. In Chapter 6, strands of hair are painted along the selection outline to replicate the soft appearance of hair falling out of focus at the edges.

A possible stumbling block in the retouching work is that the grayscale copy of Lee contains less visual information than the color original, especially around the edges of her hair. To avoid this potential stumbling block, you begin the selection definition work by opening a copy of the *original* color image from the Companion CD. Because Photoshop enables you to copy a mask from one image to another, provided that the two files have identical pixel dimensions, you define the selection on the image that shows the clearest detail, and then copy the saved mask to the grayscale image.

Here's how to begin the selection definition:

QUICK MASKING AT DIFFERENT OPACITIES

1. Open the Lee.tif image from the CHAP05 folder on the Companion CD. Save the color image to your hard disk in the TIFF file format, as Original color image.tif. (Windows 3.1 users: the file name is limited to a maximum of eight characters.)

2. Zoom in to 300% viewing resolution in the document, and maximize the document window so that it takes up the full screen. Hold the spacebar to toggle to the Hand tool, and pan your view so that you can clearly see the right side of Lee's hair.

3. Click on the Quick Mask mode icon, choose the Paintbrush tool, and then choose the second row, third-from-left tip on the Brushes palette. Press **D** (Default colors) to ensure that the current foreground color is black.

4. Drag the Paintbrush along the outside edge of Lee's hair. Don't hesitate to overlap the edge, traveling toward the inside of the hair. Because the edge of the tip is soft and anti-aliased, and the hair is out of focus, areas at the edge that display Quick Mask are partially selected (see fig. 5.11).

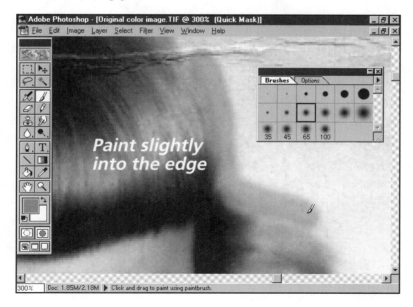

figure 5.11
Work toward the inside edge with the Paintbrush tool. The edges of the hair are soft, as is the Paintbrush tip.

5. When you finish Quick Masking the edge as far as you can with this view of the document, hold the spacebar and drag upward in the document window to see more unmasked areas.

6. Continue painting the outside edge of the hair. When you reach the area shown in figure 5.12, press **5** on the numeric keypad to decrease the opacity of the Paintbrush tool to 50%. Each keypad number represents 10% increments of Opacity on the Options palette, and zero equals 100% Opacity. Stroke the faint areas of Lee's hair. Hair that is light and out of focus should be partially selected, using the opacity setting for the Paintbrush tool, because you want only part of this hair to be visible after you replace the original backdrop with a new image.

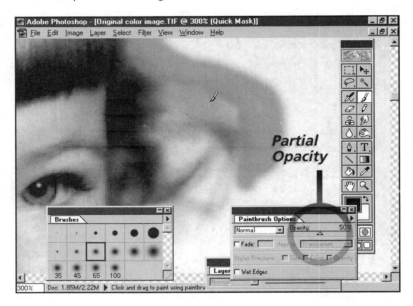

figure 5.12

Use partial opacity with the Paintbrush tool to partially mask faint, partially transparent areas of hair.

7. Continue to partially select the hair in Quick Mask mode. Remember that there are different opacities of hair in the image, and that Quick Mask represents the inverse areas of the image you want to keep. Therefore, use low Paintbrush opacity (such as 20%) for darker fringe areas of the hair, and high opacity (such as 80 or 90%) for masking lighter areas of the hair. Although this is the opposite of what intuition tells us, it makes more sense when you see the finished Quick Mask.

8. After you finish masking around the hair next to Lee's left eye, choose the Smudge tool from the toolbox, set the mode to Darken on the Options palette, and then set the Pressure to 50%.

Because the 10% increments for opacity have left hard demarcation in zones of the Quick Mask, you need to soften the transitions between, say, 70% opaque Quick Mask and 20% opaque Quick Mask. Although Quick Mask is only a preview mode for selection marquees, it can be affected by Photoshop's paint and editing tools.

9. Drag from a more opaque area of Quick Mask to a less opaque area (see fig. 5.13). This smears the Quick Mask and softens the transition between regions with different opacity.

figure 5.13
Create soft transitional areas in Quick Mask opacity by dragging the Smudge tool over them.

10. Choose File, Save to save your work.

Unlike other image-editing programs, Photoshop writes an alpha channel to hold Quick Mask information, and presents the channel selection information as a Quick Mask when you reopen a document saved in this state. You can close this document at any time, but do not try to open it in *another* image editor. You will fail. Many image editors cannot interpret a Quick Mask saved selection as an alpha channel.

In the following steps, you continue to refine the Quick Mask selection, but use the Navigator palette to help you move around the edge of Lee in the image. The Navigator palette works faster than the Hand tool, and is ideal for design situations in which an irregular outline wends through the entire image.

USING THE NAVIGATOR PALETTE

1. Choose Window, Show Navigator from the menu. The palette is displayed with the current view framed with an outline.

2. Drag the highlight box (the outline frame) down until you can see on-screen areas that have not been painted with Quick Mask.

3. Press o on the numeric keypad to set the Paintbrush tool opacity to 100%, and then continue masking the edge of Lee. The masking procedure goes faster in areas of her dress and arm because they display better focus around the edges.

4. After you finish the right edge of the mask, drag the highlight box in the Navigator palette to the top left, and continue masking the edge (see fig. 5.14).

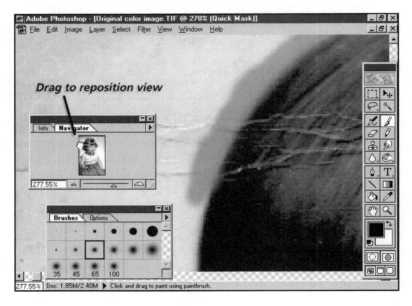

figure 5.14
The Navigator palette provides a quick way to zoom and pan to the area in which you need to work.

5. When you reach the curly hair on the left of the image, use the partial opacity/keypad shortcut to mask the hair (as you did on the right side of the image in steps 6–8 of the preceding example).

6. When you finish the edge outline, double-click on the Hand tool to zoom out to full image without scroll bars.

7. Choose the Polygon Lasso tool from the toolbox. On the right side of the image, carefully click points that fall within the width of the Quick Mask edge work you created. Close the Polygon Lasso path to encompass the backdrop by clicking once on the beginning point of the selection you defined. When the marquee appears, press Alt (Opt)+Delete (Back-space) to fill the selection with foreground color (Quick Mask tint); then press Ctrl(⌘)+D to deselect the marquee selection (see fig. 5.15).

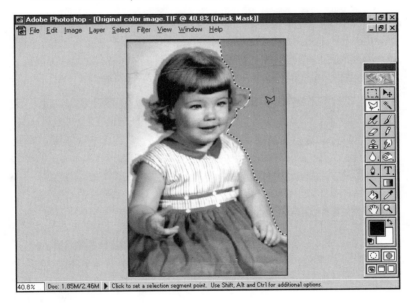

figure 5.15
You can add to or subtract from a Quick Mask by filling a selection marquee with the current foreground color.

8. Perform step 7 with the left side of the image.

WARNING

If you're not certain that your Polygon Lasso definition falls within the width of the Quick Mask edge, close the selection to produce the marquee, but do *not* fill the selection. Instead, zoom into a questionable area; when you're using the Polygon tool you cannot zoom in or out of the document until you have closed the selection.

Hold Alt(Opt) and trim away areas of the current selection you do not want included, or hold Shift and add to the selection marquee. Then you can safely fill the marquee areas with Quick Mask. When you apply Quick Mask to an area that already has Quick Mask, you lose the original selection unless you immediately press Ctrl(⌘)+Z to Undo the previous operation.

9. Click on the Standard editing mode icon to the left of the Quick Mask icon. If the Channels palette is not on-screen, press F7 and click on the Channels tab to display it. Then click on the Create a new selection icon at the bottom of the Channels palette.

10. Press Ctrl(⌘)+D to deselect the marquee, and press Ctrl(⌘)+S to save your work.

11. Open the Lee.tif grayscale image you worked on earlier (it's on your hard disk), and then click on the Original color image.tif title bar to make it the foreground document in the workspace.

12. On the Channels palette, right-click (Macintosh: hold Ctrl and click) on the Channel #4 title, and choose Duplicate Channel from the Context menu.

13. In the Duplicate Channel dialog box, choose Lee.tif from the Document Destination field (see fig. 5.16) and click on OK to add the channel to Lee.tif.

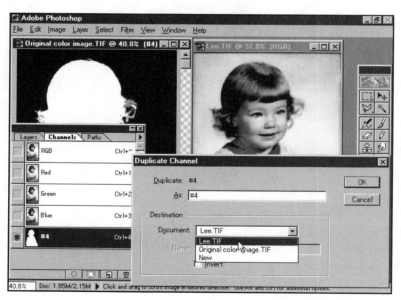

figure 5.16
Duplicate saved selections across documents of equal size.

14. Press Ctrl(⌘)+S to save the Lee image with the new channel. Close the Original color image.tif file (or whatever eight-character name Windows 3.1x users have chosen) without saving changes.

Creating a Rough Sketch for a Client

If you were to add a new backdrop to the Lee image right now, the picture would not represent a finished image. The hair needs some refining (as mentioned earlier), and the grayscale image lacks a certain warmth—precisely because it's still a grayscale image!

To conclude the restoration process—before getting into the retouching techniques in Chapter 6—it would be nice if you could walk away with a rough sample of what you can accomplish, and an idea of where this image is going. If you were retouching this image for a client, all you would need to do now is a little cleaning up, and you could show it around as a "work in progress."

These steps will not alter the image in such a way that anything you want to do in the future is affected. You add an impromptu backdrop (one that you will replace in Chapter 6) so that you can compare the original to your work, and see the dramatic change you have made in image quality.

ADDING A PROXY IMAGE BACKGROUND

1. Press Ctrl(⌘) and click on the Channel #4 title on the Channels palette to load the alpha channel you duplicated (in the previous section) as a selection marquee.

2. Choose the Gradient tool.

3. Hold Alt(Opt) and click at the top of the backdrop in the image. Your cursor toggles to the Eyedropper tool, and the current foreground color for the gradient is the color you clicked on in the image.

4. Press **X** to switch foreground and background colors, and then press Alt(Opt) and click over an area of the backdrop toward the bottom of the Lee.tif image. Press **X** now to switch foreground and background colors, making the darker tone the foreground.

5. On the Options palette, choose Foreground to Background from the Gradient drop-down list. Choose Linear from the Type drop-down list. Make sure that Opacity is 100% and that the mode for the Gradient tool is Normal.

6. Drag from the top to the bottom within the image with the cursor. This adds a transitional blend of tones to replace the background (see fig. 5.17), whose brightness values were sampled from the original image content. You have kept the "feeling" of the original lighting in the image.

7. Press Ctrl(⌘)+D to deselect the marquee and press Ctrl(⌘)+S to save your work. You can close the image at any time now.

figure 5.17
Add a gradient fill in the selection area to replace a damaged backdrop with a fresh Photoshop creation.

In figure 5.18 you can see the result of this chapter's efforts to restore life to the image. Does the Lee image require more work to bring it to completion? Definitely. But right now is a good time to pause and reflect upon what you have accomplished so far.

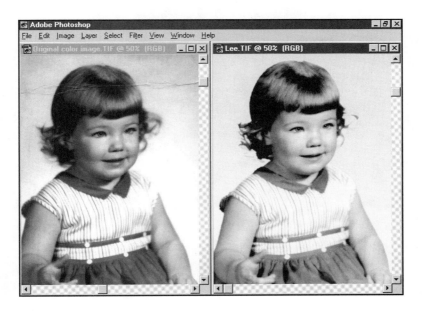

figure 5.18
Image restoration is part detective work, part selection work, and much inspired use of Photoshop's painting tools.

Summary

If you're interested in restoring monochrome images, this chapter has shown you most of the tools for completing the assignment. Restoration involves both image content and the "feel" of the image. A good practice is to always begin restoration work by examining what is beneath the surface, and to figure out how to copy undamaged image areas to fill areas that have been obscured. A "worst-case scenario" image was used in this chapter to give you real world experience in restoration and an opportunity to learn not one, but several restoration techniques. Hopefully, images you want to restore will never be in such poor condition as Lee's.

In Chapter 6, "Retouching an Heirloom Photograph," you will see how to put color back into the image, how to make the image look more dimensional, and in short, you will take about 20 years of grime, neglect, and wear-and-tear off of the photo. Let's give the little girl something to *really* smile about.

CHAPTER 6

RETOUCHING AN HEIRLOOM PHOTOGRAPH

In Chapter 5, "Restoring an Heirloom Photograph," you learned some techniques that transformed a water- and fire-damaged picture from an unacceptable image to a pleasing one. You can also perform some important post-restoration steps on this or another image to enhance the picture and bring it to nearly new condition. This chapter shows you how to add lifelike color tones to the Lee.tif image, replace the background, and add dimension to the image. When the distractions of the current background and surface flaws have been retouched away, the audience will discover the content and emotional qualities within the image.

Adding Original Colors and Tonally Correcting the Image

In Photoshop, everything you paint, and every selection you composite with other image areas, is performed in a mode. Modes specify how layer pixels and the pixels you paint into an image are combined with existing image pixels. The Layers palette and the Options palette feature a mode drop-down list for specifying how a foreground element is merged to a background element. Understanding modes is the key to making photographic corrections in Photoshop.

In the following sections you learn how, by merging a copy of the original color Lee.tif file into the grayscale image you created in Chapter 5, to produce a color image without restoring the surface damage and noise that you removed. This is accomplished through assigning the original image the color mode when added as a layer to the retouched image. Modes will also play an important part in the addition of elements that help bring out the dimensional quality of this photo.

Understanding Modes

Before you acquired Photoshop, you might have had some bitmap art experience in another program whose features were quite limited. Traditionally, a pasted selection on top of another image has one compositing mode—opaque. The pixels that make up the selection in this case simply *replace* the pixels on the underlying image. In Photoshop, however, you can adjust the opacity of a selection so that only some of the selection's pixel colors replace the underlying image area; the result is a blend of selection pixels and base-image pixels. When a floating selection of 50% opacity is merged with base-image pixels, every pixel color in the combined area is a color composite. For example, a 50-percent-opaque blue selection merged with a red image area produces a purple area, whose color components are a fifty-fifty blend.

A merge in Photoshop's Normal mode produces the example described in the preceding paragraph. But a normal-mode merge might not be suitable for compositing images. You might want to accentuate some of the colors in the selection to be merged, or you might not want to include all the colors in the base image as part of the merge operation.

The following sections briefly describe the modes Photoshop offers for both paint application and for layer compositing. When you paint or merge image layers, always consider the *way* in which the pixels in both areas come together.

Normal Mode

Because you manipulate colors as light (and not as physical pigment) in Photoshop, none of the subtractive properties of color pigment apply to compositing or painting work done in Normal mode. In Normal mode, a 50-percent-opaque blue selection on top of a 100-percent-opaque red selection produces a light purple, for example, rather than the rich purple you expect when you mix physical pigments. As you increase the opacity of the blue selection, the resulting color becomes more blue and less red until—at 100% opacity—blue is the color of the combined colors. Painting blue with the Paintbrush tool at 50% over a red area does the same thing; the more you stroke over the red area, the more the blue foreground color becomes the final color within the area. Therefore, in Normal mode, you can never attain a darker mixture of pixels than the darkest component of the two colors you mix.

Dissolve Mode

Dissolve mode produces unpredictable results when specified as a blending mode for layers; therefore, this mode is best used with paint-application tools in Photoshop. Dissolve mode applies 100-percent-opaque foreground color (or sampled pixels, when used with the Rubber Stamp tool) that alternates with underlying original colors to create an effect similar to diffusion dithering. The less the opacity with which you apply color or image samples in Dissolve mode, the less frequently the color or sample is interspersed with the original image pixels. Dissolve mode can create a fringe around image edges if you stroke a path at 50% opacity or less. This effect is great for simulating worn paper edges or creating a "splatter" type of artwork.

Behind Mode

This blending mode is available for paint-application tools but not for a layer-compositing property. In Behind mode you can paint only on transparent and partially transparent pixels on a layer; fully opaque pixels are not affected in this mode. In Behind mode, you can achieve the effect of filling in gaps in layer content, or applying foreground color (or sampled images, with the Rubber Stamp tool) to the back of a sheet of acetate.

Clear Mode

Clear mode is similar to the effect of erasing nontransparent areas on layers. This mode cannot be applied to a layer; only the Stroke command, the Fill command, and the Paint Bucket tool can clear pixels on a layer. You may never have to access Clear mode, because you can perform equivalent edits (with more predictable results) with the Eraser tool and Photoshop's many masking features.

Multiply Mode

This mode is available for painting and as a mode for an image layer. Multiply mode subtracts, from the background image, brightness values of the *source material* (whatever you paint or place on a layer) to arrive at the final composite pixel colors. Lighter colors you apply in Multiply mode have no effect on the final pixel color in the image. Multiply mode is excellent for simulating shadows. Shadows in real life never feature a color or tone lighter than either the source material (the shadow) or the background (the area that receives the shadow). You will use Multiply mode in this chapter to add a drop shadow to Lee in the restored image.

Screen Mode

Screen mode is the inverse of Multiply mode. Whether you apply a color with a paint application tool in Screen mode, or assign a layer to Screen mode, the result of merging the source and the background is always the same composite color or a lighter color. Screen mode is useful for creating neon glows in images. If you paint white (or any light color) on a layer around the edge of a background object, and then assign the layer Screen mode, you can achieve a fat or subtle glow effect by playing with the Opacity setting for the layer.

Overlay Mode

This mode blends colors that you apply or place on a layer with the background colors in a way that is not artistically logical; however, interesting effects can be achieved. Areas of pure black and pure white in the background image will fail to display Overlay paint or image areas on a layer in Overlay mode. Areas on the background that fall between black and white in brightness value are mixed with the colors of the Overlay material to produce the final composite color. Overlay is useful for painting a design or text on a background image to make it appear as though the background image was photographed with the design or text.

Soft Light Mode

Soft Light mode applies color to either darken or lighten the background image, depending upon the tone of colors in the background. For example, if you paint 50% black on a background image that is a gradient from black to white, the darker areas of the gradient turn darker as you paint, whereas the lighter areas take on a lighter tone.

Hard Light Mode

This mode is essentially the same as Soft Light, except that the background color is multiplied or screened, depending upon the colors in the background. It's a more intense effect than Soft Light mode, and like Overlay, this mode can be useful for simulating a pattern or text on the surface of a background object. Say, for example, that you want to change the text "STOP" to "GO" in an image of a traffic sign; use Hard Light mode on a layer with text to help integrate the text with the lighting conditions in the image.

Color Dodge Mode

Color Dodge mode creates an effect similar to that of Screen mode, except that the edge areas are sharper on layers assigned to—and paint strokes performed in—this mode. Also, dark areas on the background image tend to disappear whenever you specify Color Dodge to blend foreground with background pixels.

Color Burn Mode

The effect created by Color Burn mode is similar to the one created by Multiply mode, except that lighter areas in the background disappear, and the image areas in Color Burn mode take on a hard-edged quality.

Darken Mode

In Darken mode, only the tones in colors on a layer (or in paint you apply in Darken mode) that are darker than background colors are applied. This mode causes colors lighter than background colors to drop out of the composite image.

Lighten Mode

In this mode, the inverse of Darken mode, lighter areas of color predominate in the composite image; darker areas on a layer, or in paint you apply in Lighten mode, do not appear in the merged image.

Difference Mode

Difference mode works best with medium tones on a layer or with paint of medium tone. Difference mode creates the chromatic opposite of the background color. Blue colors in Difference mode, for example, will produce a cyan composite color when applied to a green background. Difference mode is useful for simulating a film negative of original designs, and is particularly useful for creating callouts in images whose background changes color from area to area.

Exclusion Mode

This mode produces a softer, brighter effect than Difference mode. Neither Difference nor Exclusion modes are capable of producing realistic or flattering image composites of people or images of nature scenes.

Hue Mode

In Hue mode, the color value of the layer, or the color of paint you apply replaces the hue of the underlying background image. It is helpful to think of the Hue, Saturation, Brightness (HSB) color model when you use this mode. Hue mode replaces the primary color component but does not affect the saturation or brightness of the background image.

Saturation Mode

This mode uses the color strength (*color purity*) of the colors on a layer (or the color you apply with a paint tool), and accentuates color on the background image according to the color strengths. When you apply pure blue to a dull background image, for example, you bring out the original pure colors in the background, but the blue color is not added to the composite image. If you choose a neutral color (one that does not display a predominant hue), no change is made to the background image. Saturation mode is useful for bringing out the underlying color in an image whose color strengths have been dulled by age.

Color Mode

This is the mode you use in the following examples to merge only the color information in the original Lee.tif file with the grayscale version you edited in Chapter 5. Color mode adds the predominant hues to the background image while preserving the saturation and brightness of the background image. Color mode is useful for hand-tinting photographs, but the tones in the grayscale image have an effect on how much color can be composited into the finished, merged image.

Luminosity Mode

Luminosity mode enables colors to remain in the background image, but replaces the saturation and the brightness of the background with the saturation and brightness of image content on a layer, or the color you apply when a paint tool is in Luminosity mode.

The Color and Multiply modes of image compositing are used in this chapter to integrate new image detail with the grayscale version of Lee.tif, the image restored in Chapter 5.

Copying Color Information to an Image

To recolor the image of Lee would present somewhat of a chore if done entirely manually. As you will see in Chapter 11, "Black and White…and Color," you can use samples of real-world colors to hand-tint an image that contains only neutral values. With the Lee image, however, a much simpler method is to copy the original image information to a layer in Color mode. In this way, you do not change color values from those of the original image, and the corresponding areas of color align precisely to the edited version of the photo.

Follow these steps to add color to the edited image of Lee.

USING MODES AND IMAGE LAYERS

1. Open the Lee.tif image you saved in Chapter 5. If you didn't complete the steps in that chapter, you can open the Lee.tif image from the CHAP06 folder on the Companion CD. (The authors created this version of the image.) Choose Image, Mode; then choose RGB Color from the menu.

2. Open the original color image you saved in Chapter 5, or use the Lee.tif image found in the CHAP05 folder on the Companion CD. The color image should now be the current foreground image in Photoshop.

3. Click and drag the Background title of the original color image from the Layers palette, and drop it into the document window of Lee.tif (see fig. 6.1). Now, having added the color image as a new layer in Lee.tif, you can close the original color image window at any time.

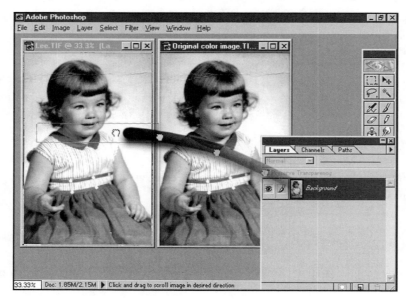

figure 6.1
Drag a copy of the original color image into the Lee document to add a copy of the color information as a new layer.

4. With the new layer as the current editing layer in the Lee image, choose Color from the mode drop-down list on the Layers palette. The image springs to life. The new layer contributes only color information to the composite image. Information about cracks and water stains is not included because these flaws are composed primarily of brightness and saturation—not color (hue)—information.

5. On the Channels palette, press Ctrl(⌘) and click on the #4 channel, which contains the saved selection area you created in Chapter 5.

6. Press Delete (Backspace). The areas of background outside the selection of Lee have been removed (see fig. 6.2), and with them, the discoloration on the backdrop in the image.

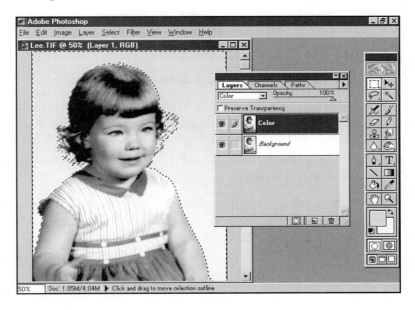

figure 6.2
On the layer on top of the image, keep only the color areas that represent the final colors you need in the image.

7. Choose File, Save as, and then save the image to your hard disk in the Photoshop file format, as Lee in Color.psd. (Windows 3.1x users should save the file with a name of eight characters or less).

Because you will add other layers to the document it would be a good idea to label the Color mode layer for easy reference later. Double-click on the layer title on the Layers palette, and type **Color** in the Name field of the Layer Options box. Click on OK to apply the name change.

Adding a color copy of the original image to a layer in Color mode is a pretty neat trick, although the previous steps don't add even shading of color to the image because color is not evenly distributed in the original image. In the following sections, you modify the grayscale background image to produce more interaction between the Color mode layer and the background one, and modify the color content of the Color layer to produce more even, consistent color values in the image.

Mapping Tonal Levels in the Image

Color mode doesn't touch the brightness values in the underlying layers. It simply adds the hues found in the source layer, to create a composite of layer color and background tone in the image. The brightest and darkest tones in the background image of Lee fail to display color, however. Color mode cannot add color to areas that lie in the tonal extremes of an image.

The solution to adding original color to these areas is to redistribute tones—brightness values in the background image—so that every area in the background has enough neutral tone to mix with the Color mode layer information. Actually, professionals who hand-tint grayscale photos make a photographic copy of an image that lacks contrast, so that the physical tints are displayed more predominantly. What you will do in the following steps is the virtual equivalent of preparing a "duller than life" version of the background image to bring out the colors on the color layer.

MODIFYING TONES WITH THE LEVELS COMMAND

1. Click on the Background layer on the Layers palette, and press Ctrl(⌘)+L to display the Levels command dialog box.

2. Drag the midpoint slider to the left until the Input Levels center field reads **1.08**. This reduces the contrast in the midtones of the background image. All the controls in the Levels dialog box are labeled in figure 6.3.

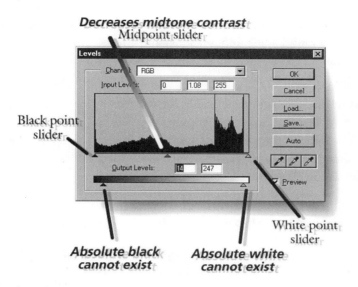

Decreases midtone contrast
Midpoint slider

Black point
slider

White point
slider

**Absolute black
cannot exist**

**Absolute white
cannot exist**

figure 6.3
The Levels command changes the tonal distribution of pixels in an image.

3. In the Output Levels area, drag the black slider to the right until the value in the left Output Levels field is 14. This action reduces contrast in the image by specifying that absolute black (0 on a brightness scale of 0–255) doesn't exist in the Lee image. The darkest tone in the image will now be 14, which will enable some of the color on the color layer to show through at the darkest points in the image.

4. Drag the white slider to the left until the corresponding Output Levels field reads **247**. You have now specified that absolute white is not reached in the image—that 247 is the brightest area in the image in a range of tones whose maximum is 255. By increasing the white point, the colors in highlight areas in the image mix with neutral tones and become apparent when the layers are eventually merged in the document.

5. Click on OK to apply the tonal changes, and press Ctrl(⌘)+S to save your work.

The terms "Input" and "Output" in the Levels command might not adequately describe their function to many designers. Some of Photoshop's controls don't have explicit names that indicate their purpose because some of the features have no real-world equivalent. Think of the controls for the Levels Input sliders as options that compress the dynamic range of tones in an image. By dragging the black point slider to the right and the white point slider to the left, you add contrast to the image because you are compressing the breadth of all tones that can appear in an image to a narrower range. The midpoint slider also affects contrast, but in the isolated area of midtones in an image, where much of the visual detail in a picture is located. By dragging left you decrease midtone contrast, and by dragging right you increase it.

The Output Levels controls enable you to *expand* the dynamic range of tones in an image. In the preceding steps you created less contrast, thus allowing a greater range of tones at the upper and lower tonal limit to the image. By decreasing the *absolutes* (the extremes in tonal regions) you allow the headroom for color to become noticeable in these areas.

Evening Out the Colors in the Image

The color copy layer in the document is only a "primer coat" of color for the finished, retouched image. The colors are unevenly distributed on Lee's skirt because the original image colors were partially destroyed by age and handling of the image. The solution to retouching this area is to sample the original colors, and then simply paint them into areas that appear too dark, light, or washed out. Because the Color mode active on this layer doesn't display tones—the aspect of color that creates image detail—you can "pour it on," using the Paintbrush tool, without fear of losing image detail. The detail of Lee is on the Background layer.

Here's how to even the color distribution in the image's skirt area.

APPLYING FLAT COLOR IN COLOR MODE

1. Click on the layer title on the Layers palette to make it the current editing layer. Uncheck the Indicates Layer Visibility icon (the eye icon) for the Background layer. The Color layer ceases to display a merge property, and you can now see the layer's contents without interaction with the background.

2. Choose the Paintbrush tool, choose the tip at the far right of the second row on the Brushes palette, and then hold Alt(Opt) while you click over an area of the skirt that contains the greatest amount of color. You might need to click two or three times and check the Foreground color selection box on the toolbox to confirm that the color you have sampled is the most "colorful."

3. Release Alt(Opt) and begin painting over the skirt (see fig. 6.4). Yes, you are ruining image detail on this layer, but it is color (and not the details of the skirt) you need on the Color mode layer. Work carefully around Lee's left hand, and change to a smaller tip to get into the smaller areas.

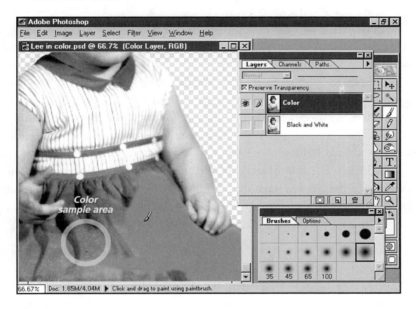

figure 6.4

Fill the skirt area with a solid color, which will then be composited with the grayscale background image.

4. At regular intervals, check the Indicates layer visibility icon for the background to see how the color you add to the Color layer composites with the background image.

5. When the skirt has been completely painted over, press Ctrl(⌘)+S to save your work. Keep the document open in Photoshop.

Although the authors did not find other areas in the image where the preceding steps were necessary, you might want to scout around the image. Perhaps the collar of Lee's dress could stand some color renewal, and areas of her hair might benefit from adding flat color.

Applying color is only phase one of the retouching process. The next section shows you how to control the *saturation* of color in the picture.

Purity of Color: Saturation

Humans have created many user-friendly descriptions for the components of color, and thus we can pinpoint a specific color. The Hue, Saturation, Brightness (HSB) color model consists of three components through which we can accurately describe colors we see. *Hue* is the wavelength of light that gives a color its distinguishing characteristic. *Brightness* is the amount of light reflected in proportion to the amount absorbed by a material. Highly reflective objects are bright, whereas rough objects absorb light and are seen as dark. *Saturation* is the relative purity of an individual hue. Most objects we see are composed of several hues, and the hue *strength* in the color is what determines whether we say something is bluish-green, or greenish-blue, for example. When many hues are present in near-equal amounts, the color of an object is dull and grayscale in content.

In the following steps you use Photoshop's Hue/Saturation command to alter the saturation of the Color mode image layer. By exaggerating the hues in the layer—emphasizing existing hue strengths—you make the layer blend with the background image in such a way that the colors make a more significant contribution to the image detail.

STRENGTHENING HUES

1. Press Ctrl(⌘)+U to display the Hue/Saturation dialog box.

2. Click and drag the Saturation slider to about +33, (see fig. 6.5).

    By default, the Preview box is checked in all Photoshop adjustment and filter dialog boxes, so that you can see your changes before you apply them. If the image looks fine, click on OK. You might want to decrease the Lightness by −2; use your own artistic taste. By decreasing the Brightness you make the colors on the layer look richer and slightly duller.

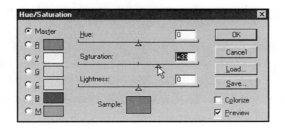

figure 6.5

The Hue/Saturation command enables you to adjust color properties independently of one another.

3. Press Ctrl(⌘)+S to save your work.

The color and tonal properties of Lee's image have now been optimized. As mentioned in Chapter 5, you might want to go into the Background layer now, and remove pinholes that are not covered by the Color layer information. In the next sections, you will add a new background to the image, and evaluate the composition as it comes together, to see which other areas need to be addressed.

Introducing New Image Elements

Care should be taken when adding a new element to an heirloom photograph. Clearly, you don't want to add something that does not fit the time period in the image—a digital clock, for example, would be a giveaway that something in the Lee.tif image has been retouched. Equally important when you add something to an image is not to disturb the balance, the amount of visual interest the new element creates versus the original image area. The backdrop in Lee's image is stark and plain. To keep the little girl as the center of attention, you can afford only marginal improvements to the background.

Adding a Fractal Background

Three D Graphics originally created a program called TextureMaker for Aldus, Inc. This fractal-generation program for the Macintosh synthesizes remarkably photorealistic textures of rocks, wood, and other organic materials. You can still buy the program from Adobe Systems. The same program is licensed and distributed (as CorelTexture) by Corel Corporation in the CorelDRAW 7 bundle for Windows, and the CorelDRAW 6 bundle for the Macintosh.

Because a truly photographic image would detract from Lee in the picture, the authors used TextureMaker to create a large image of some wispy clouds for you to use in the following steps. The lens and the focus of the original image could not compete for visual attention against a digitized photo, and there is simply something nice and abstract about a backdrop of "painted" clouds. The colors complement the subject in the image. You can experiment with textures and filters in your own work to produce stylized backdrops.

And you will add a drop shadow to the image by copying the selection defined by Lee's outline. The drop shadow helps bring out the interaction between the foreground and background in the image, and forces the viewer to look *into* the image.

For every solution, however, there is a problem. Because Lee's current backdrop is white, the introduction of a darker color (through the use of the sky image and drop shadow) causes fringing to appear around Lee's image. The fringing, which occurs because of a slightly imprecise definition of the selection around her, is almost impossible to avoid.

Here's how to add layers of interest to the heirloom image.

ADDING DEPTH TO THE IMAGE

1. Open the Clouds.tif image from the CHAP06 folder of the Companion CD.

2. Drag the Background title on the Layers palette into the Lee in color.psd image (see fig. 6.6). You can close the clouds image at any time to conserve memory.

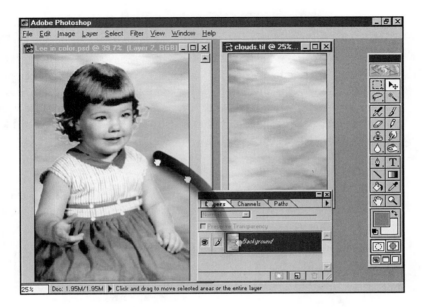

figure 6.6
Drag the cloud image into the Lee in color image to add a new background.

3. Double-click on the Background title on the Layers palette for the Lee image.

4. Type **Black and white** in the Name field of the Make Layer dialog box, and click on OK. The Background is now a Photoshop layer, and as such, you can erase the layer's pixels to transparent. Background layers cannot be erased to transparency, which is why the conversion needed to be made.

5. Double-click on the layer that contains the cloud image, type **Clouds** in the Name field of the Layer Options dialog box, and click on OK.

6. Hold Ctrl(⌘) to toggle to the Move tool. Drag the contents of the Clouds layer until it is centered in the image and the edges of the contents are not visible in the document window. When you finish, release Ctrl(⌘).

7. Click on the Create new layer icon on the bottom of the Layers palette.

8. Choose Multiply from the modes drop-down list on the Layers palette, double-click on the layer title, type **Shadow** in the Name field, and then click on OK to apply the change to the layer name.

9. On the Channels palette, press Ctrl(⌘) and click on the #4 channel to load the information stored in this channel as a selection. (The Lee.tif image on the Companion CD has this channel already created for your use.)

10. On the Layers palette, click on the Black and White layer title, and then press Delete (Backspace). You have removed the backdrop from this layer, which was created in Chapter 5. Drag the Clouds title on the Layers palette to the bottom of the layers list, and release the cursor. This re-orders the layers so that the clouds copy is on the bottom.

11. Click on the Shadow layer title, press **D** (Default colors), press Ctrl(⌘)+Shift+I to make the selection inverted, and then press Alt(Opt)+Delete (Backspace) to fill the current marquee selection with foreground black color.

12. Press Ctrl(⌘)+D to deselect the marquee, hold Ctrl(⌘) to toggle to the Move tool, and then drag the layer contents to below and to the left of Lee by the amount shown in fig. 6.7.

figure 6.7
Move the shadow to a location opposite the light source in the scene.

13. Choose Filter, Blur, and then choose Gaussian Blur.

14. Type **19** in the Radius field, and click on OK (see fig. 6.8). In this figure, the fringing (from the original white backdrop) displayed along the selection edge of Lee is painfully obvious against the dark background.

figure 6.8
Apply the Gaussian Blur filter at a high level to create a subtle shadow.

15. Drag the Opacity slider for the Shadow layer to 80%, and then press Ctrl(⌘)+S to save your work.

In step 15, opacity was reduced on the Shadow layer so that some of the Clouds image can show through. (Real-world shadows are never 100 percent opaque.)

It's time to experiment with two new techniques to remove the fringe from Lee's picture in the image.

Using the Contract Command

Often, the Select\Modify menu's Contract and Expand commands are used to create special effects, such as glowing edges around elements on layers. But you are going to leverage a less obvious capability of the Contract command. Because the Contract command (and the Expand command) feathers the new edge created from an existing selection marquee, you can use it to retain a soft edge (such as the edge between Lee and the backdrop in the original image) while the selection marquee eliminates the white fringing on the Black and White layer. Usually, the Defringe command can remove fringing, but always at the price of creating harsh edges around the area. The Defringe command replaces pixels at the edge of a border with colors found inside a selection. It's a useful command for some assignments, but not usually in intricate retouching work.

Used correctly, the Contract command does not totally remove the white fringe; it leaves a trace of a white pixel edge that can be dealt with by using different Photoshop tools. The trick in the following steps is to remove a significant amount of, but not the complete white fringe. Here's how to use the Contract command to accomplish this task.

REDUCING THE WHITE FRINGE

1. Click on the Black and White layer title on the Layers palette to make this the current editing layer.

2. On the Channels palette, press Ctrl(⌘) and click on the #4 channel title; then press Ctrl(⌘)+Shift+I to make the marquee selection an inverse selection, one that describes Lee's outline rather than the backdrop.

3. Drag the #4 channel title into the trash icon. You no longer need the saved selection information; by getting rid of it, you make the image's saved file smaller (and that's good).

4. Choose Select, Modify, and then choose Contract. The Contract Selection dialog box appears.

5. Use your judgment here when you specify the pixel amount. If the fringing around Lee seems to be two pixels wide, type 3 in the field. The reason you type a value slightly greater than the number of pixels displayed is that the Contract command feathers the selection; that is, the outermost edge of the new, contracted selection will be only partially opaque. Why not do what we did—go with 3 pixels in the Contract Selection entry field? Then click on OK to apply the Contract command?

6. Press Ctrl(⌘)+Shift+I, press Delete (Backspace), and then press Ctrl(⌘)+D to deselect the marquee.

7. Press Ctrl(⌘)+S.

If all that is left of the fringe is a trace of white, you're in good shape, and can proceed to the next section, which shows you how to blend away the remainder of the fringe. If you still have a visible fringe in the image, use the Contract command again.

The Blur Tool and Sample Merged Mode

A natural question arises when you work with an image whose elements are spread across different layers: "How can I blend stuff between layers?" With paint-application tools such as the Paintbrush, the Pencil tool, and the Paint Bucket, the answer is simple: You can't. Editing is usually, but not always, reserved in Photoshop for the layer currently highlighted on the Layers list.

The exception to this rule is that you can *move* pixel colors between layers if you use the Rubber Stamp, Smudge, Sharpen, and Blur tools. These are not paint application tools per se; instead, they move samples of image areas around.

As you may recall, Darken mode applies only pixels of darker color than that of the background image—and Darken mode is available for use with the Blur tool. In the following set of steps, you blur the remaining fringe edge on the Black and White layer. And because the options for the Blur tool include Sample Merged, you can blur the Shadow layer's contents with the Black and White layer, using the same strokes to soften the edge and remove the fringe.

Here's how to remove the remaining fringe from the image.

USING THE BLUR TOOL

1. Type **200** in the Zoom Percentage field in Photoshop, and press Enter (Return). If your retouching work looks good at twice the normal viewing size of the image, it will look flawless at 1:1 resolution.

2. Hold the spacebar and pan your view until you can see the left side of the document, where Lee's hair is curly.

3. Choose the Blur tool from the toolbox, and choose the third-from-left tip in the second row on the Brushes palette to use with the tool.

4. On the Focus Tool Options palette, drag the Pressure slider to about 90%, choose Darken from the mode drop-down list, and check the Sample Merged check box.

5. Click on the Black and White title on the Layers palette.

   Although with Sample Merged checked, all visible layers are sampled by the Blur tool, the *result* of the Blur tool will be located on the current editing layer. You probably don't want the blur effect on other layers; it would ruin the Clouds image for example, and you could not use the image layer again in a different assignment.

6. Click on the shadow area, and then drag into the fringe area around Lee's hair. Only the areas lighter than the point at which you first clicked become blurred along the fringe of the hair. By using Darken mode, you're selectively blurring the edges to remove an unwanted area (see fig. 6.9).

figure 6.9

With the Blur tool in Darken mode, brightness in areas decreases when you move the cursor from dark areas to light ones.

7. With the Blur tool, work your way around the outline of Lee, beginning in dark areas, and stroking into light fringe areas. When the fringe is gone, move to a different area; you want to remove just enough detail to blend the Black and White layer contents with other layer contents.

Spend only the time needed to Blur away the fringe in areas where Lee's hair was truncated by the selection border in Chapter 5. Remember—our intention here is to extend the "choppy" parts of Lee's hairdo with painted strands of hair.

8. Press Ctrl(⌘)+S.

Now that all the layers contain integrated areas of the individual elements, it's time to put the finishing touches on the image. In the following sections, you learn how to perform a virtual hair weave.

Completing the Retouching Assignment

Hair that has been styled to create thin wisps along the edges of one's head, or hair that is out of focus in a photograph, displays less detail than you might imagine. Quite often, traditional retouchers have painstakingly added strand after strand of brushstrokes to an image, only to create a hairdo that looks artificial. The secret to effective retouching (effective because it's invisible) is to simulate what you see in an image, and not what you *think* you see.

In the following sections, you add the suggestion of hair to the edges of the selection on the Black and White layer, and then further integrate these strokes with the out-of-focus edges by using the Blur tool.

Reconstructing a Hairstyle Through Imitation

In the following steps, you need to follow a specific procedure for adding edges of hair to the image. First, on the Black and White layer, you must paint the hair strands to be added; this gives detail to the image. Then you need to use a similar color to paint the hair on the Color layer, so that the color component of the image is (mostly) continuous throughout the picture.

Here's how to make the hair edges look as though they are a natural part of the overall image.

RETOUCHING A HAIRSTYLE

1. At 200% viewing resolution, hold the spacebar to access the Hand tool and then pan your view of the document so that you have a clear view of the right side of the image.

2. Press **D** (Default colors), and choose the Paintbrush tool.

3. Press **5** on the numeric keypad to decrease the Opacity of the Paintbrush tool to 50%. Make sure that the painting mode is Normal on the Paintbrush Options palette.

4. On the Brushes palette, choose the third from left, second row tip. This tip might seem large for restoring strands in the image, but you are painting the *shape* of the missing hair. The audience will mentally integrate your strokes with the out-of-focus original hair in the image.

5. Click on the Black and White layer to make it the current editing layer, and then make a single curved stroke, starting at an area where the hair shows a sharp edge, and ending in a curl downward. If this doesn't look right to you, press Ctrl(⌘)+Z and try this step again.

6. Make another curved stroke in a neighboring area where the hair edge is too sharp. Because the Paintbrush tool is at 50% opacity, you can build up an area without complete coverage, and this will look like different densities of hair flowing naturally (see fig. 6.10).

figure 6.10

Don't "paint" hair. Instead, suggest it with a loose stroke or two of foreground color at partial opacity.

7. When an area calls for a smaller brush, switch to the second row, far left tip on the Brushes palette. It is a mistake to calculate the size of the tip to the width of the hair you are painting. Go larger with the Brushes tip, and let the anti-aliased property of the tip create a narrow, dense stroke.

8. When you complete work on the right side of Lee's hair, click on the Color layer title on the Layers palette to make it the current editing layer.

9. Uncheck the Indicates layer visibility icons (the eye icons) on every layer except the Color layer. You need to sample some hair color, and while the Color layer is displayed as a part of a composite image (one composed of many layers), the Eyedropper tool merges color information from every layer, unless you hide the layers from which you *don't* want samples.

10. Click on a medium brown hair area, press F6 to display the Swatches palette, and then click over a vacant area of the palette to add this color. Doing this saves you from hiding layers in further steps.

11. Display the other layers by checking the Indicates layer visibility icons. Then, on the Color layer, press o on the numeric keypad to make the Paintbrush tool apply foreground color at 100% opacity, and stroke over the hair areas you added in step 6.

12. Repeat steps 6–12 with the left side of the image.

13. Press Ctrl(⌘)+S to save your work.

You're almost finished. The original hair in the image displays less focus than the hair you have added with the Paintbrush tool. This calls for a little additional softening of these areas before you can call the image complete.

BLURRING THE BRUSH STROKES

1. Click on the Black and White layer title on the Layers palette, and then choose the Blur tool from the toolbox.

2. Using the same Options palette settings you specified for blurring the edges of Lee's profile, click and drag on the areas you painted in (see fig. 6.11).

figure 6.11
Blur the hair areas you added to display the same lack of focus as neighboring original areas, and areas you softened earlier.

3. Zoom out to 1:1 viewing resolution on the image. This is the only way to tell whether your technique has been effective. If you can detect no artificial qualities in the hair areas, you're finished. If some areas still stand out, use the Blur tool for a few more strokes. Focus is an image quality you do not want, when original image quality is of poor focus.

4. Choose File, Save a Copy, and save a copy of this picture to your hard disk in the TIFF file format, as Done-Lee.tif (see fig. 6.12). When you save a copy of a layered image in any file format other than Photoshop's PSD, Photoshop automatically flattens the image, and you can show it to people who might not own Photoshop.

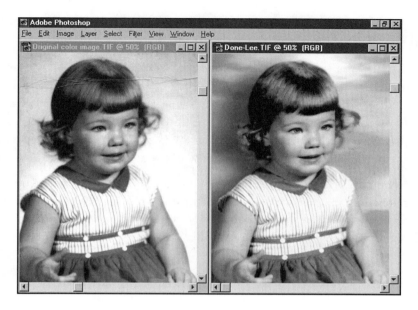

figure 6.12
Sit back and admire your restoration of Lee's image!

5. Press Ctrl(⌘)+S to save the Lee in color.psd image in the workspace a final time, and close the image.

Hopefully, you have seen more in the past two chapters than merely how Photoshop's tools are used to restore and enhance an heirloom photograph. Every picture is different in many respects, and an approach to each damaged, worn, or faded photograph must be designed before anyone touches the image. The best approach is usually based on examining the how's and why's of the photograph's appearance in the here and now, and at the time it was taken.

Clearly, different circumstances might ruin your photographs or a client's, and you might need to use tools other than those presented here. But although the tools may change, the procedure remains the same: uncover, discover, and then retouch and enhance.

Summary

Whether the assignment that lies ahead of you in Photoshop is to restore an image or integrate a new image with an old one (see Chapter 14, "Special Effects with Ordinary Photographs"), continuity is the key to successful image integration. Allow some of the original image's areas to blend with new ones, and you will find that as a retoucher of professional level, the best work is that which goes unnoticed. If you provoke a smile through your work, you have been artistically rewarded.

Chapter 7, "Combining Photographs," continues the spirit and tone of these retouching chapters. Its goal is not to disguise restoration work, however, but instead to make an absolutely *impossible* scene look authentic, plausible, and quite matter-of-fact. Did you ever see a car fly? Turn the page, and we will start the engine!

CHAPTER

COMBINING PHOTOGRAPHS

As you have seen in other chapters, if you have the patience, techniques, and time, you will be able to modify images to present a photography reality, whether it's restored or invented. The art of combining photographs, however, entails a wider scope of creative expression than fixing what occurred (or should have occurred) within an image. This chapter shows you how to create a vision that cannot possibly happen on earth. And yet—because photographs don't lie—you not only will discover another path to attract viewers to your work, but also in the process you will learn the ins and outs of realistically conveying the stuff that dreams are made of.

How Do You Make a Car Float?

First, you add two scoops of ice cream, and then you slap the author for trying to revive this ancient riddle. Seriously, the first time you saw a magician perform a feat of levitation—making his costumed assistant or even a building rise off the ground—your first reaction was probably one of disbelief. Your second reaction was to look for the wires or the hydraulic lift suspending both the object and your disbelief. The fantasy factories of Hollywood and the advertising trade, until recent years, were still resorting to wires to make things hover and fly—a practice that requires careful post-production performed by gifted image retouchers.

This chapter's assignment—to make a car float—doesn't require wires, and if you have read the previous chapters, and you can perform a little preproduction work, it's easier to accomplish than you might imagine. Planning the photography that goes into a composite picture is a critical element that makes the difference between a productive time in Photoshop and a frustrating experience. The following section discusses the photographic elements and considerations that go into the automotive levitation assignment.

Matching Image Properties

Even the most uninteresting image tells a story, perhaps not of obvious activity within the image, but of several camera and scene conditions at the time the image was photographed. Before you accept an assignment to meld two images into a single composition, you should consider the following less-than-obvious properties a digital photo can display. Matching not only the element of central interest, but also the *way* a photo was taken, the time, and other aspects can eliminate unnecessary effort in Photoshop to correct image differences. In some cases, identical image properties make the difference between creating something inspirational, or failing to make your vision appear on-screen.

Filling Identical Portions of the Frame

Suppose that you have a stock photo of Rockefeller Center, and you want to put your family in the scene. The distance that you pose your family from the camera is critically important. If you snap their picture at a typical distance to fill the film frame with family, they will probably be too large to copy and paste into the

Rockefeller Center scene. Most buildings are photographed at a distance, to include pieces of the architecture in the frame; that same distance must be used for other elements you want to add to the building scene. Enlarging or reducing the family image as a preproduction workaround is not acceptable for two reasons:

◆ Any time you change the number of pixels in an image, by reducing or enlarging it, Photoshop must recalculate the color pixels in the resulting image. This diminishes the focus of the image. It is far better to capture the element in a photo at the final size at which you will use the element.

◆ Film grain is not always perceptible, but it carries over to digitized images. If you make an element larger or smaller than the original in order to better fit into a composition, there's a strong chance the grain in one photo will not match the grain in the other. This is something the audience might not recognize, but it will register on a subconscious level, and people will suspect photographic manipulation.

Matching Lighting Conditions

If you want to add an element to a photograph of a building or city that was taken on an overcast day, you must photograph your subject on an overcast day. Similarly, if the building was photographed at 3 p.m. from the north, you must capture the elements you want to add to the image at approximately the same time, from the same direction. For example, we once received a pizza delivery brochure that had obviously been retouched in Photoshop. The reason it was obvious was that the elements were composited from different images, each with a unique lighting angle, and shadows cast every which way! Again, although these image properties might not always strike the viewer of the image at first glance, they often indicate a certain artificial quality. Your greatest editing work is that which calls no attention to itself.

Matching Camera Angles

When designers attempt to add one image to another, they seldom consider the angle formed between the height at which a camera captures a subject, and the ground plane.

Why does Godzilla look so small in the movies? Not because his proportions are wrong, compared to the toy buildings; rather, the classic flaw in photographic effects occurs because of the angle at which Godzilla is filmed. The "creature" is an almost six-foot-tall guy in an uncomfortable suit, being filmed by a camera that is "man height," also about six feet off the ground. As a result of the misplaced camera angle, the audience looks down at the city (something you rarely do in real life), looks at Godzilla eye-to-eye, and then intuitively scours the scene for other clues that support the hunch that all is not as it seems.

Never give the audience an opportunity to question the reality of your work, unless it is your deliberate intention. In this chapter's assignment, the photography has already been done for you, and the images are in the CHAP07 folder of the Companion CD. The scene of the parking lot (Parknlot.tif) was photographed at about 3 p.m. in the summer, with the camera facing north at a camera height of about six feet. The car image (Car.tif) was photographed at about 3:30 p.m. in the summer, camera facing north at a height of about four inches. The reason for capturing the images at different heights is that when you step out the door to your driveway, this is the natural height at which you would photograph the outdoors. And if a car were hovering about five to six feet above the ground when you walked out, you would realize two things:

◆ This is probably not your own car.

◆ Your view of the car, relative to your own height, is equivalent to a situation in which you are four inches tall and viewing the car, which is on the ground.

In figure 7.1, you can see two perspective views of a photographer and a car. Notice that when the photographer is standing, the car's hood becomes the focal point of the image. When the photographer is lying on his elbows, more of the front of the car is captured, and less of the hood is visible.

Figure 7.2 shows the images used in this chapter's assignment. The glowing arrows indicate the degree of inclination of the camera when the images were captured. To make the perspectives in these images consistent, the car has to be located somewhere in the air in the Parknlot.tif image.

The following sections take you through the positioning, retouching, and enhancement steps needed to build a convincing photographic composition of a floating car.

figure 7.1

If a car were to float, and you were standing, what parts of the car would you see?

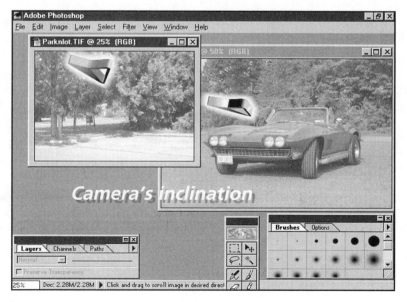

figure 7.2

Photos taken at different heights suggest different ground planes.

Adding the Car to a New Background

Because the emphasis of Photoshop 4's interface is on image layers, copying and refining the border around the image of the car is much easier than in earlier versions. The Layer Mask feature is more conveniently located, the Polygon Lasso tool makes straight-edge selections a snap to create, and the Car.tif image has intrinsic properties that help you integrate the two images.

Be sure to read Chapter 4 before you work with this chapter's example. Many of the techniques used in this chapter will go more quickly, and you will get more professional results if you're already comfortable with Photoshop's selection tools.

Copying and Positioning the Car

Notice that both the Car.tif image and the Parknlot.tif image sport the same type of foliage. This news means a significant reduction in time spent creating an accurate selection around the car. If you examine the two images, the only dissimilar quality is the type of pavement—the car is parked on quarry rock, and the parking lot is coated with blacktop. In the following steps, you copy the car to the parking lot and position it relative to the ground.

Here's how to make the floating car fly across document windows:

PLACING THE FLOATING AUTOMOBILE

CD-ROM

1. Open the Parknlot.tif image from the CHAP07 folder of the Companion CD. Type **25** in the Zoom percentage field, and then press Enter (Return). Drag the document window by the title bar to the upper left of the workspace.

2. Open the Car.tif image from the same folder as Parknlot, double-click on the Hand tool to display the complete image within the document window, and position the image window to the right of the Parknlot image so that you have a clear view of both document windows.

3. Choose the Lasso tool and drag a selection border around the car in the Car.tif image. The selection doesn't have to be precise, but the more background you eliminate from the selection, the less you will need to mask in future steps. Take care to include the antenna on the car in your selection. Without it, the car won't be able to receive FM.

4. Hold Ctrl(⌘), and then drag inside the selection marquee into the Parknlot image (see fig. 7.3). The Ctrl(⌘) keyboard toggle cuts a marquee selection's contents (usually an image area); however, when you drag between document windows, the contents of the selection are copied, and no change occurs to the source document. The copied selection is now a new layer in Parknlot.tif.

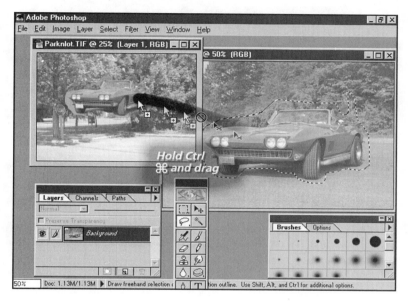

figure 7.3

Hold Ctrl(⌘) and drag inside a selection marquee to copy the area to a different image window.

5. Close Car.tif without saving it, type **50** in the Zoom percentage field, and press Enter (Return).

6. Drag the document window edges away from the picture so that you can see the image, from one edge to the other.

7. Close palettes (press Tab) or move them so that you have an unobstructed view of the entire image.

8. Hold Ctrl(⌘) and drag the car selection to its final position in the composition (see fig. 7.4). It might help to align the right edge of the car's hood with the left curb in the image, and then drag straight up (or use the Shift+up-arrow key combination to nudge the layer's contents). Because you are going to blend foliage areas of the layer with foliage areas on the Background in this chapter, now is a good time to decide on the car's final position.

figure 7.4
To suggest that the car is not touching the ground, drag it into the tree area of the Parknlot image.

9. Choose File, Save As, and save your work to your hard disk in the Photoshop file format, as Float.psd.

Now you can work with Photoshop's Layer Mask feature to hide the areas of the car selection that do not belong in the finished image.

Using the Layer Mask Feature

Often, having worked carefully to define a selection area in an image, you place the selected area in a different image and discover that fringing has occurred. There is no chance of this happening in the floating car assignment, however. Now, using the Layer Mask feature, you can preview the way the composition comes together while you remove (up to the edge of the car) the excess background area you copied to the parking lot image. You can make as many photo flubs as you like, because the Layer Mask is a "preview" state in the document for editing changes—nothing is final until you apply the mask.

Here's how to refine the car on the layer to remove unwanted layer content:

DOING THE TRIM WORK

1. Type **300** in the Zoom percentage field, and press Enter (Return).

2. Hold the spacebar to access the Hand tool, and pan your view of the document until you see the car's left tire in the center of the window. You will work counterclockwise around the car to remove unwanted layer areas.

3. Press F7 if the Layers palette isn't already on-screen, click on the Layer 1 title to make it the current editing layer, and then click on the Add layer mask icon (the far left one) at the bottom of the palette.

4. Press **B** (Paintbrush tool) and choose the second tip from the left in the second row on the Brushes palette. On the Options palette, make certain that Opacity is 100% and mode is Normal.

5. Press **D** (Default colors) and then stroke, starting from the edge of the nontransparent area on Layer 1, toward the wheel of the car. When you reach the edge of the wheel and can see no more ground areas beneath it, move on to areas to the right of where you began (see fig. 7.5).

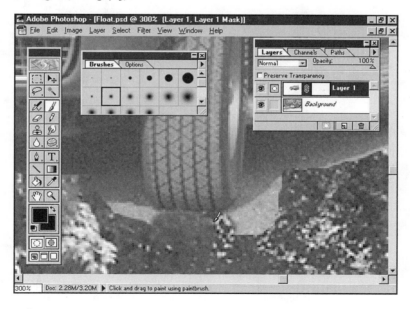

figure 7.5
Layer Mask mode hides layer areas covered with black foreground color; work from the edge of the image area toward the edge of the car.

6. When you finish masking an area, hold the spacebar to toggle to the Hand tool, and then pan your view to an unedited area to the right of the image. Continue masking from the edge of the opaque contents of the layer to the edge of the car.

In certain areas, it's easier to mask (hide) an area, particularly those areas of the car that have a concave outline, and then restore the areas. It's easier, for example, to hide the complete edge of the wheel well and then restore only the areas you want to show; restoring convex outline areas by painting is faster than hiding small, concave outline areas. In figure 7.6, you can see the wheel being restored after a large part of this area was hidden. Here's how to do this:

7. Press **X** to switch Foreground/Background colors on the toolbox. White restores masked areas of a layer (see fig. 7.6).

   The use of white to restore areas that are hidden is also good for mending mistakes you make in your masking work.

figure 7.6

To reach an accurate selection of the car's outline, alternate between hiding and restoring image areas in Layer Mask mode.

8. When you reach the car's exhaust pipe, press **D** (Default colors), choose the Polygon Lasso tool, and then click points around the edge of the tail pipe, closing the selection to

the outside of the tailpipe (see fig. 7.7). When the selection is closed, press Alt(Opt)+Delete (Backspace) to fill the selection with the current foreground color, thus hiding the image area encompassed by the selection. Press Ctrl(⌘)+D to deselect the marquee.

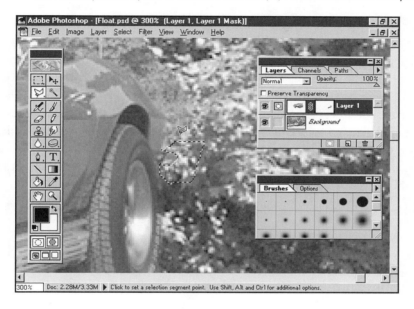

figure 7.7
Hide large unwanted areas by selecting them and then filling them with foreground color.

9. When you reach the edge of the grass and foliage in your masking work, press Ctrl(⌘)+S to save your work. You will continue masking the layer in future sections, but the Layer Mask mode is preserved even if you need to close the image and Photoshop between editing sessions.

Airbrushing a Layer Mask

As designers, we frequently choose the Paintbrush and Pencil tools by instinct because these tools provide totally anticipated, real-world results. You can make a stroke with these tools and paint a color shape whose edges are defined according to the tip you use. In certain design situations, however, you absolutely do *not* want an edge to your strokes, and the Airbrush tool becomes indispensable. The Airbrush tool applies foreground color in an extremely diffuse pattern, much softer than the Paintbrush tool with the softest tip.

Photoshop's Airbrush tool is used in the following steps to remove some areas of the foliage on the car layer, while leaving other areas intact. As you work through these steps, you will see that the leafy clumps of foliage on the car layer integrate quite well with the leafy clumps on the background parking lot layer. The two areas on different layers display a random distribution of leaves, and the Airbrush tool can make the integration between masked and untouched areas seamless. The additional benefit of working in Layer Mask mode with the Airbrush tool is that you get immediate visual feedback as to how the two foliage areas come together. The amount of car layer you mask is not what's important here; your goal is only to blend the areas so that they *look* right.

Here's how to integrate the foliage on Layer 1 with the background image:

LAYER MASK AND THE AIRBRUSH TOOL

1. Double-click on the Zoom tool to change your viewing resolution to 1:1. Scroll the window to center the foliage area of the car layer.

2. Choose the Airbrush tool, and on the Brushes palette choose the second tip from the right in the second row. The Options for the Airbrush tool should be Normal mode and 50% Pressure.

3. Drag over an edge of the foliage on Layer 1. Notice that there is no streak or edge to the Airbrush tool. Stop dragging with the tool when the foliage on Layer 1 appears integrated with the background foliage (see fig. 7.8).

4. Some Layer 1 foliage areas might look fine as is. Again, hide only those areas that display an edge, or whose foliage pattern is distinctly different pattern from that of the Background layer foliage. In some areas, simply click with the Airbrush—don't drag—to hide an area with a "burst" of foreground color. Increase the size of the Brushes tip for the Airbrush tool when necessary.

5. Press Ctrl(⌘)+S, but keep the document open in Photoshop.

figure 7.8
Hide only those areas of Layer 1's foliage edge that don't integrate well with the Background foliage you see.

There is no need to run through identical steps to hide the left edge of the areas surrounding the car on Layer 1. When you finish hiding the areas in Layer Mask mode, it's time to *apply* the Layer Mask—to actually remove from the document (and not merely hide) the areas you masked. Follow these steps to permanently remove the superfluous areas on Layer 1:

APPLYING THE LAYER MASK

1. On the Layers palette, click on the thumbnail image to the right of the chain link icon to select the Layer Mask for the next action.

2. Drag the thumbnail image into the Delete current layer icon (the trash icon) at the bottom of the Layers palette. If this sort of action leaves you a little nervous, an alternative is to right-click (Macintosh: hold Ctrl and click) and then choose Remove Layer Mask from the Context menu. Before you do *either* procedure, make sure that the mask icon (not the paint icon) is displayed to the left of the thumbnail image for Layer 1.

3. An attention box that asks whether you want to apply the mask to the layer appears (see fig. 7.9). The Apply option deletes the masked area from the layer, whereas the Discard option removes the mask and restores the layer's contents to their pre-edited state. (In effect, Discard means "forget my masking work, and don't make permanent changes to the layer.")

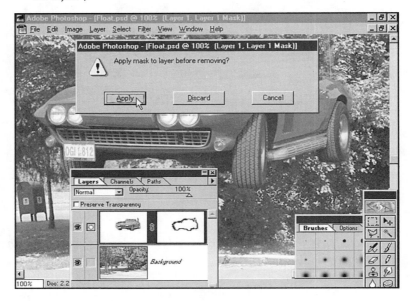

figure 7.9
Discard a Layer Mask to remove your masking work from a layer; apply a Layer Mask to remove the hidden areas from a layer.

4. Press Ctrl(⌘)+S to save your work.

Color Correcting the Composite Image

During the half hour that elapsed between photographs (of the parking lot and the car), the sun sank ever so slightly in the sky, changing the colors of the outdoors. This sort of thing happens. Fortunately, it's easy to correct with the Color Balance command. The Color Balance command gives you precise control over color found in ranges of tone—Highlights, Shadows, and Midtones. The Color Balance dialog box opens by default to change the Midtones; you can choose other options to select any range of tones to color balance. The sliders represent *complementary colors* (color opposites on a traditional color wheel).

If you look closely at the document on-screen, you can see that the foliage on the background layer is a lighter, warmer green than the foliage on the car layer. Part of the reason for the difference is that the foliage in the two pictures is different, and the digitized film came from two different rolls. Mainly, however, the reason for the difference is that lighting in the two images is close, but not identical. You can spend more time masking the car before you launch the Color Balance command, to ensure that the command affects only the shrubs on Layer 1, but the Color Balance command will have only a marginal effect on the color of the car. Viewers will not criticize your work if the red paint on the car casts slightly warmer than the original photo, because the finished image will contain nothing to which the original color of the car can be referenced. Therefore, you can save time and wind up with a better overall image by applying a color shift to the entire contents of Layer 1. Here's how to add color integration to the composition:

CORRECTING COLOR BALANCE

1. Press Ctrl(⌘)+B to display the Color Balance controls.

2. Position the dialog box so that you have a clear view of the remaining foliage on Layer 1; then click and drag the Yellow/Blue slider until the far right number field at the top of the dialog box reads about −5. Use your own judgment on color balancing; the image might display differently on your system than on ours!

In the image, notice that the foliage on Layer 1 is basically composed of midtones, with a few highlights. The shadow areas do not need to be color balanced because the shaded regions on both layers are similar in color. The color balancing should be accomplished by step 2; to finalize it, you need to address the color balance in the highlight areas.

3. Click on the Highlights button at the bottom of the dialog box and drag the Yellow/Blue slider to the left until the top right number field reads about −13 (see fig. 7.10). The car will lighten in color; shifting the highlights on this layer toward yellow removes some of the blue sky color.

4. Press Ctrl(⌘)+S to save your work.

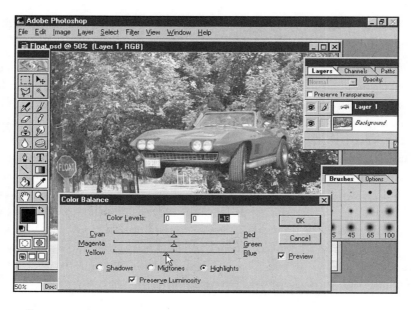

figure 7.10
By selecting a tonal range within which to shift colors, you can preserve some original image areas while creating warmth or coldness in other areas.

The integration of the car with the parking lot image is complete at this point. But an element is missing from the picture that indicates image editing, which is *not* the goal here! The car lacks a shadow. The next part of this chapter discusses ways to create photorealistic shadows.

TIP

Users of earlier versions of Photoshop will soon discover that Ctrl(⌘)+B no longer displays the Brightness/Contrast command.

To access Brightness/Contrast, go to Image, Adjust, and then choose Brightness/Contrast. You can assign this command a hot key from the Actions list palette if you use Brightness/Contrast a lot. Also, Windows users can access the hot key command by pressing Alt+I, A, and then C.

What's in a Shadow?

Shadows occur in a photograph when an opaque, or partially opaque, object blocks light from the background. But subtle natural phenomena that react with the shadow, the viewpoint from which the photo is taken, and with light itself make the "material" of a shadow more complex than you might imagine.

Shape, color, opacity, and sharpness are all properties of a shadow. You learn about these properties in the following sections, as you get hands-on experience creating a shadow for the car that looks as realistic as if the car itself were creating it.

Creating the Proper Shadow Shape

The outline of a shadow is determined by three things: the angle at which the light source is casting upon the object, the *attitude* (the degree of rotation and position) of the object relative to the light source, and the orientation and position of the photographer relative to the scene.

The orientation of the "photographer" of this simulated scene is a given; you cannot change the orientation because the photograph's contents are now established. Similarly, the source of light casting into the scene is established and cannot be altered. You can see elongated shadows of trees and the traffic sign pointing toward the image's lower-right corner in the Background layer.

Because the car's shadow in the Car.tif image has many characteristics of the shadow needed in Float.psd, you can trace over the existing shadow from the original car image, making this the general shape for the artificial shadow needed in the fantasy scene. Because of problems connected to using *exactly* the same shadow shape as that found in the Car.tif image, however, you must *modify* the shape after you trace it and before you use it in the Float image.

Shadow Sizes

If you place your hand between a table and a light bulb, the shadow cast on the table becomes larger, lighter, and fuzzier at the edges as you move your hand toward the light. This transformation occurs because light waves bend around shapes in the form of *diffuse lighting* characteristics—how light spreads on a surface according to the smoothness or roughness of the surface.

Therefore, a tracing of the same size shadow as the car resting on the ground in the Car.tif image fails to describe a shadow cast on the ground when the car is closer to the sun, about 6 feet in the air. The shadow needs to be slightly larger than the one in the Car.tif image to convey the feeling that the car is casting a shadow from a distance.

Shadow Sharpness

When you work with bitmap images, starting with a sharp image that contains sharp color transitions is always better than trying to resample (resize) a bitmap to suit a specific design need. Resampling causes loss of original image detail.

Here is a simple method for creating a larger-than-original shadow for the floating-car composition:

1. Using the Pen tool, trace the original outline of the shadow; then convert the path to curves and save it as a selection in an alpha channel.

2. Load the channel as a selection; choose Select, Modify, and then choose Expand.

3. Save the new expanded marquee selection in an alpha channel and use it as the template for the floating-car shadow.

The problem with this technique is that the Expand command is limited to expanding selections to 16 pixels outside the original marquee edge, and you might need a larger amount. Additionally, because the Expand command uses feathering, as do most of Photoshop's transformation features, you will no longer have control over the sharpness of the shadow you create.

Shadow Detail

Real shadows are better defined than those created by illustrators. We have all seen the artist's concept of a shadow in the Gaussian blur shadow effect on magazine covers. But on a sunny day like the one on which the images in this chapter were taken, the shadows cast in the images are quite well-defined. The car, for example, casts a shadow not only of the body, but also of the exterior rear view mirror and the tail pipes.

Unfortunately, because the car is perched on the ground, the angle of the photograph does not display the "top" of the shadow; it's hidden by the car. When tracing over the shadow in the original car image, you will need to fake some of the detail you cannot see.

Before you begin the shadow-creation steps, here's the method we recommend for creating the shape of the shadow:

1. Trace the shadow in the car image, using Photoshop's tools.

2. Export the path you traced to a drawing program capable of performing an offset (contour) function to make the shadow larger than the original.

3. Import the larger shadow design to Photoshop to use as a selection.

Here's how to create the shadow template for the image, using Photoshop's Pen tool:

TRACING A SHADOW

CD-ROM

1. Close the Float.psd image, and then open the Car.tif image from the CHAP07 folder of the Companion CD.

2. Type **200** in the Zoom percentage field, and press Enter (Return) to zoom into the document.

3. Hold the spacebar to access the Hand tool, and then pan your view in the window to the left until you can see the car's right wheel and license plate.

4. Choose the Pen tool from the toolbox, and then click and drag on the point where the back of the wheel touches the ground. Without releasing the cursor, drag the cursor away from the point in the image at which you first clicked. You will see direction points on the end of direction lines sprout from the origin anchor point; the goal here is to drag the cursor so that the direction lines lie flush with the side of the tire. Imagine that the direction lines represent a path segment between the first anchor point and the point you will create next.

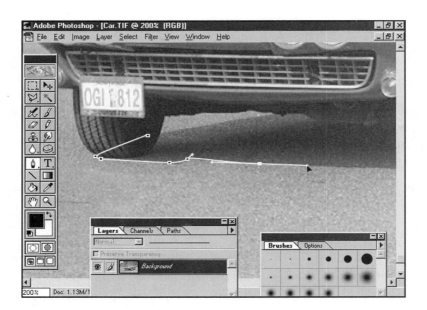

figure 7.11
Click and drag with the Pen tool in the direction of the path you want to create.

5. Click and drag a second point where the shadow curves toward the front of the car wheel (see fig. 7.11). A path segment is created that follows the outline of the shadow. When two or more anchor points have been defined in an image, the direction of the path is decided and cannot easily be changed. Continue making anchor points counterclockwise around the shadow.

6. For sharp turns in the shadow path, you need to click, but drag a short distance. If you think your path is going off course, continue anyway; you will see how to edit direction lines at the end of this section.

7. When you reach the back, right edge of the shadow, where the car obscures your view of the shadow, click and drag anchors to the left, estimating where the upper-left edge of the shadow falls. Also, you might want to create a left tail pipe shadow outline at the top left of the path (see fig. 7.12). This Corvette has dual tail pipes, and the additional shadow detail, real or imagined, gives the shadow more interest and complexity, further disguising its artificial origin.

8. Trace over the shadow area at the left of the image, and make a final click at the beginning of the path to close it.

9. Drag on the Pen tool on the toolbox to reveal the tool flyout, and then choose the Convert Anchor Point tool.

figure 7.12

Where you cannot see the shadow edge, imagine what it looks like and draw the detail with the Pen tool.

10. If any area in the image does not closely follow the shadow edge, click and drag on the anchor point closest to that area. Do not release the cursor; instead, drag the direction point to steer the path segment so that it closely matches the outline of the shadow.

11. If an anchor point needs to be repositioned, hold Ctrl(⌘) with the Convert Anchor Point tool to toggle to the Direct Selection tool, and then drag on the anchor point (but not the direction point or direction handle to the anchor point).

12. If you need to change the viewing resolution of the image, hold Ctrl(⌘)+spacebar to access the Zoom-in tool while any of the Pen tools are chosen, or hold Alt(Opt)+spacebar to toggle to the Zoom-out tool.

13. When the path is the way you want it, choose File, Export, and then choose Paths to Illustrator (see fig. 7.13). In the Export Paths dialog box, name the file Shadow. (Windows users should add the AI extension to the file name (Shadow.ai). On your hard disk, find a convenient folder for the path, and then click on OK.

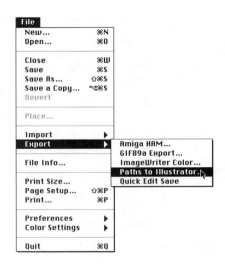

figure 7.13

Saving a path to Illustrator format enables you to modify the path as a resolution-independent shape in a drawing application.

14. The following sections require that you have access to Adobe Illustrator or another drawing program. If you have Illustrator, FreeHand, CorelDRAW, or CorelXARA, close the Car.tif image without saving your path-creation work. If you do not have a vector drawing program, with the path selected, press Ctrl(⌘)+C to copy the path, close the Car.tif image without saving, open the Float.psd image you created, choose Ctrl(⌘)+V to paste the path into the image, and then save the image.

The preceding steps might seem the long way around for defining the shape of the car's shadow, and indeed, if you are an accomplished artist, you might want to draw the path for the shadow directly in the Float.psd image, by eye. But it's important to understand that the shadow in the image is the only artificial creation; the car is photographic, and so is the parking lot. The best synthetic creations have as much realistic detail in them as your skills and time can afford. And tracing a photographic element brings you one step closer to your goal.

Offsetting a Path in a Drawing Application

Different applications have different terms for the act of duplicating a path, with every point along the duplicate path an equal distance outside, or inside, the original. Adobe calls this action *offsetting a path*, Macromedia FreeHand calls it the *Inset Path Operation*, and Corel products offer the *Contour effect*.

When you simply scale an object in a drawing program, the increase in width and height of the scaled shape is *relative* to the original dimensions. This is why a rectangle scaled to 200 percent of the original cannot surround the original on all four sides with an equal amount of distance. In the following steps, you scale *dis*proportionately the path you saved in the preceding example, so that the shadow path is larger in *absolute* dimensions at every point along the path. By doing this, you create a larger shadow whose height and width are synchronous with the dimensions of the car that is casting the shadow in the fantasy image.

RESIZING THE VECTOR SHADOW

1. In Photoshop, with the Float.psd image in the workspace, choose Image, Mode, and then choose Grayscale. Click on Yes in the attention box that asks whether you want to lose the color information from the image.

2. Choose File, Save As, and then save the grayscale image to your hard disk in the TIFF file format, as Template.tif. This image is one-third the final file size of the fantasy composition, and as such, is less taxing to system RAM when you import it to your drawing application. You don't need a color image as a reference for the shadow-editing work.

3. If your system does not have the resources to have two large applications open at the same time, close Photoshop and then launch your drawing application.

4. Open or import the path you saved in the preceding example, and place it on a unique design layer.

5. Create a new layer and import the Template.tif file. (In Illustrator and FreeHand, use the File, Place command.) Lock this new layer, and make the layer that contains the path the current editing layer.

6. Align the path to its position on top of the shadow in the image. Copy the path and locate it directly above the original path.

7. Use the Scale, Offset, Inset, or Contour feature in your drawing application to create a larger duplicate of the path, whose border is about 20 percent larger than the original. Figure 7.14 shows the Scale tool, used in its default setting in Illustrator to enlarge the duplicate path so that the distance between every point along the paths is equal. You can drag away from the center of the path to scale it disproportionately. FreeHand and CorelDRAW offer a dialog box to accomplish the offset command.

figure 7.14
Use a Scale or Offset command in combination with your drawing program's editing tools to make a larger copy of the path, equidistant from the original.

It might take some finessing of individual anchor points to get the larger duplicate exactly the way you feel is right for the image. Because vector paths retain visual information when scaled, however, the path you create will be crisp and sharp when you import it to Photoshop.

8. Assign the duplicate path a black fill and no outline property. Delete the original path from the document.

9. Delete the layer that contains the grayscale image, and then save the file in illustrator as Shadow.ai, overwriting the original file you exported from Photoshop. In other drawing programs, choose File, Export, and then export your work in the Illustrator 3.x (or later) format to your hard disk. Close the drawing application at any time now; you might want to save a copy of your work in the drawing program's native file format for future use.

Importing and Placing the Shadow

Photoshop will not import vector information that has neither fill nor outline properties, which is why you were asked to fill with black the shape you created in the preceding example. This was done to read the path information—not as an image element you place on a layer to represent the shadow, but instead as *selection information* from an image alpha channel in Photoshop.

Here's how to import the path file and use it to shape a marquee selection of the shadow, to which you add color, opacity, and other photorealistic properties:

PLACING AN ILLUSTRATOR FILE

CD-ROM

1. In Photoshop, open the Float.psd image you saved earlier, and then open the Shadow.ai file you created in the drawing application. If you didn't work through the previous steps, you can use the Shadow.ai file in the Companion CD's CHAP07 folder, created by the authors.

2. In the Rasterize Generic EPS Format dialog box, the specs for the Illustrator file should be close to 551 pixels in Width, and 119 in Height by 72 pixels/inch Resolution. If the default values in this dialog box are close, choose Grayscale from the Mode drop-down list, and then click on OK to convert the vector path to bitmap format. If the values are not even close to 551 by 119 by 72 pixels per inch, type these values and then click on OK. Occasionally, Photoshop offers you values for importing vector files, based on information you used in previous sessions.

3. When the image appears in the workspace, press Ctrl(⌘)+A to select all, press Ctrl(⌘)+C to copy the image, and then close the file without saving.

4. On the Channels palette (press F7 if it isn't currently on-screen), and click on the Create new channel icon at the bottom of the palette.

5. Double-click on the channel title (channel #4), click on the Colors Indicate Selected Areas button if it is not already chosen, and then click on OK.

6. Press Ctrl(⌘)+V to paste the image from the clipboard into the channel.

7. Click on the Layers tab on the grouped palette, and then click on the Create new layer icon at the bottom of the palette.

8. Drag the layer title on top of the Background title. This places the new layer between the car layer and the Background.

9. Choose Multiply from the modes drop-down list on the Layers palette.

10. With any selection tool, drag inside the marquee to place it beneath the car. The selection should be located horizontally, so that it spills onto the curb and about $1/8$ of a screen inch into the lawn. This is accurate placement because the sun is casting into the scene, and shadows will be displayed behind the object casting them. Additionally, the shadow calls less attention to itself in the image if it's not perfectly cast on the parking lot pavement.

11. With the Eyedropper tool, click over an area of shadow on the parking lot (see fig. 7.15).

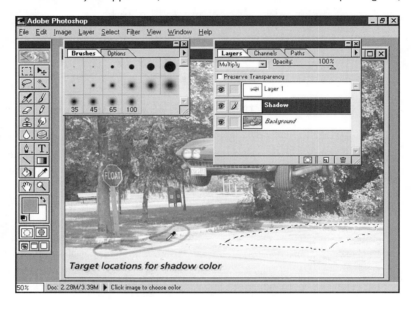

figure 7.15
Choose a color from the image to use for filling the shadow marquee selection.

12. Press Alt(Opt)+Delete (Backspace) to fill the selection marquee, and then press Ctrl(⌘)+D to deselect the marquee.

13. Press Ctrl(⌘)+S to save your work, but keep the image open in Photoshop.

If you're not quite happy with the shadow's location in the image, you can reposition the nontransparent pixels (the shadow) on the layer. Choose the Move tool and then drag in the document window.

Also, it might be a good idea to label the layers, now that you have three of them in the Float.psd document. Double-click on a layer, and then type the name for the layer in the Name field. This makes it obvious, from moment to moment, which layer contains the elements that can be edited.

Refining the Shadow

As mentioned earlier, a shadow has many properties; you have the shape and the color now, but the shadow's look and feel also need addressing. In the following sections, you add the photorealistic qualities that will make the shadow in the image truly become part of the scene.

Shadow Density versus Shadow Color

In a way, the real shadows casting on the Background image are natural "layers." They subtract from the color of the curb and the lawn at partial opacity, and cast a color into the shaded areas. The Photoshop equivalent needs to be performed now to the Shadows layer to balance the opacity of the shadows with the density—the darkness of the tonal property of the color you added to the layer in the previous section.

BALANCING THE TONE AND OPACITY OF SHADOWS

1. With the Shadow layer as the current editing layer, drag the Opacity slider on the Layers palette to about 70%. It's okay that the shadow is now lighter than the shadows on the Background. The intention here is to allow some of the background pavement to show through the shadow.

2. Press Ctrl(⌘)+L to display the Levels command. Position the dialog box so that you have an unobstructed view of the shadow you created, and of the natural shadows on the pavement.

3. Drag the black point slider to about 26 (see fig. 7.16). Use your artistic taste to decide when the tone and color of the shadow on the layer match the color of the real shadows on the Background layer; then click on OK to apply the change.

4. Press Ctrl(⌘)+S to save your work; keep the image open in Photoshop.

With shape, tone, color, and opacity down with the shadow, it's time to address the more subtle details.

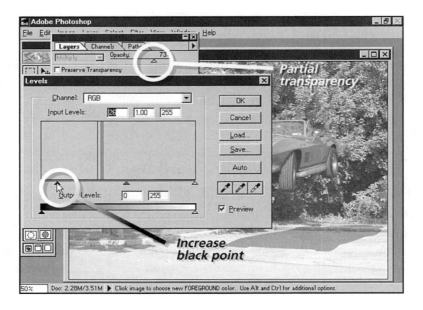

figure 7.16

To create a convincing shadow you must blend opacity with the tonal density of the color.

Blurring the Shadow

Oddly enough, now that you have a nice, sharp shadow in the image, you need to soften the edges through the use of the Gaussian blur filter. The shadows cast upon the parking lot by the trees, weeds, and other objects appear to be sharp because they are cast on an even surface, and because they are close to the surface that receives the shadow. Even on the clearest of days, however, an object *in the air* does not cast a sharp shadow because diffuse light bounces off the object, scattering light around the edges of the shadow on the ground. If an airplane ever flies directly over your company parking lot, and you're in the correct position to look closely at the shadow, you will notice that the edges are not sharp at all. The edges aren't fuzzy, either; they're simply slightly out of focus.

In the following steps, you *slightly* blur the shadow on the layer to introduce a photographic, real world effect:

USING THE GAUSSIAN BLUR FILTER

1. Move the Layers palette and other palettes out of the way of the shadow in the image. You cannot move palettes while a dialog box displays.

2. Choose Filter, Blur, and then choose Gaussian Blur.

3. Move the Gaussian Blur box to a side of the workspace so that you can preview the effect in the image.

4. Drag the Radius slider to about 1.2 pixels (see fig. 7.17), or enter this amount in the number field. This amount of blurring does not affect the general shape of the shadow; it simply softens the edges.

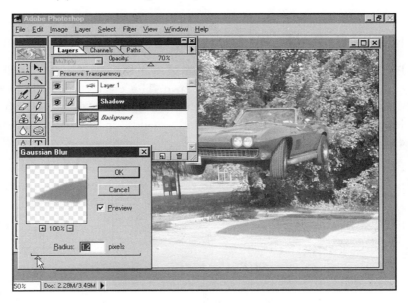

figure 7.17
Use the Gaussian blur filter to soften the shadow's edge slightly.

5. Click on OK to apply the filter, and press Ctrl(⌘)+S to save your work.

TIP

The Gaussian blur filter does not perform the same type of averages of pixels in a selection as the other blur filters. This filter distributes a *weighted* average of pixel colors within the selection area. The distribution pattern is a bell-shaped curve; pixels toward the edge of the blurred selection are most visibly affected, whereas pixels toward the center of a selection are the least blurred.

When high levels of Gaussian blur are applied to the nontransparent areas of a layer, you will see the image areas shrink inward as more pixels take on the layer's transparent property, while central pixels tend to remain the same color.

Merging Real Shadows with Fake Shadows

Earlier, we recommended placing the shadow in this image so that it spills onto the curb in the parking lot, and into the lawn. This creates a problem in the image, though, because there is already natural shading on the face of the curb facing our view of the image. To have shading and a shadow on the curb would suggest two different light sources in the scene.

Because it's easier to remove part of the artificial shadow than the *actual* shadows, the following steps show how the Quick Mask tool can be used to quickly define the areas to be lightened on the Shadows layer, to blend your creation with the photographic elements.

QUICK MASK EDITING THE SHADOWS

1. Type **200** in the Zoom percentage field and then press Enter (Return). With the Hand tool, drag inside the document to pan your view to the area where the artificial shadow meets the curb.

2. Click on the Quick Mask mode icon toward the bottom of the toolbox, and then press **B** (Paintbrush tool). Use the same Brushes tip you have used throughout this chapter.

3. Paint strokes where the curb shows shading, but do not paint over the weeds or the cracks. These are illuminated elements in the Background image, and should be shaded by the Shadow layer. You only need to stroke over areas where there is already shading on the curb (see fig. 7.18).

figure 7.18

Use Quick Mask to designate selection areas in the image where the shadow on the layer should not be present.

4. After you mask the areas in the image where there is a "redundant shadow," click on the Standard editing icon to the left of the Quick Mask icon, and then press Ctrl(⌘)+H to make the marquee lines disappear. The selection marquee is still active, but the distracting "marching ants" are gone.

5. Double-click on the Hand tool to zoom out of the image to a full-frame view.

6. Choose Image, Adjust, and then choose Contrast/Brightness.

7. Drag the Brightness slider to the right until the tone of the shadow on the Shadow layer matches the tone of the other shaded areas of pavement (see fig. 7.19). Click on OK to apply the changes.

8. Press Ctrl(⌘)+D to deselect the invisible marquee, and then press Ctrl(⌘)+S to save your work.

figure 7.19
Increasing the Brightness of the selected areas brings the shading to the same level as the natural image shadows.

The shadow now has the look, tone, and color of the shadows in the Background layer. If you call it quits with this assignment right now, you have achieved a photorealistic effect in a surrealistic image. One tiny detail is missing from the shadow, however, a detail that can become obvious when the image goes to print. Let's check out one of Photoshop's new filters in the next section to "dirty up" your work a little.

Adding Film Grain to the Shadow

With the exception of images captured with digital cameras, all digitized images today—PhotoCD images, scanned images, and scanned negatives—display *film grain.* The Background image contains "noisy" areas you can see when you zoom in to 200–300%, as does the layer that contains the car image.

The shadow, because it's a "pure" Photoshop creation, does not contain the film grain characteristic. Before version 4, Photoshop users had to purchase a special-effects filter, such as Gallery Effects' Film Grain, to achieve an authentic photographic grain look with Photoshop illustrations, rendered models, and other computer designs. Fortunately, this filter is included with Photoshop 4. If you have ever wondered why someone would want to add noise to an image, here's the perfect occasion. You can preserve the continuity between the created and the photographed when you match the Film Grain filter to the naturally occurring grain in the digitized photos. Unlike Photoshop's Noise filters, the Film Grain filter creates *patterns* of grain in the image, which faithfully reproduces the uneven distribution of grains in the photographic emulsion of film and prints.

Here's how to put the finishing touches on the floating car design:

USING THE FILM GRAIN FILTER

1. Zoom in to 300% viewing resolution of the Float.psd image, and then pan or scroll the window so that you have a clear view of both the shadow and the natural shaded parts of the parking lot.

2. Choose Filter, Artistic, and then choose Film Grain. The Film Grain dialog box appears.

3. Move the dialog box to a corner of the screen so that you still have a good view of both the artificial shadow and the natural shadows in the composition.

4. Click the + button beneath the preview window twice, to bring the preview window to the same 300% viewing resolution as your view of the document. You can pan the preview window at any time to see various parts of the shadow affected as the Film Grain Options are defined.

5. Drag the Grain Option slider to 3. The Grain slider controls the amount of the effect; its maximum setting is 20 (which you would never use for photographic image retouching).

6. Leave the Highlight Area slider at 0. The Highlight Area control introduces light colored specks to areas; the slider sets the tones at which the white specks are introduced. The shadow you are working with here is composed of a basically uniform color, with no highlights to accentuate.

7. Similarly, leave the Intensity slider at 0. The Intensity control determines how bright the Highlights are in the image. Set the controls to look like those in the dialog box in figure 7.20, check one last time to ensure that the grain effect in the preview window looks similar to the grain in the original image areas, and then click on OK.

figure 7.20
The Film Grain effect imitates the characteristics of particles in photographic emulsion.

8. Press Ctrl(⌘)+S to save your work; then choose File, Save a Copy, and save a copy as Float.tif in the TIFF file format, without alpha channels (make sure that this option is unchecked in the Save As box). You now have a working piece you can come back to, as well as a copy on hard disk that can be shared with a commercial printer, friends, and that wise guy at the auto shop who keeps telling you that your car needs more air in the tires.

In figure 7.21, you can see the completed assignment. There is something about this image that provokes a number of reactions, from laughter to awe. In your own assignments, you now have the skills and the knowledge to create floating people and floating logos, and to do it with photographic integrity that hides traces of editing work.

figure 7.21
To learn how the "Float" traffic sign was created, see Chapter 12.

Summary

In this chapter, you have seen how to combine two ordinary images to create an unlikely scene that looks absolutely correct. This twisting of reality performed with Photoshop can take your work to unparalleled artistic heights, or can be used simply to attract attention. You now have another trick in your creative bag for those times that a client calls and asks, "Can you do something interesting with this picture?" And you also have an understanding of the physical reasons that light illuminates scenes in a certain way, what goes into a re-creation of a shadow, and how camera angles affect the compositing of a scene.

If you need to *reverse* the process followed in this chapter—that is, if you want to make a scene with a misplaced element appear "normal"—then Chapter 8, "Correcting Images," is your next stop.

PART

PART IV: ADVANCED IMAGING

CHAPTER

8

CORRECTING IMAGES

The perfect image is what we all strive for in our work, but attaining the perfect image is a relative notion; one that is meaningless without putting the word "perfect" into context. Perfect for what? For printing? For the Web? For a child's birthday card?

Seldom, if ever, do you receive an image that is already perfect, in any context, in every respect. Almost every image you capture or receive from a client needs some kind of correction or adjustment. Typically, you need to integrate the image with other elements to precisely express the creative idea you have in mind.

Sometimes an image needs color correction, brightness, or contrast adjustment because the method used to digitize the image introduces color or shifts tone from the original image. Images might be the wrong size, have the wrong aspect ratio, or an image might "face" in the wrong direction. There are a million and one possible reasons that an image may not be perfect to your eye, your client's eye, or for its intended purpose.

This chapter covers some of the workarounds and correction methods you can tap into in Photoshop 4. You will learn how to make a picture "perfect" for its intended purpose, and in the process you will discover valuable techniques that you can apply in Photoshop to any image in a variety of design situations.

Creating a Portrait Image from a Landscape Image

A fundamental quality to consider about any image, whether digitally created or photographed, is its *orientation* and *aspect ratio*. Whenever you specify a Canvas Size for an image in Photoshop, or snap an image with a camera, you determine the image's height and width proportions (a *portrait orientation*) or if it is wider than it is tall (a *landscape orientation*). *Aspect ratio* describes not only the orientation, but also the relative dimensional relationship between the height and the width.

For example, an image that is 2 inches tall and 3 inches wide has an aspect ratio of 2:3, and is described as having a landscape orientation. An image that is 2 inches wide and 3 inches tall has an aspect ratio of 3:2, and a portrait orientation. A picture taken with 35mm film also has a 2:3 aspect ratio and a landscape orientation when the picture is taken with the camera held in its normal position. But if you rotate the camera 90° and then take the picture, the resulting image has a 3:2 aspect ratio and a portrait orientation. Aspect ratio and orientation are important to understand for image output (see Chapter 16, "Outputting Your Input"), and also for successfully communicating with a client about the proportions an image should have.

A common imaging problem is that the ideal photo needed to complete your client's project has the wrong orientation. Sometimes, if only a small part of the original image is needed, you can reorient the composition by cropping it to the correct aspect. More often, however, you are faced with the need to *add* to the image to increase its width or height. In the following example, you do just that; you take a stunning *landscape* photo and turn it into a stunning *portrait* photo.

Two of the sample images in this chapter, Sunset1.psd (1.13 MB) and Sunset4.tif (4.5 MB), are identical in visual content—only the files sizes are different. The images are copies of two different PhotoCD base resolutions (sizes) from a single PhotoCD image pack. (See Chapter 18, "3D and Photoshop," for more information on working with PhotoCD images.)

TIP

If you scan a photograph or negative instead of using a PhotoCD image, it pays in the long run to scan the image at several different file sizes, all in the same scanning session. You should always acquire an image at, or slightly larger than, the size you need for your finished image. You never know when you will need to repurpose an image for another assignment. When you need to create a Web version of a printed piece, or when a Web element needs to become a printed piece, you will be glad you had the foresight to scan and save your images at different sizes. It is far easier to retrieve an image from your hard disk or backups than it is to find the physical media again and rescan it.

Use a single image and sample it at many different resolutions to match the many different uses you may have for an image.

Sunset1.psd has a landscape orientation (see fig. 8.1). The image is composed of reeds in the foreground, a pond, a house in the middle of the image, and a spectacular sky at the top.

Giving this image a portrait orientation is relatively easy; the image content that lies next to the top and bottom edges contains natural elements. Natural elements such as grass, sand, leaves, and sky don't have a discernible pattern, and viewers tend to accept additions to the overall image as natural. Whenever possible, however, you should extend an image with material obtained from a copy of the same image, or from a similar one. Although viewers don't mind variations in a pattern or composition of natural elements, any variation in lighting, color, or tonal balance will strike a false chord with them.

figure 8.1
Images sometimes have the correct visual composition, but the orientation of the image needs to be changed.

The size of the image you copy from also plays a role in how credible the finished image looks. When you copy elements from a larger version of an image, the copied elements are larger than their counterparts in the smaller version of the file. This size difference is a definite *advantage* when you need to copy foreground elements into an image. Why? Because the closer objects are to the camera, the larger they should be. Adding larger reeds to the bottom of the image is good because they are in the foreground. Also, larger clouds work visually because a view of the sky from the ground shows clouds of many sizes. Clouds placed near the horizon tend to seem more distant than the clouds viewed straight above you. Therefore, larger clouds added to the image will not look out of place; in fact, they will make the sky more interesting. The larger reeds and clouds will also "frame" the center of the composition. In figure 8.2, you can see the target orientation for the finished image, and the two images used to create the composition.

figure 8.2

This image is easy to convert from landscape to portrait orientation because the top and bottom of the picture contain natural elements that can be extended without looking false.

Before you change image orientation, you must first examine the image to see how its width can be cropped (see fig. 8.2). In this example, it was not possible to use the entire width of the original image to create a portrait-oriented image. If you use the entire original width of the picture, for example, you must add *massive* areas of supplemental image to the top and bottom of the finished image. It is usually the center of a picture that holds the interesting elements, and the center elements should be larger than those in the rest of the image. If you add too much to the top and bottom, the foreground visual element is overwhelmed by the surrounding additions.

To avoid this pitfall, you should use only a *portion* of the original picture when you change the orientation of the entire image. How much you use depends on the answers to these questions:

◆ How much of the picture can you lose from each side and still have a pleasing composition?

◆   What are the dimensions and file size of the finished image compared to the original image?

The client in this example has quite specific (but not unusual) needs. The client's layout calls for a portrait orientation, and image dimensions of about 2.5" high and 1.75" wide. The image needs to fit a magazine column that is printed by using a 133 *line per inch* (lpi) screen. As you will see in Chapter 16, to optimally print an image, that image must have a resolution of one and one-half to two times the line screen used to print the image. In this example, therefore, you need to produce an image with a resolution of 266 *pixels per inch* (ppi) to meet the client's requirements. The current image, Sunset1.psd, is 7.11" high by 10.667" wide, and has a resolution of 72 ppi with a file size of 1.13 MB.

To meet the client's specifications, you need to take into consideration the relationship between resolution and image dimensions. As discussed in Chapters 3 ("Personalizing Photoshop: Preferences and Options") and 16, image resolution and image dimensions are inversely proportional. When you increase the resolution (the number of pixels per inch, or *ppi*) and keep the file size the same (in this case 1.13 MB), the image's height and width dimensions decrease. When you maintain the original file size in megabytes, but change the dimensions of an image by changing resolution (ppi), you do not degrade the image in any way. When file size is maintained and dimensions are changed, no pixels are added or lost, nor do they undergo any color or tonal changes. What *does* happen is that all the pixels in the image become larger or smaller. The term *pixel* is a *relative* measurement of a *pic*ture *el*ement.

If, however, you allow the file size (as measured in megabytes) to change, image quality *is* affected. The image will suffer some focus loss because pixels must be added or deleted in the image to attain the new file size. Changing the number of pixels (*pixel count*) in an image to achieve a different file size is called *resampling*. In other examples in this book, resampling is used to change an image's dimensions, but in this example, you do *not* want to change the number of pixels in the image. You simply want to change the dimensions of the file, as measured in inches.

In the following steps, you use the Image Size dialog box to maintain Sunset1.psd's file size while making changes to the image dimensions and the resolution.

WARNING

Users of earlier versions of Photoshop should be aware that the Image Size command dialog box has undergone *significant* changes. *Be careful:* the familiar Constrain File Size check box is gone, and has been replaced with the Resample Image check box. The Resample Image check box must be *unchecked* to constrain the file size. The first time you use this command after installing Photoshop, the Resample Image check box is checked. We recommend that you *un*check the box; it will remain unchecked until you change the option in future Photoshop sessions. If it is not your intention to change the number of pixels in an image, the Resample Image check box should be checked; otherwise (and a more foolproof state for this option) the box should be unchecked when you need to increase or decrease image dimensions while increasing image resolution and maintaining original image content.

CHANGING IMAGE DIMENSIONS AND RESOLUTION

CD-ROM

1. Open Sunset1.psd from the CHAP08 folder (directory) on the Companion CD. Double-click on the Hand tool on the toolbox to get a complete view of the image without window scroll bars. Then click on the Minimize/Maximize box (Macintosh: drag the Size box) to expand the window to display the neutral-colored document window background around the edges of the image.

2. Choose Image, Image Size. The Image Size dialog box (see fig. 8.3) reports that the current image size, in pixels, is 768 × 512, and it has a file size of 1.13 MB. The Print Size field says that at its current resolution of 72 pixels per inch, the image will print or appear in an electronic document with a width of 10.667" and a height of 7.111".

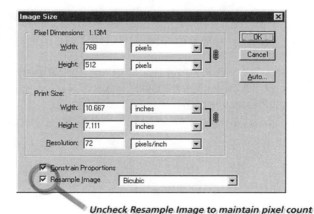

Uncheck Resample Image to maintain pixel count

figure 8.3
The Image Size dialog box is used to change the resolution and the dimensions of an image.

3. *Uncheck* the Resample Image check box. (It is checked by default.)

   Note that when you uncheck this check box, the fields in the Pixel Dimensions section become dimmed and that Width, Height, and Resolution in the Print Size section are connected to each other with link brackets. This is a visual clue that file size will remain constant and that a change made to image Width, Height, or Resolution will automatically cause the other two file properties to change. When the Resample Image box is *un*-checked, unwanted resampling of the image will *not* take place.

4. Place the cursor in the Resolution entry box in the Print Size field and type **266**. Notice that the file size remains the same, but that the width and height have changed to 2.87″ and 1.925″. Click on OK to apply the change to the image.

5. Press Ctrl(⌘)+S (File, Save) to save your work.

Although you can perform these steps to change the resolution or dimensions of an image at any time, it is important to do so as a first step when you need to edit an image's dimensions. Because resolution is the measurement of how many pixels fit within an inch, you need to establish the resolution first. Otherwise, making accurate measurements becomes a mathematical nightmare.

When the image resolution is set to the resolution needed for final output, you can skip the math and take advantage of the many measurement-related tools Photoshop puts at your disposal. The image you're working with needs to be cropped to change its aspect ratio to one that is closer to a portrait landscape. In the next set of steps, you use Photoshop 4's new guides feature, along with rulers and the measurements displayed on the Info palette, to figure out how much, and where, you should crop.

MEASURING AN IMAGE FOR CROPPING

1. Press Ctrl(⌘)+R to display the rulers. By default, the 0,0 origin point for the rulers is set to the upper left corner of the image. Press Shift+Ctrl(⌘)+; (semicolon) to enable the Snap-to Guides feature.

2. Press F8 to display the Info palette if it is not already on-screen.

3. Press **V** (Move tool). The Move tool can be used to drag guides out of the rulers, and is the *only* tool that can reposition a guideline.

4. Drag a guideline from the vertical ruler and place it at .5 inches. The X field on the left panel of the Info palette will tell you when you are at exactly .5 inches.

   If you waffle back and forth between a value a little more or less than .5 inches, zoom in to about 300%. The closer your view of the document, the more control you have over placement.

5. Drag another vertical guide and place it at 2.25 inches.

   The 1.75" wide section between the two guides is the area that defines the width of the new portrait image. The areas to the right and to the left of the guides will be cropped off. If you want to crop the image differently, use the Move tool to move the guides, but make sure that you maintain the 1.75" distance between the guides.

6. Press **M** (Marquee tool) to choose the Rectangular Marquee tool; press M as many times as necessary to choose the tool. The tool toggles between selection types. The settings on the Marquee Options palette should be set to Shape: Rectangular; Style: Normal; and Feather: 0 pixels.

7. Place the cursor near the top of the left guideline, making sure that the cursor is outside the image area, and then drag to the bottom of the right guide. By starting and stopping the selection on a portion of the guideline in the document background area outside the image, you avoid the possibility of making a selection that stops one or two rows short of selecting the entire top-to-bottom image area (see fig. 8.4).

8. From the Image menu, choose Crop. The image is altered so that only the image area contained within the Rectangular Marquee tool remains.

9. With the Move tool (press **V**), click and drag the guides back into the vertical ruler. You can tell you're about to move a guide (and not the layer) when the Move tool cursor changes to the shape shown in figure 8.5.

10. Press Ctrl(⌘)+R to hide the rulers; you don't need them any more.

11. Press Shift+Ctrl(⌘)+ S, and save the cropped image to your hard disk as Sunset.psd, in the Photoshop file format. Keep the image open in Photoshop.

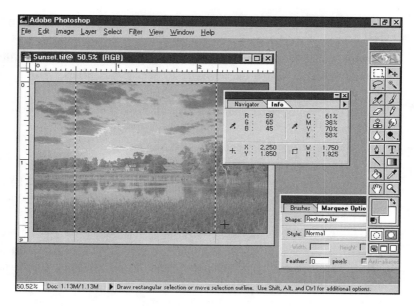

figure 8.4

When you must make an accurate crop and you don't know the pixel dimensions of the area to be cropped, use guides, rulers, and the Info palette to mark off the area.

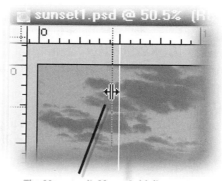

The Move tool's **Move Guideline** *cursor*

figure 8.5

You can be assured that you are about to move a guide—and not a layer—when the Move tool cursor looks like this.

TIP

Windows users of Photoshop have a status bar at the bottom of the workspace that displays information about which keys to hold to modify the actions of a tool. The status bar doesn't always tell the complete story, however. Take the Shift key, for example.

In both the Macintosh and Windows versions of Photoshop, if you hold Shift and click and drag with a selection tool, you add an area to an existing selection. If you change the order in which you do things, however—clicking and holding with the (left) mouse button and then pressing and holding the Shift key while you drag, for example—the Shift key will constrain the movement of a marquee selection to a straight line. The order in which you release the mouse and the Shift key is also important. When you use the Shift key to constrain movement, always release the mouse button first, and then the Shift key.

Next you will work with the Canvas Size command and the Sunset image. With the Canvas Size command, the pixels that make up the existing image are not changed; instead, new pixels are added to the border of the image to *extend* the overall image area. Photoshop's Canvas Size command is a bit like transferring an image to a different-sized piece of paper or canvas. The pixels in the new area(s) of the image are assigned the current background color.

The Canvas Size dialog box is where you specify how much space is added to (or removed from) an image, where pixels are added (or deleted), and to where, of nine locations in the modified image, the existing image should be placed. In the following steps, you use the default location of the center of the new image.

CHANGING THE CANVAS SIZE

1. Press **D** (Default colors), and choose Image, Canvas Size from the menu bar.

2. In the Height entry box, type **2.50**; make sure that the units are set to inches in the drop-down box. Do *not* change the Width value. Click on the center button in the Anchor field if it is not already selected (see fig. 8.6). These settings will increase the height of the canvas from 1.925" to 2.5" by adding equal amounts of blank, background-colored canvas (new image area) above and below the current image.

3. Click on OK to create the larger-size canvas.

4. Press Ctrl(⌘)+S to save your work. Keep the image open in Photoshop for the following steps.

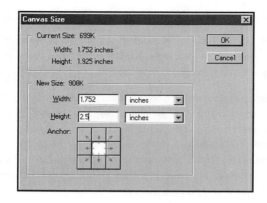

figure 8.6

Additional image area, or canvas, is added to a file by using the Canvas Size dialog box.
Use the Anchor field setting to determine where the existing image is placed on the
enlarged canvas.

TIP

When working with the Canvas Size command, you may want an existing image in a custom
location. Your own assignments might also require you to define and save a selection so that
you can make changes to the new canvas areas without affecting the original image areas, or
vice versa. To do this, you need to create and save a selection that encompasses the entire
image before you enlarge the canvas. When you change the canvas size, Photoshop automatically alters the location of saved selections so that they match the new location of the areas
they originally encompassed. You can then load the selection and, with the Move tool, move the
original image to a new location on the enlarged canvas.

Now that the image's canvas is of the final dimensions and resolution for the client,
the next step is to add top and bottom areas to the picture to make it portrait-
oriented.

Using Quick Edit and the Rubber Stamp Tool

Unlike vector design applications such as Illustrator and CorelDRAW, the product
of Photoshop is always a bitmap type of computer graphics. This means that the

larger the bitmap image you work with, the larger the saved file size—and the more system resources needed to edit, display, and write the image to disk.

The authors have kept the example file sizes on the Companion CD to 1–2 MB on most occasions, not only to demonstrate a Photoshop principle, but also so that readers with 20 MB or less of system RAM can work quickly with images. The Sunset4.tif image is necessarily larger than most of the example files, however, because this reorienting assignment requires larger areas of an identical sunset image as source material to complete the image. Sunset4.tif is 4.5 MB, and it's estimated that Photoshop requires an average of four times a file's size to hold the image in memory and to save multiple versions as temp files on disk.

You don't need to be concerned about Photoshop's memory requirements, however, when you understand the Quick Edit feature in Photoshop. Quick Edit can open an *area* of a file, thus saving the system overhead of opening a complete, large image. The only requirement for an image to be opened in Quick Edit mode is that of file format: Quick Edit candidates must be in either TIFF or Scitex CT (*.SCT) format. (That's why the authors saved this section's example images from PhotoCD to TIFF format instead of to Photoshop's PSD format.)

In the following steps, you open the reeds area of Sunset4.tif and use it as a Rubber Stamp tool cloning source, to add reeds to the bottom of your Sunset.psd image.

QUICK EDIT IMPORTING AND CLONING THE REEDS

CD-ROM

1. Choose File, Import, Quick Edit; then choose Sunset4.tif from the CHAP08 folder on the Companion CD. Click on Open after you select the image from the directory window.

2. In the Quick Edit dialog box, uncheck the Grid box (which forces you to select image areas from a predetermined grid), and drag a marquee around the reeds area of the image (see fig. 8.7).

   The Selection field of the Quick Edit box displays information about how large a section you have selected in the image. Notice that the selection in figure 8.7 is only 1 MB. This means that Photoshop will request a maximum of 3–5 MB from your system RAM and hard disk space to hold the image in the workspace as you edit.

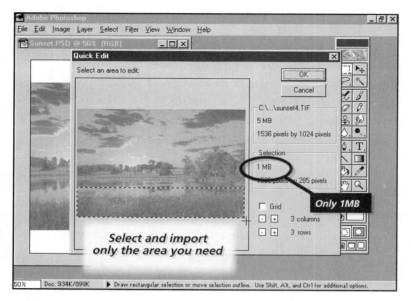

figure 8.7
Quick Edit enables you to open only the area you need of an image in TIFF or Scitex CT format.

3. Click on OK to import the selected portion of the Sunset4.tif image.

4. Arrange the workspace so that you can work between the bottom of Sunset.psd and the reeds portion of Sunset4.tif. Zoom to 100% viewing resolution of your Sunset.psd image and drag the window borders (Macintosh: drag the Size box) so that only the bottom third of the image is showing. With the Quick Edit portion of Sunset4.tif in Photoshop's foreground, Press Ctrl(⌘)+– to zoom out of the image until the entire contents of the window can be seen.

5. Choose the Rubber Stamp tool. Make sure that the Options palette settings are Mode: Normal; Option: Clone (aligned); and Opacity 100%. On the Brushes palette, choose the second row, far right tip.

6. With Sunset.psd in the foreground in Photoshop, click on the Create new layer icon on the Layers palette.

7. Press Alt(Opt) and click on a brown area of the reeds in the Quick Edit portion of Sunset4.tif to specify the initial sampling point for the Rubber Stamp tool. Using the Clone (aligned) option for the Rubber Stamp tool makes the sampling point move in parallel to wherever you apply the sample.

8. Click and then drag, beginning a little beneath the brown reeds in the center of the
    Sunset.psd image (see fig. 8.8). Although it might appear that you will run out of sampling
    area in the Sunset4 image, remember that this Quick Edit view is of an image *four times*
    the size of the image in which you're working (twice the height and twice the width).

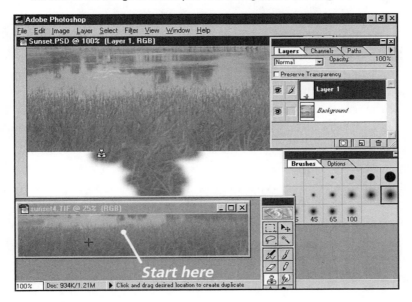

figure 8.8

Begin sampling the larger Quick Edit view of the Sunset4.tif image in the brown areas;
then work across and downward in the Sunset.psd image.

9. Because the brush tip for the Rubber Stamp tool is so large, you can cover the bottom of
    the portrait version of the Sunset image in only five or six strokes. Take your time cloning
    at the edge between the original reeds on the Background layer and the cloned reeds
    you're adding. The idea here is to stop dragging the tool when a cloned area closely
    matches the original reed areas in color and texture.

10. Press Ctrl(⌘)+S to save your work; you can close the Quick Edit Sunset4.tif window at
    any time without saving, but keep Sunset.psd open in Photoshop's workspace.

Because the Rubber Stamp tool is used to both sample and to paint, it's easy sometimes to mistakenly click and drag when you intended to press Alt(Opt) and click to sample an image area. If you ever accidentally edit a Quick Edit portion of an image by dragging the Rubber Stamp tool through it, or painting foreground color, or changing it in any way—*do not* click on OK in the dialog box Photoshop displays when you close the Quick Edit image window. Quick Edit enables you, as the title indicates, to edit a portion of a large TIFF or Scitex CT file; our use of the Quick Edit feature in the previous example was merely as a sampling source for cloning. If you confirm changes made in a Quick Edit window, Photoshop writes the changes to the larger image file on disk. Although Photoshop cannot write to a CD, large images on your hard disk can indeed be spoiled by accidentally allowing Photoshop to graft the edits you have made back to the larger image.

In figure 8.9, you can see the work in progress. We have made the preview thumbnails on the Layers palette larger than their default size to show you where the cloned reeds have been added. The uneven, opaque strokes on Layer 1 are a result of carefully matching cloned image areas to original ones on the Background layer.

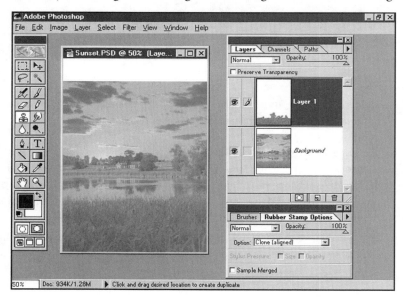

figure 8.9

Your cloning work of the reeds into the composition should be evaluated by the image content, not the geometry of the strokes you use.

Having completed the reeds area of the new Sunset image, it's time to address the clouds area. Instead of using the Rubber Stamp tool, the best way to fill this area is simply by adding a whole section of the larger Sunset4 image to a layer on top of the white area in your composition. This presents unique editing advantages to draw the composition to completion, but also creates an artistic stumbling block or two, which will be solved through the Layer Mask feature in Photoshop. You begin by copying the larger sky into the smaller, portrait-oriented image.

NOTE

If you're unhappy with any of the reed areas that should be blended together, in the following section you will see how the Layer Mask feature can be used to erase unwanted areas on a layer. Apply what you learn to the areas you might not be happy with at present.

Copying and Positioning Quick Edit Image Areas

Before proceeding, it's best to evaluate which part of the larger Sunset image will fill the top of the Sunset.psd image. The visual composition of the Sunset image suggests that more clouds should be a predominant element because there are more clouds toward the top of the original image than toward the sunset in the middle of the picture. Also, the top of the image displays light falling off in the sky, and a shift in color from the warm sunset at image center to the cold tones of dusk toward the top.

Therefore, the upper left of the Sunset4.tif image appears to fit the bill as an additional element to the portrait image you're creating. In the following steps, you use Photoshop's Quick Edit feature to select the upper left of the larger Sunset4 image and copy it to a layer in the current composition. Again, because Sunset4 is much larger than Sunset.psd, the fractional area of Sunset4 will amply cover the area that is presently white in Sunset.psd.

COPYING FROM A QUICK EDIT IMAGE WINDOW

1. Choose File, Import, Quick Edit, and click on Sunset4.tif in the directory window. Click on Open to display the preview dialog box.

2. Drag a marquee in the preview window of the area you want opened (see fig. 8.10). Click on OK after you make the selection.

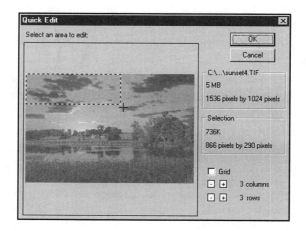

figure 8.10

Choose an area in the Quick Edit window that is tonally consistent with the image area you want to add to and contains visual interest that enhances your composition.

3. Position the Sunset.psd image in the workspace so that you have a clear view of the top, white area of the picture. Then zoom out of the Sunset4 Quick Edit window until the whole Quick Edit document fits in the workspace without window scroll bars. On a monitor running 640×480 video resolution, the Sunset4 window should be at about 33% viewing resolution.

4. With Sunset4 in Photoshop's workspace as the foreground document window, and using the Move tool, drag the contents of the Sunset4 window into the Sunset.psd image window (see fig. 8.11). The copied layer will not "land" correctly in the window because only images of equal dimensions and resolution maintain the relative positioning of copied elements.

5. With the Move tool, drag the copied sky area around in the Sunset.psd image until it covers the entire white area at the top of the document. You will most likely have a little "play" to the copied sky area—it will be a little taller and wider than the area you need to cover. Therefore, compose the visual content, the clouds, to display the most interest within the composition. Figure 8.12 shows an eye-pleasing placement of the copied clouds.

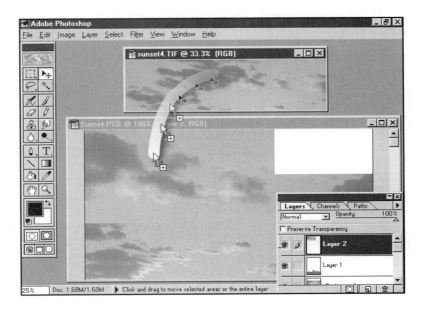

figure 8.11
Copy the sky area you need from the Quick Edit document by dragging with the Move
tool between windows.

figure 8.12
Position the copied clouds on the Sunset.psd image layer in such a way that they look
natural and attractive in the composition.

6. Press Ctrl(⌘)+S to save your work. Keep the composition open in Photoshop (but you can close the Quick Edit document at any time now, without saving it).

Naturally, there is an unsightly edge in the image now, where the bottom of the copied clouds crop your view of the underlying layers. In the following section, you use the Layer Mask feature to blend the copied clouds with the original image details.

Layer Masks and Blending Across Layers

The Layer Mask feature in Photoshop serves as a special eraser-type tool. You can completely remove areas on a layer by hiding them, and then restore areas you have hidden—which makes this feature an *extremely* useful eraser! Nothing you do with the Layer Mask mode of editing is permanent, however; Layer Mask is a preview mode for editing, which shows potential changes that become permanent only after you apply the editing changes.

The Layer Mask operates according to the tone of the current foreground color on the toolbox. As an analogy, think of a traditional school eraser as you brush a chalkboard. The harder you brush, the more completely you hide the chalk writing on the board. The hardest you can brush with a paint tool in Layer Mask mode in an image is specified by choosing a black foreground color. Strokes made with black completely erase layer content, whereas lighter shades of black partially hide layer image areas. If you specify a shade of black that is less than 50 percent, you begin to restore hidden layer areas, until with white as the current foreground color, you completely restore areas you have hidden in Layer Mask mode.

It's important to note that there is an extended function for Layer Masking that creates a variation on this hiding and display of image areas. The Opacity of the paint application tool also creates partially hidden or partially exposed areas in Layer Mask mode, but this extended feature does *not* operate identically to the foreground color you specify while applying or removing the Layer Mask.

If you apply black at 50% opacity to a layer while in Layer Mask mode, for example, you make the nontransparent pixels on this layer 50% opaque. The visual effect is equivalent to applying 50% black to the layer at 100% brush opacity. To *restore* visibility of partially hidden layer areas, however, you always need a foreground color lighter than 50% black, regardless of the current brush opacity, to partially, or completely, restore layer image areas.

In other words, applying black or white at 0% opacity does nothing to restore or hide layer image areas. White restores and black hides. The opacity setting for the brush, which is something you will use in the following steps, simply provides additional control over which areas are displayed in the finished image.

In the following steps, you selectively hide areas on the copied cloud layer, finesse these areas a little by partially restoring and hiding them, and then apply the mask to further the integration of clouds on two different image layers.

HIDING AND RESTORING THE CLOUDS

1. Double-click on the layer title for the reeds, and type **Reeds** in the Name field of the Layer Options dialog box. Rename the layer that contains the clouds as **Clouds,** using the same procedure. Later in this chapter, you will add another layer to the Sunset.psd image, and by giving the current layers user-friendly names, you will save time navigating the different layers later.

2. Double-click on the Zoom tool to move your viewing resolution to 100% of the Sunset document. Then drag the image window borders away from the picture to maximize your view, from edge to edge, of the image.

   Windows users can double-click on the image window's title bar to automatically maximize the window view.

3. With the Clouds layer as the current editing layer, click on the Layer Mask icon on the Layers palette.

4. Press **B** (Paintbrush tool) and choose the **35** pixel diameter brush from the Brushes palette. In proportion to the overall target image size, this is a relatively large brush. Your masking work will go quickly, and because larger brushes on the Brushes palette have the soft tip attribute, the edge between masked and unmasked areas will be seamless.

5. Drag the Paintbrush across the bottom edge of the clouds area on the layer (see fig. 8.13). If you begin to see the white background, this is okay, and expected. In Layer Mask mode, you can restore these areas when white is chosen as the current foreground color.

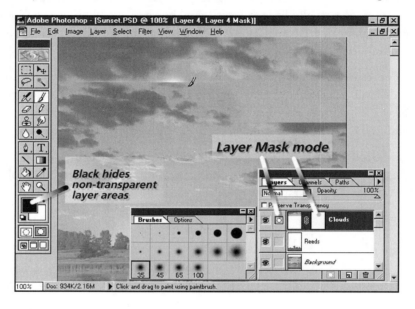

figure 8.13
Use the Layer Mask feature to hide the edge between the clouds on the Clouds layer and those in the Background image.

6. When the edge of the clouds image area has been completely hidden, it's time to restore areas that show the white of the Background areas. Press **X** (Switch Foreground/ Background colors), press **5** to make the current opacity of the paint application tool 50%, and then stroke over the white areas until the restored areas on the Clouds layer merge visually with the Background layer clouds.

You might want to increase the opacity for the Paintbrush to more completely restore certain areas, and press X to switch colors to hide other areas on the layer, to complete the visual integration of the clouds on the two layers. You will not achieve a *completely* seamless blend because the color of the sky on the two layers is different. Simply try to attain the closest match you can. There's a trick in the next section that disguises the layer edge where colors don't precisely match (see fig. 8.14).

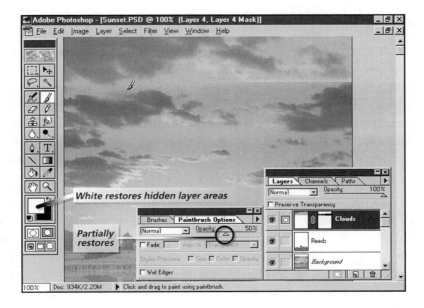

figure 8.14

Use white foreground color and the Paintbrush at partial opacity to partially restore cloud areas you have hidden.

7. When you're confident that the integration of the clouds is complete, click on the thumbnail of the Layer Mask (the far right thumbnail on the Clouds layer title) and drag the thumbnail into the Delete current layer icon (the trash icon) at the bottom of the Layers palette. Don't worry—the layer will not be deleted—it's the Layer Mask that is the current element in the document.

8. In the attention box that pops up when you drag something into the trash, click on the Apply button. This action confirms that hidden and partially hidden image areas on the Clouds layer will be deleted from the picture. You're making a permanent change to the contents of the layer.

9. Press Ctrl(⌘)+S to save your work; keep the sunset image open in Photoshop.

Using Color Balance to Match Layer Content

The RGB color mode (the arrangement of colors used to display the Sunset image on-screen) expresses both pixel color and pixel tone (how bright or dense a color is) with a single mathematical expression. You cannot adjust the component colors in an image (the reds, greens, blues, and mixtures of these primary colors) without changing the tone of the colors a little. Fortunately, Photoshop's Color Balance command has the Preserve Luminosity feature. This check box enables you to change the color cast of a selection or entire image, according to color opposite values, without disturbing the relative brightnesses with which colors are displayed.

As mentioned in the previous section, the goal was to get a tonal match between the Clouds layer and the Background layer. Now it's time to further the integration of the layers' visual content by correcting the colors on the Clouds layer to match the clouds and sky on the Background. Let's think about the problem for a moment. The clouds on the clouds layer show some warm colors, due to their proximity to the sunset in the original Sunset4.tif image. The color cast of the sky looks wrong, positioned against the original Background layer sky and clouds, because the position in the sky of these elements is toward the top, where there is less warm-colored illumination. Therefore, to match the color cast so as to create a seamless integration between the layers, the image areas on the Clouds layer need to be a little colder. Here's how to use the Color Balance command to achieve this goal.

COLOR BALANCING THE CLOUDS LAYER

1. Make sure that the top of the sunset image is in clear view in Photoshop's workspace, by scrolling and widening the window borders to display some of the neutral-colored document background. Press Ctrl(⌘)+B to display the Color Balance command.

2. Check the Preserve Luminosity check box if it's not already checked, and then click on the Shadows radio button. The darker tones in the image display the most predominant color values because it's a sunset picture; adjusting the colors in this tonal range will produce the most dramatic results.

3. Drag the Cyan/Red color slider to about −3 and then drag the Yellow/Blue slider to about +18 (see fig. 8.15). By moving reds and yellows on the clouds layer with cyans and blues, you make the image layer colder in color cast, decrease brightness only slightly, and make the layer look appropriate from a color standpoint in its current position in the document.

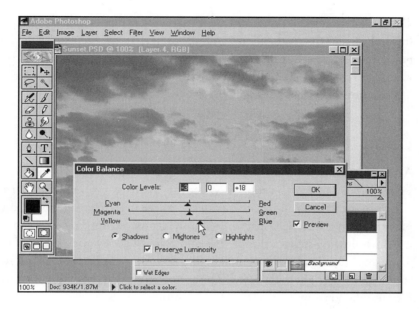

figure 8.15
Moving specific color values toward their color opposites changes the color cast (the degree of warmth or coldness) that the colors display.

4. If the seam is still apparent in the image, click on the Midtones radio button, and then balance this tonal range more toward blue and cyan. When the seam is basically invisible, click on OK to apply the changes.

5. Press Ctrl(⌘)+S to save your work; keep Sunset.psd open in Photoshop for further editing.

TIP

The Color Balance command is the only feature in Photoshop that does not progressively change the color properties of pixels in an image. For example, the application of a different hue from the Hue/Saturation command cannot be "undone" by taking a second visit to this command and choosing options that are the inverse of the original settings you made. Similarly, the Levels command progressively adds or removes contrast, and two applications of specific settings will never return an image to its unedited state.

The Color Balance command, however, affects the *relative proportions* of primary color opposites, and the proportions can be restored at any time by using inverse amounts of color settings from the first time you apply the changes in the Color Balance command.

There is one thing that tonal and color balancing the clouds layer cannot correct in this image, and that is the natural fall-off of light in the scene. Notice that the sky becomes exceptionally dim at the top of the original image. To create in this picture what nature did not, we need to play with adding some Photoshop colors to the top of the composition, to complete the assignment.

Using the Gradient Tool in Multiply Mode

As the sky makes the transition in this image from horizon to the top of the frame, we see more and more evening sky, yet the clouds are still visible. Currently, the clouds in the sky you added are identical to those in the original image, but the fall-off of light in the scene is interrupted from center to top. To correct this, you will use the following steps to sample the cold color of the evening sky, and then apply a foreground-to-transparent gradient fill to the top area of the document to simulate the diminishing light in the scene. The bonus here is that the gradient fill will further disguise the bottom edge of the clouds on the Clouds layer.

Now you will make the Sunset image picture perfect by manually adjusting the lighting.

CORRECTING THE EDITED LIGHTING CONDITIONS

1. Click on the Create new layer icon on the Layers palette. This adds a layer named Layer 1 to the image. Photoshop's auto-numbering of Layers and Channels starts with "1" if the application detects user-titled layers or channels in the current image.

2. On the Layers palette, choose Multiply as the merge mode for the new layer. Darker colors you add to this layer will multiply the density of the color with all colors displayed on layers under Layer 1, whereas lighter colors will disappear.

3. With the Rectangular Marquee tool, drag a selection to encompass the entire area of clouds on the Clouds layer, plus about one screen inch (at 100% viewing resolution) of Background sky area. The current editing layer should still be the new Layer 1, and *not* one of the layers you created in previous steps.

4. Double-click on the Gradient tool to choose it and to display the Options palette for the tool.

5. Hold Alt(Opt) to toggle to the Eyedropper tool, and then click over the sky area in the image. This defines the cold, bluish color as the current foreground color on the toolbox. Release the Alt(Opt) key at any time now to return to the Gradient tool.

6. On the Options palette, choose Foreground to Transparent from the drop-down list; make certain that Opacity is set to 100% and that paint application mode is Normal.

7. Drag a line straight down, beginning about 10 pixels from the top of the document, to about 10 pixels short of the bottom of the marquee selection (see fig. 8.16). The marquee selection keeps the gradient fill from flooding areas of the picture you don't want shaded.

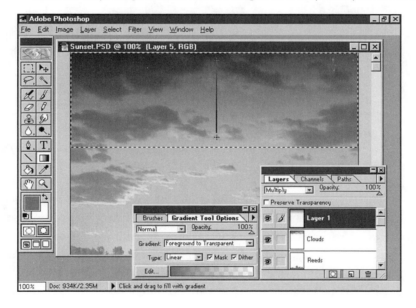

figure 8.16

The Foreground to Transparent Gradient tool option fills the selected area of the layer with color that vanishes toward the bottom of the selection.

8. Press Ctrl(⌘)+D to deselect the marquee in the document.

9. Double-click on the Hand tool to zoom out to a full view of the Sunset picture in the workspace; then drag the Opacity slider on the Layers palette for Layer 1 down to about 40% (see fig. 8.17). As you can see, the artificial light fall-off you created completely removes any seams from the image, and also directs the audience's attention to the star of the image, the bright sunset.

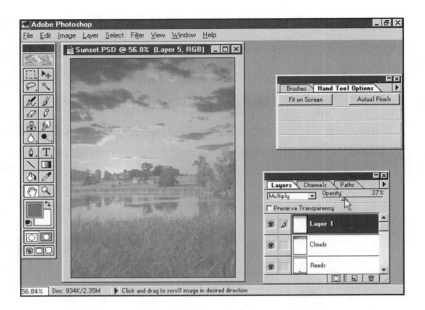

figure 8.17
You can "tune" the sunset by adjusting the amount of opacity the gradient fill displays in the composite image.

10. Press Ctrl(⌘)+S to save your work. You're finished; mission accomplished!

In figure 8.18, you can see the rewards of your hard work. The image at left is the original Sunset image; the one on the right is the edited version. The scenes look as though two different orientations of the camera were used to take two pictures of the same scene. But *you* know that with the kind of post-production work outlined here, you can use one photograph to create several "different" ones.

The "problem/solution" methodology you have learned in this chapter so far is terrific when you need to change the orientation of a photograph but want to keep the central elements of visual interest in the image. But what does a designer do when the image aspect is fine, the orientation is cool, but the background of the image is unacceptable? Again, the answer lies in Photoshop—and in the following section.

figure 8.18
You can create different orientations for a single image after you master the layers and cloning features in Photoshop.

Correcting a Problem Background

Well-composed, pleasing images contain foreground elements that exist in an environment which complements, but doesn't detract from, the central element. If you look through almost any collection of pictures, you are sure to find a perfectly wonderful moment frozen in time that suffers from a busy or inappropriate background. Many informal portraits are spoiled because the image background makes the star of the picture look as though a heating pipe is impaled in his head, or the sports car in a distant parking lot is growing out of her ear.

Photoshop puts an arsenal of tools at your disposal to correct backgrounds that steal the show from the intended subject. With Photoshop, you can turn an awkward-looking background into one that complements and supports the focal point of your image. There are a number of different routes you can take when you're working with problem backgrounds:

◆ You can alter the existing background to make it more harmonious with the subject.

◆ You can paint in a new background.

◆ You can remove the existing background and replace it with a new image, as shown in Chapters 6, "Retouching an Heirloom Photograph," and 7, "Combining Photographs," as well as in Chapter 18.

The approach you decide to take depends in part on your image, and how the final image will be used. There is no right or wrong way to go about correcting backgrounds. You will usually want to try several approaches, to determine which creative solution produces the results that are most pleasing to you or to your client, and which technique brings a graphical idea closer to your intended goal.

The following sections explore some quick methods for modifying an existing image background. The image you use is of a carousel horse. As you can see in figure 8.19, the background surrounding the horse is a beautiful carousel—and that's exactly where the problem lies. The carousel is *so* attractive that it competes for attention with the area of foreground interest, the horse.

figure 8.19
The busy carousel background distracts the viewer's eye from the horse.

Defining and Separating the Foreground Image Element

Before you begin to correct the background, you need to create and save a selection that separates the horse from the background. Ordinarily, when you separate images from their background you want to take your time and make a very precise selection by using the Pen tool. In this example, however, you are looking for a *quick* solution that creates a more aesthetically pleasing finished image. Because the background and the horse share a similar color scheme, and because the edits you make to the background will *not* remove the background or change its color composition, you don't need to spend a lot of time defining an elegant, flawless selection of the horse.

Making extremely accurate selections is one of the most time-consuming tasks performed in Photoshop. The key to increasing your productivity in Photoshop is to understand *when* you have to make precise selections and when you can save time by creating a less refined selection. Usually, when you are combining photos or performing operations that create hard-edged transitions along selection borders, the Pen tool is the best choice of edge-definition tools. In the following steps, however, you can use the Lasso and Lasso Polygon tools and Quick Mask mode to quickly select the horse from the background.

Before you begin, if you're more comfortable with alternative methods of selection, feel free to follow the steps, using any of Photoshop's tools. Additionally, Horses.psd contains a saved selection of the horse in channel #4 if you prefer to move straight to the editing techniques in this assignment. The selection steps will probably take longer to read than to perform—so if you haven't used this method of making quick selections before, please read on, and let's get to the task at hand.

Using the Lasso Tools and Quick Mask Mode to Make a Selection

CD-ROM

1. In Photoshop, open Horse.psd from the CHAP08 folder (directory) of the Companion CD. Double-click on the Hand tool to zoom in to the Fit on Screen view.

2. Click on the Maximize button in the upper right corner of the image window. Macintosh users can drag the Size Box to expand the window so that there is some neutral document background color around the image.

3. Double-click on the Quick Mask mode icon on the toolbox to put the current image into this special selection mode and to display the Quick Mask Options box.

4. Click on the Color Indicates Selected Areas button if it is not already selected; then click on OK to exit the Options box and return to the image in Quick Mask mode. Press **D** (Default colors), and then press **X** (Switch Foreground/Background colors), so that the current foreground color is white, and black is the background color.

5. Press **L** (twice, if necessary) to choose the Polygon Lasso tool. Click just outside the bottom edge of the image at the point where the horse's chest touches the bottom of the image. Then click in the document background outside the image, just past the lower left corner.

6. Click a third point in the document background slightly outside the left side of the image where the horse's mane enters the picture. Click a final time back at the first point at which you clicked.

   The Polygon Lasso tool cursor display a small circle next to it when you are over the starting point of a selection marquee. When you start or finish a selection on the document background outside the image, you are assured of including the outermost edge pixels of the image in the selection.

7. Press Delete (Backspace) to fill the selection with Quick Mask, and then press **L** to change from the Polygon Lasso tool to the Lasso tool. Press Ctrl(⌘)+D to deselect the current marquee in the image window.

8. Drag the Lasso tool along the horse's mane. Try to stay right on the edge of the mane (but don't worry if you miss a little). If you feel that you are going *way* off-course, release the mouse button; the selection will close automatically. Press Delete (Backspace) to fill the selection with Quick Mask. Look ahead to figure 8.20 to see the general shape of the area you should select.

   Because marquee selections vanish the moment you start to define a new marquee, you don't have to press Ctrl(⌘)+D to deselect the current marquee in this example. You should make it a practice, however, when you're working in Standard editing mode, where image areas can be lifted and deleted from image layers.

9. Work your way around the edge of the horse, creating selections and filling with Quick Mask. Zoom in to image areas, if necessary. Don't worry if you have covered some of the background with Quick Mask, or if the center of the horse is not completely filled with Quick Mask. When you have traced all the way around the horse, the image should look like figure 8.20.

figure 8.20
Use the Lasso tools in combination with Quick Mask editing overlay to mask the horse.

10. With the Lasso tool, draw selection areas around any of the interior areas of the horse that are not covered by Quick Mask. It's okay to include in the selection areas that are already covered with Quick Mask. Press the Delete key to fill the selections with Quick Mask.

11. If the current Quick Mask tint overlay is too far from the edge of the horse in any area, leaving a gap of unmasked areas, use the Lasso tool or the Paintbrush with a small tip chosen from the Brushes palette to add Quick Mask, using black as the foreground paint color.

    Conversely, if there are areas you have masked that *shouldn't* be there, press X to switch foreground/background colors, and paint over these areas with white to remove the Quick Mask.

12. When you finish masking the horse, click on the Standard mode icon on the toolbox. A selection marquee (marching ants) appears around the horse where the edges of the Quick Mask overlay were located in the image.

13. On the bottom of the Channels palette (press F7 if the palette isn't currently on-screen), click on the Save selection as channel icon.

14. Still on the Channels palette, double-click on the #4 channel title to display the Channel Options dialog box. Type **Horse** in the Name field of the dialog box (see fig. 8.21), make sure that the Color Indicates Selected Areas radio button is chosen, and then click on OK.

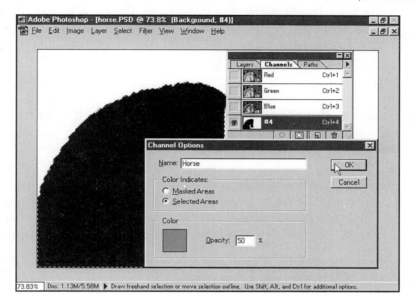

figure 8.21
Go ahead and name the saved selections in the Channel Options dialog box, which is accessed from the Channels palette flyout menu.

15. Click on the Layers tab of the Layers/Channels/Paths palette, and then click on the Background layer title to return to the composite view of the image.

16. Choose File, Save As from the menu; then save the document as Horse.psd in the Photoshop file format to your hard disk. Leave the image open; you will use it in the following sections.

Now that you have a reasonably close selection around the horse's head, you're all set to experiment with different approaches that will diminish the visual prominence of the background.

Editing the Image Background

When you work with an image, color and tonal adjustments are usually performed to make image areas more realistic. These same adjustment commands can also be used (and misused) creatively to play down image areas, or to create artistic effects. In the following steps, you will see how the Image menu's Hue/Saturation command can be used to make the background less distracting.

REMOVING DISTRACTING COLORS FROM THE BACKGROUND

1. Press Ctrl(⌘) and click on the Horse title on the Channels palette. This loads the selection information you saved earlier.

2. Press Ctrl(⌘)+Shift+I (Select, Inverse). This command inverts the selection marquee so that the background, not the horse, is now the area that will be affected by any editing you do. Press Ctrl(⌘)+H (View, Hide Edges) to hide the distracting marquee selection above the image.

3. Press Ctrl(⌘)+U (Image, Adjust, Hue/Saturation). The Hue/Saturation dialog box appears. Drag it by the title bar down into the lower left corner, so that it doesn't obscure the image you're retouching.

4. Put a check mark in the Preview check box if it is not already checked. When Preview is checked, changes made in the dialog box are shown in the image as they will appear when you apply the changes. Put a check in the Colorize check box. When this check box is checked, Photoshop applies tints and shades of a single hue to the selected image areas.

5. Drag the Hue slider to the left until you find a pleasing blue color (−155 is good). By changing the background to shades and tints of one color, attention is drawn to the more colorful horse.

6. Drag the Saturation slider to the left to −43. This decreases the uniqueness of blue in all colors displayed that make up the color image. In English, other colors are introduced into the selection, in amounts that increasingly compete with the blue you specified, to create a duller and less attention-getting background.

7. Drag the Lightness slider to the left to −70 (see fig. 8.22). Decreasing the Lightness clips the brightness component of the blue color in the background. The background will be much less intrusive, and will allow the stallion to be the focal interest in the picture.

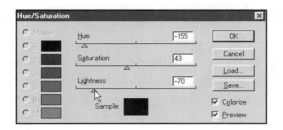

figure 8.22

Darkening and desaturating a background forces the viewer's attention to lighter-colored foreground elements.

8. Click on OK to apply the change to the image background.

9. Choose File, Save As and then save the image to your hard disk as Horseblu.psd. Press Ctrl(⌘)+ W or choose File, Close from the menu.

The more you move the Hue/Saturation Lightness slider to the left, the more a background appears to be in shadows. In this example, if you specify a –30 value, the image background is still light enough to be easily identified. A –30 Lightness setting would be a good one to use if it were important for the viewer of the image to have a fairly accurate impression of the actual carousel that the horse is part of. This setting would diminish, but not eliminate, the visual importance of the background areas. If it is only important that the viewer see a carousel horse and have a vague *impression*—a "sense"—of the carousel, then decreasing the Lightness value to around –70 forces the audience's attention squarely upon the horse.

All the values in the previous steps are purely subjective; if you experiment with the sliders, you may find a combination that is more visually appealing to you. Additionally, because the focus of our attention in this image is a white horse, a negative Lightness value was chosen to provide foreground/background contrast. If the image were of a black carousel horse, increasing the Lightness value would provide the best overall image contrast. In either event, the only way to decide upon the Hue/Saturation values is through experimentation.

Adjustment Layers as a Composition Editing Option

When you experiment with the changes you can create in an image by using Photoshop's tonal and color image-adjustment features, you can work directly on the image or an image layer (as you did in the preceding example) or you can take advantage of a new Photoshop feature—Adjustment layers. Adjustment layers are similar to Layer Masks in that they allow you to specify and view proposed changes to your image without causing permanent changes.

You can continue to refine adjustments, or discard the changes at any time. When an Adjustment layer is in place, you can turn its visibility icon on and off. With the visibility icon on, it is as if you were viewing the underlying image layer through a special camera lens filter. After you have created an effect you like with an Adjustment layer, you can make the change permanent by merging the Adjustment layer with the underlying image layer or the background. You can have as many different Adjustment layers as your system resources can support. Be sure to check out Chapter 9, "Working with Adjustment Layers," for more information about how and when you might incorporate this new feature into your work.

Using Filters to Alter Backgrounds

Tonal controls, such as Levels or Brightness/Contrast, and color controls, such as Color Balance and Desaturate, can also be used to alter intrusive backgrounds. Changes made with these adjustment controls push an image area in or out of the limelight while still maintaining the image's photographic legibility and plausibility.

As you will see in Chapter 13, "Creative Plug-Ins," however, Photoshop also offers a plethora of special effects plug-ins that can be used to play up or play down an image background through *non*-photorealistic filtering. In the next set of steps, you get a sneak peak at how one of these filters can transform the visually distracting background around the carousel horse into a very painterly, fantasy background. Not only will filtering the background make the audience focus on the horse, but the contrast between the fantasy background and the photographic realness of the horse will make this a visually compelling image.

The new version 4 Paint Daub filter, along with many other Photoshop filters, does its transformation magic by looking on both the inside and outside of marquee lines when it calculates what to do with pixels that are on the edge between the selected and masked areas. Most of Photoshop's filters do *not* see a selection marquee as a limiting border. Clearly, this is not a problem when you are applying filters to an entire image, but it can be one when you're applying a filter effect to a selected area. Depending on the filter and on the settings used (usually the amount of filter strength setting you specify), an unwanted fringe can appear around the masked area.

To prevent fringing around areas where a filter is *not* to be applied, use the Paintbrush and Rubber Stamp tools to *extend* the area being filtered into the unfiltered area. Then, when the filter is used, the edge pixels on the selection will be composed of the background pixels—and not the unfiltered ones. Extending the background area will, of course, ruin the area you are not filtering. But if you have copied to a layer the area that will remain *un*filtered, you can merge it back into the scene *after* you have used the filter on the background. In essence, you are not so much preventing the unwanted fringing effect from occurring, as you are forcing it to be created in an area that you can easily cover with a saved copy.

In the following steps you will see how to use the Rubber Stamp tool in concert with Photoshop's layers to help produce a stunning image without a telltale edge effect. And best of all, the effect only takes a few moments to accomplish.

EXTENDING A FILTER EDGE SELECTION

1. Open the Horse.psd file you saved to your hard disk. Drag the Background title on the Layers palette into the Create new layer icon at the bottom of the Layers palette. This copies the contents of the Background to a layer named Background Copy.

    You made a copy of the background so that if you make a mistake in any of the following steps, you won't damage the original image.

2. Choose a selection tool (the Lasso tool is good), and then with Background Copy as the current editing layer, press Ctrl(⌘) and click on the Horse channel title on the Channels palette. The image area on the Background Copy that contains the carousel horse is selected (see fig. 8.23).

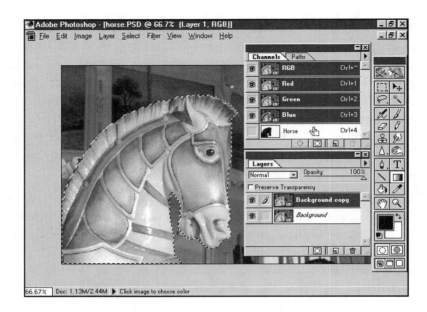

figure 8.23
To load a selection you defined and saved to an alpha channel, press Ctrl(⌘) and click on the Channel's title on the Channels palette.

3. Right-click (Macintosh: hold Ctrl and click) and choose Layer via copy from the Context menu. The new layer, Layer 1, contains the horse surrounded by transparent pixels. This layer will be used in a later step to restore an unfiltered copy of the horse to the image.

4. Click on the eye icon next to the Layer 1 title to hide Layer 1 from view. Click on the Background Copy title on the Layers palette to make it the active layer.

5. Double-click on the Rubber Stamp tool on the toolbox. Then, on the Options palette, make sure that the mode is Normal, Opacity is at 100%, and that the Option is set to Clone (aligned).

6. On the Brushes palette, choose the third tip from the left on the second row. This is a fairly small, soft-edged brush.

   In the next step, you use the Rubber Stamp tool to extend the background area into areas currently occupied by the horse. Figure 8.24 shows the direction in which you should move the Rubber Stamp tool. Be sure to start your strokes at the edge of the horse. The beginnings of the arrows mark good places to define the sampling point for the Rubber Stamp.

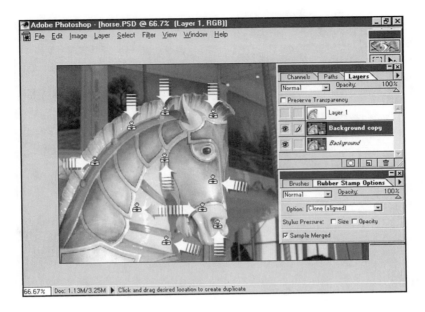

figure 8.24

Set the sampling point of the Rubber Stamp about half an inch from the horse, and then clone in the direction in which the arrows point.

7. Set the sampling point of the Rubber Stamp tool by pressing Alt(Opt) and clicking in the blue area at the bottom of the image, about half a screen inch from the front of the horse. Move the Rubber Stamp to the left, to the point where the front of the horse starts, and then drag the Rubber Stamp into the horse image about half an inch.

8. Continue cloning around the perimeter of the horse. Reset your sample point as often as necessary, and make sure that you make your strokes in a direction that follows the apparent direction and angle of the background image elements. When you finish, the image should be similar to the one in figure 8.25.

9. Choose File, Save As. Name the image Daub.psd and save it your hard disk. Don't close the image. You need it for the next set of steps.

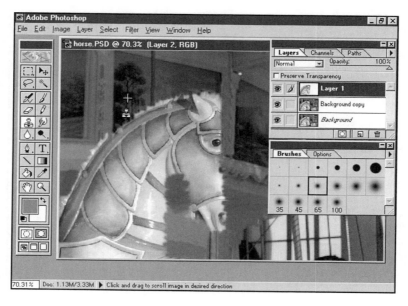

figure 8.25
To prevent a fringe around a nonfiltered area, use the Rubber Stamp tool to extend the background into the nonfiltered area.

TIP

If you would like to try out a number of artistic filters and you have adequate system resources, you might want to make copies of the Background Copy layer by right-clicking (Macintosh: hold Ctrl and click) on the Layer 1 title, and choosing Duplicate Layer, and then apply a different filter to each copy of the background image.

Now you are ready to filter the background with the filter of your choice.

APPLYING THE PAINT DAUB FILTER

1. Daub.psd should be open and Background Copy should be the active layer. From the Filter menu, choose Artistic and then choose Paint Daub. The Paint Daub dialog box appears.

2. In the Options field, use the slider or click in the entry box and set the Brush Size to 30. The larger the brush, the more abstract the Paint Daub effect.

3. Set the Sharpness to 4. Use low sharpness settings to avoid harsh, posterized edges in the effect. Then, from the Brush Type drop-down list, choose Dark Rough; this will darken and increase the abstract effect (see fig. 8.26). Click on OK to apply the effect.

figure 8.26

The Paint Daubs filter can remove selection area details to provide an abstract image quality that moves attention toward foreground composition elements.

4. If you like the effect that has been created on the image layer, press Ctrl(⌘)+ S to save your work. If you want to see what other effects can be created by using different brushes or settings, press Ctrl(⌘)+Z to undo the application of the filter, and then press Ctrl+Alt+F (⌘+Opt+F) to reopen the Paint Daubs dialog box.

5. Click on the visibility icon next to Layer 2. The unfiltered horse on Layer 2 appears on top of the filtered background. Voila! You have created a stunning image, just by "correcting" the background (see fig. 8.27).

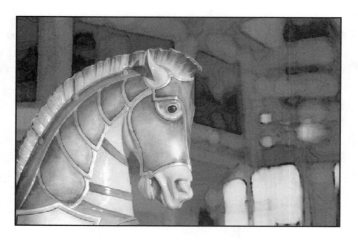

figure 8.27

The application of the Paint Daubs filter has darkened and abstracted the background, making it a good supporting element for the image.

6. From the Layers Palette flyout, choose Flatten Image. This combines all visible layers into one. If you had the visibility icon turned off for the Background layer, you will be asked whether you want to discard hidden layers; because you don't need the hidden layer, click on OK.

7. Choose File, Save As and save the image to your hard disk as a TIFF format file called Daub.tif. TIFF format files are easily imported into a wide variety of desktop publishing and electronic document preparation programs.

T I P

Unlike many of Photoshop's dialog boxes, the Paint Daub filter box does not display a preview of the changes you make in the document window in Photoshop's workspace. The preview (*proxy*) window in the filter dialog box does, however, show how your image will change if you apply the filter. You can move your view to different parts of the image in the preview box by clicking and dragging in the preview box, and you can zoom your view of the image in and out by clicking on the + and − buttons below the dialog box's preview window.

The Paint Daub filter is not the only filter or effect that requires extending the background to prevent unwanted fringing at selection edges. Use the techniques you learned in the previous steps when you use other Artistic filters or the Blur filters. In figure 8.28, you can see four background "corrections"—the two you have performed and two others that we tried.

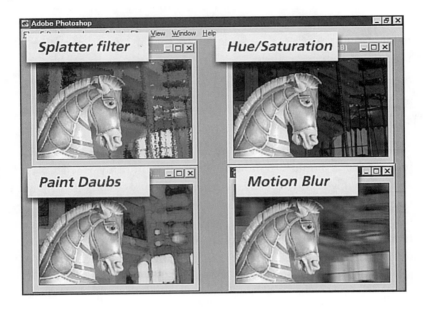

figure 8.28

Photoshop offers many plug-in filters, and a multitude of ways to edit an image background to accentuate the foreground elements.

If you want to try the other two effects for yourself, here are the settings that we used:

◆ For the Motion Blur background, use the Motion Blur filter set to an Angle of 0° and a Distance of 60 pixels.

◆ For the pebbled glass look for the background, use the Splatter filter with a Spray setting of 12 and a Smoothness setting of 4.

You can, of course, take background correction a step or two farther and use several filters on the background instead of just one. For example, To reinforce the idea that the background is a painting, for example, you can apply the Texturizer filter (Filter, Texture, Texturize), using sandstone, burlap, or canvas Texture settings, to the background after you use one of the Artistic filters, such as Paint Daubs or Watercolor. Use your artistic instincts and above all, use a little of the "less is more" philosophy. Don't go overboard with filter effects—after all, when your goal is to reduce the importance of the background, then using too many filter effects might produce the opposite effect!

Summary

This chapter showed you how the evaluation process—what is missing from an image, or what should be removed—determines not only which tools you select, but also which of your own creative techniques you use to correct an image. Hopefully, you have also seen that there is no absolute, proper, or even "professional" way to take a visual diamond in the rough and polish it to the point of commercial success. In a very real way, the understanding of the visual content of an image you bring to Photoshop is more important than the image itself, when your goal is to edit an image from "what it can be" to "what it is."

In Chapter 9, you will see how to use Photoshop's Adjustment layers feature to preview tonal and color corrections to an image before you finalize your work. It's as easy as painting on a layer, and offers the control over an image that selections and masks only hint at.

CHAPTER 9

WORKING WITH ADJUSTMENT LAYERS

Image layers can have properties beyond the visual data you see in them—they can have opacity and a merging mode, such as Multiply or Overlay. Photoshop 4 extends the capability of image layers in the form of Adjustment layers, "special instance" layers that are intended to hold color and tone information, but not necessarily image information.

If you want to preview corrections or enhancements without permanently altering an image, Adjustment layers give you that capability. This chapter takes you through the process of making extensive color and tonal refinements in an image in a special preview mode through the use of Adjustment layers.

Painting Your Way to Color Changes

Adjustment layers are a unique on-screen application of any Image, Adjust command. Instead of applying an Adjust command to an entire layer, you first define the options of, say, the Levels command. Suppose, for example, that you want to decrease the white point in part of an image to 225 (to brighten the image). After you have specified this setting for Levels, you then paint on the Levels Adjustment layer over the areas in the image that you want to make brighter. The Adjustment layer feature saves you the time of masking the area you want to change in the image; you simply paint the changes you want to make.

The following sections show you how to use contrast, saturation, and many other tonal variations in the same way that you presently use foreground color.

Colorizing an Image with Adjustment Layers

One of the controls in the Hue/Saturation command is called Colorize. Instead of shifting the original hues in the image independently of one another, Colorize defines a base hue for the entire image, and then assigns shades of the same hue throughout the image, based on original brightness strengths. The effect is similar to looking at an image through colored cellophane, and Colorize is particularly well-suited to change the color of an image area that is largely monochromatic. Hard candy, brushed steel, and many types of flowers display strong monochromatic color properties; Colorize enables you to completely change the color of such objects without losing photographic realism.

Suppose that a prop designer comes to you with an image of a pot of geraniums, and wants you to illustrate that their service includes silk flowers, in any color, to order. The Flourpot.tif image in the CHAP09 folder on the Companion CD is a study in monochrome composition—strong in design elements, but lacking in color diversity (the geraniums are all red). Follow this set of steps to leverage the power of the Adjustment layers and add a different color to one of the geraniums.

USING ADJUSTMENT LAYERS IN HUE/SATURATION MODE

CD-ROM

1. Open the Flourpot.tif image from the CHAP09 folder on the Companion CD, type **50** in the Zoom percentage field, and press Enter (Return). Drag the document to the upper left of the workspace so that your view of it is unobscured when you work with different dialog boxes in these steps.

2. Press F7 to display the Layers/Channels/Paths palette (if it is not already on-screen). On the Layers palette, click on the menu flyout and choose New Adjustment Layer.

3. Choose Hue/Saturation from the Type drop-down list (see fig 9.1), and click on OK.

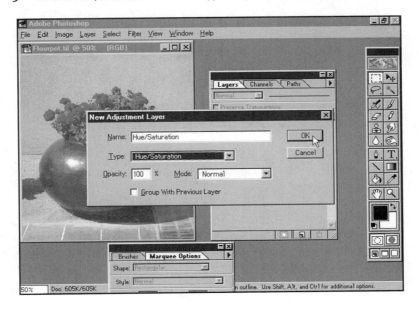

figure 9.1

Choose from any of Photoshop's Adjust menu items to assign to an Adjustment layer.

4. In the Hue/Saturation Layer dialog box, click on the Colorize check box, and drag the Hue slider to –86 (see fig 9.2). In the image window you will see a purplish cast over the entire image. Click on OK to return to the workspace.

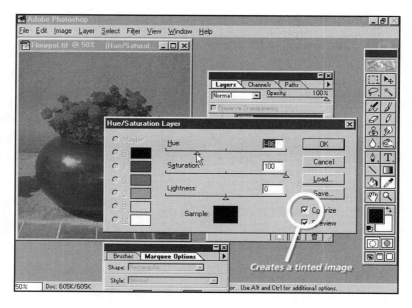

figure 9.2
Apply the Colorize option to the Adjustment layer and specify a hue with which image areas will be shaded.

5. Press **D** (Default colors), press Ctrl(⌘)+A to select the entire Adjustment layer, and then press Alt(Opt)+Delete (Backspace). Filling the Adjustment layer with black removes the effect of the Hue/Saturation command and the Colorize option (see fig. 9.3). Press Ctrl(⌘)+D to deselect the marquee.

6. Press **X** (Swap Foreground/Background colors), and double-click on the Paintbrush tool to select it and to display the Options palette.

7. Specify 100% Opacity, and Normal paint mode. On the Brushes palette, click on the second row, third from left tip.

8. Stroke over one of the geraniums (see fig. 9.4). Because you're applying white to the Adjustment layer, the effect of the Hue/Saturation command is applied to only those areas in which you paint.

9. Press Ctrl(⌘)+Shift+S (File, Save As), and save the document to your hard disk as Flourpot.psd. Keep the image open.

figure 9.3
Fill the Adjustment layer with black to remove the effect of the Hue/Saturation command across the entire image.

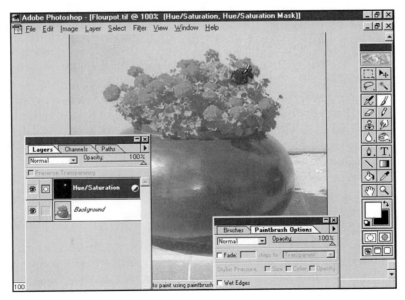

figure 9.4
Applying white to the Adjustment layer activates the Adjust menu command you specified for the layer.

The preceding example is as complicated as setting up and using an Adjustment layer gets. You have no option as to how tones are defined on Adjustment layers; black is always, "apply no effect," and white is always, "apply the effect at 100% strength." All shades between black and white apply a partial amount of the Adjust menu command you specify for a layer. In the following sections, you see how to work with several Adjustment layers on an image, and how to change and manipulate the contents of these layers.

Duplicating and Modifying an Adjustment Layer

Properties of Adjustment layers are very similar to those of ordinary image layers. You can re-order them in an image, duplicate them, and change their function with only a click or two. The picture of the geraniums looks interesting now, but the odd purple geranium doesn't really show the diversity of the client's silk flowers. In the following steps, you add a different color to one of the other flowers by stacking an additional Adjustment layer on top of the first one. Although this can be accomplished by going through the steps in the previous example, let's work a little more with Photoshop's other features to show the flexibility of its icon-driven interface.

Here's how to copy and edit the original Adjustment layer:

DIFFERENT ADJUSTMENTS FOR DIFFERENT EFFECTS

1. Drag the Adjustment Layer title on the Layers palette into the Create new layer icon at the bottom of the palette. A new layer, Hue/Saturation copy, appears at the top of the Layers palette list; it is the current editing layer.

2. Double-click on the Hue/Saturation copy layer title on the Layers palette to display the Hue/Saturation Layer dialog box.

3. Drag the Hue slider to +72 (see fig. 9.5). In the document, the geranium you colored is going to look awful, but this is okay. It has a coat of green on top of a coat of purple, but you will change the location of the white on the new Adjustment layer shortly. Click on OK to apply the change to the layer.

4. With the background color still defined as black from the previous steps, press Ctrl(⌘)+A, and then press Delete (Backspace) to erase the contents of the Adjustment layer to black. Press Ctrl(⌘)+D to deselect the marquee now.

5. Zoom in to 100% viewing resolution; then, with the Paintbrush tool, stroke over a different geranium (see fig. 9.6). Because areas outside the area in which you're painting are black, the purple geranium is still purple. Only those areas to which you apply brightness take on the green shade.

6. Press Ctrl(⌘)+S to save your work; you can close the image whenever you grow weary of painting flowers!

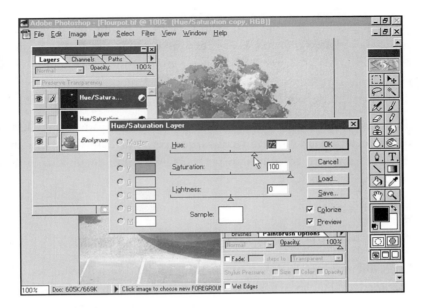

figure 9.5
Access Adjustment layer settings by double-clicking on the title on the Layers palette.

figure 9.6
Each Adjustment layer affects the base image according to the type of Adjustment you specify, and by the amount of brightness you paint into the layer.

In the preceding example, you "wiped clean" the information on the duplicate Adjustment layer, and then began fresh by defining the area to be shaded in the composition. At any time, however, you can use the Move tool to *reposition* the existing light areas on an Adjustment layer. Click on the layer to be edited, and then drag in the image window with the Move tool.

The previous examples show you only the most basic Adjustment layers' editing techniques. In the following sections, you get some hands-on experience making extensive, dramatic edits to an image by using some undocumented features of the Adjustment layers feature.

Getting Creative with Adjustment Layers

Do you remember those clay tablets that came with a dull stylus and an overlay of acetate, that you played with as a child? If so, you will recall that you could doodle away, and when you decided that you didn't like your composition, you pulled up on the acetate sheet and started fresh with a blank slate. Adjustment layers provide the same sort of flexibility in image composition: you can play—that's right, simply experiment—with design elements and modifications until something strikes your fancy.

In the following sections, you play with a photo of a classic 1957 Chevy and some poor lighting conditions in the image, to see where all this Adjustment layer stuff can take you.

A Little Color Correction, a Little Enhancement

The Classic.tif image in the CHAP09 folder was a "spur-of-the-moment" photograph. The authors were out snapping images of textures, a gentleman who owns a mint-condition car drove by, we flagged him down, and he was gracious enough to stop and pose his auto in the street. Unfortunately, the sun was behind the car and the sky was overcast when we took the image. This situation, in which only part of the image is "right," creates a wonderful opportunity to correct and enhance the image by using Adjustment layers.

To begin with, the car is a pale blue, but the photograph depicts it as dull and institutional in color. Additionally, the color in the sky is a little flat. Let's see what can be done to bring a little life to those areas.

SELECTIVELY SATURATING AN IMAGE

CD-ROM

1. Open the Classic.tif image from the CHAP09 folder of the Companion CD. A 50% viewing resolution is good for these steps.

2. Click on the Layers palette's flyout menu button, and choose New Adjustment Layer.

3. Choose Hue/Saturation from the Type drop-down list, and click on OK. The Hue/Saturation Layer dialog box appears.

4. Drag the Saturation slider to +47 (see fig. 9.7). The grass is going to turn an artificial, electric color, but don't mind this. Your only concern is that the car and the sky look more appealing; you will tone down the grass later. Click on OK to add the Hue/Saturation layer.

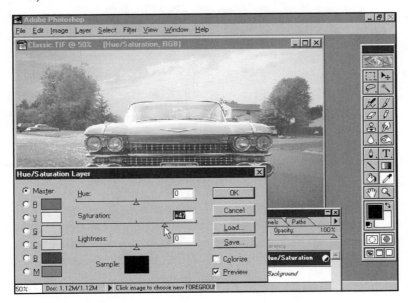

figure 9.7
Don't consider the overall image; instead, define the Adjustment layer according to the way it affects an image area.

5. Press **D** (Default colors), press **B** (Paintbrush tool), and then choose the far right, second row Brushes tip.

6. Paint over the grass areas in the image (see fig. 9.8). You do not need to take extreme care and make completely accurate strokes that cover the entire grass and tree areas. Simply paint until you see that the image is coming together; this is what Adjustment layers are for.

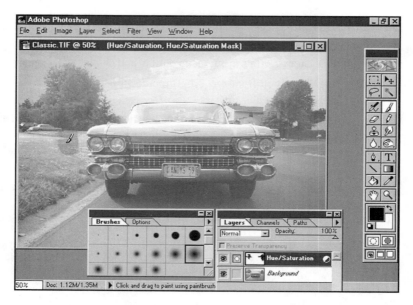

figure 9.8

Tone down the saturation of the trees and grass by applying black foreground color to the Adjustment layer.

7. When you get to the street, which probably shows visual *clipping*—an overconcentration of color or tone—you can decrease the saturation in this area in one fell swoop. With the Rectangular Marquee tool, select the street, and then press Alt(Opt)+Delete (Backspace) to fill the area with black foreground color (see fig. 9.9). Press Ctrl(⌘)+D to deselect the marquee now.

8. Press Ctrl(⌘)+Shift+S (File, Save As), and save the image to hard disk as Classic.psd, in the Photoshop file format. Keep the image open.

The image is definitely more colorful, but that sky is still a little wimpy. It needs more contrast. In the next section, you add a Levels Adjustment layer to correct this.

figure 9.9

Fill large foreground areas by selecting them and then pressing Alt(Opt)+Delete (Backspace).

Reusing Layer Transparency Information

Perhaps the only departure from the on-screen visualization of Adjustment layers, compared to standard layers, is that tones that appear on the thumbnail icons for Adjustment layers are more than tones. The tones represent transparency information; light shades represent opacity, whereas darker (and black) tones represent transparency. This transparency information can be "lifted" as a selection marquee, and reused as a border into which you can add transparency information on a different Adjustment layer.

Tally-time here. You already have a Hue/Saturation Adjustment layer in the image, that defines the car and the sky. In the next set of steps you will add a Levels layer to the composition, and use the car and sky transparency information on the Hue/Saturation layer as a template for making Levels adjustments. Then you can mask the car on the Levels layer, in less time than if you were to start anew with masking work on the Levels layer.

LIFTING ADJUSTMENT LAYER INFORMATION

1. Click on the Layers palette's menu flyout button, and choose New Adjustment Layer. In the New Adjustment Layer dialog box, choose Levels as the Type in the drop-down list, and click on OK.

2. In the Levels box, increase the black point to +42 and decrease the midtones to .79 (see fig. 9.10). (For both operations, drag the sliders to the right.) The car is going to look awful, but again, you're correcting only for the sky in the image—and not for any other element. Click on OK to apply the Levels adjustment to the layer.

figure 9.10
Correct the tonal distribution of the sky by increasing the overall contrast in the Levels command.

3. Right-click (Macintosh: hold Ctrl and click) over the thumbnail, not the title, to the Hue/Saturation layer (see fig 9.11), and choose Select Layer Transparency from the context menu to load the white areas of the Hue/Saturation layer. Although these are the opaque areas, not the transparent ones as this menu command indicates, you now have a marquee in the document that can be used to mask the foliage areas.

4. Press Ctrl(⌘)+Shift+I to invert the selection marquee, so that the grass and trees (and not the car and sky) are selected. Press Alt(Opt)+Delete (Backspace) to fill the selection with foreground black color, and then press Ctrl(⌘)+D to deselect the marquee (see fig. 9.12).

5. Press Ctrl(⌘)+S to save your work; keep the image open.

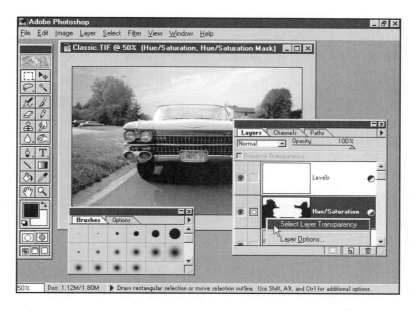

figure 9.11
Load the edited areas on an Adjustment layer through the Context menu option.

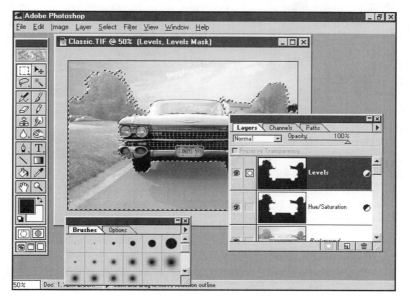

figure 9.12
Remove the effect of the Levels command for the selected areas on the layer.

Depending upon the accuracy with which you paint in the car and sky Hue/ Saturation Adjustment layer, there should be very little work to do at this point to remove the Levels adjustment to the car. To help speed up completion of the editing in the following steps, the authors created a selection in the form of a saved path in the Classic.tif image.

Here's how to brighten up the car:

SUBTRACTING FROM THE LEVELS ADJUSTMENT LAYER

1. Click on the Paths tab on the grouped palette, and then click on the Car path title. Click on the Loads path as selection icon at the bottom of the palette; then press Ctrl(⌘)+H to hide the selection marquee.

2. Click on a blank area of the Paths palette to hide the path.

3. With the Paintbrush tool, stroke over the car (see fig. 9.13). Alternatively, you can press Alt(Opt)+Delete (Backspace) to fill the entire area with foreground black.

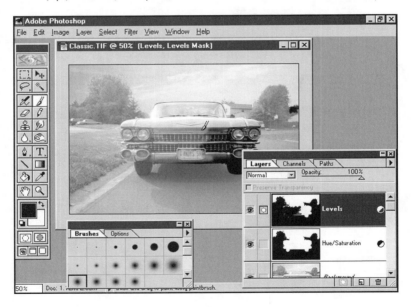

figure 9.13
Adding foreground black negates the effect of the Levels changes you specified for the Levels layer.

4. Press Ctrl(⌘)+D to deselect the marquee (if you chose to load the path as a selection); then press Ctrl(⌘)+S to save your work.

Admittedly, the time it took to create the path around the car strongly indicates that there are methods *other* than the Adjustment layer feature for correcting the tone or color balance in a scene. When you have a selection defined, you always have the option to copy or cut the selection to a different, standard layer in an image, and then perform *any* type of image correction you need. Adjustment layers are not for precision work; instead, the way they define and correct is equivalent to a physical pen and paper "rough" of a design. When precision definition of an image area is necessary, you have more editing flexibility if you put the time into using Quick Mask, the Pen tool, or other methods for defining the geometry of an area you want to edit. You can then use any feature, including the Adjustment layer, to perfect the image. Adjustment layers are a combination of selection definition and editing features you can perform.

Abstract Effects and Adjustment Layers

You can use Adjustment layers also to "dirty up" an image; their use is not reserved for photorealistic image editing. Because the Classic.tif image is very strong in geometric content, it would be fun to see the image highly posterized, accentuating the sleek lines of the car in contrast to the busy, uneven outline of the trees. In the following example, you put a Threshold Adjustment layer between the Hue/Saturation and the Levels layers to create a high-contrast, black-and-white version of the scene. The order of Adjustment layers can affect the view of the entire composition. We chose this order for the Threshold layer in this example because we wanted the Levels layer to affect the Threshold layer, adding contrast to the Threshold effect.

And as mentioned earlier, you can assign opacity and mode to a layer to create a complex, sophisticated composition.

Here's how to get creative with the right image, mode controls, and Adjustment layers:

ADDING DIGITAL GRIT TO THE IMAGE

1. Click on the Hue/Saturation layer, click on the menu flyout on the Layers palette, and choose New Adjustment Layer. Choose Threshold from the Type drop-down list, and click on OK to display the Threshold dialog box. Threshold evaluates the image in areas of black *or* white only; there are no other tonal values.

2. Drag the Threshold level slider to 121 (see fig. 9.14), and then click on OK. This setting appears to give the best balance between black and white in the image; you can read the license plate, and much of the chrome detail in the car is apparent.

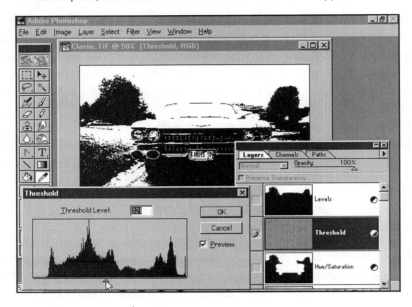

figure 9.14

Choose a Threshold setting for the Adjustment layer that shows the most clearly defined image detail.

3. Drag the Opacity slider on the Layers palette to about 30% (see fig. 9.15). Partial opacity for the Threshold layer allows some of the underlying image to be seen and creates an interesting posterized effect (better than the Posterize Adjust command).

4. On the Layers palette, choose Color Burn from the Modes drop-down list (see fig. 9.16). Color Burn is a new Photoshop mode that multiplies layer information (in this case, black and white) with underlying layer areas to create an intense Multiply mode-type effect. White areas are ignored in Color Burn mode.

5. Press Ctrl(⌘)+S to save your work.

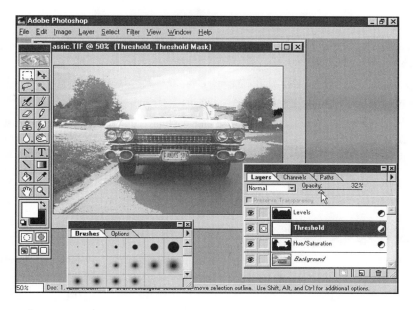

figure 9.15
Use partial opacity on the Threshold layer to blend the effect into the other layers.

figure 9.16
Apply a Photoshop mode to the Adjustment layer to further modify its appearance
when combined with a view of underlying layers.

TIP

You can add grayscale information to an Adjustment layer by using the Pattern fill command to create an advertising effect.

Create a grayscale logo or slogan about one-twentieth the size of the target image, make the logo white on black, select the entire logo, and choose Edit, Define Pattern.

Then create an Adjustment layer in the target image. Choose Edit, Fill, and then choose Pattern in the Use drop-down list. This trick works particularly well with the Levels and Hue/Saturation adjustments; you can create different patterns for different Adjustment layers to show your client variations on the design.

Using Tone Transitions on Adjustment Layers

The Paintbrush is only one of the many tools you can use to apply and remove grayscale content on an Adjustment layer. One of the interesting effects you can create is a grayscale-to-color effect (achieved by dragging the Gradient tool across a Hue/Saturation layer). Transitional areas also can be created by using a high Feather value; areas around the edge of a selection then make a gradual transition between filtered and original areas on the layer.

In the following example, you create a frame for the classic car composition. The outside border displays the posterized effect, and the center of the image contains the less stylized, color-corrected car.

Here's how to work with soft-edged geometric areas on an Adjustment layer:

FRAMING THE PIECE WITH A POSTERIZED LOOK

1. Double-click on the Rectangular Marquee tool to display the Options for the tool.

2. Type **12** in the Feather field, and drag a rectangle in the image to surround the car (see fig. 9.17). The marquee might take a moment to display; Photoshop must calculate the feather selection.

3. Press **X** (Swap Foreground/Background colors) so that black is the current background color, and then press Delete (Backspace). Press Ctrl(⌘)+D to deselect the marquee. You now have a full-color car fading out of a stylized background (see fig. 9.18).

4. Press Ctrl(⌘)+S to save your work. You can close the image at any time.

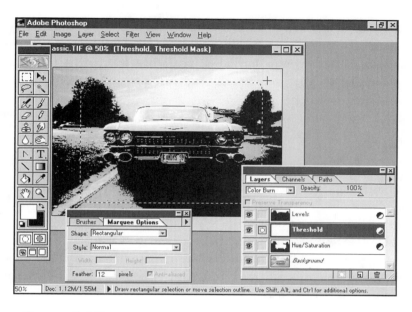

figure 9.17
Have Photoshop automatically feather selections you define by choosing the Feather option on the Options palette.

figure 9.18
Apply feathering before you fill an Adjustment layer to create a gentle transition between edited and original image areas.

Both the Flourpot and the Classic images can be further modified. You can turn Adjustment layers on or off (click on the visibility icon to the left of the layer title), and stack layers any way you choose; no changes are made to the image until you choose Merge Layers from the Layers palette's menu flyout.

Summary

Adjustment layers can be a useful editing option when you want to perform several modifications to an image, review them, further change them, but *don't* want the underlying image to be permanently changed. Adjustment layers are yet another Photoshop feature that enables you to see and work with visual data in many ways. In Chapter 10, "Enhancing Images," we move from one new Photoshop feature to another, as you work with the Free Transform command. You will see how to bend and shape selection areas in a bitmap image to arrive at photorealistic effects that were never photographed!

CHAPTER

ENHANCING IMAGES

Previous chapters have taken you through the procedures needed to correct an image, to restore an image, and to use Photoshop to "put back" something that's missing from a photograph. There will be times in your imaging career, however, when you come across an image that has absolutely nothing wrong with it—but that is not eye-catching.

This chapter explores why light behaves the way it does, how you can simulate lighting effects to create reflections, and how to work with tones in an image in order to create special effects. Additionally, you will see how to enhance one of the most common photographic elements over which you, the photographer, have very little control—how to make the sky in an outdoor scene look every bit as attractive as the landscape.

Reflections

There is something subconsciously attractive about a scene that contains a reflection. Whether it's a soft drink can on a stainless steel tabletop, or a ship, or a cloud reflecting into a cool lake, our attention drifts from object to reflection and back again. The bottom line is that, most of the time, an image that contains an interesting reflection will hold the attention of the audience longer than the same scene without a mirror-like element or two.

There will be occasions in your design work when you might want the star of a scene to cast a reflection, but a reflective surface is unavailable for the photographic session. At other times, you might need to add an element to a scene (as you have in earlier chapters), and you want that element to cast a reflection in its new environment. The following sections discuss how reflections are cast in the real world, and how you can successfully create reflections by using Photoshop.

Understanding a Mirror Plane

If you have a hand-held mirror, place it on a desk or tabletop, and then place a small object on it. With the mirror resting on the tabletop, move your head from left to right, and then up and down, and notice what happens to the object's reflection. From the left-to-right viewpoints, the reflection is fairly large and complete, but as you elevate your view, much of the reflection disappears from sight as the reflection moves beneath the object.

The most common and straightforward approach to adding a reflection to an image is to use a duplicate of the image. How successful you are at creating a realistic reflection depends on three things:

◆   The shape of the object, and whether it has lettering on it. Text necessitates flipping a duplicate of the original object, which can affect the geometry, or shape, of the reflected object. Generally, the best candidate for a reflected shape is round, with little discernible surface detail (patterns, text, and so on). Reflections are also easier to create when the reflected objects have no noticeable sides (*facets*).

◆ The angle of the camera as it captures a scene. Generally, it is better to take a photograph at eye level (the horizon is straight ahead) than to look down at a scene. When you look down at an object and its reflection, the reflection diminishes in perspective in the same way that the object casts its reflection. Simply flipping a copy of the object to create the reflection produces mirrored lines of perspective, but does not diminish the lines of perspective. In this chapter you learn how to *force* an image duplicate to display correct perspective lines. The technique is important to learn because "horizon" photography is not very interesting, visually, and because most commercial photography is set up with the camera above tabletop scenes and products.

◆ The angle, if any, of the object as it rests upon the surface that will display the reflection. Creating a reflection by mirroring a duplicate of an object is difficult when the camera angle is above the horizon of a scene. When an object such as a child's spinning top or a piece of fruit rests at an angle on a surface, for example, estimating what a reflection's shape should look like is very hard to do.

The image in the following example is almost a worst-case scenario for creating a reflection—Soda.psd is a picture of a soda can resting on a tabletop. Because the camera angle is superior to the horizon, the image shows the top edge of the can. The image clearly contains perspective lines, and the can has some distinctive text that naturally would show in a reflection.

Figure 10.1 shows two versions of the Soda.psd image; the one at left has been clumsily retouched to feature an awkward-looking, not-at-all-plausible can reflection. The image at right displays a photographically accurate can reflection. Notice that perspective lines in the image continue to diminish from can to reflection.

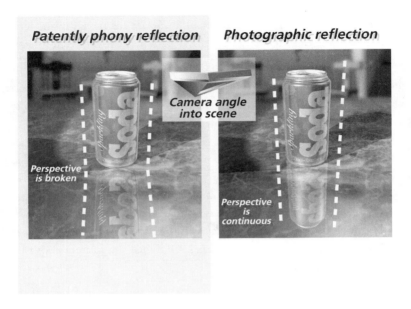

figure 10.1
When you view reflections from an angle above the horizon, perspective lines in the image continue into the reflection.

Additionally, the reflection can's top in the image at right is hidden from view; the can is tilted away from the camera. The task of creating a convincing reflection, using only original image areas, seems impossible—but Photoshop handles impossible tasks very well.

The observations made so far are important not only for evaluating the editing complexity of this section's assignment, but also for understanding optics. To create a convincing reflection of the soda can, you must understand how the *mirror plane* in a photograph works, for the following reasons:

◆ It's not worthwhile to create a fun-house mirror version of a reflection in an image.

◆ You can avoid problems when you create reflections in images if you plan the photographic session (or piece of artwork) in advance, eliminating overly complex scenes that don't lend themselves to the creation of reflections.

Figure 10.2 illustrates a side view of the soda can scene; you can see the location of the camera in relation to the scene, as well as the extent of the camera frame. From the camera's view, a real reflection recedes in perspective from view, from top to bottom, as does the can creating the reflection. When mirrored objects are viewed at an angle, the angle of perspective is one quality of optics that is *not* "mirrored."

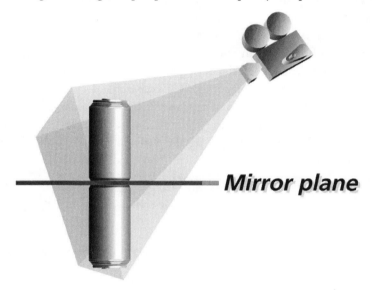

figure 10.2
The appearance of a reflection depends upon the viewing angle relative to the mirror plane that created the reflection.

Let's move from theory into practice, as you create a reflection in the Soda.psd image by using Photoshop's features.

Preparing the Image for Reflection Editing

The Soda.psd image you will work with has been edited so that the can in the image is on its own layer. When you use the techniques shown in this section on your own assignments, the first step is to mask and copy the object to be reflected to its own layer. (See Chapter 4, "Using Paths, Selections, and Layers," for an in-depth discussion of how to use Photoshop's selection tools.)

Here's the game plan: to show the text on the can as mirrored, you must duplicate the can and flip it vertically. Notice (in fig. 10.1) that in the image on the right, the vertical curves in the reflection are similar to those of the can. The text dips downward in both the can and its reflection; this is a minor detail that can be addressed before you correct the perspective lines of the duplicate can. Photoshop's Shear command distorts images along a user-defined curve, unlike Photoshop's Free Transform functions. You will use the Shear command to add the right amount of curvature to the duplicate can. There's a catch, however—the Shear command distorts selections and images along the horizon only, but the direction of the reflection distortion needs to be vertical. You need to reorient the image after you create and flip the duplicate of the can.

Here's how to prepare the image for some serious, yet fun, editing:

PERFORMING REFLECTION GROUNDWORK

CD-ROM

1. Open the Soda.psd image from the CHAP10 folder of the Companion CD. Double-click on the Hand tool to change the viewing resolution so that you can see the entire image in the workspace without scrolling the document.

2. Press F7 to display the Layers palette if it's not already on-screen, and then drag the Can title into the Create new layer icon at the bottom of the palette (see fig. 10.3). This creates a duplicate of the Can layer on a layer above the original Can layer.

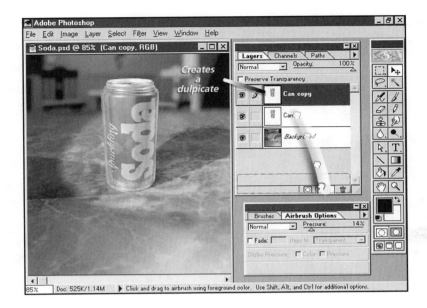

figure 10.3
Dragging a layer title into the Create new layer icon duplicates the layer.

Photoshop automatically appends "copy" to the title of the duplicate layer; this automatic labeling feature pays off when you are editing multilayer images, if you make it a practice to label layers shortly after their creation.

3. Choose Layer, Transform, Flip Vertically from the menu.

4. With the Move tool, drag the duplicate on the Can copy layer straight down, until you can see the top of the original on the Can layer.

5. Choose Image, Rotate Canvas, 90°CW (clockwise). Drag the borders of the document window away from the image so that you can see the entire image in the workspace (see fig. 10.4).

figure 10.4
The Rotate Canvas command applies to all layers within the document; you need to reorient the image to use the Shear command.

6. Choose File, Save As, and save the image to your hard disk, in the Photoshop file format, as MySoda.psd (or a similarly evocative name).

As mentioned earlier, the Shear command performs its work on the image from left to right. Now that the can is oriented from left to right, it's time to try out the Shear filter.

The Shear Filter—Local Image Displacement

If you have experimented with Photoshop's Displace filter (shown later in this chapter), tried out MetaTools' Goo, or the Valis Group's Flo', the Shear command produces similar effects. In addition to straight-line *italicizing* (skewing) of selections along the horizontal axis of an image, the Shear command can also *bend* or warp an image as though it were made of silly putty. The extent and the type of distortion effect created depend upon how you manipulate anchors on a graph on the Shear command's dialog box.

Here's how to bend the duplicate image so that it looks consistent with the curvature of the original can:

USING THE SHEAR COMMAND

1. With the Rectangular Marquee tool, drag a rectangle around the duplicate can, leaving a little more room toward the bottom of the can than toward the top (see fig. 10.5). It is important that you leave the *same* amount of vertical space (image top and bottom in this rotated view) surrounding the can in your marquee selection. Doing so makes controlling the anchor points on the Shear path a predictable adventure. The Shear command displaces the location of a selection in addition to the shape of the selected image area. You will be distorting the can toward screen left.

figure 10.5
Marquee select the area on the layer to which you will apply the Shear command.

2. Choose Filter, Distort, Shear. The Undefined Areas option is not relevant to this example; you can leave either option chosen. Drag the top anchor to the third vertical grid line, and do the same with the bottom anchor point.

3. Click on the center of the path on the grid; this creates a new anchor point. Drag this anchor toward the second vertical grid, keeping it on the middle horizontal grid line. Stop dragging when the top of the can bends inward.

   Notice that there is a dramatic distortion to the can, but the top of the can is V-shaped, and not curved, as is the bottom of the original can in the document. The next step smoothes out the distortion.

4. Click a point midway between the top and middle anchor, and then drag the anchor toward the center of the grid and to the right. Click another point midway between the bottom anchor and middle anchor; then drag this anchor to the right until the distortion of the can you see in the preview window looks symmetrical (see fig. 10.6).

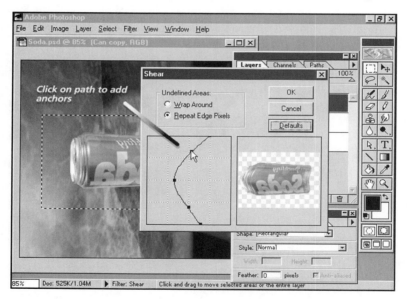

figure 10.6
The Shear path in the grid in the dialog box determines the shape of the distortion you create.

Note that the path you create in the Shear dialog box does *not have* to look like that in figure 10.6 to be correct for this assignment. The marquee you created around the soda can determines the relative positioning and subsequent repositioning and distortion of the can through the use of the Shear filter. *Do not* concern yourself about the reality of the fact that the can is narrower on its bottom than its top. Later sections of the chapter address the perspective of the can; your only concern here is the bending of the can along its horizon. Go by your eye, and when the can looks horizontally mirrored, compared to the original can, follow the next step.

5. Click on OK to apply the Shear filter, press Ctrl(⌘)+D to deselect the marquee, and then choose Image, Rotate Canvas, 90°CCW (counterclockwise).

6. Press Ctrl(⌘)+S to save your work.

The Shear filter and other Distort filters perform some intense calculations to reassign image pixels; as a result, you will notice some image quality loss in the duplicate can now. There really is no other way to reshape a selection area in a bitmap than by changing pixels, however, and you will apply a subtle amount of sharpening to the duplicate can at the end of this section to restore some of its focus. Additionally, your audience will never see the can at 100% opacity. Reflections are a combination of mirror plane material and reflected light. Therefore, the reduced opacity of the reflection duplicate can will disguise the imperfect image focus.

The Free Transform Functions

We often refer to *progressive changes* in this book as a creative weakness of working in the bitmap format of computer graphics. Quite simply, progressive changes are changes made to an area of an image to which one or more changes have *already* been made. For example, whenever you stretch a selection area to 200 percent of its original size and then shrink it to 50 percent as a second step, you are *not* returning the selection to its unedited state. In fact, you're pushing the current selection two steps away from its original condition.

Progressive changes in bitmap images are caused by *averaging*. When you stretch or otherwise distort an image, Photoshop must calculate new pixel colors within the image to represent the changes. And Photoshop does this by averaging neighboring pixel colors to arrive at a final pixel color everywhere in the affected image area.

To make a relevant analogy, suppose that you collected gas receipts every day, for a year. If you then averaged the bills by 52, you would have a weekly average for gas. But if you then averaged the average weekly amount by 12, you would *not* arrive at the same number for a monthly average that you would get if you divided the total by 12 in the first place—an average that's based on *another* average is not accurate, whether you're dealing with gas bills or edited pixels.

To reduce the number of times Photoshop averages pixel transformations, the Free Transform feature was added to version 4. You no longer have to make Perspective, Rotate, Scale, Distort, and Skew commands as separate steps: you can work between these commands until the selection area has been shaped the way you want it. And then, only a single pixel transformation is calculated. In the following sections you use the Free Transform feature to mold the duplicate can to conform to the perspective of its original.

Shaping the Soda Can Reflection

Before beginning the following steps, you should decide upon a method for accessing all the Transform features; Photoshop offers several ways to execute the same commands. In Free Transform mode, you have the opportunity to work between these commands by using Photoshop's keyboard extender keys, by choosing from the Context menu, or from the Layer main menu. By default, when you use the Free Transform command, you are in Scale mode, but you can change the function of the Free Transform box surrounding a selection area. To access the other functions, you can use the following steps:

◆ Drag on a corner Free Transform handle to rotate the selection.

◆ Hold Ctrl(⌘) and drag on a corner handle to access the Distort feature.

◆ Hold Ctrl(⌘) and drag on a middle Free Transform handle to access the Skew feature for one side of the selection.

◆ Hold Ctrl(⌘)+Alt(Opt) and drag on any handle to perform the Skew function to all four sides of the selection. The Free Transform box will move the edges of the selection in opposite directions, parallel to one another.

◆ Hold Ctrl(⌘)+Alt(Opt)+Shift (yes, this does take your whole hand!) and drag on a corner Free Transform handle to create the Perspective effect. Drag on a middle handle while you hold down these keys to access the four-sided Skew effect.

TIP

To constrain the movement of Free Transform's Perspective, Distort, and Rotate selection handles to 45°-angle increments in a document, hold Shift. When you use the Scale Free Transform feature, holding Shift constrains scaling to proportional scaling. With the Skew feature, holding Shift constrains a skewed selection to only one axis (height or width).

In Scale Free Transform mode, holding Alt(Opt) scales the selection from the center of the selection.

To cancel a Free Transform distortion at any time, press Esc or select a toolbox tool (you will be asked whether to apply or to cancel the current Free Transform effect).

In the following steps, you switch between Free Transform effects in a more conventional way. When you right-click (Macintosh: hold Ctrl and click) over a Free Transform box, the Context menu offers all the previously listed options; you can pick them and change between them as easily as if you were selecting from Photoshop's main menu. Here's how to transform the duplicate can to conform to the correct perspective for the soda can reflection:

Using the Free Transform Feature

1. With the Can copy layer as the current editing layer, choose Screen mode from the drop-down list on the Layers palette. This creates a ghostly, semitransparent duplicate can on-screen; it looks very much as it will when you finish the composition. But you need to reduce the opacity for reasons other than appearance—in Screen mode, you can compare the can's shape to the underlying original on the Can layer, and use the original as a guide for Free Transform effects.

2. Press Ctrl(⌘)+T to display the Free Transform bounding box around the can. Free Transform automatically recognizes nontransparent areas on the layer.

3. Right-click (Macintosh: hold Ctrl and click) over the Free Transform box, and then choose Perspective from the Context menu.

4. Drag the bottom-left corner handle of the Free Transform box toward the center of the image (see fig. 10.7). Photoshop takes a moment to display an in-place, low-resolution preview of the proposed Perspective change; wait a moment between editing moves. See how closely the perspective lines match the perspective lines of the can on the Can layer.

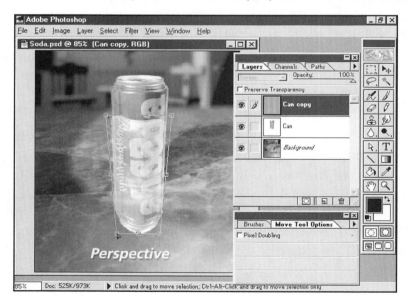

figure 10.7

Drag a corner Free Transform Perspective handle in the direction in which you want to change the selection's perspective.

5. Click in the center of the Free Transform box and then drag the bounding box down below the can on the Can layer. Areas inside a Free Transform box are used for relocating the selection (see fig. 10.8). Move the duplicate can so that it is more or less in its final, reflection position.

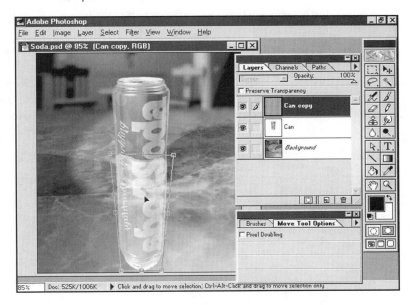

figure 10.8
You can drag anywhere within the Free Transform box to relocate the selection and the Free Transform effect.

The can selection will most likely be too tall to represent the original can's reflection; the combination of Perspective and Shear command accounts for this. No problem: Free Transform can scale the duplicate can disproportionately, and because Free Transform is a multipurpose feature, pixel transformations are calculated a single time only.

6. Right-click (Macintosh: hold Ctrl and click) and then choose Scale from the Context menu.

7. Drag the bottom-right corner handle up until the can's bottom is about $1/4$ screen inches from the bottom of the document window. Then drag the upper-right corner handle down until you can see the topmost edge of the selection touching the bottom lip of the original can.

This scaling maneuver might throw the perspective editing off by a little; scaled objects do not retain absolute perspective lines. This is okay, however—again, Free Transform transforms pixels once only.

8. Right-click (Macintosh: hold Ctrl and click) and then choose Distort from the Context menu. Distort enables you to work with the corners of the Free Transform box, independently of one another.

9. Drag, one at a time, the corners of the Distort Free Transform box so that the selection's perspective lines (the right and left edges) are parallel to the original can's edges. It is a mistake to use the Free Transform box's edges as a guide; they do not correspond to the edges of the can selection. Instead, make an edit, and then wait for the screen to redraw before you make the next edit. When the can resembles the one shown in figure 10.9, either press Enter or double-click inside the Free Transform box to apply the changes.

figure 10.9
Use Scale and Perspective to make gross changes to a selection, and then switch to Distort mode to make small corrections.

10. Press Ctrl(⌘)+S to save your work.

Now, to finalize the piece, you will make some minor cosmetic edits to the can on the Can copy layer.

TIP

There are instances in Photoshop where clear pixels on a layer are treated as selectable image content. One such instance is when you use the Free Transform feature. If you select an area on a layer and then go to Free Transform mode, the Free Transform mode box will *not* shrink to conform to the nontransparent pixels only; instead, it will maintain the proportions of the selection at the time you made the Free Transform command. Because this can mess up the accurate evaluation of Free Transform functions, such as Distort and Perspective, we recommend that you always load the nontransparent image content on a layer before issuing the Free Transform command.

NOTE

You cannot access the Layers palette's modes or Opacity controls from Free Transform mode, nor can you choose a toolbox tool. You can adjust your view of the active document, however.

Use Ctrl(⌘)++ to increase viewing resolution, and press Ctrl(⌘)– to zoom out of the document. You can also use Ctrl(⌘)+spacebar to toggle to the Zoom (in) tool. Ctrl(⌘)+Alt(Opt)+spacebar toggles to the Zoom (out) tool.

When the document displays scroll bars, you can hold the spacebar to toggle to the Hand tool, which can be used to drag your view within the document window.

Using the Smudge Tool

The Smudge tool might be best described as the graphical equivalent of mumbling. "Senator, are you for or against the proposed legislation?" "Ahem—my constituency nums frums forgrumble neps. That's all I can say at this time."

Seriously, the Smudge tool is quite versatile in a number of design situations where an image area absolutely cannot be duplicated or restored, but needs to be filled in with something. The Smudge tool treats underlying image areas as though they were wet paint, producing results somewhere between the Blur tool and the Shear command. You can move areas of image into other areas, which makes the total area covered look like a soft-focus streak of image detail.

As you might have noticed, the top edge of the reflected can and the bottom edge of the original don't quite meet. This problem is easily solved by smudging duplicate can areas upward to meet the bottom of the original can. The audience won't see this editing because you are going to move the duplicate behind the original, and decrease its overall opacity.

Here's how to finish editing the reflection:

APPLYING THE FINISHING TOUCHES

1. Drag the Can copy layer title to beneath the Can layer title on the Layers palette.

2. With the Move tool, move the Can copy to its final position relative to the original can. Because the Smudge tool will make permanent changes to the layer's contents, make sure that you won't want to move the can's reflection again.

3. With the Can copy as the current editing layer, type 5 on the numeric keypad to make the opacity of the layer 50%. In Screen mode, this diminishes the reflection's strength in the composition and makes your editing work less obvious!

4. Choose the Smudge tool; then, on the Brushes palette, choose the second tip from the left in the second row.

5. On the Smudge tool Options palette (double-click on the Smudge tool to display the palette), make sure that the Sample Merged option is unchecked, and drag the Pressure slider to 70%. The higher the Pressure value for the Smudge tool, the farther a stroke made with the cursor moves the pixels.

6. Drag from the aluminum lid part of the can reflection (on the left side of the image) into the original can's aluminum bottom. Then drag from the can reflection's aluminum bottom on the right side into the original can bottom (see fig. 10.10). Two or three strokes, maximum, should extend the aluminum lid to meet the bottom of the can on the Can layer.

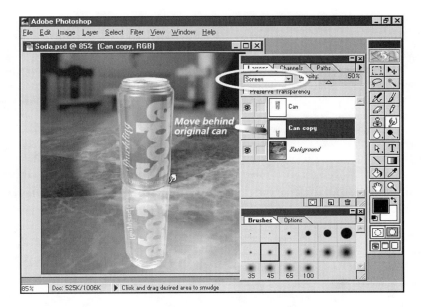

figure 10.10
Use the Smudge tool to blend areas of opaque image content into transparent layer areas to make the cans meet.

7. Choose Filter, Sharpen, and then choose Sharpen Edges. The Sharpen Edges filter (new to version 4) emphasizes areas of color contrast in an image, while leaving areas of little contrast intact. Sharpen Edges is like the Unsharp Mask filter, but without user-defined options. It produces a more subtle sharpening effect than the Sharpen and Sharpen More filters.

8. Press Ctrl(⌘)+S to save your work. Close the file at any time now.

NOTE

If you use a digitizing tablet instead of a mouse, additional control for the Smudge tool is available. In addition to Pressure, which you can change dynamically during a stroke, you can control the size of the Smudge stroke. The size option is not displayed on the Smudge tool Options palette if Photoshop does not find a tablet attached to your system when you launch Photoshop.

TIP

New to Photoshop 4 is the capability to specify the precise amount of Opacity by using the numeric keypad. For example, when a non-painting tool is active, if you type 78, the Opacity slider on the Layers palette will change to 78. When a painting tool is the current tool, typing two digits on the keypad changes the Opacity (or Pressure with the Airbrush and other tools), to exactly the amount you want on the Options palette.

In figure 10.11 you can see the finished Soda.psd image and an image of the same can with a photographic reflection cast into the marble. The two images are pretty similar; without the image at right for comparison, the audience would never notice the artificial reflection as anything other than a natural image element.

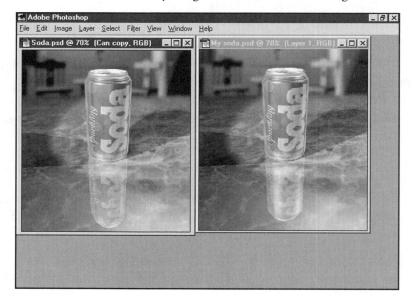

figure 10.11
A reflection you add to an image will go unnoticed if you keep perspective, mirror planes, and other optics principles in mind while you edit.

If you wanted to be extremely picky about this assignment, you might want to use Photoshop's Layer Mask mode on the Can copy layer, and remove a little of the lid of the can at the bottom of the image. The transformations you have applied to this layer have distorted most of the lid's visual content beyond recognition, but the *amount* of lid is a little more than one would see from the camera angle suggested in the image.

Small tabletop scenes are only one type of image that can benefit from Photoshop enhancement. The next section shows you how to make extensive changes to an outdoor scene, discovering in the process how to edit photographic reality to present a beautiful, natural-looking image.

The Do-It-Yourself Scene Kit

Traditional photographers have been obliged through the years to *stage* (or choreograph) the eye-pleasing images you see on posters, postcards, and other commercial media. And the more elements the scene comprises, the greater the chance that one element will not be at its photographic prime. For example, a simple scene of a sailboat on a lake can suffer from the sun suddenly going behind a cloud, the sailboat making a sudden change in direction so that the sail is not at its fullest, or a tourist sticking his face into the scene.

As is mentioned in Chapter 15, "The Artistic Side of Photoshop 4," a good idea for the ambitious imaging professional is to acquire as many stock photographic elements as possible, because the time will come when a great photo needs to be *manufactured*, not necessarily photographed, on a single frame of film.

The authors took three separate photographs for the next example: one of a sailboat in San Francisco Bay, one of an island among Ontario's Thousand Islands, and one of a bright sky with clouds. Each of these images lacks a certain something, but together they can represent an ideal photograph that captures a moment in time—one that *might* have been taken if the photographer had sufficient patience! Let's see how a photo can be enhanced through the addition of other photographic elements, as well as some elements that are purely from artistic imagination.

Improving a Sky in an Image

Lakes, oceans, and other aquatic tourist attractions are all glorious sites, and often are impossible to capture with a brilliant sky. For example, open water causes evaporation, air current and temperature changes cause clouds—and there goes the opportunity to photograph what we see in our mind's camera.

Fortunately, the duller the sky, the easier it is in Photoshop to accurately select the sky and replace it with one that makes a more significant contribution to the overall scene.

N OTE

The more image data you have to work with, the easier it is to modify the elements. It is difficult to accurately select elements that are made up of only a few pixels. The resource files for the following examples were created at two different resolutions; the larger images weigh in at about 4.5 MB, and the smaller images are a little more than 1 MB in file size.

If you have more than 32 MB of RAM on your computer, you might want to try editing the images in the larger files. The names of the files are identical, except that the file names of the smaller images include the letter *s* (for *small*). If your system resources prohibit your working with images greater than 10 MB or so, you can still complete the examples by using the smaller files.

In the next set of steps, you use Photoshop's Color Range command to select most of the sky in the island image; then you perform a little manual clean-up work on the selection to make way for a replacement sky to enhance the picture.

S ELECTING AN O VERCAST S KY

1. Open the Boring.tif image from the CHAP10 folder on the Companion CD. This is an image of a beautiful island with a dreadfully overcast sky. Type **50** in the Zoom percentage field, and press Enter (Return) to show the full image on-screen. Then drag the window borders away from the image to expose some of the document window's background.

2. With the Rectangular Marquee tool, drag a selection that includes all the sky in the image, but none of the water.

The selection must include some of the trees, but it's important to keep the water out of the image. The sky casts color into the water, and the Color Range command will select the water in addition to the sky unless the water is not selected.

3. Choose Select, Color Range. In the Color Range dialog box, choose Sampled Colors from the Select drop-down list, click on the Selection radio button, and choose None from the Selection Preview drop-down list. The areas you click on in the image to select will appear as white in the preview window in this dialog box.

4. With the Color Range eyedropper, click on an area of sky in the image in Photoshop's workspace—*not* the preview window—as shown in figure 10.12. Drag the Fuzziness slider to about 88; this increases the selected areas in the image, based upon color similarity. The higher the Fuzziness option, the broader the range of colors selected.

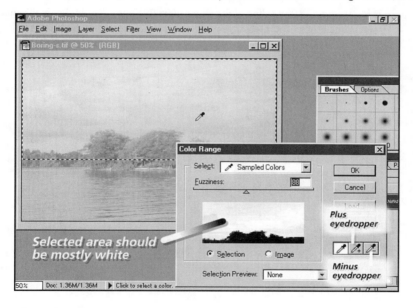

figure 10.12

The Color Range command locates and selects similar colors in an image. The selected areas do not have to be neighboring, as they do with the Magic Wand tool.

The trick to using the Color Range command is to keep the Fuzziness as low as possible while still selecting the area you want. Values that are too high select *everything* in the image.

5. If, the first time you click the Eyedropper in the image, the trees are not clearly defined as unselected areas (unselected areas appear in black in the Color Range preview window), try clicking in a different area in the document.

6. If you need to add a sky area to the selection, but cannot do so by clicking in a single area, click in the document to select most of the sky, and then click on the other areas, using the plus eyedropper tool. If you have selected areas you don't want selected, choose the minus eyedropper in the Color Range dialog box, and click on the areas to remove them from the selection.

7. Click on OK to confirm your selection and to return to the document.

8. On the Channels palette (press F7 to display it if it's not on-screen), click on the Save selection as channel icon at the bottom of the palette (see fig. 10.13). Selections saved as *image maps* (often called *alpha channels* in this book) are easier to edit than marquee selections. Press Ctrl(⌘)+D now to deselect the marquee in the image.

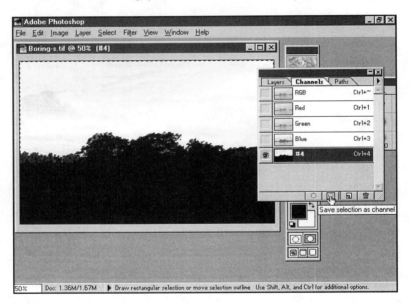

figure 10.13

Save the Color Range selection in an alpha channel; you can refine the selection by using any of Photoshop's paint tools.

9. Click on the #4 channel title on the Channels palette to switch your view in the document to the selection information.

10. Choose the Eraser tool, choose Block as the type of eraser from the Options palette, and Press **D** (Default colors). The Eraser tool now erases to white in the alpha channel.

11. Drag over areas in the sky that are not completely white (see fig. 10.14). The Color Range command selects areas in degrees of opacity; those areas not entirely selected appear in the alpha channel as light gray.

figure 10.14
Use the Eraser tool to make lighter areas in the sky completely white. When loaded as a selection, these areas will be completely selected.

Notice that the edge of the trees is a little fuzzy in the alpha channel. It is very difficult to precisely select the edges of trees, particularly when an overcast sky casts similar colors into the leaves. The tree edges need to be clearly defined, however; otherwise, some of the original sky will remain in the image, and will contrast sharply with the replacement sky you will add. To fix this, use these steps:

12. Press Ctrl(⌘)+L to display the Levels dialog box.

13. With the white-point eyedropper (see fig. 10.15), click on an area in the alpha channel that is very close to (but not exactly) white. This creates a new white point in the alpha channel. The edge of the trees will sharpen up in the alpha channel because light gray areas in the trees are now assigned to white.

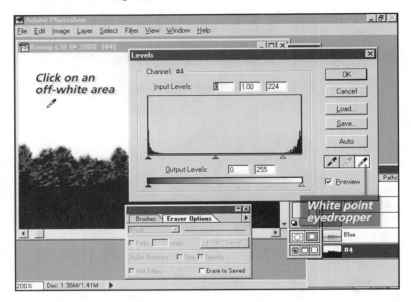

figure 10.15

By specifying in the channel a white point lower than the current white, contrast is added to the information in the channel.

14. Click on OK to apply the Levels command to the channel, and then choose File, Save As. Press Ctrl(⌘)+~ (tilde) to return your view to RGB color composite view. Save the image to your hard disk in the Photoshop file format, as Island.psd, and keep the image open in Photoshop.

Even though you have defined this selection precisely, a little additional editing of the tree edges will be necessary after you add the new sky to the document. Trees are perhaps the most difficult geometric areas of a photograph to define, but the Color Range feature takes the bulk of the manual labor out of the process.

Background Replacement and Integration

A bright sky can be a surprising complement to colors that appear dull simply because there is nothing in an image to compare them to, visually. In the Island image, the trees and surrounding foliage are actually quite lush, but they look dull because the sky is dull. In the following steps, you add a more visually interesting sky to the composition, and then use the Layer Mask feature to visually integrate the new sky with the rest of the image.

COPYING AND MASKING IMAGE LAYERS

1. If you're working with the large files, open the Cloud.tif image from the CHAP10 folder on the Companion CD. If you began this section by editing Boring-s.tif, open the Cloud-s.tif image from the CHAP10 folder.

2. Drag the Background title on the Layers palette into the Island image (see fig. 10.16). You can close the Cloud image now.

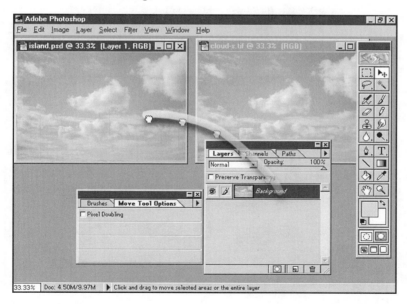

figure 10.16
Copy the cloud image to the island composition by dragging its title into the Island document window.

3. Click on the visibility icon (the eye icon) for the new Layer 1 on the Layers palette to hide the cloud layer for the moment. You need to focus your attention on the outline of the trees in the following steps, without the distraction of the clouds layer.

4. Double-click on the Background title on the Layers palette. This displays the Make Layer dialog box. Click on OK to accept the default name (Layer 0). The Background is now an editable Photoshop layer that you can mask and reposition in the document.

5. Drag the Layer 1 title to below the Layer 0 title.

6. On the Channels palette, press Ctrl(⌘) and click on the #4 title to load the contents of this channel as a selection marquee in the image.

7. Press Delete, and then press Ctrl(⌘)+D to deselect the marquee. The dull sky is gone from this layer. Click on the visibility icon for Layer 1 on the Layers palette to see the new sky contrasted against the island scene in the picture.

8. Click on the Layer 1 title to make it the current editing layer. Then, with the Move tool, drag the sky upward until the bottom edge of the image is slightly below the tree edge in the document. Clouds diminish in size as they approach the horizon, and large clouds in the sky should be at the top of the image.

9. Zoom in to a 200% viewing resolution of the Islands image, and then scroll the window so that you have a close-up view of the weeping willow to the right of the house on the island. As you can see in figure 10.17, there is a mass of original, dull sky at the edge of the willow tree, and a light fringe of original sky elsewhere in the trees.

figure 10.17
Lighter fringe areas around the trees do not play well against the darker sky.

One possible solution to eliminating the fringe is to use the Defringe command. This command replaces the edge pixels between nontransparent and clear areas with pixel colors found toward the inside, not the outside, of layer contents. This would create a harsh, pixellated edge to the trees, however, which is not what you want. Trees in the distance of an image should blend somewhat into the atmosphere. The solution to removing the fringe is to follow these steps:

10. Click on the Layer Mask icon on the bottom of the Layers palette. Press **B** (Paintbrush tool); then, on the Brushes palette, choose the far left tip on the second row. On the Options palette, make certain that 100% Opacity, Normal mode is set.

11. Brush short, precise strokes into the fringe area of the trees to hide the original sky (see fig. 10.18). It's okay if you change some of the geometry of the trees; in fact, you should completely lop off the area of the willow that displays the most original sky. This is an original composition, and there's no one in the audience who can attest to the original geometry of the tree edges!

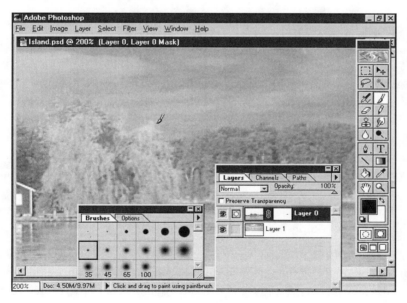

figure 10.18
Keep the Paintbrush strokes short, and try to follow, or mimic, the flow of the tree edges to hide the original sky fringe.

12. Hold the spacebar to toggle to the Hand tool, and then drag in the document window to pan your view of the image to an area where there is still light fringe in the tree edges. Paint over these areas to hide the fringe.

13. When you have finished hiding the fringe, it's time to make your edits permanent in the document. Click on the Layer 0 Layer Mask thumbnail icon on the Layers palette, and drag the thumbnail image into the trash icon. This causes an attention box to be displayed.

14. Click on Apply in the attention box to remove the areas that are hidden on Layer 0.

15. Double-click on the Hand tool to move the viewing resolution of this document to 100% (1:1). Press Ctrl(⌘)+S to save your work.

The image looks more attractive now; so much so, in fact, that it looks like a perfect day for sailing. Let's make this idea one that is "photographed" in the following section.

Adding a Sailboat to the Composition

The difficult part of the next set of steps has already been done for you. Sailboat.tif (and its smaller file counterpart, Smalboat.tif) are images that have been carefully masked. All you need to do to add the boat to the Island image's waters is load the selection saved in the boat image's alpha channel, and copy the boat. If you read Chapter 4, you understand the usefulness of partially masking image areas so that partial opacity is present in certain image areas. This technique was applied to the waters in the boat image because the wake around the boat should be copied to the Island image (but not the still water). The water in San Francisco Bay is clearly a different color than Thousand Islands' water, and color matching the two different waters in the composition would take too long.

The following sections show you how to *integrate* the boat with its new surroundings. If you look at the waters in front of the island, you can see that the foliage is clearly reflected in the water, and the water is slightly choppy. Therefore, a variation on the reflection technique is needed to make the boat appear to be sailing through the Thousand Islands. The first step is to get a copy of the boat from its original image into the Islands' picture.

Copying and Positioning the Sailboat

1. Open the Sailboat.tif image from the CHAP10 folder on the Companion CD. If you're using the smaller set of files, use the Smalboat.tif image here.

2. On the Channels palette, press Ctrl(⌘) and click on the #4 title to load the selection of the boat. Make sure that you have a view of both the boat and the Island document window in the workspace. If you don't, reposition the image windows before proceeding.

3. With the Move tool, drag inside the marquee of the boat, into the Island image (see fig. 10.19). A new layer, labeled Layer 2, is created in the Island image.

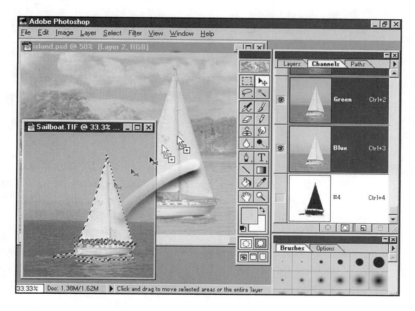

figure 10.19

Drag inside a selection marquee to copy the image contents to a unique layer in a different image window.

4. Drag the boat around in the water until it visually integrates with the scene. The authors chose the right of the image; this location helps disguise the virtual hedge work performed on the tree edges, particularly on the weeping willow (see fig. 10.20).

figure 10.20

Position the boat in the water where the visual continuity between its wake and the surrounding water is the greatest, and where it fits compositionally into the scene.

5. Drag the Layer 2 title on the Layers palette into the Create new layer icon. This duplicate boat layer will be used to create a reflection of the boat in the water (see fig. 10.21).

6. Double-click on the Layer 2 copy title on the Layers palette, type **Reflection** in the Name field of the Layer Options dialog box, and click on OK to apply the name change.

7. Drag the Reflection layer title beneath the Layer 2 title. This positions the layer to be used as the boat's reflection beneath the boat you copied to the document.

8. Choose Layer, Transform, Flip Vertical. Using the Move tool, drag the boat so that it is mirrored vertically with the original boat, with the wake of the reflection partially hidden by the wake of the original boat (see fig. 10.22).

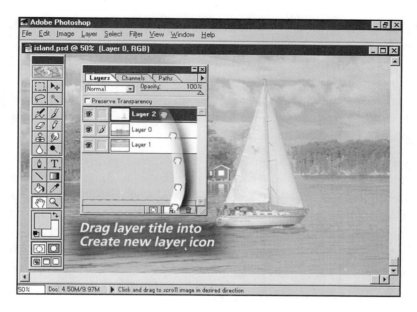

figure 10.21
Copy the layer of the boat by dragging its title into the Create new layer icon.

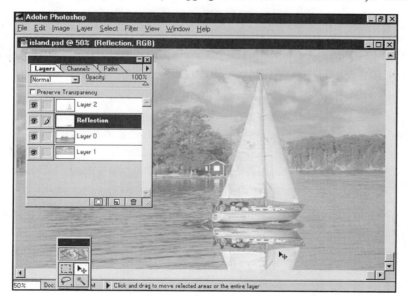

figure 10.22
Move the image contents on the Reflection layer so that the boat is centered vertically, relative to the original boat.

9. Close the sailboat image without saving it. Press Ctrl(⌘)+S to save your work. Keep the Island image open in Photoshop.

Unlike the soda can example, there is no perspective on the view of the boat; both the island scene and the boat were photographed with the camera angle close to the horizon. Therefore, the Free Transform editing steps are not required in this composition.

Here's where the editing process gets complicated—and interesting. With the soda can scene, there were no reflections in the image to compare to the can reflection you created. There is, therefore, some artistic liberty in the reflection of the soda can. The boat reflection is another story, however. There are reflections of trees all over the Island image; to make the boat truly integrate with the scene, you have to create a reflection for the boat that matches the characteristics of the tree reflections.

Using the Displace Command

The Displace filter can be used to shift the location of pixels in an image by an amount that corresponds to the brightness values in a different, user-created image. The user-defined image must be in the Photoshop PSD format, and you can use either single or multiple channel files to control the distortion created by this filter. In the following example, you use a grayscale copy of the area in the Islands image where the reflection of the trees is visible.

When a grayscale image is used as the source file for the distortion, the Displace filter pushes the target image's pixels vertically or horizontally by an incremental amount, according to the options you specify in the Displace filter's dialog box. The lighter the tones in the resource file, the more pixels in the target image will be moved (*displaced*). An authentic rendition of water displacing the reflection of the boat is created when you use an image of choppy, reflecting water as the resource file.

Here's how to make the reflection of the boat look as though it's distorted by the Island waters:

Displacing a Reflection

1. Zoom out of the image until you can see all the reflections of the foliage in the scene—50% viewing resolution is good.

2. Hide the boat and the duplicate boat by clicking off the visibility icons to the left of their titles.

3. Click on the Layer 0 title on the Layers palette. Using the Rectangular Marquee tool, drag a selection around the reflection area in the image (see fig. 10.23).

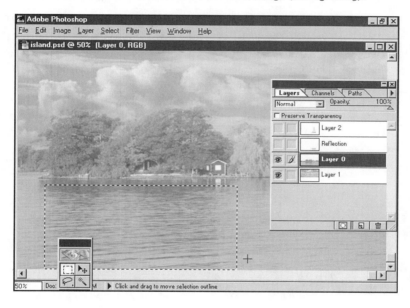

figure 10.23

Select an image area to copy that is the size of the layer area you want to displace, and that contains the visual information to create a choppy water effect.

4. Press Ctrl(⌘)+C, and then press Ctrl(⌘)+N.

5. In the New dialog box, leave all the settings at their defaults, except the Mode. Choose Grayscale, and click on OK to display the new document window.

6. Press Ctrl(⌘)+V, and then choose Edit, Purge, Clipboard.

7. Choose Flatten Image from the Layers palette's menu flyout. Save this new image to your hard disk as Warp.psd, in the Photoshop file format. Keep the image open in the workspace.

You can close a Displace resource file and still use it on a target image, but you will reuse the Warp image in this example to create an additional effect later in this chapter.

8. Click on the title bar of the Island image to make it the foreground document. Unhide the Reflection layer; click on the visibility icon on the Layers palette next to the title for Reflections. Click on the Reflections title to make this the current editing layer.

9. With the Rectangular Marquee tool, drag inside the marquee selection to reposition it over the reflection boat area. If you accidentally deselected the marquee, drag a new one to encompass the boat.

10. Choose Filter, Distort, Displace. In the Horizontal Scale field, type **10,** and then type **0** in the vertical Scale field (see fig. 10.24). This displaces the boat pixels (on the Reflection layer) that are 10 percent the maximum horizontal amount achieved by using the visual information in the Warp image, and displaces no pixels along the vertical plane of the image.

figure 10.24
Choose the amount by which you want target image areas displaced along the image's height, width, or both dimensions.

Because the marquee in the image is about the same size as the displacement map (the Warp.psd image), the Displacement Map and Undefined Areas options in the Displace dialog box are not relevant in this example. With image areas larger or smaller than the resource Displace file (the PSD file), you might want to choose Stretch to Fit, and Repeat Edge Pixels to make the resource file conform more to the dimensions of the target area for displacement.

11. Click on OK to display a directory box. Choose the Warp.psd image you saved in step 7, and click on Open to apply the Displace effect. The way the Displace filter distorts the boat is almost identical to the way the waves in the water distort the tree reflections (see fig. 10.25).

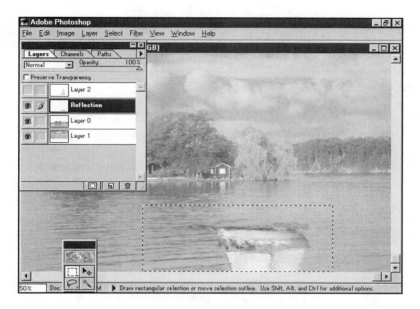

figure 10.25

What better resource is there for displacing a boat reflection than an image of waves?

12. Press Ctrl(⌘)+S to save your work. *Do not* deselect the rectangular selection in the image yet.

Reflections in any outdoor body of water show highlights and areas where the reflection hides from view, according to the way light is reflected toward the viewer. The next section shows you a quick, easy way to mix visible reflections of the boat with some areas hidden in the water.

Loading a Selection in Layer Mask Mode

Chapter 4 discussed the many ways Photoshop displays selection areas. Foreground color, for example, is the color of Quick Mask overlay, which becomes a marquee selection when you edit in Standard editing mode. The converse is also true—marquee selections can be displayed as a color in Photoshop, and this color, used in combination with Layer Mask mode, can hide selected image areas in a document.

Here's how to remove selected areas of the boat reflection, based on the visual information in the Warp.psd image:

USING SELECTION INFORMATION AS A MASK

1. Click on the title bar of the Warp document to put it in the foreground in the workspace.

2. On the Channels palette, click on the Black channel title and drag it into the Island.psd image window (see fig. 10.26). This creates a new channel in the Island document, automatically assigns white as the selection color for the channel, and places the copied Warp channel within the active marquee selection you made in the previous section.

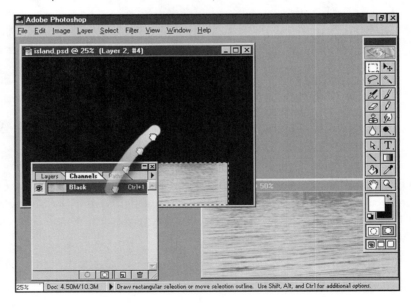

figure 10.26

To copy a channel and position it in a document of a different size, create a marquee in the target file and then drag the channel title into the target document window.

3. You can close the Warp image at any time now.

4. Press Ctrl(⌘) and click on the new channel title on the Channels palette for the Island image to load the visual information contained in this channel as a marquee selection.

5. Click on the Reflection title on the Layers palette to make this the current editing layer, and then click on the Add Layer Mask icon at the bottom of the palette (see fig. 10.27). The Layer Mask hides all the selected areas in the image, which correspond to the highlights in the waves of the Warp image you copied to the alpha channel.

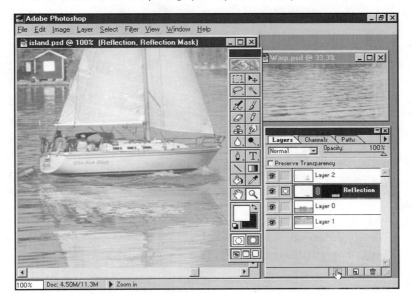

figure 10.27
Areas that would be partially hidden in the water's highlights are hidden with the Layer Mask.

6. Click on the Layer Mask thumbnail image on the Reflection layer title, and drag the thumbnail into the trash icon. In the attention box that asks whether you want to Apply or Discard the Layer Mask, click on Apply.

7. Press Ctrl(⌘)+S to save your work. You're finished!

Figure 10.28 shows the completed scene (see also the color signature in this book). Who would imagine that the "gifted photographer" who captured this image is actually a gifted Photoshop imaging expert?

figure 10.28
The correct balance of image composition and techniques for enhancing an image can make a beautiful composition from stock photographic elements.

To conclude this chapter's theme of enhancing images, the next section shows how to create a quick, effective, and subtle text effect for occasions in which you want to preserve image composition and detail, but need some text.

Creating Overlay Text

Perhaps you have seen advertisements in which a headline whose point size would ordinarily be overpowering actually complements the design, through the use of transparency. You can control the text's opacity, and integrate the text with an image behind it, by creating a copy of the text and then altering the copy's tonal values.

The Levels Command and the "Glass Look"

The Island image looks picture postcard perfect, and seems to call for the addition of some text. The integration of text with a well-composed image should be done in such a way that the text complements the image, however. The visual effect you will create in the image is similar to the effect of looking through a glass paperweight at papers, a design, or a photograph. You get the sense of the shape of the paperweight, but it doesn't really intrude upon your view of the papers. Both the paperweight and the papers share a visually harmonious importance.

Here's how to add text to practically any image, while maintaining the focus of the composition:

TEXT ENHANCEMENTS

1. Press Ctrl(⌘)+Alt(Opt)+S to display the Save a Copy dialog box. Save a copy of your work to your hard disk in the TIFF format, as Island.tif. Check the Don't Include Alpha Channels check box in the Save A Copy dialog box; you no longer need the alpha channel of the Warp image.

2. Close the Island.psd image and open the Island.tif image you saved in step 1.

3. Press Ctrl(⌘)+R to display rulers around the Island document window.

4. Double-click on either ruler to display the Units and Rulers preferences.

5. From the Rulers Units drop-down list, choose Points, and click on OK to exit the Preferences box. The Island document appears to have about 200 points of sky area into which you can add text.

The text we chose for this image is "Weekends!" And we used Neuland as the font. If you don't have Neuland, Lithos is a good font; it works well with images of vacations and oceans.

6. Drag on the Type tool on the toolbox to access the Type Mask tool. Click in the document to specify where the text should begin, and to display the Type tool dialog box.

7. Type **WEEKENDS!** in the text field, specify the Font from the drop-down list of installed fonts, type **200** in the size field, and click on OK.

8. Drag inside the text marquee to center the text at the top of the image (see fig. 10.29).

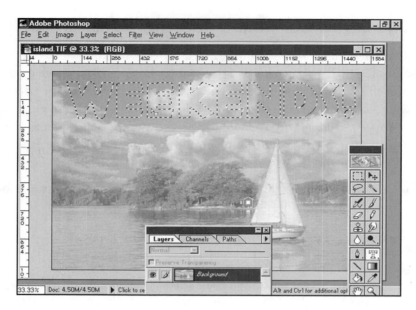

figure 10.29

Drag the selection marquee of the text to its position in the composition.

9. Right-click (Macintosh: hold Ctrl and click) and then choose Layer via Copy from the Context menu. Layer 1 appears in the document window, and the marquee disappears; Layer 1 is the current editing layer in the document.

10. Press Ctrl(⌘)+L. Then, in the Levels dialog box, drag the white point slider left to about 164 (see fig. 10.30). By lowering the white point in the image, you increase the brightness and the contrast of the copied text on Layer 1. The image *content* is the same; you can still see the clouds, but the text is brighter than surrounding areas, and subtly presents itself to the viewer.

figure 10.30
Change the tones in the copied text areas to create a faint design, slogan, or other text message.

11. Choose File, Save. You can close the image at any time now.

With areas that are lighter than the sky in the Islands image, the same glass look for text can be created by making a darker version of the image area. You can do this by increasing the black point—by dragging the black point slider to the right in the Levels command.

TIP

For more techniques on working with text as a graphics element, check out Chapter 12, "Working with Text as Graphics."

Summary

Of all this chapter's tricks for enhancing images, perhaps the best—the one that will serve you time and again in your own assignments—is how to examine real-world images for details. Reflections, composition, and the visual effect created when surfaces display light through and around them are elements that Photoshop simulates well (but only if you know what a surface is *supposed* to look like, to begin with). Then you can enhance a photo by adding what is missing to its appearance.

Now we will move from optics and enhancing images in this chapter to examining the color aspect of images in Chapter 11. That chapter, "Black and White…and Color," contains many of the secrets of effective filter use, color conversion and grayscale printing techniques, and the principles behind making images look their finest in any color mode.

CHAPTER

11

BLACK AND WHITE...AND COLOR

*Color imaging is emphasized in this book because color is the way people see
the world. The capability of the personal computer to display 24-bit color and
the development of software such as Photoshop to work with these images are
fairly recent events in the history of publication, however. As exciting as color
photography and imaging is, black-and-white photography still has a place in
the world of media. You may need to produce black-and-white work when
preparing a newsletter, flyer, or other promotion. The black-and-white
medium gives you not only a photographic purism, but also economy (in the
size of saved files).*

This chapter is a potpourri of techniques and special effects you might want to adopt in your own work with monochrome (also known as grayscale or black-and-white) photographic images. For example, an image created or photographed in color can be manipulated as a grayscale, and vice versa. In this chapter, you learn the best way to convert a copy of a color image to grayscale, how to sample colors from an image to tint a grayscale image, how Photoshop filters can be used to produce grayscale masterpieces, and how duotones can enhance a print of your monochrome images. Photoshop handles image data adeptly, regardless of color mode. You will learn how to get the most out of *any* type of image you have to work with.

Sampling Original Colors in an Image

Your introduction to the wonderful world of black and white begins, paradoxically, with the color image Laurie.tif on the Companion CD.

Before you convert the Laurie image, you will sample and preserve some of the original colors from it. Photoshop provides a quick, easy way to sample an image's colors automatically, as well as a way to sample individual pixel colors manually. By sampling and saving a number of unique colors from an RGB image, you can apply the saved colors to an image that has only grayscale values, thereby performing the digital equivalent of hand-tinting an image.

Copying and Saving Image Colors

The Swatches palette in Photoshop can theoretically hold an infinite number of color samples, limited only by your system resources. The 122 default colors on the Swatches palette are only one of several collections of colors you can display; PANTONE, TRUMATCH, and other digital color-matching systems can be loaded by clicking on the Swatches palette flyout and choosing Replace Swatches. If you specify in the Load dialog box the path to the Photoshop\Palettes folder on your hard disk, you will see the different palettes you have to choose from.

When you want to sample only a few colors from an image, you might choose to "hand pick" them by sampling a photo or illustration and then adding (*appending*) the colors to Photoshop's default color swatches. Clearly, this process can become tedious. If you want a large sampling of colors, however, don't despair; the next section shows you learn how to auto-load colors from an image.

Right now, let's walk through the process of saving a color to the Swatches palette, so that you can reuse that color in other images.

MANUALLY SAMPLING COLORS FROM AN IMAGE

CD-ROM

1. Open Laurie.tif from the CHAP11 folder of the Companion CD.

2. Press F6 (Window, Show Swatches) if the Swatches palette isn't already in the workspace.

3. Press I (for Eyedropper tool) and then click anywhere on the image (see #1 in fig. 11.1). Notice that the foreground color on the toolbox has changed to reflect the sample you have clicked on.

figure 11.1
Colors can be added to the Swatches palette by sampling them with the Eyedropper tool.

4. At the end of the color swatches on the Swatches palette, click over an empty area to the right of the last swatch. The color you sampled is appended to the default swatches palette (see #2 in fig. 11.1).

As was mentioned earlier, the manual process of sampling and saving colors on a palette is time-consuming (and usually unnecessary) in Photoshop 4. *Indexed color images* are composed of a limited palette of colors (usually no more than 256 unique colors), and Photoshop can write a palette from an indexed image to a file that you can load into the Swatches palette. It should be stressed here that if you seek absolute color fidelity in sampled colors, copying the color index from an image is not the way to go. When Photoshop creates an indexed palette from a 24-bit color image, many colors are discarded, and colors kept in the image file are actually an averaged color blend of original colors. If, however, you are looking for lifelike tones but not necessarily absolutely precise samples, this is how the procedure goes:

◆ Choose Image, Duplicate and accept the default name in the Duplicate Image dialog box by clicking on OK. To create the color palette, you have to convert the image from RGB color to Indexed color. Because this process alters the original file, you should always make your custom color palette from a copy of the original image.

◆ Choose the Rectangular Marquee tool from the toolbox (press M to toggle between the Rectangular and the Elliptical Marquee tool on the toolbox), and then click and drag in the duplicate image to create a frame around our model Laurie's face. Leave a little room on the right side so that some background colors of the trees are included in the selection (see fig. 11.2).

figure 11.2
Select an area of the image that contains most of the colors found in the entire image.

The operation for creating an indexed color image from an RGB image examines all the pixel colors in an image window. If you were to sample the entire Laurie.tif image to create a palette, that palette would contain a great many greens. The green background of Laurie.tif takes up almost 50 percent of the total number of pixels in the image—and, unfortunately, an indexed palette for an image can contain only 256 unique colors. Because the foreground subject is more important than the soft-focus background in this image, you need to crop away the exterior of the selection marquee. This forces Photoshop to average more flesh-tone pixels for the image, yet by leaving some background area within the marquee selection, you enable the program to create some green pixels for the indexed palette.

CREATING AN INDEXED PALETTE

1. Choose Image, Crop. If you look at the cropped image now for color content, you see many more flesh tones than superfluous background colors in the image window.

2. Choose Image, Mode. Then choose Indexed Color to display the Indexed Color dialog box.

3. Choose Adaptive from the Palette drop-down list. An *adaptive palette* is one composed of the most frequently occurring pixel colors in an image. Photoshop intelligently searches the image for the most commonly occurring 256 colors, and then analyzes the rest of the colors to see how many are close in value to the top 256. Photoshop then takes the information it gathered and calculates a weighted average to determine which 256 colors (out of 16.7 million possible colors) will most accurately approximate the original image.

4. Leave the Color Depth and the Colors drop-down lists at their default settings of 8 bits/ pixel and 256 colors, respectively. Note that there is no option in Photoshop for creating an indexed palette of more than 256 colors.

5. In the Options field, the drop-down list of dithering options contains three methods— None, Pattern, and Diffusion—for giving the indexed color image a different look. Because you want to generate an indexed palette (not change the appearance of the cropped duplicate image), leave the option set to Diffusion (see fig. 11.3), and click on OK.

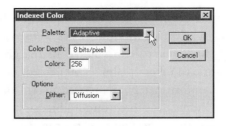

figure 11.3

The Indexed Color options box enables you to specify the number of colors in an indexed palette and the type of color reduction performed on the image.

You might not even notice at this point that the copy of the Laurie image has been reduced from 24-bit color to indexed, 8-bit color. Diffusion dithering and adaptive color reduction help disguise the reality that the image contains fewer unique colors than the original. And the 122 default colors in the Swatches palette for the duplicate image have changed to 122 of the 256 colors that make up the color index for the image. The colors on the Swatches palette are unique to the current foreground image in Photoshop, and the color palette for the indexed, duplicate image will disappear when you close the duplicate image window. To create, for future use, a permanent set of Swatches colors from the palette of colors in the duplicate image, follow these steps:

Saving a Custom Color Table

1. Choose Image, Mode, Color Table. On the Color Table box, you can see the palette Photoshop has created for the image. Click on Save to save this palette for future use. Specify the path for the saved color palette to the Photoshop/Palettes directory on your hard disk and name the file Laurie.act, as shown in figure 11.4.

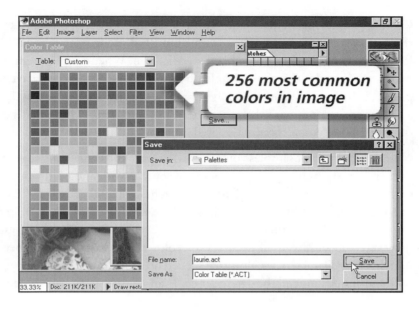

figure 11.4
Save the color table for an indexed color image to a file that can be loaded in
Photoshop later.

2. Click on OK to save the color palette, and then click on Cancel to leave the Color Table
   dialog box. Close the copy of the Laurie image without saving it, but leave the
   Laurie.tif image open for the examples that follow.

TIP

On the Macintosh, Photoshop does not distinguish between a Photoshop color table (palette)
and a color table that can be used by the system and other applications. Windows users have
the option of saving a color table to Photoshop's ACT format, or to Microsoft's PAL format,
chosen from the Save As drop-down list in the Save dialog box. A few Windows applications can
read and use a palette written in the Microsoft color palette format.

Custom palettes are an invaluable addition to your other Photoshop tools because the color characteristics of colors sampled in RGB mode from real-world pictures look more natural than a home-brew specification. When people attempt to color-match a digitized image, for example, they tend to pick colors that have too much pure hue. In nature, colors generally contain several primary values, with one value a *little* more predominant than the others. In an amount of light that's composed of several hues, you recognize the predominant hue as a shade of color.

Notice that the color samples you took earlier from the Laurie.tif image are slightly muted. Compositionally, they support and contrast with one another in the context of the photo, although at first glance they might look like the "wrong" colors to use in hand-tinting a black-and-white image. By sampling color values from an image instead of specifying them in the Color Picker or Photoshop's Color palette, however, you ensure total accuracy in color replacement. Remember that the human eye is distracted by colors that are too brilliant and pure to be natural. If you doubt it, think about all the detergent boxes and flashy sports cars sold in America!

TIP

To remove a color from a palette loaded into the Swatches palette, hold Ctrl(⌘) and click over the swatch.

From 24-Bit Color to 8-Bit Grayscale

Now that you have sampled the colors from the Laurie image, it's time to remove the color from the image to create a good-looking grayscale version. Color reduction generally *shouldn't* be performed at the digital image acquisition phase because scanners and other input hardware typically don't use a color model that can adequately handle conversion from RGB image information directly to grayscale. Grayscale is a single-channel format, whose visual information is displayed as brightness, whereas a scanner and a film recorder operate around the RGB color model.

Color Models

If you intend to manipulate images in different Photoshop color modes, you need to understand a little about color theory. This section describes how digital images get their color, and how we humans describe this color.

Color channel digital images are those whose file format enables Photoshop to read the image by assembling component channels to create a *color composite* image. The content of the channel components is typically a red channel, a green one, and a blue channel; the composite of these channels is called an *RGB color image*.

RGB Color

Although the human eye and the phosphors on a monitor receive red, green, and blue image information, the RGB color model is *not* the easiest to work with when you specify color or convert a color image to grayscale. A *color model* is an invention that enables those of us (artists and designers) who are not mathematicians to work with data that would otherwise be difficult or impossible to manipulate. Often, looking at the *structure* of data to examine why things work—or why they *don't* work—is useful. By examining a model of the RGB color space, you can quickly see why converting a color image straight to grayscale from this color model is not a good idea.

The triangular plane shown in figure 11.5 represents a color image in RGB mode. In the corners of the color model are the red, green, and blue components. At the edge of the color model, none of the component colors contributes to the composite blend of colors—and equal amounts of absence of the component colors produces black. Toward the center of the model, each component displays a greater brightness value until the color white is achieved.

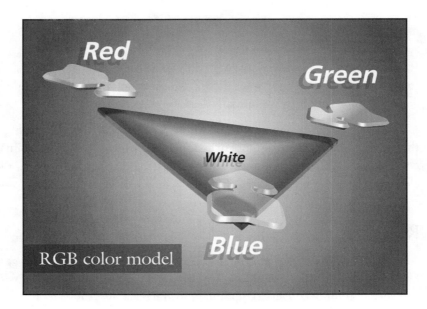

figure 11.5
The RGB color model consists of red, green, and blue components whose relative strengths combine to create a composite color.

Photoshop and other design programs usually offer a brightness slider in a color picker to enable the user to specify a neutral shade by moving the red, green, and blue strengths in a color toward or away from the center of the model. When red, green, and blue colors are present in a pixel in equal amounts, the result is a shade of gray. When component colors are present in a pixel within an image in *unequal* amounts, you see color. The hue you see is measured by the relative difference in the contributions of the component colors.

HSB Color

An easier way to describe color is the *HSB color model*, which describes color according to the *qualities* of visible light rather than the mix of component colors.

Images in Photoshop cannot be broken into discrete Hue, Saturation, and Brightness channels, but you can indeed specify colors according to this model by using the Hue, Saturation command (under Image, Adjust). Understanding the HSB color model makes it easier to grasp the LAB color model, which will be used to convert the Laurie image to grayscale.

Hue is the frequency of light wave that reflects from an object you see. It is the primary quality of light that distinguishes one particular color from another. Shocking blue or electric green might be said to have a strong hue. These strong colors are a result of a high saturation of a color.

Saturation is the relative strength of one hue compared to others in a specific color. High saturation is also referred to as *color purity*. You have often seen a color that's a mixture of say, blue with green, with a little yellow added to it. The reason we wouldn't call such a color a highly saturated one is that all the hues present in the color are competing for predominance. When several hues are present in near-equal amounts, you see a grayscale color.

Brightness, the third component of the HSB color model, is sometimes referred to as *lightness* or *value.* It is the color quality that determines the apparent reflectivity of a color. A bright purple object and a deep purple object can have the same hue and saturation, but the amount of brightness the objects display is different.

In figure 11.6 you can see the arrangement of color qualities in HSB color as a model. Hue is described as a ring at the base of a hexagon; as you travel around the hexagon, you move to different hues. Toward the outside of the hexagon is saturated color; as you move to the center, colors lose their distinguishing predominance. When you travel upward within this model, colors become brighter until the point of the model, white, is reached. Everywhere you travel inside this model is a specific color, and all colors in the HSB color model can be created through the use of different brightnesses of red, green, and blue (RGB) colors.

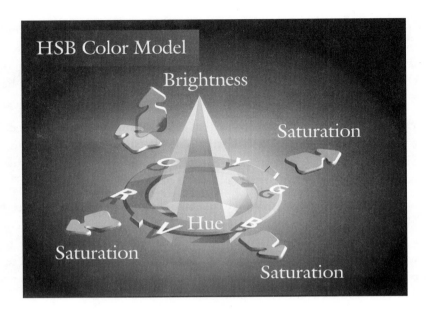

figure 11.6
The HSB color model is a more user-friendly description of light than the RGB color model.

No matter which specifications (RGB or HSB) you decide to use for describing color in your work, neither model provides an adequate description of light components that will enable you to successfully strip color from an image and arrive at a faithful grayscale equivalent. The reason for this inadequate description lies in the way the human eye perceives color; color strengths are unevenly distributed. The photo receptors in our eyes are more sensitive to green than to red, and more sensitive to red than to blue.

Have you ever photocopied a magazine cover and been disappointed by the results? Those results are disappointing because when the photocopier exchanges color information to an equivalent percentage of black, its selection of tones is heavily influenced by the brightness inherent to a specific color. Blues appear as white areas on the photocopy, and reds appear darker than you might expect them to translate. Brightness—the amount of illumination an image area displays without regard to any specific color contribution—is a key phrase here. The human eye and photocopiers cannot see the brightness quality in an image without being influenced by the accompanying color. Fortunately, Photoshop offers a color model that keeps the brightness quality separate from color information.

LAB Color

The LAB color model (also called *CIELAB*) was created as an international color specification standard by the Commission Internationale d'Eclairage (CIE). Instead of using red, green, and blue like the RGB color model, or the hue, saturation, and brightness of HSB models, *LAB color* is built around the models of lightness and chroma. In a LAB image, the L channel contains all the information about the luminance in the image, the A channel stores information about hues from green to magenta, and the B channel holds information about hues from blue to yellow (see fig. 11.7).

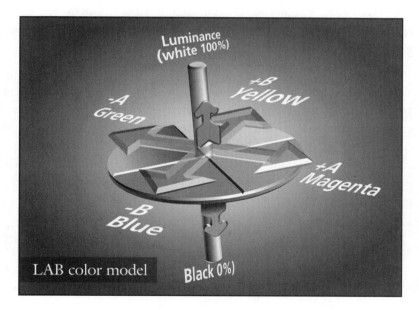

figure 11.7
The LAB color model separates chromacity (pure color information) from the brightness values found in an image.

NOTE

For designers, one of the advantages of the LAB model (compared to the RGB color model) is that it is device-independent. For example, the same values of LAB's color components can be used to describe both printed color and colored light emanating from a monitor. The ability to specify color in a way that can be used by all kinds of devices has long been needed. The LAB color model is a way to accurately specify color to anyone in the world, for users to work with any kind of output, display device, or material. Its use is similar to the widely accepted use of PANTONE swatches to specify exactly the color of ink you want a printer to use.

Translating RGB Values to LAB Values

LAB color is a superset of all other digital color models; the range of color expression is greater than RGB or CMYK (the color model for specifying printed inks). All the other color models Photoshop uses are subsets that fit within the gamut of color that can be defined with the LAB color model. Because LAB color encompasses the RGB gamut, you can convert an RGB image (such as the Laurie.tif image) to LAB color without any translation or loss of image data.

You saw the visible effects of going from a wider color gamut to a narrower one when you indexed the copy of the Laurie image. An indexed color mode has fixed, limited color values; when you limit the unique colors in an RGB mode image to indexed color, the color reduction displays dithering (the *simulation* of additional unique colors) and image content is compromised (lost). When you convert an RGB image to the LAB color model, however, no loss of image information occurs in the translation process.

Here's how to convert the color image of Laurie to a grayscale equivalent:

◆ Choose Image, Mode and then choose LAB Color from the menu bar. If you keep the Channels palette in the foreground, you can see that the Red, Green, and Blue color channels have been exchanged for Lightness, A, and B channels.

◆ Choose File, Save As, and save the image as Laurie.psd to your hard disk.

TIP

The TIFF file format also supports images arranged according to LAB color channels, as do the Encapsulated PostScript (EPS) and RAW image formats, but because Photoshop *uses* the LAB model in conversion processes, Photoshop's proprietary PSD format is a good file format in which to save the converted image.

Now that the copy of the Laurie image is arranged according to LAB's method of specifying color, you can isolate only the brightness characteristic in the image. By isolating the Lightness (luminosity) channel of an image, you have the image information you need to obtain a detailed, tonally balanced grayscale image.

Using a Single LAB Color Component

If you have experimented with Photoshop channels and copied a single RGB channel to a new file, you know that the result is a grayscale image. Because a single RGB color channel contains information about the relative strength of one color component, no single grayscale representation in a channel contains accurate grayscale information about a photo. The A and B chromatic components in LAB color are fairly meaningless as artistic, visual information in a Photoshop channel because the A and B channels each represent proportions of primary and secondary colors to define a specific color value.

Now, having saved the Laurie.tif image in a mode that arranges color information according to LAB specifications, you can use a copy of the Luminance channel in the LAB image to create a new, Grayscale mode image. The new grayscale image is the most accurate depiction you can get, using Photoshop's color modes, of the original image's light characteristics.

Here's how to perform an accurate and pleasing color-to-grayscale transformation, using the Laurie.tif image:

ACCURATELY REMOVING IMAGE COLOR

1. If the Layers/Channels/Paths grouped palette isn't currently on-screen, press F7 and click on the Channels tab (or choose Window, Show Channels).

2. Click on the Lightness channel title. It will display a view of Lightness (Luminance) on the Channels palette channel within the image window as 8-bits-per-pixel information.

3. Choose Image, Modes, and then choose Grayscale. Photoshop displays a boxed message asking whether you want to discard other channels.

4. Click on OK to lose the A and B channels and convert the image to Grayscale mode. The Lightness channel becomes the Black channel.

5. Choose File, Save As, and save the image to your hard disk in TIFF format (as Liteness.tif). Keep the image open in Photoshop for examples to follow.

If you still have doubts as to whether the last exercise is the best method for extracting ideal grayscale information from a color image, check out figure 11.8. On the left is the Laurie.tif RGB image, converted straight from RGB color to Grayscale mode through the Image, Modes command; on the right is the Liteness.tif image.

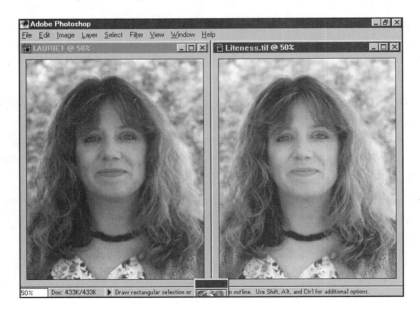

figure 11.8
The Lightness channel in an image in LAB mode contains only the luminance qualities corresponding to the colors in the image.

So, a little color theory pays off, eh? As a computer graphics designer, your ability to understand color depends upon viewing color data in a visually meaningful context. Fortunately, Photoshop can display a wide range of on-screen options for viewing visual data according to your artistic needs.

Liteness.tif might not be an award-winning grayscale image right now, for reasons unrelated to the procedure you have learned. First, the image had good lighting, but Laurie.tif does not contain excellent separations of different tonal regions—English translation: the photograph was not taken on a brilliant day. Generally, photographs of people are unflattering when you use harsh lighting that produces a great deal of contrast and clear tonal variation. Second, our eyes are influenced by color, and our perception of image quality revolves around information gleaned from both color and tone. Without the color, we see that something is *missing* from the image.

In either case, if you read Chapter 5, "Restoring an Heirloom Photograph," you saw how to redistribute the tonal values in an image by using the Levels command. With the Levels command at your disposal, you have the ticket for tweaking the Liteness.tif image or any other grayscale image you have created by copying the L channel in a LAB color image.

With the Liteness.tif image the active window in your Photoshop workspace, Choose Image, Adjust, Levels—Ctrl(⌘)+L is the shortcut—and then experiment with the midrange control (the middle triangle directly beneath the histogram). Depending on your monitor calibration, you may want to increase the midrange contrast to add a little snap to the midrange of the image. Because a grayscale image does not depend on color information to represent visual content, the Levels command is the ideal choice of tools for modifying such images. The Levels command's only purpose is the redistribution of brightness values across a grayscale, color, or other mode of image.

Creative Uses of Filters and Grayscale Images

As mentioned earlier, the human eye is attracted subliminally to a color image rather than a grayscale one, often for the wrong reasons. The eye is attracted to bright pastels and saturated colors, and often overlooks poor composition in a color image.

When you look at a grayscale image that contains no distracting color information, you are forced to analyze the image solely on its visual content. The special effects you work with in this chapter are particularly effective when applied to an image that contains only visual detail, without the distracting element of color.

Photoshop's Filters work as artistic enhancements in grayscale images for the following reasons:

◆ Shifting the focal point in a color photo by adding a special effect is almost impossible. The eye is drawn primarily to an interesting color area and registers an effect as a secondary consideration.

◆ Blending a special effect into a grayscale image is much easier to do than blending it into a color image. Because there are no hues, you don't have to worry about matching saturation and hue values between special and not-so-special areas of the image.

Think about the uses you have for black-and-white photography in everyday assignments. When the budget is tight for a flyer or newsletter, for example, process color printing is out of the question. The brunt of the printed material's attraction then lies in the composition of art and photographic images. Why not make them as eye-catching as possible by using a few Photoshop effects?

The Filters menu in Photoshop comes packed with many dramatic, processor-intensive effects you can apply to selections or to entire images. Although these effects are useful for distorting and randomizing simple still-life images, they are absolutely inappropriate to apply full-force to a portrait image. Later in this chapter you will explore some creative uses of Photoshop's more powerful filters, which are more suitably applied to still-life images.

Adding Noise to a Grayscale Image

Noise, in the context of digital imaging, is the random dispersal within an image of pixels that have different brightness levels. Because the connotation of noise is generally unpleasant (except when the noise comes from your stereo, and not your neighbor's), you might think that one's ultimate goal in digital imaging is to *remove* noise from an image.

But noise is neither good nor bad. Treated as a design element, video noise is a quality you can add to a grayscale image to create a stunning effect. When the Noise filter is applied, it removes some of the original image detail (as do all Photoshop filters). The real trick to working successfully with the Noise filter is to strike a balance in the image between the effect and the way it interacts with the original image.

In the next set of steps, you use the Noise filter to modify the visual information in the Liteness.tif image. You use the Uniform Noise option in the Add Noise dialog box because Uniform Noise can create an interesting texture in an image in which many areas gradually move into deeper and lighter brightness values. Digital grit is often an attention-getting enhancement for images that lack contrast. Noise is not a substitute for improving contrast in an image, but it can add interest and complement original image detail.

In this example you create a look that's popular in magazines—they use it to make portrait photography resemble a graphic design.

Using Noise as a Design Element

1. Type **200** in the Zoom percentage box (bottom, left of status bar or document window) and then press Enter (Return).

   Unlike many Photoshop filters, Noise needs at least a 1:1 view of the target image to accurately view and assess the effect. A 2:1 viewing resolution ensures an accurate view of the effect. Noise randomly disperses single pixels throughout an image, and although Photoshop can zoom a view to any percentage, it cannot offer you a precise view of this effect because of the on-screen interpolation it performs to offer stepless zoom levels.

2. Choose Filter, Noise, Add Noise to display the Add Noise dialog box.

3. Click on the Uniform radio button. Uniform noise is softer in appearance than Gaussian noise, the other option.

The Monochromatic check box doesn't affect the outcome of the Liteness.tif image because the Liteness image itself is monochromatic. When you work with a color image and the Monochromatic check box is not checked, the Noise filter disperses color pixels throughout the image. With the box checked, various amounts of gray component are randomly added to pixels. Adding gray component to the image pixels creates different shades of the original color and creates the appearance of noise.

4. Place your cursor inside the preview window, and then click and drag until you have scrolled to an image area with visual detail.

    By default, Photoshop offers *preview windows* (sometimes called *proxy boxes*) that show a limited view of the center of the image in the workspace. Often, this is not an area of interest in an image, so you can always click and drag to pan your view to a different area of the image.

5. Click on the plus button under the preview window to zoom into any area of interest in the image.

6. Click and drag the Amount slider to about **47** (or enter this value in Amount field), as shown in figure 11.9, and then click on OK.

    The Amount slider offers a blend of Noise with original image information in exponential (not linear) increments from 1 to 999. The halfway mark on the slider is 100. Amounts you specify in excess of 100 tend to ruin image detail.

7. Choose File, Save As, and then save the image to your hard disk in the TIFF format, as Dusty.tif. You can close the document at any time now, and reopen Liteness.tif to run through the examples in the sections that follow.

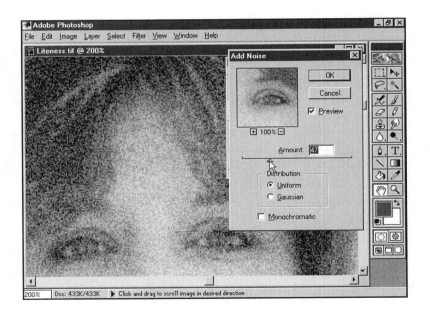

figure 11.9
The Add Noise filter can help soften and remove unwanted image details.

NOTE

The Add Noise effect actually displays in the document window while the Filter command is in the foreground if you take more than three or four seconds to specify Add Noise options. This display happens if the target image is smaller than 1 MB or so, and you are using a 486 or Quadra machine or higher, with about 32 MB of system RAM. Hence the suggestion that you zoom into the 200 percent viewing resolution before entering the command.

TIP

Although you cannot use a document's scroll bars to move around the document or to access the Zoom tool, you can manipulate your view through shortcut key commands while a Filter or other command box is the foreground application interface element.

To zoom into a document while a command box is in the foreground, hold Ctrl (⌘)+spacebar to toggle to the Zoom tool; then you can click in the document, or marquee an area with the Zoom tool to move to a specific image area. When you hold Alt (Opt) +spacebar, the tool toggles (changes) to the Zoom out tool, and you can zoom out of the image in Photoshop's workspace.

The Hand tool can be accessed from within a Filters or other box by holding the spacebar.

An extra perk that comes with noisy images is that they print well to low-resolution laser printers. The Noise filter breaks up continuous tone regions in an image, and 300–600 dpi printers have less difficulty plotting this information than they do reproducing smooth shades of gray.

Unlike Uniform noise, Gaussian noise tends to deposit a clump of random pixels in the target image. For this reason, Uniform noise is the best choice for creating an effect in an image whose subject is a person. You might want to experiment, however, with images of landscapes, still-life scenes, and the Gaussian noise filter.

Creating a Crystallized Image

The more dramatic an effect you create in an image, the more original image detail you lose, but that shouldn't stop you from applying a fairly intense effect to *part* of an image.

The Crystallize filter creates a pebbled effect in an image that can simulate a painted image, contrary to some of the other new filters, such as Artistic and Brush Strokes, which are a little too overwhelming to make a convincing piece. Although the Crystallize filter destroys much original composition detail, the effect can be worked into a portrait image in such a way that the Crystallize filter enhances, rather than disrupts, a pretty picture.

To create the next effect, you have a two-part assignment. First you follow a set of steps to apply the Crystallize filter. Then, using the Eraser tool in its Erase to Saved setting, you restore image areas, creating a smooth transition between crystallized areas and original image.

To begin: with the copy of Liteness.tif you saved earlier as the current document in Photoshop, choose Filter, Pixelate, and then Crystallize. Now, set Cell Size to 10 (or leave it set at 10) and click on OK to apply the effect. The Cell Size value roughly corresponds to the average of the height and width of individual crystals produced in the image by averaging the pixel values found in the corresponding original image area. Figure 11.10 shows the preview of the Crystallize effect; a cell size of 10 looks pretty dramatic. Crystallize, like most Photoshop filters, is extremely processor-intensive; even PowerMacs and Pentiums can take a while to execute a filter when it's applied to an image larger than 500 KB. Why not read ahead while you wait?

figure 11.10
The Crystallize filter creates shapes of solid color in the image, based upon an average of original area's colors.

The Crystallize filter produces an interesting, abstract effect, you want to *augment* Liteness.tif with the Crystallize effect, not let the effect become the main visual attraction. By restoring some of the original image details with the Erased to Saved mode of the Eraser tool, you can preserve some of the original Liteness.tif image in a very dramatic, artistic fashion. Because you applied the Crystallize filter to an image that was saved *before* you applied the effect, Photoshop can read into memory the saved version from your hard disk. The Eraser tool looks at the "before" copy of the image in memory, and changes the areas it passes over in the current image to their pre-Crystallized state.

Okay. Your processor has probably finished processing the Crystallize effect by now, and if your screen looks like figure 11.11, you're ready to try image restoration.

figure 11.11
Some images look more inviting when a filter is applied to only a portion of the image. Use the Eraser tool to restore filtered areas.

RESTORING WITH THE ERASER TOOL

1. Double-click on the Eraser tool. Double-clicking displays the Options palette for the Eraser tool.

2. Choose Paintbrush from the drop-down list on the Options palette, drag the Opacity slider to 100% if it isn't already there, and click on the Erase to Saved check box in the lower-right corner of the Options palette.

3. Press **D** (Default colors) to return your previous foreground/background selection boxes on the toolbox to a black foreground and white background. The Eraser tool now erases back to the previously saved version of the image at full power—100 percent strength (completeness).

4. Click on Brushes tab on the Brushes/Options grouped palette, and then click on the second row, second-from-the-right tip.

5. Click (don't drag) on Liteness.tif to instruct Photoshop to read the previously saved copy into memory for the Eraser tool.

WARNING

Photoshop takes a moment or two to read a saved version into system memory. Clicking and dragging with the Eraser tool set to Erase to Saved is a futile effort because Photoshop needs to read that saved image copy first. You stand a chance of making a mistake on the image if you immediately click and drag because Photoshop needs to catch up with your last input. Therefore, when working with the Erase to Saved option, it is best to click once, wait for Photoshop to load a copy of the original image, and then proceed with your work after the Photoshop cursor has returned from the system working cursor.

6. Click and drag over the facial areas of Liteness.tif, working from the inside toward the hair.

7. When the face area has been restored, press **5** on the keyboard. This decreases the opacity of the Eraser tool to 50 percent; further strokes will not completely restore the image.

8. Click and drag around the edge of the face, into the hair, until a blend between the Crystallize filter and original image information has been achieved.

9. When you have a masterpiece (see fig. 11.12), choose File, Save As and then save the image to your hard disk as Crystal.tif.

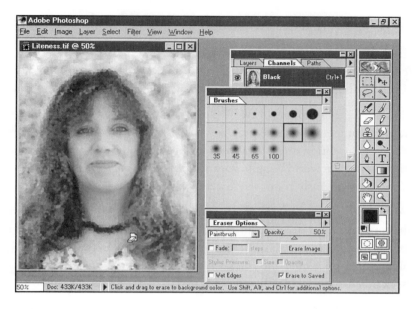

figure 11.12

Unimportant areas of an image, such as backgrounds (and sometimes hair), can have suggestions of painterly detail added through the use of a good filter.

The Eraser tool's work would be obvious if you had chosen Block or Pencil from the drop-down list of options. But the Paintbrush option made the blending of original and crystallized areas perfect because larger Photoshop default brushes have soft, semi-opaque edges. And the 50 percent Opacity setting for final detail work gives you the option of using multiple strokes to vary the amount of coverage or, as in this case, of erasure.

This book often stresses that partial opacity, pressure, and intensity really have the same effect when you set a percentage for a painting tool. The Options slider controls how completely an effect or color is applied with a Photoshop tool, and you gain overall artistic control when this slider is set to less than 100 percent.

The Zoom Blur Effect

In other chapters, you have seen how to use the Gaussian blur effectively to create convincing shadows in images. Photoshop's other Blur filters also come in handy. Each can be applied in different ways to achieve a special look.

The Radial blur comes in two flavors—Spin and Zoom. The Zoom re-creates a faithful simulation of the rack/zoom effect that photographers use to focus the center of attention on an area in an image. This effect is difficult to achieve in real time in the real world because your subject doesn't always remain motionless while you simultaneously zoom the lens and squeeze off a relatively long exposure time.

Although you can pick the focal center of a Radial blur, the Radial Blur dialog box has no option for defining an area that remains in focus; only a small central area of the image is left intact. The next exercise shows you how to manually adjust the image area on which the Radial blur concentrates—it's as simple as creating a selection area with a feathered border.

Here's how to draw the viewer's eye into the Liteness.tif image in a very compelling way by using the Radial blur filter:

CREATING THE ZOOM BLUR EFFECT

1. Press **L** (for Lasso tool).

2. On the Options palette for the Lasso tool, type **12** in the Feather field, and make sure that the Anti-Aliased box is checked.

    One way to feather a selection is to right-click (Macintosh: Ctrl+click) and then choose Feather from the Context menu. You should acquaint yourself with the Lasso tool's Feather feature, however. When you need to do feathered selection work on many images, this feature can save countless steps.

3. Click and drag a very loose selection marquee around Laurie's face area to include her neckline and part of her hair. The feathered selection created makes a gradual transition between the masked and selected area, beginning six pixels inside the marquee and ending six pixels outside the marquee (see fig. 11.13).

figure 11.13

Feathering a selection creates transitional areas of partial *selection, making an area you edit fade into unedited areas.*

4. Press Ctrl(⌘)+Shift+I (Select, Inverse). This inverts the marquee so that Laurie's face is protected from the filter, but areas on the other side of the marquee are available to change.

5. Choose Filter, Blur, and then choose Radial Blur.

6. Click and drag the Amount slider to **20** (or type **20** in the field), click on Zoom in the Method field, and then click on Best in the Quality field.

   This is an incredibly processor-intensive filter, but it's worth the wait. If you want to see a crude version of the effect in significantly less time, you can choose Draft or Good mode Quality. Photoshop has a massive amount of pixel reassignment to do with any type of Blur filter.

7. Click and drag upward inside the Blur window to set the origin of the zoom blur. Doing this moves the center of the zoom blur so that the effect appears to be emanating from Laurie's face, not from the center of the image, which would be her neck (see fig. 11.14).

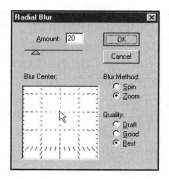

figure 11.14

Define the center of the blur effect within an image or a selected image area.

8. Click on OK and then check the fridge or do something else while Photoshop processes this complicated command.

9. Press Ctrl(⌘)+D (Select, None) to deselect the marquee in the document.

10. Choose File, Save As and save this image to your hard disk as Windy.tif.

11. Press Ctrl(⌘)+W (File, Close) to close the image window. You have finished with the image.

As you can see in figure 11.15, the selection area in the original image took most of the Radial zoom blur effect. The effect diminishes as it reaches the feathered masked area of Laurie's face.

WARNING

After you finish an assignment that calls for the use of the Feather option with the Lasso tool, be sure to set the Feather option back to 0. If you don't, and you don't have the Options palette displayed, you are in for an unpleasant surprise when you use the Lasso tool for regular freehand selection work.

figure 11.15
A soft, yet powerful aim of focus in an image can be attained by using the Zoom setting in the Radial Blur filter.

To avoid a telltale selection border when you applied the powerful Radial blur effect to the image's background, the Feather command came to the rescue again. The option to Feather a selection is available also on the Options palette for the Polygon Lasso, the Elliptical, and Rectangular marquee tools. If you have already created a selection, but have not specified a feather amount, you can always add a feather amount by choosing the Feather command from the Context menu or from the Select menu.

WARNING

The Radial blur, like the Gaussian blur and all the Stylize filters, needs to use as many of your system's resources as possible to execute an effect. Some heavy-duty interpolation is going on behind the digital scenes—yet another reason that grayscale images and special effects go hand in hand. Executing this sort of filter on an RGB image requires much more processing power, and possibly swapping out to hard disk if you don't have a great deal of system RAM. Whenever you swap to hard disk, the time needed to accomplish the effect increases substantially.

Creating Duotone Images

As mentioned earlier in this chapter, you can cut expenses significantly by using black-and-white printing for designs envisioned or edited to grayscale mode. Should you have a few cents left over in a budget, however, you can put the cash to good use by creating a duotone image of your work.

A Duotone is considered to be a color mode in Photoshop (as are Grayscale, RGB, and other color models). Because a duotone is actually a print specification, and not really a mode of color you would work with directly in Photoshop, your RGB monitor might not display an image in Duotone mode with absolute fidelity when compared to the printed result.

In commercial printing, a certain "gap" exists between the way brightnesses are reproduced in a digital image and on paper. Because a single application of pigment can cover only a limited area of the surface in a single pass, you might not see the rich tonal variations in a print of your grayscale work. The sad reality in digital press work is that a single pass of black cannot achieve the simulation of 256 shades of black.

One of the creative solutions the commercial printing industry discovered is the application of a second, colored ink to a black-and-white print to accentuate the tones that might be too faint to recognize with the first pass of black ink. The result of this process is called a *duotone*. The effect is a subtle tinting of an image to fill in areas of the image; however, do not expect a posterized print, or a sepiatone, from the process of creating a duotone—these are created by entirely different processes, and are much less subtle than a duotone.

The following sections take you through the creation of a duotone, and how to incorporate the image in a page layout.

Choosing the Right Image for a Duotone

Although subject matter is a question of personal preference, the authors believe that some of the best subjects for duotone are still life, not human, in their visual content. The reason for this belief is that although a duotone is subtle in its rendering of image content, there is still something stylized, something artificial, that can look unflattering when applied to images of people. In other words, a duotone can add interest to images of inanimate objects, but can steal something from pictures of people (which, ideally, should have enough innate visual interest to sustain the medium of black-and-white photography).

The example in this section is based on an assignment for a fictitious financial institution, the Banker's Loan & Trust. This mock client has come to you and wants a handsome cover designed for the cover of the annual report. They don't have the money for four-color process printing, but they *will* spring for two printing plates—giving you the perfect opportunity to check out this Photoshop Duotone feature.

Hurdle #1 in this assignment is that photo-finishing places can usually meet quick turnarounds for color—not black-and-white—film. (Even *purchasing* mono-chrome film at the usual stores is difficult these days!) You already know how to make the accurate conversion from RGB color to grayscale, however, so you snap your roll of film, get it written to PhotoCD disk or use a negative scanner, and the assignment continues.

For the cover of a bank report you might consider a carved stone pattern, such as the Bankwall.tif image in the CHAP11 folder of the Companion CD. Most carved stone architecture looks dignified, is easy to capture anywhere near a city, and because buildings on public thoroughfares are deemed fair game for commercial photography and display, you don't need to waste time and energy on release forms—absolutely no release forms are necessary.

In the steps to follow, you open and convert the Bankwall image to LAB color mode, and then use the Levels adjustment to bring out a little more detail in the image, which separates nicely to two duotone printing plates. The only disadvantage to photographing stone carvings is that they don't display many different tones; the stone, especially stone carved during the past 50 years, lacks the character that comes with weathering.

Here's how to convert and tonally adjust the Bankwall image:

COLOR CONVERSION AND TONE OPTIMIZATION

CD-ROM

1. In Photoshop, open the Bankwall.tif image from the CHAP11 folder of the Companion CD.

2. Choose Image, Modes, and then choose LAB Color.

3. Press F7 if the Channels palette isn't in the workspace at the moment, and then click on the Channels tab to make it the foreground palette in the grouped palettes.

4. Click on the Lightness channel on the Channels palette, and then choose Image, Mode, Grayscale. Click on OK in the attention box (see fig. 11.16) to reduce the image from color to grayscale information only.

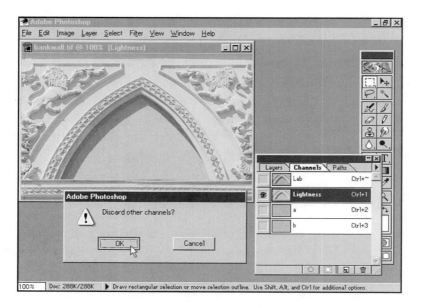

figure 11.16

Remove the color influence from the image by saving only the Lightness channel in LAB color mode.

Usually, you want to brighten the whites, add contrast by increasing the midtone frequency, and perhaps add a few black tones to a grayscale image that you plan to print from a laser printer. Duotones, however, involve a second application of ink along a different distribution curve than simple grayscale images. In essence, the second color plate in a duotone does not represent accurate grayscale information; rather, it is used to enhance the grayscale content. Therefore, you need to widen the midtone range a little for the specific duotone formula used in this example, increase the black point in the image (because the image is lacking in overall black tones), and decrease the white point in the image. Because every image is unique, you won't use these next steps for every image that you want convert to a duotone—but follow along, and you will see the rationale...

5. Press Ctrl(⌘)+L to display the Levels command.

6. Click and drag the right Output Levels slider until the number field reads **243**. This reassigns the absolute white value (the white point) in the image to a much higher level; therefore, the resulting image will contain no absolute white pixels.

   This is good; it gives the black and color plates that make up the duotone image an opportunity to display some pigment in the finished, printed image. If too much of the image were pure white, the paper color of the printed piece would show through, which is not the intention here.

7. Click and drag the black point triangle on the Input slider until the left Input Levels number box reads about **22**. This setting specifies a higher black point in the image than is in the original.

   If you look at the Levels command on your monitor, you can see that not many pixels in the image are toward black; the *histogram* (the graph) on the Levels command shows many more pixels toward darker tones, but only a smattering at the black point. By increasing the black point, more pixels will fall into a darker range, but not enough to flood the printed image (when it's printed with ink to paper). This correction is necessary because of the deficiency of the image—you might not have to adjust the black point with your own images. (For an illustration of the Levels command box, check out fig. 11.17.)

8. Click and drag the midpoint triangle until the center Input Levels box reads about **1.05**. This setting increases the range of midtones. If the Levels command looks like figure 11.17, you are in business and should click on OK.

   Although increasing the range of midtones means slightly less contrast in the image, it's a good move for final printing because it permits more individual midtone values to be printed. Contrast in a printed image is gained by the action of printing it—printed images have higher contrast than the digital equivalent displayed on your monitor.

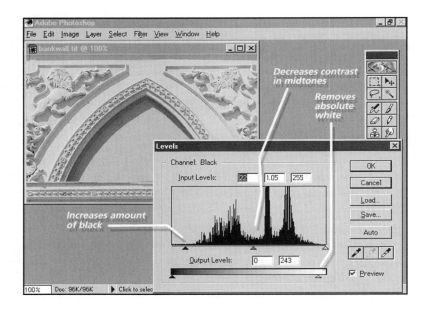

figure 11.17
The Levels command can reassign pixels in an image to different brightness levels, and create an image ideal for a duotone.

9. Choose File, Save As and save the image to your hard disk in the TIFF format as Bankwall.tif. Keep the image open in Photoshop for further steps.

The image is going to look fine as a patterned tile on the report cover. Bankwall was retouched so that it will tile seamlessly in a document window that's larger than Bankwall. (To learn how to clone your way to seamless tiling images, see Chapter 19, "Web Site Construction.")

Using the Define Pattern Feature to Create a Cover

As mentioned at the beginning of this chapter, grayscale images, because they contain one-third the number of color channels as RGB images, also take up one-third the saved file size. The Banker's Loan & Trust report cover needs to be 8 1/2" by 11", and obviously, this tiny Bankwall image won't fill the cover dimensions. The solution is to use the Define Pattern command, to sample the Bankwall image, and then fill an new document.

The only hitch in the following exercise is that your system might not have enough RAM or free hard disk space. Although grayscale images are smaller than their RGB counterparts, an 8 $\frac{1}{2}$" by 11" grayscale file is still 2 MB when these dimensions are specified to 150 pixels/inch resolution. For more information on the optimal resolution for printing to film or paper, see Chapter 16, "Outputting Your Input." Briefly, images of 150 pixels/inch in resolution output well to printers capable of 1,200 dots per inch (dpi), the equivalent of about 75 lines per inch on the printed page. You can do the following exercise if your computer has 20 MB of RAM, and equal amount of hard disk space, and is at least a 486 or Quadra machine. You might need to specify a lower resolution for the target file; by doing so, you reduce not only the maximum printing resolution, but also the system requirements.

Here's how to create the cover of the bank report:

CREATING A TILING PATTERN COVER

1. With BANKWALL as the current image in Photoshop's workspace, press Ctrl(⌘)+A to select the entire image.

2. Choose Edit, Define Pattern. Photoshop now copies the image into memory, so that it is available as a Fill option.

   If you don't have a lot of system RAM, you can close Bankwall.tif at any time. Otherwise, you might want to keep the image open so that you can compare it to the pattern-tiling effect to follow...

3. Press Ctrl(⌘)+N (File, New). In the New dialog box, type **Duotone** in the Name field; in the Width field, type **8.5** and specify Inches from the drop-down list; type **11** in the Height field (and specify Inches); then type **150** in the Resolution field. (On systems with less than 20 MB of RAM, consider typing **72** in the Resolution field; remember—this is an example, and the Banker's Loan & Trust won't hold a low-resolution cover image against you.)

4. Choose Grayscale from the Mode drop-down list, and then, if your screen looks like figure 11.18, click on OK. A 2 MB blank document is created in your workspace.

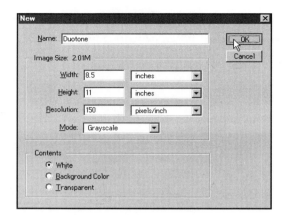

figure 11.18
Specify the color mode, the dimensions, and the resolution of the file you intend to create.

5. With the Duotone document window in the foreground, choose Edit, Fill; in the Contents field, choose Pattern from the drop-down list, leave the other options in this box at their defaults, and then click on OK. The new Duotone document tiles the sampled Bankwall image to fill it.

6. Choose Edit, Purge, and then choose Pattern. This new Photoshop feature empties your system RAM of the Bankwall sampled image, decreasing the system requirements of Photoshop as you continue working.

    Placing any text on this patterned cover image will be difficult because the variation in tones would prevent white, black, or any one shade in-between from visually separating from the image. To get around this problem, you are going to design a clean, semitrans-parent shaded rectangle in the lower right corner (the side on which the report opens) of the image so that some image background shows through, and so that white text can separate from the design.

7. With the Rectangular Marquee tool, click and drag toward the bottom right of the image window a rectangle that's about five inches wide and one inch tall (high). If you like, press Ctrl(⌘)+R to display rulers around the document, so that you get a better idea of the size of the rectangle you need here.

8. On the Layers palette, click on the Create new layer icon at the bottom of the palette. Layer 1 is now the current editing layer.

9. Click on the foreground color swatch on the toolbox, and then choose 50% black from the Color field. You can either drag the circle in the field all the way to the left, and then halfway up the vertical side of the field, or type **128** in the red, green, and blue number fields. Click on OK to confirm the foreground color change and exit the Color Picker box.

10. Press Alt+Delete (Macintosh: Opt+Backspace) to apply the foreground color you chose as the fill for the rectangular selection, as shown in figure 11.19. Press Ctrl(⌘)+D to deselect the marquee now.

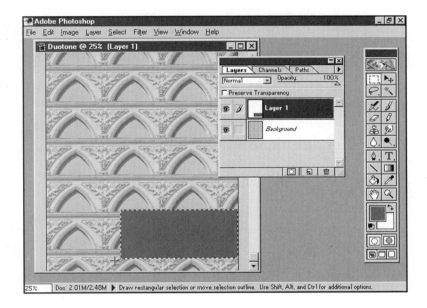

figure 11.19
Fill an area on a layer to create room for text in the image, without the visual distraction of the intricate pattern.

11. Click and drag the Opacity slider on the Layers palette to about 75% (see fig. 11.20). Now some (but not much) background image can show through the rectangle. This treatment of an image area that will contain text is much preferred to outlining the text, or using an opaque color field. Not only does it help make the design look more open, but it also helps draw the text element into the background image.

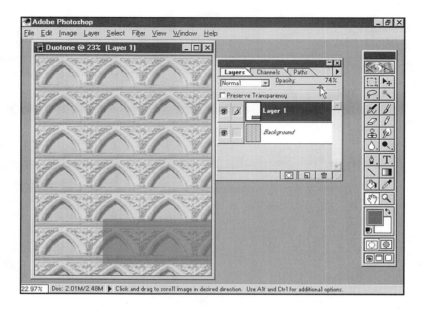

figure 11.20
If you need to darken an image area for the placement of text, but want a subtle look,
decrease the opacity of a geometric design overlay.

12. Click on the Layers palette's menu flyout and choose Flatten image. The document is
     once again in standard bitmap type that can be saved to several file formats.

13. Press Ctrl(⌘)+S, and then save your work in the TIFF format as Cover.tif. Keep the
     document open; you haven't finished yet.

You must use grayscale images to create duotones; color images don't qualify for this
unique structure of digital image data. In the next section, you will walk through
the process of converting the grayscale image to a duotone image, and explore the
options for saved file format (in case you have desktop publishing needs).

Color Curves and the EPS File Format

The color plate that makes up a duotone must complement, not duplicate, the black
image plate, or you won't achieve a duotone effect at all—instead, you will get a
muddy blob on paper. For this reason, Adobe Systems shipped scores of PANTONE
presets for duotone, *tritone* (two color and one black plate), and *quadtone* (three

color and one black plate) creation in Photoshop. Tritones and quadtones are not discussed in this book because the process is identical to that for creating duotones; it simply involves more plates, more complicated color curves for ink distribution, and it results in a more sophisticated-looking grayscale image.

The *color curves* are small files located in the Duotones folder in the Photoshop folder on your hard disk. If you chose not to install the Duotones folder during Photoshop setup, you can create your own duotone ink specification by following the next set of steps—but it is not recommended. The PANTONE color-matching and color specification firm spent a great deal of time carefully creating the best distribution curves for their process and for other inks. If you are serious about this duotone stuff, run Photoshop setup again to install these files.

PageMaker is used to compose the report document in this example. Don't worry, you don't need PageMaker to complete this example; it's used so that you can see how easily you can bring duotone information into a desktop publishing program, and what needs to be done when you save the duotone file, to make it legible to other applications.

Here's how to specify a greenish cast to the Cover.tif image, using the Duotone image mode, and then save your work to EPS format:

SPECIFYING A DUOTONE IMAGE

1. Choose Image, Mode. Then choose Duotone from the menu to display the Duotone Options dialog box.

2. Click on the Load button. From the directory box, scout down the Duotones folder in the Photoshop folder on your hard disk.

3. Specify the path to (Photoshop\Duotones)\Duotone\PMS, and then click on 3405-1.ADO. Click on Open to load the file and exit the directory box.

4. As you can see from figure 11.21, a color swatch and graphical curve have been added to the slot beneath PANTONE Process Black on the Duotone Options dialog box. Notice that the curve associated with the PANTONE green color is an inverse of the black color curve. This means that midtones will be accentuated in green in the duotone, whereas black predominates around the image's white and black points.

5. Click on OK to return to Photoshop's workspace; a duotone image has replaced the grayscale Cover image.

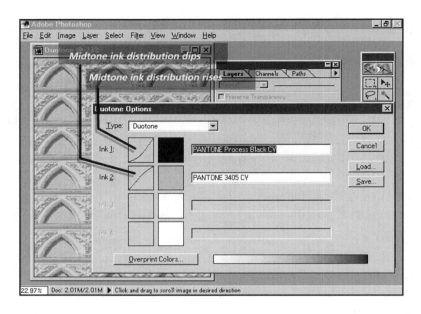

figure 11.21

When the Cover image is printed, the inverse distribution of inks will cause it to show different color tones at different brightnesses.

TIP

The names of the PANTONE duotone curves are not likely to remind you instantly of the shade of color you seek. The name PANTONE 3405, for example, doesn't really tell you that the second plate should be a mint green. All the curve files are similarly named. The same ink is specified with file numbers before the hyphen, but the numbers at the end pertain to the type of distribution curve the ink uses; some curves peak at the midtones, and others peak at the black and white points for different looks.

A good investment for designers is the PANTONE color-matching swatch book, which is available at art stores in many different flavors for different types of inks and surfaces. (It typically costs about $90.) Digital color simulations you see in Photoshop and other programs are close (but not identical) to ink on paper because illuminated phosphors cannot display the gamut of color found in a subtractive color model, such as the CMYK or Duotone formats.

WARNING

When you click on a distribution curve or on the color swatch, Photoshop displays a related dialog box in which you can choose a custom color or design a curve of your own for the second ink. Again, we advise against doing this. What looks like simple interface controls is actually carefully planned math for output to physical media.

Notice that the Black channel has been replaced by a Duotone channel on the Channels palette. This means that you cannot edit the color in the image; its on-screen display is for visual reference, and the color part of the image is being held in memory until you write the image to a format that can hold this proprietary Duotone information. A duotone cannot be saved in any format other than EPS, Photoshop's native PSD, or the RAW image file format.

Here's the story and the plan: the Encapsulated PostScript format is a perfect vehicle for transporting duotone images to other applications. In the following steps, Pagemaker is used as the target application to create the bank's report cover. The choice was made for the following reasons:

◆ The cover needs clean text. Because Photoshop renders text as a bitmap graphic, the text cannot be edited after you add it, nor is it crisp around the edges (as vector Type 1 text is when sent to a printer).

◆ PageMaker can read color information embedded in an EPS Duotone file, and accurately output the first and second color plate that you have defined.

EXPORTING A DUOTONE TO EPS FORMAT

1. Press Ctrl(⌘)+K (File, Preferences, General) and make sure that the Short PANTONE names box is checked. Photoshop ships with the most current PANTONE specifications, which might be newer than those in other applications. By checking this option, you can be sure that another application will read the PANTONE name in the EPS file correctly.

2. Choose File, Save As and then the Photoshop EPS format from the Save As (Format) drop-down list. Name the file COVER.EPS and click on Save to display the EPS Format options box.

3. In the Preview drop-down list, choose TIFF (8-bits/pixel). This setting specifies that a color copy of the graphic information in the EPS file will be included in the file header, which is displayed on-screen when you place (import) an EPS file into another

application. The other option (1-bit/pixel) provides a poor view of the document for placement, but takes up less space in the file.

4. In the Encoding drop-down list, choose ASCII.

   ASCII encoding of PostScript information is "verbose." Although it's not nearly as compact as Binary, the other option, ASCII does provide for universal portability of the image document. Binary encoding requires that you know in advance which imagesetter or other output device will be used, and you might not have a PostScript printer attached to your system, or want to out-source the actual printing of plates. ASCII encoding is plain-text encoding and is accepted by every type, make, and model of computer in the business world.

5. Leave the Include Halftone Screen box unchecked (empty). If you check the Include Halftone Screen box, any information you specified in the File, Page Setup, Screen dialog box will be included in the EPS file. This is not the best thing to do at this point because you might not have set up this option yet in Photoshop, don't care to print from Photoshop, or don't know the screen angle and frequency of an outside source who is imaging your file. By leaving this option unchecked, you can always specify the screen angle of the image from, in this example, PageMaker.

6. The Include Transfer Function includes information about any dot gain or dot loss you have specified in the File, Page Setup, Transfer dialog box for a specific output device. This is useful when you go to film with an imagesetter whose calibration is off; however, you don't have that information in this example. Furthermore, the best advice when engaging an outside service to image your work is to insist that the device is output-corrected, and not to depend on Photoshop's output correction options. Leave this box unchecked, as shown in figure 11.22.

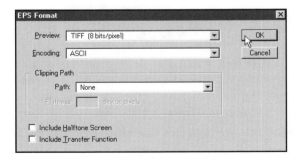

figure 11.22
The options you decide upon in the EPS Format dialog box determine how the EPS is viewed for placement, and the portability of the document.

7. Click on OK, and Photoshop will write the file to hard disk. The file size will be approximately two times the size of the file that is held in memory in Photoshop's workspace. (Check out the document sizes line on the Status Bar or the bottom of the document window).

If you'd like to draw this assignment to its conclusion, and you have a copy of PageMaker or another desktop publishing system, you can close Photoshop now. If you'd simply like to see how an EPS file can carry the complex Duotone information to another application, read on and keep Photoshop running.

TIP

For more detailed information about outputting your Photoshop work, see Chapter 16, "Outputting Your Input."

EPS and Portable Output

The whole thought behind Encapsulated PostScript is that you are not bound by an operating platform or output device to receive high-fidelity work, whether it's a duotone, grayscale, or color image. EPS bundles all the information about the file's contents into a parcel that can be placed within the page of almost any application. When the document is then rendered to a printer or imagesetter, the embedded EPS file conducts a dynamic exchange with the output device. "What resolution are you capable of rendering?" "What type of PostScript printer are you?" The EPS file, having acquired this information, then adjusts the data that is sent to the printer, automatically tuning the printing information in the EPS file to produce the best-looking image from a specific output device.

Figure 11.23 shows the COVER.EPS file as placed in the PageMaker document for the Banker's Loans & Trust Report, with white text placed on top of the file. The command to perform EPS import to PageMaker is as simple as File, Place. As you can see, the Colors palette is open in PageMaker, and the information about the Duotone plate arrived intact; when printed, the PANTONE 3405 color—and its unique distribution curve—will render to paper or film as was specified in Photoshop.

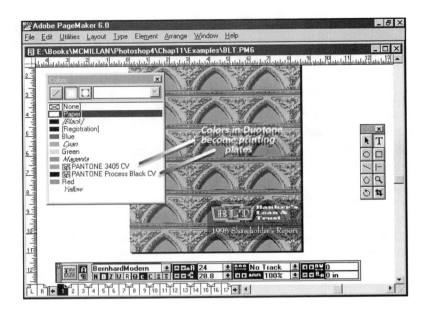

figure 11.23

Separation plates for commercial printing can be made in any program that can import the EPS format of files.

TIP

If you like the look of duotone images, but do not intend to produce printing plates, you can come close to the appearance of the image anyway. If you are printing outside of Photoshop from an EPS image to a PostScript color printer, use your host application's features to rename the PANTONE colors to the color the second ink should represent. For example, in PageMaker, rename the PANTONE 3405 color to "Green." This eliminates the link between the named color duotone plate and the specific pigment to be used; the overlay upon the base color of black will simply print the green in the document.

A simpler method is to convert the Duotone image in Photoshop to RGB color and print it to a personal color printer. Color information between Duotone and RGB color modes is retained, and printing RGB images to an inkjet or other type of color printer does not require PostScript capability.

The most valuable tip you can learn in this chapter is a simple one: For the best output of duotones from Photoshop, talk to the people who are printing your plates. They know better than you about their presses and how they receive certain line frequencies and angles. Even if you insist on outputting the files to make the plates from your office printer (unless you *work* at a commercial printer, of course), ask the professionals about any specific requirements they might have for reproducing your work. It's a shame to be able to tap into all these wonderful Photoshop features, only to have the process thwarted by a lack of communication between you and the firm that makes your digital images into ink on paper!

Full Circle: Converting Grayscale to Color Images

You have seen in this chapter how to work with color, remove color from an image, and play with the flexibility of images as a datastream. Now it's time to turn this monochrome show back into a format that displays color the way we see it in life. The following section takes you through a process by which you can hand-tint a grayscale image to give it a more inviting, familiar appearance. For video slide shows, avant garde presentations, and the simple pleasures of restoring a monochrome family photo, Photoshop is the key.

Converting Grayscale to RGB

At the beginning of the chapter, you sampled the predominant colors in the RGB version of Laurie.tif, and learned how to save the collection as Photoshop Color Table. These colors are good for tinting the grayscale version of the original, Liteness.tif, because the colors are the same as those in the original image.

In the next exercise, you need to convert the grayscale Liteness.tif image back to RGB mode. Although the Liteness image won't spring back to its original color values when you switch modes here, you nevertheless need the color capability found in the RGB mode to add colors to the image. The Grayscale file format does not support unique color values.

By switching from Grayscale to RGB mode you enable Photoshop to express as many as 16.7 million possible shades of color, including the 256 grayscale tones already in the image. You will also create a new layer on the image (in Color mode), and you will paint on this, not the Background image, when you apply any of the colors from the color palette you defined earlier. Color mode affects the hue and saturation of the pixels you paint over, but it does not affect the *luminosity* (the measure of brilliance) in the pixels. In other words, the brightness levels in the Liteness.tif image are preserved when you tint them.

TINTING A GRAYSCALE IMAGE

CD-ROM

1. Open the Liteness.tif image from your hard disk. This is the image you converted to grayscale earlier in this chapter. If you didn't perform the steps, open Liteness.tif from the CHAP11 folder of the Companion CD; this is a copy of the file, created for this example.

2. Type **50** in the Zoom percentage box, and then press Enter (Return) to zoom out to a comfortable view of the entire image.

3. Choose Image, Mode and choose RGB Color. If you have the Channels palette open, you can see that the image now has the three RGB color channels, in addition to the color composite channel.

4. On the Swatches palette (press F6 if you have closed this palette), click on the flyout menu button and choose Replace Swatches (see fig. 11.24). Click on the down arrow in the Files of type: field and choose Color Table (*.ACT). Replace Swatches is a misnomer in Photoshop, because you are actually swapping—not replacing—color palettes; but this command takes you to a directory box, where you need to find the location of Laurie.act. Find it, click on the title, then click on Open to load it into the Swatches palette.

   The Replace Swatches command is better to choose than the Load Swatches command in this example because Load simply appends the loaded colors to those currently in the Swatches palette. Then you have a billion colors to scroll through! At this time, Laurie's color table is all you need on this palette.

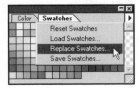

figure 11.24
Colors you have saved in Adobe's Color Table or Swatches format (ACO or ACT) can replace your current colors on the palette.

5. Click on the Create new layer button on the Layers palette and then choose Color from the modes drop-down list at the top of the palette.

6. Press **B** (for Paintbrush tool). On the Brushes palette, click on the second row, far-right tip. Depending upon the size of your own images that you want to hand-tint, you might need several tips of different sizes to cover uniquely shaped areas. This tip is good for the large areas in the Liteness image; feel free to change tip sizes as necessary.

7. Click over a flesh tone on the Swatches palette. The eyedropper cursor appears when you cross into this palette, and the flesh color is the current foreground color in Photoshop.

8. Click and drag over facial areas in the Liteness.tif image until you have covered the entire facial area.

Before you get into sampling too many different colors and applying them to the image, an explanation of Color mode is in order here, and why "you can't get there from here" is in effect with the application of darker colors on the Swatches palette.

If you uncheck the visibility icon for the Background layer, you will see the true color content of the layer upon which you are painting. The reason dark colors composited above the grayscale image when the layer is in Color mode don't register is that, in order to display hue and saturation, Photoshop masks the brightness values out of the colors you apply. The presumption is that the tonal information on the background image will contribute to the darkness or lightness of the color composited with the image. Therefore, the following steps are "workarounds" to complete the hand-tinting work.

Workarounds for Color Tinting

1. When you have colored the facial area to your satisfaction, click on a hair color on the Swatches palette, and color the hair areas in the image.

2. If the color you chose is not producing a color effect on the image, click on the foreground swatch on the toolbox and increase the brightness and saturation component of the color by moving the circle in the color field of the color picker to the right and upward. Click on OK to return to the document and try again to paint with this color. You might also want to add this color to the bottom of the Swatches palette by clicking over a vacant area of the palette.

3. Still no results? Choose white as your foreground color, paint into the area, and then try painting with a lighter shade of brown. This essentially removes the current color from the area into which you paint white because white displays nothing in Color mode on a layer, and it removes darker tones that might be hiding any color values in a specific image area.

   Finally, if you cannot display a color by painting into the Color mode layer, perhaps the underlying image area contains tones that are too dark or too light to support the addition of color. As you may recall from the decryption of the HSB color mode, earlier in this chapter, hue has difficulty registering visually if brightness overwhelms the content of the composite color.

4. Click on the Background layer on the Layers palette, choose the Burn tool from the toolbox, specify the second row, far-right tip on the Brushes palette, and choose Highlights from the Options palette. Then brush a few strokes in light areas of the image to darken them. Conversely, if areas are too dark to support color, use the Dodge tool with the Shadows option to lighten the Background image layer area. When your editing work is finished, switch back to Layer 1 as your current editing layer and try applying color.

CD-ROM

5. Complete as much, or as little, of the hand-tinting as you like in the Liteness image. Figure 11.25 doesn't really show much in the way of color application because this book is in grayscale, but if you open the Handtint.tif image from the CHAP11\GALLERY folder of the Companion CD, you will see what the authors designed. Laurie's face and hair are colorized, but are colorized the background and her dress remain in grayscale. Creating an image composite of both grayscale and color information is an attention-getter, and it helps draw the subject toward the viewer—we are all attracted by color.

6. Choose File, Save As and save your work as Handtint.psd to your hard disk.

TIP

To instantly turn a grayscale image to a digital sepiatone, define both the foreground and background colors in Photoshop as a medium, warm brown. Then choose the Gradient tool and select Color mode for a layer on top of the Background image. Click and drag across a portion of the image. (The Gradient tool fills an entire selection area, regardless of how far you click and drag.)

Voilá! Instant sepiatone—or any other color you want to define as the foreground and background color.

figure 11.25

Color layer mode registers only the hue and saturation of the foreground color, in combination with the underlying brightness values, to display the composite color in an image.

Working with grayscale images doesn't have to be an uninspired task, as this chapter has shown you. And if you have a laser printer capable of at least 600 dpi, the printed results of your labors can be immediately gratifying. When your client has a modest imaging need, you now have the tools—and some understanding of techniques—to far surpass your client's expectations. If you are a dyed-in-the-wool photographer just adopting some of the new computer-imaging powers, Photoshop might be your very last stop for digital equivalents of familiar real-world imaging tools. And the crossover between color and grayscale is effortless with Photoshop. Most of the tools and effects featured throughout this book can be applied identically to both grayscale and RGB images.

Summary

This chapter has been a small sampling of the creative possibilities that lie ahead for you when you understand how to leverage the power of Photoshop's capability to display image data in different structures.

Chapter 12, "Working with Text as Graphics," looks at another of Photoshop's powers: to create and import text for use as a graphical element in your design work. If you have a production photo of a package with no label, or need to edit signage in an image to convey a unique text meaning, look no further than just around the page.

PART  V

PHOTOSHOP SPECIAL EFFECTS

CHAPTER

WORKING WITH TEXT AS GRAPHICS

If you're familiar with a word processor, a desktop publishing application

such as PageMaker, or a vector drawing program such as Illustrator or

CorelDRAW, you're in for a surprise when you work with text in Photoshop.

Because Photoshop's painting tools belong to the bitmap family of computer

graphics, everything you create with the Type tool is a bitmap, not a scaleable

vector display, such as Type 1 and TrueType fonts. This factor may limit the

way you manipulate text in Photoshop, but it also opens up some wonderful

creative possibilities.

In the following sections, you work with both native and imported text in

Photoshop to get a feel—and some ideas—for adding type as a design element

in your Photoshop compositions.

Creating Your Own Virtual Billboard

Almost every aspiring creative talent at one time or another has taken to heart the phrase, "I want to see my name in lights." In the literal sense, this means that they want to have their title emblazoned on a movie or theater marquee in 15,000-point type in Times Square or on a billboard on Sunset Boulevard for the world to see. Photoshop cannot help you get your name posted on Broadway, but it can be used to *simulate* a name or phrase as it might be displayed in any locale you can imagine. In concept, this is as simple to do as taking a picture of a billboard, removing the original text, and then replacing the text with your own. The following sections take you through the process by which Photoshop's Type tool and other features create a unique message that looks as though it's a legitimate sign on a San Francisco trolley car.

Introducing Photoshop's New Type Tools

Before we deal with this section's assignment, a brief explanation of Photoshop 4's Type tool features is in order. Unlike earlier versions of this program, Photoshop 4 now sports two Type tools, with different behaviors to address different design situations. In figure 12.1, you can see the Trolley.tif image (the target image used in this section) in Photoshop's workspace, along with the Type tool flyout. By default, the Type tool is the current text-creation tool in Photoshop; when you need the Type Mask tool, drag the button to expose the flyout, and then click on the tool you need.

The Type tool essentially creates an insertion location in the current image window. By clicking in the image, you display the Type tool dialog box; only after you quit the dialog box, however, can you see the text in the image. Unlike previous versions, any visit to the Type tool dialog box adds a new layer to your document; the text is *not* contained in a floating selection. This is a boon to designers who in the past have accidentally deselected text in a Photoshop document after creating it—you cannot do this by mistake in version 4, because each time you use the Type tool you add an image layer. If a design calls for several lines of text in different sizes, colors, and font styles, the best approach is to collapse the additional layers to a single layer as you work with your image. Otherwise, the file can grow too large in system memory for you to work efficiently with it. Layers do increase the size of a working file. Later in this chapter you learn how to merge layers when you work with text.

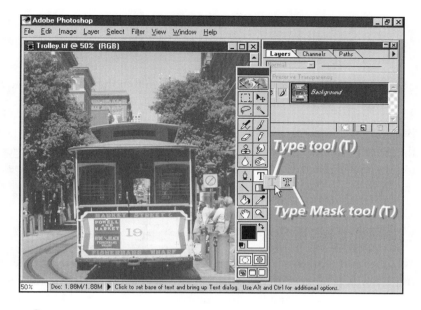

figure 12.1

The Type tool, like all the tools that offer additional flyout options in Photoshop, is marked on the button face with a triangle.

The alternative to creating a layer with text in the current foreground color is to use the Type Mask tool. You use the same procedure to create text with the Type Mask tool, but the result within the image is different than that produced by the Type tool. The Type Mask tool produces a marquee outline selection of the text you specify, floating above the current image layer—no new layer is created in Type Mask tool mode. When the marquee selection based on the text outline appears in the image, you have the following options:

◆ Moving the selection to an appropriate place in the document, and then filling the selection with any of the painting tools (or pressing Alt(Opt)+Delete). When the Type tool is active, clicking outside the marquee does not deselect the marquee; rather, it displays the Type tool dialog box again. To move the marquee, click and drag anywhere inside the marquee selection, using the Type tool or another selection tool. The unique "arrow with a selection box" cursor tells you when your cursor is located inside the marquee.

◆ Saving the marquee to a channel as a selection that can be loaded at any time in the future. To do this, click on the Save Selection as Channel button on the Channels palette.

◆ Adding a new layer to the document and filling the marquee of the type before deselecting the marquee.

Because anything on a layer can be loaded as a selection (press Ctrl(⌘)and click on the Layer title on the Layers palette), you may not need to work with image channels to save a selection. For this reason, the following examples use the Type tool, not the Type Mask tool, for the creation of text.

Working with Resolution-Dependent Type

Whether you want to add text to an image of your own or to the Trolley image in this example, you need to be fairly accurate in your *measurements* for defining the text. Text becomes a graphic the moment you deselect it in Photoshop; for this reason, you must check your own spelling, and also make sure that the text is the right size for the image. Although Photoshop has some wonderful image resizing options, such as Perspective and Scale, you should not create text of any size in an image and then depend on the Transform tools in Photoshop to make corrections. Later in this chapter we discuss why transforming text is a poor technique, and the workarounds for scaling text.

Here's this chapter's first assignment. Suppose that a client runs Lobster World, a restaurant and museum on one of San Francisco's piers, and she wants to advertise the attraction on the back of the trolley that goes from downtown to Fisherman's Wharf. The advertising space is booked for more than a year, however. Because advertising real estate on these vehicles is fairly precious, as you will see in the Trolley image, your client will settle for the next best thing: a photo of the trolley with her ad on it that she can hang on the wall of Lobster World. This retouching task is a natural for Photoshop's Type tool.

In the following set of steps, you customize Photoshop's Rulers option to specify points as the unit of measurement, measure the Trolley image's free space for placement of text, and then specify and place on a layer the first line of the Lobster World advertisement type.

SPECIFYING TYPE DIMENSIONS

CD-ROM

1. In Photoshop, open the Trolley.tif image from the CHAP12 folder of the Companion CD. Type **200** in the Zoom percentage box, and press Enter (Return) to zoom into the image so that you can see the blank sign area on the right of the trolley. This is the working area for the advertisement. Hold the spacebar to access the Hand tool, and then drag to center the blank area of the trolley's back in the window.

2. Press Ctrl(⌘)+R to display rulers around the document window. By default, inches appear on the ruler, which doesn't really tell you how many points (units used to specify type sizes) you need to use with the Type tool.

3. Double-click on either ruler to display the Units & Rulers preferences box.

4. In the Rulers, Units drop-down list, choose points (see fig. 12.2). Click on OK to confirm this preference and return to the workspace.

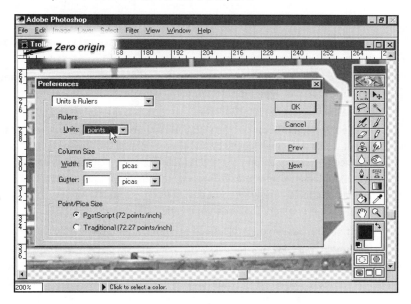

figure 12.2
Photoshop's rulers can be used to specify picas, pixels, points, inches, or other increments for your design needs.

Notice that where the rulers converge, there is a small square, called the Zero origin box. By dragging it into the image window, you can change where the tick marks and the zero begin on both rulers. Double-clicking on the Zero origin box resets the rulers to zero in the upper left corner of the image window.

5. Drag the Zero origin box to the upper right of the white area on the trolley sign, so that the zero point for the rulers is about 12 points below the center of the word "Street" in the title *Market Street &* at the top of the sign.

The phrase "Visit Lobster World Pier 41 ¹/₂" can be broken into four lines of text, arranged vertically to fit in the area between the four bolts on the right side of the trolley sign. By measuring the height within the bolts, we can see that it's about 48 points. This means that with no *leading* (interline spacing), each line of text can be 12 points tall. Setting type in a word processor at 12 points with no leading is probably not a good idea, because word processors have a special way of calculating interline spacing. But it's a little-known fact that typefaces, even Adobe Type 1 fonts, do not occupy the full "grid size" in a digital typeface. Of a possible 1,000 units, most fonts occupy only 500–600 units in height, and therefore contain a sort of interline spacing within the font. Therefore, it's okay to "spec" type for this assignment without accounting for leading. In fact, text larger than 16 points or so looks awkward when an average amount of leading is used.

6. Press **D** (Default colors) and click on the Type tool.

7. Click the Type tool at the convergence of the horizontal and vertical rulers' zero mark to display the Type tool dialog box.

8. In the Font field, choose a font you have installed on your system. Photoshop will read both TrueType and Type 1 font formats, but will not display proprietary fonts you might use in CAD or drawing applications.

We used Benguiat for part of the sign you're creating in this example. Benguiat has the correct flavor and "feel" of the hand-lettered text on the trolley sign. If you're going to convince an audience that your text retouching work is authentic, you should keep to a style established elsewhere in the original image. If you don't have Benguiat, good alternative choices are Windsor, Century Condensed, ITC Algerian, or another Roman, serif font that does *not* look fresh or clean.

9. Type **12** in the Size field, and leave the Leading and Spacing fields blank.

Unless the font you use here is extremely ill-constructed, the Spacing option isn't necessary. In assignments of your own, you might want to increase the Spacing value to create widely kerned text (wide spaces between characters). This field takes both positive and negative values. Leading is not a concern in this example because you will use different fonts for each line of text, and will be able to adjust leading manually later in this section.

10. Make sure that the Anti-Aliased box is checked in the Type Tool dialog box, and click on the left Alignment button to make the text appear to the right of the insertion point you clicked in the document.

11. Type **Visit** in the text field at the bottom of the dialog box. You have the option of seeing the approximate size and font style—check the Font and Size check boxes at the bottom of the screen (see fig. 12.3). When working at smaller point sizes, it can be useful to

uncheck these boxes to see the default font and have a larger size appear in the text field. You can easily make typing errors in this box, and because fonts are rendered to noneditable bitmap areas in the image, there's no Backspace key in Photoshop to correct such errors!

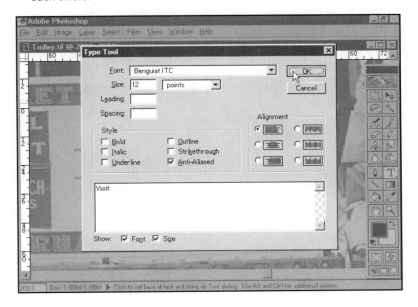

figure 12.3

Specify the font style, attributes, alignment, and other text characteristics in the Type Tool dialog box.

12. Click on OK to apply the text to the document.

13. Press Ctrl(⌘)+S and save your work to your hard disk in the Photoshop file format, as Trolley.psd.

The text is approximately where it should be in the image (see fig. 12.4). Because it's the right size, and it resides on a layer of its own, repositioning is easy. By default, Photoshop also applies the Preserve Transparency feature to the new text layer. The Preserve Transparency feature prevents you from making errant paint strokes on the text layer. The text can be repositioned by using the Move tool, but paint cannot be applied anywhere except within the text when Preserve Transparency is checked. Leave this feature checked for the moment, but remember that it stops you from working on transparent areas of a layer.

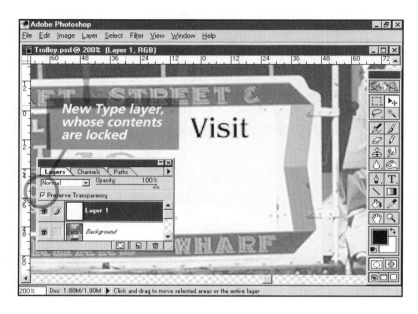

figure 12.4
Text added to an image always appears on a unique layer when you are using the Type tool.

Coloring and Outlining the Type

Images we see in the real world consist of two basic properties: the shape, and the texture you see on the surface of the object. The text outline looks okay—Benguiat is a timeless font that works well with every period—but the default black interior of the text shapes contrasts too harshly with the surrounding, original text in the image.

One of the best tricks to know when you attempt to paint something into an image is that the Eyedropper tool can provide you with color-matching. Even though it's unlikely that you will have a font that closely matches the *Market Street &* text on the trolley sign, you can come very close to convincing observers with your type creation by sampling and using the *colors* used in the Market Street text. If you're reading this without the image on-screen, the Market Street text is a pale gold, with a black outline, and a faint lilac drop shadow of the text at its lower left. In the following steps, you re-create this look with the *Visit* text you created in the previous section.

MATCHING TEXT EFFECTS TO THE ORIGINAL SIGN

1. Hold the spacebar to toggle to the Hand tool; scroll the screen so that you can see both your *Visit* text and the number *19* original text in the image window. Release the spacebar. Due to its size, the number 19 in the image is a much easier target for sampling than the Market Street lettering, and it is basically the same color as the Market Street text.

2. Press I (Eyedropper tool) and click in the gold area of the 19 lettering in the original image. The Eyedropper tool disregards layer information, and samples the first nontransparent area that you click over in a document.

3. With Layer 1's Preserve Transparency check box still checked, press Ctrl(⌘)+A (Select, All), and then press Alt(Opt)+Delete (Backspace). This fills only the nontransparent areas of Layer 1 (the text layer) with foreground color.

4. Press Ctrl(⌘)+D (Select, None), and then uncheck the Preserve Transparency check box for Layer 1. You can now apply paint to transparency areas of the layer.

5. Press Ctrl(⌘) and click on the Layer 1 title on the Layers palette. This loads all the nontransparent areas on Layer 1 as a marquee selection.

6. Press D (Default colors) to restore black as the current foreground color on the toolbox.

7. Right-click (Macintosh: press Ctrl and click) over the Layer 1 title on the Layers palette to display the Context menu. The Context menu commands displayed when the cursor is over a palette are different from those displayed when the cursor is over an image window (see fig. 12.5).

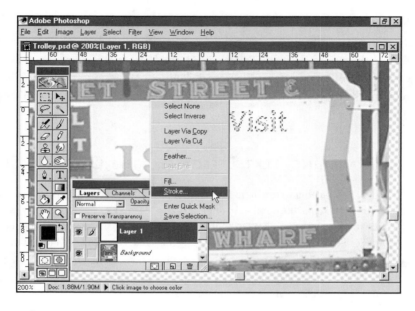

figure 12.5
The Context menu offers options for the selection, not the current tool, when your cursor is over the Layers palette.

8.   Choose Stroke from the Context menu to display the Stroke dialog box.

9.   In the Stroke dialog box, type 1 in the pixel Width field. In the Location field, click on the Outside button; leave the other options at their defaults, and click on OK. Now the selection marquee based on the opaque text on Layer 1 has a black outline around it, similar to the original text on the trolley sign.

10. Press Ctrl(⌘)+D to deselect the marquee, and then press Ctrl(⌘)+S.

Now you're going to create the lilac-colored drop shadow text effect.

ADDING A DROP SHADOW TO THE LETTERING

1. Right-click (Macintosh: press Ctrl and click) on the Layer 1 title on the Layers palette, and choose Duplicate Layer from the Context menu. The Duplicate Layer dialog box pops up.

2. Name the Layer **Drop shadow** (see fig. 12.6) and then click on OK.

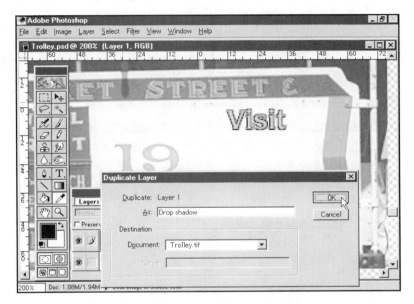

figure 12.6
Duplicate the contents of a layer, on a new layer, through the Duplicate Layer command.

3. Click and drag the Drop Shadow layer title on the Layers palette to beneath the Layer 1 title. The duplicate layer now resides under the original layer and on top of the Background image.

4. Check the Preserve Transparency check box for the current layer (the layer title is highlighted), the Drop Shadow layer.

5. With the Eyedropper tool, click on the lilac drop shadow color of the original trolley sign text. If 200% viewing resolution is too low for you to accurately select it with the Eyedropper tool, hold Ctrl(⌘)+spacebar to toggle to the Zoom in tool, and then drag a

marquee around the image area that features the lilac drop shadow text. Release the Ctrl(⌘) and spacebar keys to return to the Eyedropper tool. To zoom out again after you sample this color, type **200** in the Zoom percentage field, and press Enter (Return).

6. Press Ctrl(⌘)+A (Select, All), and then press Alt(Opt)+Delete (Backspace). This fills the nontransparent pixels in the Drop Shadow layer with the color you sampled with the Eyedropper tool.

7. Press Ctrl(⌘)+D (Select, None), press **V** (Move tool), and then use the arrow keyboard keys to nudge the lilac text down and to the left of the original (see fig. 12.7). Notice that in the original text the drop shadow is offset only one or two pixels from the gold text; you should be able to duplicate this effect with only one or two nudges of the arrow keys.

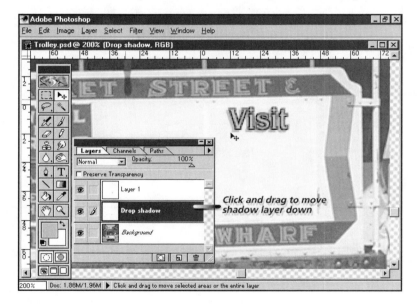

figure 12.7
When the Move tool is the current tool, you can move the contents of a layer by dragging with the tool or using arrow keystrokes.

8. Click on the Layer 1 title on the Layers palette to make it the current (active) layer.

9. Click on the Layers palette's flyout menu button (the triangle to the right of the Paths tab) and choose Merge Down from the menu (see fig. 12.8). This option merges the contents

of Layer 1 with the contents of the Drop Shadow layer, making the saved file size of the Trolley.psd image smaller (and saving resources and hard disk space). You can no longer edit the two layers' contents as individual elements, but this is as far, artistically, as we need to take the *Visit* lettering.

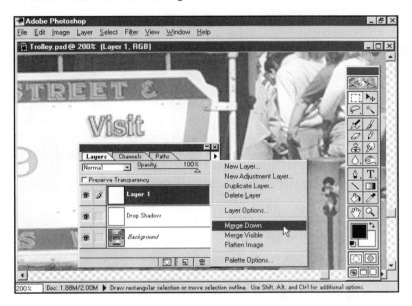

figure 12.8
By merging layers you eliminate the possibility of individually editing layer contents,
but you conserve saved file size.

10. Double-click on the Drop Shadow title on the Layers palette to display the Layer Options box. Type **Visit** in the Name field and click on OK. With an appropriate name, this layer will be easier to identify later.

11. Press Ctrl(⌘)+S to save your work.

Editing Text that Is Too Wide

Getting the word *Visit* into the composition at a legible type size was no problem; because the word is only five characters long, you have the luxury of using a 12-point font height. To keep *Lobster World*—the next two lines of text, which are wider than the *Visit* line—within the width of the area in which you're adding text, however, you need a little strategy:

◆ Use a smaller font size. When text is already small, however, less than 12 points would become illegible, especially with a decorative typeface.

◆ Use a condensed font. This is usually the authors' preference for sign-making because you can get more characters per line at a good font height with condensed fonts. See how they get all that text on an aspirin bottle?

We play "worst-case scenario" in the following set of steps and assume that you don't own a decorative, condensed font. In figure 12.9, you can see that the authors used a typeface called Algerian to create the Lobster World text, and that it overlaps the area reserved for the advertisement in the image.

figure 12.9
The borders of the advertising space on the trolley demand a condensed font. What do you do when you don't own one?

The authors do not recommend the next set of steps for any reason other than desperation; you're going to use Photoshop's Transform feature to scale the text horizontally to fit within the border of the trolley sign. Although the Transform feature produces smoothly distorted selections, it also degrades the sharpness of original image content. If you perform this more than a few times, you will lose the crispness of the text, and it will become illegible. The reason for the loss of visual quality is explained in detail later in this chapter, and we offer some workarounds for situations you might run into in your own work.

Here's how to make text fit into an image area when you cannot find the correct font for the assignment:

CONDENSING TEXT

1. With the Eyedropper tool, click on any of the dark red areas on the Background image to sample this color for use as the Lobster World text.

2. Press **T** (Type tool), and click an insertion point below the *Visit* lettering to display the Type Tool dialog box.

3. Choose any font you like for this step. Algerian is a nice font, but you could stick with Benguiat, or use another decorative font in the Font drop-down list.

   Because Photoshop retains, in a single user session, information about the last-used font and other attributes in the Type Tool dialog box, the type attributes you used to create the *Visit* lettering are still in operation in this dialog box.

4. Type **12** in the Leading field and click Center in the Alignment field. The *Visit* text required no leading value because it was a single line of text. As mentioned earlier, you can use a very "tight" leading value for more than one line of Photoshop text because most fonts don't occupy their entire character grid space within the font.

5. Type **LOBSTER**, press Enter (Return), and type **WORLD** in the text field at the bottom of the dialog box.

6. Click on OK to add a new layer with the text you added to the document. (The new layer automatically becomes the current editing layer.)

7. Choose the Move tool. Using the arrow keyboard keys, nudge the text until the left side of the text falls inside the sign area on the trolley.

8. With the Rectangular Marquee tool, drag a selection around the Lobster World text.

9. Right-click (Macintosh: press Ctrl and click) on the selection to display the Context menu, and choose Free Transform from the menu.

10. Click on the right, middle handle of the Free Transform box and drag to the left until the Lobster World text fits inside the trolley sign area. The lettering has become a *floating selection* (see fig. 12.10); the text doesn't actually belong to the layer in the image while it is being transformed. This is why it's critical to remember to deselect a selection after you transform it; otherwise, it can accidentally be lost or deleted in future editing steps.

figure 12.10
The Free Transform feature enables you to scale, shear, rotate, perspective, and distort a selection area.

See Chapter 2, "Leveraging Photoshop's New Capabilities," for a more detailed explanation of the Free Transform tool and the extended functions of this feature.

TIP

If you make a mistake with the Free Transform tool, and you want to quit the feature, either press Escape or choose a different tool from the toolbox. If you switch tools, Photoshop pops up an attention box that offers Apply, Don't Apply, and Cancel options; click on Don't Apply to make the transformation box disappear, leaving you with only a selection marquee and the unaltered image.

WARNING

If you have many open palettes on-screen, clear them away from the target area you intend to edit with the Free Transform feature, or close them altogether. The selection handles on the Free Transform box can be moved behind and past a palette or the toolbox, but neither palette nor toolbox can be moved while the Free Transform box surrounds a selection. And with palettes in the way, you might not be able to see an area of the image that you need to see.

11. When the text has been scaled enough horizontally to fit within the trolley sign, double-click inside the Transform box to apply the scaling.

    Notice that the text looks a little more refined after you apply the transformation than it did inside the box as you moved the Transform handles. The reason is that Photoshop calculates a rough on-screen preview when you edit, and recalculates only the selected pixels after you apply the transformation. So don't trust the on-screen display within a selection for final image quality while editing the selection.

12. Press Ctrl(⌘)+D (Select, none) and then press Ctrl(⌘)+S to save your work.

As you might have noticed, the lettering isn't exactly running at the same angles as the horizontal lines of the trolley in the image. When the image was taken, the authors had the choice of making either the background or the trolley crooked; trolley cars simply don't remain absolutely perpendicular to the ground in San Francisco. Therefore, to integrate the text you have added to the image with the image itself, you need to apply a transformation to the finished text. Generally, the best approach is to apply as few transformations as possible to pixel-based text, so you should lay out and center all the text before you make any transformations.

In figure 12.11, a new layer of text has been added to the image. You already know what steps to take to add this text; add it, nudge the text on its own layer if necessary to align it to the Visit layer's text, and then use the Merge Down command on the Layers palette's flyout menu to make a single layer containing the four lines of text. Then you might want to double-click on the merged layer's title and rename the layer "Text" (its name in the following figures). In the next section, you will work on transforming the text so that it has the same angle of inclination as the rest of the trolley.

figure 12.11
Add the final line of text, use the Move tool and the arrow keyboard keys to center it,
and then use Merge Down to arrive at a single text layer in the Trolley image.

Distorting a Selection Area on a Layer

Although the edge of the sign may not show up well on these pages, the delineation
between the placard and the rest of the trolley sign should be quite clear on your
monitor. We use the outline of the placard in the following steps to define an outline
that encompasses the text you have created. By stroking the outline you define, the
image content on the text layer will be a rectangle surrounding the text, which makes
the layer's contents easier to distort in keeping with the slant of the original text in
the image. Because the edge of the nontransparent image areas will be rectangular,
and the Free Transform bounding box is rectangular, the distortions you perform
on the text and rectangle will be predictable.

The Free Transform feature is new to this version of Photoshop. Free Transform enables you to perform skewing, scaling, and other manipulations of a selection in a single editing session. The advantage to this is image fidelity; multiple pixel transformations in an image lead to a loss of image quality.

Here's how to use the placard on the rear left of the trolley as a template for the Free Transform feature, and how to make the text look like a real-life advertisement:

USING FREE TRANSFORM AND A TEMPLATE

1. With the Rectangular Marquee tool, drag a rectangle around the text on the Text layer. The rectangle will not align perfectly to the placard area on the trolley image because the placard is rotated slightly, relative to the window edges. That's okay; approximate the height and width of the placard with the rectangular selection.

2. Press **D** (Default colors) to ensure that black is the current foreground color on the toolbox, right-click (Macintosh: press Ctrl and click) to display the Context menu, and choose Stroke (see fig. 12.12).

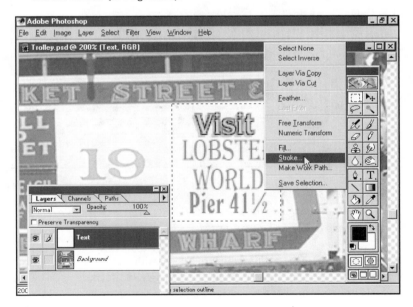

figure 12.12
Drag a Rectangular Marquee selection around the text in the image. This will serve as the outside dimensions of the advertisement.

3. In the Stroke dialog box, leave the options at those you last chose for this command: 1 pixel in width, and Outside Location for the foreground color stroke. Click on OK to apply the paint stroke.

4. Press Ctrl(⌘)+D to deselect the active marquee in the document, and then press **V** (Move tool).

5. Click and drag the Text layer's contents so that they rest on top of the placard on the left of the back of the trolley (see fig. 12.13). Notice that the rectangle you stroked on this layer falls slightly outside the "Powell and Market" sign. This is okay. Next, you use the Free Transform feature to match the edges of the layer rectangle (and the text it contains) to the corners of the placard on the Background layer.

figure 12.13
Use the slant of the original placard on the Background layer as a guide for modifying the text and rectangle on the Text layer.

6. Press Ctrl(⌘)+T to surround all opaque pixels with the Free Transform box. The Transform bounding box appears around only the rectangle and its contents on the layer. When only a few nontransparent areas are on a layer, the Transform box shrinks to encompass only the contents of a layer. Note that this activity will *not* occur if there is an active marquee selection in the document.

7. Hold Ctrl(⌘) and then click and drag the upper-right corner of the Transform box so that it touches the upper-right corner of the Powell and Market sign (see fig. 12.14).

figure 12.14

In Transform mode, the Ctrl(⌘) key toggles the function of the cursor to move bounding box corners freely.

Note that the Free Transform bounding box operates differently according to which extender keys you use with the cursor. (See Chapter 2 for more information.)

8. While holding Ctrl(⌘), click and drag the three remaining corners to match the corners of the Powell and Market sign.

9. Double-click inside the Transform bounding box to apply the distortion you have specified.

10. With the Move tool, drag the distorted text to its original position on the right side of the trolley.

11. Double-click on the Eraser tool to choose the tool and display the Options palette for the Eraser tool.

12. Choose Paintbrush from the drop-down list on the Options palette, click on the Brushes tab on the grouped palette, and click on the third tip from the left in the top row. We ungrouped the palettes (by dragging the tab away from the palette) to show you the tip in figure 12.15, but this step is not necessary here.

13. Carefully drag over the rectangle outline areas in the layer (see fig. 12.15).

figure 12.15
Choose a small tip for erasing the rectangle from the layer; the Paintbrush Eraser tool mode enables you to decide on a tip size.

14. Press Ctrl(⌘)+S to save your work.

Improving Image Focus

If you look carefully at the text in the image, you can see that it's fairly crisp; there is perhaps only a pixel in width of transitional color between, for example, the red lettering and the white background. Unfortunately, the text you have created does not display the same clarity and sharpness along the edges because it was transformed (the Lobster World text was transformed twice, in fact). Whenever transformations are performed, edge crispness is lost because Photoshop must average new pixel colors around areas that have been changed. Photoshop uses *bicubic interpolation* by default to maintain a semblance of original image quality when you distort things. Although this is a remarkable feature, it cannot accurately calculate new pixels from original pixels when the size of the sample area contains only a handful of pixels, as this text does.

One way to put better focus into the text is to use the Unsharp Mask feature. The Unsharp Mask intelligently improves the contrast along areas in a selection that display some sort of color contrast; in other words, Unsharp Mask works best on improving edge crispness in an image.

Here's how to use the Unsharp Mask filter to bring the distorted text into focus so that it looks more like the original text on the trolley:

SHARPENING THE TEXT

1. With the Rectangular Marquee tool, drag a rectangle around the text on the Text layer. Although the text is surrounded by transparent pixels that are unaffected by filters, by defining your target area for Unsharp Mask, Photoshop can apply the effect more quickly. Photoshop has less calculating to do when it knows the defined area for the filter. If you don't select an area on a layer for filter application, Photoshop takes a moment to calculate which pixels are affected, and which aren't (the transparent masking pixels on the layer).

2. Press Ctrl(⌘)+H to hide the marquee selection. The marquee is still active; it simply doesn't appear on-screen to hinder your view of the image.

3. Double-click on the Zoom tool to bring your view to a 1:1 resolution (100% Zoom) of the Trolley document.

4. Choose Filter, Sharpen, and then choose Unsharp Mask. The Unsharp Mask dialog box appears.

5. Drag the Amount slider to about 65%. The Amount setting determines the strength of the Unsharp Mask filter. The maximum is 500%; the 65% setting is a mild, subtle amount of sharpening.

6. Type .9 in the pixel Radius field. You can define a fractional amount in this box, and Photoshop, depending on the imaging operation, sometimes calculates filtering on a subpixel level.

The Radius option determines how far from an edge in an image Photoshop searches for other pixels to sharpen. This setting should increase as the size of your image file increases. Because this Trolley image is less than 2 MB, and only a small amount of sharpening is required, .9 pixels does the trick. In your own work, with extremely blurry images of 4 MB or more, you might want to increase this value.

7.   Specify 1 in the Threshold field to apply sharpening that is very pronounced around image edges. The scale for this effect is 0–255, which corresponds to similar brightness values in the image. If you need to *gently* sharpen edges in an image that contains people or other soft, natural shapes, use a higher Threshold to retain tonal smoothness as you sharpen areas.

8.   When the settings on your monitor look like those in figure 12.16, click on OK to apply the Unsharp Mask.

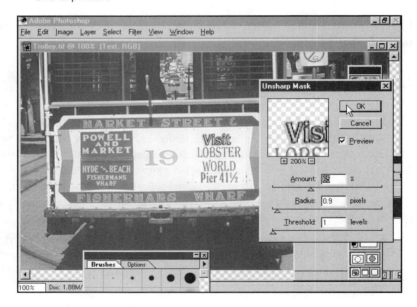

figure 12.16
The Unsharp Mask filter applies contrast to sharpen edges in an image to any amount you specify.

9. Press Ctrl(⌘)+D to deselect the hidden marquee, and then press Ctrl(⌘)+S to save your work.

The trolley is almost at the end of the line, and the text needs only one more edit to make it look as though it was actually painted on the sign in the image. The next section looks at the Multiply compositing mode as the answer to this problem.

Painting "into" an Image

Retouchers occasionally make the fundamental mistake of applying text on top of an image, and then ask the viewer to suspend disbelief. Text doesn't really look as though it's *within* an image unless it reflects some of the same lighting conditions present when the image was taken. You sampled the colors in the original image and used them for the advertisement text, and you slanted the text to make it fit the image better. You will find, however, that 100% opaque color on a sign lasts about five seconds in the outdoor environment, and lettering on a white sign in broad daylight fades into the surface, and also fades from your own view, the text pale in comparison to the brilliant reflectance of background white.

The Multiply mode of image compositing in Photoshop calculates the base color in an image—pixel colors on the bottom-most layer— with the color pixels on layers above, and then multiplies the tonal value of the combination of pixels. (The Adobe documentation calls this the *result color*.) The artistic effect is that darker pixels on a layer turn very dark in areas above dark pixels on the Background layer, whereas light layer pixels do not affect the Background pixels at all.

We need a minor amount of Multiply mode for the Text layer, to suggest that the white background has absorbed the "painted text," as it would in real life. In the following steps, you adjust the Layer mode to create this effect.

BLENDING TEXT INTO THE BACKGROUND

1. With the Text layer highlighted on the Layers palette (it's the current editing layer), click on the modes drop-down list (there is no label on this drop-down list) and choose Multiply. Notice that the on-screen text gets darker and loses some of its color.

2. Click and drag the Opacity slider to about 90% (see fig. 12.17). This reduces the amount of pixel color displayed on the Text layer and allows some of the white background to show through.

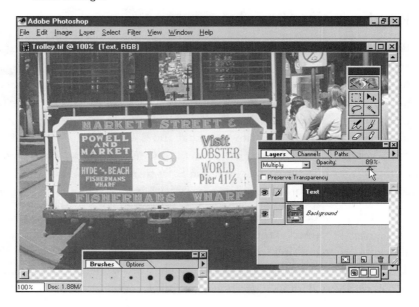

figure 12.17

Text actually painted on a sign displays wear and takes on a pastel look through time. Fade the text you add to a photo accordingly.

3. Press Ctrl(⌘)+S to save your work, and then choose File, Save A Copy.

4. Choose the TIFF file format from the Save A Copy's Save As (Macintosh: Format) drop-down list, and save the copy to your hard disk as Lobster World.tif.

    Because the TIFF format cannot contain a layer, the Flatten Image option is dimmed in the dialog box. Photoshop merges layers in their current opacity and mode settings to the Background layer.

5. Click on Save. With the finished image saved to your hard disk, you can send a copy to your client, keeping the editable version ready for further modification. Who knows? Perhaps other clients will want their advertisement on the back of a San Francisco trolley. There might be a rice manufacturer right around the corner.

When you need a minor transformation on text to make it fit an image better from a compositional standpoint, Photoshop's Type tool and the Transform effect provide professional results. When you need to bend and stretch text by a significant amount, however, you should look to an application other than Photoshop for help. The next section shows you how to use Adobe Illustrator or another vector drawing program to generate text that you can bring into Photoshop and meld seamlessly with an image.

Text and Package Design

If part of your profession involves commercial package design, or even the minor addition of text to an image, this part of *Inside Adobe Photoshop 4* is your ticket to better visualization solutions. Adobe Systems' intention was to create different communications and graphics products that excel in a particular area; the *line* of products overlap, and each product's output can be easily exchanged through common file formats. Photoshop's Type tool is not the end-all for creating typographic effects, but Illustrator's feature set is more than capable of stretching and distorting text and graphics designs. In the following sections, we take a look at working *between* applications to create a label in a photographic image. If you use FreeHand, CorelDRAW!, or CorelXARA, many of the steps used in Illustrator will seem very familiar. And if you're not familiar with the type of drawing application that works with vectors, read on and discover some secrets to creating better images using different tools.

The Gold Fruit Assignment

The imaginary list of clients in this book includes a manufacturer of fruit drinks who wants a visual example of a new label on an orange drink container. The boys at the Gold Fruit Production Department have modeled a nice scene (see fig. 12.18). As you can see, the label area on the container is blank. It needs a package design, and unlike the trolley example, the label area is rotated and skewed along a dimensional axis in space.

TIP

The **"Boys in Production"** is a *nom de plume*. The Gold Fruit image was created in Macromedia Extreme 3D. (To learn more about modeling and rendering, check out *Inside Macromedia Extreme 3D*, New Riders Publishing.)

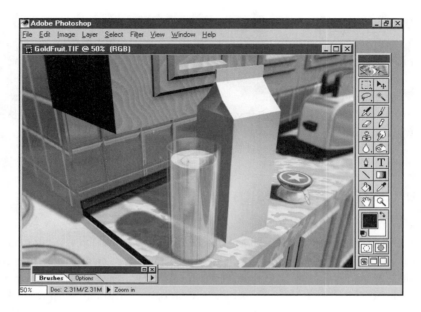

figure 12.18
Because using the Type tool to create text for the container label would be difficult, we suggest using a supplementary set of tools.

The Problem with Skewing Bitmap Images

In the trolley example, the Transform feature was used to a *minor* extent to change the border of the text so that edges do not meet at 90° angles. As you can see with the Gold Fruit example, however, the front face of the container is severely skewed toward our viewing angle. To change the sides of text so that they are no longer at right angles, to an extent that they match the edges of the container, would distort the pixels in the text to a point where they lose legibility.

Try this simple experiment as an example you can perform to decide for yourself how acceptable text distorted in Photoshop will be.

AN EXERCISE IN FUTILITY

1. Open a new image window that is 300 pixels in Height and 300 pixels in Width. Choose Grayscale mode in the New Image dialog box—this experiment doesn't need to be in color.

2. Click the Type tool into the new image. In the Type Tool dialog box, choose an ornamental font (Goudy Handtooled is used in our figures), specify about 70 points in Size, and then click on OK to add the text to its own layer in the image.

3. Press Ctrl(⌘)+T, and the bounding box for the Transform effect will surround the text.

4. Hold Ctrl(⌘) and drag on either of the middle handles on the sides of the bounding box until the text is skewed to an extent that seems to match the skew of the front face of the Gold Fruit container in figure 12.18. Figure 12.19 shows the extent of the skew.

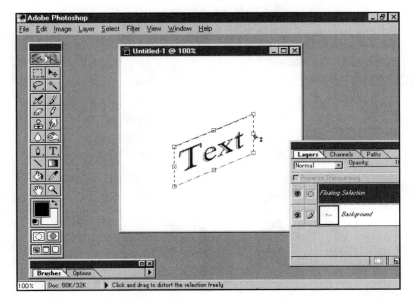

figure 12.19
Hold Ctrl(⌘) to access different types of transformations when the Free Transform effect is chosen.

5. Double-click inside the Transform bounding box to apply the Skew transformation, press Ctrl(⌘)+D to deselect the current marquee selection, and then use the Zoom tool to zoom in to about 300% on the text you distorted.

You can close the file at any time now without saving; these steps simply served as a way to give you a qualitative view of text that is dramatically distorted in Photoshop.

If much of your work in Photoshop includes applying text to an image, and you want the text to look as refined as the objects you place it on, we recommend that you try a "helper" application to Photoshop to complete your tasks with text. For example, the left window in figure 12.20 shows a close-up of text to which the Shear tool has been applied in Illustrator; the text was then imported into Photoshop in EPS format. On the right is the same text, skewed by using the Transform feature. Notice that the interior of the decorative font is muddy, the edges display several tones (not one or two that anti-aliasing provides), and the overall quality of the text will look out of place in a photographic image.

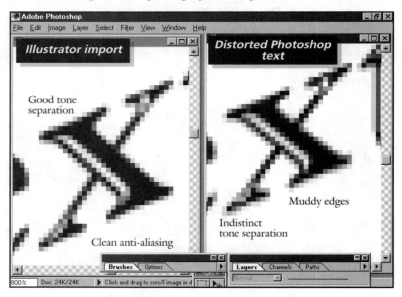

figure 12.20
It is better to distort text in a vector drawing application than to apply effects to bitmap text in Photoshop.

We want to stress here that we are not criticizing Photoshop's capabilities; you simply need specialized tools sometimes to perform what seems to be a simple task.

Anti-Aliasing and Text

If you have ever wondered why some text looks smooth on-screen, but other text looks coarse and harsh, *anti-aliasing* is typically the reason. Pixels on your monitor's screen and pixels written to file format are arranged in a building block or grid fashion, and there is always a stair-step pattern where the foreground color of the text meets the background color. To eliminate some of this *aliasing* harshness, several mathematical schemes have been employed to create a transitional color between the foreground and background colors around the edge of text, to smooth the appearance of the pixel "stair steps" caused by aliasing. Acrobat Reader 3 uses anti-aliasing methods to produce on-screen font displays that look smooth and quite like text you would print to a laser printer. Most of the text you see on HTML pages, however, looks aliased and harsh because it is your system that is displaying the text, and not a helper application or special plug-in that provides anti-aliasing.

In figure 12.21, you can see a split-screen example of anti-aliased and aliased text. If this figure were viewed at a high resolution, you would see percentages of black filling the areas of the anti-aliased text where it curves or makes a diagonal ascent, or in other areas where pixels are forced to display a non-right-angle design.

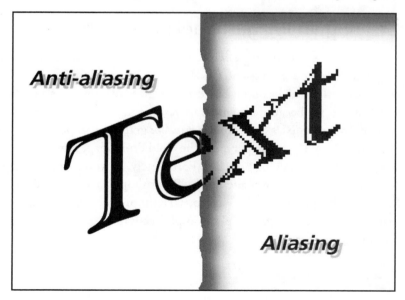

figure 12.21
For text to appear crisp and legible on-screen or in a saved file, the correct amount of anti-aliasing needs to be added to the edges.

Photoshop is almost entirely geared toward anti-aliasing, which is why it's important to use anti-aliasing and the correct drawing program when applicable. Photoshop uses sophisticated *algorithms* (math procedures) to attempt to maintain a smooth edge to image areas that you distort, but with text, particularly small text, Photoshop has only a limited number of pixels with which to recalculate new pixels, based on the changes you make to a selection. It is far better to bring distorted text into Photoshop in Illustrator's EPS format (Windows users are more familiar with the *.AI extension for Illustrator files), than to make several changes to achieve a certain look, and subsequently lose the focus of the text in the Photoshop process.

The following sections are a brief set of procedures that describe how to make a label that looks like part of the Gold Fruit container image. If you do not have Illustrator or another vector drawing program, Goldmold.ai is provided in the CHAP12 folder of the Companion CD, and you can use this file in Photoshop to complete the assignment. Additionally, if you want to use the design from the following examples, Goldfrut.ai is also on the CD. Goldfrut.ai is an undistorted copy of the label design that can be used in Illustrator and can be imported to most other drawing packages quite easily.

Creating an Image Template for Labels

Vector art is *resolution-independent*; that is, you can make it any size you like by simply scaling the artwork—no visual content is lost through scaling. To create the vector artwork in this example, however, you need to know the size of the image into which it will fit, because bitmap graphics have a *fixed resolution*—they contain a finite number of pixels (*resolution-dependent* graphics). With a file size of 2.3 MB (7.3" by 4.9" by 150 pixels per inch) the Gold Fruit image is much too large to serve as a template in a drawing program. Fortunately, however, you can make a smaller copy of this image to use as a template. Photoshop's Image Size command is useful for resizing images; although image focus is compromised when you eliminate pixels to decrease image size, the template simply needs to be suitable for tracing over, and not for image clarity.

Here's how to reduce the size of Gldfruit.tif, the sample image on the Companion CD, for use as a template:

SCALING AN IMAGE TO SERVE AS A TEMPLATE

CD-ROM

1. Open the Gldfruit.tif image from the CHAP12 folder of the Companion CD.

2. Choose Image, Image Size to display the Image Size dialog box.

3. Make sure that the Constrain Proportions and Resample image check boxes are checked, and that the resampling method displayed in the drop-down list is Bicubic. Bicubic interpolation is processor-intensive, but provides the best quality resampling of an image when you need to add or remove pixels from an original.

4. Click on the drop-down box to the right of the Width field in the Pixel Dimensions field, then choose percent.

5. Type 50 in the Width field. Notice that the final file size for the Image size operation is 592 KB—one-fourth of the original 2.3 MB size—because you're decreasing both the Width and the Height of the file by a factor of 2. Click on OK to apply the new size.

If the image seems to be lacking in focus, to the extent that you cannot clearly see the edges of the front face of the container, the following step is optional.

6. Choose Filter, Sharpen, and then choose Sharpen. The default sharpening feature in Photoshop increases the contrast in the image in areas where different colors meet (seen usually as an edge in bitmap images). Although it's not as artistically pleasing in image content now, this image will serve you well as a tracing guide, which is all that matters.

7. Choose File, Save As, and then save the image to your hard disk in the TIFF format, as Small.tif.

We turn now to the drawing application portion of the assignment. Again, if you have a drawing application and want to use the Goldfrut.ai file from the Companion CD, import the file to your program, and you will see how the text effect is created.

Designing and Distorting a Label for Photoshop Import

Designs you create in Illustrator (or drawing applications that can read and write the Illustrator format) are most useful to your final Photoshop design when done in grayscale. Illustrator writes, and Photoshop reads, Illustrator graphical information in CMYK color mode for accurate process color printing, but you don't always want process colors defined. The Gldfruit image, for example, is in RGB color mode. This reality requires a certain strategy for you to design a label, distort it to match the angle of the container in the image, and import it for use in Photoshop.

If you stick to only shades of black in your drawing application design work, the resulting file can be imported and placed in an alpha channel in the Gldfruit image. At that point, you can define selection areas within the image and paint in the colors you like.

Figure 12.22 shows the container design (in Illustrator) in the CHAP12 folder of the Companion CD. If you have third-party plug-ins for Illustrator, such as Letraset's Envelopes, or if you use CorelDRAW!'s native Envelope Effect, you can make the text on the container label arc or swoop, in addition to distorting the label to conform to the container in the Gldfruit.tif image.

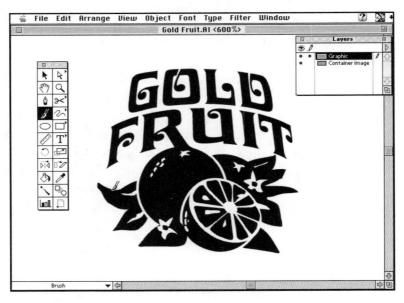

figure 12.22
Keep a logo text design clean and in monochrome. You can add color later when the design is loaded as a Photoshop selection marquee.

Unfortunately, Illustrator for Windows has not kept pace with the Macintosh version, and Windows Illustrator version 4 users do not have a Free distort filter. Users of FreeHand for the Macintosh or Windows can accomplish the following steps by using the 3D-Rotation Xtra. Windows users who own CorelDRAW! or CorelXARA can use the Perspective effect or the Mould tool's Perspective setting, respectively, to accomplish the following steps.

Macintosh users can follow these steps in Illustrator 6 to distort the label design to conform to the top portion of the container in the Gldfruit image.

USING FREE DISTORT IN ILLUSTRATOR 6

1. In Illustrator, with either your own design or the Gldfruit.ai file as the current document, choose Window and then choose Layers. Click on the menu flyout on the Layers palette, and choose New Layer. In the Layer options box, type **Container Image** in the name field and click on OK. Other drawing applications have a similar layer feature and naming convention.

2. Click and drag the Container Image layer title on the Layers palette to a position under the layer with the design on it. (In the Goldfrut.ai file on the Companion CD, its title is "Graphic.") Now the Small.tif image you import will reside underneath the graphic.

3. Click on the Container Image title to make it the current editing layer in Illustrator. Choose File, Place, and then choose Small.tif (the file you created earlier in Photoshop) from your hard disk. Click on Place. Other drawing applications might use the Import command instead of Place.

4. Position the image anywhere you like on the printable page, and then lock the layer from further movement or editing by unchecking the pencil icon to the left of the layer title on the Layers palette.

5. Click on the Graphic title on the Layers palette to make it the current editing layer.

6. Press ⌘+A to select all the objects that make up the Graphic design, and then press ⌘+G to group the objects so that they can be moved as a single unit.

7. With the Selection tool, drag the grouped graphic so that it rests on the top portion of the container's front face in the image.

8. With the Scale tool, hold Shift and then drag the grouped design toward the design's center, so that the design roughly fits the top portion of the container image.

9. With the Zoom tool, zoom in to about 300% resolution in this area. Then hold the spacebar to access the Hand tool, and pan your view so that the design on top of the container is to the left of the screen. This makes room for the filter box in the next step, so that neither the box nor the document is obscured.

10. Choose Filter, Distort, and then choose Free distort to display the Free Distort dialog box.

11. With the cursor, drag on each corner of the Free distort box, one at a time, until the angle of each of the bounding box's sides matches the sides of the top portion of the container (see fig. 12.23).

figure 12.23
Match the angle of the sides of the container top to the bounding box of the Free distort filter.

12. Click on OK when you finish distorting the proxy design in the Free Distort dialog box; then use the Selection tool to reposition the grouped graphic, centering it in the top of the container image (see fig. 12.24).

figure 12.24
The graphic will serve as a selection after you import it into Photoshop.

13. Press ⌘+S and then name and save the file to your hard disk.

Creative Use of Type in a Design

To create the bottom of the front label for the orange drink container you need a different aspect ratio for the design than the one used for the top of the container. Plan your design to about 3:1 proportions; this is the approximate measurement of a traditional half-gallon container of juice, milk, and malted milk balls.

As an informational aside here, the fonts used in the Goldfrut.ai file are Helvetica Condensed for the volume text on the container, Davida for the Gold Fruit logotype, Goudy OldStyle for the Orange Drink title, and Kabel Hairline for the description of the drink at the bottom of the package (see fig. 12.25). Font specifications are an art. With so many typefaces to choose from, you can easily mismatch styles and wind up with an unprofessional-looking package design. The fonts recommended here are time-proven and effective for design situations in which you want to suggest an established, slightly "country-style" food or drink.

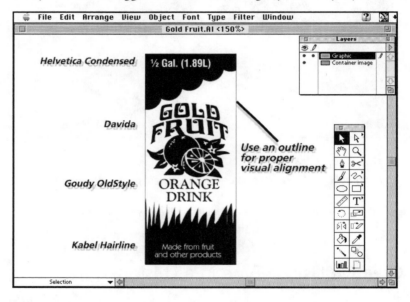

figure 12.25
Choose fonts in a design sparingly, and make certain that they visually complement one another.

Notice also in figure 12.25 that an outline has been drawn around the container design. This outline, like the one you drew around the text in the trolley example, makes it easy for you to visualize the perspective you need to apply to the container design with the Free Distort filter.

In figure 12.26, the Free Distort filter is used to slant the grouped design to conform to the lower portion of the container. It is not easy to exactly match the angle of distortion in a proxy window, however; if the distortion doesn't match the container image exactly, correct it by using the Shear toolbox tool.

figure 12.26
Match the Free Distort bounding box to the shape of the lower, larger part of the container in the image.

In figure 12.27, you can see the effect of the Free Distort filter on the remainder of the package design. The grouped objects have been aligned to the underlying container image areas, and you're all set now to save the design and bring it into Photoshop.

figure 12.27
When a text-and-graphic design seems overly complex to create in Photoshop, use the proper tool: a vector drawing program.

To Windows users, the Illustrator interface and the procedures for creating the distorted text might seem a little mysterious. In figure 12.28, you can see the CorelXARA workspace, and the perspective mode of the Mould tool's function is being used to create the distortion of the label. CorelXARA and CorelDRAW!'s tools work very similarly—to define a distortion box to conform to the container shape, drag the corner points (as you would in Photoshop) to correspond to the corners of the container image.

figure 12.28

In some drawing applications, you can distort a grouped vector design through in-place editing of the bounding box's control points.

Having completed the distortions to the vector design, it's time to get to some compositing work in Photoshop to complete the visualization of the mock-up for your client.

Import/Export Procedures for the Illustrator Format

If you're using Illustrator for this design work, all you have left to do in Illustrator is delete the Container image layer from the document. With the Container image layer highlighted, click on the Layers flyout menu button, and choose Delete Layer "Container Image." Save the file a final time, and quit Illustrator.

T I P

Illustrator 6 (featured in these figures) and Photoshop 4 support inter-application drag-and-drop capabilities. If your system has enough RAM (at least 32 MB) to keep both applications open, you can drag the design from Illustrator to Photoshop and into a new document window. We do not recommend this dynamic exchange of data for systems lower than the Power Macintosh series. Data exchanged in this way is converted automatically to PICT image format when it arrives in Photoshop.

For users of drawing applications other than Illustrator, the design data must be in the Illustrator format for Photoshop to import it correctly. In FreeHand, choose File, Export, and then choose the Adobe Illustrator 5.x format from the List Files of Type drop-down list. CorelDRAW! users should choose the Adobe Illustrator, *.AI, *.EPS file type when exporting, and use the *.AI file extension for the export, and not EPS. In Windows, this file extension should always be AI, and not EPS, because the EPS extension is usually reserved for file formats that contain printer data, and not editable vector shapes.

If you haven't created an Illustrator file yet, use the Goldmold.ai file in the CHAP12 folder of the Companion CD to follow the next steps.

Converting Vector Information to Bitmap Format

The data stored in an Illustrator file is resolution-independent—it can be scaled to any dimension you like before Photoshop translates the visual information to bitmap format, to be placed in any bitmap file. The following sections show you how to complete the design, color it, and make a vector text creation an integral part of a bitmap image.

Importing Your Text Design to Photoshop

The process by which Photoshop converts image data it reads in the Illustrator format to bitmap format is sometimes called *rasterizing,* or *parsing. Parsing* is the action of an application understanding data it opens or imports. *Rasterizing* is the display of data in pixel format, usually on-screen, but it also applies to vector information that is converted to bitmap image format. In reality, when you work in a drawing program, the visual data is constantly being updated on-screen through the process of rasterization.

In the following set of steps, you import the Gold Fruit label into Photoshop and then add the design to a channel in the Gldfruit.tif image. The only way to affect the import process unexpectedly is to forget that this design was scaled to the Small.tif image (exactly 50 percent the size of Gldfruit.tif). Photoshop knows the physical dimensions of an imported Illustrator file because this information is written into the header of Illustrator files, but the resolution needs to be *twice* that offered in Photoshop's Rasterize EPS Format dialog box (because Gldfruit.tif is twice the height and width of your template, Small.tif).

Here's how to import and place the Illustrator design:

IMPORTING THE TEXT DESIGN

1. In Photoshop, with the Gldfruit.tif image open, press Ctrl(⌘)+O (File, Open). Windows users can double-click on the workspace to display the Open dialog box.

2. Choose Goldfrut.ai in the directory box, from your hard disk or from the CHAP12 folder of the Companion CD. Photoshop then displays the Rasterize Generic EPS Format dialog box.

   Illustrator's PostScript descriptor language for files is actually a *subset* of Encapsulated PostScript files (EPS). Not all EPS files are Illustrator files, but Illustrator files can generally be thought of as EPS files. Files created in Illustrator, or written to the Illustrator format by other applications, qualify for parsing here.

3. Leave the Width and Height fields alone in this dialog box; Photoshop has read the Illustrator information correctly. Type **300** in the Resolution field. The resolution of the Goldfrut.tif image is 150 pixels per inch, and you need the imported design to be twice the resolution of the template image, Small.tif. Alternatively, you can click on the increments drop-down list for either Width or Height, specify percent, and then type **200** in either field. With Anti-aliased and Constrain Proportions checked, click on OK (see fig. 12.29).

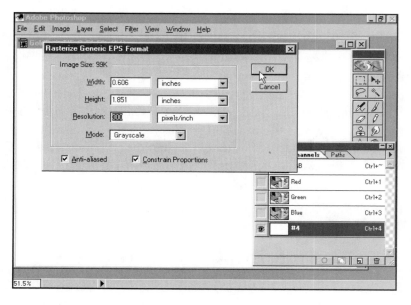

figure 12.29
Increase the size of the imported Illustrator file to reflect the dimension you need in the high-resolution, original image.

4. Press Ctrl(⌘)+A to select the entire image window of the imported graphic, and then press Ctrl(⌘)+C to copy it to the clipboard.

    Notice that the areas outside the graphic, and areas in which you didn't design, are marked with Photoshop's transparency grid (the checkered pattern). If your design contained no white elements (Gldfrut.ai does, around the shape outlines), you could easily drag the design into the Goldfruit.tif image window while holding Ctrl(⌘) to copy the design to a new layer. Removing the white areas would take time, however; white and transparent aren't the same imported Illustrator property. You will do the next best thing—copy the design to a channel in Goldfruit.tif, where white represents masked areas, black represents selected areas, and there is no transparent property.

5. Click on the Gldfruit.tif image's title bar to make it the current, active image in the workspace, and then click on the Channels tab on the Layers palette.

6. Click on the Create new channel button at the bottom of the Channels palette, and then double-click on the new channel title on the Channels palette's list.

7. Click on the Color indicates selected areas button, and click on OK. Now, every colored area you copy into the channel will represent a selected area, and every white area will be masked when the channel is loaded in the document.

8. Press Ctrl(⌘)+V to paste the copy of the design into the new channel, and then press Ctrl(⌘)+D to deselect the floating selection. The design is now selection information in the new channel (see fig. 12.30).

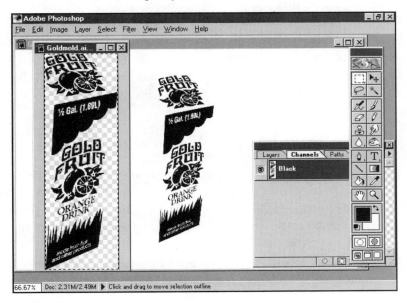

figure 12.30
The copy of the Illustrator design now serves as selection information you can paint into within the image.

9. Close the Illustrator import file without saving it, and save the Gold Fruit image to your hard disk in the Photoshop file format, as Gold Fruit.psd. Long file names are okay for saving to your own hard disk; we cannot use them for the Companion CD because of the bi-platform file-naming conventions used for writing CDs.

If you zoom in now to the new channel in the Gold Fruit image, you see the correct amount of anti-aliasing surrounding curved and diagonal design areas. Rotating or otherwise distorting a bitmap would cause too much anti-aliasing. Photoshop intelligently anti-aliases imported Illustrator-type files to any dimension you specify.

Repositioning and Painting the Label

Chances are slim that you pasted the Illustrator design exactly into the channel where it would correspond to the label in the color composite channel of the Gold Fruit image. No problem. In the following set of steps, you load the channel as a selection, fill it with default foreground color, and reposition the design on its own layer, where you can paint it the color of your choice and finish the assignment. Here's how to complete the Gold Fruit visualization assignment:

ADDING AND POSITIONING THE LABEL

1. On the Channels palette, press Ctrl(⌘) and click on the new channel title; its default name should be #4. This loads the grayscale information in the channel as a selection.

2. Click on the Layers tab on the grouped palette. Then click on the Background title on the Layers palette to force your view of the document back to color composite view, and not the alpha channel view.

3. Click on the Create new layer button at the bottom of the Layers palette. You will now be working on the new Layer 1, and not on the Background image.

4. Choose any of the selection tools from the toolbox (the Rectangular Marquee tool is fine) and drag inside the marquee selection toward the front face of the container label (see fig. 12.31). The marquee's final position should be directly on top of the container.

   In Photoshop 4, unlike earlier versions, you cannot remove the image *contents* of the marquee by using the selection tools for marquee selections—you simply reposition the marquee.

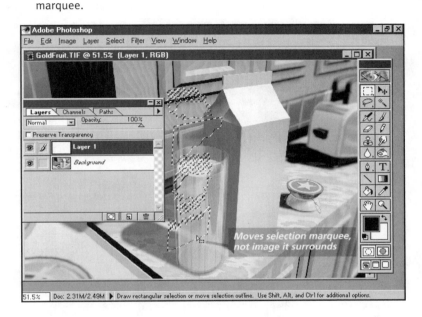

figure 12.31
Use a selection tool to reposition the marquee, but not the underlying image areas.

5. When you think you're close to the intended destination for the marquee, press **D** (Default colors), and then press Alt+Delete (Macintosh: Opt+Backspace) to fill the marquee with foreground black (see fig. 12.32). Press Ctrl(⌘)+D to deselect the marquee. You now have a nice stencil of the design on Layer 1.

6. Zoom in to one of the corners of the design on Layer 1; then use the keyboard arrow keys to nudge the design into exactly the correct position above the container.

7. On the Layers palette, click on the Preserve Transparency check box for Layer 1. Now, if you paint into the image, only the black areas will be recolored.

   You can choose any color you like for the next step. You can even choose to fill Layer 1 with a custom gradient fill, but it might hinder the legibility of the design. The authors chose a grass green for the label because green is an appealing dark color that contrasts nicely against the pale orange container.

figure 12.32

Fill the marquee selection above the layer with foreground color to better see the design, and to position it.

8. Click on the Foreground color selection box on the toolbox to display the color picker. On the color picker, choose a color (hint: choose green) and then click on OK to change the foreground color and return to the workspace.

9. Press **B** (Paintbrush tool). Pick the second from right, first row brush on the Brushes palette for the Paintbrush tool, make certain that Opacity is 100% and the mode for the brush is Normal on the Options palette, and then paint away in the image (see fig. 12.33).

figure 12.33
By checking the Preserve Transparency option, you can now replace the colors on the layer with color of your own within the design.

10. After you replace the black on Layer 1 with your custom color(s), press Ctrl(⌘)+S to save your work. If you want to make a copy that can be shown in programs other than Photoshop, use the Save a copy steps described earlier in this chapter. You can close the Goldfruit.psd image at any time and exit Photoshop.

In figure 12.34, you can see the completed design. We got a little creative and used different shades of green on the package design. (You might not be able to see them in the grayscale figure.) Many times, you are limited to spot colors or a single color plate for packages as disposable as drinks; a monochrome design must really work hard to call attention to itself on a supermarket shelf.

figure 12.34
The image was not complete without a text design. How many of your own Photoshop images can benefit from creative text?

Summary

Hopefully, this chapter has shown you that text not only has its place in Photoshop design work, but also that it can indeed be the focal element of your creations. For simple text replacement assignments, you have the trusty Type tool, and for more ambitious endeavors, we have explored how well Photoshop imports vector designs. Other chapters of this book also contain examples of text as graphics.

In Chapter 13, "Creative Plug-Ins," we kick into high gear and describe how to use some of the most popular plug-in filters to enhance and catapult your designs from the extraordinary…to the sublime.

CHAPTER

13

CREATIVE PLUG-INS

The Adobe Photoshop Help System includes pictorial examples and a brief explanation of the 14 categories of program extensions called plug-ins. Although the documentation is useful as a quick reference, the authors take an "applied" approach to examining plug-in filters in this chapter. Everyone feels that plug-ins are cool, and that they're good—like owning every Type 1 font in existence—but what are plug-ins good for? How can you make the most creative use of them in real-world assignments? Can some plug-ins be used more often than others? This chapter walks you through the process of creating extraordinary effects using the filters native to Photoshop 4.

Using Combinations of Plug-In Filters

Users of previous versions of Photoshop will find a different organization to the Filter menu in version 4. The Artistic, Brush Strokes, Sketch, and Texture menus contain many of the Adobe (formerly Aldus) Gallery Effects plug-ins, and the Filter menus from version 3 of Photoshop also contain new plug-ins. One property Photoshop users will appreciate about the new plug-in filters is that Adobe has re-engineered all of them to be 32-bit. There are no longer the system halts and limitations, especially among Windows Photoshop users, that were found with 16-bit plug-ins running under Photoshop 3.0.x.

Plug-ins are actually mini-applications. You cannot run the filters outside Photoshop. And although each filter can produce a unique effect on an image, you might find that the options for plug-ins are somewhat limited. A specific plug-in simply might not provide you with the exact look you envision for a composition. In the following sections, you will see how to create specific, exotic, fantastic special effects by using *combinations* of Photoshop filters, both old and new.

TIP

Plug-ins require memory resources. If you have added several third-party plug-ins to Photoshop, you can work faster, with more resources dedicated to your imaging work, if you load only those filters you expect to use.

Windows users can limit the number of filters loaded into Photoshop by moving the *.8bf files out of the Plugins folder; third-party filters are installed to the Plugins\Effects folder, and Photoshop's native, shipping filters are located in the Plugins\Filters folder. Create a unique folder (called "unused") in the Photoshop directory to keep filter files you don't want present in Photoshop during a particular Photoshop session. To enable or disable filters, Windows users must physically move the plug-ins in or out of the Plugins folder, and then restart Photoshop for the change to take effect.

Macintosh users can use a similar strategy to limit the number of plug-ins that are loaded. Create a folder that holds the filters you use most often and another for the ones you use less frequently. Then, to choose which plug-ins folder to use in a Photoshop session, hold the ⌘+Opt keys as you launch Photoshop.

Using Gaussian Blur to Prepare for Poster Edges

The Poster Edges plug-in is one of Photoshop's new Artistic plug-ins that can turn a photographic image into a handsome, turn-of-the-century Art Nouveau-type poster. The Poster Edges filter is best used with images that display sharp color contrast between areas and are free of subtle variations in tone. Image noise, for example, or small textures within the target image, will produce dark lines and blobs—where you might not want them.

The Poster Edges filter reduces the number of unique colors in an image. The Poster Edges dialog box offers three controls:

◆ **Edge Thickness.** A slider whose scale is from 1 to 10. The number 1 produces thin edges in the image, whereas 10 creates fat, bold strokes around edges in the image.

◆ **Edge Intensity.** You can choose values from 1 to 10, to control the visual predominance of edges in the image. The number 1 creates a subtle effect, whereas 10 produces clearly visible poster edges.

◆ **Posterization.** Available in values from 1 to 6, this option controls the number of unique colors rendered to the filtered image.

Depending upon the visual content of the image you want to process through a plug-in filter, some images work better than others. In general, images with brilliant, saturated colors and sharp-edged detail work best for all Gallery Effects filters. We make specific recommendations in this chapter on image content as well as on how to prepare images for filtering.

CD-ROM

The Nicknack.tif image on the Companion CD is a good (but not perfect) choice for filtering with Poster Edges. The image contains bright colors, clearly defined edges in its content, and a limited number of unique colors; Poster Edges will preserve many of the original color values. Shortly, however, you will see that the speckle design on the butter dish in the Nicknack image would filter through the Poster Edges plug-in to produce very unappealing splotches in the design. The solution? Photoshop's Gaussian blur filter is a good choice for softening the contrast between the green and the speckle finish of the butter dish, and because the dish is mostly consistent in color value, the Magic Wand tool is used to select only this area in the image. It's important to understand that all filters change image information; most of them reduce the amount of original image content to create a stylized look.

Therefore, you can dramatically edit an image destined to become a "Gallery" masterpiece, and the audience will never see your editing work in the finished image.

Let's work through the process of editing and then apply Poster Effects in the image.

Creating an Optimal Poster Edges Image

1. Open the Nicknack.tif image in Photoshop from the CHAP13 folder of the Companion CD.

2. Choose Filter, Artistic, Poster Edges to display the dialog box in the workspace.

3. Drag inside the preview window to see what the image looks like with the default settings specified for the effect. As you can see in figure 13.1, much of the image will filter nicely, except the butter dish, whose finish would create ugly blobs if filtered in an unedited state.

figure 13.1
Filter preview windows give you the chance to see an image before you apply the effect.

4. Now that you have surveyed the potential changes that Poster Edges will affect, click on Cancel.

5. Double-click on the Magic Wand tool to select it and to display the Options palette for this tool.

6. Type **32** in the Tolerance field, and check the Anti-aliased check box. At this setting, the Magic Wand tool will select much of the green butter dish from the image, and the anti-aliasing option will include the light specks in the butter dish.

7. Click on the top of the butter dish to select it; then choose Filter, Gaussian Blur.

8. Drag in the preview window to hone in on the butter dish. Drag the slider to about 2.2 (see fig. 13.2), or to a value at which the preview window displays no speckles in the selected image area.

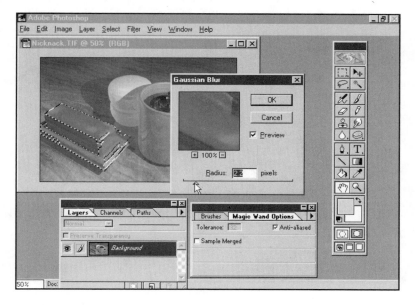

figure 13.2

Specify for the Gaussian blur filter an amount small enough to eliminate the speckles but retain the color variations in the selection.

9. Click on OK to apply the Gaussian blur, and press Ctrl(⌘)+D to deselect the selection.

10. Choose Filter, Artistic, and then choose Poster Edges.

11. The specific settings are your decision; the authors went with the default settings. If you decide to change the Edge Intensity, for example, drag the slider, wait until the preview shows in the preview window of the dialog box, and then click on OK to apply the effect.

12. Press Ctrl(⌘)+Shift+S (File, Save As), and save the image to your hard disk as Niknack1.tif, in the TIFF file format. Because we use the original Nicknack image in this chapter to show you other effects, adding a number to the file name is a good idea. You can close the filtered image at any time now.

In figure 13.3, you can see the result of reducing noise in the original image, and how the Poster Edges filter creates an eye-catching version of the file's original contents. Note that, unlike Photoshop's original filters (such as Gaussian Blur, Unsharp Mask, and others), the Gallery Effect filters that ship with Photoshop 4 do not allow you to preview the effect as it will be applied to the entire image in the workspace. Nor can you "step outside" the dialog box to zoom in or out of the image in the workspace, as you can with the non-Gallery Effects filters. You must use the zoom in and out controls in the dialog box to preview areas of the image.

figure 13.3
The Poster Edges effect can create interesting, illustration-type renditions of a photographic scene.

In all plug-in filters in Photoshop 4, the preview window for a filter can provide "before and after" views of the effect. Click and hold in the preview window to see the current image, and then release the cursor to see the proposed filtering changes. Note that the Gallery Effects filters take a moment or two to display a preview, and that with some effects, it's difficult to distinguish between the filtered image and the original, seen in the preview window. Adobe provides a visual clue as to when a preview window is actually showing the preview. Beneath the zoom percentage (directly beneath the preview window) you will see a blinking underscore. A slowly blinking underscore means that Photoshop has almost prepared the preview image; when the underscore disappears, you're looking at the proposed filter effect.

One of the best possible uses of a plug-in is to edit only part of an image. In this way, you can direct the focus of an image by accentuating only certain elements in a composition. In the next section, you learn how to create a selectively (partially) filtered image.

Creating an Abstract Composition Background

There are various ways to force the foreground focus in an image to better convey to the audience that only part of the image is relevant or important. Many techniques are discussed in Chapter 8, "Correcting Images," but in this section, we show you how to highlight the "hero" in a picture by making the elements in an image abstract.

Suppose that you were handed the Nicknack image as part of a commercial brochure, and that your client wants to call attention to the coffee mug. Now, there's nothing more boring in a composition than cropping an image from a complete scene; it ruins the balance of a well-composed image, and steals visual interest added by the other elements. The creative way to highlight the coffee mug in the Nicknack image is to remove detail and color from the surrounding image areas. In the following set of steps, you use the Palette Knife Artistic filter, in combination with Photoshop's Hue/Saturation command, to play down all areas of the scene except the coffee mug.

FRAMING REALISM WITH AN ABSTRACT BACKGROUND

CD-ROM

1. Open the Nicknack.tif image from the CHAP13 folder of the Companion CD. Windows users can access the file from the four last-used files list (under File).

2. With the Rectangular Marquee tool, drag a rectangle around the coffee mug in the image. Press Ctrl(⌘)+Shift+I to invert the selection. Now, everything except the coffee mug is selected.

3. On the Channels palette (press F7 if it's not in the workspace), click on the Save selection as channel icon at the bottom of the palette. You might want to save the selection for later editing of only part of the image.

4. Choose Filter, Artistic, Palette Knife. The Palette Knife effect averages the colors in a selection and creates a highly representational version of original image data.

5. Drag the Stroke Size slider to 5. The Stroke Size determines how much averaging the filter performs. At a low setting, the original image content looks less stylized.

6. Drag the Stroke Detail slider to 3. Stroke Detail determines the fidelity with which the Palette Knife renders areas of edges it detects in the image.

7. Drag the Softness slider to 0. Softness determines the complexity of edges in the filtered image. You want to retain the greatest edge detail for the purpose of abstracting the selected areas in Nicknack.

8. Click on OK to apply the filter. The photographic reality of the coffee cup is in sharp contrast against the stylized selected areas (see fig. 13.4).

figure 13.4

The Palette Knife filter creates a soft-focus, artistically primitive rendering of selected image areas.

9. Press Ctrl(⌘)+U (Hue/Saturation). If you're performing these steps, notice that the Palette Knife creates a brighter, more contrasting version of original image information. This is not the effect you want in this assignment; the content is good, but the bright colors are much too distracting.

10. Click on the Colorize check box, and then make the settings shown in figure 13.5: Hue:–149 (a steel blue color), Saturation: 32, Lightness: 0. Although you cannot see the color in this figure (see the color signature), we recommend a cold, steel tone to contrast with the bright table top and dusty rose coffee mug outside the selection.

11. Click on OK to colorize the selected areas, press Ctrl(⌘)+D to deselect the marquee, and then save the image to your hard disk as Nicknak2.tif, in the TIFF file format. Keep the image open for the moment.

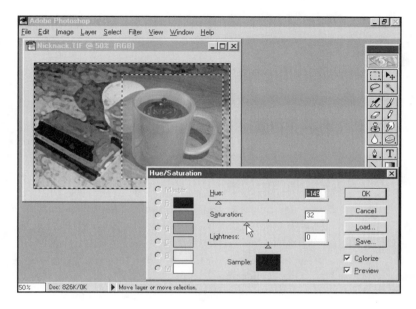

figure 13.5
Use the Hue/Saturation command to create monochrome areas and to decrease the color importance in selected areas.

You can see the finished image, with a drop shadow added around the original selection area of the coffee mug, in figure 13.6.

figure 13.6
The foreground element in this composition is clear; you removed realistic qualities from the surrounding areas through the Palette Knife effect.

To create this effect, you could use a third-party plug-in filter, or one of the techniques shown in Chapter 20. Briefly, these are the steps for making a drop shadow:

FRAMING SELECTION WITH GAUSSIAN BLUR

1. Load the selection of the coffee cup by pressing Ctrl(⌘) and clicking on the channel #4 title on the Channels palette; then press Ctrl(⌘)+Shift+I to invert the selection (the saved selection was the background, not the cup).

2. On the Layers palette, right-click (Macintosh: hold Ctrl and click) over the image title for the Background, and choose Layer via Cut from the Context menu. When you click on a layer title, it makes no difference which tool is currently selected.

3. Drag the Layer 1 title into the Create new layer icon at the bottom of the Layers palette to duplicate the layer; click on Layer 1 to make it the current editing layer, then check the Preserve Transparency check box.

4. Press D (Default colors), press Ctrl(⌘)+A (Select, All), and then press Alt(Opt)+Delete (Backspace) to fill only the nontransparent area of the duplicate layer. Uncheck the Preserve Transparency check box now.

5. Press Ctrl(⌘)+D (Select, None), choose Filter, Blur, Gaussian Blur. Specify a 3 to 4 pixel setting for the effect, and click on OK.

6. Choose Multiply from the drop-down list on the Layers palette for this blurry layer. Then choose the Move tool, press Shift+down arrow once or twice, and press Shift+right arrow the same number of times. (Shift, in combination with the arrow keys, performs "power nudging"; the nontransparent areas on a layer move by 10 pixels per stroke.

Think of the variations you can perform by using other filters and the same techniques. You can apply feathering to a selection, to make a gradual transition between filtered and original image areas. You can also create different visual impressions by using different filters to abstract the background. For example, select the background and apply Filter, Stylize, Find Edges to surround the foreground area of interest with a pencil sketch. This technique works nicely when your foreground subject is a person.

Hopefully, you understand now that it is not the filter, per se, but the appropriate use of it, that can turn a still life into a more visually interesting piece. In the following section, you use a combination of filters to make a table top scene an "unfinished symphony."

Using Virtual Oils, Charcoal, and Chalk

The American painter Gilbert Stuart is perhaps best remembered for his unfinished rendering of George Washington. Although Stuart and his daughter created several versions of this classic piece, the version with the unpainted, roughed-out corner has become an icon among masterpieces.

There is something fascinating about viewing both a rendering and the preliminary sketches beneath an artistic work. In the following steps, you learn how to emulate the look of the Stuarts using Photoshop's Quick Mask selection feature and some other new filters.

Here's how to use the Chalk & Charcoal filter, in combination with the Dry Brush effect, to turn a scene of fruit into an ambitious, artistic design.

Creating Quick Mask Brush Strokes

CD-ROM

1. Open the Fruit.tif image from the CHAP13 folder of the Companion CD.

2. Double-click on the Quick Mask icon toward the bottom of the toolbox, and then click on the Color Indicates: Selected Areas button (if it is not already selected). Click on OK. The current image is in Quick Mask editing mode now; the dimmed titles on the Layers palette confirm that this mode is active.

3. With the Rectangular Marquee tool, select the top third of the image, and press Alt(Opt)+Delete (Backspace) to fill the selection with foreground color (Quick Mask tint overlay, in Quick Mask mode). Press Ctrl(⌘)+D to deselect the marquee.

4. Press **B** (Paintbrush tool). On the Brushes palette, choose the second row, far right tip. On the Paintbrush Options palette, the current painting mode should be Normal and Opacity should be 100%.

5. Create brush strokes in a painterly fashion around unmasked areas in the image (see fig. 13.7). Create a stroke or two along the edge of the bowl, outline a piece of fruit with a single stroke or two, and press **X** to switch foreground/background color so that you can erase Quick Masked areas (if you feel that doing so contributes to the piece). All the areas covered with Quick Mask will be filtered, using the Dry Brush effect; the "unfinished areas" will become a Chalk & Charcoal rendering.

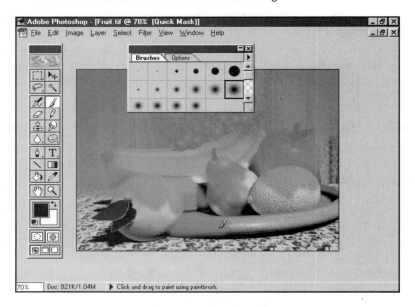

figure 13.7

The Quick Mask strokes you paint into the image will serve as a selection area for the Dry Brush effect.

6. Click on the Standard editing mode icon to change the areas of Quick Mask in the image into a selection marquee, and then press Ctrl(⌘)+Shift+I to invert the selection.

7. Click on the Foreground color selection box. In the Photoshop color picker, choose a dark, warm brown and click on OK. The Chalk in this effect is drawn with the current background color (white), and the charcoal is rendered by using the current foreground color. Areas that are not "drawn" are rendered to 50 percent black.

8. Choose Filter, Sketch, Chalk & Charcoal.

9. Drag the Charcoal slider to 5. This determines how much of the total selection area receives charcoal (foreground color). The maximum setting is 20.

10. Drag the Chalk slider up to 10, to create more white areas of rendering than brown in the image.

11. Drag the Stroke Pressure slider to 1. This creates a subtle rendering effect; too high a setting makes the effect look as though an auto-drawing application (not an artist) created the art. Click on OK. The piece should look like figure 13.8.

figure 13.8

Create a soft, hand-rendered style for the selections by using the Chalk & Charcoal plug-in.

12. Press Ctrl(⌘)+Shift+I to invert the marquee, and choose Filter, Artistic, Dry Brush. The Dry Brush filter simplifies selected areas in much the same way the Palette Knife filter does, but Dry Brush faithfully renders much more original image detail into the selection.

13. Drag the Brush Size slider to 2. This controls the detail in the image, the maximum size being 10. The smaller the brush, the more representative the effect is of original image detail.

14. Drag the Brush Detail slider to 10, the maximum for image intricacy.

15. Drag the Texture slider to 2. This is the middle ground for smoothness settings for the effect. Click on OK to apply the filter.

16. Press Ctrl(⌘)+D to deselect the marquee, stand back to admire the piece, and then save it to your hard disk in the TIFF format, as Fruit1.tif.

As you can see in figure 13.9, the still life looks as though the artist went out for a lunch break, and not at all like the synthetic composition from which it began. The author created the still life in a modeling application; if you use a modeling application, Photoshop effects can enhance your work, and sometimes disguise its origin! Although Fruit.tif is somewhat passable as a photorealistic image, the plug-in effects replace "fake photography" with fairly authentic paint strokes, and make it a more attractive piece overall.

figure 13.9
If you have a still life scene (and about five minutes to spare), you can turn it into a work of art by using Photoshop's plug-ins.

T I P

Unlike the commercial Gallery Effects plug-in filters, the native Photoshop filters do not allow you to save specific settings. You might want to write down (in a plain text file) the settings you really like, for future use. If you purchased Gallery Effects before you bought Photoshop 4, you can still use them—but you will find many duplicates, and Photoshop's native versions will run faster.

Although Adobe has organized the plug-ins into aesthetic categories, intimating types of artistic impression, there are similarities between plug-in effects that might not be obvious from the filter's name. The Watercolor, Dry Brush, and Fresco filters all produce similar artistic effects, for example. The differences between these filters are nominal. If you cannot achieve precisely the effect you seek, try a "related" plug-in.

The authors have a personal preference for the Dry Brush filter, especially used in combination with other filters, for the soft yet accurate interpretation of image content. In figure 13.10, you can see a close-up of the original Fruit.tif image compared to a Dry Brush application across the entire image. This is a good filter to use when the focus is poor in the original image, or the image contains a misplaced element, or the content of the image is simply not interesting enough to stand on its own.

figure 13.10
Soften an image with creative flair by using the Dry Brush or similar plug-in effects.

Multiple Applications of a Plug-In

As mentioned throughout this book, a filter, a tonal or color correction, or anything else you do to an image is a *progressive change.* You cannot return to an original image by applying a negative amount of correction to a previously corrected image. Sometimes this truth can lead to some wonderful effects.

The authors were once faced with a design situation in which the client wanted a picture of "a guy in a suit." Our client wasn't fussy about who "the guy" was—he simply wanted a placeholder in a publication to show to his boss; the actual guy in the publication would be photographed later. If you need a "generic" human illustration, and an illustration from a drawing program doesn't suit the purpose, consider running a Photoshop plug-in over a photo a number of times to achieve an image of someone whose features are indistinct. In figure 13.11, the original image is on the left; the copy on the right was processed by using the Dry Brush plug-in two times in succession. Then the image was converted to a Duotone to remove unique colors from the image, dulling down the visual interest. (Duotones are discussed in Chapter 11, "Black and White…and Color.")

figure 13.11
If you definitely don't want a person to stand out in a crowd, consider using a Photoshop plug-in at least twice on an image.

Fading an Effect

Photoshop 4 now sports a Fade command similar to that found in Fractal Design Painter; you can decrease the amount of filtering after applying the effect by partially restoring original image content. To add to the versatility of this feature, you have a choice of modes in which to fade a filter effect. And you can also use the Filter, Fade command after you apply any of Photoshop's Image, Adjust commands.

Clouds.tif is a nice image of a cloudy sky—but a piece of art, it isn't. Let's walk through the following steps to see how the Fade command can be used to make the best use of Photoshop's Reticulation filter—normally, at full strength, it's an overpowering effect.

USING MODES TO FADE AN EFFECT

CD-ROM

1. Open Clouds.tif from the CHAP13 folder of the Companion CD.

2. Click on the Foreground color selection box, define a dark purple in the color picker, and then click on OK. Click on the Background color swatch, choose a tangerine color in the color picker, and click on OK. The Reticulation effect uses Photoshop's Foreground/Background colors to create the effect.

3. Choose Filter, Sketch, Reticulation. The Reticulation filter simulates the effect of distorting film emulsion. Dark clumps of emulsion and patterned film grain are the result.

4. Drag the Density slider to 14 (50 is the maximum). This creates a fair amount of simulated grain in the image.

5. Drag the Black Level slider (which controls the point at which image areas are 100% black) to 40. Drag the White Level slider (which determines how much background color will be rendered into the image) to 5 (see fig. 13.12).

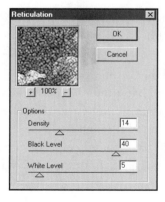

figure 13.12
The Reticulation filter creates the effect of controlled distortion and shrinking of physical film emulsion.

6. Click on OK to apply the effect, and then press Ctrl(⌘)+Shift+F (Filter, Fade).

7. Choose Soft Light from the Mode drop-down list, and drag the slider to 72 (see fig. 13.13). The original image takes on some of the color and texture of the Reticulation plug-in, and you have a striking photographic distortion of a cloud scene. Click on OK to apply the Fade command.

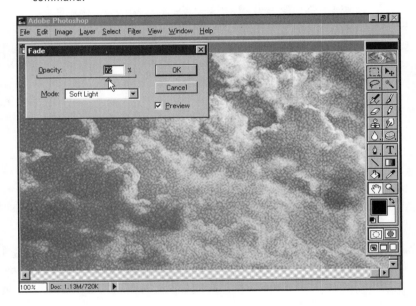

figure 13.13

The Fade command performs no fading at 100%, to 100% of the original image at 0%. Use this command and the Photoshop modes to blend an effect into the original image.

8. Press Ctrl(⌘)+Shift+S (File, Save As), and save the image to your hard disk in the TIFF format, as Clouds.tif.

With the exception of the Chrome plug-in, all of Photoshop's Sketch filters use the current foreground and background colors to render a variation upon an image. This is why you can create an interesting effect by combining original colors with the colors the plug-ins use, through the Fade command. It's also a good idea to define foreground and background colors before you launch any of these filters; otherwise, all the effects will be in unexpected shades.

TIP

To further modify the Reticulation effect, try using Photoshop's Minimum and Maximum filters (on the Other menu) to shrink or grow the size of the emulsion and grain.

WARNING

If you choose the Fade command and then press Cancel, the command is no longer available for use in the current image. If you have made a mistake, press Ctrl(⌘)+Z to undo the filter, reapply the filter, and then choose the Fade command again.

For all the wonderful, natural media-type effects at your disposal with plug-ins, there is a real-world property that no single filter provides. When you paint with oils, *build-up* (texture from applying coats of thick oils) becomes visible in the design. In the following section, you see how to simulate the build-up of oils in your work.

Lighting Effects and the Watercolor Filters

If you have experimented with the Lighting Effects filter in Photoshop 3.0.x, the current version has not changed. You can still define surface lighting color, scene lighting color, type of light, and most important, the Texture Channel. The Texture Channel feature enables the user to define any grayscale channel in the image (Photoshop 4 now allows the use of a color channel without an alpha channel defined in the image) as a relief map to filter the color composite of the image. In *relief mapping*, a feature typically found in modeling and rendering applications, the brighter areas of the image map appear to push corresponding areas of the color image upward, while darker areas of the map push corresponding color areas downward.

The Watercolor filter, used as a stand-alone filter, produces exquisite results. When the filtered image is then processed through the Lighting Effects filter, however, the dimension of the watercolor strokes is made more apparent, and the overall effect more closely resembles an oil painting or a hand-tinted mold of a sculpture. Here's how to take an ordinary scene and turn it into a timeless classic.

PRODUCING A 3D PAINTING

1. Open the Glen-inn.tif image from the CHAP13 folder on the Companion CD.

2. The Watercolor filter typically works best with images that display bright colors which are light in tone. The Glen-inn image is light enough, but the sky and river front are dull and monochromatic. With the Magic Wand tool (at its current tolerance of 32), click in the sky area of the image to select it.

3. Click on the Foreground color selection box, choose a light blue from the color picker, and then click on OK to return to the workspace.

4. Click on the Background color selection box, choose white from the color picker, and click on OK.

5. Choose Filter, Render, and then choose Clouds. The Clouds filter uses the foreground and background colors to render fractal math that simulates soft clouds into the selected area (see fig. 13.14). Do these look like real clouds? Not at all. But after the Watercolor filter is applied, the audience will never detect the truth!

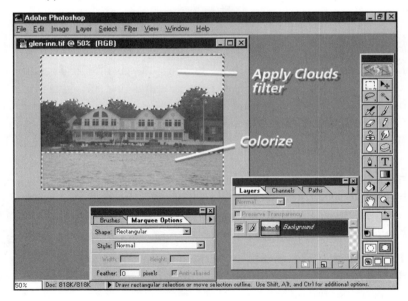

figure 13.14
Edit the colors and tones in an image before you use a filter.

6. Press Ctrl(⌘)+D to deselect the marquee. Then, with the Lasso tool, hold Alt(Opt) and click around the water area to select it.

7. Press Ctrl(⌘)+U to select the Hue/Saturation dialog box. The water in this image will never show pure color (it's simply too gray); therefore, you can use the Colorize feature to simulate a pleasing water color in the image.

8. Click on the Colorize check box, drag the Hue slider to –112, and then drag the Saturation slider to about 11. Click on OK, and press Ctrl(⌘)+D to deselect the active marquee.

9. Choose Filter, Artistic, Watercolor. The Watercolor filter is one of the more processor-intensive effects; wait a moment for the preview window to display the proposed changes.

10. Drag the Brush Detail slider to 14, the maximum (see fig. 13.15). Drag the Shadow Intensity slider to 0. Shadows are created in areas to simulate the drying effect of actual watercolors, an effect you don't want in this assignment. Drag the Texture slider to 2, to add a moderate amount of distortion to the color edges in the effect, and then click on OK.

figure 13.15
Use the Watercolor filter's controls to specify high detail with a minimal amount of image shading.

The Watercolor effect is a nice artistic touch and adds interest to the image, but the image is a little flat now, and needs additional texturing (see fig. 13.16).

figure 13.16

Photoshop's Watercolor effect is a flat treatment of the traditional application of paints to a surface.

11. Choose Filter, Render, and then choose Lighting Effects. By default, the light casting into the preview window is Spotlight.

12. Change the Spotlight to a Directional light by choosing this from the Light type drop-down list.

13. Drag the light source dot—the dot at the end of the line in the preview window—to 12 o'clock, and position it slightly outside the preview window (see fig 13.17). Click on the Texture Channel drop-down list and choose Green. Then drag the Height slider to about 12. You might need to drag the Directional light dot farther from or closer to the preview image window, to match the overall lighting in the original image. When things look right, click on OK to apply the filter.

14. Press Ctrl(⌘)+Shift+S and save the file to your hard disk in the TIFF file format, as Glen-inn.tif. You can close the image at any time now.

As you can see in figure 13.18, a combination of Watercolor and Lighting Effects has taken this image away not only from the photographic medium, but also from preconceived notions of "computer art." It's simply "Art," and through your knowledge of plug-ins you have given this piece a feeling.

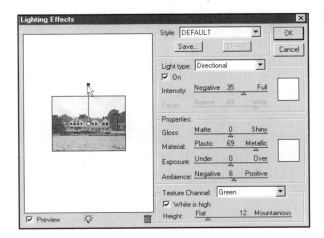

figure 13.17

Use the Lighting Effects filter's controls to apply a small amount of embossing to the image, based upon the Green channel's relief mapping information.

figure 13.18

The Watercolor and Lighting Effects plug-ins can only be considered "instant art" tools when you understand the options and use the right source material.

The Green image channel was used in this example because (for this image) it contains the best tonal blend of image information to use as a relief (texture) map. In photos of your own, check out the Channels palette before you apply Lighting Effects, to see which channel has the greatest number of unique tones. Also, consider making a grayscale copy of the color image and placing it in an alpha channel, if none of the channels contain a good mix of tones.

Also, you should be aware that all the settings recommended for the images in this chapter depend not only on color and tone, but also on file size. Most of the images in the CHAP13 folder are approximately 1 MB in file size. If you used an Edge Thickness of 4 in the Nicknack assignment earlier in this chapter, you might want to increase that amount to 5 or 6 when filtering an image of 2 MB or more.

Other Embossing and Relief Techniques

Apart from good composition and use of colors, audiences respond positively to a "3D" look, whether it's created with geometry or with a filter that suggests 3D texture. The following sections explore more of the texture-creation and embossing engines you have at your disposal under Photoshop's Filter menu.

Using Photoshop's Patterns Folder

For at least three years now, Photoshop has shipped with a collection of patterns in Illustrator format, which many users have overlooked as an important art resource. Although the patterns were of limited use in earlier versions, several filters at hand today can use these patterns as a 3D texture resource for embossing and making simple scenes look more dimensional. One such filter, the Texturizer plug-in, can be used to create dimensional images whose surfaces look like canvas, burlap, or any grayscale image you save to Photoshop's PSD format. In the following steps, you see how to create a quilted wishing well, or any image you choose to use as image stock.

THE TEXTURIZER PLUG-IN

CD-ROM

1. Open the Wishwell.tif image from the CHAP13 folder of the Companion CD. This image is about 450 pixels in height. You should know the dimensions of the target image before you define a texture pattern for the file.

2. Open the Mayan.ai file from the PATTERNS folder where Photoshop 4 is located on your hard drive. If you chose not to install this folder with Photoshop, create a new grayscale image about 50 pixels wide and high, and add some foreground detail in black to the image. You will see the principle for working with a user-defined pattern in the steps to follow.

3. In Photoshop's Rasterize Generic EPS Format dialog box, type **50** in the height field. This will create an image in bitmap format that will tile 9 times vertically when the Texturizer filter uses the image as source material. Type **72** in the Resolution field (see fig. 13.19), choose Grayscale image Mode, and then click on OK for Photoshop to import and convert the vector Illustrator information to bitmap format.

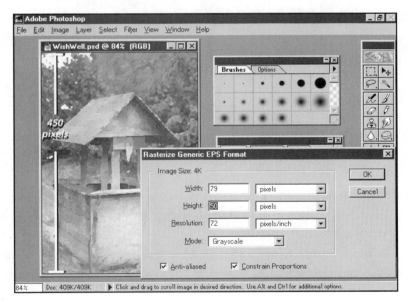

figure 13.19
Choose a resolution for the Texturizer pattern that will tile many times in the target image.

4. After the image appears (see fig 13.20), choose Flatten Image from the Layers palette's menu flyout, and save the file as Mayan.psd to your hard disk. Illustrator files can contain transparency information; by flattening the file, you remove a potential problem with the Texturizer plug-in reading the image. You can close the file at any time now.

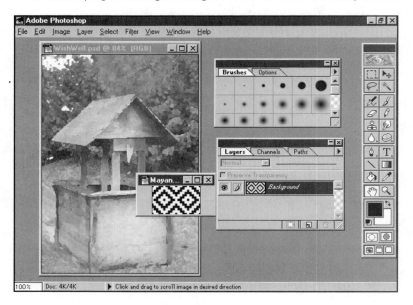

figure 13.20
Photoshop's PATTERNS folder contains many useful seamless, tiling patterns for use in designs and as texture maps.

5. With Wishwell.tif as the current image, choose Filter, Texture, Texturizer.

6. In the Texturizer dialog box, choose Load Texture from the Texture drop-down list. This displays the Open dialog box.

7. Choose the Mayan.psd file you saved, and click on Open to load the file.

8. Any amount of Scaling, Relief, and any light direction you choose for this example is fine. These are options you might want to specify in work of your own to achieve a special lighting effect or amount of texturizing (embossing). Click on OK to accept the defaults and apply the Texturizer filter.

9. Press Ctrl(⌘)+Shift+S. Save the file to hard disk in the TIFF format, as Wishwell.tif.

In figure 13.21, you can see the effect of the Texturizer filter.

figure 13.21
When you need to blend image detail with surface detail, the Texturizer filter is your ticket.

Qualitatively, there is little difference between the Texturizer filter and the Lighting Effects filter's Texture Channel feature, although you cannot accidentally create an under- or overexposed piece by using Texturizer. Nor can you scale a texture, as you can with Lighting Effects.

Underpainting and Conté Crayon also offer the option to map a grayscale image as the basis for the embossing work they perform. These filters also offer foreground/ background color shading, and when used with Photoshop's Fade command, you can wind up with a *very* complex artistic piece!

As mentioned earlier, the image used by the Texturizer and other relief-mapping filters can be of anything. In the following section, you see how image content can become visually subordinate to a very intricate Texturizer relief map.

Creating Your Own Texture Maps

Chapter 20 describes how to use Photoshop's Offset filter to create a seamless tiling image for Web use, but right now is a good time to cover the topic briefly. An effective way to make the emboss effect created by plug-in filters seem both natural and prominent in the image is to slightly blur the relief map you intend to use. This enables the filter to read the transitional tones in the relief map image as heights that progress gradually from shallow to steep, and gives the impression of a rounded edge to the embossed areas.

Figure 13.22 shows Pattern.psd, an image in the CHAP13 folder that was created by simply mixing Adobe's Wood Ornaments characters together into a pattern. This font comes with many of the Adobe applications, as well as with Adobe Type Manager; virtually any symbol font is a good candidate for pattern making. Type a few characters, use the Offset command to move the design relative to the document window, and then type a few more characters. Because Photoshop 4 adds text to a document (by default) to a new layer, after you type the text, you can easily move the layers around to arrive at an aesthetically pleasing composition.

figure 13.22
Use a symbol font as a resource for an elegant pattern.

Striking the right compositional balance between an elegant emboss effect and the visual elements in a photo is not the easiest of tasks. Think about this one for a moment: if Pattern.psd is to be the "star," and you use the Fruit.tif image as the host for the emboss, then the Fruit.tif image needs to be reduced in visual complexity so that the *colors* become the visual contribution to the finished piece.

In the following steps you use one filter to make way for the effect created by another one.

C REATING C OMPOSITIONAL B ALANCE WITH F ILTERS

CD-ROM

1. Open the Pattern.psd image from the CHAP13 folder on the Companion CD.
2. Choose Filter, Blur, Blur More. The Blur More filter applies four times the strength of the Blur filter.

3. Press Ctrl(⌘)+F to apply the last-used filter. Filtering the image twice by using Blur More creates about the same effect as applying the Gaussian Blur filter once at a specific strength (but the authors needed to work this shortcut command into the book someplace).

4. Press Ctrl(⌘)+Shift+S, and save the file to your hard disk as Pattern.psd, in the Photoshop file format. You can close the image at any time.

5. Open the Fruit.tif image from the CHAP13 folder of the Companion CD.

6. Choose Filter, Artistic, Palette Knife, and drag the Stroke Size slider to about 25.

7. Drag the Stroke Detail to 3, and then drag the Softness slider to 1. Click on OK to apply the effect.

8. Choose Filter, Texture, Texturizer. Click on the Texture drop-down list, and choose Load Texture.

9. Choose the Pattern.psd file you saved to your hard disk, drag the Relief slider to 11, and choose Top Right (the same angle at which light is cast into the Fruit picture) from the Light Direction drop-down list (see fig. 13.23). Click on OK to apply the effect.

figure 13.23
Specify the pattern you saved as the relief map for the Texturizer filter.

10. Press Ctrl(⌘)+Shift+S, and save the image to your hard disk as Fruit2.tif, in the TIFF file format.

In figure 13.24, you can see the visual correlation between the blurry pattern and the effect it created in the Fruit image. Dark areas created recesses, and light areas in the pattern created bumps because Top Right was defined as the Light Direction. If you want the bumps to be recesses and vice versa, check the Invert check box before you exit the Texturizer dialog box.

figure 13.24
When a pattern contains clear, intricate composition, let it dominate the piece by reducing the original visual content first.

The Craquelure and Mosaic Tiles Texture filters also can create an embossed look, but you cannot define a user-created image to use with these effects. Perhaps the best use of Craquelure and Mosaic Tiles is to apply them to a color gradient-filled image. The visual effect of most of the texture filters can overwhelm a composition. By adding these effects to simple blend fields such as those created by using the Gradient tool, you can make a beautiful background to which you can add image elements from other pictures.

The Patchwork filter also creates an emboss effect, but this filter can create a more pleasing "fly's eye" interpretation of a scene than the Extrude/Stylize filter. If you begin with a scene with rich colors and simple geometry, you can make a piece of tapestry with the Patchwork filter. In figure 13.25, you can see the effect of the Patchwork filter on a copy of the Fruit image, which had previously been filtered with the Palette Knife.

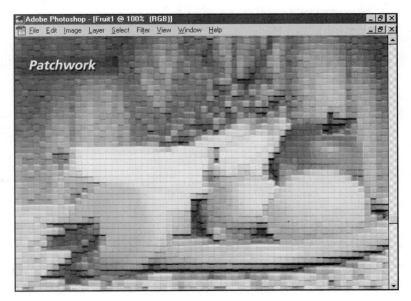

figure 13.25
The Patchwork filter produces the best results when applied to a simple color field.

You have seen how to create unusual, attractive results with many of Photoshop's filters by using them in combination, using the right target image, and adding your own creative input. The plug-in collection also includes "special purpose" filters that, because they frequently don't produce the effect you anticipate, are often dismissed as design tools. In the sections to follow, you apply a little "artistic pressure" to some of the more esoteric plug-ins, and see how they can suit a vertical design need.

NOTE

For techniques and secrets in the effective use of third-party plug-ins, such as Kai's Power Tools and Andromeda filters, check out *Photoshop 3 Filters and Effects*, another book we wrote for New Riders Publishing.

Specialized Plug-Ins

Several Photoshop plug-ins produce cool effects, but the effect itself might not fit into the context of a design. It's always a wise artistic choice (one that we might not always listen to) to forego the cool effect for the betterment of the overall composition. In several instances, however, you can—and should—opt for an exotic, strange sort of effect. In these instances, you simply need to decide whether you're controlling the effect or it's controlling you!

The following sections cover some of the filters you might not use often, but whose effects can add a novel look in exceptional design situations.

Creating "Wet" Lettering

The Plastic Wrap filter is definitely not a good choice to apply to photographic material. The result—whether moldy-looking objects or moldy-looking people—is not an appetizing image! But when the Plastic Wrap filter is applied to a graphic that contains sharp edges (such as one created in Illustrator or another drawing application), or to text, the resulting image looks more dimensional, and takes on a "wet" look.

In the following steps, you create some text and use the Plastic Wrap filter, in combination with the Lighting Effects filter, to produce a greeting with both texture and dimensions for an advertisement or a Web page.

CREATING "WET LOOK" TEXT

1. Press Ctrl(⌘)+N to display the New document dialog box. Windows users can press Ctrl and double-click on the workspace as a shortcut.

2. Define the new document as 450 pixels Width by 100 pixels Height, at 72 pixels/inch Resolution, in RGB color mode. Click on OK to create the new document.

3. Press **D** (Default colors), click on the Background color selection box, choose a gold color from the color picker, and then click on OK.

4. Press Ctrl(⌘)+A, press Delete (Backspace), and then press Ctrl(⌘)+D. The background is now gold.

5. Click in the document, almost at far left, with the Type tool. This defines the starting point of the text and displays the Type tool dialog box.

6. Choose a rounded style of font for this assignment; the Plastic Wrap filter produces nice, prominent highlights in areas of the image that are rounded. Frankfurter is used in the following figures, but Kabel, VAG Rounded, and Rockwell work well, too.

7. Type **100** in the Points field, type **GREETINGS!** in the text field, and click on OK to apply the text on a new layer in the document.

8. Uncheck the Preserve Transparency check box for the new layer, and choose Filter, Artistic, Plastic Wrap. The Plastic Wrap filter creates highlights in a selection area, and also renders shading outside the selection. Because the text is on a layer, surrounded by transparent pixels, no shading will be rendered outside the text.

9. Drag the Highlight Strength slider to 20 (the maximum). This setting will render strong, white highlights in the filtered image. There is no option in this filter to alter the color of the highlights.

10. Drag the Detail slider to 12. This slider controls the intensity of the highlights. Lower settings result in thin, subtle highlights.

11. Drag the Smoothness slider to 12. When the target for the Plastic Wrap filter contains many colors, low Smoothness settings produce many highlights in the image, based upon color changes in the image. The text in this example is composed of only one color, however, and lower Smoothness settings would make the effect look faint and lacking in visual impact. You can see the preview image and the recommended settings for this example in figure 13.26. Click on OK to apply the effect.

12. Press Ctrl(⌘)+S, and save your work to your hard disk as Greeting.psd, in the Photoshop format. See the filtered text in figure 13.27. Keep the image open in Photoshop.

TIP

To increase the complexity of the Plastic Wrap effect, try adding noise to a selection before you launch the Plastic Wrap filter. Noise causes the Plastic Wrap filter to wend and weave highlights in patterns that look like highlights on ocean waves.

figure 13.26
The Plastic Wrap filter applies a smooth highlight to selection areas, which simulates cellophane on a surface.

figure 13.27
The Plastic Wrap filter does not produce pleasing results with *every* image, but stylized, highly graphical compositions can benefit from its use.

WARNING

Many native Photoshop filters, and almost all third-party plug-ins, do not understand transparency and layer information. If you are not getting the effect you want, or an error message pops up in Photoshop while you're trying to apply a filter to a layer, add nontransparent areas to the layer, and then try the filter again.

The Preserve Transparency check box should also be unchecked when you use plug-ins, unless you want an effect confined to only nontransparent areas of a layer. Occasionally, plug-ins must access data outside a selection; the Preserve Transparency option diminishes the visual effect of such a plug-in.

The foreground of the composition looks dimensional now, but you need to embellish the background to make the text look as though it's embedded in the background. Here's how to use the Lighting Effects filter to accomplish the task:

EMBEDDING TEXT IN THE BACKGROUND

1. Press Ctrl(⌘) and click on the Layer 1 title on the Layers palette to load the nontransparent areas (the text) as a selection marquee.

2. On the Channels palette, click on the Save selection as channel icon at the bottom of the palette.

3. Click on the Channel #4 title to move your view to the saved selection information. Then press Ctrl(⌘)+D to deselect the marquee.

4. Choose Filter, Blur, Gaussian Blur, drag the slider to about 2, and click on OK to apply the effect to channel #4.

5. Press Ctrl(⌘)+~ (tilde) to move back to the RGB view of the document, click on the Background layer title on the Layers palette, and then choose Filter, Render, Lighting Effects.

6. Choose Spotlight from the Light Type drop-down list, choose Channel #4 from the Texture Channel drop-down list, drag the Height slider to 9, and then drag the light source dot to an 11 o'clock position (see fig. 13.28). Because White is high is the default setting for the Texture Channel, the channel information is producing a dent, not a bump, from the blurry text. The light angle will further reinforce, visually, that the Background layer is denting inward.

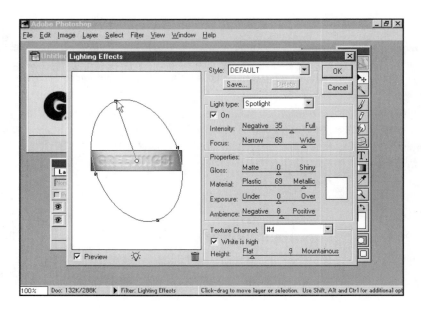

figure 13.28
Create bumps or dents by using the Lighting Effects' Texture channel.

7. Click on OK to apply the Lighting Effects filter. The simple text greeting now looks dimensional (see fig. 13.29). This technique can also be used to create authentic-looking license plates.

figure 13.29
Mix and match design properties through the use of several Photoshop plug-ins.

8. Press Ctrl(⌘)+S to save your work. Keep the document open.

It should be noted that the Material Properties slider in the Lighting Effects filter is, by default, turned toward Metallic. This worked well in the previous example, but you might want to move the slider to the center in your own pieces. The

Metallic/Plastic slider affects the highlights in an image that is filtered by using the Texture Channel feature. In metallic renderings, highlights are the same color as the primary hue in an image area, whereas Plastic settings turn highlights to white.

The Plastic Wrap filter can render white highlights only, but you can edit the highlights after you use the filter, tinting them any color you like. In figure 13.30, you can see the Hue/Saturation command being used to colorize the Layer 1 text to make the highlights blue. This trick works in this particular example because the text is black, and will receive none of the Colorize feature.

figure 13.30
Change the color of the Plastic Wrap's highlights by using the Hue/Saturation command's Colorize feature.

Working with the Cutout Filter

Although there is a wonderful demo version of Alien Skin's Cutout filter on the Photoshop installation CD, the Cutout filter covered in *this* section is one of the Gallery Effects plug-ins; the two filters produce entirely different effects.

The Gallery Effects Cutout plug-in changes a selection, or an entire image, in two ways. It *posterizes* (averages) colors to a much greater extent than any of the other Photoshop filters, and it creates silhouette shapes based upon color edges detected in the image. Cutout is the most processor-intensive of Photoshop's filters—you need a very special image to make it worth the wait. It's often processing time well spent, however. The Cutout filter generates a design that looks as though you painstakingly trimmed colored pieces of paper and fitted them together to create a composition.

The choice of images is the most important aspect of getting an interesting image from the Cutout filter. The Lwnchair.tif image on the Companion CD is not a *perfect* candidate for this filter, but it has many good qualities:

◆ The image has a limited color palette. Basically, there's a white chair, green foliage, a blue sky, and a little shading. The Cutout filter can easily posterize the colors in this image down to a handful of unique values.

◆ Geometry is clearly defined in the image. The chair separates nicely from the background, and the Cutout filter can speedily trace around the geometry.

◆ The geometry in the image is simple. Except for the foliage, which will cause the filter to take a while calculating the intricate outlines, the geometry of the image is pretty simple.

Because you have control over both edge fidelity (accuracy) and edge complexity in the Cutout filter's dialog box, you can simplify the foliage outline and still get a pleasing image. Here's how to change the medium of the Lwnchair image from photographic to construction paper.

USING THE CUTOUT FILTER

CD-ROM

1. Open the Lwnchair.tif image from the CHAP13 folder on the Companion CD.

2. Choose Filter, Artistic, Cutout.

3. Drag the No. of Levels slider to 5. This specifies how many levels of brightness are used to determine unique colored "papers" in the image. This control is *not* equivalent to the number of posterization colors. The minimum/maximum settings are 2 to 8, with 8 producing the greatest variety of colors from different brightnesses in the image.

4. Drag the Edge Simplicity to 4 (10 is the maximum). This setting will produce a somewhat faithful rendering, mainly because the geometry in the image is not very complex.

5. Drag the Edge Fidelity slider to 2. This medium setting is a compromise between accurate edge tracing (which would take an eternity because of the foliage line) and inaccurate tracing (less visually interesting than the original image). Figure 13.31 shows the preview of the image with all these settings.

figure 13.31
The Cutout filter creates a stylized scene, reminiscent of construction paper designs.

6. Click on OK to apply the filter, and save the image to hard disk as Lwnchair.tif in the TIFF file format.

In figure 13.32, you can see the finished image. Although the design is fine as is, you might want to use the Lighting Effects Texture Channel feature on similar images to create relief. You might also want to add Noise to the image to suggest sandpaper instead of construction paper as the medium.

figure 13.32
The Cutout filter is good for cleaning up an image whose geometric content is simple,
and whose color palette is small.

The Chrome Filter

At first, the authors spent a lot of time with the Chrome filter, which seemed to hold wonderful possibilities with the right image. As it turned out, we were simply trying too hard—the filter will not produce a cyborg version of a photograph, and it seems that the photo dictates almost entirely the Chrome filter's design efficacy.

If you need a wild texture, something from out of this galaxy, the Chrome filter can instantly generate an abstract image if you use a high-frequency image as the target material. A high-frequency image is one that contains visual information whose color and tonal values shift abruptly from pixel to pixel. Examples of high-frequency images you might consider for use with the Chrome filter are wood, rough stone, and other nature photographs.

In figure 13.33 is a photo of driftwood (Drftwood.tif in the CHAP13 folder), with the chrome version on the right. The Detail and Smoothness settings in the Chrome filter's dialog box can be used to alter the amount of detail rendered (at the price of processing speed), and the characteristic of the chrome (high Smoothness values work well with most images).

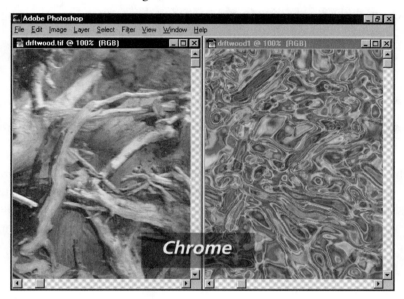

figure 13.33
The Chrome filter can turn a high-frequency photograph into a view of a shattered thermometer!

Typically, the effect of the Chrome filter leaves the image looking dull; you might want to try increasing the contrast of the image for a finished piece. Also, the Chrome effect is *mono*chrome: it removes the color from color images. Consider using the Colorize feature in the Hue/Saturation command, or adding a layer of color fills (in Color or Overlay mode) to the image after you apply the Chrome effect.

Summary

This chapter is an "idea book" for the creative use of filters, but you shouldn't confine your private experimentation to only those listed here. Certainly, there are other filters yet to explore, and there will be third-party offerings in the near future to increase the listing on the Filter menu! You will have expanded your creative horizons and your capability to design things that look fresh and new when you approach the *use* of a plug-in as described in this chapter, that is, when you do the following:

◆ Dictate the effect through the creative use of a filter. (Always remember that the filter has no intrinsic artistic talent.)

◆ Apply filters in combination to arrive at a graphical idea you seek.

◆ Use post-production techniques and other Photoshop color and tone features to refine a filtered design.

In Chapter 14, "Special Effects with Ordinary Photographs," we return to the human element in Photoshop, both in design content and artistic sensitivity, to show you how 30 years between photographs can be brought to a single, seamless captured moment. You will see how to create special effects, using ordinary photographs of your family and friends.

CHAPTER

14

SPECIAL EFFECTS WITH ORDINARY PHOTOGRAPHS

Over the years, we all amass a collection of snapshots of family members and friends. Your collection of photos undoubtedly holds a great deal of emotional attachment and sentimental value for you and your family. In the event of a disaster such as a house fire, this collection of photos (your history of family, relatives, and friends) cannot be replaced by insurance.

Although it is unlikely these photos will ever hang in an art museum, you already have the ingredients to create a very special, private masterpiece. With Photoshop as your tool, you can cook up virtually any image from your collection of photos, to stir memories and evoke emotions.

This chapter's assignment is to reunite a father and son through the digital manipulation of two photographs. Jim's father passed on early in life, and Jim does not have any photographs of the two of them together. This reality can be changed, as you will soon see; in this chapter, you will produce a touching image for Jim and his family. An interesting element of this virtual reunion is that Jim and his father were the same age (34) when their photos were taken. A reunion, and also a spanning of generations, will be accomplished in Photoshop.

Combining a badly deteriorated, 30-year-old photograph of Jim's dad and a recent photo of Jim requires a very special concept and artistic approach. A great deal of detail and color is missing from the old photo, whereas the new photo is rich with detail and color. By using techniques that are the complete opposite of those found in Chapters 5 and 6 ("Restoring…" and "Retouching an Heirloom Photograph," respectively), you are going to age the new photo to blend in with the photo of Jim's dad.

Setting Up the Source Images

CD-ROM

To give a composite image a sense of reality, you must pay careful attention to detail from the moment you get the idea. In this example, the first step is to examine the scanned photo of Jim's dad. (This image, Jimsdad.tif, is in the CHAP14 folder on the Companion CD if you want to take a look at it now.) Where can we put Jim in the photo of his father? What should Jim wear?

There are two possible areas where we can add Jim to the Jimsdad.tif photo—standing in front of the jeep looking at his father, or standing behind his father. The first of these possibilities would leave Jim's face obscured. If Jim stood behind his father, however, not only would Jim's face be visible, but he could put his arm over his dad's shoulder, creating interaction between the two. As for clothing, we want Jim to blend in as much as possible; a service station uniform similar to the one his dad wears in the photo is in order.

Lighting, posing, and type of lens must also be considered. In Jimsdad.tif, it is a sunny day, and the two clocks in the photo show 10:00 a.m. On a day with similar conditions, Jim and the author went to a parking lot. With the sun crossing Jim's face at the same angle as his father's, Jim put his arm over the author's shoulder and looked at him as though his father were actually there. A little coaching was necessary, because Jim is not an actor; to evoke an expression and pose of familiarity and affection, the author asked Jim to envision his father standing next to him. Then, while Jim held that pose, the author stepped away and took the photo of Jim with a normal focal-length lens (50 mm). A wide-angle lens was not used because it would have created a distortion especially evident at the edges of the photo. A telephoto lens also was unsuitable for capturing the resource image for this assignment, because it would have created a compressed look between the foreground and background. When you match different photographic images, your choice of lenses is as critical as lighting and image content are.

Using the files on the Companion CD, which were acquired through scanning both the new and old photographs, you will begin the composite photograph by performing a technique to make the older photograph shed some years of deterioration. As mentioned earlier, you are not going to completely restore this image, but there are some problems with it that can easily be fixed.

Using Curves for Tonal Adjustment

When we discuss qualities in a digital image, we often describe *tones* (the neutral components of an image that determine brightness) as a property separate from the *hue* (the wavelength of light that gives an image area a predominant color quality). The Curves dialog box enables you to adjust the tonal range with the highest degree of precision. Unlike the Levels command, which gives you only three tonal ranges to work with, Curves enables you to adjust as many as 16 ranges in each of the separate color channels that make up an image; Curves also enables you to adjust the tones in the composite color image. If you need to add contrast to a photo, for example, the results you can achieve by adjusting the Curves are far superior to those achieved by using the Contrast command. Increasing the contrast in the Brightness/Contrast dialog box causes middle tones to drop out, and causes loss of image detail in those areas. Increasing contrast by using Curves, on the other hand, not only retains the detail, but actually increases it. If you spend time working with Curves and become proficient with it, your images will benefit greatly.

A visually pleasing photograph should contain at least one black and one white area to give the eye points of reference for the complete tonal range of the image. Master black-and-white photographers such as Ansel Adams and Edward Weston labored intensely to achieve the darkest blacks and the whitest whites when they printed their work. The photo of Jim's dad contains neither a black not a white area; and a yellowish cast is the dominant color in the photo. A quick trip to the Curves adjustment will provide the tonal range we want, and selective sharpening of the contrast in image areas will restore some original color to the photo. Muddy tonal ranges in an image often obscure true color content.

RESTORING CONTRAST WITH CURVES

CD-ROM

1. Open the Jimsdad.tif image from the CHAP14 folder on the Companion CD.

2. Press Ctrl(⌘)+M to open the Curves dialog box.

3. Choose the black eyedropper, and then click inside the jeep, through the back window. This defines the black point for the image; now no other image area can display a darker tone than the area you have clicked in the image. Choose the white eyedropper and click on the sign to the right of the gas station door. You have now defined the whitest point in the photo (see fig. 14.1).

4. Click on OK. Then press Ctrl(⌘)+S, and save the image as Reunion.psd to your hard disk. Leave the image open for the steps to follow.

figure 14.1
Use Curves to create a new white and black point in a low-contrast image.

The image of Jim's dad now shows a full range of tonal values. The yellow color cast is removed, and you have a quick, acceptable restoration. Notice, however, that the blacks and many middle tones have deteriorated to a reddish color. No problem. Photoshop has a way to create a selection of those reddish pixels, thus enabling you to edit them.

The Color Range Command

If you are familiar with the Lasso, Magic Wand, or Marquee selection tools, you know that they select only pixels adjacent to the point you click over, or those contained within a marquee in the image. A bright white shirt is easily selected with the Magic Wand, for example, and a road sign can be selected with the Polygon Lasso tool. But what about similar pixels that are located in different places throughout an image? With the Color Range command you can select a specific color anywhere in the entire image.

In photographic images especially, any particular color may also contain many variations of that color. For example, to make a partly cloudy sky more dramatic, you might want to increase the saturation of blue. A blue sky contains numerous shades of blue—darker toward the zenith and lighter at the horizon. To select all the blue areas and compensate for the changes in color, use the Fuzziness slider in the Color Range dialog box to increase the selection criteria.

In the following set of steps, you take the Color Range command out for a spin to see how it can be used to select only the reddish cast in the image.

EDITING BY USING COLOR RANGE

1. Choose Select, Color Range from the menu bar.

2. With Sampled Colors as the Select method, click just above the door handle on the door of the jeep.

3. Drag the Fuzziness slider to 50. Click on the +Eyedropper to add to the current selection, click on the jeep to the left of the door handle, and then click on OK.

4. Press Ctrl($\mathcal{H}$)+U to access the Hue/Saturation dialog box. Drag the Saturation slider to −100 to remove the color from the selected pixels. Click on OK.

Step 4 is an artistic call. Another way to eliminate the red is to add cyan, but you are going to insert a color image, and matching the new image to gray is easier than matching it to a specific shade of cyan.

5. Press Ctrl(⌘)+D to select none; then press Ctrl(⌘)+S to save the changes.

Resolution and Image Size

All *bitmap images* (digital photos, or artwork created in Photoshop and other programs) are composed of *pixels* (picture elements). The dimensions of bitmap images can be measured in either a relative or an absolute way. Designers frequently specify image dimensions in inches, a *relative* measurement because there can be any number of image pixels per inch—the user decides. Image dimensions, whether described in inches, picas, or other physical measurements, do not indicate the *resolution* of the image—the number of pixels per inch (or other unit). The *absolute* measurement of a bitmap image is described in pixels, with no reference to physical dimensions, because image resolution is inversely proportional to physical image dimensions. The higher the image resolution, the smaller the number of inches, picas, points, or other physical unit that describes the image.

For example, a 4"×6" RGB image with a resolution of 300 ppi has a file size of 6.18 MB, whereas another 4"×6" RGB image with a resolution of 72 ppi has a file size of 365 KB. As you can see, the 300 ppi image contains far more image information (more detail) than the 72 ppi image.

Jimsdad.tif has a resolution of 72 ppi, and Jim.tif's resolution is 150 ppi. Before you insert Jim into the other photo, the resolutions must match or an unpredictable sizing problem will occur. After the resolutions are the same, you need to check Jim's dimensions to make sure that he doesn't stand 10 feet tall!

Adjusting Resolution and Image Size

1. With Reunion.psd open, press Ctrl(⌘)+R to show the Rulers. By default, the units will be in pixels. If you need to change the units, press Ctrl(⌘)+K. Then press Ctrl(⌘)+5, and choose pixels in the Units drop-down list.

2. Press **Z** (Zoom tool) and marquee zoom around the father's head. You need to get a facial measurement as a guide for sizing Jim.

3. Place the cursor in the upper-left corner of the window, directly below the Close box. Click and drag the cross hairs to a point on his nose, between his eyes (see fig. 14.2), and then release the mouse button. This changes the zero origin of the rulers.

figure 14.2

Drag the zero origin point of the Rulers into the image to help measure the distance between two points.

4. Again place the cursor in the upper-left corner of the window, click and drag to the bottom of his chin, and do *not* release the mouse button. Note that the measurement on the y-axis is roughly 30 pixels. Release the mouse button and press Ctrl(⌘)+W to close the document.

5. Open Jim.tif from the CHAP14 folder on the Companion CD. Choose Image, Image Size, and uncheck the Resample Image check box. With this option turned off, decreasing image resolution increases the physical dimension of the image (as it would be printed), but maintains the number of pixels in the image of Jim; no image content is recalculated. In the Print Size field, change the resolution to 72, and click on OK.

6. Marquee zoom around Jim's head, drag the ruler cross hairs to the point on his nose between his eyes, and release the mouse button. Measure, as you did in step 4, the distance to the bottom of his chin.

The measurement from Jim is 40 pixels, and from his dad, 30 pixels. If you were to drop Jim into the other photo at this point, he would stand abnormally tall. The percentage difference between 30 and 40 is 75 percent, but we do not want the men to be the same size because Jim is slightly farther away. Based on experimentation, Jim.tif needs to be reduced by 62 percent.

7. Choose Image, Image Size. Check the Resample Image check box. In the Print Size field, change the Width to 62 percent. If percent is not currently the selected unit, click on the drop-down menu and choose percent. Click on OK to apply the resampling.

8. Double-click on the Hand tool to display the full document view. Press Ctrl(⌘)+R to hide the rulers.

9. Press Ctrl(⌘)+S and save the image as Jim.psd (in Photoshop file format) to your hard disk. Keep the document open for the steps to follow.

The two images contain the same resolution, and Jim is scaled to the photo of his father. But before you combine the images, you need to separate Jim from the background. Creating the marquee around Jim requires more than one selection tool.

Creating Selections from Complex Shapes

As you may recall from Chapter 4, "Using Paths, Selections, and Layers," a *selection* is an area designated by a marquee, within which only those pixels contained therein can be edited. Photoshop has eight ways to create a selection in one step, and numerous other methods to create a selection in two or more steps. With this many techniques, you can create a selection of any shape.

You need to select Jim so that none of the background is added to the other image. You will use a variety of methods to select Jim accurately from the background of the image.

SELECTING A COMPLEX SHAPE

1. With Jim.psd open, click and drag the Background layer to the Create a new layer icon at the bottom of the Layers palette to create a duplicate layer in the document. Click on the Indicates layer visibility icon (the eye icon to the left of the Background layer title) to hide it from view.

2. Choose Image, Adjust, Brightness/Contrast. Drag each slider to +30, and click on OK. By increasing the contrast and brightness, you make it easier to select specific areas in this image, and by creating a duplicate layer you preserve the original.

3. Double-click on the Magic Wand to activate it and to display the Magic Wand Options palette. In the Tolerance field, enter 40.

4. Click on the sunny street area to the left of Jim's legs, and then press the Delete (Backspace) key. Repeat this procedure with the remaining street areas (see fig. 14.3). Do not select Jim's shadow; it is needed for the target image. You will remove any small remaining sections in another step.

figure 14.3

Use the Magic Wand as a quick way to select areas surrounded by contrasting pixels.

5. Reduce the Magic Wand tolerance to 10, and click in the sky area just above Jim's head; then press the Delete (Backspace) key. Press Ctrl(⌘)+D to deselect the sky area.

6. Press **M** (Rectangular Marquee tool). If the Elliptical tool becomes active, press **M** again. Place the cursor about one screen inch above Jim's head, click and drag straight down to his hand, and then drag directly left to the edge of the image. Release the mouse button.

7. Press **Z**, and marquee zoom to this new selection area (approximately 120%).

8. Press **W** (Magic Wand tool) and enter 26 in the Tolerance field for the tool on the Options palette. Hold down the Alt(Opt) key and click near the left edges of Jim's hair, face, and uniform (see fig. 14.4). Holding down the Alt(Opt) key removes these areas from the current selection.

figure 14.4
Press and hold Alt(Opt) and click with the Magic Wand to remove areas of hair, skin, and clothes from the rectangular selection.

9. Double-click the Quick Mask mode button toward the bottom of the toolbox to display the Quick Mask Options box. In the Color Indicates field, choose Selected Areas and click on OK. Quick Mask enables you to create, add, or subtract from a selection by using any of Photoshop's paint application tools. Press **B** (Paintbrush tool) and choose the top right brush on the Brushes palette. Press **D** (Default colors), and then press **X** to switch the foreground and background colors.

10. Paint over the Quick Mask areas that cover Jim. You are removing Quick Mask because you set white as the foreground color. At this point, you don't need to take great care with the edges.

11. Press **X** to switch black to the current foreground color, and then paint Quick Mask over background areas in the rectangle that do not contain the mask, such as the area over Jim's shoulder.

12. Press **Q** to return to Standard editing mode. The areas that displayed Quick Mask are now defined by a marquee selection, and should be saved. Click on Save selection as channel icon at the bottom of the Channels palette. Press Ctrl(⌘)+D to deselect the marquee.

13. Use the horizontal scroll bar to move the view to the right side of the image. Repeat steps 6 through 12 with the right side of Jim and the background. When you have finished masking, click on the Save selection as channel icon; the two alpha channels containing

the left and right selections are named channels #4 and #5. Figure 14.5 shows the areas in which you need to add or remove Quick Mask.

14. Press Ctrl(⌘)+S to save the changes.

figure 14.5
You can see Quick Mask areas that need to be edited on the right side of the image.

You have used three tools to create a complex selection. Now you will use the selection to separate Jim from the background.

MANIPULATING SELECTION INFORMATION

1. Press Ctrl(⌘) and click on the #5 Channel to load the selection you created for the right side of the image, press the Delete key, and then drag this channel to the Delete current channel icon (the trash icon) at the bottom right of the Channels palette. Repeat this procedure with the #4 Channel. Press Ctrl(⌘)+D to deselect the #4 selection.

2. Double-click on the Hand tool to get a full window view, click on the Layers tab, and then press Ctrl(⌘) and click on the Background copy layer. You now have a near-perfect selection of Jim and his shadow.

3. Press **Q** to turn the marquee selection to Quick Mask mode; then paint to remove from the image any mask that is not over Jim and his shadow. (Press **X,** if necessary, to switch to add or remove Quick Mask.)

4. Press **Q** again to return to Standard editing mode. If you see a selection marquee anywhere in the image except around Jim, return to Quick Mask mode and remove the mask in those areas.

5. Click on the Delete current layer icon at the bottom of the Layers palette, and choose Yes in the confirmation box that appears.

6. Press **Q**, and then press Ctrl(⌘)+spacebar; marquee zoom Jim's outstretched arm.

7. By using the techniques you learned for adding and subtracting Quick Mask, touch up the edges throughout Jim and his shadow. The smaller brushes on the second row of the Brushes palette will serve you best. Use the scroll bars or Hand tool to move the image around in the window.

8. Press **Q** to return to Standard editing mode, press Ctrl(⌘)+J to copy this selection to a new layer, and then press Ctrl(⌘)+S, saving this document to your hard disk as Jim.psd. Leave the image open in Photoshop.

In your adventures with Photoshop, do not limit yourself to creating any selection with just one tool. Early in our Photoshop career, a friend showed us his method for selecting an area such as a face—using the Magic Wand, and holding down the Shift key to add to the selection, he clicked inside the face about 100 times to complete the selection! A much quicker method, but by no means the only one, is to use the Magic Wand for large areas of similar tone, add to the selection with the Lasso tool, and clean the edges with Quick Mask.

NOTE

On the toolbox alone, you have eight tools for creating a selection: Rectangular Marquee, Elliptical Marquee, Single Row, Single Column, Lasso, Polygon Lasso, Magic Wand, and Quick Mask. Spend time working with these tools. Learn how they function, separately and in combination with one another. Save a selection in the Channels palette, apply one of Photoshop's many filters on it, and then load it into the image for creative effects. When you master the concepts of selections and channels, you harness one of Photoshop's most powerful features.

Layers and Compositing

In addition to Channels, one of Photoshop's most powerful features is Layers. Layers, as described in Chapter 4, are analogous to the animator's cells. You can keep areas on one layer separate from those on another, and reposition elements such as backgrounds, text, and foreground elements (such as Jim), as you would scraps of paper on a physical drafting table. All your composition work is live, and can be changed indefinitely until you merge layer elements together.

The two images you have been working on are ready to be combined. You will take full advantage of the Layers feature, without which the following steps would be tedious and time-consuming.

COMPOSITING AND USING LAYER MASK

1. With the Jim.psd image open, press Ctrl(⌘)+O (another method to access the Open dialog box in Windows is to double-click in the workspace), and open Reunion.psd.

2. Click on the Jim.psd title bar to make it the active document; then click and drag Layer 1 (from the Layers palette) onto the Reunion.psd image.

3. Click again on the Jim.psd title bar, and press Ctrl(⌘)+W to close it.

4. Press Z (Zoom tool), and click once over Jim's dad. Press V (Move tool), and click and drag Layer 1, Jim, to the left side of his father (see fig. 14.6).

figure 14.6
Position Jim's head between the clock and the door frame, and his foot just outside the jeep's shadow.

5. Choose Layer, Add Layer Mask, Reveal All.

   The Layer Mask, on which you will use the Paintbrush, is now active. The object is to hide areas of Jim in such a way as to create the illusion that he is standing behind his father. In other words, you will add Mask to any area of Jim that obstructs the view of his father.

6. Press **B** (Paintbrush tool); then press **D** (Default colors), and paint mask over all areas of Layer 1 that cover Jim's father and the jeep.

   You will need to change brush sizes and zoom percentages when you detail the edges. If you apply mask into areas that do not require it, press X to switch from add Layer Mask to remove Layer Mask. Because Jim's outstretched hand will have to be repositioned in a future step, there is no need to be precise with the mask on his hand. Figure 14.7 shows the image after step 6 has been completed.

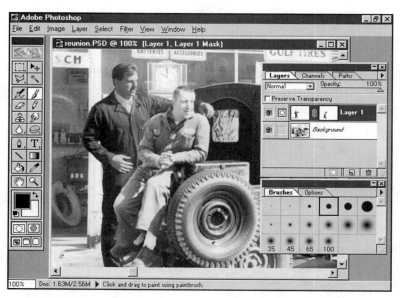

figure 14.7
Apply Layer Mask as shown to create the illusion that Jim is positioned behind his father.

TIP

If at some point of applying Layer Mask you need to see the layer without the entire mask, press Shift and click on the Layer Mask thumbnail. A red X will appear, indicating that the mask is turned off.

7. From the menu bar, choose Layer, Remove Layer Mask, and then click on Apply in the dialog box.

8. Press Ctrl(⌘)+S to save the changes.

You have almost finished integrating Jim into the Reunion.psd; only one area—Jim's outstretched hand—still requires additional editing.

NOTE

Starting with version 3, Photoshop included the power of layers, a feature that has proven invaluable to most Photoshop users and has revolutionized the way many of us work. In version 4, instead of providing a single new feature that, like layers, appeals to the masses, Adobe Systems (apparently taking to heart the many suggestions of Photoshop users) has programmed many smaller changes to accommodate the way many users work. For example, whenever you created a new layer in version 3.x, a dialog box requested a name for that layer. This redundancy (the thumbnail shows you the contents of that layer) no longer occurs in Photoshop 4. Also, because Photoshop is the tool of choice for most prepress work, the Actions palette was developed to enable the user to create scripts to run in Photoshop. With scripts, Photoshop can perform the repetitive steps on one image or a batch of images, often more quickly than the operator.

If you are familiar with Photoshop 3.x, look for changes in menu items, palette drop-down menus, right mouse clicks, and Ctrl(⌘), Shift, and Alt(Opt) features to add power and speed to your imaging techniques.

The Layer menu item is new to version 4; with it come some speed-enhancing features—one of which you use in the next set of steps.

EDITING JIM'S HAND

1. With the Reunion.psd image open, and Layer 1 active for editing, press **M** (Rectangular Marquee tool).

2. Click and drag a selection around Jim's outstretched hand.

3. Right-click (Macintosh: hold Ctrl and click), and then choose Layer via cut from the context menu. Notice that Jim's hand is cut to a new layer, and the marquee area is deselected.

4. Press **Z** (Zoom tool), and click and drag an area that encompasses Jim's upper body and his right hand.

When you edit a small area, especially when that area is a part of a person, it is best to keep the surrounding area in view. In this way, you can make accurate judgment calls by comparing your edits with the rest of the immediate area.

5. Press **V** (Move tool), hold down the Shift key, and press the down arrow once. This key combination moves the layer's contents in 10-pixel increments.

6. Click on Layer 1 in the Layers palette. Press **M** (Marquee tool) and select the white area located where Jim's hand was. Press the Delete key; then press Ctrl(⌘)+D to deselect the area.

7. Click on Layer 2 in the Layers palette, and drag the Layer Opacity slider to 60% so that you can see the position of the hand relative to the Background layer(see fig. 14.8).

8. Press **V** (Move tool). Using the arrow keys, nudge Jim's hand down to the position shown in figure 14.8.

9. Choose Layer, Layer Mask, Reveal All from the menu. Press **B** (Paintbrush tool) and apply Layer Mask to any areas of Jim's sleeve that cover his father's face.

figure 14.8
Reducing the layer's opacity enables you to edit more precisely.

10. Choose Layer, Remove Layer Mask, and click on Apply.

11. Drag the Opacity slider on the Layers palette to 100%. Press Ctrl(⌘)+S to save the changes. Leave the document open in Photoshop.

Jim's hand is now positioned and edited to look as though it is on his dad's shoulder. To complete this illusion, one element needs to be added—a shadow.

Creating a Shadow

During the past few years, adding a shadow to anything and everything has become very popular. Graphics and text now seem to float above the page. One small concern prevails when you create this effect—whether to put the shadow directly below the source casting the shadow, or slightly to the right or left? You determine the angle of the apparent light source when you place a shadow in an image.

With photographic images, shadows are not that simple to simulate. You must work with the given angle of the light source. Sometimes you have to distort a created shadow to a precise shape by using existing shadows as your visual guide.

The shadow for Jim's hand must be distorted so that the shadow at the finger tips is not as long as the one at the cuff of his sleeve. After creating a shadow (using his hand as a template), you will use a new feature called Free Transform to make the necessary adjustments, and then add some final touches.

CREATING AND DISTORTING A SHADOW

1. In the Reunion.psd image, press Ctrl(⌘) and click on Layer 2 in the Layers palette. This action creates a selection around all nontransparent pixels on the layer.

2. Click on the Create new layer icon at the bottom of the Layers palette; then press Ctrl(⌘)+Shift+[to move the layer down in the order of layers in the document.

3. Press Shift+Backspace to activate the Fill dialog box. Choose Black from the Use drop-down list, and Normal from the Mode list. Click on OK to apply the fill.

4. Press Ctrl(⌘)+D to deselect the current selection marquee. Press **V** (Move tool), and then press the down arrow two times.

5. Press Ctrl+T to activate the Free Transform box.

6. Hold down the Ctrl(⌘) key to constrain the Free Transform to Distort mode, and drag the upper-left anchor straight down to half the height of the box (see fig. 14.9). Either press Enter (Return) or double-click inside the box to apply the effect.

For most photographic purposes, a black or gray shadow is sufficient, but all the shadows on Jim's dad are grainy and have a green tint. To keep the look consistent, you will copy from the existing shadow on the left side of the chest area.

figure 14.9
Press Shift and drag the top left anchor of the Free Transform box to distort the hand's shadow

7. Double-click on the Rubber Stamp tool, and click to check the Sample Merged box on the Options palette. Also click to check the Preserve Transparency box on the Layers palette.

8. Choose the fourth brush on the top row on the Brushes palette. Press Alt(Opt) and click on the Background layer uniform in the shadow area of the middle of the chest, just left of center.

9. Click and drag over the shadow of the hand on Layer 3.

10. You need to add "grit" to the new shadow to simulate the deteriorated shadow areas. Choose Noise, Add Noise from the menu bar. Enter 7 for the Amount, choose Uniform for Distribution, and leave Monochromatic unchecked (see fig. 14.10). Click on OK.

11. Choose the Blur tool, press 3 for 30% pressure, and choose the first brush on the second row of the Brushes palette. Use the keypad to quickly define Option palette strengths for tools in 10-percent increments.

12. Uncheck Preserve Transparency on the Layers palette, and apply the blur only to the bottom edges of the shadow. One careful stroke should be enough.

figure 14.10
Add noise to simulate the grainy effect of the Background layer.

13. Press Ctrl(⌘)+Shift+[to move to the layer above the Background layer; then press Ctrl(⌘)+E (Layer, Merge Down) to merge the shadow with the Background layer.

14. Click on Layer 2, and press Ctrl(⌘)+E to merge Jim's hand layer with the layer that Jim is on.

15. Press Ctrl(⌘)+S to save the changes.

While you are working with shadows, notice that Jim's shadow on the ground does not extend to the edge of the image as it should. In the following set of steps, you add length to Jim's shadow.

ADDING TO AN EXISTING SHADOW

1. Type **230** in the Zoom percentage box, and press Enter(Return). Use the Hand tool or scroll bars to move the view to the far bottom left of the image.

2. Press **L** once (or twice) to choose the Polygon Lasso tool.

3. Click a point on the top edge of the shadow, about half the length of the shadow. Click a second point directly to the left at the edge of the window, letting the marquee follow the line of the shadow until you return to the first point; click to close the path and create a marquee selection (see fig. 14.11).

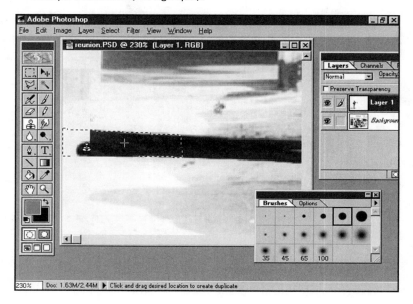

figure 14.11

After you use the Polygon Lasso tool to create a selection, the Rubber Stamp will clone only within the marquee.

4. Press **S** (Rubber Stamp tool) and choose the fifth brush on the top row of the Brushes palette.

5. Press Alt(Opt) and click at the right side in the rectangle; then drag from the center bottom to the left edge of the rectangle, following the lower edge (see fig. 14.11).

6. Repeat the click-and-drag procedure for the upper half of the selection.

7. Press Ctrl(⌘)+D to deselect the marquee, double-click on the Hand tool to get a full image view, and take a moment to appreciate your handiwork.

8. Press Ctrl(⌘)+S to save your work.

At this point, the composite image you have created by using various Photoshop features is almost finished. At first glance, Reunion.psd is an impressive image, but the credibility of this edited image will be evaluated by the detail work you add to it. Layer 1 needs to be aged, or deteriorated, to show the same characteristics as the Background layer.

Applying the Effects of Age to a New Photo

Analyzing the characteristics of a photo that has deteriorated over time is the first step in re-creating the effect. Notice that there is a striking difference between the two uniforms in Reunion.psd. The new photo on Layer 1 retains detail in the areas exposed by the direct sun, the color is rich, and transitions from shade to shade occur very smoothly. The uniform on the Background layer has very little detail in the sunlit areas, and the saturation of the color is low.

Look at the men's heads and hands on each layer. The sunlit areas on the Background layer are almost completely devoid of color and detail, and where there is color, it has very little saturation. Also, there are white spots that indicate physical damage to the photo. You must apply each of these characteristics to Jim, to the *same degree* displayed in the photo of his father.

In the following set of steps, you create one selection, the hands and head, and adjust its image quality to resemble that of the Background layer. Then you invert the selection and make numerous changes to the uniform.

REDUCING THE INTEGRITY OF AN IMAGE

1. Press **Z** and marquee zoom to Jim's upper body.
2. Double-click on the Magic Wand, enter **52** in the Tolerance field on the Options palette, and click on the shadow area of the left hand. Hold down the Shift key and click in the sunlit area of the same hand to add to the selection. To select the entire hand, you can press Shift and click in the unselected areas or apply Quick Mask (as you did earlier in this chapter).

3. Press **L** (Lasso tool), hold down the Shift key, and drag marquee selections around Jim's head and his other hand (see fig. 14.12).

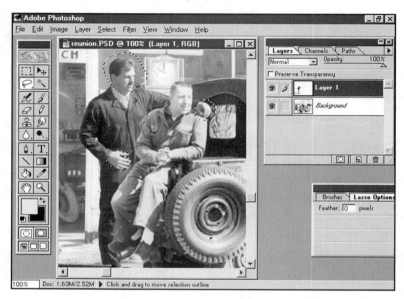

figure 14.12
Create a selection around the hands and head.

4. Choose Select, Feather, enter **1** for the Feather Radius, and click on OK. (Without feathering, a sharp edge would become visible as you apply the changes in the following steps.)

5. Press Ctrl(⌘)+U for the Hue/Saturation dialog box, and slide the Saturation to –80. Click on OK.

6. Press Ctrl(⌘)+M to display the Curves dialog box. Drag the middle tone point of the curve up and to the left (see fig. 14.13). Click on OK.

7. Choose Filter, Noise, Add Noise from the menu, enter **7** in the Amount field, and click on OK. (Distribution should be Uniform, and the Monochromatic box should be unchecked.)

8. Choose Image, Adjust, Brightness/Contrast. Enter **+8** in both fields, click on OK, and then choose Filter, Blur, Blur.

9. Press **Z**; press Alt(Opt) and click once in the center of the image to zoom out and see more of the uniform. Press Shift+Ctrl(⌘)+I to invert the selection. Now you will alter Jim's uniform and shadow.

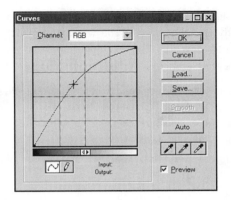

figure 14.13

Adjust the curve to increase the brightness values of the midtones.

10. Choose Image, Adjust, Brightness/Contrast. Slide the Brightness to +21, the Contrast to +41, and click on OK.

11. Press Ctrl(⌘)+U for the Hue/Saturation dialog box, and enter **–38** for the Hue and **–80** for the Saturation. Click on OK.

12. Press Ctrl(⌘)+M for Curves, and drag the white point directly left three-quarters of the grid space. Drag the middle tone point up 45° to the left, to the center of the first grid space it enters, and click on OK (see fig. 14.14).

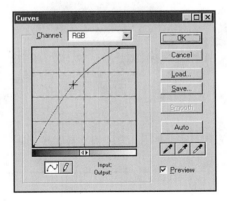

figure 14.14

Adjust the curve for the uniform to increase the brightness values of the highlights and midtones.

Now that the highlights and midtones (with some modification to the shadows) are adjusted to match those in the Background layer, you need to return to the Curves dialog box and make adjustments to the shadow area. These settings have been saved as a file on the Companion CD to demonstrate another feature of the Curves dialog box.

13. Press Ctrl(⌘)+ M, and click on Load. From the CHAP14 folder on the Companion CD, load Jimscurv.acv. Now, if you click on the Channels drop-down menu, you can inspect the changes to the Green and Blue channels that cause the shadows to look similar to those on the Background layer. Click on OK.

14. Choose Filter, Noise, Add Noise, enter +7, and click on OK.

15. Choose Filter, Blur, Blur.

16. Press Ctrl(⌘)+D to deselect, double-click on the Hand tool to zoom to a full image view (see fig. 14.15), and press Ctrl(⌘)+S to save.

figure 14.15

An almost completed Reunion.psd. Can you find the last significant area that needs editing?

Having undergone some serious changes in the preceding steps, the photo of Jim more closely resembles the old photo of his father. Reunion.psd does seem to be completed, but a close inspection is always a good idea before you call any image a masterpiece.

NOTE

The very first composite image one of the authors created in Photoshop was of his baby daughter crawling over some buildings in a city scene. The proud parent (of both the baby and the edited image) proceeded to show the piece to everyone he knew. Unfortunately, he did not give the image a final, close once-over. Between the baby's arm and her body, you could see a mirror reflecting the author's face (wearing one of those goofy expressions you make only to a baby!)

The most obvious edit needed in the Reunion.psd image is of Jim's shadow. Jim's shadow is uniformly dark, whereas the shadow from the jeep progresses from dark to very light. To match the jeep's shadow, you apply Layer Mask with the Gradient tool.

Also, a by-product of all the editing of Jim's image is a thin white edge along his silhouette. This halo effect tells the viewer, "This image is a fake!" You need to remove the white pixels; fortunately, removing them is easy to do with the Defringe command.

One last detail you need to address is the dust and scratches on the photo of Jim's dad. These white spots appear intermittently throughout the image, and you need to simulate them on Jim's image area.

In the following steps, you make Jim's shadow fade in the same way the jeep's shadow fades, you remove the white edge surrounding Jim, and you add a few white specks.

THE FINAL TOUCHES

1. With Reunion.psd open and in full image view, press **Z** and click two times over Jim's shadow to zoom in about 70%.

2. Click on Layer 1 to make it the active layer, press **D** (Default colors), and double-click on the Gradient tool to choose it and display the Options palette.

3. The following default settings are used: Gradient is Foreground to Background, Type is Linear. Press **9** to reduce the Opacity to 90%.

4. Hold Shift to constrain the tool to 45° increments, click at the far left edge of the image, and drag to an area directly below the right side of the door frame (see fig. 14.16).

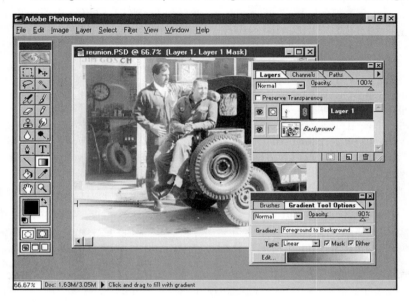

figure 14.16
Use the Gradient tool to make Jim's shadow fade in the same way the jeep's shadow fades.

5. Choose Layer, Remove Layer Mask, and click on Apply.

6. Press **Z** and marquee zoom to Jim's upper body. At this view (approximately 200%), the white edge pixels are evident.

7. Choose Layer, Matting, Defringe, and enter 1 for the Width (see fig. 14.17). Click on OK. This step replaces the color of the fringe pixels (white) with the colors of adjacent pixels.

8. Press **B** (Paintbrush tool), click on the Brushes tab, and choose the first brush on the top row.

9. Press **X** to make white the current foreground color, and then add a few spots and lines to Jim's uniform. Try to make these strokes geometrically consistent with the actual flaws in the 30-year-old photo.

10. Choose Layer, Flatten Image to merge Layer 1 with the Background layer. Press Ctrl(⌘)+S to save your work. Your image should look like figure 14.18.

Congratulations on completing an image that transcends "eye candy" and touches the heart!

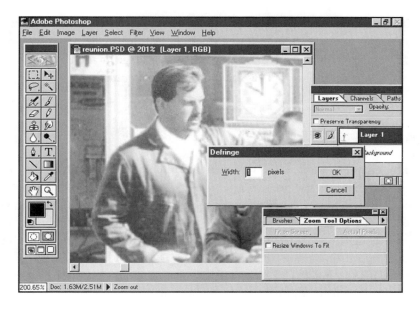

figure 14.17
Use the Defringe command when you want to replace the pixel color at the edges of an area.

figure 14.18
The finished piece, authentic aging and all!

In this section, you aged a photo rich in color and detail so that it looks at least 30 years old. As you learn more about what Photoshop can do to improve your images, don't forget that features can be used to *reduce* image fidelity, to keep a consistency between old and new images that you want to combine.

Summary

This chapter demonstrates that ordinary photos can be combined to create a very special image. In the process, attention to detail is the key to making a convincing composited image. When you take a photo that you will combine with an existing one, be sure that the new photograph matches the properties of the old one in areas such as lighting, camera angle, type of lens, clothing, and anything else you find important. The more attributes that work together in each photo, the more plausible the image you create. If you ever doubt the emotional impact you can create with image editing and Photoshop, remember this "Jim and Dad" image. Jim was so touched by the sentiment in the image that he gave it to his mother on Mother's Day.

The next chapter takes us deeper into the artistic side of Photoshop—from developing a concept, preplanning, photographing the scenes, and executing the concept of a surrealistic scene.

CHAPTER

THE ARTISTIC SIDE OF PHOTOSHOP 4

In Photoshop, you have at your command not only the most powerful image editing application, but also perhaps the greatest fine art tool for creative expression. Your imagination is your only limitation. Like all art tools, when you grasp the functions of Photoshop, you are free to create whatever you want. After Michelangelo understood how to use his paintbrush, chisel, and other tools, his vision of the finished piece was foremost in his thinking, not the tools themselves. It's well within your reach to become so familiar with Photoshop that it becomes as unnoticeable as the pen in your hand.

This chapter explores the methods and artistic decisions that go into creating a surrealistic image called Water Street. Most of Water Street is a city scene of buildings, cars, and, of course, a street. The street, though, is submerged under about five feet of water. This image challenges our mental paradigms of what something should be. Sometimes the audience doesn't immediately see the water because of their mind-set. When you look at this scene, mostly composed of very familiar objects, the mind fills in the entire image with what it *should* look like, not what it *does* look like. Interestingly, teenagers who saw this image recognized the water and rocks immediately, whereas older folk (40+) did not—even when someone put his finger right on the water area to point it out! It seems the older we get, the more prone we are to rely on our mental paradigms than on what we *actually* see.

In your Photoshop adventures, it is a good idea to develop your own unique style of images, one that shouts, "This was created by [insert your name here]." Let your creativity guide you. Not only will your work be your own, but you will have an artistic and marketing edge over all the Toms, Dicks, and Harrys. To help cultivate your style, look at work by accomplished artists and examine the strengths of their images.

One approach to creating images is to search through your stock photographs for elements that would work together in a surrealistic fashion. The more photographs you acquire, the more material there is to work with.

Stock Photography: Too Much Is Never Enough

Jerry Uelsmann is a master at combining elements of different negatives in the darkroom to create surrealistic images. For decades, he has been creating photographs that catch the eye and generate astonishment—hands breaking through a paper-like sky, or a dolphin swimming in the palm of a hand. Mr. Uelsmann shoots between three and forty rolls of film every week and has accumulated possibly one-half million negatives to date! This enormous collection gives him plenty of material to work with to create his stunning images. It is interesting to note that he realizes 99 percent of the final image in the darkroom, not in the camera.

To acquire your own collection of stock photography, particularly if your background is in photography, you must start looking at potential subject matter in a different way. You will want to photograph or scan scene elements, rather than entire scenes. Therefore, the background you see in a viewfinder is not a concern; similarly, the car entering the picture from the right is no big deal because you will be using a different portion of the photo. This does not mean that you should photograph in a haphazard manner. Instead, create some guidelines for consistency in your shooting, particularly methods that reflect your style.

Guidelines for Photographing Elements

To combine objects from different photos and make them relate to each other in a logical manner, you need to strive for consistency in the following areas:

◆ **Film speed and brand.** If you use Kodak 200 ISO, for example, stay with it. Grain size varies from speed to speed, and color varies from brand to brand. If you photograph a person with Kodak 400 speed film, and then subsequently digitize the photo and insert or paste it into a scene that was shot with Fuji 100 speed film, discrepancies between the two films will be evident. The large-grain pattern on the person will contrast dramatically with the small, smooth grain structure of the 100 speed film. Fuji films tend to amplify the saturation of colors, making them bold and rich, whereas Kodak films are more realistic in color representation.

◆ **Focal length of the lens.** Each focal length of a lens has its own characteristics. A telephoto lens gives the illusion of compression, with the background proportionately larger than foreground objects. A wide-angle lens distorts the image, particularly at the edges of the frame. A box located in the lower left of the viewfinder, for example, distorts very differently than if it were located in the upper right. If you plan to use a wide-angle lens exclusively, you may want to photograph a particular element in several locations within the viewfinder. A normal lens (approximately 50mm) exhibits no visible distortion.

◆ **Lighting.** The importance of consistent lighting is mentioned in Chapters 7, "Combining Photographs," and 14, "Special Effects with Ordinary Photographs." You may, however, want to adopt some personal guidelines with respect to building a photo stock—shoot mostly on sunny days (or cloudy days), for example, shoot mainly when the sun is at its zenith, and so on.

◆ **Exposure.** Most cameras determine the exposure by averaging all the light that enters the lens. This technique works for a low-contrast scene, but not for a high-contrast scene. For example, shooting the full moon at night will render it pure white with no detail. Set the exposure on your camera for the amount of light reflecting off the subject you want, not the entire scene.

For example, we presently shoot most of our stock when the full sun is low in the sky and either directly behind or in front of the camera, using Kodak 100 and a 28mm lens. Often, the axis of the lens will be either parallel to the ground or in 30° increments. With subject matter taken within these guidelines, it's easy to combine several elements out of hundreds of photos so that they logically relate to each other, yet in a surrealistic manner.

Finding Clues to Elements that Work Together

After you establish photographic guidelines and build your collection of photos, you need to think like Sherlock Holmes when you look over your collection. Your intuition and creativity are your best guides for identifying which pieces will look best when assembled in a composition. Because each person has his or her own unique vision, artistic ability, and approach, we will limit our discussion to how Water Street was "discovered."

Of the 1,000 or so thumbnail images from 10 Photo CDs spread out on a table, approximately 50 photos of city streets were of possible interest for this chapter's composition. Because of our familiarity with buildings, asphalt, cars, and sidewalks, using one of these areas to depart from reality provides a visually interesting image. One photo in particular was chosen for its simplicity of composition and straight-forward viewpoint (see fig. 15.1). The lines of cars and building tops form an X and attract the viewer's attention toward the center of the picture. Something subtle outside the center was needed, but what?

figure 15.1

This street photo is very simple in composition and has potential for manipulation.

When the street scene was photographed, the axis of the lens was perpendicular to the ground, a 28mm lens was used, and there was full sun. The scene has four distinct triangular areas you can work with (see fig. 15.2). The next step was to find an element that worked within any of the zones in the image. The element had to be symmetrically located in the same area of the frame as the area intended for manipulation. The street was chosen as a good starting point, because any element located toward the top or bottom of a horizontal picture would be distorted (by the wide-angle lens) in the same way as the street.

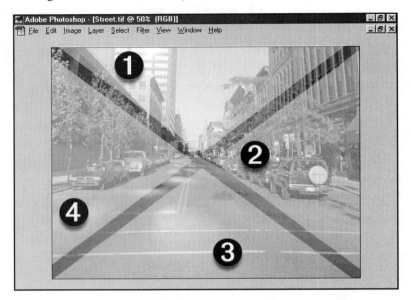

figure 15.2
The composition of the city street photo can be defined by an X.

After a time-consuming search for a workable piece to play into the street area, it became clear that the obvious is sometimes the hardest thing to find—the name of the street is Water Street, and there were at least 100 images of water from which to choose! The photo shown in figure 15.3 was chosen because of the gentle waves and soft lighting—characteristics that would create a "dynamic tension" against the physically hard subject matter and harsh lighting in the Street image.

figure 15.3
The gentle waves and soft lighting will play nicely against the harsh-looking city street.

Because the photo of the street is the background for the finished composite, this target image should be fine-tuned before adding the water to it.

Adding to the Mood of an Image

The subject of an image greatly influences the mood of the image. Glamour photography uses a diffusion filter to accent the beauty of the woman. Documentary photography, in an attempt to accurately record reality, uses no filters or special effects at all. Photoshop has many features that enable you to adjust an image to visually support the tone of your image.

In this set of steps you bring the photo of the city street into Photoshop and apply some subtle adjustments to accentuate the physical hardness of the subject matter.

FINE-TUNING THE BACKGROUND IMAGE

CD-ROM

1. Open Street.tif from the CHAP15 folder on the Companion CD. (Windows users: to access the Open dialog box, you can double-click in the workspace.)

2. Press Ctrl(⌘)++ to zoom to 50%. Press F to access Full-Screen mode with Menu Bar, and then press the Tab key. When you perform image-wide adjustments, a full, unobstructed view helps you see the corrections you are making.

3. Press Ctrl(⌘)+L (Image, Adjust, Levels) and drag the Midpoint slider (the middle slider) so that .82 shows in the Input Levels midpoint field (see fig. 15.4). Click on OK. Lessening the midpoint value increases the contrast in the middle tones of the image.

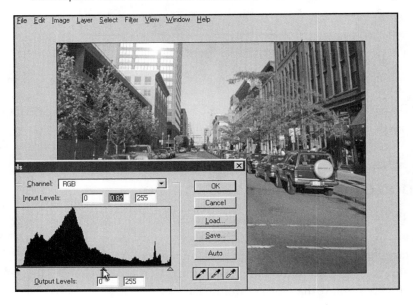

figure 15.4
Adjust the midpoint to increase contrast in the midtones without altering the shadows and highlights.

4. From the menu bar, choose Filter, Sharpen, Unsharp Mask. Drag the Amount slider to 94%, drag the Radius slider to 1.9 pixels (Threshold should be 0 levels), and click on OK. Most scanning softens the image, and the Unsharp Mask restores the sharpness quite nicely.

5. Press Ctrl(⌘)+U (Hue, Saturation), drag the Saturation slider to +28, and click on OK. Increasing the saturation increases the purity of the colors, thus lowering the gray components within the image.

After you increase the saturation, the yellowish cast from the setting sun is amplified too much and must be corrected. Yellow is the color opposite of blue (just check out the traditional color wheel). By increasing the strength of the blue color channel in the image, you move the overall color cast of the picture from yellow to a more pleasing neutral color.

6. Press Ctrl(⌘)+M (Curves), and then Ctrl(⌘)+3, to choose Blue from the Channel drop-down menu. Place the cursor slightly above and to the left of the middle of the curve line (the midtones). Slowly move the cursor until the Input reads about 118 and the Output reads about 138 (see fig. 15.5). Click the mouse button to adjust the curve, and click on OK.

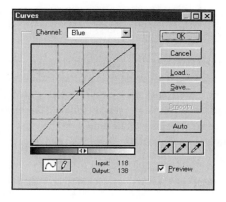

figure 15.5
Remove the yellow cast by adjusting the Blue channel.

7. Press **F** twice, and then press Ctrl(⌘)+−. Press the Tab key to return to Standard Screen mode and to restore the visibility of the tools and palettes.

8. Choose File, Save As from the menu, and save this image to your hard disk as Water Street.psd. (Windows 3.x users: pick an eight-character name.) Leave the image open for the next set of steps.

By adjusting the levels and saturation, among the other corrections, you add to the "hardness" of the subject matter. The street photo is now ready for the water image.

Image Compositing with Layers

Because the details and method of combining two photographs are well documented in Chapter 7, this chapter does not elaborate on the process. Suffice it to say, no other imaging program has a better feature for compositing than the Layers feature in Photoshop.

TIP

Before proceeding with the composite, you might want to customize an option on the Layers palette. The thumbnails of the layers can be made larger than the default size, or turned off completely. To access this option, click on the Layers palette control menu icon and choose Palette Options (see fig. 15.6). The larger the thumbnail, the easier it is to see the layer contents, but you sacrifice screen space and memory for the view. On the other hand, if your system resources are low, you can turn off the thumbnail and free up some memory. Be sure to name all your layers first!

Hint: Hold down the Ctrl(⌘)+Alt(Opt) keys, and access the Palette Options; then, after a couple of seconds, release the two keys for an undocumented feature in Photoshop.

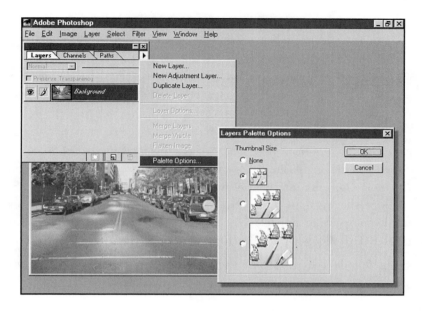

figure 15.6
The Layers Palette Options provide you with the capability to customize the view of the
thumbnails.

Okay, back to the composition. You're going to combine the city street and the
water.

MERGING TWO IMAGES

CD-ROM

1. Double-click on Water Street.psd's Background layer in the Layers palette, name this
   layer City, and then click on OK. The water layer must be placed under this layer, which
   is not possible while it is named Background.

2. Open Water.tif from the CHAP15 folder on the Companion CD, and drag the image window
   by the title bar off to one side, so that most of the Water Street image can be seen.

3. From the Layers palette, drag Water.tif's Background layer into the Water Street image window. Click on the Water.tif title bar to make it the active image, and press Ctrl(⌘)+W to close the document.

4. Click and drag Layer 1 down below the City layer, and release the mouse button.

5. Press Ctrl(⌘)+S to save the changes you made to Water Street.psd to your hard disk. Leave the image open for the next set of steps.

You may have noticed that Water.tif is dimensionally larger than Water Street. When you dragged Water.tif's layer into the other document, Photoshop retained the image information that lies outside the document window. In Photoshop 4, unlike earlier versions of Photoshop, the "outside" image areas are never clipped until you decide to crop a layered image. This new Photoshop capability gives you greater flexibility when you position the water layer after masking the street area.

In the following steps, a Layer Mask is created to allow the water to be seen in the street area, and then the water layer is repositioned.

MASKING AND MOVING LAYERS

1. With Water Street open, press Ctrl(⌘)++ twice and F once. This zooms the image to 50% magnification and changes the view to Full Screen Mode with Menu Bar.

2. Click on the City layer to make it active; then click on the Add Layer Mask icon at the bottom of the palette.

3. Press D (Default colors), press B (Paintbrush), Shift+], and then press the right square bracket [. Pressing Shift+] selects the largest brush on the Brushes palette, even when the palette is not in view. Pressing [selects the next smaller brush. By default, the 65-pixel brush is now the current brush.

   If, after you press D, black is not the foreground color, press X to switch the foreground and background colors.

4. Press o for 100% Paintbrush opacity, and paint just inside the street area (see fig. 15.7). If you accidentally paint into the cars or curbs, press X to switch the foreground and background colors, and then paint to remove the Layer Mask.

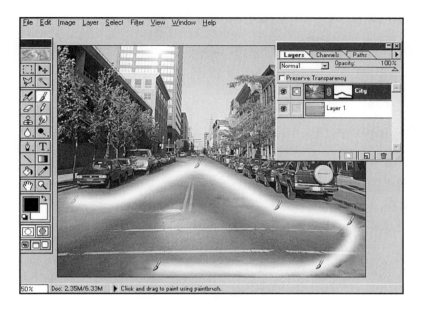

figure 15.7
Outline the street area with Layer Mask.

5. Press Alt(Opt) and click on the Layer Mask thumbnail. The image window now shows the entire Layer Mask.

6. Press **L** (once or twice) to activate the Polygon Lasso tool, and click a selection marquee that follows the border of Layer Mask (see fig. 15.8).

7. Press Alt(Opt)+Delete to fill the selection with the black foreground color; then press Ctrl(⌘)+D to deselect the active marquee in the image.

8. Press Alt(Opt) and click on the Layer Mask thumbnail again to return to the document view.

9. Click on Layer 1 in the Layers palette, press **V** (Move tool), and drag the document Layer 1 to the location shown in figure 15.9.

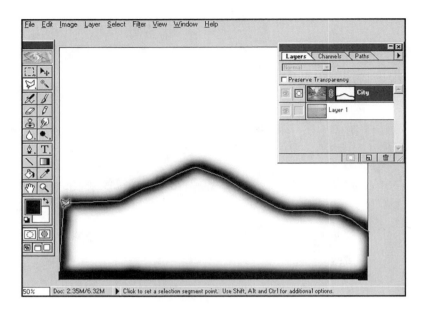

figure 15.8
With the Polygon Lasso tool, create a selection inside the line of the Layer Mask border.

figure 15.9
Move the layer containing the water to this location.

10. Press Ctrl(⌘)+S to save the changes.

In terms of surrealism, a beneficial aspect of the water is that the color is very close to that of asphalt, which is why it is not readily recognizable. To finish this stage of the composite, you need to do one last edit to remove the branch and rock—we want to see only water. In the next set of steps, you remove the branch and rock.

STAMPING OUT DEBRIS

1. Press **S** (Rubber Stamp), and then F5 (if the Brushes palette is *not* on-screen). Choose the 45-pixel brush.

2. Clone water over the branch in the lower-right corner of the image and the stone in the bottom center of the water. Follow the color and direction of the different shades of the water (see fig. 15.10). Fortunately, the subject matter does not have a great deal of detail and is not well-defined, and precision is not a big concern.

figure 15.10
Use the Rubber Stamp to remove the rock and branch.

3. Click on the Standard Screen Mode button at the bottom left of the toolbox, and then press Ctrl(⌘)+– twice. This organizes the screen space for the next set of steps.

4. Press Ctrl(⌘)+S. Don't close the image just yet. You need it open for the next enhancement you add to the scene.

Although Water Street is not finished, at this point it could stand on its own. Initially, feeling that the image was complete, we did stop here. Yet, after many days spent considering the design, we felt it needed more. Having one element (the water in the street) show a departure from reality is okay—but *two* elements would make the image even more intriguing. The water area is the best place for additional manipulation because the rest of the image needs to retain the truth of reality. Again, back to the stock of photos for ideas.

How about the photo of a colorful inner tube? Hummm, that seems a little too goofy. A boat? Nope, the street is too small for the ocean liner. Instead of something on top of the water, how about something under the water? This creates a surrealist image that remains subtle in its artistic statement, and is in keeping with the style used so far. There is a photo of the rocky bottom of a lake that looks promising!

The following set of steps closely resemble the method you used to flood the city street with water.

MERGING, MASKING, AND MOVING LAYERS

CD-ROM

1. Open Bottom.tif from the CHAP15 folder on the Companion CD, and drag it so that you can see most of the Water Street image.

2. Click and drag the Background layer from the Layers palette into the Water Street document window. The Bottom image becomes Layer 2 in the Water Street image, and should be between Layer 1 and the City layer. If it is not, click and drag the Layer 2 title on the Layers palette to move it to create the desired layer order.

3. Make the Bottom.tif image active, and close it with Ctrl(⌘)+W. (Windows users: Ctrl+Tab will toggle between all open documents.)

4. Press Ctrl(⌘)++ twice to zoom in (to about 50%), and then resize the document window to view the entire image.

5. Press **V** (Move tool) and drag Layer 2 to the bottom of the image (see fig. 15.11).

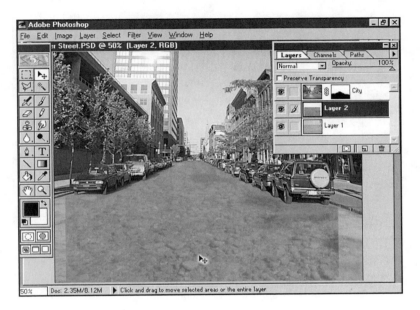

figure 15.11
Move Layer 2 to the bottom of the image window.

6. On the Layers palette, click and drag Layer 2 down below Layer 1.

7. Click on Layer 1 to make it active for editing, and then click on the Add Layer Mask icon at the bottom of the palette.

8. Press **B** (Paintbrush) and Shift+] to directly select the 100-pixel brush.

9. With black as the current foreground color, apply the color to the Layer Mask to roughly define a triangular shape (see fig. 15.12).

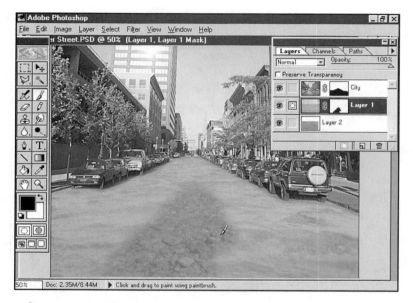

figure 15.12
Paint Layer Mask in a shape similar to, but inside, the water area.

10. Press **5** to reduce the opacity of the Paintbrush to 50%. In one stroke, follow the outline of the triangle shape you created in the previous step, to make the edge much softer.

11. Press **2** to reduce the opacity of the Paintbrush to 20%, and again in one stroke, follow just outside the border you created in the previous step, to make the edge even softer. The border now has an almost undefined edge.

12. Right-click (Macintosh: Ctrl+click) over the Layer Mask thumbnail on Layer 1, and choose Remove Layer Mask from the menu. Click on Apply in the confirmation dialog box.

13. Press Ctrl(⌘)+S.

TIP

When you work with partial opacity, use the tool once in any specific location to achieve that opacity. The more you apply the tool in one area, the more you increase the opacity.

WARNING

The keyboard shortcuts for applying partial opacity to paint application tools do not work if a paint application tool (such as the Paintbrush, the Gradient tool, the Pencil tool, and so on) is not your currently chosen tool.

When selection tools or editing tools are chosen, the keyboard shortcuts for opacity apply to the Layers palette's opacity for the current editing layer. Pressing 2 when the Rectangular Marquee tool is chosen, for example, reduces the opacity of the current image layer to 20%.

Water Street is almost complete. Placing Bottom.tif into the water area added a sense of dimension, but the image needs one more edit.

In your image-creating career, you will know without a doubt that the image in certain projects is finished. At other times, though, the place at which you call an image completed can be very unclear. Try setting the image aside for a few days or weeks, and then come back to it with a more objective viewpoint. You might be surprised at how quickly the solution to finishing the project will come to you. Water Street, at this stage, was just such an image—we set it aside for about two weeks before continuing.

You might remember from school that when you are going to make an argument for a particular point of view, you can solidify your point by listing three reasons. Two reasons leaves your argument too weak, and four reasons is overkill. In Water Street, so far, we have two reasons (the water and the rocky lake bed) to support a surrealistic point of view. We need one more element to make the image complete.

After looking over the stock photos for about an hour, the authors remembered that the obvious is sometimes the hardest element to find. Instead of playing to the water concept a third time, why not use something from the original street? The double-line traffic divider would work quite nicely!

The lines could "float" on top of the water, or appear to lie on the bottom. The artistic call was to paint the river floor with the yellow traffic lines. To create believable lines, you use the lines on the City layer as a guide. Creating the selection of this area is best accomplished with the Pen tool.

Painting the Bottom of a River

No need to hang a "Caution: Wet Paint" sign here! Having made the decision to lay some yellow lines on the river bed, all you need is a little help from the Pen tool to bring the image to near-completion.

N O T E

The Paths feature can be essential in your image editing. Therefore, a good understanding of its functions is important. Be sure to read Chapter 4, "Using Paths, Selections, and Layers."

The following steps show you how to use the Pen tool to accurately trace the outline of the yellow traffic lines and make a selection from the path.

C R E A T I N G   A   S E L E C T I O N   F R O M   A   P A T H

1. With the Water Street.psd image open, press Shift and click on the City Layer Mask thumbnail in the Layers palette. A large red *X* appears on top of the Layer Mask preview, indicating that the mask is turned off. The street is now visible.

2. Press Ctrl(⌘)+spacebar to toggle to the Zoom tool, and click once anywhere inside the document window. If you closed the image after the previous set of steps, type **50** in the Zoom percentage box, and press Enter. Resize the document window by dragging on the sides of the window (Macintosh: use the Size box) until you can see the entire image.

3. Press the PgDn key to move your view to the bottom of the image.

4. Double-click the Pen tool to make it active and to display the Options palette. Place a check in the Rubber Band box, and click on the Close control button to hide the Options palette.

5. Make your first click with the Pen tool at the top left edge of the yellow lines, just in front of the car (facing the camera) in the left lane as you look at the street.

6. Bring the cursor to the bottom of the image. Before you click the mouse button, make sure that the path segment is on top of the left edge of the left yellow line. See the completed path in figure 15.13 for the location of this segment.

7. Click about $1/4$ screen inch directly to the right, and then click immediately to the right of your *first* anchor point at the far end of the street. Caution: do not close the path! Your cursor should remain as cross hairs. *Do not* click if the cursor changes and a small circle appears next to it—this indicates that the cursor is over the first anchor point and a click will close the path.

8. Click another anchor immediately to the right of the last one; then follow down the left side of the right yellow line to the bottom of the image, and place another anchor point there.

9. Continue this procedure until you reach the top right side of the yellow lines. For this point, click just above and to the right of the top group of anchor points.

10. Click the last point on the first anchor point to close the path (see fig. 15.13). Note that the image is lightened here, to make the path more visible in the figure.

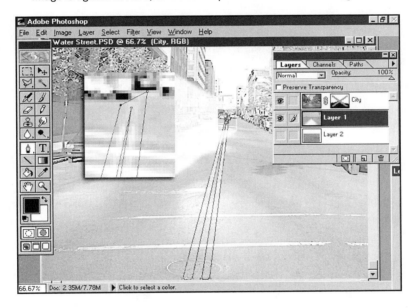

figure 15.13
The completed path uses the yellow lines as a guide.

11. Click on the Paths tab in the Layers\Channels\Paths palette; then click on the Loads path as a selection icon (third from the left) at the bottom of the palette.

12. Drag the Work path to the Delete (trash) icon at the bottom right of the palette. Then click on the Channels tab and click on the Save selection as a channel icon (second from the left) to save it.

13. Press Ctrl(⌘)+S to save the changes.

TIP

When an image is too large to display full-size, you can use Photoshop's shortcut keys to navigate your view, without having to display the Navigator palette. The PgUp key moves the view up incrementally, whereas the PgDn key moves downward in the same manner. The Home key moves the view to the upper left of the window, and the End key moves it to the bottom right. Photoshop is a very "deep" program, with many features and different ways to perform the same function.

The yellow lines selection was moved to the very bottom of the image to make the lines a visually stronger element. After all, although we know that this is the end of the street, the viewer doesn't have to!

Now that we have the lines selection, it's time to fill it with a yellow color on a new layer.

PAINTING TRAFFIC LINES FASTER THAN THE DOT

1. Press Ctrl(⌘) and click on the #4 channel in the Channels palette to load the selection. (This step is not necessary if you are performing these steps directly after the preceding set of steps.)

2. Click on the Layers tab, click on Layer 2, and then click on the Create new layer icon at the bottom of the palette. Layer 3 is created, and positioned between Layer 2 and Layer 1.

3. Press Shift and click on the City Layer Mask thumbnail to deactivate the mask and make the street visible.

4. Press I (Eyedropper) and click near the bottom end of the right yellow line to sample the official DOT yellow.

5. Click on the Layer 3 title to ensure that it is the active layer. Press Alt+Delete to fill the selection with the new foreground color.

6. Right-click (Macintosh: hold Ctrl and click) on the City Layer Mask thumbnail, choose Remove Layer Mask, and click on Apply.

7. Press Ctrl(⌘)+D to deselect the yellow lines. Click on the Channels tab, and drag the #4 channel to the Delete (trash) icon at the bottom of the palette.

8. Press Ctrl(⌘)+S to save the document. At this point, your image should look like figure 15.14.

figure 15.14
Water Street with no passing on either side of the shore.

Water Street is near completion—all the elements are in place and the composition is good. The image just needs a few last minute touches before you can call it a finished masterpiece.

The Finishing Touches

When you think you have finished creating an image, take a good, long look at it. Look at the whole picture and examine the details. Is the composition strong? Are the colors correct? Does something need just a slight nudge to the right? Are the edges of all layer contents perfect? Does the image contain any unnecessary pixels?

After taking a good hard look at Water Street, we can see two areas that need attention. The yellow lines should look submerged under the water, and the river bottom should be slightly darker. Let's begin editing the yellow traffic lines you created.

Creating the Underwater Look

To create the illusion that the yellow lines are underwater, keep two things in mind. First, you need to imitate the attributes of the existing river—notice how light, dark, or faint different sections are. Second, you must alter the shape of the object to mimic the visual distortion created by the refraction of water.

In the following steps, you match the yellow lines to the river bed's attributes.

MATCHING IMAGE CHARACTERISTICS

1. Click and drag Layer 3, which contains the yellow lines, to a position immediately below Layer 1 (which contains the water). Notice that the far end of the lines already looks submerged.

2. With Layer 3 active, drag the Opacity slider on the Layers palette to about 66% (see fig. 15.15). This reduces the opacity and saturation of the yellow, and enables some of the rocks to show through the paint.

figure 15.15
Reduce the opacity of the lines so that the rocks can partially show through.

3. Click on the Add Layer Mask icon to add a Layer Mask to Layer 3.

4. Press **B** (Paintbrush). To set up the brush, press Shift+] for the 100-pixel tip. Press **7** for 70% pressure. If black is not the foreground color, press **X**.

5. Place the cursor over the far end of the double lines, and click once to apply Layer Mask. This makes the lines and rocks fade out.

6. Click and drag the Layer Mask icon into the Delete (trash) icon, and click on Apply.

7. Press Ctrl(⌘)+S to save the changes.

Now the lines appear to rest on the rocks. You need to distort them slightly, so that they seem to be viewed through water.

Imitating Distortions Caused by Water

Adobe packed this version of Photoshop with filters—more than 90 of them! All the filters are 32-bit native, thus providing greater processing speed. Almost all the filters have a dialog box to allow customization of the effect, and the settings you choose within the filter dialog boxes are previewed in real time. The Distort filters do exactly what the name implies—they distort the image. Although there is a filter called Ocean Ripple, it is not appropriate for use here because this is a river. Seriously, this new filter leaves something to be desired when you work with a partially opaque layer. The filter of choice in this situation is the Ripple filter.

Because the river bed has no straight lines to show you what the distortions should look like, the way you apply the Ripple filter is an artistic call.

APPLYING THE RIPPLE FILTER

1. With Layer 3 active, choose Filter, Distort, Ripple.

2. Drag within the preview window, panning the image to bring the yellow lines into view.

3. Click on the – button to zoom out to 100%.

4. In the Options field, drag the slider to 28, and choose Large in the Size drop-down list (see fig. 15.16).

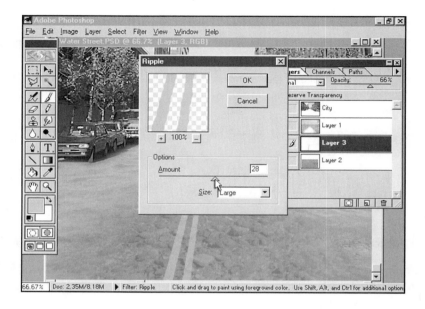

figure 15.16
Set up the Ripple filter dialog box as shown to best imitate the waves in the water.

5. Click on OK to apply the filter.

6. Press Ctrl(⌘)+S to save the changes.

The last detail to work on is the floor of the river, which you want to look more consistent with the rest of the image.

Creating a Consistent Lighting Effect Between Layers

If you used the recommendations at the beginning of this chapter for building a collection of compatible images, you still might need to make a few small adjustments to make the different elements more cohesive. In Water Street, the two photos of different bodies of water were shot under slightly different lighting conditions. The photo of the river bed is actually a shot of a very clean lake, taken with the sun fairly high in the sky. The other photo of water reflects a great deal of the sky, and just happens to be one of the world's most polluted lakes!

The following steps show how to make the river bed more consistent with the other layers and add a finished, presentation look.

THE FINISHING TOUCHES

1. With Layer 3 active, click on the Layers palette control button and choose Merge Down. This command merges the active layer with the layers below it on the palette. Layer 3 is incorporated into Layer 2, and Layer 2 becomes the active layer.

2. With Layer 2 active, choose Image, Adjust, and then choose Brightness/Contrast from the menu bar.

3. Enter −8 in the Brightness field and −47 in the Contrast field (see fig. 15.17). Click on OK.

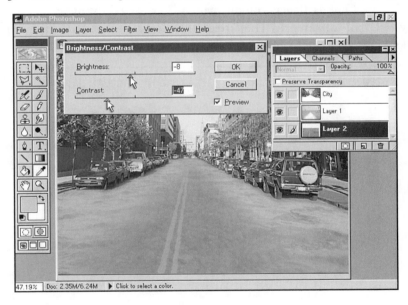

figure 15.17
Reduce the brightness and contrast in the Brightness/Contrast dialog box.

4. From the menu bar or the Layers palette flyout menu, choose Layer, Flatten Image.

TIP

In your own work, you might want to save a layered version of your image with a different name in case you want to edit the image in the future.

5. Type **30** in the Zoom percentage box, and press Enter (Return).

6. Click on Window, Show Actions on the menu bar.

7. Click on the Actions palette control button, and choose Button Mode if the palette is not already in Button mode.

8. Click on Drop Shadow (full image). Choose OK for the two dialog boxes that appear during the drop-shadow process.

9. Choose Layer, Flatten Image from the menu bar. Press Ctrl(⌘)+S to save your masterpiece.

Figure 15.18 shows the finished image created with Photoshop and a little imagination. The twist of surrealism can draw some interesting remarks from viewers. One particular comment on Water Street, "Why aren't the cars under water, too?" is flattering. The surrealistic image is a success when the audience stops looking *at* the image and starts looking *into* the image.

figure 15.18
The finished Water Street!

Summary

The focus of this chapter might not have been what you expected. Instead of talking about flashy filters and undocumented commands, we focused on the way you, the artist, interact with Photoshop to make it a tool that's an extension of your eyes, your hands, and your imagination. Water Street is not a facade behind which the electronic wizardry of Photoshop claims credit for the piece. It is always you, the artist, who uses a tool, or a suite of tools, to create art.

After you have poured your talent, Photoshop skills, and time into creating an impressive piece, you might want to make a hard copy of it or bring it into the physical world in some other way. Read about outputting your masterpiece in the following chapter.

"GAMES"

This image was created using Macromedia Extreme 3D as the modeler. The surface textures were painted using Fractal Design Painter 4, and the playing card design was illustrated in CorelXARA. The composition was assembled in Photoshop 4. In Chapter 4, you see how to use layers and selections to make significant changes to the image.

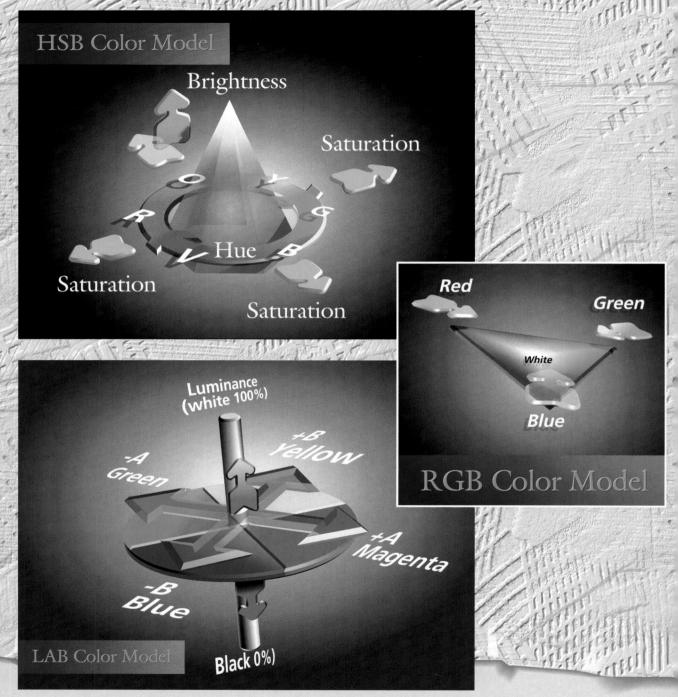

Color models are used throughout this book to describe and match specific colors used in imaging, in on-screen presentations, and in traditional print. Each color model has a *color space*—a limited capability to represent unique colors. The illustrations on this page show a dimensional relationship between the components that, together, represent a color.

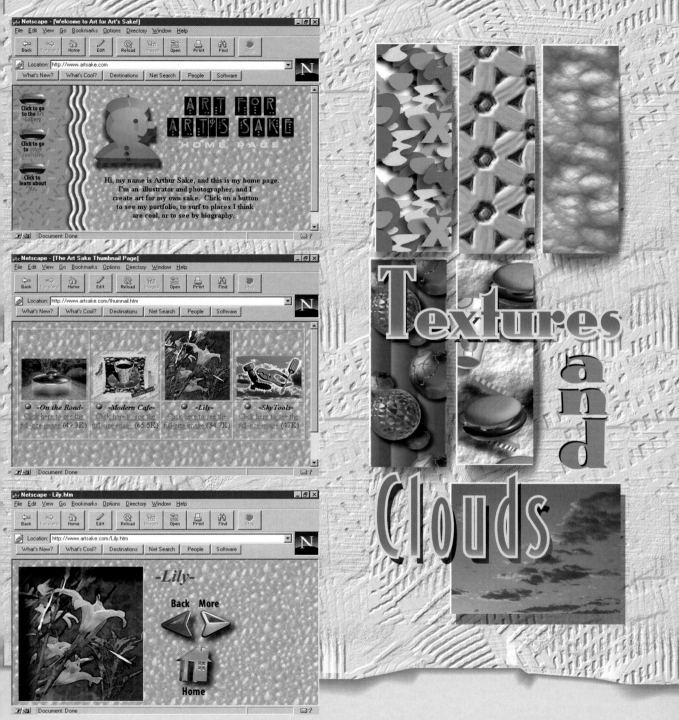

On the *Inside Adobe Photoshop 4 Companion CD*, you will find resource materials for both Windows and the Macintosh, for creating Web sites, interactive presentations, and other image compositions. Chapters 2, 19, and 20 show you how to create interface designs and navigation buttons. The Companion CD contains more than 100 high-quality seamless tiling textures, and a collection of high-resolution cloud images, perfect for use as backgrounds in compositions.

"Lee"

The top left image is a scan of an original picture that most professional retouchers would dismiss as hopeless. In Chapters 5 and 6, you learn the key techniques for Photoshop image restoration, and work with the original image. The main image on this page was restored entirely in Photoshop; the step-by-step procedures and the reason *why* areas of damaged areas deserve special editing procedures are discussed, also.

"Sunset"

This image was originally taken in landscape orientation— the width of the image far greater than its height. The image was *not* cropped to change its orientation, however. Chapter 8 shows how Photoshop's tools and filters can be used to alter digital photography so that images don't *look* retouched.

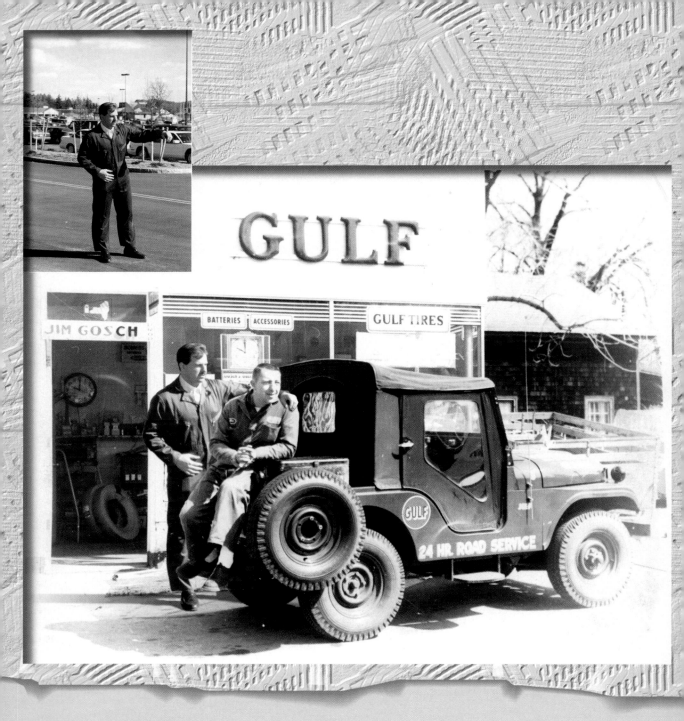

"Jim and Dad"

Photoshop is a very popular tool for restoring age-worn photos. But, how about manipulating a new photo to look 30 years old? Learn the techniques in Chapter 14 to age a photograph and create a reunion of a son and his long-deceased father, to create a very special moment.

"Toaster"

This image is a rendered model, created in Extreme 3D. The reflections are image maps, and the tile floor was created in Photoshop. *"Toaster"* is highlighted in Chapter 16 as an example of how to prepare images for traditional printing.

"Island"

The background in this image was photographed on the Canadian side of the Thousand Islands, the boat was photographed in San Francisco Bay, and the clouds were captured in Syracuse, New York. Chapter 10 shows you how to create a scene from different elements, add accurate lighting qualities, and present an image that people will assume came off a roll of film.

"Floater"
Photoshop has excellent tools not only for correcting images, but also for creating a complete fantasy that looks photorealistic. Chapter 7 provides the information for making a car, a flying saucer, or even your Uncle Fred appear to be lighter than air.

"Fruit"

The title of this image and the composition are far from captivating, but in Chapter 13 you see how to apply some of Photoshop's new Gallery Effects, and create artistic variations on this piece (or on your own work). Learn how to express yourself using digital charcoal or a palette knife, and create your own effects by using filters in combination. Also learn how to find the most suitable image for filtering— plug-in filters are *not* "instant Art" program extensions!

"NickNack"

This image, like "Fruit," is a still life study transformed through the use of Photoshop filters. Both images were created in a modeling program, rendered, and then retouched and enhanced in Photoshop.

"Carousel"

In Chapter 8, this picture and others are refined in the quest for proper dimensions, a balance between foreground and background image interest, and other qualities that separate a good picture from a great one. Stunning photography is not always captured through a lens. Sometimes, you need to "create" great photographs in Photoshop.

"Inside Photoshop 4"

This book's cover image was created by using scanned images, textures built in Photoshop and Fractal Design Painter, and modeling resource files. The concept was to blend new and traditional imaging technology to represent the new wave in visual communications. Is it a photo? Is it a painting? The answer today is, "It's a Photoshop image."

(top) *"OceanSide"*
The foreground of this image was modeled in Extreme 3D, rendered using trueSpace, and then composited with photographs of clouds in Photoshop.

(bottom) *"Morning"*
In Chapter 2, you see how to change the lighting in an image to create more atmosphere, interest, and drama. The image shown here was originally rendered without the venetian blind shading. See how to accomplish this effect manually, along with a host of other photorealistic retouching.

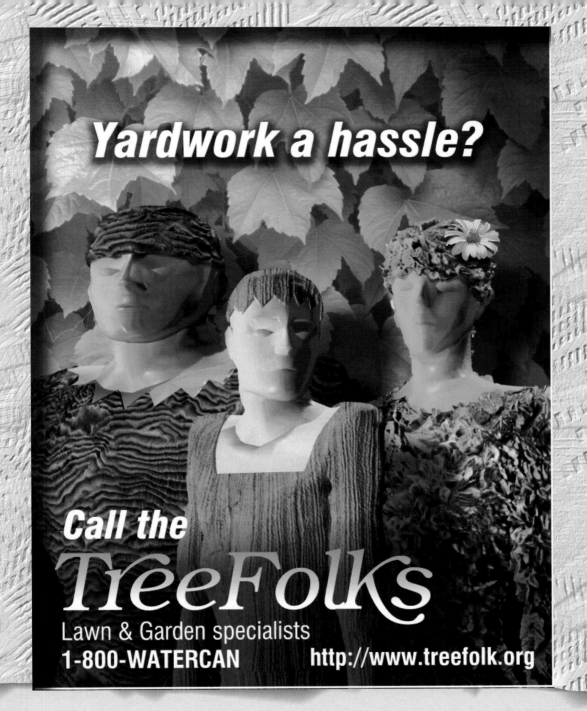

"The TreeFolks"

In Chapter 18, Fractal Design Poser is used in combination with Photoshop to produce this advertisement, without a casting call, a costume designer, and without having to leave your chair. "3D and Photoshop" explores some of the easiest methods for complete scene creation, and how applications can work together to produce a compound document.

"Water Street"
Three photos of everyday subjects were used to create this surrealistic image. In Chapter 15, you'll see how this composite was made and take a look "behind the scene" at the artistic decisions used in the design.

PART

PRODUCTION, WEB-WORTHY IMAGING, AND BEYOND

CHAPTER

OUTPUTTING YOUR INPUT

For all the novelty, speed, and ease of publishing the World Wide Web offers, the classic art form of creating an imprint on a physical surface still remains the primary vehicle of popular communications today. Unless every client you have owns a personal computer, or your monitor has an infinitely long cable—and neither situation is likely—you frequently need to produce a hard copy of your Photoshop work. This chapter is an excursion into the routes you can take to achieve the best-looking output from your creative input. From ink on paper, to 35mm film, to color separations, physical output requires that specific translations, and sometimes accommodations, be made to a copy of your original work. Rule number one in publishing is to decide upon the output device before you compose your image. Let's take a look at the WYSIFO (What You See Is Faithfully Output) considerations that go into making a traditional rendering of your designs, using state-of-the-art equipment.

The Many Routes to Physical Output

Although some proprietary printing methods are available to computer graphics artists, output options fit into a handful of basic categories. The following options are covered in this book:

◆ **Home or small office personal printing.** Typically the output is to paper using a black-and-white laser printer, or a thermal wax or inkjet color printer.

◆ **Service bureau printing.** Depending on the size and specialty of a service bureau, you can order anything from dye sublimation prints to 35mm and larger format film-recorded slides of your Photoshop images.

◆ **Commercial printing.** Of all the categories of output media, commercial printing of color separations offers the highest-resolution work. It is also one of the least familiar processes to many graphics designers.

◆ **Electronic publishing.** Preparation of your work is required to optimize it for on-screen display, but electronic publishing (in-house presentations or work on the Web) is a medium that does not use traditional printing color spaces or image resolution. Chapters 19, "Web Site Construction," and 20, "Animations and SFX on the Web," are devoted to electronic publishing techniques and specifications.

In figure 16.1, you can see the areas of output most commonly used today.

Publishing—the art of outputting your input—is a dynamic education, one that changes in its technology almost daily. The *scope* of the topic of output cannot possibly be documented in this chapter. This chapter covers some of the basic stumbling blocks to, and solutions for, accurately representing your work in a physical medium. As a Photoshop designer or artist, you should become familiar with the many kinds of output for digital work.

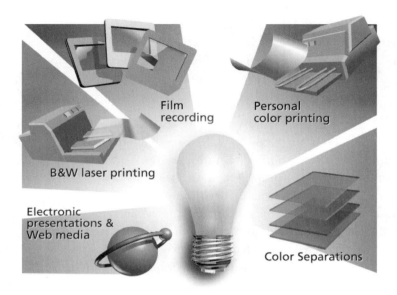

figure 16.1
When you need to publish a graphical thought, you have many options for the media used. Choose the one that best suits your audience.

Personal Printing

In 1997, the small office and home market for personal printing can be divided into two distinct categories: black-and-white laser printing and color printing. As designers, we might immediately conclude that color and black-and-white output are completely different media of artistic expression, but there is also a *technical* aspect that separates color output from black and white.

Inkjet and other types of color printers output a finished product only; that is, output from personal color printers can be used to produce short, low-budget print runs. The color produced is nowhere near equal to that produced by a printing press in terms of quality or durability, and your choice of papers is limited. Nevertheless, personal color printed output may fit the bill when you are faced with a limited budget and color quality is not paramount.

On the other hand, high-resolution black and white laser prints can serve as both hard copy proofs of your work *and* as camera-ready prints. Because the capability of a black-and-white laser printer is extensible, this chapter looks first at personal color output, and then at the direction of black-and-white printing.

Personal Color Printers

There has been much talk in trade magazines and computer publications about "affordable" color printing from the desktop. Today, color printers that cost less than $500 put color printing well within the reach of anyone purchasing his first computer system. Personal color printing is an exciting concept, but "affordable" shouldn't become synonymous with "professional," if you're serious about your craft. The personal color printer is on the verge of becoming a mature market, but at present its output pales in comparison to the product of a color printing press or a photographic print. The personal color printer cannot be used for color-critical work.

Advantages and Disadvantages of Personal Color Printers

If you compare a personal color print output to what it looks like on your monitor or to the output produced by a commercial press or a film recorder, the magnitude of difference in image quality and accurate color reproduction is similar to comparing a Polaroid snapshot to an 8×10" transparency. Personal color printers have much smaller color *gamuts* (the range of colors they can reproduce) than a monitor, film, or printing press. Typically, there is a significant drop-off in a specific hue within the printable range of colors. A personal color printer might, for example, print rich violets and blues, while subtle turquoises color cast to green, and golds turn to orange. How do you correct a particular fall-off in the color spectrum? Sometimes, you can correct the color balance of a print from the printer's proprietary print driver controls (but not using Photoshop's print options). Most of the time, however, a noticeable color cast in a printed image *cannot* be totally corrected.

If you cannot print colors as you see them on your monitor to a personal color printer, the workaround is to balance the color of a *copy* of a specific file. Rule number two in digital imaging is that when the end product is a printed piece, the colors in the printed piece are all that matter. This means that the colors you see on the monitor might look grossly inaccurate, but if the file looks correct when it's printed, it is the file or the monitor that displays "wrong" colors, and not the color printer. This might seem a strange philosophy, particularly when color management systems come with almost every graphics product, and Photoshop itself has a handsome set of calibration controls. If a color print looks wrong, however, and you cannot significantly change the printer's color options, it is the *file information* that must be changed to arrive at the printed colors you envision. And this is always best done with a copy of your work; you might decide in the future to render a design to several different output devices, all of which will certainly have different color gamuts.

To the serious professional designer, personal color printing should be both personally gratifying (see the printed product without leaving your desk!) and a way to send a rough idea of the finished product anywhere you can mail or otherwise send a piece of paper. Despite the inherent color inaccuracy of personal color printers, they are simply nice to have around for a quick hard copy, a greeting card, or other final product purposes. Additionally, many media manufacturers for color printers offer acetate, label stock, business card stock, and even small swatches of fabric. The media becomes part of the art form with color printers and carefully chosen paper, film, or cloth stock. For the artistic purist, these options take you far away from the image you see on-screen, but there is a definite cottage industry possibility for the combination of creative talent, Photoshop, and a color printer.

To ensure the best output when your finished design is to be rendered to a personal color printer, you should do two things:

◆ Print all your images in RGB (Red, Green, Blue) color mode from Photoshop. Although most personal color printers use a combination of cyan, magenta, yellow, and frequently black, color mode conversion circuitry in these printers is designed to internally convert RGB images to CMYK (Cyan, Magenta, Yellow, Black). Check your documentation for specific printer instructions, but most of the time, inkjet printers require RGB color input.

◆ Gather a representative sampling of your imaging work, use Photoshop's Eyedropper tool to create color samples of about 100 different colors in your images, and then paint these colors as swatches into a new image document. Print this document to your color printer and compare the swatches to the color areas in your work.

The color swatches that are not even remotely similar to the colors you see on-screen are your "problem colors" with respect to your printer. These are colors you should avoid using when your final output is this specific printer. You should use Photoshop's Color Range command to select these areas in copies of the original files, and change the colors to ones that will print accurately.

As color-capable beings, we tend to be forgiving when it comes to evaluating a poor design done in color, or color accuracy; "some color is better than none" might be the best observation regarding color printing that is within the financial reach of most designers and many of their clients. Even though quality of a piece printed on a personal color printer cannot be considered equal to that printed on a four-color press, that *doesn't* mean that professional-quality output cannot be generated.

Professional quality *black-and-white* desktop output is within the reach of almost everyone. Black-and-white output is a stable, mature medium in the computer graphics community. The following sections concentrate on printing specifics and the techniques you can use with Photoshop to produce high-quality professional black-and-white output from your desktop.

Black-and-White Output: Personal and Professional

Computer and printing technologies have advanced in recent years to the point at which a black-and-white laser proof can legitimately serve as a camera-ready piece of artwork. The physical line screens and halftone dots used in traditional printing can now be simulated with laser printers and digital imagesetters to provide quality printed copies of your work to suit design, publication, presentation, and "send one to your mom" needs.

All digital imaging hardware must convert color information to whole, quantified amounts of pigment (called *dots*). Different kinds of dots are used; the two primary types are halftone and non-halftone dots. The type of dot used can significantly impact whether you can have your work printed commercially. Let's take a look at the physiology of electronic dot-making and examine the methods by which every rendered electronic image can look as faithful to your on-screen display as possible.

Using a Printer Command Language (PCL)

The technology that drives Hewlett-Packard's LaserJets, the *Printer Command Language* (PCL), was quickly adopted by the business community and became an industry standard that other manufacturers emulated. PCL-based printers are noted for their speed and the rich blacks they produce.

Grayscale images, however, have a gamut much wider than a laser printer can express with its limited palette of available tones. Laser printers can place a dot of colored toner (usually black) on a surface (usually white paper). The gamut of color for laser printer output is exactly 2—black and white—with no percentages of black in between. PCL-based printers simulate the appearance of continuous tones in an image by using a technique similar to what commercial printing presses use to create tones. Both use dots arranged on a page in such a way that your eye integrates the dots and your brain "sees" them as a continuous, tonal image. In figure 16.2, Pushpin.tif is a grayscale image in Photoshop, and LaserPrint.tif is a file that was created by scanning a laser copy of the same image.

figure 16.2

Laser printers can only render a single color to a page, and therefore must use halftones to simulate grayscale images.

Because *Inside Adobe Photoshop 4* is itself printed, we have exaggerated the examples in the figures in this chapter. The scans of the printed artwork were acquired at 35 pixels/inch, about one-fourth the sampling rate required to produce a medium-quality print.

How faithfully a laser copy represents the original image depends on three factors:

◆ The accuracy with which the printer places dots on a page

◆ The organization or pattern of the dots on the page

◆ The resolution of the printer (size of the dots, as expressed in dots per inch)

Laser printers that use the PCL technology have a resolution of either 300 dpi or 600 dpi. Although 300–600 dpi is an adequate resolution for producing a business letter or a chart, you might be disappointed by the limitations of these resolutions when you try to reproduce a Photoshop masterpiece. The human eye easily perceives the dot patterns in a grayscale image that has been printed at 300–600 dpi. A laser printed continuous-tone image must meet or exceed 1,200 dots per inch before a viewer's eye focuses on its composition and tonality rather than on the toner dots that make up the image.

Disadvantages of PCL Printers

PCL printers are more than suitable if you're printing correspondence, an invoice, or a simple graphic to show to a client. The drawback to PCL printers is that they fail to interpret tonal information that directly corresponds to the pattern of a printing press. Faithful copying of the way a printing press places dots of ink requires more information, processing power, and precision than the PCL technology and the printer's controller circuitry are designed to handle.

If you have a 300–600 dpi PCL printer hooked up to your computer, and you want to print a grayscale picture from Photoshop, there aren't any options you can choose to increase the quality and accuracy of the printed piece. Because a PCL printer cannot accurately arrange dots into traditional line patterns, Photoshop's Screen options in the Page Setup dialog box are, by default, dimmed. You can uncheck the Use Printer Defaults box and enter a (line) Frequency and Angle of your choice, but this will not improve the quality of a PCL print. A stylized version of your work will appear, but your work cannot print more accurately than the printer's language can understand.

Error Diffusion Printing

Error diffusion, as the name implies, uses a mathematical formula similar to Photoshop's Indexed Color Mode Dither Option to soften the harsh areas of contrast when an image goes from a high color capability to a much lower color capability—black toner on white paper. Unfortunately, error diffusion is not a Photoshop option. Adobe Systems is trying to encourage users to follow the professional route with imaging, and error diffusion printing is often met with gentle smiles and occasional laughter when mentioned in publishing circles.

Error diffusion printing using a PCL-based printer requires a proprietary *printer driver.* A printer driver is a software program on your computer that takes information from an application and converts the information to machine code that a printer can understand. Windows 95 natively supports error diffusion dithering for non-PostScript printers (Print, Setup, Properties, Graphics, in Photoshop and other applications). If you have Photoshop and a 300-dpi PCL printer and are not using Windows 95, think about investing in an error diffusion printer driver. The error diffusion printer driver intercepts the information an application sends to your system and instructs the printer to follow its own instructions rather than the instructions in the default printer drivers that were installed when you installed your printer. Figure 16.3 shows an error diffusion print placed next to a PCL print.

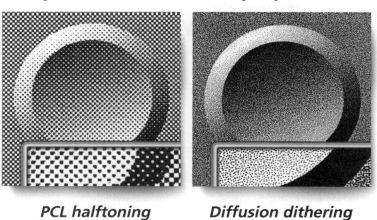

PCL halftoning   **Diffusion dithering**

figure 16.3
Error diffusion printing creates a disorganized arrangement of toner dots, which can look more visually appealing than PCL prints.

The most notable disadvantage to error diffusion printing is imprecision. Error diffusion takes into account the inability of the printer to represent original image areas as different tonal values. As a result, dots of toner are spread in a random fashion on the page; denser areas receive more toner, and lighter areas receive less. There is no organization of dots in an error diffusion print, which makes it unsuitable for commercial camera-ready artwork. If you are not concerned with producing camera-ready artwork, error diffusion printing creates a smooth, eye-pleasing image from a printer that has limited resolution.

PostScript Printers

PostScript personal printers aren't news to Macintosh users; one of the first high-quality printing specifications for the personal computer came along with the Macintosh operating system years ago. Compared to PCL laser printers, PostScript printers are very slow, but their results are astoundingly faithful to original imagery. The method PostScript printers use to organize and place toner dots is almost identical to output of physical screens used by commercial printers.

Unlike PCL, Adobe System's PostScript descriptor language is a complete, complex programming language that was designed to be platform- and device-independent. Imagesetters, laser printers, film recorders, fax machines, and equipment that hasn't even been invented yet can all "read" a PostScript-standard file or image if their manufacturers outfitted them with PostScript interpreters. Therefore, one of the benefits of PostScript printing is a consistent standard of quality. You can rest assured that your image will reproduce as accurately as possible when it's translated from pixels to dots.

Because PostScript printing technology can simulate the screen patterns of traditional printing presses, hard copy can serve as camera-ready artwork. If you think about this, how would any of the images you have created in the assignments in this book be reproduced? As recently as the 1980s, an image created in a computer would have to be imaged by a film recorder, the resulting photographic negative then printed, a physical line screen dropped over it, and finally the image copied again to a photographic press plate. Generations of image quality are recaptured with the advent of the digital halftone, and Adobe's PostScript technology provides the means to create dots from printers and imagesetters that can faithfully hold up to traditional methods of imaging.

Examining a Digital Halftone Image

Continuous-tone images, such as photographs, have a *gamut* (a color or tonal breadth) so close to that of the human eye's perception that *banding* (the demarcation of solid color values between transitional shades) is not seen. In other words, the tones in an image are *continuous,* without a beginning or end to a shade's component colors. A Photoshop gradient fill is a good visual example of a design element that displays continuous tone characteristics. In contrast, you can clearly see where the chocolate ends and the vanilla begins in Neapolitan ice cream; as long as the ice cream is kept frozen, it does not display continuous tone characteristics.

As described earlier in this chapter, the color gamut of black-and-white printed material is limited to foreground color and background color; to express the brightness values in a grayscale image, dots of different sizes are arranged in a precise pattern to correspond exactly to the values they represent in the original image. Figure 16.4 shows a PostScript printed image with the PCL print next to it. As you can see, the dots in the PostScript copy are of different sizes and are consistent in their shape. The quality is good enough to give to co-workers or clients, and also is invaluable in commercial printing.

Non-PostScript halftoning   **PostScript halftoning**

figure 16.4
Most laser printers can produce halftones; PostScript's photographic halftones are of publication quality.

Figure 16.5 gives you a better idea of how the PostScript dots correspond to their tonal equivalents in a digital image. As you can see, areas that are roughly 50 percent black in the original are represented in the PostScript print by halftone cells that occupy half the "white space." Each dot you see is a *digital halftone cell* within an invisible grid that contains all the halftone dots.

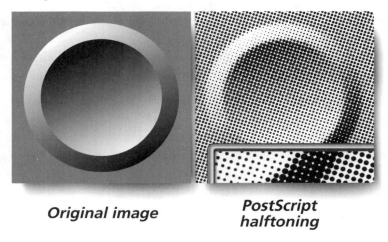

Original image   **PostScript halftoning**

figure 16.5
PostScript halftone dots represent equivalent, continuous tones by their size, as arranged in a pattern.

Try a little experiment. Hold this book about four feet in front of you and look at the halftone example in the last figure. Try the same thing with the PCL and error diffusion figures. You will see that the consistency of the dot shapes, size, and organization (called *line screens*) is such that your mind easily interprets what you see as an image of a button. This is the primary difference between halftone screening and other technologies. Our next stop—the organization of dots that compose a halftone image, and how to optimize your Photoshop designs so that they will print their best.

Understanding the Halftone Cell, Resolution, and Other Factors

Printer resolution and on-screen resolution are measured differently and have different capabilities for expressing tones and colors. Unlike image *resolution*, you define resolution for PostScript printing in *lines per inch* (of halftone dots), not in dots per inch. You need to understand the relationship between the halftone frequency (lines per inch) used to print the image and the image's resolution to evaluate how good the image will look when commercially printed. You'll learn how these inter-relate in later sections of this chapter.

To get a better idea of how halftone printing works, imagine a grid that covers the area on the printed page where you want an image. This grid, or *line screen*, is composed of *cells*. Each cell in the line screen is composed of a small grid of toner dots that collectively make up the larger dot. The number of slots in the halftone cell's grid that are filled with toner determines the density of the individual halftone cell. The more filled grids in the halftone cell, the darker the cell, and the larger the digital halftone dot. The size of a single PostScript halftone dot has a direct relation to the *shade*, or degree of density, in the original image. Figure 16.6 is a representation of this halftone screen with halftone dots placed inside. The percentages of coverage at the bottom of the figure correspond to the size of the halftone dot in the cell. You can see the relationship in this figure between the traditional, physical halftone screen, the digital halftone, and a continuous-tone source image that has the same halftone values. Arranged in a line and viewed from a distance, halftone dots convey the feeling of continuous tones in a grayscale image.

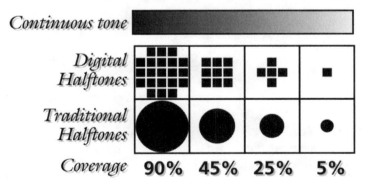

figure 16.6
A digital halftone is today's equivalent of a halftone screen applied to continuous tone photographs.

Halftone dots on an invisible grid are not the only factor that determines good printed output. Other important factors are line angles and the number of spaces on a line that are available for the halftone dots.

Line Angles

The halftone dots need to be arranged on the page in lines that collectively form the *line screen*. The angle at which the lines are positioned is called the *line angle*.

In nature, continuous-tone images contain many right angles, such as the sides of buildings and the stripes in a shirt. For this reason, setting a halftone line angle at zero or 90 degrees is not a good idea. You should specify a halftone line-screen angle that's *oblique* to the elements in a digital image—45 degrees works in most cases. Line-screen patterns that closely resemble the patterns in images *resonate* visually, creating unwanted *moiré* patterns. Figure 16.7 illustrates the way different-sized halftone dots are arranged in a 45°-angle screen.

figure 16.7

Lines of halftone dots arranged at an angle help prevent unwanted patterning in the printed design.

Photoshop and many other applications offer a default line angle of 45 degrees for halftone dots. In Photoshop, you have the option of adjusting this angle, but you would only need to do this if you had photographed an image containing strong diagonal stripes.

To define specific halftone screens for printing, use Photoshop's File, Page Setup, Screen command to display the Halftone Screen dialog box shown in figure 16.8.

Although the same Halftone Screen options appear when a PostScript printer or a PCL printer is defined as the Specific Printer, the shape and frequency of dots are not rendered as true halftones when printing to a non-PostScript (PCL) printer. To achieve a true digital halftone effect, you must use a PostScript-capable output device. If you check the Use Printer's Default Screen check box in the Halftone Screen dialog box, the options for screens dim to indicate that these user-defined options are now unavailable and won't be used. Generally, when outputting to a non-PostScript printer, it's best to allow the printer to render by using its own, internal screening process.

The options in Photoshop's Halftone Screen dialog box include Frequency and (dot) Shape, in addition to halftone Angle.

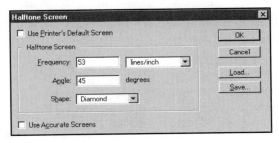

figure 16.8

Photoshop's Halftone Screen dialog box options are useful for PostScript output only.

TIP

The Use Accurate Screens option in the Halftone Screens dialog box refers to an Adobe technology designed for very high-end PostScript Level 2 printers and printers with Emerald controllers. PostScript Level 2 interpreters without Emerald controllers are installed in most of the newer PostScript printers, and they produce better and faster halftone prints than the older PostScript standard.

Accurate Screen technology is usually found on imagesetters and not on personal laser printers, but it's worth checking the documentation for your printer to see whether it supports PostScript Level 2 and Accurate Screens. If it does, be sure to check this box so that you can benefit from this feature. If you're not sure whether your printer supports Accurate Screens, check the box anyway. If your printer doesn't support Accurate Screens, the information will be ignored.

Halftone screen frequency is another option to specify when you print from Photoshop. The *frequency,* or number of lines per inch used when printing halftone dots, has a direct correlation with *the number of unique tones* you can simulate in a print. There's a simple way, using your eyes and a little math, to achieve the best line frequency for a grayscale image.

Line Frequency

The default setting for a 300 dpi laser printer is usually about 45 to 60 lines per inch; for 600 dpi printers, it is about 85 lines per inch. The actual lines-per-inch capability of any given printer is determined by the manufacturer. The basic truth about medium- to low-resolution laser printer output is that when you *increase* lines per inch, you *decrease* the number of grayscale values you're simulating on the printed page. There is a direct correlation.

Two factors govern the maximum number of tonal values that laser printing can simulate:

◆ The resolution of the digital image, expressed in pixels per inch

◆ The number of densities that can portray the gray shades in the printed image

The Times Two Rule

An accurate halftone print of a grayscale image should have a lines-per-inch value no less than half the pixels-per-inch value of the original file. For example, many of the example images on the Companion CD have a resolution of 150 pixels per inch. To print these images with any sense of aesthetic value, the halftone screen should be no less (or more) than 75 lpi.

TIP

Keep this rule in mind when you specify image dimensions and resolution for a copy of an image you want printed. When you create an image, "shooting for the stars" is good practice. If you're particularly proud of some work you have done in Photoshop at 300 pixels/inch, save it this way. You might get to print it at a high resolution some day. But then make a copy of it, keeping in mind the resolution of your present target printer. You can use Photoshop's Image, Image Size command to specify a lower resolution for an image.

To calculate the optimal resolution for printing a digital image, use this mathematical formula:

Printer Line Frequency (in lpi) $\times$ 2 = Image Resolution (in pixels/inch)

If you print an image with a resolution of more than two times the current line screen defined for a printer, you are creating a productivity bottleneck. You cannot squeeze more visual detail out of an image than the printer is capable of producing. Excess image information is spooled to the printer and then discarded at printing time, creating an unnecessary waste of time before you receive your hard copy. You have two alternatives if your image contains a higher resolution than your printer is capable of outputting:

◆ Choose Image, Image Size, check the Resample Image check box, and enter a resolution in the Print Size field. The resolution you enter should be two times the Frequency of the Halftone Screen in the Halftone Screen dialog box in the Page Setup command.

By using this option you physically change the arrangement of pixels to create a new resolution. If you choose this option for printing, remember to save the resulting image file to a different file name, and remember to uncheck the Resample Image box before you use the Image size command again. The Resample Image check box usually should remain unchecked to prevent inadvertent distortion of images you work with in the future.

◆ If you have no particular image dimensions in mind for your laser copy, you can also choose Image, Image Size and then reduce the Resolution to less than two times the Halftone Screen Frequency value with the Resample Image box *unchecked*. Unlike most Windows and Macintosh applications, Photoshop does *not* offer sizing options from the Print command dialog box; image dimensions should be checked to make sure that the image will fit on the page before you print. Because image resolution is inversely proportional to image dimensions, this approach does not change any visual content within the image; after you print the piece, resolution can be restored to the file's original resolution.

When you print from Photoshop, the active document is printed in the center of the page. A useful feature in Photoshop is the image preview box, which can be displayed at any time by clicking on the Document Sizes box to the right of the Zoom percentage field. As you can see in figure 16.9, the image oceanside1.tif falls outside the currently defined print page in Photoshop. The white area of the page preview box is the live area of the printed page, and the box with the "x" inside it is the document. In its current orientation, this image needs to be resized so that the entire "x" is visible in the image preview box; otherwise, the print will be clipped on the left and right sides. If you want the image placed on the page in some other position, you will have to import the image into a DTP program, such as PageMaker, and then print from there.

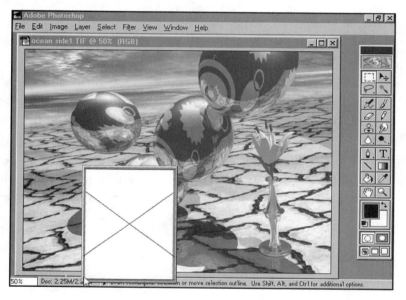

figure 16.9

The pop-up image size box will tell you whether the image is too large to print to the currently defined page size.

In addition to displaying the image preview box, Photoshop alerts the user prior to printing if an image is too large to print to the currently defined page size. The warning shown in figure 16.10 was displayed when we attempted to print the Oceanside image.

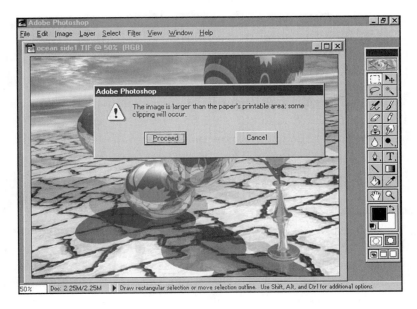

figure 16.10
Photoshop alerts you when the resolution and dimensions of the image are too large
for the currently defined page size.

If this happens to you, you have three alternatives, besides letting the printer crop
your work:

◆ Rotate the printable page, with images where possible, by using the File,
Page Setup command, so that the widest side for the image falls within the
new printable page orientation.

◆ Choose Image, Image Size from the menu, *check* the Resample Image check
box in the Image Size dialog box, and enter smaller values in the Height and
Width boxes of the Print Size field to create a smaller image. Click on OK,
and then print your image. This is *not* a recommended course of action
because it changes image qualities, as described earlier.

◆ Choose Image, Image Size. With the Resample Image box *un*checked,
increase the pixels/inch amount in the Resolution field. This will decrease
the physical dimensions of the image.

Even though no change to file content is made when you increase image resolution in the Image Size dialog box while the Resample Image check box is unchecked, Photoshop sees this as a change in the file. Photoshop will flag you if you have respecified an image's dimensions/resolution before you close the image.

The reason Photoshop asks about dimensions/resolution is that image resolution is a property specific to some, but not all file formats, and applications that can import images often use resolution information to determine the dimensions of an image placed within a document. The Tagged Image File format (TIF, or TIFF), for example, keeps image resolution information stored in the header of the file. A 2" by 2" image with a resolution of 150 pixels/inch will usually import as 2" by 2" to an application such as PageMaker. If you were to increase the dimension of this file in Photoshop while the Resample Image check box is unchecked, the resolution of the image would decrease, and although the *content* of the image would not change, it would be imported to other applications as a dimensionally larger file that might not print at its best. The reason that output would look poor is that the file would cover a larger area, with fewer pixels per inch.

You're not quite ready to print from Photoshop yet. You hold some of the keys to printing the correct image resolution, but you still don't know how to achieve a balance between Halftone Screen Frequency and the number of unique shades your printer can handle. The Times Two Rule is only half the equation for printing a grayscale image from a laser printer.

As mentioned earlier, you have some flexibility in determining the lines-per-inch value when you use a PostScript printer. You can adjust the coarseness of the lines (the space between them) by specifying a lower line frequency, but depending on your printer's resolution (measured in dpi), you may not get a very good-looking print. The print may look blocked in or muddy and lack refinement. This is why you need to determine *how many unique tones* in a grayscale image can be represented by halftone lines.

The Number of Tones in a Grayscale Image

An 8-bit grayscale image can contain as many as 256 unique tones. A laser printer has a definite threshold for expressing all the grayscale information; this may become painfully obvious when you print to a low-resolution printer. Occasionally, you will need to strike a balance between line frequency and the number of shades the halftone dots can represent. The balance is expressed as this mathematical equation:

Printer Resolution (in dpi)/Printer Line Frequency (in lpi)= n (squared) = shades of gray

You will "plug and play" with this equation shortly in this chapter to see how faithfully a printer can represent the tonal values in a grayscale image.

Using Calculations to Determine Image Quality

Suppose that you have an image with a resolution of 150 pixels/inch, such as the one used earlier as an example. You know from the first equation that the setting for the halftone screen's lines-per-inch frequency should be half the image's pixel-per-inch resolution, or 75 lines per inch. The following calculation is for a 300 dpi printer:

300(dpi)/75(lpi)= 4, then

4^2 = 16 shades of gray

Pretty pathetic, right? When a 256-shades-of-gray image is reproduced at 75 lpi on a 300 dpi printer, all the tonal information is reduced to 16 shades! This is unacceptable for the serious imaging-type person.

To be fair, a 75 lpi halftone screen is way too high a value for a 300 dpi printer. Most manufacturers recommend a value between 45 and 60. The line screen frequency you should use with a printer, then, is really a question of aesthetics. The fewer lines per inch used to express the halftone patterns, the more shades they simulate, but the more visible the lines are in the image. A line screen frequency of *less* than 45 per inch is apparent on a printed page to the extent that the line pattern overwhelms *the composition* of the printed image.

Higher-Resolution Printers

To get a reasonable facsimile of your digital image, a printer capable of 600 to 1,800 dpi is more in keeping with hard-copy proofing needs. Many professional black-and-white publications, in fact, can be sent to press from a camera-ready 1,200 or 1,800 dpi laser print. Several add-in cards are available now that can step a 600 dpi printer's resolution up to 1,200 dpi PostScript output, and Lexmark, LaserMaster, NewGen, and others make fairly affordable, high-resolution laser printers that can produce good camera-ready copy. So don't compromise the quality of your printed piece; instead, improve the capability of your output device. The following equation shows the gamut of grayscale that a 1,200 dpi PostScript printer can simulate with a halftone line screen of 85 lpi:

$$1,200(dpi)/\ 85(lpi)=14.12$$

$$14.2^2 =199.37$$

Not bad! Of the 256 possible shades in a grayscale image, 199 can be represented at 1,200 dpi with an 85 lpi line screen.

But what happens when you use these settings for a grayscale image that contains *more* than 200 shades? You do lose some control over the finer visual details in the image, and you leave the extra shades to chance. And if your print is to serve as camera-ready art for commercial printing, you run the risk of a final, ink-on-paper print that has harsh, contrasted areas where you least expect them because you gave the machine more visual information than it could handle.

Consider an alternative to letting a machine dictate the quality of your finished print. Although you cannot change the screen, you *can reduce* the number of tones in a *copy* of the image, with such subtlety and finesse that viewers will never notice that anything's missing. To reduce the number of tones in your image to match the printer-imposed limit, you first must determine how many shades are in your image, and then use Photoshop's Levels feature to eliminate as many shades of gray as necessary. In the following section, you will see how to calculate the number of tones in an image.

The Photoshop Method of Counting Colors

Photoshop can be used to determine the number of unique shades in a grayscale image. The approach you must take is not straightforward, however, and before you try this you should definitely have a copy of the image saved under a different name. When you convert an RGB image to Indexed mode, the Indexed Color dialog box's Colors field, beneath the Color Depth drop-down list, reports the number of colors in an image. If Photoshop does not offer the Exact Palette and the Other Color Depth, it means that the image contains more than 256 colors.

To make the best use of the Indexed Color mode's report of the unique colors in an image, you should first convert a color image to Grayscale mode, and then back to RGB Color mode to determine the unique number of tones in the image. Use the techniques in Chapter 11, "Black and White…and Color" to convert a copy of your color work to LAB mode, and then save the Lightness channel as the Grayscale mode image you want to use for printing.

In the following example, you use the Toaster.tif image in the CHAP16 folder on the Companion CD to have Photoshop calculate the unique tones in the image. This image was originally a color image, converted to Grayscale mode. Let's see how many unique tones the image contains.

CALCULATING UNIQUE GRAYSCALE TONES

CD-ROM

1. Open the Toaster.tif image from the CHAP16 folder on the Companion CD.

2. Choose Image, Mode, and then choose RGB Color from the menu.

3. Choose, Image, Mode, Indexed Color from the menu. Photoshop calculates that an exact match of unique values can be made and saved to a custom color palette consisting of 238 colors (see fig. 16.11).

figure 16.11
When an image contains fewer than 256 unique colors or tones, Photoshop calculates an Exact palette containing only those colors.

4. Click on Cancel and then choose File, Revert. Click on Revert in the attention box that pops up, and save the image to your hard disk as Toaster.tif.

As discussed in the previous section, at 1,200 dpi and using an 85 line-per-inch screen, you can faithfully output 199 unique tones. To print the Toaster image successfully, 39 of the unique tones (238–199) in the image must go!

But which ones? This is where you should pick up the telephone and learn the specifics of the commercial press used to output the image. Your printer (the human, not the machine!) knows the capability and limitations of printing from a plate made from your camera-ready image, using their printing presses. In fact, as you will see in the next section, you might want to reduce the tonal information in an image to *less* than what your laser printer can handle, to create an image that can be successfully transferred to the ink-on-paper medium.

Ink Is Different from Toner

A print press and a laser printer are two different *physical* ways of rendering a halftone image. Halftone dots of ink on paper soak into the medium, whereas laser toner dots rest on top of the paper. Experienced commercial printers will often tell you to avoid shades that approach absolute white and absolute black in the camera-ready print you give them. The reason for this is that although a halftone screen printed from a laser is capable of fusing a 100 percent dense, black area *onto* a page, print press inks soak *into* a page and spread. Depending on the paper, the ink, the presses, and the line screen used, a digital halftone containing halftones that represent the extreme ends of possible brightness values will not "hold." For example, an area that screens at, say, a 90 percent or 95 percent density might completely saturate the corresponding printed area with ink. When a screen doesn't "hold" on the press, the darkest areas become black and bleed together, creating a puddle that eventually dries to create a misrepresented area of your original design.

Design misrepresentation can also occur in light and white areas. A no-coverage area on a laser copy sent to a commercial press sometimes results in an image area that contains a "hot spot," caused by an absence of halftone ink dots in the image. Zero percent and one percent densities in an image, expressed as ink halftone dots, create an unwanted border in the image. Think about this for a moment. The one-percent dots have to *start* someplace, don't they? The idea is to cover even totally white areas in the original image with at least a one-percent density of halftone dots.

Decreasing Contrast in the Laser Copy

To handle image tonal extremes, go back to your original digital image and make a *copy* of it for modification. Then, in the copy, reduce the contrast of the image so that there are no absolute blacks or whites. Although the modified image will look flat and dull on the monitor, the image will snap up when printed from a plate made from your laser hard copy. Again, the "correct" rendition of your image, when paper is the final output, is the paper, and not what you see on the monitor.

For the purposes of this Toaster example, let's suppose that after your talk with the commercial printer, you learn that the press doesn't handle halftone percentages of less than 12 percent density. The solution is to change the distribution of tones in the image so that the first 12 percent (the very light tones) are reassigned to darker values. This shifts the tonal range of the image into a printable range of tonality. Don't think of it as degrading your work, but instead as optimizing the image for display in a different medium.

The first thing to do is calculate which tones in the image are located in the upper 12 percent of the image. A brightness gamut that ranges from 0 to 255 doesn't correspond directly to a density percentage that ranges from 0 percent to 100 percent, so we need to use the following equation:

$$256 - [\text{Halftone Density (in percent)} \times 2.56] = \text{Brightness Value}$$

Now plug the 12 percent minimum density value for the print press into the equation:

$$12(\text{percent}) \times 2.56 = 30.72$$

$$256 - 30.72 = 225.28$$

The solution, then, is to bring the output level for an image's upper range down to 225.

Similarly, if the commercial printer tells you that 90 percent black is *the densest* halftone dot the press can render, you should apply the same rule, as follows:

$$90(\text{percent}) \times 2.56 = 230.40$$

$$256 - 230.40 = 25.60$$

In this case, you would enter **26** in the left Output Level field in the Levels command dialog box.

In the next set of steps, you reduce the number of tones in the Toaster.tif image to optimize it for a camera-ready print that will reproduce accurately from a commercial press.

DECREASING IMAGE CONTRAST FOR THE PRINT PRESSES

1. Open the Toaster image you saved earlier to your hard disk.

2. Press Ctrl(⌘)+L to display the Levels command.

3. Enter **225** in the right Output Levels box.

4. Enter **26** in the left Output Levels box (see fig. 16.12).

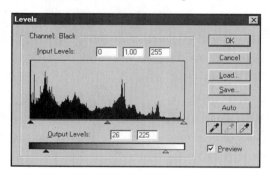

figure 16.12

Decrease the Output Levels for the image to reduce extreme blacks and white for black-and-white output.

5. Click on OK to apply the tone changes, press Ctrl(⌘)+Shift+S (File, Save As), and then save the file as Output.tif to your hard disk.

If you perform the steps outlined in the previous section for converting the Grayscale mode image to RGB, and then check out the potential Indexed color palette for this image, you will discover that the Output.tif image now contains 189 unique tones. This is within a 1,200 dpi printer's tonal gamut at 85 lpi, so you can successfully print this image, and it can serve as an optimized, camera-ready print for commercial printing in this example.

WARNING

If your commercial printer specifies only a high- *or* a low-density threshold, *don't* use Levels to redistribute both the bottom and top tonal extreme in the target image. Photoshop recalculates and redistributes *all* the pixels in an image when you make a change in a specific brightness area. Photoshop's capability to redistribute the scheme of tonal values so that they look smooth can wreck your chances of an optimal print if you specify an Output Level that the commercial printer has *not* specified!

After you finish printing, you can free up hard drive space by deleting the copy of the Toaster image or any images of your own that you have optimized for camera-ready printing. After you degrade an image by reducing the tones, you can never retrieve the pixel information that has been simplified for printing purposes. That's why you should always specify digital image dimensions and resolutions for printing from a *copy* of your work.

Photoshop's Printing Options

To bring the discussion back to the application you will most likely use for output, the following sections describe how Photoshop's output options are used for rendering images to paper. When you believe you're all set to press Ctrl(⌘)Shift+P to access Page Setup, the following sections walk you through the options you will encounter.

Using the Page Setup Dialog Box

When you choose Page Setup from the File menu, the Page Setup dialog box appears (see fig. 16.13). The Page Setup screen always looks the same, regardless of which printer driver you have loaded on your system.

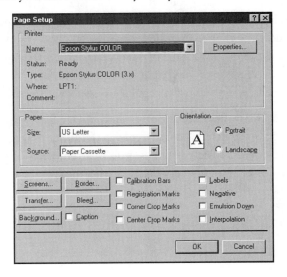

figure 16.13
The Page Setup dialog box.

In this dialog box, you have the option to print from the default printer (the one currently defined for your system), or you can choose another printer from the Printer name drop-down list, a list of all printer drivers currently installed on your system. Although there are many buttons and check boxes in this dialog box, most of them usually can be left at their default settings. The next few sections explain these settings so that you will know which settings to change when you have a special application or printing need. For the following examples, the authors have chosen an Epson Stylus color printer driver. If your own printer is a black-and-white laser printer or a different output device, some of the options might not be available to you.

Screens

Like commercial printing presses, personal color printers use three colors (cyan, magenta, and yellow) or four colors (cyan, magenta, yellow, and black) to produce the colors in your image. These pigments can be in the form of wax, ink, toner, or dye. Printers that use four colors usually produce better results than three-color printers because pigments contain many impurities, and blacks in an image need a reinforcing pass of black pigment from the printer so that darker areas in the printed image will not display a greenish color cast.

The screen angles for each color the printer uses are defined at angles that do not cause resonating lines relative to each other. The use of different screen angles greatly reduces the chance that the cyan, magenta, yellow, and black pigments will build a moiré pattern into your printed image when they are printed to the same page in successive passes. A *moiré* pattern is the result of screen lines (lines composed of halftone cells) overlapping at regular intervals within the image.

When you click on the Screens button in the Page Setup dialog box, the Halftone Screens dialog box is displayed (see fig. 16.14). Notice that the Use Printer's Default Screens check box is selected. Unless you're attempting to achieve a special effect with your color print or are very familiar with the specifications for your machine, this is a good option to leave checked.

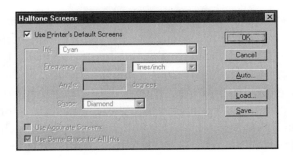

figure 16.14

Unless you understand the screen specifications for a specific output device, allow Photoshop to render to the device's internal screen settings.

Personal color printer manufacturers have built the optimal screen angles right into the machine—there's really no need to change them. When you enable this option, all other options are dimmed, and you cannot change the Halftone Screen settings.

Border

A click on this button accesses a dialog box that enables you to place a black border around the edges of your image. You can specify the width of the border, but you cannot choose a color other than black.

Transfer

Transfer functions are designed to compensate for a miscalibrated imagesetter. These functions are *not* used with the typical personal color printer, and should be used only when you create black-and-white camera-ready art. A click on the Transfer button displays the Transfer Functions dialog box, where you can adjust the values used to compensate for dot gain. *Dot gain* is the growth in the size of halftone dots that occurs when the ink used to print an image on a printing press expands as it is absorbed into the paper. Imagesetters compensate for dot gain by reducing the size of the halftone dots they put on the film from which the press plates are made. Exactly how much imagesetters reduce the size of the dots is determined by the settings you make in the Printing Inks Setup dialog box (which you access by choosing File, Color Settings, Printing Inks Setup). The information needed to determine the values you enter in the Printing Inks Setup dialog box *must* come from the commercial printer. Only the commercial printer knows what the appropriate value is for the paper, ink, and press on which your image will be printed. If all this sounds complicated, it is. It is far better to insist that an imagesetter be properly calibrated than to "guesstimate" the Transfer function or the Printing Inks Setup equations.

Bleed

If you intend to physically crop the printed image, you can have Photoshop insert crop marks in the image to guide the person who runs the paper cutter. You can specify how far into the image the crop marks appear.

Background

If your image doesn't fill the page, and you want color around the image, you can choose a color here. A click on the Background button displays Photoshop's color picker, or the color picker you have chosen in Photoshop's Preferences. Be aware that choosing a background color for output really eats up the costly ink, wax, or toner the printer uses, and increases print time dramatically. You should not choose this option frivolously.

Caption and Labels Check Boxes

Check the Caption check box if you have already made a caption entry in the Caption field of the File/File Info dialog box. The caption will be printed in nine-point Helvetica in the margin of your printout. Put a check in the Labels check box if you want the file name and channel name printed on the image in nine-point Helvetica. The size and typeface for these options cannot be changed. You might want to enable the Caption and Labels check boxes if you're sending a hard copy proof to a service bureau or other organization that handles massive numbers of images from different clients.

Registration Marks

When you print color separations for spot color, process color, or duotones, check this box to place bullseyes in the margin around the image to enable the commercial printer to align the printing plates. Registration marks are not used for printing a composite image to a personal color printer; only a single page is printed.

Calibration Bars

Enabling this feature causes a gradient-filled rectangle to be printed in the margin of the page. This is used by commercial printers to check that their press, or printer, is producing the proper density of color. The 10 percent part of the calibration bar, for example, actually should be 10 percent when the commercial printer measures it with a device called a *densitometer*. Densitometers are precision instruments designed to measure the tonal values in printed material. If you are printing CMYK separations, the Calibration Bar feature adds a progressive color bar. Progressive proofs are used at commercial printers to check the alignment and density values of the C, M, Y, and K values of pigments as they are applied in combination on the printed page. To see an example of a calibration bar in action, take apart a cereal box or other printed package. Usually calibration bars are printed on the inside flaps as a method for proofing a production run as it comes off the presses.

Corner and Center Crop Marks Check Boxes

If your image does not fill the page and will be trimmed physically to the edges of the image, you can specify that Corner or Center crop marks be printed. Check both boxes to print both kinds of crop marks.

Negative and Emulsion Down Check Boxes

You use these options when you print film to make printing plates. Check with your printer to determine how these options should be set for the printing press that will be used. *Don't* guess or make an assumption based on something you might have heard or read, or you might go to the expense of producing film that is unusable. When you are printing a complete, finished image on paper, however, these check boxes always should be left *unchecked*.

Interpolation Check Box

This option applies only to some PostScript Level 2 printers. If you are printing a low-resolution image, a check in this check box instructs the printer to increase (sample up) the resolution of the image. The advantage to using this option is that interpolation reduces a low-resolution image's tendency to produce stair-step, aliased edges. The disadvantage is that overall image quality is reduced, and the focus of the image will not be as clear as it is on the monitor. If you feel that interpolation of the image is necessary for final output, choose Image, Image Size in Photoshop and then increase the Print Size dimensions or resolution with the Resample Image box checked. In Photoshop, you have the opportunity to see what the effect of the interpolation will be; when the printer does it, you pay for a print with which you might be dissatisfied.

Using the Print Command from the File Menu

After you have set all the Page Setup options, it's time to actually print the image, using Photoshop's File, Print (Ctrl (⌘)+P) command. This dialog box usually looks the same, no matter what kind of printer you are printing to. The important settings are Print Quality, Print As, and Encoding (only available with PostScript printer drivers). Print Quality should be set to the highest level your printer is capable of producing. The color mode chosen in the Print As field should match the color mode of the printer. As noted earlier, most personal color printers expect RGB input and not CMYK.

Printing to Different Color Modes

Photoshop is capable of printing a color image to a black-and-white printer, and although the authors recommend grayscale mode images as the best visual data to send to a black-and-white printer, there will be times when your intended final output is to color separations, not as a single image that represents a monochrome copy of your original color piece. If you have a PostScript printer driver defined as your intended output device, Photoshop's Print dialog box looks a little different than when a non-PostScript printer is defined. Only with PostScript output do you have a complete set of output options. The bottom of the Print dialog box has a Print As field that contains Gray(scale), RGB, and CMYK options (see fig. 16.15).

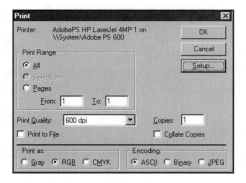

figure 16.15
Photoshop enables you to send to the printer information that's organized in different color modes.

These Print As options appear in the Print dialog box for all kinds of printers when the image you're printing is a color image, but are not displayed when you print a grayscale image. Although these options are convenient for default printing to a personal printer, they aren't really acceptable if you want to get the best possible black-and-white print from an image.

Choosing RGB

A black-and-white printer doesn't understand color information; its only concern is the way black toner is distributed. When RGB is chosen in the Print As field, Photoshop sends all color information in the file to the printer. The printer discards most of the information, processing only what it thinks is pertinent to printing the image as black dots of toner on the page. When you print a color image to a grayscale printer, the results are never optimal, and the process is slow because the printer must figure out what information to discard and what to keep, based on a pre-established set of rules programmed by the printer manufacturer. A similar printer "bottleneck" is created when you try to print an image with a resolution higher than that of the printer.

Choosing Grayscale

If you choose Gray(scale) from the Print As field, Photoshop decides what information is used to produce the print. Photoshop makes an internal copy of your color image and converts it to Grayscale, using its normal method for converting color images to Grayscale mode. Although this is a better course of action than choosing RGB information to send to the printer, Photoshop's Grayscale mode conversion methods are *not* the best way to produce a grayscale image. See Chapter 11 for information about accurate RGB-to-grayscale conversions. The best quality laser prints are produced from images that start with good tonal separation of image areas, have been manually converted to the appropriate grayscale file format, and in which the grayscale image has been adjusted to bring it in line with the capability of the printer.

Choosing CMYK

Of all the modes for output, Print As CMYK is most likely to get you into trouble unless you understand what outputting to this mode actually does. It takes your image and converts a copy to CMYK, using the same process Photoshop uses when you choose Image, Mode, CMYK color from the menu. When you print using this method, you're working blind—you cannot preview the changes or see whether colors are out of gamut. Additionally, if you are printing to most personal color printers, the results will not be the best you can get because the printer and its drivers are optimized to handle RGB data from you, not CMYK. This method also produces a composite color image, not color separations.

When you want color separations, you must first convert a copy of your work to CMYK mode (Image, Mode, CMYK color), and then check the Print Separations check box to begin the separation printing process. The authors do not advise that users without an extensive background in color printing create their own separations. If you must produce your own separations, see the following sections on color separation specifics.

When you print to a personal color printer, you are unlikely to need to print to CMYK or to convert the image you want to print. Most affordable inkjet color printers insist on using their own internal conversion circuitry to read image data in RGB mode to print CMYK inks.

It should be noted here that PostScript Level 2 color printers actually prefer to take LAB Color data. You will get crisp colors and a better image if you send a LAB color mode image to these types of printers. PostScript Level 1 printers (found in older personal printers and imagesetters) do not handle LAB color gracefully. Use RGB for personal color printers and CMYK for imagesetters.

Encoding Options

An additional field, Encoding, sometimes appears at the bottom right of the Print dialog box, depending on the printer driver you are using. When Encoding is an option, the print should be set to ASCII for greatest compatibility when printing over a network. Binary is the option of choice if your printer supports binary mode and is attached to your computer. Binary prints about twice as fast as ASCII. JPEG encoding is useful when you want to print very quickly and are willing to put up with the information loss associated with JPEG compression.

Finally, the Print to File option should *not* be checked if you expect a hard-copy version of your work to come out of your printer. Later in this chapter we discuss Print to File options as a strategy of getting your work to a service bureau.

After you decide on all the settings on this dialog box, click on OK and wait for your image to come out of the printer. You might have to be patient; large, photorealistic images, printed at high-quality settings, can take a long time to print.

TIP

If you want to print only part of an image, use the Rectangular Marquee tool to select the area you want to print. All the pixels within the marquee must be opaque. Press Ctrl (⌘)+P. In the Print dialog box, choose Selection in the Range field and click on OK.

Increasing Print Quality, Decreasing Artist Involvement

You have seen in this chapter what you can do by yourself with a high-resolution laser printer and Photoshop methods that optimize an image for the best reproduction. As you gain experience with imaging, however, you will find that you are spending equal amounts of time at your computer and at the commercial printer. You will become familiar with the special requirements of a specific printing press and learn to trust the people who render your work as ink on the printed page.

This is also the time when you might consider abandoning the "home brew" halftone from your laser printer and letting the commercial printer render your computer file directly to an imagesetting device. Instead of depending on toner dots to render halftones, you may want to turn your work out on your service bureau's imagesetter. Imagesetters produce high-resolution film positives and negatives from digital files. The film produced by an imagesetter can be made into printing press plates. Some imagesetters skip the film step altogether and instead create a printing plate directly from your digital file.

Many of the formulas and techniques you have learned in this chapter also apply to work that is sent to an imagesetter. If you are producing images that will be part of a color printing run, there are additional Photoshop features you can take advantage of to ensure great work. If you are ready to take the plunge into other types of output, the next sections are for you.

Prepress and the Service Bureau

Most people don't have a commercial printing press hooked directly into their computer. They need to establish a link between the ethereal nature of digital images and such physical, tangible things as press plates and ink on paper. Your allies in bridging the gap between your artistic input and physical output are the prepress service bureau and the commercial printer.

A service bureau prepares and transforms your file into a form and a format that can be used to produce physical output. Service bureaus use expensive, complex equipment—imagesetters, film recorders, high-resolution color printers, and proofing devices are all the tools of high-quality output trade. The output from these devices might be all you need, as in the case of color laser prints or slides, to make your image come alive. On the other hand, to bring your images to the world, you might need to have film *separations* made, which any commercial printer can then use to make printing plates. If color printing from a commercial press is your goal, you will need the services of a prepress service bureau's imagesetter as the intermediate step to the printing press.

Service bureaus and commercial printers are not always two separate businesses; sometimes you find them under one roof. And even when they are separate businesses, the services they offer might overlap. Both a commercial printer and a service bureau might own imagesetters, digital color printers, and proofing devices. The difference between service bureaus and commercial printers is that the commercial printer makes printing plates from negatives and mass produces your work on high-speed presses that apply ink to paper. Regardless of whether your service bureau and commercial printer are at the same location, the roles that both firms play, and their knowledge of a specialized craft, are vital to successfully producing beautiful printed copies of your work.

How Prepress Savvy Do You Need to Be?

As a computer imagist, your first responsibility is to devote yur skills, talents, and time toward producing outstanding work. Like artists who seek mentors to help them refine their skills, you need to send your creations to people who are experts in their line of work. Although your level of involvement in producing a finished, printed copy of your imaging work is limited in some respects, you should understand a *few* things about the printing process. There are things you can do with a digital file before you send it to the service bureau or commercial printer that will make your business partner's work go more smoothly, and you will be happier with the completed image.

Although you certainly don't need to acquire all the skills and knowledge that these folks have, you *do* need to know how to deliver digital copies of your color and grayscale work to them so that they can be successful in transforming your digital image into a physical image. You also need to know what kinds of services they provide, what to expect when you engage their services, and how their equipment affects many of your most basic design decisions.

If you're reading this chapter in sequence, you already have begun the process of learning what you need to know to be able to make the service bureau and the commercial printers your partners. PostScript technology, the way halftone cells and screening work, and the relationship between resolution and file dimensions are all as important to the production of commercially printed output as they are to personal printed output.

Strategies for Getting Your Work Out the Door

To increase the distribution of your work in a high-quality medium, you need to give a commercial printer a copy of your digital image file. Up to this point we have provided one of two ways to accomplish this goal—by creating an in-house camera-ready hard copy of your work. But because not all commercial printers are computer-equipped, and partly because properly preparing photographic images for reproduction on a printing press always has been highly specialized work, the service bureau was born. The service that the staff at a prepress service bureau performs is to take your files and prep them for printing. Preparing your files for printing entails, at the very least, the use of an imagesetter or film recorder that renders digital files to film. After your image is on film, any printer can make the printing plates for the press.

So the real trick to producing high-quality output is how you go about bundling your work and getting it to the service bureau in a format they can render to camera-ready format. The following sections discuss the special processing and saving you will need to perform on copies of your Photoshop files.

Working with CMYK Images

If the intended output for your Photoshop work is a four-color printing press, you need to send your images to the service bureau in CMYK color mode. This color model uses four color channels to produce the colors that can be printed on a printing press. CMYK's gamut of colors is smaller than that available in RGB mode; our eyes can see a wider gamut of color than can be reproduced by using subtractive, reflective color pigments.

When the three process colors (cyan, magenta, and yellow) are mixed, they produce other colors. When the colors are mixed in equal proportions, black *should* be produced. Impurities in ink pigments usually make it impossible for perfect black (absorption of all light) to be achieved, however. To circumvent this problem, an additional black color plate is used to apply black ink. A black separation plate is made from the weighted average of the three other color plates used to produce CMYK process color images.

Because the monitor you use to display your work uses a combination of additive red, green, and blue colors, you can never truly see on-screen what a CMYK color image looks like. For this reason, and because the extra channel the CMYK model uses creates much larger files, most image editing should be done by using the RGB color model. When editing is completed, convert a *copy* of the image to the CMYK model. Image quality is lost when you convert the same file from RGB to CMYK and back several times; always keep an RGB copy, and only convert duplicates to CMYK.

Using the Gamut Warning Feature

When you're working in RGB mode, it's easy to specify colors that cannot be faithfully reproduced in the CMYK model. These colors are said to be *out of gamut*. Happily, Photoshop provides you with several ways to identify and correct out-of-gamut colors, the easiest being Photoshop's Gamut Warning feature, found on the View menu.

In the following steps, Photoshop's Gamut Warning is used to identify any colors in the Flowers.tif image that cannot be converted faithfully to a CMYK color formulation.

DISPLAYING OUT-OF-GAMUT COLORS

CD-ROM

1. Open the Flowers.tif image from the CHAP16 folder of the Companion CD.

2. Double-click on the Hand tool to make the image display at a viewing resolution that is full screen without window scroll bars.

3. Press Ctrl(⌘)+Shift+Y (View, Gamut Warning). Suddenly the brighter flowers in the image have spots of flat color all over them (see fig. 16.16). These specks mark the colors that are out of gamut.

   Don't close the image; you use it in the next set of steps.

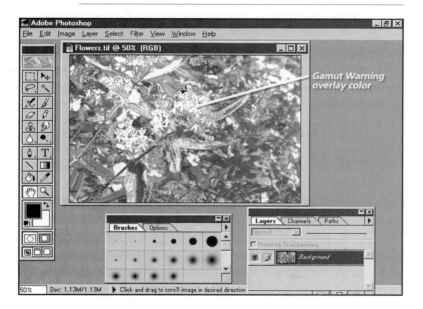

figure 16.16

Photoshop displays a Gamut Warning overlay in the image window to indicate which areas of the image cannot be printed to CMYK inks.

You set the color used to mark out-of-gamut colors by choosing Preferences, Display and Gamut. Depending on the colors in the image, you might want to choose a Gamut Warning color that contrasts against the original image information. White was chosen for the Flowers.tif image because white is not found within the image.

To correct out-of-gamut colors in the image, you need to change the highlighted areas to similar colors that are CMYK-legal. The Sponge tool can be effectively used to bring colors back into gamut in isolated image areas; the Gamut Warning colors provide an in-place marker in the image for only those areas that require color changing.

BRINGING COLORS BACK INTO GAMUT

1. Choose the Sponge tool from the toning tools flyout on the toolbox.
2. On the Options palette, choose Desaturate from the drop-down list. A 50% Pressure setting is good for this example.
3. On the Brushes palette, choose the 35-pixel diameter tip.
4. Carefully drag back and forth over an area that displays the Gamut Warning color (see fig. 16.17). A second application of the Sponge tool might be necessary in some areas that display the greatest concentration of the Gamut Warning color.

figure 16.17
Use the Sponge tool in its Desaturate setting to remove some of the out-of-gamut colors from the image.

5. Press Ctrl(⌘)+Shift+S (File, Save As) and save the image to your hard disk as Flowers.tif.

Many times, as in this example, images that are fairly bursting with color cannot be successfully printed to CMYK because of the saturation of colors—the purity and strength of a hue as compared to other hues present in certain colors. Although the

Sponge tool does a remarkable feat reducing the amount of saturation in local areas within the image, it also makes the areas look visually duller. This can be corrected to a certain extent after the image has been converted to CMYK mode, as discussed in the following section.

Converting RGB Images to CMYK

Converting an RGB image to CMYK is simple to do. Choose CMYK Color from the Image Mode menu. You should not click on the menu option without first ensuring that your monitor is correctly calibrated, however. Calibration is important because Photoshop uses the RGB values it finds in your image and builds equivalency tables that convert RGB colors to the appropriate CMYK formulations. If your monitor is not calibrated properly, you will not get what you expect when your image rolls off the presses. Before proceeding, be sure to see Chapter 3, "Personalizing Photoshop: Preferences and Options," for tips and steps to using Photoshop's calibration features.

Photoshop *also* considers the settings in the Printing Inks Setup and the Separation Setup dialog boxes found on the File, Color Settings menu. The only person who can tell you what the Printing Inks should be is the commercial printer on whose presses this particular image will be printed. All these values depend on the kinds of paper, ink, and printing presses used. The choices you make in the Separation Setup dialog box require you to know which method—GCR or UCR—the printer plans to use, and what the settings for each should be. GCR *(Gray Component Removal)* and UCR *(Undercolor Removal)* are strategies that printers use to reduce the amount of process colors used in areas that are neutral or black, and then replace them with black ink. This is done to prevent muddiness and to prevent more ink from being applied in one area than can be absorbed by the paper. In the Printing Inks Setup dialog box, there is a huge laundry list of different kinds of paper and printers. Additionally, Photoshop compensates for the percentage of expected dot gain—the amount of spread a dot of ink will take on when applied and absorbed into the paper fibers.

Never guess about these settings, and don't waste your time and money converting RGB images to CMYK and then printing separations unless you have thoroughly discussed these settings with the commercial printer.

WARNING

If you change any of these prepress settings, including Monitor Calibration settings, after you have converted an image to CMYK, you will have to throw out the image and create a new one from a saved RGB copy of the image. *You should never convert an RGB image to CMYK and then convert it back.* You will lose a great deal of color information because the CMYK color gamut is smaller than the RGB color gamut. After the color information has been converted to CMYK, it cannot be returned to its original RGB values, and you are stuck with CMYK colors.

Always make a copy of an RGB image and convert the copy to CMYK. Then, if you have to make adjustments, you still have the original RGB image from which a new CMYK file can be created.

If you're certain that Photoshop's File/Color Settings have been defined correctly, choose Image, Mode, and then choose CMYK color to convert the Flowers.tif image to printing color mode. To enhance the image's colors at this point, you might opt to use the Levels command to increase the contrast slightly in the image. Doing this assigns more neutral, tonal image information to areas in the image that lack contrast, and reinforces the presence of underlying colors. This action does change original image content, but if your goal is to create the best hard copy of a digital file, the appearance of the printed copy is what matters (and not a copy of the file as you see it on your monitor).

Printing Color Separations

When you have a properly made CMYK image before you, you can print color separations if you know exactly what printer settings to make. (These settings are described in the personal color printing section earlier in this chapter.) To make a perfect CMYK file, you need to have long conversations with your commercial printer. To print color separations, you need to know everything there is to know about the printer that will be used to create the separations. Most likely, if you are going to the expense of printing the image to a commercial color printing press, you will need better resolution than you can get from any personal printer you own. You need the services of an imagesetter. Imagesetters have resolutions that span the range from 1,200 dpi to more than 3,000 dpi, and can cost up to $500,000.

If you are having a service bureau print the separations to paper or film, give them the CMYK file and let them set it up for their imagesetter. Make sure that they know who the commercial printer for this project is, and encourage them to discuss the assignment with the commercial printer if they have any questions. You are expected to supply at least the following standard information about the commercial printer's requirements:

◆ Whether the image should be negative or positive

◆ Whether the image should be imaged emulsion up or down

◆ The optimal screen frequency for the printing press, the paper, and the inks that will be used

◆ The shape of halftone dots that should be used, and the screen angles for the plates that the commercial printer finds work best with the printing press

◆ The expected dot gain on the press

If, by chance, you have a PostScript printer that you want to use to create the color separations, you would make these settings—along with settings for crop marks, registration marks, and calibration bars—for your printer in the Page Setup dialog box, as discussed earlier in this chapter. Because you probably will be printing to paper and not to photographic film, leave the Negative and Emulsion Down options unchecked. Then you choose Print from the File menu and enter the necessary print quality value. Click on the Print Separations check box, and then click on OK. Four black-and-white prints will come tumbling out of your printer. The printer can use these paper print separations as camera-ready separations from which to make the printing plates.

Deciding Whether to Do Your Own Color Separations

You now know that Photoshop has the *capability* to generate color separations from an image. This means that the cyan, magenta, yellow, and black plates a commercial printer runs on a press can be made from laser camera-ready art you can provide. But the fact that Photoshop gives you the tools to generate the separations *doesn't* mean that you necessarily want to—or *should*—do this.

In addition to being the application of choice for artists on both the Macintosh and Windows platforms, Photoshop is a magnificent tool for commercial printing houses to use in their work. Many copies of this program are used in production departments, service bureaus, and advertising agencies because the *other* half of creating digital artwork is *printing* an image. And Photoshop has features to do both.

But color printing is a science, and as such, it is best left to professionals. For this reason, we recommend that artists and designers *not* use the bulk of Photoshop's color prepress features. Let the people who know best about the medium of *publishing* handle your work. You might go through two or three commercial printers or service bureaus before you settle on one that you can work with, who understands the style or look you want to convey in an image. You will learn much by working with a good prepress service bureau or printer, but why do what someone else is already doing well? (Unless you want to switch careers?)

A good commercial printer or service bureau that is wise in the ways of Adobe Photoshop can guide you and your work through the world of process printing. Only they know the best line screens, ink coverage, dot-gain settings, and emulsion placement needed to yield optimal results with the presses and the papers used to bring your work to life.

When you know how the assignment will be completed after it leaves your hands, you can plan your work (file size, color capability, resolution, and so on) in a way that ensures the best possible finished output.

Print to File Options

Occasionally, you will want to pack off your work for a service bureau or commercial printer as a "predigested" *Print to File* document. The advantage to printing an image to file is that all the recipients of this document have to do is load the file to a specific output device, and you can receive the work. Because you specify the printer settings and other options exactly as you would to a local printing device hooked up to your machine, you eliminate the guesswork—and the possibility of errors introduced by the party performing the rendering work. The receiving party doesn't even need to have Photoshop installed on the machine that drives the imagesetter.

The disadvantage to sending a Print to File document to a service is that they cannot tweak the piece, should there be any errors in dot-gain, image cropping or sizing, or other aspects of the image as sent to a printer.

In general, we advise against using Photoshop's Print dialog box's Print to File option as a means for transporting a design to a service bureau or commercial printer. The file will typically be larger than a TIFF equivalent of the same digital information, and Print to File documents require that you use the specific print driver used by the service bureau's imagesetter, or you're out of luck. If you have a compelling corporate or personal reason to choose the Print to File option, please run through the following checklist before you deliver the document to the service that will render the file:

◆ *Do you have the exact printer driver installed on your system that the service bureau or commercial printer uses?* Often, a service bureau will gladly copy its printer driver to a floppy disk for you to install, free of charge. This prevents headaches and ensures that the file is written in a way the service bureau's imagesetter will understand.

◆ *Do you know the type of encoding the service bureau uses?* If not, play it safe and encode the Print to File to ASCII encoding. ACSII is a universally understood printer language; it's slower and produces larger files than the Binary option in the Print dialog box, but Macintosh, DOS, Windows, and Unix machines can understand print commands as ASCII.

◆ *Are you certain that the file information is correct?* Print to File documents cannot be changed, except by a handful of individuals who can hack a PostScript file.

You might save spooling time at a service bureau by printing to file, but in many cases this option causes more headaches than you can imagine.

Printing to PDF or EPS

Because PostScript is platform-and device-independent, there have been numerous implementations of PostScript in different printers, and different interpreters for applications created that take advantage of this page description language. Unfortunately, this also leaves in question the "standard" for a specific design rendered to PostScript; often, a PostScript file will fail to render because of an illegal operator (a function that describes part of the PostScript code to the output device).

There are two ways to output a Photoshop piece to PostScript—to essentially print the design to file—that minimize possible PostScript errors and make your experience with the service bureau a hassle-free one.

When you print to file using a PostScript printer driver, you are locked into the specifics of the output device. It is almost as though you are printing by proxy. The Encapsulated PostScript (EPS) format, however, is also a PostScript page description of a file's contents; this file format can be placed in a container document for output. For example, you can place an EPS file in a PageMaker document and have the service bureau render a high-resolution imagesetter copy of the file. The benefit to writing a file to EPS format is that you have some control over how the file is written.

In Photoshop's EPS Format dialog box (see fig. 16.18) you can specify (or not specify) the screen angle used to print the image by checking the Include Halftone Screen check box. Transfer functions can also be included (or not) by checking the Include Transfer Function check box. Additionally, when you save to EPS format, you have your choice of encoding schemes (Hint: always use ASCII), the opportunity to write a low-resolution image for placement only if you decide this image should be part of a larger document, and you can specify that a path saved in the file should mask areas of the image (Clipping Path).

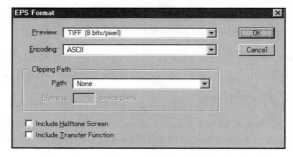

figure 16.18

Saving a file to the Encapsulated PostScript format enables you to print to file without including device-specific characteristics in the file.

The EPS format is "genuine" PostScript, and many different color and line screen properties of the design can be edited after the file has been written if you place the EPS file in a host document.

In the past year, many imaging professionals have turned to Adobe's Acrobat document format as a means for "cleaning up" PostScript files that do not output correctly to imagesetters. An EPS file written from Photoshop or another program can be converted to Acrobat format. Additionally, Photoshop 4 can save image files to Acrobat PDF format. Ask your commercial printer whether he can use an Acrobat document for final output to color printing. The Acrobat PDF file format is basically a goof-proof way to send your commercial printer a document that will output accurately.

The Film Recorder

As you have discovered throughout this book, there is a close, strong relationship between bitmap graphics and traditional photographic images. *Bitmapped images* portray graphical information as light and dark areas of continuous tones that our eyes recognize as a picture. The photosensitive grain of film and photographic paper also portray images as a wash of continuous tones. Many of the images you have worked with in this book, and many of the elements that comprise your own assignments, are traditional, photochemically based photographs that have been digitized.

Remarkable news for the digital imagist is that the conversion of photographic information to digital information is a two-way street. A device called a *film recorder* can take any image you have created or enhanced in Photoshop and faithfully render it to the familiar, aesthetically pleasing, and eminently practical medium of color film, as a film negative or transparency. You can find high-resolution film recorders at a special kind of service bureau, commonly called a *slide imaging service bureau*, or *imaging center*. Learning how to work with this type of service bureau should be high on your list of priorities because there is no greater satisfaction for the professional designer or hobbyist than to hold in your hands a photograph of your Photoshop work.

This section shows you how to prepare a digital image in Photoshop, to produce the best results on photographic film.

Formats of Film Recorder Output

The most common film recorder found at an imaging center is one that renders digital images to 35mm film. Slides are the mainstay of business presentations today, whereas a photographer gets more mileage from a 35mm negative. Each of these needs is accommodated through the use of the same film recorder. Larger-format output film recorders are also found in specialty imaging centers that handle 4 × 5-inch or 8 × 10-inch film. The 4 × 5-inch formats can be used to produce high-quality, poster-sized prints for high-quality color publishing and for the television industry. The 8 × 10 format is most commonly used to produce high-quality overhead transparencies for corporate and educational presentations. This format is also used to produce wall-size enlargements for trade shows, for motion picture industry special effects work, and to meet the demanding requirements of very high-end, color-critical publishing.

Transferring a Photoshop Image to Film

Before you start packing up images to take advantage of the digital-to-film experience, you need to explore some of the finer points of working with film and the imaging center. To ensure that your Photoshop-to-film work looks every byte as good as it does on your monitor, you need to understand the special requirements a film recorder has for the data it writes—preferred file formats, data types, aspect ratios, monitor settings, and the size of your file. These are universal considerations, regardless of the type of film recorder output you need. The following sections show you how each of these digital issues can affect your work, pleasantly or otherwise, by focusing on the most popular product of a slide imaging center: the 35mm slide.

Your Monitor's Setup

Both your monitor and a film recorder use an RGB color model. When you save a Photoshop file in a 24-bit RGB file format, such as TIFF or Targa, every color used in the file has been described in terms of its red, green, and blue values. The film recorder reads these values to determine how to expose the film. If your monitor is properly calibrated, the colors you see on-screen will be represented accurately on the slide. If your monitor is *not* properly calibrated, you might get orange instead of gold, and purple where you wanted blue, in the finished piece of film.

Color-matching is a sport to be engaged in by every individual who cares about accurate output, but it's also a game in which you can never declare a decisive "win." A monitor, a television set, film, press ink on paper, the *same* ink on *different* paper, and different printing technologies—inkjet, thermal wax, dye sublimation—all display color differently because they use different physical materials and different technologies to express color. One technology might not be able to express a color that another technology can express. Fortunately, *film* can express a wide range of colors. If you use a properly calibrated monitor to edit your image, the colors you see on-screen can be accurately rendered to film.

Matching your monitor's gamma to an individual film recorder's CRT—the *cathode ray tube*, the central imaging element in a film recorder—involves an element of trial and error. Ask your service bureau what the gamma of their film recorder is, and set your monitor to match their figure. The gamma of a film recorder's CRT will most likely fall somewhere between 1.7 and 2.1. After calibrating your monitor to match the imaging center's gamma, save the calibration settings in Photoshop and send the center an image to process as a test image. See Chapter 3 for information about calibrating your monitor, setting monitor gamma, and saving custom settings. If the slide comes back too brilliant or too dull, reduce or increase your gamma by a few tenths of a point and try again. When you find the magic gamma figure, save this setting so that you can reuse it when you create images that will be rendered to film by the *same* film recorder at the *same* service bureau.

The gamma setting that produces the best results with the imaging center's film recorder may change over time. Gamma is a somewhat elusive factor—as monitors and CRTs age, their light-producing phosphors dim, and gamma values change. The changes in gamma caused by aging phosphors happen gradually, and you may not notice that changes are occurring. It's a good idea to take a critical look at your output for signs that you and the service bureau are drifting out of synchrony. If you find that your images are coming out a tad brighter or duller than they used to, it's time to make adjustments to your gamma settings.

Sending the Right Size File

Determining the proper file size to send to a service bureau for slide-making is not as straightforward a process as determining resolution for print presses. Printing to paper and film imaging are different processes and different media. Measurements for image files rendered by film recorders are expressed in storage units (kilobytes and megabytes), not in pixels per inch. The ultimate quality of a film recorder's output is based on *how much* information the film recorder can handle *and* how much information you have given it to work with.

When service bureaus describe their services, they sometimes say that they do 2-KB (2,000-line), 4-KB (4,000-line), or 8-KB (8,000-line) imaging. These terms refer to the size of the *pixel grid* the film recorder can render. When a file is imaged at 2 KB, the "2 KB" describes a pixel grid 2,048 pixels wide by 2,048 pixels high. A 4 KB image is a pixel grid of 4,096 by 4,096. A 24-bit RGB file that is 2,048 pixels wide by 1,365 pixels high (2:3 ratio) produces an 8 MB file. A grayscale image of the same size is only 2.67 MB. A 24-bit RGB file imaged to 4 KB and in a 2:3 ratio would be 4,086 pixels wide by 2,731 pixels high, and would occupy 32 MB, whereas its grayscale counterpart would occupy only 10.7 MB.

Service bureaus usually base a large portion of their imaging fees on the size of the file you bring to them because the larger the file, the harder it is to handle. Large files also take up large amounts of the bureau's hard disk space and take longer to image than smaller files. Files under 5 MB are fairly inexpensive to image (usually under $20), but you should expect higher imaging costs for 20–30 MB files.

How Large Is Large Enough?

So how large *should* your file be? There *is* no hard and fast rule. It depends on what you want to do with the slide, how detailed the slide is, and how critical an eye your viewing audience has. Slides have nice juicy colors; when slides are projected, the difference between a "low-resolution" slide and a "high-resolution" slide is often difficult to see because of the typically low quality of the projection equipment and the screen. If you look at both slides, side-by-side, through a loupe, on a good day, in a good mood—you might see a significant difference.

Most service bureaus are willing to run a test slide or two for you or provide you with samples of slides imaged from different-sized files. Experiment with different sizes of files to find the size that suits your needs, your patience, and your pocketbook. Files that are too large to fit on a floppy disk are unwieldy to transport. Time is money to a service bureau. Large files take longer to process—and you are charged for that time.

The fundamental question of how large your image should be boils down to your definition of *acceptable*—a relative term, but we place it at somewhere between 1.13 MB and 4.5 MB. Ask your service bureau to show you slides they have made from files of different sizes so that you get the scope of the meaning of "acceptable."

Using the Proper Aspect Ratio

Aspect ratio is the height-to-width proportion of an image, as described in Chapter 8, "Correcting Images." If you want your image to fill the entire frame of the film to which it is rendered, your image and the film must have the same aspect ratio. The aspect ratio of 35mm film is 2:3; 4×5 and 8×10-inch film share the same 4:5 aspect ratio. If you anticipate sending an image to a film recorder, you should plan your composition so that the ratio of the image's height to width will match that of the film format to which you will render the image.

One of the things that sends technicians at a service bureau up the wall is a file that doesn't have the proper aspect ratio. Regardless of how artistically inclined the bureau's staff is, you probably will not be happy if the bureau adjusts your image to fit the aspect ratio. When your image doesn't fill the frame, the service bureau has a decision to make—to crop or not to crop. If they crop the image, they are forced to make an artistic decision that was *your* responsibility to make as a designer.

Achieving the Proper Aspect Ratio

You don't have to be a math wizard, or even own a pocket calculator, to ensure that your work has the proper aspect ratio. Let Photoshop do the math for you and then use your eye to decide whether to crop or to place a background around the image to make the overall image dimensions correspond to the aspect ratio of the film.

The following steps show you how to "trick" Photoshop into figuring out the dimensions your image has to have to achieve the proper aspect ratio for imaging to 35mm film.

Determining an Image's Aspect Ratio

CD-ROM

1. Press Ctrl(⌘)+N to display the New dialog box.

2. Click on the Units drop-down list for Width, and choose Inches; do the same with the Height drop-down list.

3. Click on the Mode drop-down list and choose Grayscale. Any mode can be used here, but Grayscale uses one-third the system resources of RGB mode images.

4. In the Width field, type **3**; in the Height field, type **2**; in the Resolution field, type **72**. Accept the default name of Untitled-1 and click on OK to open the new document.

   If you're sending work for large-format output (4 × 5-inch or 8 × 10-inch), put **5** in the Height field and **4** in the Width field. These two formats share the same 4:5 aspect ratio. Traditionally, 35mm work is imaged in landscape mode and larger formats are imaged in portrait mode.

5. Open the Pastime.tif file from the CHAP16 folder on the Companion CD.

6. Choose Image, Image Size; change the units to inches (if not already set that way).

7. With the Resample Image box *unchecked,* type **3** in the Width field. The image Resolution will change. The new Height for the image is displayed as 2.737 " (see fig. 16.19).

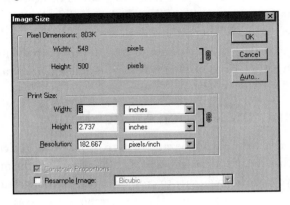

figure 16.19
Constrain the proportions of the Print Size boxes to arrive at the aspect ratio of the target image.

The Height value of 2.737 means that the Pastime.tif image has an aspect ratio of 2.737 to 3, which is not the desired 2:3 aspect ratio for full-frame rendering to a 35mm film recorder.

8. Hold Alt(Opt) and click on the Reset button (which is the Cancel button when Alt(Opt) is not held). Write (on paper) the original Width and Height values (7.611 and 6.944), and then click on Cancel.

    You pressed Cancel because you *do not* want to change the image size of Pastime.tif yet.

___

Don't close the Pastime image yet. You need it for the next set of steps.

When the Constrain Proportion box is checked in the Image Size dialog box, changing one dimension changes the other automatically to a value that retains the image's *current* aspect ratio (proportions). By setting the value to 3 in the width box, you can quickly determine whether the image can be scaled to a 2:3 proportion. In this example, the height is greater than 2, which indicates that it is not a 2:3 proportioned image. To bring this image into a 2:3 ratio without altering the design, you have to crop the image or add to it. But you might not want to crop one of your finished images *or* build more image information around one aspect of the image's borders. A good alternative, which is also image-enhancing, is to increase the size of the background canvas to create a border around the image, bringing the overall image into the proper aspect ratio.

Here's how to flesh out the image's proportions to make it suitable for a film recorder.

CALCULATING AN ASPECT RATIO

1. Click on Untitled-1's title bar (the 2"×3" blank image) to make it the current document in Photoshop.

2. Choose Image, Image Size. Type **7.25** in the Height field. 7.25" is slightly larger than Pastime.tif's 6.9" original height, but you will want a background on all sides of the image, not simply the height aspect of the picture. After you type the new Height, the Width field in the dialog box displays 10.875". Write down these numbers.

3. Click on Cancel, and close Untitled-1 without saving it. Pastime.tif is now the current image in Photoshop.

4. Press I (Eyedropper tool) and click on a dark sky area in the image. The current foreground color in Photoshop is now dark blue.

5. Press **X** (Switch Foreground/Background colors).

6. Choose Image, Canvas Size. Choose inches from the Width drop-down list and type **10.875** in the Width field. Choose inches for the Height field, type **7.25** in the field (see fig. 16.20), and then click on OK.

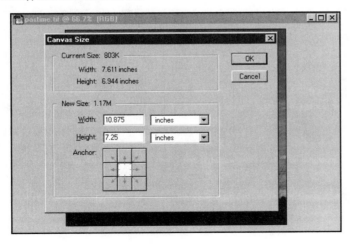

figure 16.20
Changing the size of the canvas brings the image to the proper aspect ratio.

7. Press Ctrl(⌘)+Shift+S (File, Save As), and then save the image to your hard disk in the TIFF file format. You now have a centered image with a border in a color that complements the image and can be sent to a service bureau for film recording (see fig. 16.21).

figure 16.21
Pastime.tif now has the proper aspect ratio for a slide—and also looks good.

An image's size and the way it's positioned on the canvas are design decisions you make for each image—but the math for obtaining the proper aspect ratio is always the same.

TIP

If you have a film recorder attached to your computer, and you're imaging your file from Photoshop, you could have Photoshop insert a background color for you. This option is available when you choose File, Page Setup and then click on the Background button in the lower-left corner of the Page Setup dialog box. Choose a color for the background in the color picker, and click on OK. This doesn't change the image—just the way it prints. If you use this option, you cannot preview the image to see what it looks like before you image the file. This method leaves more to chance than adjusting the canvas size does.

Making 35mm Negatives

If you plan to have a large, high-quality photographic print made from the negative, the first thing you need to consider is file size. You will want to send a larger file than you normally send for a slide. Just as you need a large-format negative to make a really large print in traditional photography, with digital photography, larger files go hand-in-hand with larger prints because they contain more information.

As with a slide, there is no hard and fast rule for what size file makes an "acceptable" print. Kodak states that photofinishers should not make prints larger than 8 inches by 10 inches from the standard version of a Kodak PhotoCD file, a special digital format whose multiple resolutions include an 18 MB BASE file. We believe that Kodak's definition of what an acceptable print looks like is a little overestimated, and that you will find a print made with a much smaller file to be "acceptable." Again, as with the slides, file size is a matter in which you have to find your own level of comfort, as you find the balance between file size and quality of the output.

If your commercial printer is not a computer "guru," and you plan to give him or her the negative for traditional prepress production and placement into a printed document, produce your negative from a larger file.

Whether it's for the printing press or for you, tell the service bureau *why* you want a negative made. If the service bureau is aware of the specific purpose for the negative, they can make tiny adjustments to the film recorder's settings and "tweak" the negative so that it is optimized for photographic printing or print press printing.

In the previous section on slide preparation, you increased the canvas size of an image to a 2:3 proportion and made that additional canvas a dark color. Dark borders on slides are good because they keep the audience's attention on the image information, and spare viewers from the brilliant light of the projector as it passes through clear areas in the slide. But on prints and negatives, the tradition is to use white borders instead of dark ones. White is the border color most people expect on a print. And if the image is to be cropped, white usually makes the "live area" (the image area) easier to crop.

NOTE

There are a few points you need to take into account if your intention is to have a paper print of your image made from the film recorded negative. When prints are made from film with automated photo-printing equipment, 3 percent or more of the image is cropped on all sides. If you go the more expensive route and have your prints custom printed by a human being using a photographic enlarger, the entire image will appear in the print.

As you've seen, an important step before you prepare your image for output is to calibrate your gamma to the film recorder's gamma, or consult with the commercial printer. Similarly, you should decide where and how (machine printed or custom printed) the negatives you have made will be printed. If you only occasionally have prints made of images you've had film-recorded, be sure to leave at least a 5-percent border of white canvas on all four sides of your image to compensate for the cropping an automated photo-printer performs.

Additionally, when you order your prints, remember that the aspect ratio of the photographic paper should closely match that of the film. In other words, when printing from a 35mm negative, have 4" × 6" or 8" × 12" prints made. The results of printing a 35mm negative to 8" × 10" paper are usually very disappointing.

Converting a Portrait Design to a Landscape Slide

Most film recorders are set up for landscape imaging, which satisfies the needs of most users. Before you save your file to disk to send to the service bureau, you might want to turn your image on its side to get the whole image in frame and avoid excessive cropping.

Photoshop makes this easy for you to do, although the process is not so easy on your system's resources. Rotating images is processor-intensive. It's a Photoshop effect, similar to the Perspective or Distort command, in that Rotate tells Photoshop to recalculate the color values for every selected pixel in the image. Before you use the Rotate command, be sure that you have flattened the image and eliminated any unnecessary channels and paths. You should also close any other images you have open and make sure that you aren't running any other applications, such as word processors or screen savers, in the background. To rotate the image from portrait to landscape, click on the Image menu, choose Rotate Canvas, and then click on 90° CW or 90° CCW.

Summary

Regardless of the route you take to get your images out of the computer and onto media you can pass around, the key to successful images is the quality of the rendered image. Use monitor calibration up to a certain point, and then depend on the principles you have learned in this chapter and your artistic eye to evaluate what makes the best image rendered to physical media.

Chapter 17, "Mixed Media and Photoshop," focuses on "new media" and the art of expressing one's concepts by porting traditional art forms, such as a pen and ink cartoon, into the digital realm of Photoshop. You will see how a simple line drawing can benefit from Photoshop's media integration capabilities, some complex fills, and artwork created inside the computer.

CHAPTER

MIXED MEDIA AND PHOTOSHOP

Although many skilled professionals depend upon Photoshop for prepress color correction and for photographic image retouching, there is a creative side to Photoshop, whose bounds are limited only by the user's imagination and ability to bring source material other than digital images into the application.

In this chapter, you experiment with the transformation of a traditional art form—a pen-and-ink cartoon—to see how different types of digital elements can be incorporated into a Photoshop composition.

Creating a Digital Cartoon

Artists from a variety of traditional disciplines approach Photoshop as the gateway for creative expression with new media—the Web, *Director!* movies, interactive titles, and desktop publishing, to name but a few. A frequent question is, "How do I make a digital cartoon?" Today, many comic books have turned to glossy, high-quality stock, and the content creators have made the move to the digital equivalents of Bristol board, brushes, pens, and permanent inks. This chapter describes an easy migration path to Photoshop cartooning from the physical drafting table.

Scanning a Physical Pen-and-Ink Drawing

No matter how good the digitizing tablet, the authors' experience is that nothing compares stylistically to a scan of a physically drawn cartoon or other type of line drawing. The expression of the lines, the way the ink takes to the paper, and other characteristics that the artist controls directly can be successfully digitized to produce a more human quality in the art.

This adventure in porting a physical cartoon begins with scanning a drawing.

Working at the Optimal Drawing Size for Scanning

As mentioned throughout this book, your final output of a design should be taken into account before you place one pixel in a document window. For digital sampling—the *acquisition phase*—you should have a sufficient amount of physical area on a piece of paper to enable you to work with the art in its digital state. Too few samples can result in a harsh, unaesthetic digital design that cannot be manipulated successfully in Photoshop, whereas oversampling a physical cartoon can create a needlessly large file that is unwieldy to work with on a system with modest resources.

In figure 17.1, you can see the TWAIN interface for the authors' Microtek flatbed scanner, with a physical cartoon sample in the preview window. If your system is configured to use a scanner, we will walk through some of the settings you will want to use for your own work. If you are working in Windows 95, you can take advantage of Photoshop's 32-bit TWAIN drivers. In either case, the command in Photoshop to activate the scanner interface is File, Acquire; options unique to your scanner can be found under this menu.

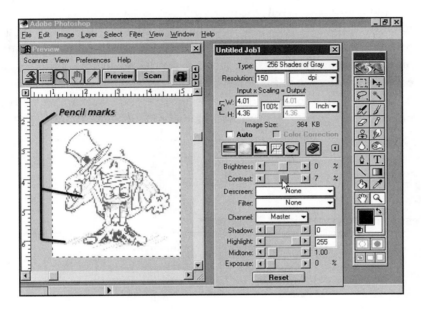

figure 17.1

Sample a physical piece of artwork from within Photoshop by using scanning hardware and software.

As you can see from this figure, the original cartoon on paper is about 4 inches on a side. If you don't like to work this small on paper, that is okay. To arrive at an optimal drawing sample, the important scanning factors are sampling resolution and color mode. In figure 17.1, you can see that the scan resolution is defined at 150 pixels per inch. This setting yields enough pixel samples of the original image information for you to work with in Photoshop and other programs. Less than this amount of resolution can result in larger, fewer pixels per inch, a smaller overall file size, and pixels that represent a coarse, artificial-looking digital version. A greater resolution for scanning is often wasted digital information because very few output devices can print more than 150 pixels per inch.

Understanding Pixel Resolution

Pixels per inch is *not* an equivalent measurement to laser printer or imagesetter *dots per inch*. The terms are frequently (and incorrectly) used interchangeably in computer documentation. Typically, imagesetters and other output devices whose resolution is greater than 600 dpi are PostScript devices, and PostScript devices measure image resolution as printed to a surface (paper, film, and so on) in terms of line frequency, not dots per inch. At this point, the math that establishes an equivalency between pixels per inch in an image and lines per inch to film or paper is not very straightforward. If you have no experience working with a commercial printer, *line frequency*—the number of lines (of dots) per inch in a printed piece—is usually, but not always, half the pixel-per-inch resolution of a digital file. Table 17.1 provides you with target sizes for image resolution, line frequency, and the dot-per-inch value you can expect from a specific image.

Table 17.1

Image Resolution Versus Printer Resolution

File	Line Frequency	Output Resolution
90 pixels/inch	45–60 lpi	300 dpi
160 pixels/inch	80 lpi	600 dpi
200 pixels/inch	100 lpi	1,270 dpi
266 pixels/inch	133 lpi	2,540 dpi

The numbers quoted in table 17.1 are a rough average of the sort of output you can expect from various devices. Line frequency can be changed, increased, or decreased at the expense of the number of grayscale tones simulated in the printed image through halftoning. For more information on output see Chapter 16, "Outputting Your Input." Right now, remember that a 150 pixel/inch sample of the cartoon will output reasonably well at 1:1 dimensions.

The Best Color Scanning Mode

The assignment in this chapter is to take the sampled cartoon to a glorious color digital version, and to do this, one or two procedures are necessary to ensure the best reproduction.

From the artistic perspective, the best way to conceive of and to prepare a physical cartoon is to draw it with opaque ink or a brand new felt marker to ensure artistic stroke density, and to thoroughly remove pencil lines from the physical image before scanning. Notice that some pencil lines are visible in the scanner preview window in figure 17.1; this happens because scanners are extremely sensitive to any variation in tone within the physical sample. Because totally removing your pencil lines from an image that is being scanned is difficult to do, you might choose a soft lead pencil, or use tracing vellum on a pencil sketch to ink the design. Unwanted pencil lines often can be eliminated by adjusting the Brightness/Contrast controls for the scanner. If your scanner doesn't offer these options, you can remove most telltale pencil strokes by using Photoshop's Image, Adjust, Brightness/Contrast command after the image has been scanned.

In designing your physical piece, try to eliminate cross-hatching from your style; this technique overcomplicates design areas that can take a color fill later in the design process. Try to "think in color, but design in black and white," in anticipation of adding color fills later.

The color mode in which you scan should be grayscale, not RGB color and not black-and-white line art (*1 bit/pixel* is another commonly used name; also, Photoshop's *Bitmap* mode). If you scan a black-and-white image in color mode, you needlessly increase the file's color capacity at the acquisition phase; note that the saved file size in figure 17.1 is only about 500 KB in grayscale sampling mode. Note that 1-bit/pixel sampling produces a black- *or* white-only digital file, which, in turn, produces harsh, aliased edges in the scanned image. Clearly, you want the most natural-looking digital equivalent of your original pen strokes, and because digital samples are rectangular in shape, black or white pixel samples of your work will fail to produce anti-aliased edges in the digital sample.

Grayscale sampling mode softens the transition between background paper white and foreground ink black with a few grayscale pixels at the edges to keep the digital scan looking like the original.

Creating "Cell" Artwork from your Scanned Design

Working with a white background and a black foreground bitmap sample of your original artwork is tedious because adding color inevitably leads to replacing some of the black edgework with color. You simply cannot afford to spend the time carefully creating color edgework! Even traditional cartoonists (*cell animators*) use clear acetate for the art to be colored; the black outlines are rendered to the front of the acetate, and the opaque colored inks are then painted on the reverse side, or on a separate sheet of acetate.

One solution to the problem of prepping your design so that coloring it in Photoshop goes quickly is to copy the grayscale cartoon to an alpha channel in a blank color image. By following these steps you can create a black and *transparent* copy of your grayscale scan that you can color in later, using a separate Photoshop layer.

CREATING A BLACK AND TRANSPARENT ILLUSTRATION

CD-ROM

1. Open a grayscale design in Photoshop. If you need a design, Tophat.tif in the CHAP17 folder of the Companion CD can be used for this example. This image has been cleaned up from the original scan, and is ready to be embellished in Photoshop.

2. Press Ctrl(⌘)+N. With the New dialog box in the interface, click on the Window menu and choose Tophat.tif. You will replace Photoshop's default New file information with the dimensions of Tophat.tif.

3. Choose RGB color from the Mode drop-down list. Click on the Transparent Contents radio button, and then click on OK. The new document window displays the Photoshop grid pattern (the checkerboard) for transparent areas in the document because the window does not yet have any image content.

4. Click on the title bar of the Tophat.tif image to make it the current document in the workspace.

5. Make sure that the Channels palette is the currently displayed palette in the Layers/ Channels/Path grouped palette. Click on the Black channel title on the Channels palette, and then drag the title into the new document window (see fig. 17.2). The new document now has design content in a new alpha channel.

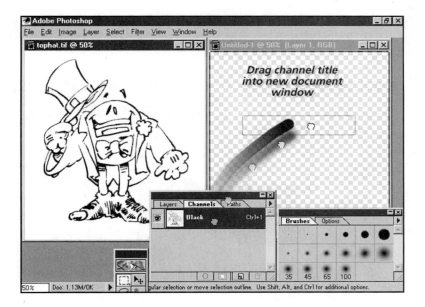

figure 17.2

Copy the channel information from the image to an alpha channel in a new document, for use as selection information.

6. With the new document currently in the foreground of the workspace, press Ctrl(⌘) and click on the #4 title on the Channels palette to load the design in channel #4 as a selection marquee.

   If for some reason you see a marquee line around the edge of the document window, the selection is inverted; this happens because the preferences for colors in the channel are reversed, to represent masking information instead of selection information. Press Ctrl(⌘)+Shift+I to make an inverse of the current marquee selection.

7. Press Ctrl(⌘)+~ (tilde) to ensure that all this channel switching hasn't accidentally moved you to a channel view instead of the main, color composite view of the new document. You can close the Tophat.tif image at any time without saving; you have the information you need from the file.

8. Press **D** (Default colors) to ensure that the current foreground color is black, and then press Alt(Opt)+Delete (Backspace) to fill the marquee selection above the layer with foreground color, as shown in figure 17.3.

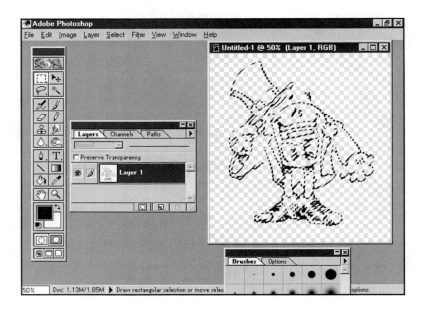

figure 17.3

Fill the marquee selection above the layer with foreground color to achieve a black and transparent version of the artwork.

9. Press Ctrl(⌘)+D to deselect the floating selection and merge the design with the layer.

10. Click on the Layers palette tab, click on the Create a new layer icon at the bottom of the Layers palette, and then drag the layer title on the Layers palette down beneath the original layer. This is the current editing layer, and color can be applied so that it appears to be filling the interiors of the cartoon design without altering the black "pen work" (see fig. 17.4).

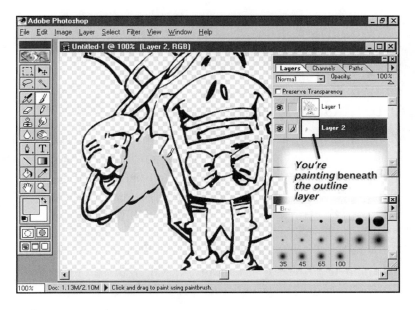

figure 17.4
Using Photoshop layers is equivalent to traditional cell animation for filling transparent interiors of a design.

11. Save the work to your hard disk in the Photoshop file format, as Tophat.psd. You can close the document now.

CD-ROM

Copying a grayscale image to an alpha channel for further loading and filling to achieve a cell of your design is perhaps the most basic technique for creating digital cartoons. After the Tophat image was scanned, it was refined by using Adobe Streamline, a bitmap-to-vector conversion utility, because the scan of the cartoon original was simply not clean enough after sampling to produce a professional quality illustration. If you open Scan-hat.tif, the original scanned image from the CHAP17 folder of the Companion CD, and try the earlier steps, you probably won't be happy with the results.

Read on for valuable information about Adobe Streamline's "clean up" powers, the resolution-independence of vector images, and how to edit the cartoon so that selected areas are transparent while other areas can have one or more colors.

AutoTracing Your Artwork

Adobe Streamline, a utility sold as a stand-alone product in addition to being part of the Illustrator bundle, intelligently examines a bitmap image based upon finding color edges in a design. Then, much like Photoshop's Pen tool, it creates a tracing along all the edges in the design by using splines (vector paths) and anchor points. The auto-trace can then be saved in Illustrator format and imported to Illustrator or any drawing program that can read this format. Then you can work with your pieces as a collection of paths, whose size on the page you can define.

"Streamlining" artwork is an additional step along the way toward creating a digital cartoon, but it might be worth your while for these reasons:

◆ Streamline is very literal in the paths it creates. Therefore, the bitmap scan of your art will look about 99 percent the way you originally drew it.

◆ A vector copy of your scanned design leaves very little "noise." Pencil lines that are not completely removed, as well as smudges and fuzzy lines that you have drawn, take on the crispness of a vector path. Your design contains only areas where you made a stroke and areas where you didn't—but no gray areas.

◆ You might or might not decide to refine your illustration as a vector design. The artist's hand is sometimes not quite perfect in the execution of lines on a physical page, but with the design in vector format, strokes can be smoothed out, and minute areas that need adjusting can be done in a click or two. Many times, though, Streamline's auto-trace procedure creates an Illustrator format file that needs no further tuning—you simply import the information to Photoshop, and it once again becomes a bitmap graphic.

◆ Vector graphics can be scaled to any size without loss of image quality. You can therefore create a very small or a very large scanned file, and adjust its size to arrive at the correct final output size.

One of the especially nice things about working with a cartoon in Illustrator format is that you have your choice not only of colors, but also for transparency in the design. For example, because Streamline leaves the exterior of a design empty, when Photoshop imports the design to bitmap format, *transparent* areas exist wherever there is an open line. Thus, you can import and then color a file from a drawing program such as Illustrator without having to go through any of the intermediate channel-selection steps.

The only caveat to auto-tracing your scanned cartoon is that shapes you draw in the original, physical cartoon should consist of short, unconnected strokes. If an area is enclosed by a pen stroke (a circle, for example), then instead of keeping the interior of the circle transparent, Streamline will overlay a white object on top of a larger, black object to represent the circle.

In figure 17.5 you can see the different results Streamline produces when you use a solid line, as opposed to a broken line, to create a shape. Don't think of this as a necessary step while you design the physical artwork, however. Breaks in the outline shapes can be made by using Photoshop's Eraser tool after the image has been scanned and saved to bitmap format, prior to using Streamline.

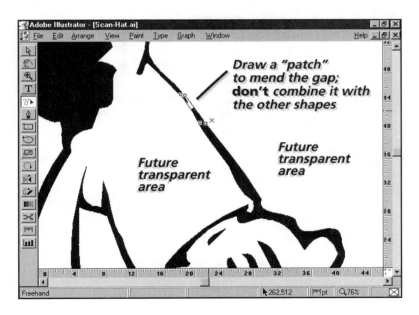

figure 17.5
A break in a design outline enables Streamline to trace around shapes, instead of stacking closed vector objects to represent the original bitmap image.

TIP

In addition to Adobe Streamline, CorelTRACE, CorelXARA, and other programs can perform auto-tracing, and save the resulting file to Illustrator format.

One of the options that Streamline features is Threshold, which decides where the edge is found in a grayscale image when a vector path is created. In figure 17.6, you can see that by reducing the Threshold on the scanned cartoon, line thickness in the original artwork can be increased with no user intervention.

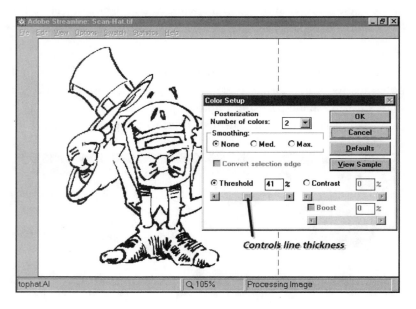

figure 17.6
Increasing or decreasing the Threshold in Streamline creates different outline thickness in the finished file.

The real trick to using an auto-tracing of your original bitmap work is to go into the file with your drawing program, combine (*compound*) objects that overlap, and make breaks in paths that have an excess of 100 anchor points (also called *control points* or *connection points*). Paths that contain too many anchor points might not import properly to Photoshop.

A good way to keep anchor point count to a reasonable number is to "patch" the breaks in an outline with a rectangle filled with the same color as the interior of an object. By doing this, you increase the size of the saved Illustrator file by a few objects, but when you import the file Photoshop interprets it as having a continuous outline with a transparent fill.

CD-ROM

If you own Illustrator, FreeHand, CorelDRAW!, or CorelXARA, and would like to perform the following steps to mend the breaks you made in the outline of an image before importing to Photoshop, use Tophat.ai from the CHAP17 folder of the Companion CD. Here's how to bring a cartoon into Photoshop as you envision it:

Editing a Vector Design

1. Open (or import) the Tophat file, or any Illustrator format design you like, in your drawing application.

2. Find the areas where you created breaks in the outline; the Tophat file has several of them on the left side of the cartoon character.

3. With the pen tool in your application, draw a series of connected lines that are located on top of the area where there is a break in the Illustrator file. In figure 17.7, you can see a path being drawn over an area of the auto-trace that did not close the drawn outline because the authors erased part of the outline before auto-tracing it. After you create the closed path, fill the object with the same color as the auto-traced outlines, and give the object no outline width.

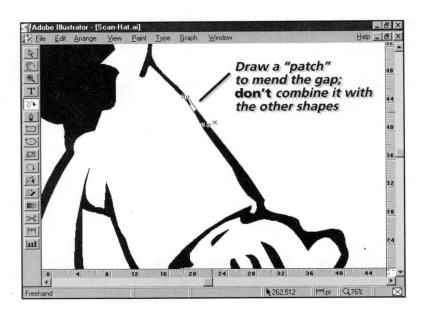

figure 17.7
Without grouping or combining, add a filled object on top of the existing trace of the cartoon outline to connect the break.

Checking everywhere in a scan of a design to see that all the pen strokes are unconnected is impractical. A better idea is to use the Eraser tool in Photoshop to *create* breaks in the scanned image so that the imported Illustrator-format design consists only of objects and empty areas in the design that are interpreted as transparent. Designs, particularly intricate ones, will contain areas, however, in which an auto-tracing utility will close a path and then proceed to create a white object on top of a black one to suggest that the interior of the bottommost shape is unfilled. If you see a design area that you want to treat as transparent in Photoshop, but a white object is on top of the design in this area, see step 4 for more details.

4. Select the bottommost object and the top, white object, and combine them. In Illustrator, you do this by choosing the first object and then, while you hold Shift to additively select the top object, choosing Object, Compound Path, and then Create. In FreeHand, you do this operation on the Arrange menu (Join Shapes); in CorelDRAW!, you choose Arrange, Combine.

   It doesn't matter whether objects are grouped before you save your edited vector cartoon; Photoshop doesn't use this information when it converts the Illustrator format of graphics to bitmap. You do have the opportunity to leave some areas of the design filled with white overlapping objects, however; this can be a time-saver when it's time to color the design in Photoshop. In the Tophat.ai vector file, the cartoon character's teeth and gloves were left filled with white; Photoshop treats these areas as filled, not transparent, and areas that will be white in the finished illustration are created in the drawing program before taking the design into Photoshop.

5. When you finish editing the file, if you're using Illustrator, choose File, Save, and then quit the application. If you use FreeHand, CorelDRAW!, or another vector drawing application, choose File, Export, and then export the file to Adobe Illustrator format. Most drawing programs are up to version 5.x of Illustrator format export; use this one. Windows users should add the two-character extension "AI" after the period in the saved file name.

You have seen two methods for getting a physical piece of artwork into the computer and into a format that can be filled with colors or patterned fills in Photoshop. Taking the design through the intermediate vector format might seem complicated and unnecessary, but the qualitative difference between "raw" scanning and refining the design before working with it in Photoshop is noticeable.

The cartoon character looks as though it's dressed up for a spectacular event, so without further delay, let's get down to the business of importing and coloring the design.

Working with Photoshop's "Acetate" Layers

Because Photoshop 4 is "layer-centric," you use the Layers feature to select, paint, and pattern-fill the design in this section to its completion. For traditional illustrators who have spent hours using white paint to remove a mistake, the steps in this example will be a pleasant change. Layers make image composition the next best thing to being "error-proof."

User-Defined Gradient Fills and Layer Selections

You deal first with the central element in the Tophat cartoon; the roundish fellow between the hat and the shoes gives you a perfect opportunity to use the custom gradient feature. From a conceptual standpoint, a nice touch is to color the cartoon by using shades of color to simulate lighting and dimension; smooth blends of color will contrast nicely with the primitive pen strokes that define the cartoon.

You probably have noticed on the Web and in printed publications that suggestions of a sphere shape (a navigation button, for example) usually include more than one light source. A primary light source provides a highlight on shapes that are supposed to look shiny, and a secondary light at a 180° opposition to the primary light is used to fill and add roundness to the surface. This effect is easy to accomplish with the Gradient tool and a multicolored fill. The fill you define and add to the cartoon character begins with a bright color for the highlight, makes a transition to a dark orange, and then becomes lighter at the end of the gradient to suggest this secondary source of illumination in the design. (This is sometimes called *catch lighting* on the edges of objects.)

Here's how to import the Illustrator design, define a new layer in the file for colors, select only the area you want to fill, and create a user-defined, multicolor gradient:

CREATING LAYERED ARTWORK

CD-ROM

1. In Photoshop, press Ctrl(⌘)+O (File, Open), and then choose Tophat.ai from the CHAP17 folder of the Companion CD. (If you have an Illustrator format design of your own, feel free to use it instead of the example file.) Photoshop now displays the Rasterize Generic EPS Format dialog box.

2. Accept the Height, Width, and Resolution offered in these fields. Photoshop reads the file's header information and offers the same size image as the one that was auto-traced and converted to Illustrator format.

3. Choose Grayscale from the Mode drop-down list. Although this image will be in color in its finished format, it takes less time for Photoshop to convert the file to bitmap format in grayscale than in RGB color. Because the file contains only grayscale information, choosing a higher color mode would delay the conversion.

4. Choose Image, Canvas Size, type **4.25** in both the Width and Height New size fields, and then click on OK. You increase the area surrounding the design so that you can work a little more freely with the design and add background elements later.

Photoshop offers a document window that precisely fits the outer dimensions only of the "live area" of an Illustrator-format design. This is why the cartoon character appears to be cramped in the document window after Photoshop translates the vector information to bitmap format.

5. Choose Image, Mode, RGB Color. On the Layers palette (press F7 if it isn't currently in the workspace), click on the Create a new layer icon at the bottom of the palette, and then drag the new layer's title on the palette to beneath the default layer.

    This is the layer upon which you will add fills. You might want to double-click on the layer title, and rename the layer **Color**; do the same with the default layer, giving it the title Tracing. By labeling the layers, you will have fewer design errors in the long run!

    Notice in figure 17.8 that Photoshop treats areas in the design that don't contain objects as being transparent.

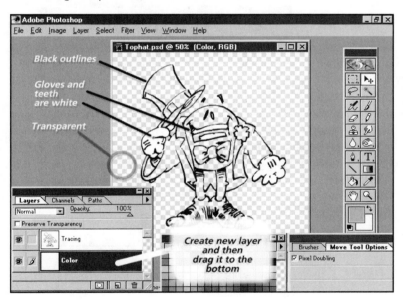

figure 17.8
The areas in the file that contain white areas are white, the black areas are black, and areas with no objects are transparent.

6. Click on the Polygon Lasso tool on the toolbox. If the Polygon Lasso tool is hidden, drag on the tool-button face to display the flyout, and then release the mouse button over the tool.

7. Click on the Color layer to ensure that it is the current editing layer, and then click points around the face of the cartoon character; see the white circle callouts in figure 17.9 for the position of your click points with the tool. When you arrive at the beginning point of the path you have defined, single-click to close the path. A marquee selection appears. Double-click on the Gradient tool to display the Options for this tool and to deselect the Polygon tool, whose properties are such that it creates lines wherever you click, whether intended or not!

figure 17.9
Single-clicking with the Polygon Lasso tool creates a selection area that describes the interior of the cartoon face in the image.

8. Press F6 to display the Swatches palette (if it is not already on-screen), and then carefully arrange the workspace so that the Swatches palette can be accessed from a dialog box. Figure 17.9 shows a good location for the Swatches palette.

Now that the document is prepared for coloring, it's time to experiment with Photoshop's new Gradient Editor.

CUSTOMIZING GRADIENT FILLS

1. Click on the Edit button on the Gradient tool Options palette to display the Gradient Editor dialog box. Click on New in this box, type anything you like in the Gradient Name dialog box (I named the cartoon character "Smirk," which is why the new gradient color is named "Smirk Skin"), and then click on OK to exit the Gradient Name dialog box. Figure 17.10 identifies the Gradient Editor interface elements discussed in these steps.

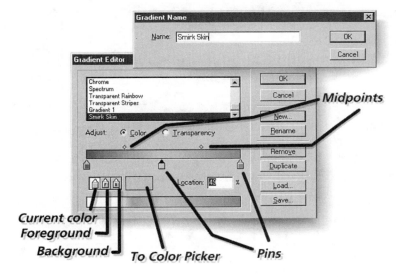

figure 17.10
The Gradient Editor dialog box.

2. Click on the far-left pin below the gradient preview strip (the current color), and then click on the yellow swatch on the Swatches palette. This specifies the beginning transition color for the gradient.

    In the Gradient Editor dialog box you can sample a color from the Swatches palette or from an open image window.

3. Click directly beneath the preview gradient strip to add another pin. Drag this pin to the right until the value in the location field is 86. With the pin highlighted, click in the Swatches palette to define this part of the gradient as orange.

4. Click on the far-right pin (see #1 in fig. 17.11), and then click on the yellow swatch on the Swatches palette (see #2 in fig. 17.11). If you click on the pins to the left of the Location field, the first applies the current color in the gradient to any new pins you add to the gradient; the "F" pin applies the current foreground color, and the "B" applies the current background color. The swatch to the right of the pins takes you to the color picker for any color you want to choose.

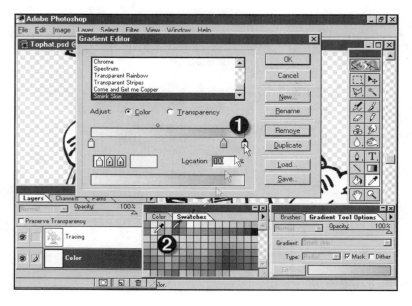

figure 17.11
Use an image in the workspace, or the Swatches palette, to define colors along the custom gradient.

TIP

To remove a color pin from a gradient, drag it in any direction off the strip.

5. Click on OK to exit the Gradient Editor; you can see that the current gradient on the Options palette has your title. Click on the Type drop-down list on the Gradient options palette, and choose Radial.

6. With the Gradient tool, drag from the upper left of the cartoon character's face to the lower right (see fig. 17.12). The selected area on the color layer fills with a transitional blend from the colors you defined, making the character look more dimensional than if you had used a uniform color fill.

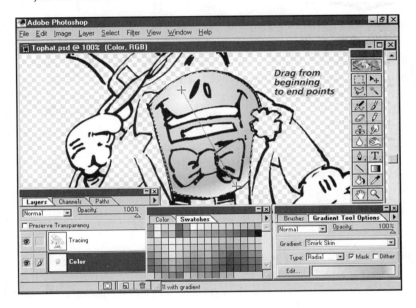

figure 17.12

Use custom gradient fills to save time in the design shading process.

7. Press Ctrl(⌘)+S, and save the document to your hard disk as Tophat.psd (the Photoshop file format). Press Ctrl(⌘)+D to deselect the active selection marquee, and keep the document open in Photoshop.

Foreground color is only one of the media types you can apply to the Color layer in the document. In the following section, you walk through the creation of a pattern that is applied to other selected areas of the cartoon.

Creating Simple Patterns

As mentioned in Chapter 2, "Leveraging Photoshop's New Capabilities," the Polygon Lasso tool is a supplemental tool that *replaces* the extended function of the Lasso tool from earlier versions of Photoshop. Alt(Opt) always enables you to subtract from an existing marquee selection, and in version 4 does not toggle the Lasso tool to straight-line marquee definition. The next set of steps illustrate the real new property of the Polygon Lasso tool, however; when you use the tool, shapes created by intersecting lines automatically define a selection marquee whose interior does not include self-intersecting areas. This makes it easy, for example, to create a five-point star shape by clicking only six points.

The pattern fill for the cartoon character should be in the same spirit as the formal attire—light but elegant. Here's how to create a star pattern fill, using the Polygon Lasso tool and the Offset Filter command:

DESIGNING A PATTERN FILL

1. In Photoshop, press Ctrl(⌘)+N to open the New dialog box. You are creating a separate document in which to make a pattern file.

2. Specify in the dialog box a width and height of 256 pixels, RGB color mode, and an image resolution of 150 pixels/inch, the same resolution as the Tophat file. Click on the White (background) Image Contents radio button. Click on OK to create the new document window, and return to Photoshop's workspace.

3. Press Ctrl(⌘)+A to select the entire new document, click on a powder blue swatch on the Swatches palette (press F6 if the Swatches palette isn't currently on-screen), and then press Alt(Opt)+Delete (Backspace) to apply the current blue foreground color to the entire new image. Press Ctrl(⌘)+D to deselect the image after applying the foreground color.

4. With the Polygon Lasso tool, click six points in the new document to define a star, about the size of the star shown in figure 17.13. You don't need to make a perfectly symmetrical star shape—this is a cartoon, and it deserves a cartoon-star pattern fill. Note that after you close the Polygon Lasso selection by clicking a final point at the beginning point, the intersections inside the star will disappear.

figure 17.13

Create a star-shaped selection in the new document by defining the points of the star with the Polygon Lasso tool.

5. Click on the bright gold swatch on the Swatches palette, press Alt+Delete (Opt+Backspace) to fill the selection with foreground gold, and then press Ctrl(⌘)+D to deselect the active marquee selection.

6. Repeat step 5, creating smaller and larger stars in other areas of the new document until you have about five stars, with approximately the same distance between the stars.

   Creating a seamless tiling pattern is difficult when you don't see in advance how the pattern tiles. The new document is bound to have an area that deserves an additional star toward the edge of the image. A generally good idea, therefore, is to shift the canvas so that you get a clear view of the edges, and then perhaps add a star or two.

7. Choose Filter, Other, and then choose Offset.

8. In the Offset dialog box, type **100** in both the Horizontal and Vertical pixels fields, and then click on the Wrap Around button in the Undefined Areas field.

   If you leave the Preview check box checked in the Offset dialog box, you can see on-screen that Photoshop "slides" the new document's canvas to the right and down (see fig. 17.14). The preview shows that the pattern you are creating might need an extra star or two—a need that shows up only when you preview the Offset filter.

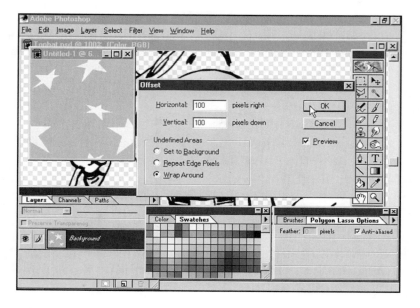

figure 17.14
The Offset filter is an invaluable tool for the creation of a seamless pattern that will tile in a document.

9. Click on OK in the Offset dialog box, and then create one or two more stars in the image to flesh out the pattern.

10. Press Ctrl(⌘)+S, and then save the document to your hard disk in the TIFF image format, as Stars.tif. Keep this and the Tophat image open in Photoshop.

Although a few twists and workarounds lie ahead in the process of coloring in the cartoon, you should understand the basic concept and approach if you have followed the steps up to this point.

What you might consider is changing the methods by which you select different areas in the cartoon design. The Polygon Lasso tool is useful for defining certain geometric areas, and the Quick Mask tool is handy for irregularly shaped, soft-edged selections, as you will soon see.

Using a Combination of Selection Tools

As a house painter works first on the trim areas and then gets out a broader brush to fill in larger areas, you need to give the cartoon character's coat and hat edge definition, and then use broader strokes to select and then fill the selections.

In the following steps, you use the Paintbrush tool in combination with Photoshop's Quick Mask mode to define the inside edges of the coat and hat; then you use the Lasso tool to fill the interior with Quick Mask. After you finish this process, filling these areas with the defined star pattern is simple.

DEFINING AREAS WITH QUICK MASK

1. Click on the title bar of the Tophat document to make it the foreground document in the workspace. Press B (Paintbrush tool) and then double-click on Quick Mask mode (below the background color selection box on the toolbox) to display the Quick Mask Options dialog box.

2. Make certain that the Color Indicates Selected Areas option is the current one; then click on OK to exit the dialog box.

3. Press **D** (Default colors) to ensure that you will be applying Quick Mask with black foreground color, and then click on the top row, far-right tip on the Brushes palette.

4. Zoom into the Tophat document to 1:1 (100%); then click and drag inside the edge of the coat and hat outline (see fig. 17.15).

   Everywhere you apply foreground color tint will become a selection marquee when you switch back to Photoshop's Standard editing mode. Notice in the figure that the Quick Mask area runs over the area you filled earlier in the cartoon character's face. This is okay, and is a time-saving step; shortly, you will apply the pattern to an individual layer underneath the color layer, so that areas filled with the star pattern appear *underneath* the gradient fill in the composition.

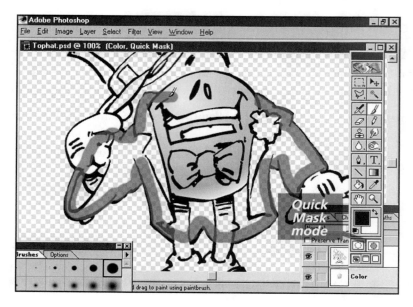

figure 17.15

Apply Quick Mask to the image in areas you want to fill with the star pattern you created.

5. To get a smaller Paintbrush tip for areas around the interior of the coat and hat, right-click (Macintosh: hold Ctrl and click), and then choose Previous Brush from the Context menu (see fig. 17.16). This command moves the current brush selection to the next smaller size displayed on the Brushes palette.

   Conversely, Next Brush moves the current tip to the next larger size displayed on the Brushes palette. These Context menu options are particularly useful when the Brushes palette is closed or hidden behind other Photoshop palettes.

6. After you outline the interior of the coat and hat with Quick Mask, choose the Lasso tool and draw a selection that encompasses the interior of the coat and encroaches on the Quick Mask areas. Press Alt+Delete (Opt+Backspace) to fill the coat area with a Quick Mask overlay.

7. Press Ctrl(⌘)+D to deselect the marquee; then repeat step 6 on the hat area in the image.

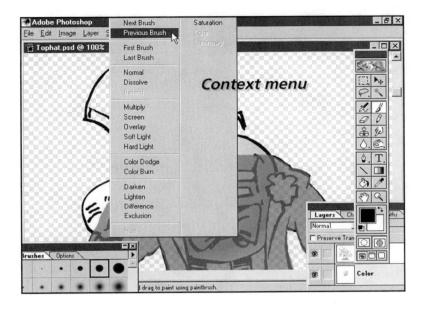

figure 17.16
The Context menu offers options specific to the current tool. When the Paintbrush is chosen, the menu offers painting options.

8.   Click on the Standard editing mode icon on the toolbox (to the left of the Quick Mask icon), press F7 to display the Layers palette, click on it, and then click on the Create new layer icon at the bottom of the palette.

9.   On the Layers palette, drag the title for the new layer down to locate it beneath the Color layer. Double-click on the title to display the Layer Options dialog box, type **Suit** in the Name field, and click on OK to close the box.

10.   Click on the title bar of the Stars image, press Ctrl(⌘)+A to select the entire Stars image, and choose Edit, Define Pattern from the menu. You can close the Stars image at any time now.

11.   With the Tophat image as the foreground image in the workspace, choose Edit, Fill. In the Fill dialog box, choose Pattern from the Use drop-down list; then click on OK. The cartoon character's new suit is shown in figure 17.17.

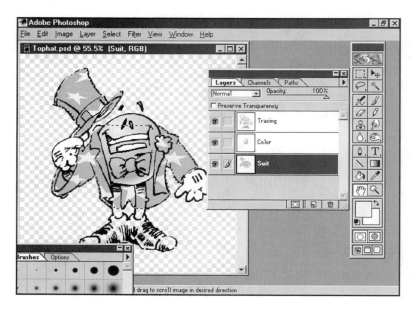

figure 17.17
Fill the selection area with the pattern you defined.

12. Choose Edit, Purge, Pattern. Photoshop discards the pattern data from system memory—now you can work faster with the image.

13. Press Ctrl (⌘)+D to deselect the current selection, and then press Ctrl(⌘)+S to save your work up to this stage.

As you work with other areas in the image, you will see that you can define selection areas that overlap filled areas on other layers. This sort of "Behind/In Front Of" layer structure is one that traditional cell animators didn't have; given the opacity factor of acetate, three or more cells stacked in a design significantly reduced overall image brightness. Photoshop layers can be 40 or 100 deep and still display 100 percent transparency in transparent areas.

Finishing the Foreground Design

Between the Polygon Lasso tool and the Quick Mask feature, you can finish coloring the character in the Tophat image. You don't need a detailed list of steps here to complete the design, but you might consider these tips as you go through the next example.

Use Photoshop's Zoom Features

Zooming into an area gives you a much better opportunity to use the Lasso tool in its default freehand selection mode to accurately define the interior of an area that needs filling. Because the outline strokes that make up the cartoon character are three or four pixels wide in most of the composition, the outlines hide fill areas whose edges are not exactly in the center of the black outline strokes. And you have the luxury of being a little loose in the way you create selection marquees for areas you will fill.

In figure 17.18, you can see the Bow.tif image (from the CHAP17 folder on the CD) being sampled as a pattern for filling the bow tie in the design. To use the Lasso tool to select the bow tie, simply drag and close an outline that falls within the outline strokes that make up the bow tie.

figure 17.18

Use the Bow.tif image on the Companion CD as a pattern to fill the bow tie area in the image.

Because the bow tie in the design goes in front of the cartoon character, you can use the Color layer as the target layer for filling this area with pattern. The bow tie pattern will replace part of the gradient fill on this layer, however, which is fine— you don't have to keep the fills for the tie and the character's face on separate layers.

Use Gradient Fills to Bring Out Dimension

Gradient fills keep the image from becoming compositionally static because light cast on real-world objects causes shading to drop off at the point farthest from illumination. Gradient fills do not have to consist of multiple colors (as in the cartoon face), however. In figure 17.19, you can see how a simple, two-color linear-type blend adds shading to the shoes in the design. After choosing brown for the foreground color (by clicking on the foreground color selection box on the toolbox), the color was specified in the Color Picker. Pale cream was defined for the background color of the gradient, the Foreground to Background Gradient option was chosen from the Options palette, and the Gradient tool was dragged from the beginning to end point in the shoes selection to create shaded coloring.

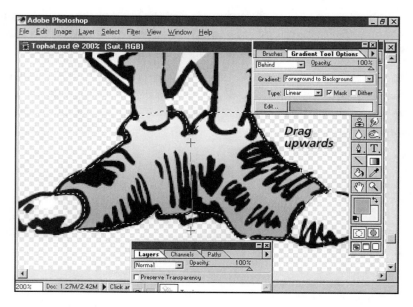

figure 17.19
Drag in the direction in which you want the gradient to make the transition between foreground and background color.

Use the Airbrush Tool for Delicate Shading

The Airbrush tool can be used effectively to apply shading to the white gloves in the image. Switch the current layer to the Tracing layer by clicking on its title, specify a small tip for the Airbrush tool, and then use a faint blue to apply shadow areas to the gloves. Pale blue is frequently used to shade whites in comic strips because natural sunlight tends to reflect the color of the sky (blue) into areas that don't face the sun directly. You can see this effect in shaded areas of white sheets hung out to dry on a sunny day.

After you completely fill the cartoon character with colors or patterns, it's time to create a background to support the cartoon compositionally. Doing so involves surprisingly little effort, now that you know some of the secrets of working with layers and defining gradients and patterns.

Building a Cartoon Background

Without an environment to support the cartoon character compositionally, he looks a little lost in space, and the shading you added by using gradients has nothing to "play" against. Creating an ornamental background that steals visual interest from the character would be a mistake, however. You need to strive for a middle ground, between compositional harmony and design focus; the following sections show you how to create a background that meets both artistic needs.

Creating Perspective with the Transform Tool

CD-ROM

One of the most important elements you can add to your cartoon work, or any Photoshop composition, is the definition of a *ground plane.* Establishing where the ground is in a picture helps the viewer relate to what is sometimes a surrealistic or light-hearted element in the scene. A wooden floor is an appropriate ground for the Tophat image, and the Luan.tif image in the CHAP17 folder of the Companion CD meets this need. Luan.tif was created in Adobe TextureMaker, a photorealistic texture-making application. TextureMaker does not create seamless tiling images, but the image was *edited* to tile seamlessly, using methods described in Chapter 19, "Web Site Construction."

As mentioned throughout this book, applying any of the Free Transform options on a selection changes pixel colors and slightly blurs image content—an acceptable phenomenon with the Luan image. The ground plays an important visual role in the composition in terms of color and texture, but the actual detail in the image is not of great visual interest, and can hold up against a transformation.

Here's how to add a ground to the Tophat composition:

CREATING FLOORS

CD-ROM

1. Open the Luan.tif image from the CHAP17 folder of the Companion CD. Press Ctrl(⌘)+A (Select, All), and then choose Edit, Define Pattern (see fig. 17.20). You can close Luan.tif now.

figure 17.20

Sample a seamless tiling image or wood, linoleum, or other material to use as a ground for a composition.

TIP

Check out the TILES folder on the Companion CD for a collection of seamless tiling textures for use in your cartoon work, Web page layout, and other situations in which you need to fill a background image area.

2. On the Layers palette, click on the Create a new layer icon at the bottom of the palette; then click and drag the layer title to the bottom of the title stack on the Layers palette. On this bottom layer, which is also the current editing layer, you will create the ground for the image.

3. With the Rectangular Marquee tool, drag a rectangle that roughly describes where a floor should go in this image. Do *not* define the rectangle so that it touches the left, right, or

bottom edges of the window, however. You need some room to stretch the image area after you fill it. Sneak a peek at figure 7.21 for the size and location of the rectangle.

4. Choose Edit, Fill, choose Pattern from the drop-down Use list, and click on OK to fill the rectangle with a tiling pattern of the Luan image.

5. Drag on each edge of the image window, one corner at a time, to expose about 2" of neutral-colored document background space. In Windows 95 and Windows 3.1x, you can click on the Maximize title bar button on the document to display the document background.

    In the following step, the Free Transform bounding box around the wood selection is stretched *way* past the confines of the image window. To do this, you need empty space surrounding the document window, and probably need to close or move palettes out of the way before you choose the Free Transform command.

6. Right-click (Macintosh: hold Ctrl and click) in the document window, and then choose Free Transform from the Context menu. The bounding box for the Free Transform command appears around the selection.

7. Hold Ctrl(⌘) and drag the bottom right corner of the Free Transform bounding box out of the document window, as shown in figure 17.21. Release the corner; an on-screen preview of the effect you have created is displayed in the image window.

figure 17.21
Distort the selection by using the Free Transform bounding box to suggest a perspective for the wood area.

8. While holding Ctrl(⌘), click and drag the bottom left bounding box handle to the left, an equal distance outside the document window.

9. Double-click inside the Free Transform bounding box to apply the distortion to the wood selection (see fig. 17.22), then press Ctrl(⌘)+D to deselect the selection marquee.

figure 17.22
The Perspective command can add dimension to your composition.

10. Press Ctrl(⌘)+S to save your work up to this stage; keep the Tophat document open in Photoshop.

The only remaining piece to add to the composition is something to support the background directly behind the cartoon character. The following section shows you how to design a theater curtain that complements the overall tone of the piece.

TIP

Although the Distort option was used with the Free Transform feature in the preceding example, you can access the Perspective option through a different combination of keystrokes, in case your work needs a precise amount of perspective.

To access the Perspective option, hold Ctrl+Alt+Shift (⌘+Opt+Shift) while you drag on a corner Free Transform bounding box handle.

Advanced Gradient Tool Options

The Gradient tool's Editor window is similar to an options box for a third-party plug-in filter in Photoshop. Now, having covered some of the basic steps for creating a multicolor blend, you see how to quickly set up a *complex* multicolor gradient blend.

Here's how to simulate a curtain effect, using the Gradient tool:

IT'S "CURTAINS" FOR THE CARTOON CHARACTER

1. On the Layers palette, click on the Create a new layer icon. New layers appear directly above the current editing layer; this new layer should pop into the Layers list, directly above the layer containing the wood floor.

2. Double-click on the Gradient tool to select it and to display the Options palette.

3. Click on the Edit button on the Options palette, and then click on New. In the Gradient Name dialog box, type **Curtains**; then click on OK to return to the Gradient Editor.

4. Click on the far-left pin below the gradient preview strip and then on the swatch to the left of the Location field; this displays the Color Picker.

5. In the Color Picker, use the color field and the color strip to define a rich purple color, and then click on OK to return to the Gradient Editor.

6. While holding Alt(Opt), click and drag the far-right pin to the left until the Location field reads 20%. This duplicates the far-right pin, and you now have a minitransition from purple to black in the gradient design.

7. Click on the far-left (purple) pin, and press Alt(Opt) and click on the pin twice. You create two duplicate purple pins, both situated in exactly the same place on the gradient strip.

8. One at a time, drag the purple pin duplicates to various points along the gradient preview strip. Look ahead to figure 17.23 for the recommended locations for the new pins.

9. Click on the pin that is at the 20% location, and then click the color swatch to the left of the Location field. In the Select Color field, click at the very bottom to choose black, click on OK, and then press Alt(Opt) and click on the black pin twice.

10. Drag the duplicate black pins to positions on the strip, to create an alternating purple-and-black-pattern for the curtain in the design. Now that you have the technique down, create as many alternating gradient colors as you like for the design. The authors called it "curtains" at four alternating gradient segments (see fig. 17.23).

figure 17.23

Pressing Alt(Opt) and clicking on a color pin duplicates it. This is your ticket to the quick creation of a color-alternating gradient.

11. Click on OK to exit the Gradient Editor. Then hold Shift while you drag the Gradient tool from the left edge of the image to the right edge, filling the new layer with the gradient you designed. Shift constrains the angle of the gradient to 45° angles, so the fill will be perfectly vertical.

12. Press Ctrl(⌘)+S to save your work up to this stage.

The gradient covers the entire image layer now—it would be nice, however, if some of the floor you carefully edited into the image showed through! In the following section, you trim the curtain by using the Pen tool to define the area that needs to be removed.

Shape versus Texture

You might not envision the gradient you added to the design as a curtain because the *shape* of a curtain is as important an element as the *shading* (the gradient texture), and there *is* no curtain shape in the composition yet.

The following example shows you how a simple edit or two on the curtain layer turns the gradient into a shape we recognize from theater productions.

SHAPE DEFINITION USING THE PEN TOOL

1. Double-click on the Hand tool to zoom your viewing resolution to fit the entire image in the workspace, without scroll bars.

2. Drag the edges of the image window out so that you can see a small area of window background on all sides of the window.

3. With the curtain image layer as the current editing layer, drag the Opacity slider on the Layers palette to about 50%. Now you can see the wood beneath the curtain layer.

4. Press **P** (Pen tool), and click a point at the right edge of the image window, at the point where you think the curtain should meet the floor in the image.

5. About the width of the cartoon character's hand, click another point directly to the left and drag upward a point in the image. This creates a path segment between the first and second anchor points, and it arcs the segment in a downward curve.

6. Alternating between dragging up and down, define points with the Pen tool across the image, at each change of color in the gradient fill. In this way you create a wavy path in the image.

7. When you reach the left edge of the document, click an anchor, then click another anchor slightly outside the document in the lower left corner. Click a point slightly outside the document at the lower right corner; then click on the beginning point of the path to close it (see fig. 17.24).

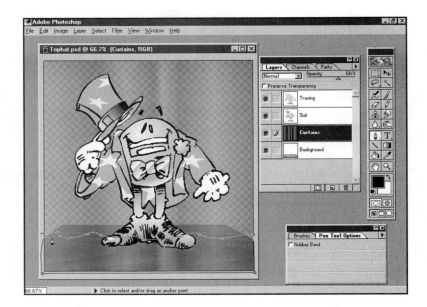

figure 17.24
Use the Pen tool to encompass the area of the curtain image layer that you want to delete.

8. On the Paths palette, click on the Loads path as selection icon at the bottom of the palette (see fig. 17.25). Press Delete (Backspace), press Ctrl(⌘)+D to deselect the marquee selection, and then drag the Opacity slider on the Layers palette back to 100%. Now you have the curtain shading *and* shape.

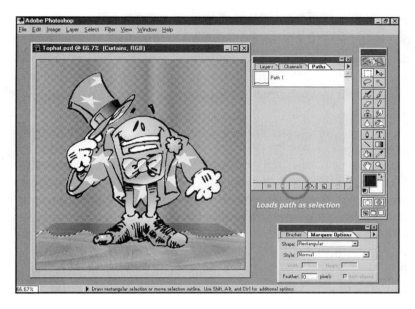

figure 17.25

Paths can serve as the basis for a marquee selection outline. Define the area you want removed, and then delete the contents of the selection.

9. Press Ctrl(⌘)+S to save your work up to this point; keep the document open in Photoshop.

A few minor edits in the cartoon, and it will be complete.

Using the Burn Tool to Enhance Shading

Chapter 11, "Black and White…and Color," touched upon the importance of viewing and working with different color models to better manipulate the components of color in an image. The Hue, Saturation, Brightness (HSB) color model is your best choice for defining the mechanics of the burn tool, which you use in the final set of steps to complete the cartoon image.

The Burn tool can be customized to affect three tonal regions in an image you drag over with the tool: Shadows, Midtones, and Highlights. In all these areas, the Burn tool decreases the brightness component of pixels while increasing the saturation of any predominant color value it finds. The Burn tool does nothing to affect the hue of pixels, but instead creates shading to produce different tones of the same colors in the image.

The Burn tool is effective for creating shadows and shading in image areas. Real shadows, which are almost never totally opaque, display some of the underlying color in an image.

In figure 17.26 you can see the Burn tool being applied to the floor layer in the cartoon. Set the tool to Highlights on the Options palette, set Exposure (strength) to 50%, and pick a medium tip from the Brushes palette to add burn areas that give a hint of shadow to the image. The right side of the hat and of the coat sleeves, and areas of the floor on which the curtain would cast shadows are all good candidates for the Burn tool. Work on one layer's contents, and then move to the next layer.

figure 17.26
Use the Burn tool to break up the monotony of solid tones in the image and to intimate a source of light cast into the scene.

After you finish using the Burn tool, you might want to choose File, Save a copy, and then save a flattened copy of the design to TIFF, PICT, or BMP file format so that you can show it around. By keeping the original file's contents on separate layers, you can come back to the piece at any time and create a different color and pattern scheme for the cartoon.

Summary

This chapter has walked you through the process of transforming your physical artwork to digital media, performing additional conversions to different digital media types, and manipulating data to reach a cartoon that expresses the best of different mixed media. Although the image in this chapter is lighthearted and fanciful, you can choose any sort of theme, and express your graphical ideas with a complement of tools from both the digital and traditional worlds of art.

Moving from the fanciful to the sublime, Chapter 18, "3D and Photoshop," investigates the creative possibilities of combining a modeling program with Photoshop's features to produce some photographic imagery that simply *cannot* be captured with a camera.

3D AND PHOTOSHOP

Everywhere you look, the term 3D *is displayed in 48-point type on magazines, Web pages, trade papers, and advertisements. For artists, this is good news. A piece of the 3D graphics action is yours for the taking when you own Photoshop, and an additional tool or two. Buzzwords such as* 3D *and* virtual reality *actually point to a type of artistic expression called* photorealism; *the more realistically you can portray a scene, the faster you can communicate a message to your audience. Although modeling and rendering applications (the programs used to create photorealistic scenes) have a steep learning curve, you can get right down to business with several programs that take the calculations out of photorealistic object creation. One in particular, Fractal Design Corporation's Poser, is demonstrated in this chapter as a helper application to create an advertisement* real *actors probably would never pose for!*

The TreeFolks Assignment

The fictitious advertisement in this chapter is for a family-run lawn-care service called "The TreeFolks." The client (like most clients) wants a sort of "larger than life" treatment of the advertisement—super heroes dressed in lavish attire—and wants it by Tuesday. And no—there's no budget.

Fortunately, you have Photoshop. And you have about $100 in your pocket to hire actors, design scenery, provide costumes, and never leave your workstation. Fractal Design Poser is a modeling program that doesn't fit the stereotype of a modeling and rendering application. Poser does only one thing, but does it exceptionally well: it creates human forms. Without any modeling skills, you can generate the TreeFolks in Poser, add costumes you design in Photoshop, and then bring the "actors" into Photoshop for some compositing work to complete a highly unusual, compelling piece of ad work.

CD-ROM

For fine artists, commercial artists, scientists, ergonomic engineering professionals, and for people who need a certain "something" to enhance their design work, it's tough to top Poser. The first part of this chapter deals with working between Poser and Photoshop to create costumes for the human forms. Although having a copy of Poser handy for the brief examples is helpful, Poser isn't a household graphics staple yet. The CHAP18 folder on the Companion CD contains the rendered Poser files. The focus of this chapter is the way different digital media can be integrated into a Photoshop composition.

Creating the Appropriate Poser Type and Costume

If you play with a modeling application for more than 20 minutes, you will quickly conclude that modeling is difficult stuff! When the authors first heard of Poser, our apprehension was at an all-time high. "It's difficult enough to model a chair—how tough will it be to model a lifelike, plausible human being?"

Fortunately, the bulk of the calculations that go into a Poser human form have been predesigned for the user. You have to specify the form's sex, choose from preset poses (or define your own), set up lighting and a camera angle, and then tell Poser to render away. In figure 18.1, you can see the first of three TreeFolks characters rendered in Poser. Notice that by adjusting the Y Scale (*Height*, in the coordinates of 3D space), you can make a human form look squat; perfect for a lumberjack-type character in this advertisement.

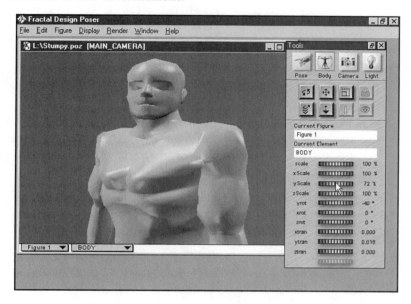

figure 18.1
Specify the human form type, and Poser fills in the details, to provide "actors on call" for your designs.

As you can see, this TreeFolks character is missing something—*clothes*! Which leads us to the first set of steps: how to design an image in Photoshop that can cloak the Poser figure in something that's in keeping with the flavor of a lawn-work ad. Poser ships with several templates that basically offer the same function: to serve as a map for the geometry of the human shapes. The mapping of colors or patterns to the templates might remind you of a paper doll cut-out, but the effect of the image, when it's used to surface the Poser model, is far from kid's stuff. Although any of these texture maps can be used as is on Poser figures, you are going to customize the LEOTARD image map to create a wood costume for one of the TreeFolks.

Here's how to use Photoshop's Pattern feature in combination with an image on the Companion CD to create the costume for a Poser figure:

CREATING A CUSTOM POSER COSTUME

CD-ROM

1. In Photoshop, open the Leotard file from the Poser Maps folder. On the Macintosh, this is a PICT file, and the folder is called Bump/Texture Maps. In Windows, the Leotards image is a BMP file. Choose File, Save As, and then save the file under a different name. ("Stumpy" is good.) Windows users should save the image in BMP or TIF format; Macintosh users, in the PICT file format.

2. From the CHAP18 folder of the Companion CD, open the Stumptex.tif image. This is a seamless tiling image of wood texture (see fig. 18.2). Press Ctrl(⌘)+A to select all; then choose Edit, Define Pattern. You can close the Stumptex image at any time now.

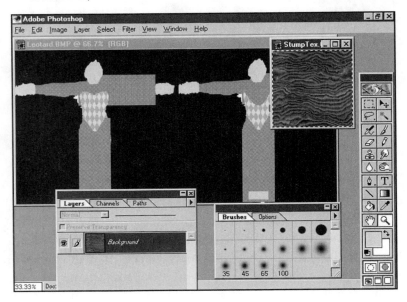

figure 18.2
Sample an image for use as a pattern. Then you can apply the pattern to the texture template to create a new costume.

3. Double-click on the Zoom tool to move your view of the image to 1:1 resolution on-screen. Then double-click on the Quick Mask mode control on Photoshop's toolbox to display the options for Quick Mask mode.

4. Click on the Color Indicates Selected Areas radio button, and then click on OK to close the Options box. Now, everywhere you apply foreground color will represent a selected area when you switch back to Standard editing mode.

5. Press **B** (Paintbrush tool), and then choose the top row, fifth tip on the Brushes palette. Press **D** (Default Colors) to ensure that you will be applying Quick Mask with black foreground color.

6. Paint over the top of the torso at the left of the Leotard image (see fig. 18.3).

   Because the lower half of the torso isn't visible in the view of the Poser figure shown in figure 18.1, you don't have to cover it with Quick Mask. And you don't have to paint over the back view of the costume—the design on the right side of the Leotard image— because the figure in this example is facing front, and you cannot see his back.

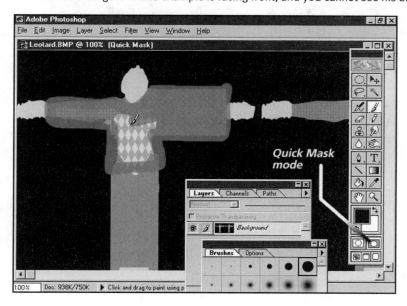

figure 18.3
Apply foreground color in Quick Mask mode to define a selection area in the image you want to fill with the pattern.

7. Hold Ctrl(⌘)+spacebar to toggle to the Zoom tool; then marquee drag a rectangle around the head portion of the costume to zoom into this area.

8. Choose the Polygon Lasso tool, and then click a zigzag pattern around the neck area of the image, closing the Lasso selection area above the chest area of the image (see fig. 18.4).

   By creating the zigzag pattern, you give this costume an unusual neck—sort of a pencil sharpener look. The idea is to leave the Poser figure's face flesh colored, but give the costume the wood texture you defined as a pattern.

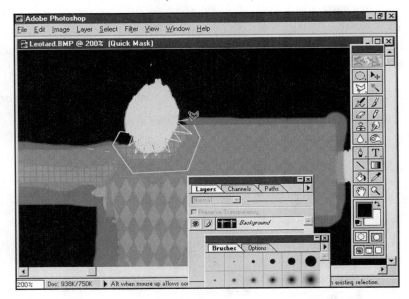

figure 18.4
Define a zigzag selection with the Lasso tool to extend the area in the image defined by the Quick Mask.

9. When the Lasso selection is closed, a marquee selection appears. At this point, press Alt(Opt)+Delete(Backspace), and then press Ctrl(⌘)+D to deselect the marquee. The area you defined is now filled with Quick Mask.

10. Click on the Standard mode control to the left of the Quick Mask icon. The areas filled with Quick Mask are now a marquee selection.

11. Zoom out to 100%, right-click (Macintosh: hold Ctrl and click), and then choose Fill from the Context menu. In the Fill dialog box, choose Pattern from the Use drop-down list, and click on OK to apply the fill (see fig. 18.5). As you can see, the tiling wood sample you defined as a pattern fills the interior of the marquee selection.

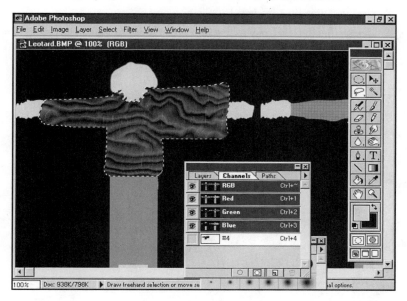

figure 18.5

Fill the selection marquee with the pattern you defined.

12. Press Ctrl(⌘)+Shift+I to create an inverse selection in the image. Now the area you filled is protected, but all other areas are available for editing.

13. With the Paintbrush tool, hold Alt(Opt) and click on the flesh-colored area at the top of the costume. Holding Alt(Opt) toggles the Paintbrush tool to the Eyedropper tool; by clicking on the flesh color, you make it the current foreground color on the toolbox.

14. Release Alt(Opt); then click and drag the Paintbrush in the image to extend the flesh color into the zigzag design at the neck of the costume, to bring the flesh color to the edge of the wood pattern fill. Also, extend the head above the original area in the image by about one screen inch.

15. Press Ctrl(⌘)+D to deselect the marquee, and then choose the Rubber Stamp tool from the toolbox.

16. On the Options palette, choose Pattern (aligned) from the Option drop-down list. This eliminates the need to create a sample point in the document for the Rubber Stamp tool; when you drag the tool, it will apply the wood pattern you defined.

17. Choose the third tip from the left on the top row of the Brushes palette, and then drag along the top of the flesh color in the image to add a cap to the costume (see fig. 18.6).

figure 18.6
Add a cap to the costume by painting the sampled pattern file and using the Rubber Stamp tool.

18. Press Ctrl(⌘)+S to save your work, and keep this file open.

Mapping a texture to a Poser figure is an imprecise art, to be sure. You really have no way of knowing (while you're working in Photoshop) precisely where the texture in the image will be located on the 3D figure in Poser. If your system has enough RAM to keep both Poser and Photoshop open, however, you can refine the image map of the wood costume by trying it out in Poser and then, based on the visual results, modifying the image in Photoshop.

You do *not* need to create multiple versions of the Stumpy file to arrive at a perfect "fit" for the costume, however. After you declare that the Stumpy image is the one to be mapped on the Poser figure, the Poser figure automatically updates as you edit the image in Photoshop. Macintosh users might want to launch Poser before launching Photoshop, because Photoshop requires a larger percentage of application RAM than Poser does.

Mapping and Rendering the Poser Model

As mentioned earlier, the rendered figures from Poser for the TreeFolks assignment are in the CHAP18 folder of the Companion CD. If you have Poser and would like the procedure for creating Poser costumes in Photoshop, the steps in this section are for you.

The following steps show you how to map the Stumpy image to a Poser figure and render the results to a file format that Photoshop can use.

Rendering a Model from Poser

1. In Poser, with the figure, lighting, and camera angle defined for the pose, choose Render, and then choose Surface Material to display the Surface Material dialog box.

2. In the Texture Map field, click on Load, select the Stumpy file you created in Photoshop, and click on OK to exit the directory box. Then click on OK in the Surface Material dialog box to return to the workspace.

3. Choose Render, from Render menu. As you can see in figure 18.7, the Poser figure is handsomely attired; it's time to perform a final render to file format.

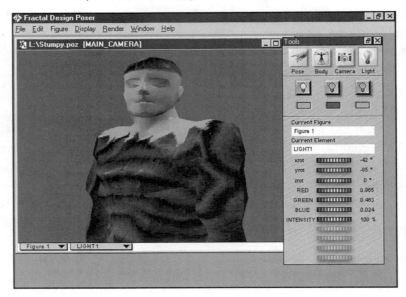

figure 18.7
By adding the texture map you created to the Poser figure, you "dress up" the character to fit your special design.

4. Choose File, Export. For the export file format, Windows users should choose TIF, and Macintosh users should choose PICT.

    Both the PICT and the TIF file formats are capable of containing an alpha channel that describes the Poser figure. After saving to these formats, you can easily separate the foreground figure from the background in Photoshop.

5. Save your Poser work, and close the application.

One detail omitted from the preceding set of steps has to do with the *output resolution* of the files you export from Poser. Poser writes TIF, BMP, and PICT files to the resolution of your monitor (72 pixels/inch), which might, or might not, be sufficient for creating larger compositions in Photoshop.

You have two basic options for outputting larger file sizes from Poser:

◆ In Poser, choose Render, Render Options, and increase the Width and Height values for rendering to a New Window. You still need to render to screen to generate the image, but then you can save the increased-resolution file to PICT or TIFF format.

◆ Choose to Export the Poser figure to DXF or RIB modeling exchange formats. This is not an option if you do not own an external rendering program, but if you do, you can render the figure to any dimension you like from outside the Poser application.

The authors chose the latter of these options to create the resource files in the CHAP18 folder of the Companion CD. We used PIXAR Showplace for the Macintosh to create the characters shown in figure 18.8. Above the figures you can see the textures used. You can use the textures, which are in the CHAP18 folder, to complete Poser costumes of your own (by following the steps described earlier) or as texture maps in modeling and rendering applications.

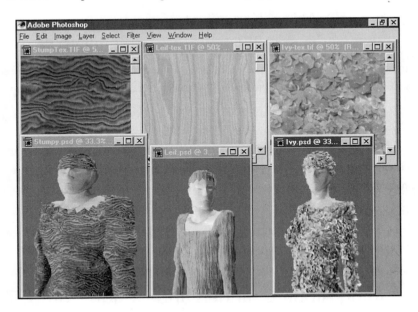

figure 18.8
Use different Poser figures and surface material textures to create a variety of characters.

NOTE

The decision to use an outside rendering application for the Poser figures was made because PIXAR Showplace performs displacement mapping. *Displacement mapping* goes beyond surface texturing to provide bumps along the *silhouette* of a 3D shape. Most rendering programs, including Poser's internal rendering engine, simply provide surface detail within the volume of a model, but not along the edges.

The qualitative difference between a Poser-rendered figure and one rendered in an outside application can be noticeable. Your choice of rendering options should depend upon your proficiency with modeling, your patience, and the budget you have for additional software programs.

Now, presuming that at this point you have the TreeFolks figures rendered from Poser, it's time to move forward to compositing work in Photoshop—to create the advertisement. Again, the files of the rendered figures are in the CHAP18 folder on the CD, and will be referenced as needed.

Creating a 3D Advertisement

Regardless of the source material that goes into a Photoshop composition, you can make a flat design, or an attractive *dimensional* design, if you understand some basic rules of lighting and how to create lighting effects by using Photoshop's features.

Poser figures are nicely shaded, but they do not cast shadows, whether grouped or rendered individually from Poser. This is one of the reasons for recommending that you render a group of Poser figures as individual poses. You can add shadows to the composition later in Photoshop, and individual Poser renderings use fewer of your system resources.

In the sections to follow, you create a composite image from the three characters rendered from Poser, manually add some lighting effects, and make the finished advertisement as three-dimensional as the individual elements.

Loading Alpha Channels and Design Composition

To help make this band of lawn-care specialists more interesting-looking, each Poser figure was created with a distinguishing characteristic. There's a brawny, squat character, a diminutive adolescent character, and a leafy female character. In the next set of steps, you separate the figures from the background by loading the alpha channels Poser writes into rendered files, and you create a multilayered, single composition from the Poser files.

COMPOSING THE POSER IMAGES

CD-ROM

1. Open the Stumpy.psd image from the CHAP18 folder on the Companion CD. The authors' rendered files were saved in Photoshop's native format to save time (by eliminating any cross-platform file-compatibility issues).

2. Open the Layers palette if it is not already in the workspace (press F7); then click on the Channels tab.

3. Scroll down to the #4 title on the Channels palette, and then press Ctrl(⌘) and click on the channel title to load the channel information as a selection marquee in the image (see fig. 18.9).

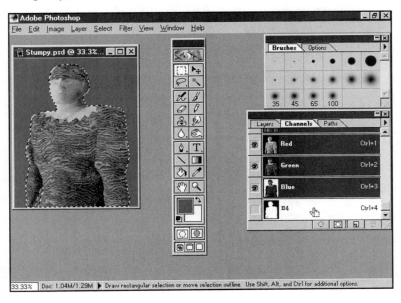

figure 18.9
Load, as a selection marquee, the information Poser wrote to an alpha channel.

4. Choose any of the selection tools, right-click (Macintosh: hold Ctrl and click) over the image, and then choose Layer via Cut from the Context menu. This creates a new layer that consists only of the figure. The Background layer is now unimportant.

5. Click on the Layers tab, then drag the Background layer title on the Layers palette into the trash icon to delete it from the document.

Because Poser writes image files to screen resolution, calculating the final dimensions of the advertisement, expressed in inches, is difficult. The screen resolution of 72 pixels/inch is almost never used in high-quality printing. Fortunately, resolution is inversely proportional to dimension, and Photoshop can therefore change the resolution without affecting the image *content* of your work.

Say that you want the finished ad to be 7" high by 5" wide at 150 pixels/inch resolution. To prepare the Stumpy.psd image for a camera-ready advertisement, follow these steps:

CHANGING IMAGE RESOLUTION

1. Choose Image, Image Size to display the Image Size dialog box.

2. Clear the Resample Image check box, and then type **150** in the Resolution field (see fig. 18.10). Note that the values displayed in the inches fields are smaller than those of the original image; thanks to the new width, you can add the extra TreeFolks characters to the file.

3. Choose Image, Canvas Size; then type **8** in the Width (inches) field and click on OK. Although this is a wider measurement than the intended final size for the advertisement, the additional width gives you some room to compose the characters in relation to one another.

4. Open the Ivy.psd image from the CHAP18 folder. With a selection tool as the active toolbox tool, on the Channels palette, press Ctrl(⌘) and click on the channel #4 title to load the selection. Then move back to the Layers palette, right-click (Macintosh: hold Ctrl and click), and choose Layer via Cut from the Context menu. At any time now you can delete the Background layer in the Ivy.psd image (see fig. 18.11).

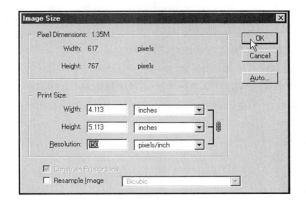

figure 18.10
Choose new dimensions for the image by increasing the resolution.

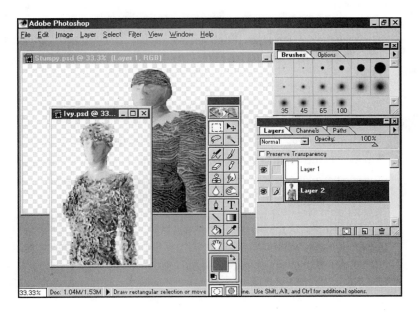

figure 18.11
Remove the background area from the Ivy image to make copying the foreground content to another image window easier to do.

Note that the Ivy image has an additional layer, Layer 1, consisting of a Black-eyed Susan located in Ivy's hair (a creative touch). To keep the flower in the final image, choose Merge Visible from the Layers palette's flyout menu.

5. Drag the Layer palette title for the Ivy image into the Stumpy.psd image window. This copies the Ivy image to a separate layer in the Stumpy image.

6. Close the Ivy image without saving it. Open the Leif.psd image from the CHAP18 folder, and repeat steps 4 and 5 to add this image to the Stumpy.psd image.

7. Close the Leif image without saving it. Now, with the players assembled, label the layers on which they reside by double-clicking on the layer title, typing a unique name in the Name field in the Layer Options dialog box, and then clicking on OK to apply the change to the Layer name.

8. With the Move tool, position the characters on their respective layers. Chances are that the copying procedure you performed did not position the characters so that the bottom of the image is flush with the bottom of the image window. You can use the keyboard arrow keys to precisely nudge the current editing layer's contents into position. See figure 18.12 for a suggested positioning of the TreeFolks.

   Although the order in which the characters appear in the image (from front to back) can be changed by re-ordering their titles on the Layers palette, the order in which you added them to the original Stumpy file seems to work (see fig. 18.12). Try to overlap the characters as much as possible without losing image details. When the image is cropped to a width of 5", you want image content to be as large as possible.

9. Choose the Rectangular Marquee tool. Then, on the Options palette, choose Fixed Size from the Style drop-down list.

10. Type **750** in the Width field, and type **1,000** in the Height field.

    The number 750 was chosen for the pixel width of the Rectangular Marquee tool because 5 inches—our target width for the ad—is equal to 750 pixels at 150 pixels/inch, the resolution of the image ($5 \times 150 = 750$). The height for the Rectangular Marquee selection is not important at the moment; the height of the image will be changed later. A good height here is 1,000; it exceeds the height of the image, and the marquee will be easy to reposition due to its height.

figure 18.12

Arrange the content of the layers to minimize the width needed to crop the image to 5 ";
you gain image size this way.

11. Click in the image window to create a marquee selection with the dimensions you
    specified.

12. Drag inside the marquee until its vertical orientation frames the characters nicely (see fig.
    18.13). It's okay if the rectangle crops slightly inside the characters; tight cropping, as it's
    called in the trade, sometimes creates a better composed framing of image content.

13. Choose Image, Crop; then choose File, Save As, and save the document to your hard
    disk in the Photoshop file format, as TreeFolks.psd.

Because more work must be done with the characters in this ad, increasing the size
of the document to its final height didn't make sense in the previous steps. Although
transparent areas in a Photoshop image contribute less than opaque image areas to
the overall file size held in system memory, creating the final dimensions for the
advertisement now would add an unnecessary "overhead."

figure 18.13
Drag the Fixed Size marquee selection around in the image window until you have the best crop for the image.

Adding Individual Drop Shadows

In the files of the characters on the Companion CD, a strong light source comes from the 10 o'clock direction. Shadows are necessary to keep the dimensional quality of the composition. Because the characters are on separate layers, creating shadows is an easy procedure. The next set of steps shows you how to manage layers and create the shadows.

ADDING SHADING TO THE TREEFOLKS

1. Click on the Stumpy title on the Layers palette; then press Ctrl(⌘) and click on the title to load the nontransparent layer areas as a marquee selection.

2. Right-click (Macintosh: hold Ctrl and click), and choose Feather from the Context menu.

3. In the Feather dialog box, type **10** in the Feather Radius field (see fig. 18.14), and click on OK. The marquee lines in the document now represent the midpoint between 100% selected areas and 0% selected areas (masked areas), the transition distance being 5 pixels inside the marquee and 5 pixels outside.

figure 18.14
Feather the selection marquee to create a transition between selected and masked image areas.

4. Click on the Create a new layer icon at the bottom of the palette, and drag the new layer title down so that it lies beneath the Stumpy layer title. The new layer should be the current editing layer now.

5. Press **D** (Default Colors) to ensure that the current foreground color is black, and press Alt(Opt)+Delete (Backspace) to fill the selection with black. Press Ctrl(⌘)+D to deselect the marquee in the image.

6. With the Move tool chosen, press and hold Shift, and then press the down-arrow keyboard key once and the right-arrow keyboard key once. This power nudges—moves the layer contents by 10 pixels—the shading on the layer to a position at which one would find a shadow in the real world.

7. Choose Multiply from the Layers palette's drop-down list, and drag the Opacity slider to about 76% (see fig. 18.15). The Multiply mode makes your hand-crafted drop shadow dense, and the partial opacity allows some background to show through, although the final background image isn't in place yet.

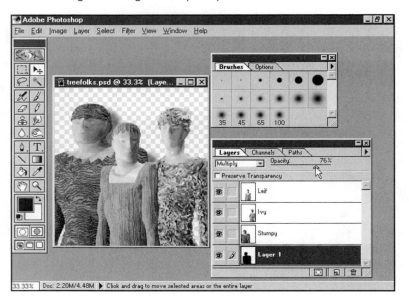

figure 18.15
Create a drop-shadow effect by filling a feathered version of a character's outline with partially opaque foreground color.

8. To keep the saved file size of this document to a minimum, click on the Stumpy title on the Layers palette to make it the current editing layer; then choose Merge Down from the Layers palette's flyout menu. Double-click on this merged layer, and retitle the layer in the Layer Options dialog box before going much further.

9. Perform steps 1–7 with the Leif and the Ivy layers in the image. When you finish, press Ctrl(⌘)+S. You should have three layers in the TreeFolks document now, each with a drop shadow attached to the character.

Because the final background image is not currently in place, we asked that you trust the "guesswork" settings for the shadow opacity in the previous steps. The reasons for recommending Multiply mode and 75-percent opacity, which generally work against medium-tone backgrounds, is simple—to conserve system resources. In the next section, you add a 4.5 MB PhotoCD image to the composition. This means that in *addition* to the amount of memory you need for holding the TreeFolks image, you need from three to five times this amount (an additional 13.5 to 22.5 MB) in application RAM and temp space on your hard disk to hold the image (PhotoCD and TreeFolk) in memory as you work. When Photoshop is deprived of actual RAM, it seeks temp space on your hard disk—and takes a lonnnnng time to execute commands.

If you have more than 32 MB of RAM on your system, however, you might want to keep drop-shadow layers separate in your own imaging work, merging the layers only after you have evaluated the background image and increased or decreased the opacity of the shadow layers accordingly. By merging the shadow layers, as you did in the preceding set of steps, you saved about 30 percent of the file size held in memory for the TreeFolks document.

Adding a PhotoCD Background

When you work with synthetic images such as those created in Poser, it's a good idea to include some sort of real-world digital photograph in the composition to root (pardon the pun) the piece in reality. This helps viewers suspend disbelief, and it's easy to accomplish if you have a collection of stock photography.

The Img0012.pcd file in the CHAP18 folder was copied from a PhotoCD created for the authors from original photographic works. Imaging your photography work to PhotoCD format presents a number of advantages over conventional scanning of photographs:

◆ The images are not on your hard disk, taking up space.

◆ PhotoCD disks have an expected life span of nearly 100 years, as compared to disks or other removable media, which must be freshened (copied to other media) every few years or so to maintain the magnetic integrity of the data.

- ◆ Because PhotoCD images come in a "pack" of five resolutions, choosing the right size for an assignment is easy.

- ◆ The images on a PhotoCD are acquired through scanning the original negative, not a print; therefore, color fidelity and detail are much higher than in an image scanned with a desktop scanner.

See the Acrobat document (*The Argyle Pages*) on the Companion CD for contact information on PhotoCD imaging services. PhotoCD images are cheap, and because the images are your own, you can use them in your work with no copyright issue.

In the following steps, you open the Img0112 file from the Companion CD and copy it to the TreeFolks composition. Here's how to achieve a blend of reality and the surreal in the advertisement:

ADDING A PHOTOCD BACKGROUND IMAGE

1. Choose Image, Canvas size; then type 7 in the Height field, click on the bottom, middle icon in the Anchor field, and click on OK. The canvas size of the document now has the final image dimensions, and you can place the background. Seven inches at 150 pixels/inch resolution is 1,050 pixels.

2. Choose File, Open. Choose the Img0112.PCD file from the Open box in Photoshop. This displays the Kodak Precision CMS PhotoCD dialog box.

3. If the Destination is not Generic Monitor, click on the Destination button and choose it. The other destinations in this dialog box pertain to different color modes for the image; Generic Monitor is the most compatible with the RGB mode image with which you're currently working. Use a profile for a specific monitor for the Destination setting only if you have a calibrated monitor that corresponds to one on the list.

You know that the TreeFolks advertisement is 750 pixels in width and 1,050 pixels in height. To fill the width of the TreeFolks image completely, you need to specify the 1,024×1,536 size for opening the PhotoCD image. The next smaller PhotoCD image size is 512×768, which is not nearly large enough to serve as a background in this assignment.

4. Choose 1,024×1,536 from the Resolution drop-down list in the dialog box (see fig. 18.16), and then click on OK.

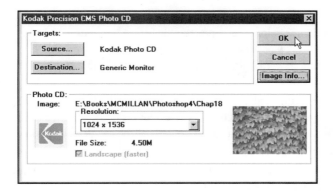

figure 18.16
PhotoCD images come in five resolutions. Choose the one that suits your design needs.

5. On the Layers palette, drag the Background title of the Img0112.pcd file into the TreeFolks window (see fig. 18.17). Chances are that the image will copy to an inappropriate order in the layers, obscuring some of the TreeFolks.

figure 18.17
Copy the PCD image to the design by dragging its layer title into the target document window.

6. Drag the PhotoCD background image layer down in the Layers palette so that it is positioned below the characters' layers. Then, with the Move tool, drag inside the document window to ensure that the entire background is covered, and that the transparency grid (Photoshop's checkerboard display for indicating transparency on a layer) is not visible.

7. Uncheck the visibility icon to the left of the PhotoCD image layer icon on the Layers palette, click on any of the characters layers titles, and then choose Merge Visible from the Layers palette menu flyout to merge all the character layers into one layer. You should see a significant decrease in saved file size on the document sizes area in Photoshop.

8. Click on the visibility icon for the PhotoCD image layer, and then press Ctrl(⌘)+S to save your work. Keep the TreeFolks image open in the workspace, and close the Img0112.pcd file without saving it.

TIP

To quickly determine the size of the current document, press Alt(Opt) and click on the document sizes field; it's on the status bar in the Windows version of Photoshop, and on the document window on the Macintosh. The pop-up box displays color mode, dimensions in both inches and pixels, and image resolution.

Although it looks appropriate in the context of the design, the image of the ivy was taken under overcast lighting conditions. Because there is no predominant lighting direction in the image, it's flat when compared to the foreground subjects. In the following section, you use the Lighting Effects filter to correct this lighting problem.

TIP

Unlike Photoshop 3, layer content in Photoshop 4 can be repositioned an indefinite number of times, with no loss of the image areas that fall outside the image window. At any time you can reposition the ivy on the layer so that the leaves fall in any pattern you like; the PCD image is much larger than the document window.

The only time you lose the areas of an image that fall outside the window when copying a layer to a different document window is after you have changed the size of the image by cropping.

Using Lighting Effects

Although you cannot change the apparent direction of strong lighting in an image with the Lighting Effects filter in Photoshop, you can indeed suggest a lighting source in an image whose original lighting is flatly lit from ambient lighting.

In the next set of steps, you use the Lighting Effects filter to perk up the background PhotoCD image, making it look as though it's actually behind the TreeFolks, who are illuminated from the 10 o'clock position in the composition.

ADDING A LIGHT SOURCE

1. With the PhotoCD image layer as the current editing layer, choose Filter, Render; then choose Lighting Effects to display the Lighting Effects dialog box.

   By default, one light (a Spotlight type) is in the proxy window of the Lighting Effects filter. The dot in the center of the ellipse that represents the Spotlight is the target area, where the light from the source lands in the image. The dot connected to the target point is the source—the light itself. You control the angle of the light—how broad or narrow it is—with the dots along the ellipse.

2. Drag the source dot in the proxy window to the 10 o'clock position.

3. If the light appears to be too intense on the proxy image, drag the source dot farther from the image (see fig. 18.18).

4. Click on OK. The Lighting Effects filter is processor-intensive; you might have to wait a moment while the command executes. (See Chapter 13, "Creative Plug-Ins," for more about this filter.)

5. Press Ctrl(⌘)+S to save your work up to this stage.

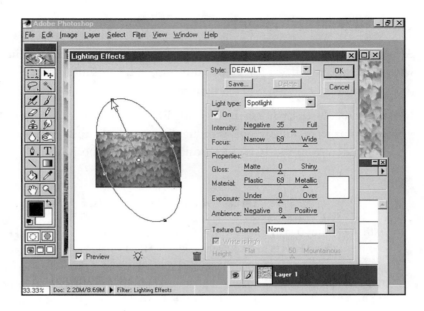

figure 18.18

The Lighting Effects filter simulates a light source in an image, or in a selected area of an image.

As you can see in figure 18.19, the Lighting Effects filter has enhanced the ivy image layer, but left the TreeFolks elements untouched. The reason is that all editing actions, including the application of filters, can be performed on the active layer only. You might want to perform Levels adjustments (Ctrl(⌘)+L) to the ivy image to get the tonal properties of the image more in line with those of the TreeFolks. PhotoCD images tend to be balanced for a number of display options: monitors on different platforms, as well as television sets, which have a higher *gamma* (signal-to-brightness ratio) than monitors. Generally, if you decrease the midtone level in the Levels command (drag the middle slider to the right), you increase contrast in the midtones enough with PhotoCD images to correct them for digital media.

figure 18.19
The Lighting Effects filter can help bring together a composition's elements.

Text: The Final Touch

As you might recall from Chapter 12, "Working with Text as Graphics," composing text in a drawing application and then importing the text to your Photoshop composition works better than trying to use the Type tool alone. To conclude the TreeFolks piece, the authors have done some of the text composition for you (using techniques from Chapter 12). In the next set of steps, you complete the work by adding a layer of text to the advertisement.

Here's how to turn this somewhat silly poster into a *commercial*, somewhat silly poster:

ADDING TEXT TO THE COMPOSITION

1. Open the Treetext.psd image from the CHAP18 folder on the Companion CD.

2. Arrange both the TreeFolks and the Treetext images so that you have a clear view of both in the workspace, in addition to the Layers palette. Zoom out of the images, if necessary. Click on the TreeFolks Layer title on the Layers palette (with the TreeFolks image in the foreground in the workspace) to make this layer the current editing layer.

3. Click on the Treetext title bar to make it the foreground image in the workspace, and then drag the layer title, "Text," into the TreeFolks window (see fig. 18.20).

figure 18.20

To complete the advertisement, copy text you have imported from an Illustrator-compatible program into the target window.

4. Position the text by using the Move tool. Unless the source document window and the target document window are of identical dimensions and resolution, the text (or layer with other content) will not land perfectly aligned to the layers in the target document.

5. The bottom copy on the Text layer is fairly well laid out, but if you want to shift the headline, choose the Rectangular Marquee tool.

6. Drag a marquee around the headline. Hold Ctrl(⌘) and drag the headline. The Ctrl(⌘) key extends the function of the marquee tools to cut the selected image area that the marquee surrounds, and it becomes a floating selection above the layer. Drag inside the floating selection to position it, and then click outside the marquee to drop the image area back onto the layer.

7. Choose File, Save a Copy, and then save the image to your hard disk in the TIFF file format, as Treefolk.tif. You now have a copy of the composition that can be shared with a non-Photoshop enabled client, and the original to use again one day when a theme park or other concern drops by for an outstanding advertisement.

Summary

You have seen in this chapter how Photoshop, once again, serves as the great integrator of different media types. Hopefully, you have seen also that "3D" is in the eye of the beholder and of the creator. You don't have to go to great expense to produce great artwork—you simply need to understand how to create some special effects manually, and observe the real-world conditions in which lighting affects objects.

Chapter 19, "Web Site Construction," takes you beyond the concerns of printed output, into the WYSIWYG environment of worldwide, on-screen presentations. You will explore the techniques and processes for generating interface elements and converting images to Internet format. You will put the imaging techniques you have learned so far to a different use as you practice "small is beautiful" in designs, file formats, and navigation link creation.

CHAPTER

WEB SITE CONSTRUCTION

When they see the propagation of home pages on the World Wide Web, most people are amazed by the diversity they encounter—both in personal expression and style of graphical content. Designers all over the world have discovered procedures with specific applications to make the most out of a limited number of pixels and other digital media, to make small wonders that pass through narrow bandwidths.

CD-ROM

When the authors finally arrived at their *own* procedures for creating multipage Web sites, Photoshop immediately became the hub around which media from other design applications (as well as designs completely created in Photoshop) became a unified composition. This chapter takes you from the ground up, with design techniques, suggestions, and styles for composing Web page elements—from background texture to creating navigation buttons. The example in this chapter is a fully functioning Web site that you can preview before you begin reading. Copy the ArtSake folder from the CHAP19 folder on the Companion CD to your hard disk, drag the Art-Sake.htm document into your favorite browser, click on the links, and we will show you how this site was created, using Photoshop.

Planning Your Web Extravaganza

Before you begin collecting plug-in filters and images, and *especially* before you accept an assignment to author a Web site, there are some conventions you should bear in mind for creating a *successful* Web site. The first guideline you should understand and adopt is that:

Everything on the Web is 72 pixels per inch in resolution.

Certain self-proclaimed experts will tell you otherwise, and high-resolution monitors for the Macintosh and Intel-based machines often claim greater resolution support, but the World Wide Web is a common ground for the display of graphical media, and the convention is that 72 pixels/inch is the resolution at which images are displayed on-screen.

Therefore, forget about *pixels per inch* as a measurement of image dimensions in this chapter; all visitors to Web sites see your images at the same resolution. In this chapter, all references to design elements are expressed as pixels. This means that if a client's image is 2" by 2", and he or she forgets to tell you that the resolution of the image is 300 pixels/inch, the client hasn't told you that the image (as it would be embedded on a Web page) is actually 600 pixels by 600 pixels. To qualify as a Web element that visitors to the site could download within a lifetime, such an image would have to be dramatically resized!

To reach your audience, keep the pixel count small in your images. A theme throughout this chapter is "Small is Beautiful." We will show you how to design the best images, and how to display the images you already have, at a compact file size.

Red, Green, and Blue Are the Colors of the Web

For designers of traditional print media, the Web as a publication environment is going to be a mixed blessing. Say good-bye to the subtractive color mode of printing inks when you enter the World Wide Web. Images that you might have saved in CMYK color mode for printing will look simply awful, embedded in a Web document, because the RGB color model—that used by your monitor—is the color space of the Web.

It's a good idea to think WYSIWYG when you design Web media; exactly what you see in preview on-screen as you design is what visitors to your site will see. This includes dimensions, as well as RGB color mode. If an image displays at 1:1 in Photoshop with scroll bars, visitors to your site will have to scroll the image, as well. Unless you have a very compelling reason for designing larger than monitor resolution, don't do it; nothing looks worse on-screen than an image divided into "Parts 1 and 2" because of its oversized dimensions. The key to conducting smart business on the Web is to understand that Web images are designed to sell something, but not necessarily the exact image displayed.

In other words, create miniature masterpiece duplicates of your larger work, optimized for the Web. If you can sufficiently intrigue visitors to a site with the miniature, they can always contact you for a larger version of the piece.

Play to the Lowest Common Denominator

Remember the last time you told a funny story to a group of friends, and forgot the punch line? Your closest friends might have stuck around as you fumbled for, "Okay, so *you* hold the chicken, and I'll take the suitcase," but in all likelihood, most of your audience drifted over to a clique whose entertainer had his or her act together. Web audiences have short attention spans.

Although designers tend to go with high-end equipment these days, *do not* presume that your audience is similarly outfitted. With respect to Web presentations, you're safe to assume that your audience in 1997 has a video card with sufficient RAM to display Indexed color (hundreds of colors, 8 bits/pixel) at 640×480 pixel resolution. Many will be able to display TrueColor (millions of colors, 24 bits/pixel) at 640×480 or higher resolutions. However, because some visitors might not know how to switch their screen modes to a higher resolution or color depth, they will see your site with the system default settings they have used since they purchased their machine—256 colors at best.

Your audience might also have a 28.8 modem or access to high-speed data lines, but don't count on it—9600 baud or 14.4 modems are hard to simply throw away, and high-speed data lines are expensive and difficult to get in most parts of the world. Remember, your audience is the entire *world*.

To play to the lowest common denominator, you would be well-advised to compose your Web pages to a maximum of 620 pixels in width by 295 pixels in height. Why this "magic" number? The authors measured the live space in Netscape Navigator and the active space in Microsoft Internet Explorer, and came up with this number—the smaller of the maximum dimensions between the two, with a few pixels subtracted to account for scroll bars. The reality is that unless you use a frame-based Hypertext Markup Language (HTML) page, neither browser will let you display page content clear to the edge of the browser window. Don't let this information lead you to compose all graphics at 620×295, however. Rather, think of this dimension as a guideline for the whole page. (Remember—you need to add navigation buttons and text to a page, also.) You might consider composing a design to be embedded in a page at half these dimensions, or less, and see how the other elements can be worked in.

It's unlikely that visitors will connect flawlessly to your site, given that most of the world connects to the Internet through Plain Old Telephone System (POTS) lines, and there is noise that reduces transfer times. But with optimal line conditions and a visitor with a 28.8 modem, you can expect a transfer rate of approximately 1.8 kilobits per second for your Web work. If you measure the file size of your images according to this optimistic rule, a 15 KB image would take 8.3 seconds to completely download, and a 50 KB image would take about 28 seconds. If visitors have to wait more than 30 seconds to see your work, they're likely to ask themselves what *other* sites they can surf today.

Use File Size as an Alternative Unit of Measurement

There is no rule of thumb for image dimensions displayed on a page as "optimal," but you can take a copy of your work and scale it in Photoshop to a fairly large size, if you're willing to compromise color depth and image fidelity. Later in this chapter, you will work with two file formats, GIF and JPEG, that reduce image file size to a fraction of the original's size by discarding image information. How much original fidelity is lost is up to you; the loss of information is more visible in some images than in others.

The bottom line is that you should check the saved file size of an image you intend to post on the Web. If it's larger than 40 KB—50 KB, tops—consider rendering a different, smaller version for Web use. For many visitors and potential customers, it's simply not worth the wait. That's why many designers strive for a maximum page size (all the text and all the graphics on a page) of less than 50 KB. In a nutshell, if you design for the screen and keep it small, you have leapt past the competition in the greatest marketplace for artwork in the world.

The following sections address the construction and optimization of the components of a Web site.

Backgrounds, Buttons, and Images

Because Photoshop has no export filters for animations, sounds, or aromas, we necessarily have to limit the discussions in this chapter to Web media that Photoshop can handle. The basic compositional elements of a Web page are the following:

◆ **Backgrounds**—Navigator and Microsoft Explorer account for the lion's share of the Web browser market, and both support the **BODY BACK-GROUND=** tag in an HTML document. These browsers will create a background for the page by tiling any JPEG or GIF graphic you specify.

◆ **Buttons**—Hypertext links are a fundamental feature of HTML, but that doesn't mean you must always click on text to automatically move to a different page or Internet resource. The same **A HREF=** tag that is used to mark "hot" text can be used also to mark a graphic as a place on a page where a hypertext link can be activated. Face it—personal computer users are more accustomed to clicking on a button to make something happen than they are to clicking on text. (That is why the following sections show you how to create images shaped like navigation controls.)

◆ **Images**—The **IMG SRC=** tag is used for placement of graphics as graphics on a Web page. GIF and JPEG file formats are supported. This chapter shows you how to access different types of these file standards to make your images look better and download faster.

The steps to building a better Web site begin with creating an appropriate background image. In the next section, you will design an intricate background for a fictitious illustrator, Arthur Sake, whose goal is to make his work, his favorite links, and his life a public matter to all "Netizens."

Creating a Wide Tiling Background

It didn't take Web designers long to figure out that displaying a 640×480 or larger image as the background to an HTML page causes a page to download *very* slowly. An alternative approach, which reduces this bottleneck, is to use a small image that has been carefully edited so that you cannot see the seams where the image repeats across the background.

Instead of using a small square tile, designers have found that by using an image that is very wide, but not very tall, they can produce a much more interesting page background, and still keep the file small. When you use this technique in background creation, you can produce patterns or zones of color across the width of the page. This effect can be seen on the top page of Arthur Sake's site on the Companion CD.

When two different types of foreground content must be displayed on a single page, a natural design decision is to create a background of two different patterns. In the sample site, Arthur Sake's welcome screen is separated from the navigational controls by wavy lines and a distinctly different background texture for the buttons.

Here's how to use a sample texture image, Stones.tif, in Photoshop to make a small, seamlessly tiling image:

CREATING WEB BACKGROUND TILES

CD-ROM

1. In Photoshop, open the Stones.tif image from the CHAP19 folder on the Companion CD. This image was created in Fractal Design Painter and does not tile seamlessly.

2. Choose Image Duplicate. Accept the Default name in the Duplicate Image dialog box and then click on OK to create the duplicate image.

3. Press F8 to display the Info/Navigator palette on the workspace, if it's not already present.

4. Click and hold on the plus-shaped icon to the left of the X and Y coordinates on the Info palette; then choose pixels from the drop-down list. Coordinates for the cursor and the measurement of selected areas in the image will be displayed in pixels on the palette.

5. Choose the Rectangular Marquee tool. While holding Shift, drag a marquee in the duplicate image window. Stop dragging and release the cursor when the W and H fields on the Info palette read 128. The Shift key constrains rectangular selections to squares.

6. Choose Image, Crop (see fig. 19.1). Although you can select a square by using the Options palette's Fixed Size Style for the Rectangular Marquee tool, this step is quicker when you have only one image to crop.

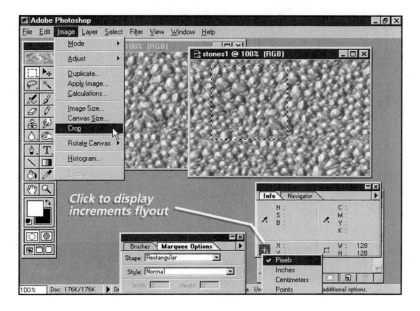

figure 19.1
Crop the duplicate image to square proportions, and make its dimensions small.

7. Choose Filter, Other, and then choose Offset. The Offset dialog box appears.

8. Type **64** in both the Horizontal and Vertical fields, click on the Wrap Around button (see fig. 19.2), and then click on OK. As you can see, the image wraps to the right and down in the image window, leaving a seam in the exact center of the image. Because the image has been turned "inside out," its current edges will tile seamlessly, but the center seam needs to be removed.

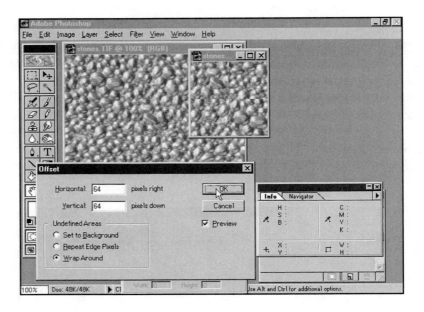

figure 19.2
Turn an image "inside out" to correct areas that will display a seam when the image is used as a tiling background.

9. Look at the seam in the duplicate image, and try to find a location in the original Stones image that has a similar pattern of stones. With the Rubber Stamp tool, in the Clone (aligned) Option mode, press Alt(Opt) and click on the area in the Stones image to set the sampling point; then put the duplicate image in the foreground of the workspace. Release Alt(Opt), choose the second row, third (from left) tip on the Brushes palette for the Rubber Stamp tool, and drag over the seam in the 128×128 image (see fig. 19.3).

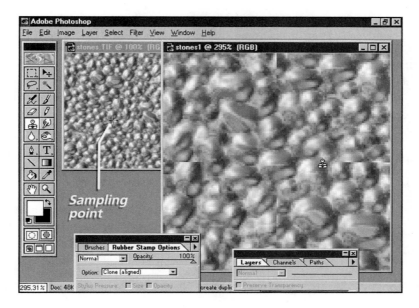

figure 19.3
*Clone away seams in the duplicate image by adding samples from the original,
larger image.*

10.   After you have removed the seam from the image, choose File, Save As, and save this
      image to your hard disk as Back01.tif, in the TIFF file format. Better yet, start a new folder
      on your drive for this image and those to follow in this chapter (the ones that make up the
      Web site).

11.   *This step is optional:* The background should not intrude upon the foreground elements.
      This means that the background should be either very light (to support black or dark-
      colored text) or dark (to support white or light-colored text). If you want to use this tile for
      other purposes in the future, do this to a duplicate of your work: Choose Image, Adjust,
      and then choose Brightness/Contrast. Drag the brightness slider to about +57, drag the
      Contrast slider down to about –60, and click on OK.

12.   Press Ctrl(⌘)+A to select all; then choose Edit, Define Pattern.

13.   Close the original Stones.tif image without saving it, and press Ctrl(⌘)+N to display the
      New (document) dialog box.

The Back01 image will serve as tiling wallpaper for the link pages for Arthur Sake's site but, as mentioned earlier, we want a wide tiling image for the top page of the site—and the new image is it. Basic math tells us that a wide seamless tiling image can be made from the Back01 image, provided that its width is a multiple of 128, the width of Back01. Seven times 128 is 896, which will cover the width of a visitor's monitor screen running 800×600 video resolution. The authors feel it's unnecessary at this date to accommodate a higher video resolution, so this number (896) covers not only the 640×480 crowd, but also all 800×600 screens.

14. In the New dialog box, type **896** in the Width field, type **128** in the Height field, type **72** as the Resolution, choose RGB Color Mode, and then click on OK to create the new document.

15. Choose Edit, Fill. Then choose Pattern from the Contents Use drop-down list, and click on OK (see fig. 19.4). Displayed as a background in a Web browser, the wide document will tile seamlessly.

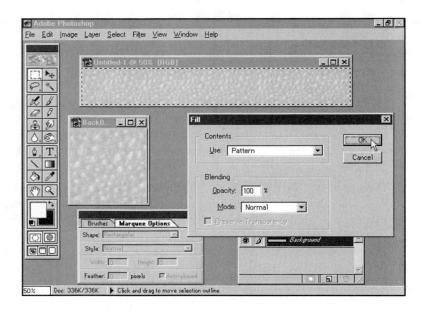

figure 19.4
If the target document dimension is a multiple of the pattern sample, it will also become a seamless, tiling image.

16. Press Ctrl(⌘)+S and save the document to your hard disk in the TIFF file format as Backwide.tif. Keep this image open for further steps. You can close the BACK01 image now.

TIP

The BOUTONS/TEXTURES folder on the Companion CD contains over 100 original seamless, tiling images created by the authors. Simply convert the TIFF images to the format you need, and you have instant background textures. Be sure to read the documentation in Acrobat PDF format in the TEXTURES folder for more information and the license agreement.

In the following section, you add a distinctive pattern to the left side of Backwide.tif. The reason you're asked to save initially in the Tagged Image File (TIFF) format instead of a Web graphic such as GIF or JPEG is that the TIFF format has a higher color capability than GIF images, and JPEG images lose some of the original image data in the conversion process. You can always go from a high-fidelity image to a low one, but you cannot recover lost image data by going from low to high fidelity. Generally, you want to save original artwork and make copies of the art for Web use.

Patterning Tricks with Quick Mask Mode

Other chapters have shown you that Photoshop's Quick Mask mode is an alternative way to designate areas in an image that you want to select or protect from editing. Like many things in Photoshop, however, Quick Mask tint overlay is also an object—it can be moved and copied, which makes it handy for advanced image selection work.

Arthur Sake asked us to design three wavy lines to separate the stones pattern on the right from a different pattern on the left. The pattern on the left, yet to be created, will serve as the background for the site's navigation controls. In the next set of steps you see how to create seamlessly tiling wavy lines by using Quick Mask selections and a new Photoshop duplicating feature.

OFFSETTING A SELECTION MASK

1. Type **200** in the Zoom percentage box, and press Enter (Return). Hold the spacebar to toggle to the Hand tool; then pan the image window until you see the left edge of the Backwide image. Release the spacebar and drag the window borders outward so that you can see from the top to the bottom edge of the document.

2. Press Ctrl(⌘)+R to display rulers around the document. Notice that when you choose a unit of measurement on the Info palette, all of Photoshop's other interface elements switch their display to use the same unit you specify.

3. Drag a guide from the vertical ruler to approximately the 128 pixel mark on the horizontal ruler.

4. Double-click on the Quick Mask mode control icon at the bottom of the toolbox, make sure that Color Indicates Selected areas is chosen, and click on OK to display the document in Quick Mask mode. Now, everywhere you apply foreground color will take on the Quick Mask overlay tint.

5. Press **D** (Default colors), and choose the Paintbrush tool and the tip shown on the Brushes palette in figure 19.5. Draw an inverted *S* pattern along the guide. Try to keep your beginning point at the same vertical position as the starting point. In the next step you will fix any imperfections to this mask.

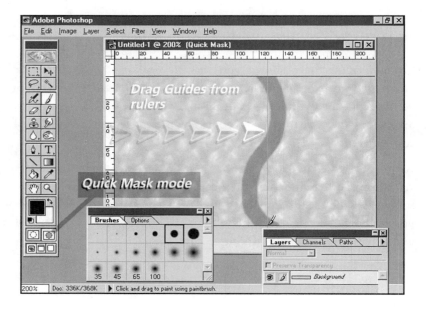

figure 19.5

Paint a stroke that will become a design element in the image by using the Quick Mask method of selecting areas.

6. With the Rectangular Marquee tool, drag an area around the Quick Mask *S* shape to select it. Quick Mask is an on-screen metaphor for a selection, but other selection tools can be used at any time to modify a Quick Mask area.

7. Choose Filter, Other, and then Offset. Type **0** in the Horizontal field and **64** in the Vertical field (see fig. 19.6). Click on OK to apply the Offset command. You can see that the author's inverted *S* pattern was close, but not perfect; the flaw in the Quick Mask's edge can be corrected.

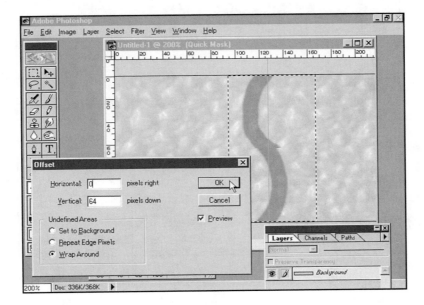

figure 19.6
Offset the selected Quick Mask to check for, and to correct, imperfections in its outline.

8. Press **X** (Switch Foreground/Background colors). Then, with the Paintbrush tool, drag around the flawed part of the Quick Mask (assuming that you did as well or as poorly as we did here). White foreground color removes Quick Mask, and black restores it. You might want to press X one final time to switch the toolbox colors to black foreground, and perform a last-minute touch-up or two to the Quick Mask pattern.

9. With the Rectangular Marquee tool, hold Ctrl+Alt (Macintosh: hold ⌘+Opt) and drag a pixel or two to the left of the pattern. This duplicates the Quick Mask as a floating selection; you cannot see the original because the interior of the selection marquee is in Normal mode at the moment, obscuring the original.

10.   *Do not accidentally click outside the marquee selection*! On the Layers palette (press F7 if it isn't on-screen), choose Multiply from the modes drop-down list. Multiply mode allows the original marquee selection to show through; now you can use the keyboard arrow keys to nudge the duplicate to a position about five pixels to the left of the original Quick Mask pattern (see fig. 19.7).

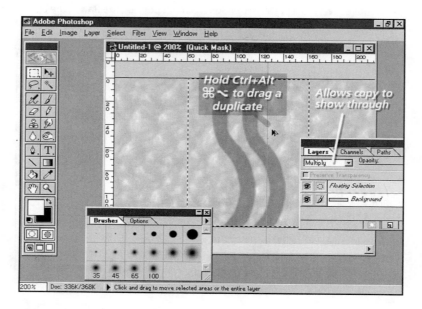

figure 19.7

Drag a duplicate of the Quick Mask pattern to the left of the original.

11.   When the duplicate Quick Mask pattern is in the correct position, hold Ctrl+Alt (Macintosh: hold ⌘+Opt) and drag the duplicate to the left. This drops the duplicate and creates a floating selection of another copy of the Quick Mask pattern in the same Multiply mode you originally specified for the floating selection of the pattern. Drag the wave to create equal horizontal spacing between all three waves. Click outside the current floating selection to drop it onto the image and complete the wavy-line pattern.

12.   Click on the Standard editing mode control on the toolbox, right-click (Macintosh: hold Ctrl and click), and then choose Layer via Copy from the Context menu. The new layer becomes the active layer and contains a copy of the background area made through the Quick Mask mode of selection.

13. Press Ctrl(⌘)+L to display the Levels command. Drag the white point slider (under the histogram) to the left until the far right Input Levels field reads about 220; then drag the black point slider on the Output Levels controls (the bottom slider in the Levels dialog box) to the right until the left Output Levels field reads about 72 (see fig. 19.8). This step lightens the image contents on the new layer enough to make the wavy lines pattern, but with the original stones pattern displayed somewhat in the lightened areas.

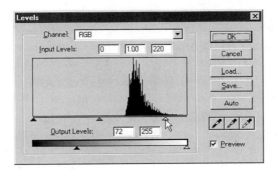

figure 19.8
Use the Levels command to apply a subtle amount of lightening to the nontransparent areas of the new layer.

14. Press Ctrl(⌘)+S to save the image to your hard disk in the only format Photoshop allows for layered images—as Backwide.psd.

Now it's time to embellish this design. In the following section, you add a drop shadow to the wavy lines, and complete the seamless, tiling background design with a secondary pattern on the left side of the image.

Working Between Design Layers

A marvelous flexibility in design options is yours when you tap into the power of Photoshop layers. The design currently needs a more dimensional look and a distinctive pattern to go behind its navigation control area. To accomplish this, you will work on different layers of Backwide.tif and use the Offset command again to create a seamless pattern from a design created by using the Paintbrush tool.

Here's how to finish the Web background image:

EMBELLISHING THE BACKGROUND DESIGN

1. Click on the Background title on the Layers palette; then click on the Create a new layer icon at the bottom of the palette. A new layer is created directly above the current layer, and Layer 2 is now sandwiched between the wavy lines layer and the background.

2. Click on Layer 1 to choose it. Then press Ctrl(⌘) and click on the Layer 1 title on the Layers palette to load the wavy lines as a selection marquee.

3. With a selection tool chosen, click within the selection (the cursor changes to a black wedge shape) and drag the selection to the left about 10 pixels so that the selection is next to, but not touching, the original location. Click on the Layer 2 title to make it the current editing Layer. Selection marquees do not "belong" to a specific layer; it's only when you copy or fill a selection that the current editing layer counts.

4. Right-click (Macintosh: hold Ctrl and click) and choose Feather from the Context menu. Type 4 in the Feather Radius field and click on OK to close the Feather selection box.

5. Double-click on the Paint Bucket tool to choose it and to force the Options palette for the tool to the front of the workspace.

6. On the Options palette, choose Multiply mode, drag the Opacity slider to about 65%, and type **255** in the Tolerance field. For transparent pixels on a layer, 255 is not really necessary, but this is a good practice to get into. For example, 255 specifies that every pixel in a selection is affected by the color or pattern the tool applies.

7. Press **D** (Default colors) and click inside the marquee selection (see fig. 19.9). Although the selection marquee is not contiguous—three enclosed areas are actually defined—the 255 Tolerance of the Paint Bucket tool fills all three areas; as long as you click in one of the marquees, a nice, soft drop shadow is created.

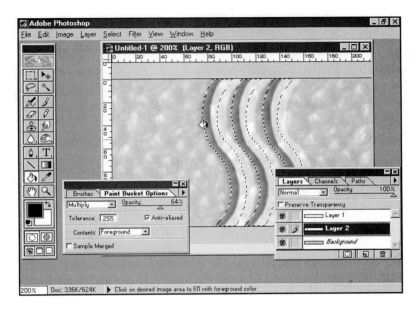

figure 19.9

Create a semitransparent drop shadow by filling a feathered selection marquee with the
Paint Bucket tool.

8. Press Ctrl(⌘)+D to deselect the marquee; then click on the Background title on the Layers
    palette to make the Background the current editing layer.

9. With the Lasso tool, click at the top center of the right wave, drag down within the wave
    to the bottom of the image, drag to the far left, then to the top, and release the cursor to
    close a selection marquee around the image area to the left of the wavy lines.

10. Click on the Foreground color selection box on the toolbox and choose a medium, neutral
    tone. (H:60°, S:5%, and B:65% is a good color choice.) After you define the color, click on
    OK to exit the color picker.

11. Press Alt+Delete (Macintosh: press Opt+Backspace) to fill the current selection with the
    foreground color you defined (see fig. 19.10). One of the advantages of working on
    separate layers is that the shadows and the wavy lines can still be repositioned, if
    necessary, and the area you filled can be restored simply by applying the Back01 pattern
    as a fill on the Background layer.

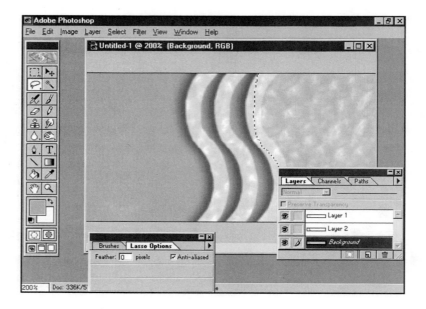

figure 19.10
Fill the selected Background layer area with foreground color.

12. Press Ctrl(⌘)+D to deselect the marquee and Ctrl(⌘)+S to save your work. Keep the file open in Photoshop.

Next, you add a painted texture to the area you just filled. It's important to keep the design muted, because the buttons and text you create later in this chapter must be legible when placed on the background in the HTML composition.

MANUALLY CREATING A PATTERN

1. Click on the Foreground color selection box on the toolbox and choose a slightly darker color than the current one from the color picker. Click on OK to exit the color picker.

2. Choose the Paintbrush tool and press **X** (Swap Foreground/Background colors); the background color on the toolbox is now the current foreground color.

3. Hold Alt(Opt) to toggle to the Eyedropper tool and click on the filled area in the image to sample it.

4. Click on the Foreground color selection box and choose a color that's slightly lighter than the current color. Click on OK to exit the color picker.

5. On the Brushes palette, choose the top row, third from left tip, and paint a short stroke in the left part of the image.

6. Paint three or four more short strokes, as though you were designing a fleck weave in a piece of clothing. Press **X** (Switch Foreground/Background colors) and continue to make short strokes, going in any direction, evenly spaced from one another (see fig. 19.11).

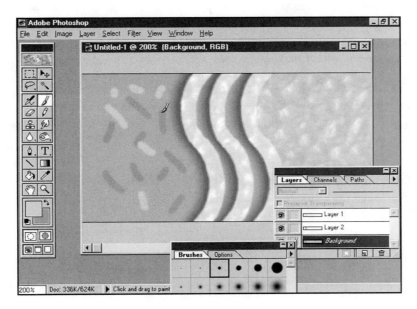

figure 19.11
Create a pattern of strokes slightly darker and slightly lighter than the color on the left of the image.

7. When there appears to be no more room to make strokes, choose Filter, Other, and then choose Offset.

8. In the Offset dialog box, type 0 in the Horizontal field, type **64** in the Vertical field, and click on OK. This displaces the pattern by half its height; now you can see the edges of the image displayed at the vertical center of the image.

9. Complete the design by filling the area at the vertical center of the area in which you're painting with a few more strokes.

10. Press Ctrl+Alt+F (Macintosh: ⌘+Opt+F) to access the last-used Filter dialog box. Unlike the Ctrl(⌘)+F command, the filter is not applied until you choose other options in the dialog box, or accept the last-used options, and then click on OK.

11. Type −64 in the Vertical field and click on OK. This displaces the image by a negative amount equal to the application of the Offset command in step 8. Now the image's Background layer is in its original position relative to the window.

12. Choose File, Export, and then choose GIF89a Export. Choose 32 from the colors drop-down list, choose Adaptive from the Palette drop-down list (if it isn't already selected), and then click on OK.

13. In the Export GIF89 box, choose a folder on your hard disk in which you intend to keep all the elements of this Web site, name the file Backwide.gif, and then click on Save. A three-character extension is necessary for exporting a copy of your work to GIF format. The World Wide Web is accessible to users of most computer platforms, but the "traveling name" for files on the Web requires this three-character extension.

14. Press Ctrl(⌘)+S to save your work. You can close the Backwide.psd image at any time.

Congratulations are in order here if this is your first export to "Web media" format! You have an editable original file, and the GIF copy will display as a tiling background element when visitors come to this site.

The Inside Photoshop HTML "Starter Kit"

This book doesn't have enough space to cover Web site *composition*. The Hypertext Markup Language (HTML) used to define where elements are placed on a Web page is documented in other books produced by New Riders Publishing. We do have some guides that can be used for placing Web elements, however; they are located on the Companion CD.

First, the Top-page.pdf file in the CHAP19 folder is an annotated HTML page. Top-page was used to generate the opening page of the Art for Art's Sake site, and because this document is in Acrobat format, both Macintosh and Windows users can access it. (You can open it in Acrobat Reader and copy the contents to a text editor.) In the Top-page document you can see text highlighted in different colors.

These sections should be replaced with the names of your own images created in this chapter. Give the text editor file a name that is no more than eight characters long, and save it (with the .HTM file extension) to the folder in which you are saving this chapter's sample files.

Better yet, if you study this Acrobat document, or understand the tagged language style of HTML, you can re-purpose the HTML documents in the ArtSake folder on the Companion CD. The Arthur Sake site includes one top-page document and seven linking documents. If you add references to your own images and strike references to our fictitious Arthur Sake, you can have yourself a pretty decent site!

TIP

Only established professionals and masochists get into writing HTML manually in a text editor. If you are a designer, you should consider any of the following HTML editing programs to add to your repertoire of Web-creation tools. These WYSIWYG programs insulate you from the often confusing language style of HTML.

Adobe PageMill is available for the Macintosh and Windows. PageMill is a graphically oriented, drag-and-drop HTML composing environment that features a full-complement of tagging and formatting tools.

Microsoft Front Page is a Windows-only application. Its features are similar to PageMill's, and it also sports a drag-and-drop environment for quick Web-page formatting.

Netscape Navigator Gold (available in Windows and Macintosh versions) contains a WYSIWYG HTML editor. NavGold's feature set is less comprehensive than the products by Adobe and Microsoft; you can download a copy from Netscape's site for free, however, and you can put NavGold's editing features to the test before you decide to purchase the application. If you are affiliated with a qualified educational institution or a non-profit organization, you can legally continue to use Navigator Gold without buying it.

Figure 19.12 shows the Backwide.gif image as a part of an HTML document displayed in Netscape Navigator. If you're serious about Web composition, consider keeping Navigator and your HTML editor running in the background while you work in Photoshop, creating the page elements. In this way, you can get visual feedback as to how your site is coming together.

figure 19.12
The wide, seamless tiling image will support black or dark-colored text, and other

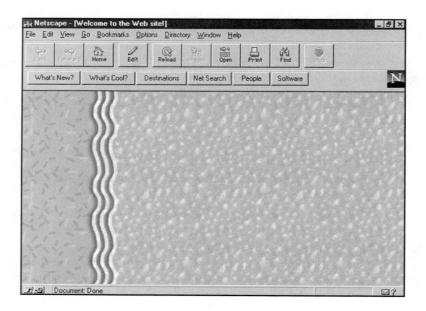

images in your composition.

The following section addresses the problem of displaying soft drop shadows and transparent objects on a Web site, and explains why 32 unique colors were chosen for the Backwide.gif image.

Optimizing Images for the Web

People like their work to look as good as possible when it's displayed on a Web site. Unfortunately, however, certain limitations sometimes seem to dampen their plans. For example, the "Gaussian blur drop-shadow" effect, which has almost become a cliché on the Web, can seldom be accomplished effectively against a pattern background such as the Backwide image. Here are some reasons this works—or doesn't work—the way it should.

"Faking" a Floating Web Element

Transparent GIF images, discussed later in this chapter, can hold open (for transparency information) only one color value of the 256 possible colors in the GIF 89a format. A Gaussian blur drop shadow, however, contains *several* intermediate transparency values around the edges, as the shadow makes the transition from shadow color to background color.

To make the signature character (a blue glasslike cartoon of an artist on Arthur Sake's Web site) appear to be floating on top of the Backwide background would seem an impossible task. The glass surface of the cartoon figure should cast a semitransparent shadow on the Backwide image, and you should be able to see some of the stone design through the character.

Here's the secret: The stone's texture is not all that clearly defined to visitors to this site. In other words, very few visitors will look to see whether the stone pattern tiles flawlessly, or (because of a trick you're about to learn) whether there's a minor interruption in the continuity of the texture. In the next set of steps, you merge the glass cartoon figure with a small version of the tiling Backwide image. Let's do this, and in the process, evaluate the quality of the results as displayed on a Web page.

ADDING FOREGROUND ELEMENTS TO A TILE

CD-ROM

1. Open the Art-guy.psd image from the CHAP19 folder of the Companion CD. This image was created by designing and then merging layers of geometry at partial-opacity settings. You can see the Photoshop transparency grid through the character and his shadow.

2. Click on the Create a new layer icon at the bottom of the Layers palette, and drag the layer to beneath the "Art Sake Age 11" layer title on the Layers palette.

3. Press Ctrl(⌘)+A to select all, then with any of the selection tools chosen, right-click (Macintosh: hold Ctrl and click), and then choose Fill from the context menu. From the Use Contents drop-down list, choose Pattern. Click on OK to apply the pattern (see fig. 19.13), then press Ctrl(⌘)+D to deselect the marquee.

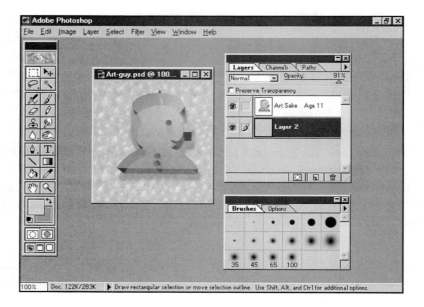

figure 19.13

Fill the layer with the same pattern used to create the background elements for the site.

4. Choose Edit, Purge, and then choose Pattern. This clears the stone pattern from system memory. (Your system will perform more quickly now.)

5. Choose File, Export, and then choose Export GIF 89a.

6. Choose Adaptive from the Palette drop-down list. An adaptive palette is a custom color look-up table for an Indexed color image (GIFs are Indexed color mode images) that contains as many of the colors unique to this image as the color table can hold. The result is a more refined image, more faithful to the original, with less dithering of pixels.

7. Choose 64 from the colors drop-down list. A GIF image can contain up to 256 unique colors, but an illustration might be conveyed in GIF format by using less. This particular image looks okay when sampled down to 64 adaptive palette colors. Click on the Preview button and see whether you agree. The file size of a 32-color version of the design is 14.6 KB, versus 29.4 KB for a 256-color-sample version. Think of the savings in transfer time to a visitor to your site!

In figure 19.14 you can see Photoshop's GIF Preview dialog box. Every image is unique, and you might choose not to sample a GIF copy of an image to less than 256 colors. Photographic images do poorly when sampled to a handful of unique colors, but illustrations tend to have colors confined to a limited range, mostly because we, as designers, don't switch colors every other brush stroke! Try previewing an image at 128 colors, then 64, then 32, until the preview looks awful, and then accept the next higher number of colors for the export.

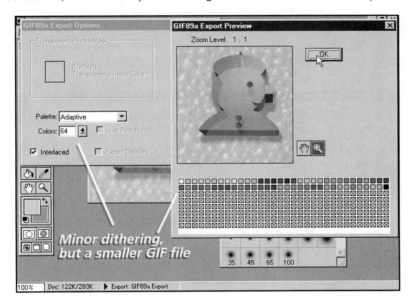

figure 19.14

Export to the lowest number of unique colors that still represents the thought behind your design.

8. Click on OK, choose a name (such as Art-guy.gif), save the file to the same folder in which you saved the background images, and then click on Save in the Save directory box.

9. Save the layered design to your hard disk as Art-guy.psd, in Photoshop's native file format, and close the image. You might want to create a folder called "Stash" or something on your hard disk for resource files for the Web site; images that are copied to GIF format, but are not used on the site. In this way, you can go back and update the full-color originals for future Web postings, as necessary.

As you can see in figure 19.15, the top page of the Web site is coming together nicely. Granted, figures in this book don't represent all the image quality of a monitor view of the document, but if you open the site in a Web browser, you will see that the experiment was a success, and you can barely detect the edges where the Art-guy element doesn't align precisely with the background pattern. Keep pattern elements small—pebbles, sand, and other indistinct textures work best—and you can get away with fancy drop shadows and transparency on your Web page that will intrigue visitors.

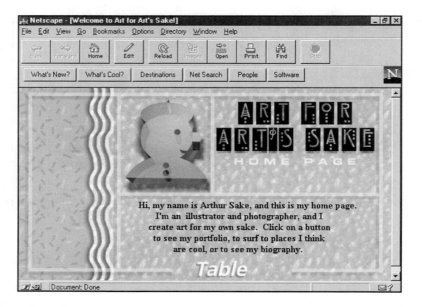

figure 19.15

Indistinct patterns help disguise elements on your Web page that are similar but not perfectly aligned.

The precision with which you can position elements in an HTML document is limited, compared to what you can do in a desktop publishing application or in Photoshop with the snap-to Grid feature enabled. In figure 19.15, a faint overlay indicates where an invisible table exists in the HTML document. All the HTML editing programs recommended earlier make the placement of a *table*—similar to a spreadsheet layout of cells—an easy task. The elements can then be dropped into the HTML table, and your Web page looks neatly organized.

Notes on Text as Graphics

The headline in this figure was created as a graphic, not as text, because of HTML's limitations in displaying a specific font. Visitors to your site receive text as ASCII code, which can contain relative fonts, sizes, and attributes (such as bold or italic). But with text as text, you cannot specify a Type 1 font such as Rennie Mackintosh (used in this example) because it is up to the individual visitor's browser program to display the fonts on a Web page. Unfortunately, many users don't own the same fonts you do.

In general, if you're creating text as a graphic element, stick to a point size (at 72 pixels/inch resolution) of 36 or less. In this way, graphics and headlines don't compete with, but instead complement, the text you add to the HTML page. Most browsers display text at 12 to 14 points for baseline body copy text, and a proportion of 12 to 36 points is more than adequate to make your headline stand out.

Image Compression and Resizing Graphics

The *Graphics Information Format* (GIF) is a technology licensed by CompuServe. There have been confusing legal stipulations, in the past, concerning a licensing fee owed to Unisys, Inc. (the creator of the format for CompuServe) by software developers who include the GIF format as an application export option. Designers can save images in the GIF format without paying a royalty; it is Adobe Systems and other manufacturers who pay a licensing fee for the GIF export technology.

The *Portable Network Graphics* file format (PNG) is a partial response by the software-creation community to offer a nonambiguous solution to compressed image creation. The developers of the PNG file format state that the technology is free and will always be free for third-party manufacturers to adopt in their programs. Like GIF and JPEG file formats, the PNG format uses compression. Additionally, the PNG file format offers 24-bit color capability with an option to save an alpha channel. In theory, images saved to this format by using Photoshop are optimized for sending across the Web.

In reality, however, the PNG file format is in its infancy; no leading Web browser on the market can read a PNG file without running a helper application (such as Photoshop). Additionally, PNG export filters currently do not compress an image to a greater extent than the JPEG file format, which *can* be used for placing images in an HTML document. In our quest for displaying high-quality images on the Web, in 1997 we have the choice of GIF and JPEG as file formats. The following sections introduce the JPEG format for creating large, quick-downloading, full-color images on a Web site.

The Joint Photographers Experts Group's Invention

Early in the technology of digital imaging, newspapers and other media publishers saw a need—to be able to compress images on the fly, for quick electronic transmission across the world. The Joint Photographers Experts Group decided upon a standard, a file format (JPEG, pronounced "jay-peg") that can compress an image down to a fraction of its original file size, while maintaining good original-image quality. Unlike the GIF format, JPEG images are color channel images—JPEG images can contain up to 16.7 million unique colors. The GIF format limits images to a color capability of 256, maximum.

The JPEG file format (Windows designers use the JPG file extension for this format) is of the *lossy* compression type; when a JPEG image is created from an original, some of the original image data is discarded. The Experts Group worked very hard to ensure that the *type* of information lost from the original image is basically unnoticeable; however, designers who are purists in their work should be advised that a JPEG copy of an original file does not contain 100 percent of the original image information. If you decide to adopt JPEG technology in your own work, the authors recommend that you perform JPEG conversion to a *copy* of the original image.

Since the invention of the JPEG format, there have been variations to the file structure, and options have been added so that users of JPEG technology can decide on how much compression and whether the JPEG image is optimized for downloading.

Exporting JPEG Images

As mentioned earlier in this chapter, you should plan your images so that they do not exceed about 620 pixels in width or 290 pixels in height, so that they can be displayed on an HTML page in a Web browser without scrolling the window. Our fictitious client in this chapter wants large samples of his artwork displayed on individual Web pages. The TIFF images in the Companion CD's CHAP19/ STOCK folder are used in the following steps to create JPEG versions of Arthur Sake's work. You do not have to convert all the images in this folder to complete an assignment in this section. We walk you through the process and explain the options you have for JPEG exports so that you can make an educated decision about JPEG exports in your own work.

EXPORTING TO JPEG FORMAT

CD-ROM

1. Open the Modcafe.tif image from the Companion CD's CHAP19/STOCK folder.

2. Choose File, Save as, and then choose JPEG (*.JPG) in the Save As dialog box. In Windows, choose from the Save As drop-down list; on the Macintosh, the drop-down list is in the Format box. Choose the folder you created on your hard disk for this chapter's image files, name the file Modcafe.jpg, and then click on Save.

3. The JPEG Options dialog box appears (see fig. 19.16). The following steps describe the options available for converting an image to the Web, while maintaining the quality of the exported JPEG file.

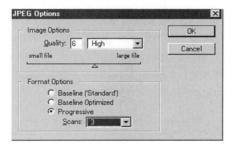

figure 19.16
The JPEG Options dialog box.

4. Drag the slider until the Quality field reads 6, or choose High from the drop-down list.

5. Click on the Progressive radio button in the Format Options field, and choose 3 from the Scans drop-down list.

6. Click on OK to save the file in JPEG format to disk. Although the Modcafe image is still in the workspace, the file's contents are being displayed from memory; the image does *not* display the quality of the JPEG file written to disk at the moment.

7. Close the file, and open the JPEG image from your hard disk so that you can see what the JPEG options have done to the copy of this file.

Understanding JPEG Compression Options

The JPEG process examines an image for color similarities, averages color values it estimates are close in hue, and writes these pixels to identical color values. This is why, for example, an image of a sunset can be faithfully written to JPEG format with a great deal of compression—a JPEG copy of the sunset could amount to one-tenth the original file size with no discernible loss of the original image content. The sunset contains a relatively small number of unique hues, and the transition in color from pixel to pixel in the image is a slight one.

The Modcafe image is unlike this sunset image, in that it contains a very "busy" textured background and a sharp transition from color pixel to color pixel. The coffee cup in the image, for example, is a dull gold, which sharply contrasts against the turquoise pattern at regular intervals across the image. Images that display high color contrast along image detail edges are called *high-frequency* images. These images are the most difficult for JPEG compression to faithfully reproduce. Therefore, it might help the overall quality of images you intend to post on the Web if you choose for "JPEG-ing" images that don't have sudden color transitions or a high number of unique hues.

Quality Settings

The setting you choose for Quality is a compromise between a compact file and a file with image fidelity. The JPEG copy of the original file is 53.3 KB, saved to disk, whereas the original image as a TIFF is 327 KB. What you have done has compromised the design content of the image almost imperceptibly, but made the JPEG copy capable of being downloaded to the visitor's browser program within 20 seconds of reaching the site (with a fast modem and clear connection). You might want to play with multiple versions of a JPEG export by using 5 or 6 as the Quality setting for the file, and see whether a specific image shows a loss of quality. If it displays poor reproduction at the 5 Quality setting, try 6 on your next Save As and see whether the image is an acceptable file size for the Web.

The Quality setting of 10 will reduce, to approximately 50 percent, the saved file size for a copy of this image, and the quality of the image will be quite good because 150 KB is an unrealistic file size for posting on the Web. The other extreme, a quality setting of 0, would result in a file size of 24 KB, more than a 10:1 compression factor, but the resulting file would look *awful*! For your own images, use a compression setting according to the frequency and unique colors in the image. Not all files are as unusual in pixel arrangement as the Modcafe image; typically, the 10 Quality setting compresses one-third to one-fifth the original file size, and 0 Quality compresses up to one-hundredth of the original file. Quality settings of 5 or 6 generally provide the best results and an acceptable image quality.

Format Options

Each of the three Format Options from which you can choose is affected by the Quality slider, discussed in the previous section. The Baseline ("Standard") option writes a file to the standard that the Experts Group originally established. The compression ratios are not as good as those of the Optimized option, but more original image content is preserved, and almost any application today, including Web browsers, can open and read a file in this format.

The Baseline Optimized JPEG format offers a little better compression, but some applications might not be able to read the file. By choosing this option, you might pick up 5 or 6 KB in saved image size for images of the same dimensions as Modcafe. Both Internet Explorer and Netscape Navigator can read an optimized JPEG image.

The Progressive JPEG format is understood by both Explorer and Navigator. This compression scheme compresses, on average, the same amount as the Optimized option. The reason we chose this option is that a Progressive JPEG is sent across the Internet as streaming data. The visitor sees the image immediately as a low-resolution image. As the file data is downloaded, the image magically increases in resolution. This is a wonderful option for keeping a visitor at your site watching what happens, and not losing interest when greeted by a blank page.

The number of scans you choose specifies how many times the image is sent over the Web at different resolutions. The default setting of 3 is fine. The number of Scans option does not affect the file size as sent across the Web, but higher numbers result in slightly better image quality (and visitors must wait longer to receive the final, high-resolution image on-screen).

Creating Thumbnail Images

"Accommodating" is the key word that can spell the difference between a popular site and an unsuccessful one on the World Wide Web. If you present your media in only one format, you risk losing business because a potential customer cannot access that particular format.

The following sections show you how to create an accommodating site by using preview thumbnails of an image. By creating very small GIF equivalents of Arthur Sake's work, you can post the entire collection of four illustrations on a single Web page. Visitors can then choose to browse to a larger JPEG copy of the image thumbnail, decide from the "Thumbnail Gallery" that they don't like the collection at all, or decide to hire you to create their Web site, based upon your innovative, accommodating approach to Web site construction.

The following sections cover the "batch mode" use of a new Photoshop feature, the Actions list. If you have more than five images that need cropping to a specific size, read on and save yourself some time.

The Actions List: A Macro Recorder in Photoshop

The Actions list, explained in more detail in Chapter 2, "Leveraging Photoshop's New Capabilities," records the actions you take to apply menu commands to an image. It does not record keystrokes or changes made to an image, using tools. As you can see in figure 19.17, Arthur Sake's images are all of different dimensions. We need to crop them to a consistent, specific width so that they can serve as thumbnail previews on a single Web page.

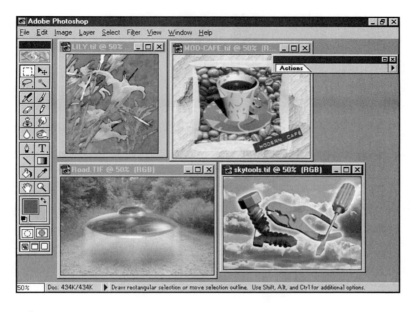

figure 19.17

The Actions list can be customized to make short work of repetitive actions in Photoshop.

Let's see—four images resized to 135 pixels in width gives us a total width for the thumbnails of 540 pixels, well within the recommended 620 pixel overall width for Web pages. With this knowledge at hand, and the information in the steps to follow, you will be able to program the Actions palette to crop 4 (or 400) images to an identical width; your role in the actual cropping process will be minimal. Here's how to create the thumbnail Web page.

BATCH IMAGE PROCESSING

CD-ROM

1. Copy the CHAP19/STOCK folder on the Companion CD to your hard disk. You can put it on the desktop, if you like. You need to do this because you need a unique folder on your drive as a target directory for performing an Actions command in batch mode. You can delete this folder later. (You will want to create a unique folder of your own in assignments that use this batch mode technique.)

2. In the STOCK folder, create an empty folder called **Finished**. You will use this as a target directory for converted files.

3. In Photoshop, open the Modcafe image from the Companion CD. You need a target file to program the Actions palette.

4. Choose Window, Show Actions. If you have experimented with the palette before reading this, click on the flyout menu button and make sure that the palette is not in Button mode. (You cannot access the recorder controls or use the Batch command in Button mode.)

5. From the flyout menu, choose New Action (see fig. 19.18).

figure 19.18
Create your own macro scripts by choosing New Action from the Actions list's flyout menu.

6. In the New Action dialog box, type the name of the action you intend to create. In figure 19.19, you can see that the author has chosen to name this **Resize Web Images**. At this time, you could assign a function key to the task; however, doing so in this step is not recommended because of the limited number of F keys on the keyboard. You might want to reserve these keys for your own Action tasks. Click on Record, but don't make any further moves until step 7, or they will be recorded.

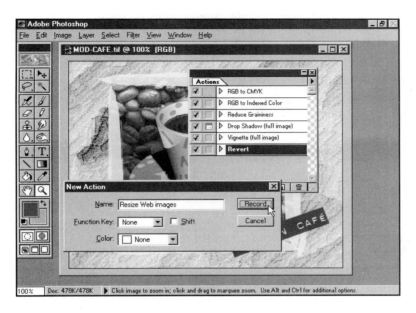

figure 19.19

Use these steps, or carefully plan your Actions list session. Clicking on Record begins the process!

7. Choose Image, Image Size, type **135** in the Width, Pixel Dimensions field, and click on OK.

8. Choose Filter, Sharpen, and then choose Unsharp Mask. Specify these settings: Amount: 89, Radius: 0.9, and Threshold: 1. Click on OK to apply the Unsharp Mask.

9. Choose File, Export, and then choose Export GIF89a from the menu.

10. The Palette drop-down list should be at Adaptive, the Colors field set to 256, and the Interlace Option should be checked. Change these options if they are not currently displayed; then click on OK.

11. Click on Save in the GIF89a Export dialog box. Photoshop writes the GIF file to the same folder where it found the original TIFF image, and automatically enters the same file name, but with the GIF extension. For Macintosh users, this file now has a different name than the original so that the original is not overwritten. On the Internet, identical file names with different file extensions are seen as different files.

12. Close the Modcafe image without saving it.

13. Click on the Stop button, the black dot at the bottom of the Actions list.

You now have the recipe for cropping all the images in the STOCK folder on your hard disk. The Actions list provides the complete details of what you did (see fig. 19.20). (Check out Chapter 2 if you want to see how to edit an Action to add, remove, or modify commands.)

figure 19.20
The Actions list provides you with a visual reference of what you did in any recording session.

The reason for adding the Unsharp Mask command in the export procedure is that reducing an image from its original size to thumbnail proportions blurs the image as pixels are assigned new values. The Unsharp Mask helps add crisp edges to image detail. Fortunately, when an image is posted on the Web, 1:1 viewing resolution is all that most browsers provide. If the image looks good on-screen, you have accomplished your goal, and visitors won't criticize your work for the slight amount of contrast that sharpening filters add to an image.

Running the Actions List

If you pay a little attention to the Actions list, both in setting up the batch editing mode and replying to questions that cannot be answered automatically in an Action script, you pretty much have your work finished for you in the following example. You will run the Action you created to convert the remaining three images in the STOCK folder to the necessary dimensions.

THE ACTIONS LIST IN ACTION

1. Click on the Actions List flyout menu and choose Batch.

2. In the Batch dialog box, choose Folder from the Source drop-down list, click on Choose, and locate and select the STOCK folder on your hard disk.

3. On the Action drop-down list, choose Resize Web Images. Be careful, always, to select the command you need. The wrong selection here will start a process that could ruin your images!

4. On the Destination drop-down list, choose Folder (see fig. 19.21). Then click on Choose, choose the FINISHED folder from the directory of your hard disk, and click on OK.

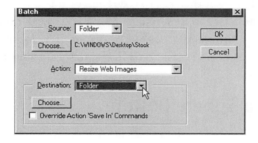

figure 19.21
Choose the Source folder, the Destination folder, and the type of Action you want performed in batch mode.

5. Click on OK. Photoshop proceeds with the custom Action, placing resized, GIF-format copies of the original STOCK image files in the FINISHED folder.

6. When the GIF89a Export Options dialog box displays, press Enter (Return) on the keyboard to accept the default options. Press Enter (Return) when the Export GIF89a directory box appears. This is required intervention that you cannot program into an Actions script. For the most part, however, you can sit back with your favorite beverage while Photoshop processes as many images as it finds in the Source folder.

TIP

If at any time the Actions process goes awry, click on the Stop button on the palette to halt the processing. If a palette covers the Actions list and you cannot move the obstructing palette, press the Escape key to halt the Action.

Now, having covered Web images both large and small, it's time to discuss the fine art of button creation in Photoshop. You need to provide your Web site with navigation controls so that visitors can move from large image to small image on the site.

Creating Navigation Controls

As mentioned earlier in this chapter, a button on a Web page is merely a bitmap image that links to another HTML document, or to a different area of the same HTML document. It can look like anything you like, although visitors are usually less confused by buttons that *look* like buttons. The following sections show you how to use Photoshop's native tools to create spectacular 3D navigation buttons.

Creating a Sphere Button

If you own Kai's Power Tools (any version), you can use the Glass Lens Bright preset command to render a shaded sphere from the contents of a selection, or an entire, unselected image file. Read on, however, if you want to know the *manual* technique for creating a shaded 3D sphere you can use as a navigation control on a Web page.

PAINTING A 3D SPHERE

CD-ROM

1. Create a texture file. Alternatively, open any of the files in the BOUTONS/TEXTURES folder on the Companion CD. In the following figures, we used the Water02.tif image, but you can use your own in these steps—256 pixels square at 72 pixels/inch is more than adequate in file size.

2. With the Elliptical Marquee tool, hold Shift+Alt(Opt) and drag away from the center of the image to constrain the ellipse selection to a circle, drawn from the center of the selection. When you have created a selection about three-fourths the total area of the image, release the cursor.

3. Right-click (Macintosh: hold Ctrl and click) and choose Layer via Cut from the Context menu.

4. Drag the Background layer into the trash icon on the Layers palette. Then choose File, Save As and save the image to your hard disk in the Photoshop PSD format.

5. Check the Preserve Transparency check box on the Layers palette. Choose Filter, Distort and then Spherize.

6. Drag the Amount slider to 100% (if it isn't there already) and click on OK (see fig. 19.22). Because the Preserve Transparency option is checked for the layer, the Spherize filter distorts the image contents without spreading the distortion outside the circle layer shape, and a more dramatic effect is achieved.

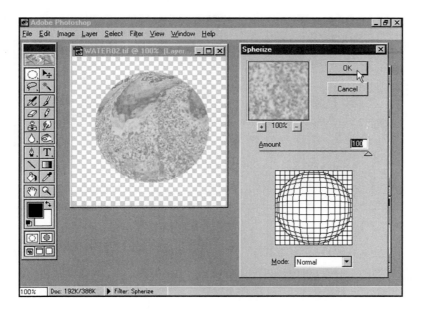

figure 19.22
The Spherize filter exaggerates the center of the selection while compressing image areas at the selection edges.

7. Press Ctrl (⌘)+F to apply the last-used filter. The second application of Spherize further distorts the image area on the layer, making the effect more visually obvious. You might not need this additional step if your texture has clearly defined image content.

8. Double-click on the Burn tool to choose it and display the Options palette. On the Options palette, choose Highlights from the drop-down list. The Burn tool will now darken highlight areas in the image, but the most *pronounced* effect will be in the darker areas; it will add shading to make the circle appear dimensional.

9. Drag several times in an arc, going from 2 o'clock to 7 o'clock in the image, until you see the shading from the Burn tool create an effect (see fig. 19.23).

figure 19.23
The Burn tool can be used to darken image areas; the most pronounced effect is on medium tones, in Highlight mode.

10. Choose the Dodge tool, choose Highlights from the Options palette drop-down list, and stroke over the upper left of the image in a circular motion to produce a bright highlight.

11. Stroke over the lower-right edge to produce what is known as a *photographer's catch light*, the intimation of a second light source in the scene, to make the circle appear more dimensional (see fig. 19.24).

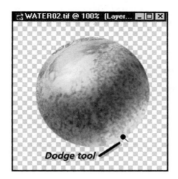

figure 19.24
Use the Dodge tool to lighten areas of the image, to produce a more dimensional, spherelike look.

12. Uncheck the Preserve Transparency option on the Layers palette, and press Ctrl(⌘)+S to save your work.

To make the image a proper size with correct file format and color mode for the Web, you need to resize the image and then use the GIF89a Export command in Photoshop. Depending upon your needs, 35 pixels on a side is more than adequate for a Web button. Be sure to use the Unsharp Mask filter before you export the resized button.

Because there is so little pixel information in a Web graphic, you might find it easier to use the steps outlined in the previous example for creating buttons than to specify a new file at only 35 pixels on a side. Working with large files and then reducing and sharpening them produces similar results to "working small," and small images don't give you the required perspective for producing work as you intend it to appear.

Making Square Buttons

The Lighting Effect filter in Photoshop can be used to add a chiseled edge to any shape; for this reason, it's ideal for creating more traditionally shaped Web buttons (if such a term applies to the three-year-old World Wide Web!). In the following steps, you use a texture to create a square button; the procedure can be used also for rectangular buttons, and even odd-shaped ones made from symbol font characters.

THE LIGHTING EFFECTS BUTTON-MAKING MANEUVERS

1. Open a texture from the TEXTURES folder or open your own.

2. With the Rectangular Marquee tool, hold Shift+Alt(Opt) and drag away from the center of the image until the selection looks like the one shown in figure 19.25. On the Channels palette, click on the Create a new selection icon, and then press Ctrl(⌘)+D to deselect the marquee.

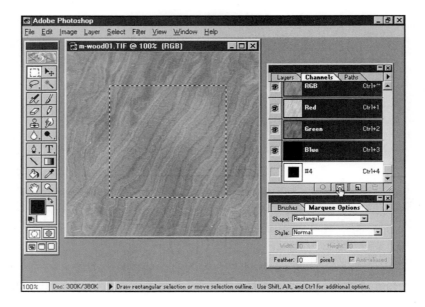

figure 19.25
Save the selection area you created in the texture file to a new channel in the image.

3. Click on the channel #4 title on the Channels palette to make this channel your current view of the image.

4. Choose Filter, Blur, Gaussian Blur. In the Gaussian blur dialog box (see fig. 19.26), drag the slider to 5 pixels and click on OK.

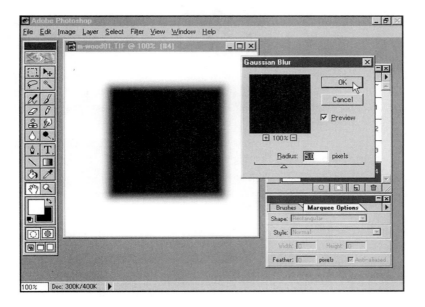

figure 19.26

Create a blurry design in the alpha channel to create transitional shades between white and black at the selection edges.

Here's the deal: The Lighting Effects filter produces a much better emboss effect than Photoshop's native Emboss filter, but the Lighting Effects filter needs a saved selection in an alpha channel (like the one you just created) to perform this emboss effect. Soft edges in color areas of the alpha channel produce a better effect, however, because too sharp a transition between black and white simply produces a sharp step when the alpha channel is used as a texture map in the Lighting Effects filter. It's important not to blur the selection too much; typically, an amount between three and five pixels for an image of less than 500 KB in file size will produce good emboss results.

5. To get extra fancy here, press **D** and then press **X** to make the current foreground color white.

6. With the Type tool, click in the alpha channel. Type **OK** in the Type tool dialog box; then click on OK to apply the text to the channel. When text is applied to a channel, the text is not written to a separate layer; instead, it becomes a floating selection.

7. Insert the cursor inside the selection marquee of the text. Hold Ctrl(⌘) and drag the selection to the center of the blurry rectangle; then press Ctrl (⌘)+D to deselect the floating text.

8. With the Rectangular Marquee tool, drag a selection around the text; then choose Filter, Blur, Blur. This applies a small amount of blurring to the text, and the Lighting Effects filter will apply a correspondingly small amount of relief to the text. Press Ctrl(⌘)+D to deselect the marquee now.

9. Press Ctrl(⌘)+~ (tilde) to move your view in the document back to color composite; then choose Filter, Render, Lighting Effects.

10. Drag the default light's target dot in the Lighting Effects box to the location shown in figure 19.27, choose #4 as the Texture Channel option from the drop-down list, uncheck the White is high check box (black in the alpha channel should represent extruded areas), and then click on OK.

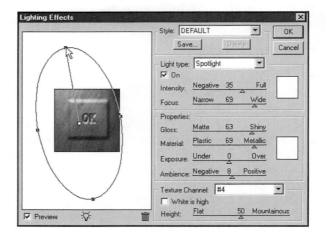

figure 19.27
Use an alpha channel as a texture channel to produce photorealistic, embossed designs.

11. With the Rectangular Marquee tool, select around only the embossed area of the image and choose Edit, Crop. Save the file to your hard disk in the Photoshop PSD format. You can apply any resizing and export a copy to GIF89a format by using the steps outlined earlier in this chapter.

As you can see in figure 19.28, the selection area in the alpha channel has been loaded and inverted, and the "OK" title for the button is being filled with white to improve its legibility. This step is optional, but clearly labeled buttons *are* an "accommodation" for visitors to your site.

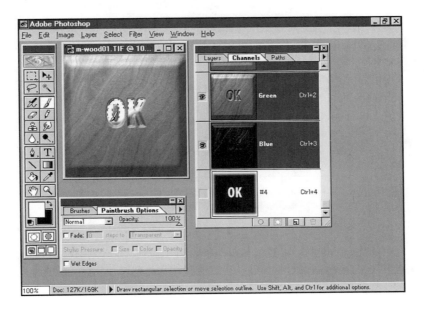

figure 19.28
Improve the legibility of text created on buttons by filling them with a solid foreground color.

Still searching for a more exotic-looking button? In the following section, we will breeze through some outside applications that can help fulfill your wishes.

Button-Making in 3D Text Programs

Adobe Dimensions, a vector modeling program that comes with Illustrator 6 for the Macintosh, is adept at extruding outline paths you import or create in the application. Part of the power of Dimensions is that you can save your work to Illustrator format and then command Photoshop to render the information to bitmap format—at any resolution. In figure 19.29, you can see the Dimensions interface, with a symbol font used for path information that Dimensions extrudes to a 3D shape.

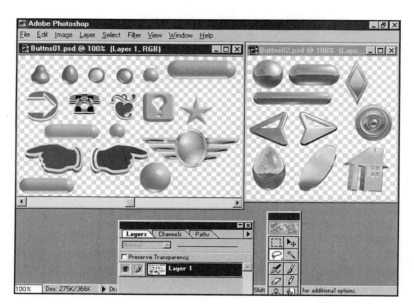

figure 19.29
3D button creation is a snap in Adobe Dimensions.

Another application, Fractal Design AddDepth, performs vector extrusions with fonts or imported artwork, and it, too, can export to Adobe Illustrator format. The suggested list price for this program is less than $50, and it's available for Windows or the Macintosh. AddDepth is also bundled with CorelDRAW 7, under the name CorelDEPTH.

CD-ROM

There are several examples of Dimensions 3D buttons in the CHAP19/BUTTONS folder on the Companion CD. To bring them into Photoshop, press Ctrl(⌘)+O, choose the files whose extensions end in AI, and then specify a size of no more than about 35 pixels in width in Photoshop's Rasterize Generic EPS Format dialog box.

Also in the BUTTONS folder are two Photoshop format files: Buttons01.psd, which has the Dimensions buttons rendered to bitmap file format, and Buttons02.psd, whose buttons were created in a modeling application. Any of the buttons shown in figure 19.30 can be copied off their layer into a composition of your own, which leads us to the next section's discussion of exporting a transparent background along with a button in GIF89a format.

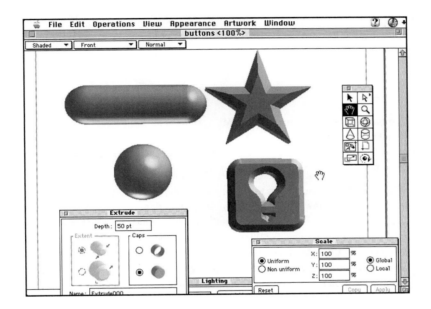

figure 19.30

Use the button images in the Photoshop files to create navigation controls for Web pages.

Button Layout and Transparency Options for GIFs

The way transparency operates in the GIF89a file format is similar to Photoshop's transparent Layers feature. When a GIF89a image is read into a Web browser, one color in the file format instructs the browser to display image information that lies underneath the image, instead of the color that is keyed as transparent. Photoshop, on the other hand, never displays a color for the masking (transparent) pixels on a layer; this makes nontransparent image areas easier to see as you are working with them.

In the following steps, you will use a button from the BUTTONS sample files (or use your own) and create navigation controls for the top page of Arthur's site. If you check out the ArtSake site on the Companion CD, as recommended at the beginning of this chapter, you will see the link (navigation) buttons for his thumbnail gallery, a list of sites Arthur thinks are cool, and a personal biographical Web page. This was accomplished through the use of an HTML *image map* tag.

Ti p

The image map tag is a reference in an HTML document to the location in a single image for multiple links. The image map tag is *not* contained within the image itself; it is the HTML document that contains the coordinates on an image that correspond to link references in the HTML document.

It is nearly impossible for designers to create the coordinates for an image map tag manually, but some applications allow WYSIWYG placement of image coordinates in an HTML document. With Adobe PageMill you can define "hot spots" in an image that are part of an HTML document by marqueeing the image areas. For Windows, there is "Mapedit," a $25 shareware utility by Thomas Boutell that can be downloaded from http://www.boutell.com/mapedit. Mapedit enables you to drag a marquee around image areas, and the image map editor saves the coordinate information to the HTML container document for the image, as PageMill does.

When the Web site game plan calls for multiple buttons, the easiest approach is to create the buttons in one image file and then use the image map tag, as described in the preceding tip. Individual buttons are difficult to align properly in an HTML document. Here are the steps for creating the three button navigation controls for the Arthur Sake home page.

CREATING A MULTIBUTTON DESIGN

CD-ROM

1. Press Ctrl(⌘)+N to open a new document; specify that the new image is 100 pixels in Width, 250 pixels in Height, RGB color mode at 72 pixels/inch Resolution, and that the background color is White. Click on OK after you have made these choices in the New dialog box.

2. Open the Buttons02.psd image from the CHAP19/BUTTONS folder on the Companion CD.

3. With the Rectangular Marquee tool, drag around the top, second-from-left capsule-shaped button.

4. Hold Ctrl(⌘) and drag inside the selection marquee into the new document window. A new layer is created for the copied button. With the Move tool, position this button in the horizontal center of the new image, at the top of the image window.

5. Press Ctrl(⌘) and click on the layer title on the Layers palette to load a marquee around the copied button. Then hold Ctrl(⌘)+Alt(Opt) and drag straight down on the area inside the marquee, to create a floating selection duplicate of the button.

6. Use the keyboard arrows to nudge the duplicate, aligning it horizontally with the original, and leaving about 70 pixels of vertical distance between the two buttons.

   If you're not sure what 70 pixels looks like, press Ctrl(⌘)+R to display the rulers around the image window. (Pressing Ctrl(⌘)+R a second time toggles the rulers off.)

7. Hold Ctrl(⌘)+Alt(Opt) and drag the floating selection to create a third button. The duplicate drops onto the layer. (There should be about 70 pixels of vertical distance between the second and third buttons.) Press Ctrl(⌘)+D to deselect (drop) the third button after you position it.

8. With the Type tool, press **D** (Default colors); then click between the first and second buttons.

9. Specify 16 as the (point) Size for the typeface used, use 17 (points) in the Leading field, and click on the justify center button in the left Alignment field. You can use any font you like in this example. (We used the Adobe Myriad Multiple Master font in a condensed style in the figures to follow.)

10. Type **Click to** ⏎Enter **go to the** ⏎Enter **Art Gallery**; then click on OK to apply the text.

11. Title the second and third buttons by repeating steps 8–10, telling the audience that the second button links to Arthur's "Cool Sites" page, and the third to his biography page.

12. Align the text on the various layers to center the buttons horizontally. Use the Move tool and the arrow keyboard keys to nudge them into position.

13. Choose File, Save As, and save the file as Button1.psd, in the Photoshop file format, to the folder you created on your hard disk for all this Web stuff.

Although the following two steps are not critical to your own image map button creations, we used them as we created Button1.gif for the top Arthur Sake Web page:

◆ Always try to crop as tightly as possible to the nontransparent areas on a layer, as a final step before exporting to GIF89a. Do this with the Rectangular Marquee tool after the image map elements have been composed, to keep the image's saved file size as small as possible. Also, by cropping tightly you can keep elements on the HTML page closer together, making more room for additional elements.

◆ Resize the image, if necessary, to keep it from overwhelming other page content. The final size of the Button1.gif image in Arthur's site is 60 pixels wide by 230 pixels high. The button used in the previous example is larger than the button used on Arthur's site. The authors wanted to offer you high-quality, large buttons on the Companion CD; you can use them as is or scale them to suit your needs.

Here's the low-down on exporting the buttons to feature transparent areas when displayed in a Web browser application: any of the 256 colors in the GIF89a file format can be specified in the Photoshop Export box, but you should determine which one you want *before* you export a file. For example, if you specify a solid color background in your HTML document instead of a pattern (as we have in this chapter), and the color is shocking pink, you need to write down the red, green, and blue components used for the background color in your HTML editor. Then you specify this color in the Transparency from Mask color selection box in the GIF89a Export Options dialog box in Photoshop.

By default, Photoshop offers Red=192, Green=192, and Blue=192 for the transparency color when a layer image is exported to GIF89a format. (This is Navigator's and Microsoft Internet Explorer's default background color.) If you simply drag a GIF89a image into either Web browser (without an HTML parent document), the background areas will show through, because Photoshop's default masking color is identical to the browsers' background color. We will stick with the default color in the following steps because it blends nicely with the stones pattern you created earlier, and you will not see any fringing around the edges of the image map buttons.

Now you are going to export the Button1 image to GIF89a format, with transparency defined as the nonimage areas that surround the buttons and text.

EXPORTING TRANSPARENCY INFORMATION

1. Choose File, Export; then choose Export GIF89a from the menu.

2. In the GIF89a Export Options box, click on the Colors drop-down list, and choose 32 (see fig. 19.31). The Transparency Index color swatch is highlighted. Click on the swatch to display the Color Picker, where you can define a custom transparency color. (This step is not required in this example because the stones pattern you worked with earlier in this chapter is very close to the Default transparency color.)

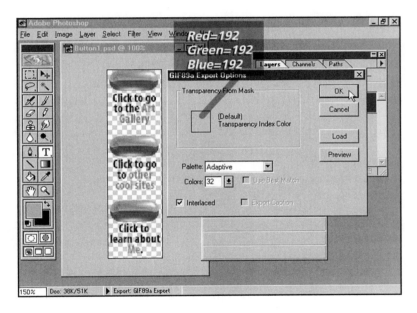

figure 19.31
If you use a custom background color for an HTML page, match the color to the Transparency swatch offered in Photoshop's GIF89a export box.

3. Click on Preview. This is the magic moment—you get to see whether 32 unique colors is enough to faithfully represent the button image, and whether the nontransparent areas blend into the edges of the opaque buttons. Figure 19.32 shows you that they do. Now click on OK.

If you could see drop-out colors in the design areas of the image in the Preview window, as well as in the transparent areas, you would have a problem. (We address that problem immediately after these steps.) For now, everything is proceeding according to plan.

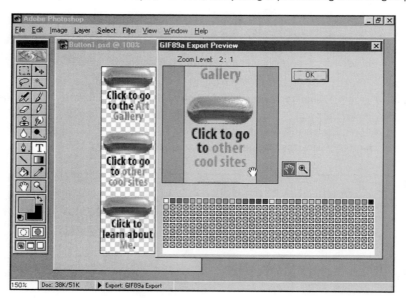

figure 19.32
Scroll and zoom into the Preview image to see whether the transparency map has any holes, or unintended areas, displaying transparency.

4. Click on OK to return to the Export dialog box, and then click on OK to display the Directory dialog box. Save the image to the folder with all the Web images, as Button1.gif. Then click on Save to save the file.

There will be occasions in your design work when a color in the design closely matches the default background color. This will create a drop-out in the design when it's displayed in a Web browser—clearly not something you want to have happen. Base your decision of which colors to use for a Web site on the concept for that site, and then define a contrasting color or pattern for the background of the site. The decision to create Arthur's site in grayscale tones was deliberate, so that the color images would stand out from the buttons and background.

If you don't use the transparency option, there's no need to be careful when you select contrasting foreground and background colors. It *is* important, however, that you match the HTML page background precisely to the color defined in Photoshop in the Transparency from Mask field; otherwise, dithering can occur around the edges of the image displayed in the Web browser—and there goes the beautiful illusion that an image or button is hovering above the Web page background.

Take notes when you define colors in an HTML editor, and bring those notes along to Photoshop when you create the Web elements.

In figure 19.33, Art's site is finished—and it looks pretty good in printed format. Why not browse the site from the Companion CD to see how the colors integrate, and to see how your own work can be professionally composed, now that you know some of the tricks of Web site construction?

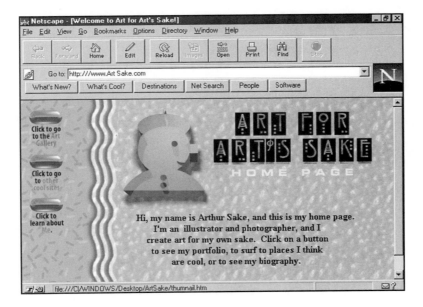

figure 19.33
From background to button, Photoshop can help create the Web media you need to build an attractive Internet site.

Summary

You now have a firm understanding of Web site construction, as well as the background necessary for you to accept an assignment from a client who wants a Web site built. The graphics are the visible part of Web construction, but they cannot leap by themselves onto the Web. Your knowledge of the correct image resolution, how to successfully resize an image, and other factors play heavily in a well-designed, quick-to-download site.

To add to your Web experiences, and to gain insight into how to outperform the competition building enhanced Web sites, move on to Chapter 20, "Animations and SFX on the Web." You will see how a series of still compositions can be put into motion by using Photoshop and a utility or two.

CHAPTER  20

ANIMATIONS AND **SFX** ON THE **WEB**

As you have already seen, Photoshop is the ideal tool for creating graphics in a wide variety of formats for print and other forms of visual communication. But what might not be obvious is that Photoshop is also an excellent animation tool for creating special effects and Web elements in motion. All you need is Photoshop, a utility or two, and your own imagination.

Palettes and Animations for the Web

Quite by accident, Mr. Royal Frazier, a programmer, discovered that the Web's ubiquitous GIF file had hidden capabilities. He found that a GIF file could be structured like a film strip—multiple images, one after another—and that Web browsers such as Netscape Navigator and MS-Internet Explorer could read the "film strip" and display it in a Web page as an animation. No one had noticed this capability before because no program had claimed the capability to read or write a multi-image file, an "animated GIF." Even today, only Web browsers can play animated GIFs (graphics creation programs, such as Photoshop, show only the first frame of the animated GIF).

To create an animated GIF, you first create the images, and then use a utility to compile the separate images into a single file. In this chapter we not only recommend Macintosh and Windows GIF animation utilities you may want to try, but also show you how to *prepare* an animation by using three different methods, each of which produces a different type of animation.

Web Animation Types

Netscape Navigator and Microsoft Internet Explorer, versions 3 and later, support three types of animation without the use of a plug-in:

◆ **An animated GIF.** This file can contain several images in indexed color format. Time delay between frames can be specified, as can the type of replacement each frame uses to cover the previous frame. Animated GIFs, like most digital animation formats, are a "flip-book," with each successive image replaced by the next image in the sequence. The GIF format offers options for image replacement by writing over the previous image, all the previous images, or by displaying images beginning with a blank image window. We make recommendations in this chapter for animated GIF replacement options.

◆ **An animated texture on a *Virtual Reality Modeling Language* (VRML) object.** Both Internet Explorer and Navigator support the display of VRML objects in Web pages. Version 1 (and later) of the VRML standard allows the application of animated GIF textures on objects within a VRML world. If you know how to write a VRML script, or if you own a modeling application that can create a VRML file, you can animate a texture created in Photoshop without using a GIF animation utility. The texture file you create has to be in GIF format, and arranged in a way you will learn to create later in this chapter.

♦ **Replacement animation.** HTML versions 2 and later enable users to offer an alternate image wherever one is located on a page. This provision was created to help speed Web traffic and let visitors see that a graphic is being downloaded. Although the LOWSRC HTML tag was intended to simply provide a replacement feature when images on a page are so large they cannot be quickly downloaded, this tag creates a short and simple animation effect when two images are specified for a single position on a Web page. Images on HTML pages are commonly in the GIF format, but JPEG file format is also accepted by most Web browsers without a helper application or special plug-in for the browser.

Two of the three animation types require the use of the GIF file format. You need to do a number of special things to a GIF file to make it look its best on-screen. The following section provides some details about GIFs and the Indexed color file format.

Indexed Colors Images

Bitmap images are composed of an invisible grid, into which you place color. We don't usually think of images as a "quilt" of color pixels, and we certainly don't create artwork by filling in each pixel, one at a time, but this structure for holding graphical data does determine how quickly, and with what sort of image fidelity, we send images across the Web.

Early in the history of computer graphics, engineers developed a way to quickly display bitmap images that take up a modest amount of hard disk space, and look near-photographic in quality. The Indexed color file format is a reference system that describes each pixel in an image according to a predefined color. Each color pixel is assigned a tag; when the image is viewed in an application, the header of the file tells the application which color values correspond to each tagged pixel in the image. The part of the image header that contains the color information is called a *lookup table* (sometimes also called a *color palette*). Because the viewing application needs to read this index of colors only once, the image loads on-screen quickly.

GIF images have a color capability of 256 unique, indexed colors. Usually, you do not create an Indexed color image, but instead perform color reduction on a color channel image to arrive at a GIF-type, indexed image. A color channel image defines each pixel color as an explicit combination of contributions of component color channels. For example, an RGB mode image shows its visual information by mapping each pixel to the sum of brightnesses in red, green, and blue color channels. In figure 20.1 (on the left) you can see an indexed color image with "shorthand" references to two colors in the image. On the right is an illustration of a color channel image. *Color channel* images are larger than indexed images because the reference system is more verbose with color channel images; they can contain many more colors than their indexed equivalent.

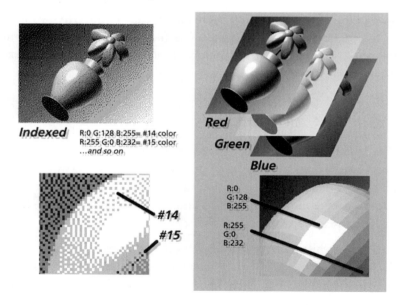

figure 20.1
Indexed color images get their visual information by reference to a lookup table. Color channel images contain explicit color values.

Types of Color Reduction

Because the color capability of color channel images is far greater than 256 colors, there are three basic types of color reduction:

◆ **Pattern dithering.** This process creates a "weave" of available colors in an indexed color image to represent the full color fidelity of the original image. Because all image content in bitmap images comes from pixel colors, pattern dithering is not usually the best choice of color-reduction methods. Small images contain fewer pixels than large images, and at a certain point, the pattern of an indexed image overwhelms the visual content of the picture.

◆ **Error diffusion dithering.** Error diffusion, like pattern dithering, looks at the original image and decides how a limited number of unique colors can represent all the colors in the original. This process assigns colors according to how closely the colors resemble original pixel colors. There is a tolerance of color matching, and wherever in an image a color cannot be acceptably matched, this pixel is moved to a neighboring pixel space until an acceptable color match to the original is found in the indexed image. Error diffusion images tend to look like a view of a scene through frosted glass, but their overall appearance is more artistically pleasing than other color-reduction methods.

◆ **Nearest match.** This color-reduction method does not use dithering to arrive at the final pixel color in an indexed color image. Instead, the application that performs the color reduction looks at a potential lookup table for the image, and then assigns the closest matches to original colors based upon the colors available in the lookup table. The results of this method usually are unacceptable.

Lookup tables are created at the time a color channel image is converted to indexed format. Photoshop offers many options for *palettizing* an image, as described in the following section.

Custom, System, and Web Lookup Tables

Creating an indexed version of your color channel image is a three-way trade-off between final image size, color fidelity (compared to the original), and dithering. It is often better to modify an image while it exists in RGB mode (a color channel mode), to reduce the number of unique colors, than to allow a dithering color-reduction procedure to take away your artistic control. Photoshop can palettize a color channel image by using one of the following three categories:

◆ **System.** The system palette is unique to an operating system. Microsoft has the Windows system palette, and Apple has the Color Look-Up Table (CLUT). Because these palettes are arranged differently, they do not bridge the gap between operating platforms. And because the system palette is a fixed one, it cannot address every unique design you might come up with. For example, the number of blues in the system palette is limited. If you need to color-reduce a picture of a sky that contains many shades of blue, the resulting image will display excessive dithering.

◆ **The Web palette.** Netscape Communications anticipated the need to standardize images for display on the Web, and created a color lookup table that displays images on systems using 256 (hundreds of) colors for monitor display. In Photoshop, you can choose to reduce colors to this color table. The Web palette is much more useful as an artist's palette, however, than a palette from which you can color-reduce an original image. If you use only Web colors in an image, for example, there will be little or no dithering when the image is palettized to the Netscape Web lookup table. But images that are color-reduced to the Web lookup table might not look very pleasing, because colors in the real world cannot be expressed, without dithering, to any sort of limited palette. The next Tip is about how to create a Web palette for use in Photoshop.

◆ **Adaptive palettes.** These lookup tables are also called *custom palettes,* because each color is custom-specified. Imagine that you want to create a tapestry of a glorious picture of a sunset. If you buy an off-the-shelf kit, its limited number of yarns probably won't include many of the colors you need to represent the sunset. If you shop for individual yarns from a selection of millions, however, you can select the 256 colors of yarn that are the closest match to the sunset picture you want to create.

An adaptive color palette is based upon approximations of the 256 most commonly found colors in the original image. Dithering is performed during color reduction, but often is not noticeable because the colors that cannot be expressed in the adaptive Indexed color file represent a small part of the overall image.

The process of palettizing an indexed color image and the type of dithering used affect image quality, but so does the unique range and number of colors in the original image. When you plan an animation, it is a good idea to plan first which colors you will use. By limiting the range of colors—by using primarily blue tones, for example—you can color-reduce the image by using diffusion dithering and an adaptive color palette, with minimal loss of image detail.

You should not think of "256" as your target number of unique colors in an indexed-color GIF animation, however. Photoshop can reduce the size of the lookup table—thereby significantly reducing the saved file size—from 7 bits/pixel (9,128 maximum unique colors) to 3 bits/pixel (8 unique colors). How small a lookup table you specify depends upon the image, how closely you want the indexed color image to represent the original, and how much dithering you can accept.

TIP

If you want to paint an image in Photoshop whose colors will display the least amount of dithering when it is color-reduced for the Web, follow these steps. Open an image of any size in RGB Color mode. Choose Image, Mode, and then choose Indexed. In the Palette drop-down, choose Web and click on OK. Choose Image, Mode, and then choose Color Table. Click on Save and save the color table as Web.act to your hard disk. Then choose Cancel to close the Color Table dialog box, and press Ctrl(⌘)+Z to undo the mode change so that you don't ruin your image.

The next time you want to work with "Web-worthy" colors, click on the flyout menu on the Swatches palette, choose Replace Colors, and then choose the Web.act file you saved.

In the following section, you work with Neon.psd, a layered image in the CHAP20 folder on the Companion CD, to create the resource material for an animated GIF. The design was carefully constructed to use a narrow range of colors; very little dithering will occur when you palettize the image, even when it is color-reduced to a small palette.

Creating an Animated GIF File

As in any art form, the *concept* behind the artistic expression dictates many of the procedures and the final form of the composition. What dimensions should the animation have? How many frames will make a suitable animation? What is the story line of the animation?

In the following sections, you learn how to create an animated neon sign that flashes "NEW" to the audience. The story line is simple: the sign flashes on and off, with a few transitional frames to make the animation less abrupt (and less visually annoying). The final size of the animated GIF will be 100 pixels wide by 60 pixels high. The reason these dimensions were chosen is that multi-image GIF files are larger than single-image GIFs. The smaller the dimensions, the smaller the saved file size, and the more quickly the file will download across the Web to the audience's browsers. Final size doesn't have to be working size, however; the Newneon.psd file is 500 pixels wide by 300 pixels high. It's easier to work with a larger image, and then resample (resize) it to final dimensions, than to work on a postage-sized document in Photoshop.

Also, because the art for the animation, Newneon.psd, is of similar colors, diffusion dithering to a small, adaptive palette will result in high image fidelity, and further decrease the final size of the saved GIF file.

Creating a "Variation" Animation

The most successful GIF animations on the Web tell a simple story in a continuing loop. The story begins and ends at the same point, the animated GIF repeats itself several times, and the audience's attention is sustained for a period that exceeds the total length of the animation.

The neon sign assignment in this section is created from a single, multilayer Photoshop image; variations to the brightness of the neon in the Newneon.psd file are created as separate frames that make up the animation. In figure 20.2, you can see the file in Photoshop's workspace; the image has a Neon layer (containing only the neon tubing), and the Background of the brick wall. The image was created in Macromedia Extreme 3D because Extreme 3D writes alpha channels to rendered images, which makes it simple to place elements on discrete Photoshop layers. In your own assignments, you can use any resource images, but usually manipulating individual elements is easier when they reside on separate Photoshop layers.

The Newneon.psd document shows the neon in a "neutral" lighting state—it is neither glowing nor completely dimmed. If you need to create a flashing sign in your own work, this is a good lighting condition to begin with, because you can then make copies of the document and alter the brightness in the image to make the object either brighter or darker.

figure 20.2
Objects that glow, move, or are animated in other ways are easy to create when they are located on a Photoshop layer.

Here's how to create the second frame in the flashing neon animation sequence—
an extremely bright version of the neon sign:

DUPLICATING AND EDITING AN ANIMATION FRAME

CD-ROM

1. Open the Newneon.psd file from the CHAP20 folder of the Companion CD, and choose Image, Duplicate.

2. In the Duplicate Image dialog box, name the new document Neon01. This will be the first frame in the animation sequence.

3. Press F7 if the Layers palette is not already in the workspace. Press Ctrl(⌘) and click on the Neon title on the Layers palette to load the nontransparent areas on the Neon layer as a marquee selection.

4. Click on the Background layer title on the Layers palette, and then click on the Create new layer icon at the bottom of the Layers palette. This creates a new layer, Layer 1, beneath the Neon layer and above the Background image.

5. Press I (Eyedropper tool) and click over the neon tubing in the image to make the bright magenta the current foreground color.

6. Choose Select, Modify, and then choose Expand. In the Expand Selection dialog box, type 12 in the number field, and click on OK.

7. Press Alt(Opt)+Delete (Backspace) to fill the marquee selection with foreground color (see fig. 20.3), and then press Ctrl(⌘)+D to deselect the floating selection.

8. On the Layers palette, choose Screen from the modes drop-down list. This accentuates the brilliance of the glow you have created.

9. Choose File, Save As, and save the document as Neon01.psd, in the Photoshop file format, to your hard disk. Keep the image open in Photoshop; you haven't finished creating the glow effect.

The shape of the glow surrounding the neon tubing is a good color and the correct shape, but there are neon properties that need to be added to make a convincing image. Here's how to edit the document to finish frame 1 of the animation.

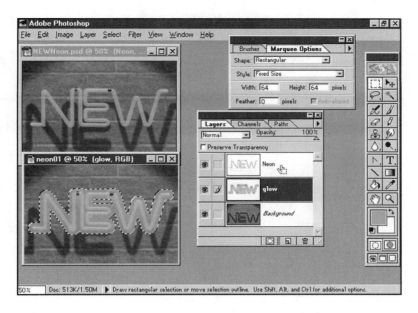

figure 20.3
Fill the expanded selection with foreground color to create the shape of the glow.

ENHANCING THE NEON EFFECT

1. Using the Neon01.psd file, press Ctrl(⌘) and click on the Neon title on the Layers palette, and then load the nontransparent areas as a selection marquee.

2. Choose Select, Modify, and then choose Expand. In the Expand Selection dialog box number field, type 4 and click on OK.

3. Click on the Layer 1 title on the Layers palette to make it the current editing layer.

4. Press Delete (Backspace), and then press Ctrl(⌘)+D to deselect the marquee.

5. Choose Filter, Blur, and then choose Gaussian Blur.

6. In the Gaussian blur dialog box, type 5 in the number field and click on OK. This creates the effect of glowing neon from the hard-edged shape on the new layer.

7. Drag the Opacity slider on the Layers palette down to about 90% so that some of the background image can show through the glow.

8. Click on the Neon layer title on the Layers palette, and press Ctrl(⌘)+L to display the Levels command.

9. The neon needs to be brighter to make a visual transition between lit and dimmed in the animation. Drag the white point slider until the right Input Levels text field reads 148. Then drag the black point slider up to about 21 (see fig. 20.4). This increases the contrast of the neon on the layer and adds visual "punch" to the animation.

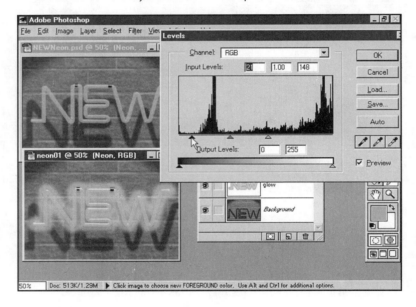

figure 20.4
Using the Levels command, increase the overall contrast of the neon on the layer.

10. Click on OK to apply the tonal change to the neon in the image.

11. Press Ctrl(⌘)+S to save your work.

The only thing missing from the glowing neon sign at this point is a brilliant core of gas at the center of the tubing. In the following section you use the Pen tool to create a glowing core effect.

Stroking a Path

Vector paths created in an image by using Photoshop's Pen tool are nonprinting "directions" in a document that can guide the creation of a selection marquee, and also serve another purpose. Vector paths can leave their mark in a composition if you stroke the path with many of the toolbox tools. For example, if you want to create a smeared effect in an image, but the smear needs to be of a precise geometric design, you can stroke a path by using the Smudge tool. The following tools can be used to create some unusual effects with Photoshop paths:

◆ The Airbrush tool

◆ The Paintbrush tool

◆ The Pencil tool

◆ The Eraser tool

◆ The Smudge tool

◆ The Focus tools: Blur and Sharpen

◆ The Toning tools: Burn, Dodge, Sponge

◆ The Rubber Stamp tool (The results of using this tool are extremely bizarre; a sample point must be defined for the tool before you stroke the path.)

If tools other than those listed here are active when you stroke a path, the effect will default to the application of the Pencil tool, using the current Brush tip and foreground color.

The goal here is to stroke a path at the center of the neon tube in the image to simulate the appearance of excited gas within the tube. The creation of the path has already been done for you in the Newneon.psd file, and the path exists in the duplicate Neon01 file, as well. Here's how to apply the glowing gas effect to the animation frame.

STROKING THE NEON PATH

1. In Neon01.psd, double-click on the Layer 1 title on the Layers palette (the layer containing the glow). Type **glow** in the Name field of the Layer Options dialog box, and click on OK to name the layer.

2. Click on the Neon title on the Layers palette, and then click on the Create new layer icon at the bottom of the Layers palette. The new layer, titled Layer 1, is now the current editing layer and is at the top of the layer stack in the document. On the Layers palette, choose Screen mode from the drop-down list for this new layer.

3. Press **D** (Default colors), and then press **X** (Switch Foreground/Background colors). White is now the current foreground color.

4. Click on the Paths tab on the grouped palette, and then click on the Filament title to display the path the authors created in the document. Press **B** (Paintbrush tool).

5. On the Brushes palette, choose the second row, first tip, and on the Options palette, specify Normal mode and about 60% Opacity for the Paintbrush tool.

6. Click on the Strokes path with foreground color icon at the bottom of the Paths palette (see fig. 20.5). Click on an empty area of the Paths palette to hide the Filament path in the document window and to see the effect created by stroking the path.

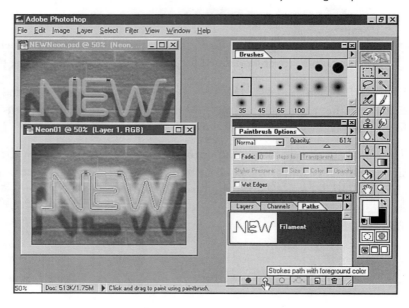

figure 20.5
Stroking a path in Photoshop is an easy way to create a precise geometric effect.

7. Press Ctrl(⌘)+S to save your work up; keep the Newneon and Neon01 documents open in Photoshop.

If you want to accent text in your own designs, check out Chapter 4 and the use of the Pen and other tools for path creation.

Creating Different Intensities of Neon

As mentioned earlier, the GIF animation should go through four frames showing on and off, to make it a more visually interesting Web element, and also to reduce the visitor's irritation with yet another "blinking thing" on the World Wide Web. Now that you have created bright, glowing neon in Neon01.psd, you can create a *copy* of Neon01.psd with all layers intact, and reduce the brilliance of the glowing neon to create the third frame used in the animation.

Here's how to use Photoshop's Layers feature to make traditional animation in-between cell rendering (*'tweening*) a snap:

CREATING A TRANSITIONAL GLOW

1. With Neon01 as the current foreground document in Photoshop, choose Image, Duplicate. Type **NEON02** in the As field of the Duplicate Image dialog box, and click on OK to create the duplicate. Neon02 is now the current editing document in the workspace.

2. On the Layers palette, uncheck the Indicates Layer Visibility icon (the eye icon) on Layer 1. This hides the stroked path you created in the previous section, and the neon sign no longer looks quite as brilliant.

3. Click on the Glow layer on the Layers palette to make it the current editing layer, and drag the Opacity slider down to about 50% (see fig. 20.6). Compare the frames in the animation. The Neon 2 image seems to make a nice transition between the original Newneon image and Neon01.

4. Choose File, Save As, and then save the image as Neon02.psd in the Photoshop file format to your hard disk.

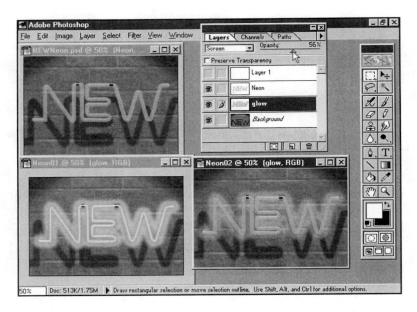

figure 20.6
Alter the opacity of the Glow layer to suggest a lower amount of glow from the neon
sign.

The fourth frame of the animation should show the neon sign completely off. Here's
how to use the Levels command to "dim the lights."

FINISHING THE ANIMATION SEQUENCE

1. Click on the title bar of the Newneon.psd image to make it the current editing document.
   Choose Image, Duplicate, type **NEON04** in the As field, and click on OK. Click on the Neon
   title on the Layers palette to make the neon tube the current editing layer.

2. Press Ctrl(⌘)+L, and then in the Levels command box, make the following settings (from
   left to right) in the Input Levels: 48, 0.56, and 255. In the Output Levels area, drag the right
   slider until the right field reads 160 (see fig. 20.7). These settings decrease the brightness
   in the Neon layer and make the tubing appear to be switched off.

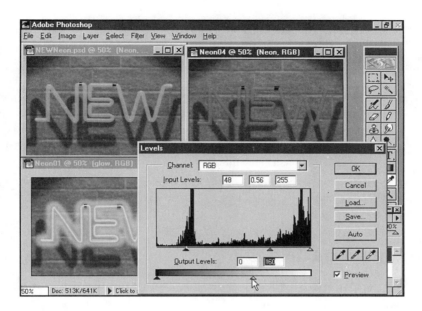

figure 20.7

Visual content on an image layer can be changed without affecting the areas on other layers.

3. Click on OK to apply the Levels command changes. Then choose File, Save As, and save the image to hard disk as Neon04.psd in the Photoshop file format.

4. It's time to flatten copies of the layered images and reduce the dimensions to the size of the final animation. Click on the Newneon.psd document title bar, and press Ctrl(⌘)+Shift+E. This is the shortcut for merging visible layers.

5. Choose Image, Image Size; then, in the Width drop-down list at the top of the dialog box, choose Percent. Type **20** in the width field and click on OK to apply the size change.

6. Choose File, Export, and then choose GIF89a Export.

7. Make sure that the Interlaced check box is checked. This option enables the file to be sent as streaming data across the Web, which means that visitors to a site will begin to receive file information (the animation) immediately upon reaching the site.

8. Choose Adaptive from the Palette drop-down list, and then choose 32 in the Colors drop-down list. This tells Photoshop to come up with the 32 best color matches to the original image. By doing this, you not only make the saved file size a little smaller, but also cut Web transmission time significantly. And because all the colors in the image are similar, dithering will not noticeably affect the visual quality of the saved GIF image.

9. Click on OK, and save the file to hard disk as Neon03.gif. Click on Save to save the file and exit the dialog box.

10. Choose File, Revert, click on Revert in the confirmation box to restore the Newneon image to its unedited size, and then close the document.

11. Perform steps 4–10 with the three remaining images in the workspace. The file sequence names are correct; simply save the GIF images with the same file names as the Photoshop originals. Remember to use the File, Revert command to restore your hard work before closing the original layered documents. You will need the layered versions of the files if you need to edit them in the future.

12. Close Photoshop. We now need to find a good GIF animation compiling program.

GIF Animation Utilities

As we write this book, there are at least four programs that can compile individual image frames into an animated GIF file. If you have a modem and an Internet connection with Web access, check out any of the following sites to download a trial or shareware copy of the utility needed in the following examples:

◆ (Macintosh) GIF Builder v.04—a drag-and-drop utility by Yves Piguet. Available at Info-Mac and its mirror sites; the best location we have found is ftp://mirror.apple.com/mirrors/Info-Mac.Archive/gst/grf/gif-builder-04.hqx. Yves doesn't specify the price of the shareware, but his documentation requests either a postcard or a bank note if you use GIF Builder.

◆ (Windows 3.1x and Windows 95) GIF Construction Set. At http://www.mindshopwork.com/alchemy/alchemy.html. Steve Rimmer's program is "bookware" (to get rid of the "nag screen" in this animation compiler, you must buy one of his fiction books).

◆ (Windows 95 and NT only) Microsoft GIF Animator. At http://www.microsoft.com/msdownload/gifanimator.htm. As this book is being written, the program is in beta; no price has been specified for the GIF Animator.

◆ (Windows 3.x, Windows 95) PhotoImpact GIF Animator. At http://www.ulead.com. This is a 30-day trial program. Retail is $29.95.

Although these animation-creation programs are platform-specific, the animations they can compile can be played on most browsers on any computer platform. Microsoft's GIF Animator and Yves Piguet's GIF Builder are highlighted in the following sections, as we walk through the steps needed to build the animated file.

Working with Animation Programs

When you launch MS-GIF Animator, you will notice that there is no program menu. This makes it a little less than intuitive for first-time animation hopefuls, but if you have completed the previous examples, or would like to use the resource files the authors have created, follow these steps:

CREATING AN ANIMATION

1. Launch Microsoft GIF Animator, and then open the folder window that contains the neon sign GIF files you created earlier. The authors' GIF files can be found in the CHAP20 folder of the Companion CD.

2. Click on the Open icon on the toolbox (second from the left), browse to the Neon01.gif image, select it, and click on Open. The image appears in the Frame #1 area in GIF Animator's workspace. After you have "primed the pump" by opening the first file, you can add the other images by dragging them from the folder into GIF Animator.

3. Drag the Neon02.gif title from the folder window into the space beneath the Frame #1 icon in GIF Animator's workspace. It is now labeled Frame #2.

4. Press Shift and click on Neon03 and Neon04 in the file folder on the desktop, and drag them into the space beneath Frame #2 in GIF Animator's workspace (see fig. 20.8). You can select as many files as you like and drag them into GIF Animator. If the files fall out of frame sequence, drag one frame on top of another (exactly as you do with Photoshop Layer titles) to re-order the sequence.

5. Because the images are already color-reduced (using Photoshop's adaptive palettization and error-diffusion dithering), there is no need to change the options on GIF Animator's Options tab. Click on the Animation tab now.

6. Click on the Looping and Repeat Forever check boxes (see figure 20.9). Animations of your own don't necessarily have to play continuously; these options depend on the story line of the animation. In this example, the animation will play as long as the page that contains the animation is loaded in the browser, or until the viewer clicks on the browser's Stop button.

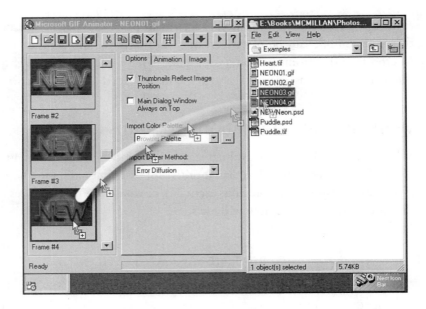

figure 20.8
Drag files from a folder window into GIF Animator's workspace to add them to an animation sequence.

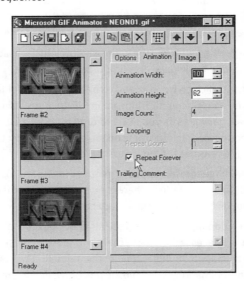

figure 20.9
Microsoft's GIF Animator enables you to specify the number of frames and the length of the animation sequence.

7. Click on the Image tab, and type **10** in the Duration field; each frame will remain on-screen for 10/100 of a second. Choose Leave in the Undraw Method drop-down list. Explanations of all the replacement (Undraw) methods (options) for animated GIFs follow this set of steps.

8. Click on the Save As button (Ctrl+A), and save the animation to your hard disk as Neonsign.gif. Close GIF Animator.

When an animated GIF arrives at a visitor's browser, the browser must decide what to do with the previous frame whenever the replacement frame appears on-screen. This is how the animation is accomplished. Here are the options for the replacement of the single frames, as listed in MS GIF Animator's Undraw Method drop-down list:

◆ **Undefined.** This option tells the browser to do nothing with the background upon which the animation is played before displaying the next frame. For most animations, this option and the Leave option produce identical results.

◆ **Leave.** This option leaves the previous graphic image as the next is drawn, to create a "stockpile" effect. This option is unsuitable for animations where elements move, although it can make smooth transitions in animations (such as the neon sign), where color, but not element positions change. A ball bouncing, for example, would look awful with the Leave replacement method chosen.

◆ **Restore Background.** This option creates a strobing or popping effect; the background of the Web page is redrawn after a frame is displayed. Typically, this attention-getting replacement effect is *extremely* annoying for the visitor to your site.

◆ **Restore Previous.** This replacement option can be used effectively in two-frame animations, to bounce back and forth between the previous frame and the frame being drawn. It produces a crude animation "look," but can help keep the overall file size for the animation to a minimum.

GIF Builder uses interface conventions similar to Microsoft's product. Here's how to compile the animation in GIF Builder version .04.

CREATING AN ANIMATION IN GIF BUILDER

1. Launch GIF Builder, and open the folder that contains the GIF files you exported from Photoshop.

2. Drag the files into GIF Builder's list (see fig. 20.10). You can drag one file at a time, or drag multiple files into GIF Builder. If the files are out of order, you can drag a file title to any position in the list.

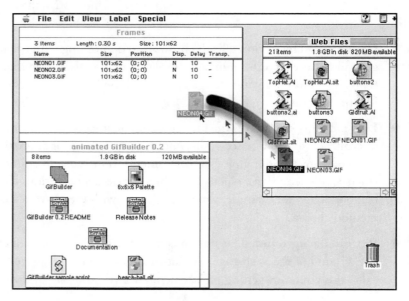

figure 20.10
Yves Piguet's GIF Builder will animate different image file types, and it provides advanced animation controls.

3. By default, the replacement method (called image *Disposal* in GIF Builder) is Do Not Dispose, equal to Microsoft's Leave terminology. Leave this setting at its default for this example. If you want to change the replacement method for your own creations, click on a file title on the list, and choose Options, Disposal Method.

4. By default, the delay time between frames is 10/100 of a second. Leave this option as-is for this example. If you want to speed up or slow down the animation, click on a frame title on the list, and choose Options, Interframe Delay.

5. Choose Options, and then click on Loop. GIF Builder offers only a single-play animation sequence, and continual.

6. Choose File, Build (⌘ +B). Name the file Neonsign.gif and save it to your hard disk. Because files for the Web need the GIF file extension, be sure to use the Internet naming convention for the file.) Close GIF Builder.

To view the animation without adding it to an HTML document, you can drag the file icon into Netscape Navigator version 2 or later, or Microsoft Internet Explorer version 2 or later.

Additional options can add to the animation features such as an embedded comment or copyright, a framing for the animation as played in a Web browser, and the palettizing of colors. The authors have found, however, that these animation program features are sometimes equal to—but in many cases not as refined as—the dithering and palettizing features Photoshop 4 offers.

Creating a VRML Animated Texture

An animated texture (as of the Virtual Reality Modeling Language version 1 specification) is a legitimate component of a virtual world composition. Both Navigator's Live3D plug-in and Microsoft Internet Explorer's VRML Add-In support animated GIF images as textures; however, an animated VRML texture is constructed differently than an animated GIF. The good news is that no special utility is required to produce an animated VRML texture; Photoshop can export one with only a little creative input on your part.

The following sections describe how to animate a virtual world texture.

Virtual World Creation

CD-ROM

A VRML file is the 3D equivalent of an HTML document. It is text-based, with fields and nodes similar to HTML's tags and attributes. Clearly, documenting VRML is beyond the scope of this book, but we have included a VRML script (VRML.PDF) in the CHAP20 folder on the Companion CD, so that after you have created an animated texture in Photoshop, you can surface the spinning cube in the VRML script and play it in your Web browser. The Adobe Acrobat file contains annotations for which text performs a specific task. The PDF document is platform-independent; both Windows and Macintosh users can copy the file's contents to a text editor document and duplicate this simple VRML world.

VRML textures will animate on a 3D object surface if the images have the following three properties:

◆ The image file must be in the GIF format. Microsoft's VRML Add-In also accepts JPEG images for surface maps, but cannot animate them.

◆ The dimension of the animation file must be 128 pixels in width, and a multiple of 128 pixels in height.

◆ The images that make up the animation must be arranged vertically in a single file.

If you have access to Adobe Premiere and any animation utility, then 90 percent of your work is done. Animation programs such as KPT version 3's Interform Designer, Adobe TextureMaker, and others can create stand-alone animations in QuickTime or Video for Windows formats, but do not offer the option to render single frames. Premiere can convert animations in either format to Adobe Filmstrip file format, and the single image file can then be brought into Photoshop to edit to a suitable VRML animated texture file.

The Filmstrip format is the underlying animation effect in the following sections; we have provided the Filmstrip in the CHAP20 folder so that you don't need additional animation and film editing applications. The concept here is to design a spinning VRML cube for the eMotion Animation Studios Web page. The visual content of the animated texture is a background of waves (the Filmstrip file), on top of which you add a stylized, pulsing heart. The heart is animated by using Photoshop's native Pinch filter.

Briefly, before getting to the Photoshop steps, here's an outline of the steps used to create the Filmstrip file. You need an animation program and Premiere to follow along.

CREATING AND CONVERTING AN ANIMATION

1. In the animation utility, specify 128 pixels in width and 128 pixels in height for the finished, rendered animation.

2. Make the animation brief, and make the first frame's visual content begin where the last frame of the animation ends. One second is a more-than-adequate duration for the animation.

3. Choose your animation program's render to file command. This option is different in every animation program.

4. Choose 8 frames per second as the speed of the animation if the animation length is 1 second. If it is more or less than a second, perform the math in the program that yields an animation of 8 frames. The maximum number of frames in an animated GIF texture should be 8; with more frames, the animation plays too slowly across the Web. The fewer frames used to express the animation's content, the better.

5. Under compression type and color options, choose the maximum color capability (16.7 million colors, Millions of colors, where offered), and choose no compression for the animation. Macintosh users should choose the QuickTime file type (MooV), and Windows users should choose Video for Windows (*.AVI). Launch the rendering command, and quit the application after the file has been rendered.

6. In Premiere, open the animation file. Choose File, Export, Filmstrip file.

7. Choose the Frame Rate in the dialog box. In figure 20.11, you can see that 8 has been chosen; the Puddle.MooV animation consists of a total of 8 frames. The Movie Analysis command gives specific file size, dimensions, and length information (see fig. 20.11).

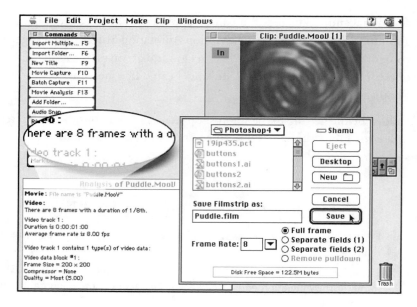

figure 20.11

Adobe Premiere can convert an AVI or QuickTime animation to a native file format that Photoshop can import.

8. Save the Filmstrip file to your hard disk. Windows users need to use the *.FLM extension for Filmstrip files. Close Premiere after you have exported the file.

The previous steps aren't the only way to quickly generate resource material for a VRML animated texture. Fractal Design Painter 3 and later versions can export still frames from an animation you create or import, as can several shareware utilities, such as Video for DOS and Dave's Targa Animator. Using Premiere's Filmstrip format to create the animated background is simply less work, as you will see in the following section.

Editing the Filmstrip File

Adobe Systems created the Filmstrip format as an information exchange between Photoshop—the program with all the special-effects filters—and the video-editing application, Premiere. As you get into the following steps, notice that the Filmstrip file provided on the Companion CD contains an alpha channel and a time marker separating the frames. When these file areas are removed to create the texture animation, the file can no longer be saved in Filmstrip format. This is okay; we have other file format options in Photoshop for saving the edited Filmstrip file, and our plans do not involve future video editing.

Here's how to prepare the Filmstrip file so that it qualifies for use as a VRML animated texture.

Film Editing, Photoshop-Style

CD-ROM

1. In Photoshop, open the Puddle.flm file from the CHAP20 folder of the Companion CD.

2. On the Channels palette (press F7 if it's not currently displayed), drag the alpha channel (#4) into the Trash icon, and then save the file to your hard disk in the Photoshop file format, as Puddle.psd.

3. Double-click on the Background title on the Layers palette, and click on OK in the Make Layer dialog box. This makes the default background into a Photoshop layer, and clicking on OK accepts the default name for the layer.

4. Press Ctrl(⌘)+" (quotation marks symbol) to display Photoshop's Grid, and then press Ctrl(⌘)+Shift+" to make the Grid snap-to.

5. Press Ctrl(⌘)+K, and then press Ctrl(⌘)+6 to go to the Guides and Grid Preferences menu.

6. In the Gridlines Every field, type **128**; in the Subdivisions field, type **8**. Click on OK. Now the grid will snap to every 128 pixels (the height and width of the Filmstrip frames).

7. With the Rectangular Marquee tool, drag a rectangle around the second frame in the film strip, hold Ctrl(⌘), and then press the up-arrow keyboard key once or twice to make the selected frame a floating selection. Drag the frame upward so that it touches the first frame in the animation, covering that frame's time-code area. The frames should be touching at precisely 128 pixels (see fig. 20.12); the snap-to Grid will guide the floating selection into position.

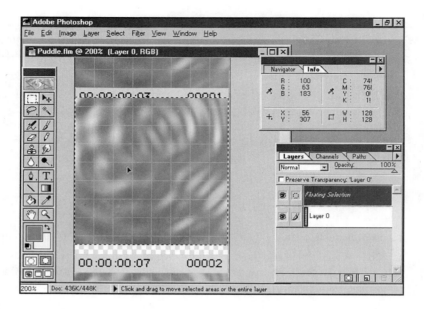

figure 20.12

Use the snap-to Grid feature to precisely align the top of frame #2 to the bottom of frame #1.

8. Press Ctrl(⌘)+D to deselect the floating selection.

9. Repeat steps 7 and 8 with the remaining frames in the film strip.

10. Marquee select the bottom time code in the image window, and press Delete (Backspace).

11. Press Ctrl(⌘) and click on the Layer 1 title on the Layers palette to load only the nontransparent pixels on the layer; then choose Image, Crop. This step removes the extra document window height and makes the image file 128 pixels wide by 1,024 pixels high. The image now qualifies, with the correct dimensions, for a VRML animated texture.

12. Press Ctrl(⌘)+" to hide the grid and automatically turn off the snap-to property in the image. Save the file to your hard disk in the Photoshop file format, as Puddle.psd.

This completes the animation of the background. In the following section, you will see how to create an animated star for the texture file.

Copying and Aligning Some Foreground Interest

The image Heart.tif was created in PIXAR Typestry for use as the foreground animation in the texture file, but you can use your own creation in the following steps, if you like. Typestry, like many other modeling programs, automatically generates an alpha channel mask; selecting an object from its background is an easy, one-step process. The plan is to put the heart in the center of every frame, but the *problem* is that with only transparency surrounding the heart, there is nothing to measure the heart's relative distance to the center of the Puddle image, from frame to frame. And consistency of object location is critical in animation.

The solution? You create a hairline border and use Photoshop's Guides feature to ensure that each heart you add to the filmstrip is centered identically in relation to the height and width of each frame.

Here's how to add some heart to the animation:

USING PHOTOSHOP'S GUIDES

CD-ROM

1. Open the Heart.tif image from the CHAP20 folder of the Companion CD. Alternatively, you can use your own image here, as long as it is less than 100 pixels in height and width.

2. Click on the Channels tab on the grouped palette. Then press Ctrl(⌘) and click on the Channel #4 title to load the channel's information as a marquee selection in the Heart.tif image.

3. Make sure that your view is of the RGB composite of the Heart image. (Press Ctrl(⌘)+~ (tilde) if you see only the monochrome channel image in the document window.) Then, with the Move tool, drag inside the heart selection and into the Puddle.psd document window (see fig. 20.13).

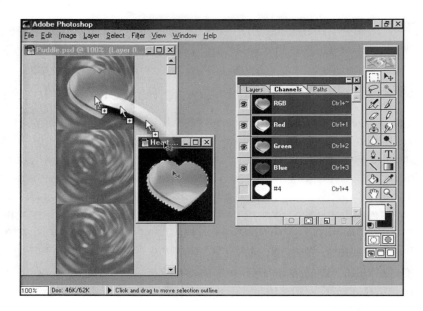

figure 20.13
Drag between image windows with the Move tool to duplicate the contents of a marquee selection.

4. Drag the heart on Layer 1 to the center of the first frame in the Puddle document.

5. Press F8 if the Info palette is not currently on-screen.

6. Press Ctrl(⌘)+R to display the rulers, and then drag down from the horizontal ruler into the document window until the Info palette tells you that the Guide is at Y: 127 pixels. If the Info palette is not displaying pixels, click on the plus symbol to the left of the X and Y fields, and choose pixels from the flyout menu.

7. With the Rectangular Marquee tool, drag a square from the guide to the top of the document window, from the left to the right edge of the window. You might want to extend the document window by clicking and dragging the window border away from its center.

8. With the Eyedropper tool, click on a light gold area of the heart. Your foreground color is now gold.

9. Choose Edit, Stroke. Type 1 in the Stroke Width field, click on the Location field's Inside button, and then click on OK (see fig. 12.14). Press Ctrl(⌘)+D to deselect the marquee now.

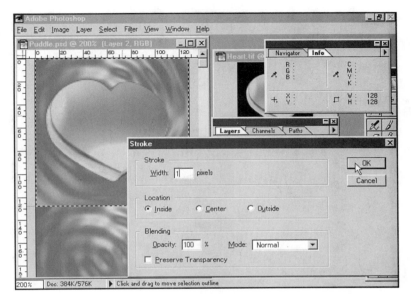

figure 20.14

Stroke the selection marquee to the inside to define a border whose outside dimensions are 128 by 128.

10. Right-click (Macintosh: hold Ctrl and click) on the Layer 1 title on the Layers palette, choose Duplicate Layer from the Context menu, and click on OK to accept the default name. Layer 1 copy becomes the current editing layer in Puddle.psd.

11. With the Move tool, drag the contents of the Layer 1 copy so that the edges you stroked touch the top of the guide (see fig 20.15). Now the heart in frame #2 is perfectly aligned with the one in frame #1.

12. Repeat steps 9 and 10 to fill the height of the document with eight hearts. Use 255, 383, 511, 639, 767, and 895 as the heights on the ruler for the guides for the remaining frames.

13. When all eight frames have hearts in their centers, uncheck the Indicates layer visibility (the eye) icon on the bottom layer (the puddle animation), and press Ctrl(⌘)+Shift+E to merge the visible layers.

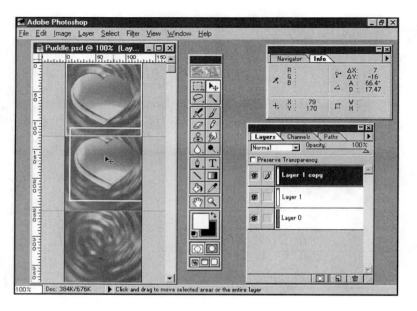

figure 20.15
The Snap To Guides feature enables you to precisely align each frame to the next in the animation.

14. Check the eye icon for the bottom layer to restore its visibility, and press Ctrl(⌘)+S to save your work. The guides and rulers can be turned off now. Press Ctrl(⌘)+R to hide the rulers, and press Ctrl(⌘)+; (semicolon) to hide the guides.

15. Press Ctrl(⌘)+S to save your work; keep the document open in Photoshop, but close the Heart.tif image without saving it.

The borders around the frames can easily be deleted now, but let's keep them as an element in the animation. The texture will be mapped to a VRML cube, and because each frame's edges are of similar colors, the gold border will help define the facets of the VRML cube. Now, using one of Photoshop's filters, you will *animate* the heart in the Puddle.psd frames.

The Pinch Filter as an Animation Tool

One of the nice qualities about performing animation with Photoshop's filters is that the amount of distortion to the still image doesn't matter. Because the collection of frames is always in motion, the audience never gets to inspect individual frames. Photoshop's Pinch filter examines the selected area in an image and then distorts the pixels inward, or outward, along the surface of an imaginary sphere. When pixels have to be reassigned to the extent of suggesting a bulge in the image, some fuzziness is introduced to the image. But again, an animation can contain flawed frames provided that the continuity of motion is preserved. Continuity is the prime compositional element.

Here's how to pinch (and punch) the heart in the animation to create a pulsing foreground element:

U S I N G   T H E   P I N C H   F I L T E R

1. At this point, you should have only two layers: one containing the heart frames, the other holding the animation frames of the background. If you have additional layers, merge them with the heart layer. The heart layer should be the current editing layer.

2. With the Rectangular Marquee tool, select the heart in the second frame in the animation. Don't select the golden border, however.

3. Choose Filter, Distort, Pinch.

4. Drag the Amount slider to 50 (see fig. 20.16), and click on OK.

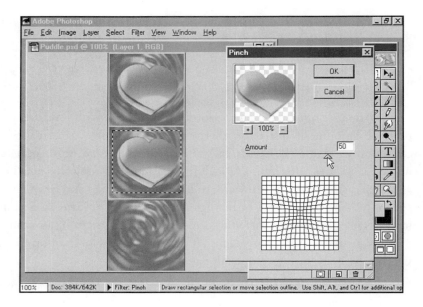

figure 20.16

The Pinch filter can pucker or bloat a selection area.

5. Click inside the selection marquee, and then move it down to the heart in frame 3. Press Ctrl(⌘)+Alt(Opt)+F to access the last-used filter dialog box.

6. Drag the Amount slider to 100 in the Pinch filter dialog box, and click on OK.

7. Move the selection marquee down by one frame, and use the following Pinch filter settings for the following frames: frame 4: 50, skip frame 5 (no distortion for this frame), frame 6: –50, frame 7: –100, and frame 8: –50. When the texture is "played" on a VRML object's surface, frame 8 makes the correct transition back to unfiltered frame 1.

8. Press Ctrl(⌘)+D to deselect frame 8. Press Ctrl(⌘)+S to save your work, and then choose File, Export, GIF89a Export.

9. Choose the Adaptive Palette from the drop-down list, choose 32 from the Colors drop-down list, and then click on the Preview button.

You will see a minor amount of dithering to the image as it is exported (see fig. 20.17). This is an acceptable amount, however. The next higher lookup table for the image (64 colors) would make the saved file 10 KB larger (51 KB)—a file of that size would make the VRML animated texture load far too slowly in a visitor's browser on a machine with a slow Internet connection. You might want to consider reducing the colors to 16 for simple, monochromatic animation files.

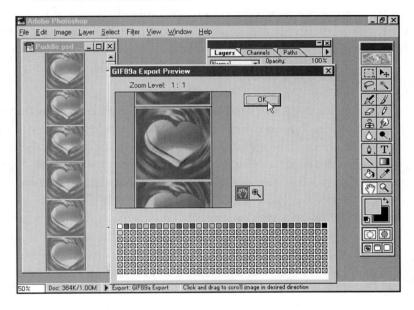

figure 20.17
Color reduction should be performed at a level that is a compromise between image fidelity and small file size.

10. Click on OK to exit the Export Preview box, and then click on OK in the GIF89a Export dialog box to export the file.

11. Choose a folder on your hard disk for the file. We suggest putting all the graphics you create in this chapter into a common folder, which makes playing the animated Web page easy to preview. Name the saved GIF file Heart.gif. After you name the file, click on Save to return to Photoshop's workspace.

12. You can close the Puddle file at any time now.

You need to build one more element for the VRML world. The spinning cube with your animated texture needs a *background* in 3D space.

Creating a VRML Background File

VRML specifications enable you to add a bitmap background within the virtual world, similar to an HTML document. VRML version 1 specifications (and the capability of today's VRML browser plug-ins) require that surface textures be in the GIF format. The background image for the virtual world, however, can be in either JPEG or GIF file format.

In the following steps, you use Photoshop's Clouds filter to generate an image of deep space as a background for the spinning VRML world. We recommend the GIF format for the saved image because JPEG images compress image information poorly when the visual content is of a high-frequency nature. *High-frequency* is an image description for visual detail that displays sudden changes in pixel colors from one area to another. For example, a smooth gradient fill from black to white is considered a low-frequency image; JPEG compression can significantly reduce a copy of such an image with good image quality. Noise, an image of sand, and the clouds that Photoshop's plug-in can render are considered high-frequency images. GIF compression creates a smaller saved file of Photoshop's clouds with reasonable image fidelity.

Here's how to create the background for the VRML composition:

CREATING A CLOUDY BACKGROUND

1. In Photoshop, press Ctrl(⌘)+N to display the New dialog box.

2. Type **256** in both the Width and Height fields, type **72** in the Resolution field, choose RGB Color from the Mode drop-down list, click on the White Contents button, and then click on OK to create the new document.

3. Press **D** (Default colors), and click on the Background color selection box on the toolbox to display the color picker.

4. Use the color field and color slider in the color picker to define a bright blue; click on OK to define this color as the current background color in Photoshop.

5. Choose Filter, Render, and then choose Clouds. A cloud pattern is created, using the current foreground and background colors.

   The effect of the Clouds filter is subtle; it needs a little dramatic enhancement, which the Difference Clouds filter provides.

6. Choose Filter, Render, and then choose Difference Clouds.

7. Press Ctrl(⌘)+F three or four times, until you see a design that's pleasing to the eye (see fig. 20.18).

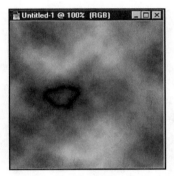

figure 20.18

The Clouds and Difference Clouds filters can create a texture that supports (but does not overwhelm) the foreground of a composition.

Ctrl(⌘)+F applies the last-used filter. The Difference Clouds color inverts current color schemes in a document; for this reason, applying it an even number of times will produce the same foreground and background colors as those you originally specified. The Difference Clouds filter does not use the toolbox's foreground and background colors; it depends upon the colors currently in the document to calculate the effect.

8. Press **D** (Default colors) and then press **X** (Switch Foreground/Background colors). White is the current foreground color.

9. Press **B** (Paintbrush tool); then, on the Brushes palette, choose the second row, far left tip. On the Options palette, make sure that mode is Normal and Opacity is 100%.

10. Click five or six dots on the clouds image. This creates stars in the cosmic background you're creating for the spinning VRML world.

    The reason 256 was chosen for the document's height and width is an undocumented property—Photoshop's Clouds filters seamlessly tile to these dimensions. Therefore, wherever visitors to your site navigate within the VRML world, they'll see a seamless tiling background. The stars you're adding should be evenly distributed, however, and as you saw in Chapter 19, "Web Site Construction," the Offset command helps create seamless tiling foreground patterns.

11. Choose Filter, Other, Offset. Type **120** in both the Horizontal and Vertical fields (see fig. 20.19), click on the Wrap Around button if it's not the current choice in Undefined Areas, and then click on OK. The design shifts down and to the right in the document window, and you can now see areas that might need a star or two.

    120 was chosen here because it is about half the dimensions of the image. This is not a "magic number"; it simply puts the edge of the image approximately in the center of the image, making editing work easier to see.

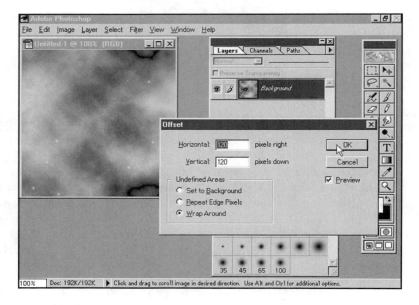

figure 20.19
In a seamless, tiling image, correct the evenness of image content distribution by using the Offset filter.

12. Paint one or two more foreground dots in the image to fill areas that do not have stars, and then choose File, Export, GIF89a Export.

13. From the drop-down list, choose Adaptive as the Palette type; choose 16 from the Colors drop-down list, and then click on OK.

14. Name the file Sky.gif, save it to the same folder that contains the Heart.gif file, and click on OK.

15. You can save the original sky image to hard disk, but for this example, it's not required (it has no further use). You can close all images and Photoshop now. The next stop is a text editor and a Web browser.

As mentioned earlier in this chapter, a VRML file is a "recipe," a collection of text references that are commands for the VRML plug-in, and references to images in the same location as the VRML file. In the following section, you see how to plug your image and animation creations into the VRML file and play the virtual world in a Web browser.

Editing the Platform-Independent VRML File

Because a VRML file consists of only ASCII (plain) text, it doesn't matter whether you run a Macintosh or a Windows system to play the VRML creation. To view and interact with the virtual world, all you need is a VRML plug-in extension for a Web browser, such as Internet Explorer or Navigator. The complete installation download of Netscape Navigator for both Macintosh and Windows contains the Live3D VRML plug-in. If you download the minimum installation of Navigator, you will need to return to Netscape's site and download the Live3D plug-in from the components page. (Choose Software from Navigator's Help Menu to link to the correct download page.) If you're using MS-Internet Explorer, you can download the VRML add-in, created by InterVista, from Microsoft's site. At the time of this writing, the file name is Vrmlocx_ie.exe (a Windows-only extension, at present). There are other third-party VRML browsers for both platforms, some of which play outside a Web browser. Virtus Corp., for example, offers a Macintosh stand-alone VRML viewer for download at http://www.virtus.com.

CD-ROM

The authors decided on Adobe Acrobat as the format in which to offer you the text needed to create a simple VRML world. Acrobat documents are platform-independent, and the Acrobat format also enabled us to annotate the VRML file so that you can customize it to create variations upon the world we have created. In figure 20.20, you can see a 100% view of Vrml.pdf, the Acrobat file in the CHAP20 folder of the Companion CD. Notice that Sky.gif, the name of the Background image you created, is enclosed in quotation marks toward the top of the document. Heart.gif, the animated texture, is also enclosed in quotation marks toward the bottom of the document.

In the next set of steps, you put the texture on a spinning cube that is the VRML scene, and add the Sky.gif background texture.

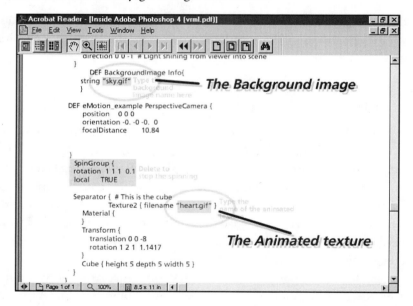

figure 20.20

A VRML document is simply a plain-text file with references to how the world is constructed and what resources need to be loaded to display materials and backgrounds.

WARNING

Special care needs to be taken should you decide to customize the VRML file by using images named differently than those specified in this chapter. Do *not* add extraneous spaces to the VRML document, do not delete brackets, quotation marks, or line spacing, and do not use a word processor to edit the document. Word processors put invisible text-formatting codes in a document; these codes ruin the Web browser's capability to accurately display plain-text commands in VRML language. Additionally, typesetter's quotation marks are not used in ASCII text; make sure that your text editor doesn't add "curly quotes."

CD-ROM

Copies of BBEdit Lite for the Macintosh, and TextPad for Windows are on the Companion CD; these are text editors, not word processors, and you should use them if you cannot find a plain-text editor on your system.

Here's how to copy the PDF document information to a text editor and display a virtual world:

CREATING AN ANIMATED VIRTUAL WORLD

1. If you do not have Acrobat Reader 3 (or later) available on your computer, install the copy from this book's Companion CD.

2. Launch Acrobat Reader, and then load the Vrml.pdf file from the CHAP20 folder of the Companion CD.

3. Scroll to the top of the document, click on the Text selection tool (the characters surrounded by a dotted outline), and then with the cursor, drag from before the pound sign (#) at the beginning of the document to the bottom of the text.

   The remarks in green in the document are graphics; you cannot copy them to the Clipboard by using the Text selection tool. The green highlights indicate where you should make edits in a plain-text version of this document to stop the cube from spinning in the VRML world, and where file name changes can be made to insert other texture files and background images, in case you want to create other VRML files (in addition to the example here).

4. Press Ctrl(⌘)+C to copy the text to the Clipboard, and close Acrobat Reader.

5. Open a text editor and choose a new file.

6. Paste the text into the file, and save the plain-text file, as Emotion.wrl, to the same folder in which you saved the GIF images. The file's name can be upper- and lowercase; if this virtual world is to be embedded in an HTML document, however, you must reference the VRML file in the HTML document with *exactly* the same case spelling. And you *must* add the .WRL extension to the file name.

7. Close the text editor and launch your Web browser.

8. Either choose to open the virtual world file in your Web browser, or drag the Emotion.wrl file into the browser window to view it (see fig. 20.21).

    The spinning cube with animated texture might be a little large in the Web browser because the camera distance in the VRML file was specified for optimal view of the world, as displayed as an embedded element in an HTML document, which you will see shortly. To zoom out from the spinning cube, you can use the navigation controls in your browser, or simply drag up or down in the VRML world to move closer to, or away from, the cube.

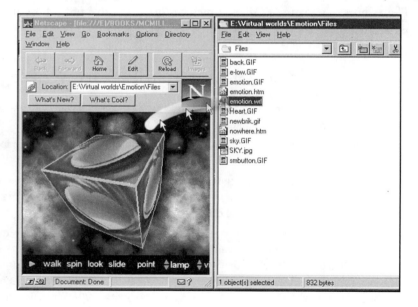

figure 20.21
If your VRML browsing plug-in or stand-alone program supports drag-and-drop, simply drag the world into the window to play it.

9. Think of other scenes you can create with the VRML text file and other textures you can create in Photoshop. Close the Web browser when you tire of watching the spinning cube!

WARNING

Web servers use file extensions (examples are MYFILE.WRL, MYFILE.GIF) to determine which MIME type to assign to the file. If you omit the file extension or if the server on which the VRML file resides is misconfigured, the browser will display only the text that makes up the VRML world, and not the 3D graphical world you expect. On Windows systems, the file extension is used also to launch the browser and the VRML plug-in when playing VRML files locally from hard disk.

The term "world" was initially confusing to us when we first discovered VRML language. "A spinning cube? That's a fairly wimpy world!" was our first thought. But when you become familiar with the VRML language and its syntax, you can build more complex worlds, full of spinning and static objects, and every one of them can have a unique Photoshop texture, animated or still, on the surface.

You now know how to use Photoshop to create two types of Web animation. If you're ready to learn a third, it's the easiest of all animation types to create and implement.

The Two-Frame LOWSRC Animation

The LOWSRC attribute for a graphics file is not a pure HTML specification; however, Navigator can read LOWSRC information correctly, as can Internet Explorer (and eventually all Web browsers that are made to compete with market leaders!). The idea behind this attribute is to load a small graphics file immediately in a Web browser, and then allow the graphic to be replaced with a larger file after the complete HTML page has downloaded.

This LOWSRC attribute provides the Web designer with an opportunity to create a short, two-frame animation on the site without any special utility or plug-in. As long as visitors to the site use one of the more popular browsers, they will be treated to whatever you choose to create as the animation elements.

In the following set of steps, you will create a two-bit-per-pixel outline version of a corporate logo. This will be the LOWSRC image; the color version will be color-reduced to comply with the GIF file format's limitations, to make up the final logo as it appears on the Web page.

CREATING A LOW-RESOLUTION ALTERNATE IMAGE

CD-ROM

1. In Photoshop, open the Emotion.tif image from the CHAP20 folder of the Companion CD. This is the image to be used for both the high-resolution and low-resolution versions of the logo on a Web page.

2. Choose Image, Duplicate, and click on OK in the Duplicate Image dialog box to accept the default name for the new image.

3. Choose Filter, Stylize, and then choose Find Edges. The Find Edges filter has no dialog box. It simply creates an outline version of an image, based upon the border of color changes in an image (see fig. 20.22)

4. Choose Image, Mode, and then choose Grayscale. Click on OK in the attention box that asks whether you want to discard color information.

5. Click on Image, Mode, and then click on Bitmap. Bitmap mode in Photoshop can be accessed only by first going through Indexed color or Grayscale.

6. In the Output Resolution field of the Bitmap dialog box, type **72.** In the Method area, choose Diffusion dither, and then click on OK to apply the change.

7. Press Ctrl(⌘)+A to Select all, and press Ctrl(⌘)+C to copy the image.

8. Press Ctrl(⌘)+N to display the New dialog box; then specify RGB color for the new image from the Color drop-down list, and click on OK.

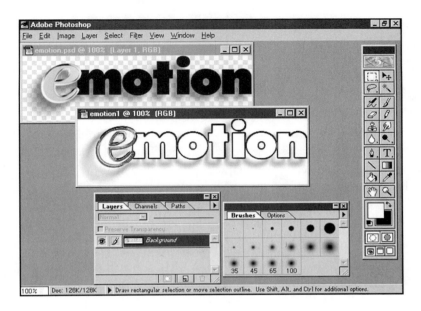

figure 20.22

The Find Edges filter reduces the graphical information in a file to its essentials, where the edges of color contrast exist.

9. Press Ctrl(⌘)+V to paste the clipboard image as a new layer in the New document.

    Photoshop will not export a one bit-per-pixel image to GIF format. By choosing to paste the dithered copy to a new RGB Color mode image window, you save the steps of converting the low-resolution file back through the color modes to RGB Color mode.

10. Choose File, Export, Export GIF 89a.

11. Leave the Color and palette drop-down lists at the currently suggested settings. Notice that the default palette is Exact, and the number of colors is 2 (black and white). This setting will produce an *extremely* small image file. This is a good example of composing image content for saved file size.

12. Click on OK and save the image as E-low.gif to the same folder as the rest of the images you have created in this chapter.

13. Export the original Emotion.tif file to GIF89a format, using the Adaptive Palette and 128 colors (follow the steps shown earlier in this chapter).

14. Close all three images in Photoshop without saving your work. You have the GIF images you need for the Web site.

To view the fictitious eMotion Electronic Motion System's Web site, drag the Emotion.htm document from the CHAP20/Emotion folder on the Companion CD into a Web browser on your machine. This site contains all three types of animations discussed in this chapter. If you were actually constructing a Web site, three animations on a single page would make the page too large (in file size) to download quickly; as a result, this company would lose business. But as an example, you can see that the page plays *fairly* quickly, for the following reasons:

◆ The VRML file, texture, and background image are as small as they can be without losing image detail. The VRML file (named Emotion.wrl in the folder) is only 832 bytes. You would be surprised at what you can display if you allow optimized graphics to represent the bulk of the visual content of a VRML world.

◆ Access from a CD to a personal computer is faster than downloading a file through a telephone line across the Internet. Do not use local hard disk or CD access as a measure for testing the speed of downloading an HTML or VRML creation. Access time from a floppy disk would be a little more representative of a slow connection on the Web, but the floppy disk would still play faster.

◆ The GIF animation and the replacement logo animation both comprise adaptively sampled (and very limited) color palettes.

If you know how to write HTML, the attributes for the logo image are, respectively:

```
EMBED SRC="emotion.GIF"
```

and

```
LOWSRC="e-low.gif"
```

Remember to write the HEIGHT and WIDTH attributes in the HTML document; this enables the browser to compose the HTML page more quickly on the visitor's screen. Your Photoshop image optimization will be thwarted if the Web browser then has to calculate how large an image you want displayed on the page.

If you're not familiar with HTML, the Emotion.htm file is on the Companion CD in the EMOTION folder; you can examine it to see how the page was constructed. Many WYSIWYG HTML editors are on the market—one of the easiest to use is Netscape Navigator Gold. In NavGold (Windows or Macintosh version), you choose Insert, Image, choose the high-resolution file for the Image File name field in the Properties dialog box, and then choose the low-resolution file for the Alternative Representations field.

You might want to enlist the help of an experienced HTML author to bring a Web site to fruition. Or better still, offer your graphics services to an HTML author as part of a freelance, collaborative effort. Figure 20.23 shows the finished Emotion Web site.

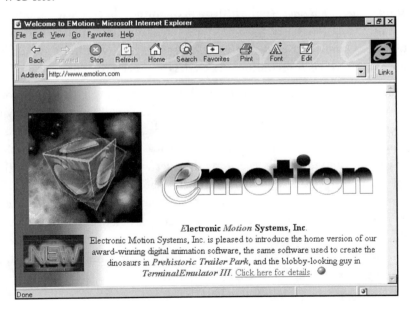

figure 20.23
There is wonderful, inexpensive support for animation on Web pages. Use Photoshop and your imagination to fill in the content!

Summary

If you completely understand animation, the Web, and Photoshop's role in advanced graphics design by now, congratulations—and your head is probably spinning like the VRML cube in this chapter!

This "new media"—HTML, the Web, animated, interactive elements, and so on—might initially be a little unsettling to traditional computer graphics designers. And certainly to *physical* media designers! As long as you understand the *principles* behind computer graphics and Photoshop's features, however, you can adapt your present skills to on-screen display fairly quickly, and bring to the Web your unique style of creative content.

Closing Thoughts

Inside Adobe Photoshop 4 is the fifth book the authors have written about Photoshop. Through the years, we have received mail from our friends and readers with questions (and a scattered complaint here and there). The most useful feedback we have received has been on the way readers approach the books.

Many readers never actually perform the tutorials; instead, they skip around in the book looking for a magic recipe or technique here and there. For many users, this approach works when they need to solve a specific problem quickly. But the most "successful" readers—the ones who have increased both their overall understanding of graphics and their skill level—are the ones who found time to sit with the book for an hour or two at a stretch and work their way through a chapter. Like most things in life, mastery of an art comes from doing. It's only then that the principles behind the steps become tangible. If you have passed over chapters on your way to this paragraph, please invest completely in your own talent and work through a favorite chapter. Follow the steps, and then do something similar with images of your own. Make the knowledge truly yours.

Also, it should be known that the authors actually read sometimes(!), and even a tutorial-based book has some "good stuff" lodged between the pages that might not be a formal set of steps to arrive at a finished piece. What we do when we discover a nugget of wisdom is outlined in (you guessed it) a numbered list:

INDEXING A NUGGET OF WISDOM IN A BOOK

1. Take out a pad of fluorescent sticky notes.
2. Detach one leaf.
3. Place it between the pages in the book that contain a morsel of interest.

Despite all the information organized into procedures in this book, however, please *don't* treat *Inside Adobe Photoshop 4* as a workbook. We have tried to make this book an excellent *resource* guide, too.

Whether you are an imaging enthusiast who simply wants to retouch photos as a pastime, a designer in a large enterprise who is forced to measure output in volume, or a fine artist who is looking for that "special something" to refine your work, we all have toolkits, both virtual and physical. Hopefully, this book has shown you that Photoshop is not only a necessary part of your computer graphics toolkit, but that it also should be located at the *top* of the toolkit. Many applications are shown in this book, but at some phase of creative imaging (concept, execution, enhancement, or final output) Photoshop proves to be the finest integrator of digital media—that any of us can possibly imagine.

INDEX

Symbols

A

magine a hidden code placed inside this photo that reveals the photographer's name, address, phone number and an instant copyright notice.

Stop imagining and start communicating your copyright with digital watermarking today!

Digimarc's watermarking preserves the creative value of your work and offers a fairer financial reward system.

Bundled in **Adobe® Photoshop® 4.0**, Digimarc's breakthrough technique instantly announces ownership of all your images. Imperceptible to the eye, our digitally embedded watermark contains vital information regarding your copyright, ownership and reproduction rights.

When you subscribe to our service, you'll receive a Creator ID code which is embedded in your watermark. Prospective clients reading your watermark are linked to your personal information by this code.

For more information or to get started, visit us at **www.digimarc.com/offer** or call **1-800-DIGIMARC** (344-4627) and mention code IAP-197.

FREE 90-DAY NO RISK TRIAL!

Try digital watermarking for 3 months, if you like it – sign up for the special low price of just $79 a year. Almost a 50% savings off the regular price!

Offer ends December 31, 1997.
For more information, visit us at: www.digimarc.com/offer

Every image you create is an ad for yourself.

REGISTRATION CARD

Inside Adobe® Photoshop® 4

Name _____ Title _____

Company _____ Type of
business _____

Address _____

City/State/ZIP _____

Have you used these types of books before? ☐ yes ☐ no

If yes, which ones? _____

_____

How many computer books do you purchase each year? ☐ 1–5 ☐ 6 or more

How did you learn about this book? _____

Where did you purchase this book? _____

Which applications do you currently use? _____

_____

Which computer magazines do you subscribe to? _____

_____

What trade shows do you attend? _____

_____

Comments: _____

_____

_____

Would you like to be placed on our preferred mailing list? ☐ yes ☐ no

☐ **I would like to see my name in print!** You may use my name and quote me in future New Riders products and promotions. My daytime phone number is: _____

New Riders Publishing   201 West 103rd Street ◆ Indianapolis, Indiana 46290 USA

Fax to 317-581-4670

Fold Here

- -

BUSINESS REPLY MAIL

FIRST-CLASS MAIL PERMIT NO. 9918 INDIANAPOLIS IN

POSTAGE WILL BE PAID BY THE ADDRESSEE

NEW RIDERS PUBLISHING
201 W 103RD ST
INDIANAPOLIS IN 46290-9058

Check Us Out Online!

New Riders has emerged as a premier publisher of computer books for the professional computer user. Focusing on CAD/graphics/multimedia, communications/internetworking, and networking/operating systems, New Riders continues to provide expert advice on high-end topics and software.

Check out the online version of *New Riders' Official World Wide Yellow Pages, 1996 Edition* for the most engaging, entertaining, and informative sites on the Web! You can even add your own site!

Brave our site for the finest collection of CAD and 3D imagery produced today. Professionals from all over the world contribute to our gallery, which features new designs every month.

Hind Fire
Copyright 1995 - John Brooks

From Novell to Microsoft, New Riders publishes the training guides you need to attain your certification. Visit our site and try your hand at the CNE Endeavor, a test engine created by VFX Technologies, Inc. that enables you to measure what you know—and what you don't!

New Riders

http://www.mcp.com/newriders